WALTER PATER: THREE MAJOR TEXTS

(*The Renaissance, Appreciations,* and *Imaginary Portraits*)

WALTER PATER: THREE MAJOR TEXTS

(The Renaissance, Appreciations, and Imaginary Portraits)

Edited with an Introduction by

William E. Buckler

New York University Press
New York and London
1 9 8 6

The publication of this work has been subvented in part by a grant from the Abraham and Rebecca Stein Faculty Publications Fund of New York University, Department of English.

LIBRARY OF CONGRESS CATALOGING-IN-PUBLICATION DATA
Pater, Walter, 1839–1894.
Walter Pater, three major texts.

Bibliography: p.
Contents: The Renaissance—Appreciations—
Imaginary portraits.
I. Buckler, William Earl. II. Pater,
Walter, 1839–1894. Renaissance. 1986. III. Pater,
Walter, 1839–1894. Appreciations. 1986. IV. Pater,
Walter, 1839–1894. Imaginary portraits. 1986.
V. Title. VI. Title: Walter Pater, 3 major texts.
PR5132.B8 1986 824'.8 85-29738
ISBN 0-8147-1088-3 (alk. paper)
ISBN 0-8147-1089-1 (pbk.)

All clothbound editions of New York University Press books are Smyth-sewn and printed on permanent and durable acid-free paper.

Book design by Ken Venezio

Contents

vi

Preface and Acknowledgments

Walter Pater: Three Major Texts is offered in partial fulfillment of a critical need. Though there is a larger and more intense interest in Pater at the present time than ever before, full and trustworthy texts of the books he published have never been harder to come by. Current library holdings are frequently spotty, individuals have increasing difficulty building their personal collections, and undergraduate and graduate courses are hampered by the unavailability to numbers of students of dependable editions. The present volume contains the complete texts of three of the five books Pater published during his lifetime, the other two being *Marius the Epicurean* and *Plato and Platonism*, and thus it should help to correct what has become a crippling situation.

In this edition, the text of *The Renaissance* is based on the 1893 text as edited by Donald L. Hill and issued by the University of California Press in 1980. The text of *Appreciations* is that of the New Library Edition of 1910 with one crucial difference: *Æsthetic Poetry* has been restored from the first edition of 1889, replacing *Feuillet's "La Morte,"* which was substituted for it in the second and subsequent editions of the work. To the original four critical fictions published under the title *Imaginary Portraits* in 1887, four other portraits that Pater thought of including in a second series have been added. The texts of the eight portraits are also those of the New Library Edition as follows: *A Prince of Court Painters, Denys L'Auxerrois, Sebastian van Storck*, and *Duke Carl of Rosenmold* from *Imaginary Portraits*; *The Child in the House, Emerald Uthwart*, and *Apollo in Picardy* from *Miscellaneous Studies*; and *Hippolytus Veiled* from *Greek Studies*.

Despite their respective dates of publication, I have discussed *Appreciations* before *Imaginary Portraits* in the introduction. Part of the rationale for what may seem to some a slight anachronism is given in section 3 of the introduction itself, "A caution about chronology." It should also be noted that Pater began as a literary critic and that half of the essays later collected in *Appreciations* had been published before he wrote the first of the imaginary portraits. The introduction is a critical statement; I have, like others, sacrificed the usual advantages of footnoting it to the interests of keeping it nonpolemical.

A passage of some three paragraphs in my discussion of *The Child in the House* appeared originally in an article on the poetics of Pater's prose published in *Victorian Poetry*. I am grateful to the journal's editor for permission to reprint it here. I wish also to thank the University of California Press for permission to use the text of their edition of *Walter Pater: The Renaissance* (1980), edited by Donald L. Hill. Copyright © 1980 by the Regents of the University of California.

W.E.B.

Introduction:
Walter Pater and the Art of Criticism

Walter Pater chose not simply to be a critic but to create a critical literature, as Plato had been not simply a philosopher but the creator of a philosophical literature. His goal was to give criticism its own formal characteristics, its own laws and limitations, that were analogous to but different from those of painting, sculpture, music, architecture, poetry, and prose fiction. In making that choice, Pater hoped to simplify his life without mechanizing or literalizing it and to achieve such unity with himself as circumstances and his personal organization—the complexion of his mind, spirit, and senses—made possible. He had neither the lyric nor the dramatic power to be a poet or a novelist, and, in his eyes, to be a historian or philosopher in the modern scientific sense was simply not enough. He was a dedicated student of history and philosophy, but in his valuation of things, they were, though indispensable, ancillary, subordinate in interest and importance to art's manifestations of the capacity of the human spirit to master its environment by creating for it an ideal form that was rooted in matter but infinitely more significant. Such supreme dénouements, such formal artistic proofs of man's ability in each age to create unified, self-validating alternatives to a life otherwise lacking in any substantial solace, were the objects of study Pater found worthiest of devotion; they included everything else and yet were greater than the sum of its parts. More importantly, they touched him at the deepest level, at the center of where he was personally organized; it was under their influence that he experienced the most elevated, spiritually suffused, imaginatively unified moments of his life. Art and poetry, Pater discovered earlier than we can specifically document, had for him a conversional power more intense, all-enveloping, and lasting than religion, and consistent with the generic self-regard he regularly practiced — his habit of "noting and distinguishing" his own "most intimate" characteristics as a way of gaining access to the "intimate recesses of other minds"—he conceived the idea that what was true for him was also true for others and, properly encouraged, could be true in varying degrees for a much larger number. Pater's vocation as an extraordinary type of critic was the result of that conception.

Like several of his older contemporaries who had contributed substantially to the aesthetic climate in which he worked—Tennyson, Browning, Arnold, and Swinburne, for example, as well as the Pre-Raphaelite poets and painters—Pater was fascinated with the *how* rather than with the *what* of poetry and art. How the artists of the various ages individually took charge of the same environment that had held others in thrall and transformed it in such a way as to give their creations a perpetual hold upon the interests, admiration, and ideals of the future—how the new "*form*" at the heart of each of those creations, "the new perspective, the resultant complexion, the expressiveness which familiar thoughts attain by novel juxtaposition," bore in itself "the life-giving principle" that gives art an inexhaustible capacity to alter people's lives—was the center of Pater's critical interest in poetry and art. It enabled him to write criticism that is "aesthetic" in a quite specific sense and, as he said of Wordsworth's poetry and influence, is "organic, animated, expressive" rather than "conventional, derivative, inexpressive."

Each of those older contemporaries had inherited the revolution in poetry for which Wordsworth was the chief exemplar and spokesman and had continued to experiment with new ways of positioning poetry as both the creation and the creator of the age, of finding for it a new voice that was true to its external circumstances as well as transformational. One was not more absolutely original than the other, for each embodied a unique temperament, mined a different specific poetic tradition, and crafted an exemplary personal style; but all of them registered a profound concern with form and sought to discover that point of perfect correspondence between fact and their imaginative sense of fact that would provide their personal moments of transcendence and show them how to do even better what they had been doing with relative success all along. What they impressed upon Pater was the truth of something he was already convinced of when he came to them, namely, that *style* in the full sense of that term is the ultimate test of art, the point at which art's means and ends become one. Style is the final proof of an artist's greatness and the source of the interest, admiration, and influence he holds for future generations. That is the truth to which Pater held most steadfastly throughout his writing career, the truth that he internalized and made functional in his efforts to create a critical literature.

2. PATER'S METHOD

If Pater internalized and made critically functional the persuasion that style is the ultimate test of art, the point at which art's means and ends become one and art's influence is passed on from generation to generation, then just how he did so is the primary question facing the critical student of his writings. How do they actually work? What is the internal evidence for claiming that Pater deliberately attempted to do for criticism something that, with one or two exceptions and then only in degree, had not been done before?

First of all, Pater valued art "at its eternal worth." In his "studies in art and poetry," he conceived of his *critical subject-matter* as a *creative subject*. That was his way of resolving the apparent conflict between criticism's need to be "*about* something other than itself" and art's need to be "autotelic," to be its own end and purpose. It also relieved him of the charge of obscuring the distinction between criticism and creation. The critical function of his essays is thoroughly intact, as identifiable and measurable as any other "fact" a poet or artist uses, and as indispensable. However, Pater conceived of the elements essential to authentic criticism—an understanding of the artists's "environment," his internal organization, and the "sensuous form" through which he exhibits his peculiar sense of the essential meaning of things—as themselves constituting an exemplary action or myth, and it was that conception or intuition and its consequences for his writings that enabled him to apprehend the creative process that is the critic's particular business metaphorically and to transform a work of criticism into an autonomous work of art. Pater's criticism is specifically aesthetic by virtue of his controlling interest in the pleasure of art's *form* rather than its *matter*; his creations are aesthetic in that the myths in which he mirrors life's best consummations are integral to his view of art's ideal way of modeling life. For Pater, the highest function of art is to help us to *become* something, the ultimate aesthetic ideal to make life itself a work of art.

The "new creation" for which the work of art was for Pater a "starting-point" is far more integral to his criticism than Oscar Wilde seemed to imply when describing it—just as integral, for example, as Browning's THE RING AND THE BOOK is with the OLD YELLOW BOOK or George Eliot's MIDDLEMARCH is with English provincial life in the years prior to the enactment of the Great Reform Bill. In his criticism, Pater used the internal evidence of the life and works of a painter, poet, or imaginary persona to form a single, unified image and "composed" an essay or story in which all the various elements are attuned to the perspective of that single image. In his imaginative creations, he used those images, supported by the same evidence, to show through mythic example how the spirit enmeshed in the "bewildering toils" of modern life can find at least the "equivalent for a sense of freedom." Only by attaining for his life in this world some degree of the distance from the chaos of detail, some degree of the ideal modeling, that form or style in art symbolizes can modern man experience some equivalent to the sense of freedom that he needs. Pater's transformation of a critical view of art into a sentiment or summary view of modern life is one of the primary bases for claiming that he converted criticism into an art form.

Inseparable from subject is treatment, the qualities of "line and color" by which Pater attempted to make his insights expressive. Language is part of it, and much of the immediate pleasure of

Pater's writings comes from the language. He so regularly avoids the vocabulary coded into previous criticism that his use of a word or phrase made familiar by a predecessor is usually a frank if indirect acknowledgment of its public source. Characteristically, he uses words of general currency in slightly altered but apt and gratifying ways, the originality of resonance and suggestiveness that results from their new contexts giving them the force of metaphors even when their figurative intent is not explicit. The individuality of his language is the result of Pater's having followed his conviction that "in aesthetic criticism the first step towards seeing one's object as it really is, is to know one's own impression as it really is, to discriminate it, to realise it distinctly." The only way a writer can show that he has done that is to show that he has found the right word to describe it, and since sincerity or personal authenticity is the issue here as surely as it is in poetry, the words cannot be conventional, merely orthodox, or facile. The question being "What is this song or picture, this engaging personality presented in life or in a book, to *me?*" the answer must come from an individual mind touched with an individual emotion and be proof of the individual's capacity for both originality and truth. Though Pater dissented from Matthew Arnold's call for classical simplicity and directness in language, urging instead a varied language befitting a varied need—"reserved or opulent, terse, abundant, musical, stimulant, academic"—he agreed with Arnold's principle of subordination and relevance. "The style is the man," but it is also the subject, and the language of criticism, like the language of creation, must serve its purpose of conveying the "inward sense" of things that are themselves, in part at least, outside. Language that calls attention to itself at the expense of function merely confesses the lack of a genuine "quickening motive within." Pater himself scrupulously observed that principle even where one may be tempted by the charm of his language to think that he has not done so.

The color of language works together with the architecture of line. Pater was an admirer of logical structure in writing as proof of its intellectual dexterity and "comprehensive reason." Such structure is, he said, a sign of wholesomeness and a source of delight; the lack of it shows that the initiating intuition was faulted and the thought structure organically incomplete. The words he used to characterize architectural design—"insight, foresight, retrospect, in simultaneous action"—are perfectly applicable to his own essays. Their endings are implicit in their beginnings, and their central turning-points look both backward and forward.

Treatment is larger than language and architecture, though they are certainly indispensable. Treatment also includes, besides its tendency in all art to absorb and be absorbed by subject itself, the angle of vision from which things are comprehended. Pater looked at art in its relation to life from a double perspective, each part of which has an inner and an outer dimension. On the one hand, he was a child of the new age, was irreversibly modern; on the other hand, he depended ultimately on an inner authority and was essentially, organically, self-referential.

From beginning to end—from, say, *Coleridge's [Prose] Writings* (1866) and *Winckelmann* (1867) to *Style* (1888)—Pater showed the keenest awareness of the spiritual condition of man in his modern situation; he acknowledged it as his own situation and accepted it as the "environment" within whose imperatives he had to work if he hoped to achieve anything constructive in criticism. Even more important to the way he practiced his craft, that acute modern consciousness actually monitored his choice of critical subject-matter and the design and purpose of his myths. Pater welcomed modernism as a challenge and an opportunity. It is, he said, "a world of fine gradations and subtly linked conditions, shifting intricately as we ourselves change and bids us, by a constant clearing of the organs of observation and perfecting of analysis, to make what we can of these. To the intellect, the critical spirit, these subtleties of effect are more precious than anything else." Pater considered Romantic efforts to harken back to a medieval worldview mere vague dreams that, if realized, would have catastrophic results, and in his first published essay, he took measure, through Coleridge, of the great current of idealist thought that had flowed into England from Germany at the beginning of the nineteenth century. He acknowledged the contribution it had made to a positivistic modern orthodoxy that, without its challenge, would have been less self-critical and more facile. But he found critically unacceptable the theoretical, meta-physical, and absolutist principles upon which, as a system of perception and thought, it was based. The Hellenism to which he did subscribe was metaphoric rather than literally historical, an ideal representation of what modern man might make of his life if he accepted his earthly estate as what *is* and used his creative human resources to become what the example of the classical Greeks shows he can *be*.

The self-referential quality of Pater's writings, already apparent in the way he presented himself as a spokesman for the modern spirit against the brilliant, exemplary, and impossible position of Coleridge, requires some delicacy of handling. That self-reference was a fundamental principle of criticism for Pater, everyone acknowledges in one form or another. It is the distinctive premise, the "first step," of the *Preface* to THE RENAISSANCE. The need for delicacy is in one's assessment of the way that premise actually works in the essays and fictions. That he did not intend to relegate criticism to the subjectivity, caprice, and mannerisms of the individual critic is clear enough. Pater was not only one of the most sensuous of critics, but also one of the most ascetic. The "vision within" that he postulated as critically indispensable operates only relatively and under the conditions of knowledge, discrimination, and distinctness. While conceding that "human language" is "evanescent and delicate" rather than absolute, Pater required that "one's own impression" be an "absolutely sincere apprehension" as judged by those sensitive enough to be critics and "by others 'who have intelligence' in the matter." Thus what appears to be permissive from a conventional critical point of view is in fact conscientious to the point of severity—more severe, for example, than Arnold's premise that it modifies and as severe as Newman's conditions for an act of religious faith. Those same conditions of knowledge, discrimination, and distinctness also undercut the applicability to Pater's critical writings of such an overinclusive term as *autobiographical*. If one is sensitive enough to be in the business of criticism and accepts those who have intelligence in the matter as his judges, then almost certainly one is going to be as much concerned that his impression be worthy as that it be his own. That means that he will make it the best he can in light of the best he can know in an environment of which he is as much the creator as the creature—an example of Arnold's "best self" in the context of "the best that is thought and known." While that does not negate the crucial subjective referentiality of criticism, it conditions or types it, pushing it toward metaphoric or imaginative representativeness.

The Pater of the literary text, as distinct from some vaguer Pater we are constantly tempted to make biographical guesses about, was intimate or self-referential by carefully calculated critical design. He was an empiricist of the critical consciousness, a Baconian of the imaginative mind, and since art is both an object and a process having the power, and with the power the duty, to "Suffice the eye and save the soul beside," no critical inventory of its data can be adequate that does not account for all of its defining properties, including its "'glory of motion.'" Criticism had customarily concentrated on "the authority of the eye"—on art as an object—and Pater's use of such terms as "sensuous form" to characterize art tends to confirm rather than challenge the art object's primary importance in both creation and criticism. But art even as an object is an embodiment of the soul's becomings, and one can know what it is only by knowing what went into the making of it, how it came to be. Evidence for any but a mechanical and irrelevant insight into that process is the internal evidence of the object itself, and our only empirical access to it is a discriminating knowlege of how it affects us—what we become, how our natures are modified, under its immediate influence. Such empiricism of the self, such subjective knowledge of what we become under the art object's immediate influence, cannot be any more arbitrary or capricious than any other inductively based knowledge. Our individuality may make it original; only practiced conscientiousness can make it valid. Unless it has about it a sort of "poetry of nature," either the art object is itself false or we have a mistaken impression of it.

Pater's self-referentiality works under such a strict critical condition. He did not become a Sandro Botticelli or a Charles Lamb, and he did not create them in his own image and likeness. He became something under their immediate influence, his nature was modified in an ideal way by the power of their presence, their ideal individuality struck such a deeply sympathetic, such an intimate, chord in his individuality that his knowledge of his best self, his own ideal possibilities, was profoundly enriched. Thus, though his response was personal and absolutely sincere, it was also exemplary and impersonal. The "poetry of nature" that the poets and painters had revealed by modeling in sensuous form their own ideal individuality had found a correspondence in the poetry of his own nature, and he knew that the more perfectly he reproduced it, the more truly and ideally critical the result would be. The demand for intimacy in its literature was a hallmark of the age; it was also a demand of its criticism for any critic who, like Pater, understood its spiritual causes and its creative possibilities. What as a critic he attempted to do was to yield to it in order to master it, to be intimate in a genuinely critical way. Thus the role he assumed is representative as well as intimate; he registers from deep inside himself the imaginative power deep inside the work of art to illustrate the spiritual modeling through self-knowledge that is the ideal result of art in people's lives.

3. A CAUTION ABOUT CHRONOLOGY

Whether or not one concludes from the internal evidence of his life and works that Pater succeeded in making a work of art of his own life—that he mastered his environment by drawing on his own creative resources refined and reinforced by close, constructive study of the legacy of sympathetic human beings in Western history and effected what was for his life an ideal or exemplary consummation—there is good reason to examine him as he examined others, namely, for the single unifying image to which everything we know about him contributes but to which everything is distinctly subordinate. Pater had a history, of course, as the chronology following this introduction shows, but its dates are less important than the unity in variety of interests it reflects. Pater was one of the least linear of writers, and though we have a dependable record of his publication dates, we know relatively little about the time at which he conceived an idea or when he actually worked at putting it into writing. After a careful study of Pater's reading program, one scholar has recently asserted that we should not look for new ideas in Pater after 1873, the year his first book was published. That may seem a startling observation about a writer who held that "what we have to do is be forever curiously testing new opinions and courting new impressions, never acquiescing in a facile orthodoxy" and who bid us to stay abreast of the perpetual changes in our environment and in ourselves "by a constant clearing of the organs of observation and perfecting of analysis," but it is probably true. During the fifteen-year period from the fall of 1858 to the winter of 1873 and more especially during the decade between his election as a probationary fellow of Brasenose College and the publication of THE RENAISSANCE, Pater undertook a wonderfully productive regimen of critical study that included everything that comes under the umbrella of the humanities. He took only second-class honors in Literae Humaniores at Queen's College, but that was largely the result of the diversity and individuality of his interests, not of any lack of capacity or discipline in the larger vocational sense. Pater was not a formal systematist or theorist, but he was an exemplary methodologist and conceptualist, and whenever he was determined to master something—a subject-matter, a style, a mode of regard—he devised a personal method for enforcing and measuring his progress. As his writings show, he was as severe in his exclusions as in his inclusions; he padded nothing and wasted nothing. But he had a highly associative mind and was perpetually making connections that boldly scaled both time and subject-matter, while at the same time he was finely critical, regularly making distinctions and differentiations worthy of a formal philosopher without any of the cold-blooded manner to which he found systematic philosophers prone in their handling of ideas. Based on the character and quality of his mind, his program of reading in the 1860s, and the wide range of reference even in his earliest writings, it is a fair speculation that Pater's writing agenda was fairly complete before his first book was published. In other words, his canon probably already existed in the seed by, say, 1869–1871 and had merely to undergo the organic process of fully flowering. New subject-matters would attract his fancy, and new narrative structures would satisfy his habit of experimenting with formal modes of imaginative and critical regard. But his summary view of modern man's condition and need had taken final shape, the acts of writing in his life being in the nature of a complex imaginative organism simply fulfilling the law of its being. One of the constituent elements in mankind's spiritual nature found, in English at any rate, its uniquely graceful expression—informed, circumspect, complete, and, in the context he supplies for it, persuasive—in the writings of Walter Pater.

4. THE RENAISSANCE

Pater's purpose in THE RENAISSANCE is to make wholly secular knowledge spiritually powerful, to contribute to a "renaissance of the spirit" of individuals and of the age by creating superbly crafted portraits of a representative number of historical personages who, each in a distinctive way, had mastered their environment and contributed to "one complete type of general culture." Neither their environment nor their particular way of mastering it could be revived, but the sustaining human *ideal* that they had realized in their lives others could realize in theirs if they would identify the choice element in their common humanity exemplified there and "be divided against themselves"—that is, struggle against their humanity's baser elements—in trying to revive it.

The Renaissance of the fifteenth century in Italy could not be revived; in fact, it had not survived the sixteenth century, having decayed into the Saint Martin's summer of du Bellay and the Pleiad. Nor indeed had it begun in the Italy of Leonardo, Michelangelo, and Raphael; it had begun in France in the Middle Ages. It had already begun when speculative humanism began to break up the narrowness, even the refined narrowness, of the medieval mind and to enlarge it; when the style of a legend began to take precedence in persons' tastes over its mere matter, such qualities as narrative strength and narrative sweetness to be more highly valued than mere story-line; when liberty of thought, feeling, and imagination—the inherent human need for intellectual experimentation, sensuous pleasure, and the unimpeded freedom to express in a great variety of ways the spirit's deepest intuitions of things—began to take a fresh hold on people's consciousness.

The Renaissance was already well advanced when *earthly passion*, a free play of *human* affections, assertions of the liberty of the *heart*, and a love of *beauty for its own sake* began to assume the character of a rival religion. It had passed into a state of decay when enthusiasm turned to melancholy, prospect to retrospect, and a once splendid grandeur, a once great revolutionary cause, became something fragile, delicate, vulnerable, and merely tantalizing. Thus the great Renaissance transformed itelf into the restless, exquisite, violent, trivial, deceitful culture of sixteenth-century France, whose spokesmen, like du Bellay, despite their "courtly and well handled" manner and their "remarkable daintiness of hand," express a "sentiment of ruins," a "sentiment of the grandeur of nothingness." But though the historical Renaissance cannot be revived—and misguided, dreamlike efforts to do so could lead to a period of cultural catastrophe analogous to that described in *Denys L'Auxerrois*—the "renaissance idea" can be revived; it is archetypal and possible in any age.

Pater reinforced the contemporary applicability of THE RENAISSANCE in numerous ways. The *Preface* is an introduction to a "complete criticism" of both art and life. In it, Pater effectively dismantles the conventional objective-subjective categories and encourages the "aesthetic critic" to give at least as much attention to how he feels or thinks about an object as to how clearly he "sees" it. Unless he knows what is going on inside him under its immediate influence, knows who he is or can be in its illuminations of the self, little that the critic sees with his scientific eye can have much meaning, for him or for those he addresses. In the most graceful manner, Pater makes it clear that abstract theories of art are "unmeaning and useless"—useful sometimes by accident, almost never by intent—and dismisses "metaphysical questions" as just as "unprofitable" in art as elsewhere. The rule he urges upon his readers is adopted from Sainte-Beuve and is as secular as it is practical: "*To confine themselves to knowing beautiful things at first hand, and to nourish themselves thereby as discriminating amateurs, as accomplished humanists.*"

The *Conclusion* is the most urgent exhortation Pater ever wrote. He reminds his readers that they are only the momentary result of a concurrence of "phosphorous and lime and delicate fibres," elements that will soon be on their way to other concurrences. People have but this "interval," this "short day of frost and sun," to experience what of the "flamelike" their life possesses—its capacity to form images, to see designs, in what appears to be a "clear, perpetual outline." Pater then implores them (the word is not too strong) to discriminate between dullness and passion, orthodoxy and eagerness, stereotyped habit and self-renewal. Citing Rousseau, Voltaire, and Victor Hugo as representative " 'children of this world' "—men who accepted their earthly interval as all human life is or means and made something spectacular out of it—he celebrates his belief that "love of art for its own sake" offers to the wisest of men the greatest chance of "success in life," their brief interval filled with the greatest number of superbly qualitative moments.

The *Conclusion* to THE RENAISSANCE is an intensely passionate, magnificently cadenced vocalization of the "good news" of aestheticism, but Pater will never again publish anything even approximately like it. Though he will continue to endorse its sentiments for the rest of his life, he will never again experience its peculiar combination of intuition and emotion. In its original form, the *Conclusion* was the last part of an essay on the "new poetry" of the Pre-Raphaelites, *Poems by William Morris*, the earlier parts of which would be revised and republished under the title *Aesthetic Poetry* in the first edition of APPRECIATIONS. Following *Winckelmann* by a year, *Poems by William Morris* contained an answer to the crucial but troublesome question that stood between the very special kind of self-modeling achieved by the eighteenth-century proto-Hellenist Winckelmann and passed on by him to the Olympian Goethe, on the one hand, and, on the other, the more general and widely accessible, the archetypal, renaissance of the spirit that could and finally did supply the motive for THE RENAISSANCE. The question was the one of revival already touched on, in its more generalized form a question of the functional relevance of a cultural past to a cultural present that in its accidents and even perhaps to some degree in its essence has undergone massive, irreversible change. The answer made not only THE RENAISSANCE but also Pater's life as a man of letters possible: "We cannot truly conceive the age: we can conceive the element it has contributed to our culture: we can treat the subjects of the age bringing that into relief." A few paragraphs later, Pater composed the original version of what is now the *Conclusion*, and its critical self-assuredness, its emotional headiness, its frank secularist alliances, and its epiphanic cadences are all the result of an intuitive breakthrough that opened the idealized past to the most thoroughly modern of idealizing presents and gave its critic a creative mission, in the best sense a religion, to which he could be ever faithful and in that faith flourish. It would require exercises of an Ignatian rigor, but it made a wholly secular ideal clear and worthy and showed him that what he had the greatest capacity and sympathy for was at one with the social and moral meaning of his life.

Leonardo da Vinci was the first fruit of the process of search and discovery that had climaxed in Pater's critical study of the poetry of William Morris. Having defined his ideal of aesthetic criticism by pinpointing the critical-creative principle that underlay that "first typical specimen of aesthetic poetry," Pater submitted both the ideal and his ability to realize it to the challenge of one of the greatest masters of the Italian Renaissance around whom a massive literature of fact and legend had been accumulating for centuries. It was adventurous to the point of foolhardiness on the part of a young Oxford fellow who had thus far published nothing under his own name and contradicts any inclination to characterize Pater as timid. He was as bold as Nietzsche, but very different in his choice of strategies. The experiment succeeded magnificently. In a relatively short essay, Pater characterized the life and works of Leonardo in a way that, according to Kenneth Clark, "even today, with access to Leonardo's notebooks and to a vast corpus of scholarship, we cannot improve on."

Leonardo da Vinci is a model of the kind of critical literature Pater sought to create. Its architecture is flawless, the gradual, perfectly scaled enlargement of an image whose essential lines are drawn in the first paragraph. The process by which the image is to be given life and carriage, made both dramatic and representative, is then given in the second paragraph. Even external evidence is to be valued only at its internal worth, and "legends" may be imaginatively valid even though no historical validity can be ascribed to them. In short, the creative burden is on the creator. The raw facts will not speak for themselves, however dramatically they may seem to do so in the finished artistic product; they must be found, penetrated, and ordered by the imagination for their inner significance to be illusively self-revealing. The language of the essay is always precise, graduating here and there into various shades and degrees of color, just as analysis assumes from time to time a more or less intense dramatic tenor, the critic identifying through feeling with the experiences he recounts. The biographical facts are narrated in such a way as to give history the character of spiritual romance, meaning, as Browning had recently said, "beyond the facts." In part, this is the result of Pater's concentration on the inner life of Leonardo, using biographical and historical facts simply to provide a chronology for the idiosyncrasies, forward movements, disgusts, ambitions, precarious gambles, exemplary self-salvation, and final self-exile of the soul; part is the effect of his having apprehended Leonardo in the symbolic role of naked, existential man—aloof and alone, wholly self-possessed, untouched by conventional opinions and by passing political events, intolerant of the prosaic aspect of things, having only an inner oracle to which to refer all ideas, speculations, and schemes. Pater calls Leonardo the representative of the true spiritual Renaissance, but nowhere else in the book does he characterize the Renaissance in Italy in the fifteenth century in such relentlessly secularist terms. Pater's Leonardo is at once fascinating and repellent as we might be fascinated and repelled by the secularist ideal of abandoning all of our conventional orthodoxies and taking our chances in a world void of all pure and applied metaphysics.

At the exact center of *Leonardo da Vinci* is the sentence that defines the crisis upon which both the critical and the creative interests of the piece turn: "This struggle between the reason and its ideas, and the senses, the desire of beauty, is the key to Leonardo's life in Milan." Leonardo has brought to the knowledge that his boundless curiosity about man and nature has enabled him to acquire a style that is no longer adequate to that knowledge. "His problem was the transmutation of ideas into images."

He is saved by a combination of secularism and aestheticism. On the one hand, he is wholly indifferent to the so-called moral and metaphysical implications of his studies; on the other, he will not compromise in any degree his faith in art for art's sake, that is, in what makes art art and not something else—the light, line, color, image, the novel impression, the exquisite effect, that *are* art's purpose. That is what enables Leonardo to survive his crisis and save himself for art; it is ultimately what gives him complete rule over his subjects, over his restless mind's remotest knowledge and lore, and enables him to bend them to "purely artistic ends." His fidelity to art for art's sake even in the midst of an almost violent discontent with the common or conventional aspects of things nurtures in him the "perfect patience" that waits absolutely on that "moment of *bien-être*" in which, the "alchemy" being complete, he sees into the heart of things and uses line, light, color, and image to refine it to "a subdued and graceful mystery."

That Pater has used his creative imagination and his superb craftsmanship to convert the subject-matter of the critic into the subject of the artist is clear. He has critically characterized the life and works of Leonardo in a way that art critics have not been able to "improve on," and he has transformed that criticism into an ascetic parable of what persons four centuries later can do to bring about a renaissance in their own lives. The critical fact has not been sacrificed to the creative intuition; both are there, and neither is obscure.

This last point is sometimes contradicted by fine critics of Pater when applying it to the most famous passage in the essay, that on *La Gioconda.* They claim for it the status of an original "poem" and, ignoring its critical function, speak of it as "Pater's vision" or "Pater's idea of Lady Lisa." (Yeats called it the first modern poem, set it up as verse, and printed it as the first piece in the OXFORD BOOK OF MODERN VERSE.) But neither the text of the essay nor Pater's distinction as a critic will sustain such a position, and the result is a serious disjunction in the fruitful integration of criticism and creation described above.

What Pater is trying to do in this passage is to bring his *understanding* of his *impression* of what the object in itself really is as close as possible to the "object as in itself it really is" without disturbing a relationship between the two that is at once crucial and appropriate. In creating one kind of art object out of the complex, concentrated stimulus of a different kind of art object, he is trying to keep free the tendency of one art form to "pass into the condition" of another and to lend to it and take from it "new forces"—what he called *"Anders-streben"*—while at the same time preserving the identity of each art form and acknowledging the dependence of the one on the other. In that way, he wishes to achieve two ends simultaneously—to assert the artistic integrity of his own critical creation and to acknowledge its dependence, even in independence, on the imaginative stimulus of Leonardo as concentrated and summarized in this one painting. Nowhere is the painting allowed to become secondary to the criticism. Pater sees everything up close and imaginatively, but all that has made the picture "refined" and "expressive," "subdued," "graceful," and mysterious is the result of Leonardo's genius, not his. All the "strange thoughts and fantastic reveries and exquisite passions" registered there so suggestively are Leonardo's, as Pater has been at pains to show in the earlier pages of the piece; all of the "thoughts and experience of the world" that have "etched and moulded" this "outward form" are the result of Leonardo's curious interests and pursuits—his obsession with the female face, his reverence for the extreme subtleties of nature, his restlessness of mind and temperament, his curiosity about everything apropos of the "mechanics" of nature and the nature of man.

Pater enters the two relevant paragraphs through the phrase "the seventh heaven of symbolical expression," and that concept conditions his remarks on the painting. It has a "subdued and graceful mystery" undisturbed by any "crude symbolism," but it employs "a cryptic language for fancies all [Leonardo's] own," not Pater's. The passage is in fact a recomposition of phrases, figures, and critical judgments from the earlier parts of the essay, and though Pater works them into new and interesting combinations, they constitute a reprise rather than a new departure. The "fantastic rocks" are echoes of Leonardo's fascination with geology and hydrology, with bizarre rock formations, especially in relation to water, and the figure "as in some faint light under sea" is an adaptation of earlier images, "as in faint light of eclipse, or in some brief interval of falling rain at daybreak, or through deep water." The face has, in a sense, already been promised by the powerful effect on Leonardo of Verrocchio, his ambitious, accomplished master, and the endless recollective reciprocation that emerged from Leonardo's apprenticeship with him.

That Lady Lisa had been a vampire, a Sappho, a Thaïs, a Leda, a Saint Anne, a Medea, a Mary Magdalen, a Lucrezia Borgia, and so forth *ad infinitum*, was one of the more obvious demands of Leonardo's imaginative conception. The really exhilarating thing about her portrait—what makes it so masterful a revelation of Leonardo's artistic genius—is the recognition that to La Gioconda herself all of this has been "but as the sound of lyres and flutes," a sort of elegant musical competition between Apollo and Pan, and that the artist has himself refined it all to "a subdued and graceful mystery . . . that pleases the eye while it satisfies the soul"—has, in other words, subjected its vast historical content to the "delicacy with which it has moulded the changing lineaments, and tinged the eyelids and hands." Even the final conceit—of Lady Lisa "as the embodiment of the old fancy" of eternal life and "the symbol of the modern idea" of mankind as a "summing up" of "all modes of thought and life"—is Leonardo's, not Pater's. That is what *La Gioconda* says insofar as a Renaissance painter could have said it, philosophy's modern extensions being only examples of time's endless ongoing variations. The idea inheres both in the painting's composite intuition and in the perpetuation statement that its very existence makes.

The conflict between knowledge and beauty that Leonardo was able to resolve by virtue of his indifference to metaphysical questions in favor of nature and man just as they are found and his uncompromising fidelity to art for art's sake has its counterparts in the other essays in THE RENAISSANCE. In *The Poetry of Michelangelo*, the poetry addressed is neither that of Michelangelo's verses nor that of the "poems in stone" he executed. The poetry is in himself, in his personal struggle for the sweetness he loved and lacked to make less barbaric the strength he possessed and feared. Michelangelo, like Goethe in a different medium, used what is now called the "journal method," seeing himself whole and mastering himself through artistic works that are the external expression of the struggle for self-conquest of a great, rugged, idealizing nature. The prayer his works project would run something like this: O Lord, let me who have known so much inner violence know inner sweetness too; let me carve sweetness out of the great block of my strength—*ex forte dulcedo! Sandro Botticelli* shows how one may deal successfully with a feeling of sympathy and affection "for humanity in its uncertain condition," how one may yet invest with "a character of loveliness and energy" one's "consciousness of the shadow on [him] of the great things from which humanity shrinks." *Pico della Mirandola* is the celebration of a great and generous faith in man, of a humanism that cannot rest content with the parochial idea that the sweet reasonableness of Christianity and "the natural charm of pagan story" cannot be reconciled in an inspired vision of man's "heart and imagination." Indeed, the true meaning of inspiration is its hidden subject and the quality of their implicit faith in man the criterion by which moral or intellectual systems as different as medieval Christianity and modern inductive science are measured. *Luca della Robbia* invokes the charm of obscure persons who stand in the trough between spectacular monuments of artistic accomplishment and who yet find in the inherited conventions of their craft a "subtler sense of originality" and capture within their "narrow limits" the "personal quality," "profound expressiveness," *intimité* or "soul" of things. *The School of Giorgione* exemplifies the call upon our interest of those who achieve their particular sense of freedom by creating an idyllic world of harmony and refinement, an earthly paradise of spun gold, with music, landscape, artistic appointments, and sensibilities the most exquisite. *Winckelmann* is the portrait of a man imprisoned in a culture wholly alien to his spirit who yet burns inwardly with such an intense intuition of a lost earthly ideal that he virtually wishes himself transported out of a dark age into the light of spiritual freedom and shows others infinitely greater than himself the way to it. These are representative variations on the "renaissance idea" that emerges through the criticism of THE RENAISSANCE. They show how Pater used criticism of art as a criticism of life, how by making the creative ends of the various essays one with their critical means, he authored a critical literature that is both about something else and autotelic, critical and creative too.

5. APPRECIATIONS

Pater's APPRECIATIONS is one of the two best volumes of literary criticism the nineteenth century produced, the other volume being Matthew Arnold's ESSAYS IN CRITICISM. Together they represent the finest thread of the English critical sensibility from the decline of Coleridge to the rise of T.S. Eliot, and their influence persists despite vigorous controversy today. Their critical emphases were different, as are the pressures they continue to exert on critical practice, but no one in the last hundred years has made a better case for the value to a modern technological society of the critical study of literature. On that subject, they were continuous with each other, and important technical differences between them should not be allowed to obscure what is vastly more important, namely, the intelligence, range, and modernity of their common faith in the humanistic ideals of which literature is the primary expression.

Arnold was the nearest and most compelling example of self-modeling available to Pater. As he sat in the Oxford theater term after undergraduate term in the late 1850s and early 1860s listening to the Professor of Poetry, Pater was in the throes of his own spiritual formation. What he was witnessing was more than ideas and arguments; he was witnessing, in words soon to be made poignantly exhilarating by John Henry Newman, a "living intelligence," a "Mind and its Beliefs and its sentiments." Pater was witnessing his own vocation taking shape, a way of life in which writing would be the essence of moral action and self-modeling the essential message. Pater was no ordinary listener and would have recognized the formal strategies, the craftsmanship and artistry, of Arnold's lecture-essays and would have been unusually susceptible to their influence. Pater knew and deeply admired Arnold the critic in poetry before he read or heard Arnold the critic in prose, and it was perhaps inevitable that he would hear in the latter the voice of the earlier poet and the "poetics" of the prose—those accents, metaphors, echoes, analogies by which a subject is elevated and enlarged beyond its factual, analytical, assertive level. Pater would have been immediately aware that the lecture-essays that make up ESSAYS IN CRITICISM, for example, belong to an order of creativity in the literary art that is more all-encompassing than literary criticism as ordinarily conceived and practiced, and would have seen that Arnold's explicit efforts to enlarge the field and to clarify and deepen the function of criticism resulted in the creation of an imaginative structure or literary text that far exceeds its working metaphor and reaches, rather in the manner of poetry, toward life itself in one of its representative aspects. Arnold treats ideas, not discursively, but, again in the manner of poetry, as imaginative processes which we as readers participate in at an experiential level that is deeper and more affective than mere intellectual participation. In Arnold's example, coming at a crucial moment in his self-formation, Pater found just the critical-creative encouragement and modeling he needed. Moreover, that influence came to him at the right temperamental and stylistic distance. He was not an Arnold nor was meant to be, but in Arnold's critical essays he saw an image of his own future possibilities, a creative activity in which he could be wholly himself, making such personal advances upon his model as his temperament, taste, and talent would sustain.

No serious student of Arnold and Pater will deny that Pater made those advances or that they needed to be made. Arnold had been a discontented modern and had not listened to the poetic voices that were new. He had not been responsive to the "*Anders-streben*"or striving toward otherness among the arts, and his emphasis had been on adequate ideas rather than on sensuous forms. His table of artistic discovery had included little or no data from the visual arts, and he had not modified his generalizations about art to include them. He had no more than a cultivated generalist's knowledge of the Continental Renaissance, and although he shared Pater's enthusiasm for Goethe, he was reverential toward Spinoza, whom Pater considered something of a cold-blooded transcendentalist, and dismissive of Hegel, to whom Pater put himself to school. Arnold had a highly refined sense of style that almost never failed him, but in ESSAYS IN CRITICISM he tended to make style adjunct to other considerations and to treat it seriously but more or less along the way; though he would not have subscribed to a twentieth-century history-of-ideas approach to literature, Arnold's leaning was toward classical ideas, "the best that has been thought and known."

Pater spoke for a generation coming on that had less faith in the efficacy of ideas and the strategy of measuring their relative adequacy. Ideas were certainly essences of the mind and one of the most distilled substances, so to speak, with which literature concerned itself, but ideas per se were not the ultimate significance of literature as a fine art. What the aesthetic critic understood by poetry was "all literary production which attains the power of giving pleasure by its form, as distinct from its matter." Direct experience of a holistic kind was what Pater sought—life's infinity of details having undergone the metamorphosis of ideal or typical form and been stripped thereby of all the primary effects of mere sectarianism. Ideas might attain that status, as they had in Plato, but then they became forms and images, rather than simply ideas. Pater spoke for a growing number of persons for whom style in this holistic sense was the raison d'être of both literature and life, and therefore style was the inevitable and controlling subject of APPRECIATIONS.

Though the book begins with the essay *Style*, Pater wrote it only after deciding to make a volume of selected literary essays written over almost a quarter of a century. Though unavoidable in light of the book's purpose, Pater found the abstract nature of the subject thoroughly taxing, and this may account for one critic's assertion with reference to the essay that "we do not believe that the style is the man when we read Pater," as it was certainly Oscar Wilde's reason for calling it "the least successful" essay in the volume. *Style* is to APPRECIATIONS what *The Function of Criticism at the Present Time* is to ESSAYS IN CRITICISM, and Pater did not like some of the ambiguities of the role it cast him in. Not only was the subject idea-centered rather than a hands-on evaluation of an individual author's life and works, but it would also inevitably seem to be a credo-manifesto and a public *apologia* for his own style. Nevertheless, it is his essay, and "the style is the man" in the circumstances in which he chose to place himself. There is not just one style that is the real Pater, though a critic may form his own ideal of Pater and "believe" him only when his style fits that ideal. APPRECIATIONS itself has several styles—the style of *Aesthetic Poetry* and *Dante Gabriel Rossetti,* of *Charles Lamb* and *Sir Thomas Browne,* and of the three essays on Shakespeare; moreover, the style of *Wordsworth* is different from that of *Style* itself and of *Postscript* (formerly called *Romanticism*). Throughout his career, Pater tended to absorb into his most sympathetic and best essays significant characteristics of the style of the subject he was writing about and to practice what he called a fine stylistic mimicry. It was a manifestation of the principle of intimacy by which he tried to achieve an insider's view of the subject while maintaining sufficient detachment to make genuine criticism possible. That was his way of proportioning the elements in what we call "empathy," a term that Vernon Lee brought into general use partially under Pater's influence. It was impossible to empathize with an eclectic idea of style, but the essay's lack of intimacy except in the several pages devoted to Flaubert, while it may make *Style* less generally representative of Pater, makes it no less credibly his own. It shows how superbly well Pater could treat a subject under the mandate of conscientiousness rather than the call of personal sympathy.

The character of *Style* is inseparable from its audience and its purpose. It is not an aesthetic reverie, an abstract philosophical meditation, or a lyrical celebration of the palpable mysteries of a great style; rather, it is an analytical, comprehensive, and graceful but tough-minded essay in practical criticism. Its subject is craftsmanship, not inspiration, and though Pater insists that nothing can come of nothing, workmanship of any worth being dependent on a "quickening motive within" the workman, he wishes to dispel untenable *a priori* assumptions and mechanical *a posteriori* conclusions about his subject and to disabuse his audience of the infatuating illusion that good craftsmanship is equivalent to great art.

Pater addresses his remarks to an audience of critical readers with more than the usual interest in literature as a fine art and some ambition to be writers. It is an audience the times themselves are likely to produce, young people caught up in the surge of modernism, with a limitless "curiosity" about the "chaotic variety and complexity of its interests"and a desire to have some say in the matter. Pater has felt very much as his audience feels; he admires the vigorous response of literary motive to the new realities of the times. It is both good in itself and a dramatic illustration of how literature has always reinvigorated itself. The harsh formal distinctions between poetry and prose characteristic of the arbitrary aesthetic psychology of the eighteenth century having been dismissed, prose in the nineteenth century entered the lists of artistic competition as a free agent of the imagination and, by virtue of its internal resources and the characteristics of the times, became "the special and opportune art of the modern world." It rejected all *a priori* efforts to limit its scope and became "as varied as humanity itself reflecting on the facts of its latest experience."

But sympathy from a conscientious teacher who knows whereof he speaks always has its price, and so does Pater's. Even welcome revolutions are dangerous, and the danger of this revolution in style is that, having been born of chaos and curiosity, it may foster only chaos and curiosity. That, Pater thinks, would be a misfortune, and the essay's implicit purpose is to remind the reader that, in the long rhythms of art and life, there are demonstrated values that the artist neglects at a very considerable price both to his art and to the artistic tradition of which he is the inheritor and, in his generation at least, the guardian. Thus the central concern of *Style*, the first essay in APPRECIATIONS, is very close to that of the last essay, *Postscript (Romanticism)*. In both, Pater casts himself in the role of a sympathetic Romantic Modernist giving his fellow Romantic Modernists some classical literary advice. Their curiosity, their "all-pervading naturalism," has served them well; it has modernized them and prepared them to deal creatively, as their prose shows to a degree their poetry does not, with the "chaotic variety and complexity" of modern life. But the creators of an age, as distinct from its creations—its artists in their active role—have a responsibility not only to mirror the age, but also to master it to some degree. As persons with a "quickening motive within," they have a gift, one of whose conditions is that the pleasures of the revel be accompanied by the responsibilities of *askesis*, which is the source of a severer kind of pleasure. In art, *askesis* takes the form of aesthetic discipline, frugality, knowledge, respect for ideal outcomes, and the willingness to go to any lengths of time, effort, and self-criticism to realize them. This is why the central movement of the essay takes the form of four propositions outlining the necessities of the subject, the most important being the "scholarly attentiveness of mind" to which Flaubert, the exemplary scholar-artist, gives such severe and personally engaged testimony.

The final paragraph of the essay, in which Pater says that "the distinction between great art and good art depend[s] immediately, as regards literature at all events, not on its form, but on the matter," has become something of a cause célèbre in the commentary on Pater. One commentator has said that it "undercuts . . . the whole of Pater's earlier insights into the nature of literary art" and another that it "astonishingly seems to repeal the special emphasis of everything that has come before." Looked at both textually and contextually, however—that is, as Pater actually phrased it and against the background both of this essay and his works generally—the paragraph justifies a very different reading. Addressed particularly to an audience of prospective young writers in the crosscurrents of modernism, *Style* insists on the austere demands of conscientious craftsmanship in an age that without it may dissipate its artistic opportunities in mere chaos and curiosity. In fact, Pater's emphasis on the severities of style and his use of Flaubert as his exemplum may, he perhaps thinks, have given rise to the misconception that mere craftsmanship is equivalent to or even a guarantee of literary greatness, and he would like to correct any such illusion. But even in a context of such important practical consequence, Pater does not "undercut" or "repeal" what was for him the operating premise of all aesthetic criticism. The key word is "immediately"—"the distinction between great art depending immediately . . . on the matter"—that is, "immediately" on the matter, but ultimately on the form.

What Pater says of the difference between great and good art is sound enough: the work of a writer who has undertaken successfully to treat "the great structure of human life" with such compass, variety, purpose, depth, and largeness of view that his work has "something of the soul of humanity in it" is to be judged greater than the work of a writer whose workmanship may be impeccable but whose aim and understanding have been conspicuously less. No deftness of technique can make great art of an essentially trivial intuition. But that leaves the issue of the ultimate significance of form untouched. Art is "inform[ed] and control[led]"—is brought into existence and enabled to hold together and exist—by form. Not only does form enable art to be distinctive and autonomous within "the great structure of human life"; it is our only universal, self-perpetuating metaphor of that great structure and the source, therefore, of such quality of pleasure as is capable of enlarging and refining our humanity. Though the relative greatness of art depends immediately on the relative greatness of its matter, matter must ultimately yield to form if we are to call it art, and the great, as distinct from the good, artist's challenge is to discover in the imagination's severest depths a form equal to the demands of the very greatest matter.

APPRECIATIONS ends where it had begun, on style in relation to the age. The final paragraph of *Postscript* was obviously an effort to adjust *Romanticism* to its new use in the volume. But it does much more than echo the language and sentiments of the opening essay and contribute to the book's coherence and shape. Written toward the end rather than the beginning of his career, the paragraph is virtually an effort on Pater's part to redirect the significance of his canon. Like *Style*, it is addressed to the producers rather than the consumers of art, telling them essentially to take heart and endure. The subjects of art are still all there, as is the need for their handling of them. Language presents a problem, requiring a special scholarly kind of attention, but "the style" is the age as well as "the man," and the nineteenth century will not only have its own style but, with a little more conscious effort on the part of its artists, it may have one of the very greatest styles of all.

Pater's tone is that of one who appears to be indifferent to critical outcomes, disposed to the view that the terms *classical* and *Romantic* as used by persons of literary experience and good sense designate equally present and valuable qualities in the history of European art, allowance, of course, being made for the special use of *classical* to identify the works of Greek and Roman antiquity. However, this appearance of indifference is by no means the critical reality. Pater turns something less than subtle irony on some of the advocates of classicism, calling them "people who would never really have been made glad by any Venus fresh-risen from the sea, and who praise the Venus of old Greece and Rome, only because they fancy her grown now into something staid and tame"; they are the people who greet every "progressive element" in literature with the lamentation, "'tis art's decline my son!'" He allows his chief internal authority, Stendhal, to describe classicism as the art of "presenting [people] with that which gave the greatest possible pleasure to their grandfathers." He characterizes Pope's poetry as exquisitely insipid and calls the "beauties" of Homer and Phidias "quiet," while allowing that they must have provoked "excitement and surprise" among those seeing them for the first time. On the other hand, Pater parades before the reader a cavalcade of admirable European Romantics—Rousseau, Meinhold, the Goethe of *Goetz von Berlichingen*, Balzac, Victor Hugo, Murger, Gautier, Senancour, Chateaubriand, Bertrand, and Stendhal, not to mention, in England, Blake, Scott, Byron, and Emily Brontë. He claims for such a Romantic writer as Victor Hugo at his best the very qualities—"energy, freshness, intelligent and masterly disposition"—that Sainte-Beuve had called "the characteristics of a genuine classic" and finds exemplary marks of Romanticism in Dante, Homer, Sophocles, Aeschylus, Euripides, and Shakespeare.

Even Pater's central thesis—that Romanticism is not a quality peculiar to a specific historical period but "rather a spirit which shows itself at all times, in various degrees, in individual workmen and their work," though it is more likely to arise in eras when the human spirit craves release from conditions of *ennui*, disillusion, and fatigue—is not quite as detached and objective as it seems. Though he makes "the desire of beauty" the common denominator of classical and Romantic art, the "fixed element in every artistic organisation," he makes "curiosity" the defining characteristic of Romanticism, leading to its "strangeness," its rebelliousness, its determination to improve man's situation, its individuality, its enthusiasm, its novelty, its excitement and surprise, its pathos, and, when curiosity and the desire for beauty are out of balance, its grotesqueness. From that catalogue of Romantic characteristics, it is clear that no new literature—no new poet, novelist, or dramatist—could hope to be interesting if the artist were not, to a significant degree, Romantic. So even if, as Pater says, artists are "born" classicists or "born" Romantics, it seems obvious that all but the most towering geniuses would be wise to be born Romantics.

Thus, toward the end of his career Pater seems to be purging some of the critical discontents he had harbored silently under the influence of Arnold. The customary critical distinction between classicism and Romanticism may do very well for consumers of art, but as guidance to its producers, it collapses by its own falseness. Artists must be both free and wise. Then, as Stendhal had said, if they have the requisite talent, their Romantic works will one day become classics.

Each of the inner essays in APPRECIATIONS has its individual way of approaching the subject of style. *Charles Lamb* and *Sir Thomas Browne* are examples of classical or Theophrastan character-writing put to modern critical uses. In *Charles Lamb*, Pater carries the critical principle of intimacy so far that the essay becomes, as he says *Love's Labours Lost* became for Shakespeare, virtually "a reflex of himself, when he has just become able to stand aside and estimate the first period" of his writing. In his estimate of Lamb's critical characteristics, we see the lineaments, not of what Pater thought he had achieved, but of the critical ideal with which he identified at a deeply intimate level. Lamb's moral effects are achieved through "a sort of boundless sympathy" for concrete details—"actual things, books, persons"—with no part of them "blurred to his vision by the intervention of mere abstract theories." He becomes for his readers the actual "creator" of the "charm of an old poet or moralist" in that what he conveys is the strength of his feeling of that charm and of its significance. He tries to be attentive and alert to "the whole process" of literary production, "tracking" it "to its starting-point in the deep places of the mind" of the artist, attempting to realize even its "half-conscious intuitions." He tries to be sensitive to every nuance or modulation in a master author's style, reaching even to the "power of delicate imitation in prose," "a fine mimicry even." His very "mission" as a literary critic is primarily concerned with fine literature's "gradations of expression, its fine judgments, its pure sense of words, of vocabulary." Like the poet of Wordsworth's *Preface* to LYRICAL BALLADS, he sees things by "the light of an understanding more entire than is possible for ordinary minds, of the whole mechanism of humanity," and he sees "also the manner, the outward mode or fashion, always in strict connexion with the spiritual condition which determined it." He is a scholar, with the scholar's retrospective vision, but the "high way of feeling developed largely by constant intercourse with the great things of literature" becomes gradually linked "in a thousand complex ways to the condition of human life," and life assumes a sort of authority from the association with such literary greats as Shakespeare. When this happens, the critic requires an atmosphere of "profound quiet . . . which has in it a kind of sacramental efficacy, working, we might say, on the principle of *opus operatum*, almost without any cooperation of one's own, towards the assertion of the higher self." The "principle of *opus operatum*" —it is the ideal form Pater seeks. Only when a work of art affects him according to that principle is he a critic in the ideal sense; when such influence is complete, the critic becomes an artist, criticism an art.

In the three essays on Shakespeare, Pater refracts the idea of style in various ways to show what a profoundly revealing mirror of human nature it is. *"Measure for Measure"* is as nearly perfect as a critical essay can be; its critical texture is as dense as poetry and demands a similar kind of scrutiny and reflection. In it, Pater makes one of the clearest, justest, most persuasive statements in English on *"poetical justice"* or the true morality of art, a statement that is wholly integral with the creative character of the essay—its design, the progress of its argument, and its expression. The "finer issues" of the first sentence grow into the "finer appreciations" of the last, and everything in between nurtures, expands, and refines that growth. The "idea of justice" involves "the idea of rights"; rights "are equivalent to that which really is, facts"; the recognition of what a person is "in his inmost nature" determines any expectation of justice at his hands; sympathy alone can discover what a person really is in the matter of "feeling and thought"; true justice, then, is "in its essence a finer knowledge through love." These are the revelations, the "finer appreciations," that true poetry "cultivates in us the power of making"; they, rather than something rougher and coarser, are poetry's natural morality.

What *"Measure for Measure"* is to style as morality, *"Love's Labours Lost"* is to style as self-criticism. In *"Love's Labours Lost,"* Pater follows the example of Shakespeare's serious playfulness in making a point whose implications modern linguistic scientists are vigorously exploring, namely, that the laws of language have "their root in the nature of things." Thus, when in the play Shakespeare stood aside and sought to estimate "the first period of his poetry," he examined his ability to handle language in action, or style, as the most revealing measure of his progress in dealing with human nature itself. Pater's subject in *Shakespeare's English Kings* is "true imaginative unity." The idea of unity, he says, is an internal property of the imagination itself, unity of effect being recognizable only according to the individual reader's capacity through sympathy to penetrate the sensuous form in which it manifests itself to the imaginative reality within. In poetry, it is the divine right of language to be that senuous form, and what Shakespeare's kings share with each other and with all persons elevated above the prosaic and the trite of the ordinary human condition is the gift of eloquence. Richard II is "the most sweet-tongued of them all," and so he is the particular embodiment of Pater's view of the English history plays' universal theme, that though we may wait upon grief to discover who we really are, when some combination of inner defect and outward circumstance brings us down, style—the language of who in truth we are—is the ultimate instrument of such redemption as, in our representativeness, we can achieve. Through it, we enjoy "something of the royal prerogative" both to reveal the innermost reality of ourselves and "to obscure, or at least to attune and soften," the extremes of our grief.

Æsthetic Poetry and *Dante Gabriel Rossetti* have as their subject the style of the "new poetry" of the age. William Morris and the mentor of his first poetic period, Rossetti, were Pater's spiritual and aesthetic contemporaries in that they practiced their craft in the first full phase of modernism as Pater defined it and took it fully into account both in formulating their idea of what a genuinely modern poetry should be and in actually selecting the subjects of their poems and determining their poetic manner. "Aesthetic poetry" was, in a general sense, the poetry that from his incapacity as a poet Pater did not write, aesthetic criticism being the alternative he adopted instead. Like Morris's and Rossetti's poetry, Pater's criticism is dedicated to the art-for-art's-sake principle, accepting frankly the artifice implicit in striving to idealize an ideal in which the spontaneity of so-called natural feeling has already been formalized and distanced, and putting the highest premium on the style in which it is executed. Shared attitudes of so fundamental a character made Pater an extraordinarily insightful critic of the poetry of Morris and Rossetti. No successor has ever come closer to seeing what their poetic goals were, how those goals worked in the making of their poems, and what the essential difference between them was. Despite the late date officially assigned to the Rossetti critique, both essays belong to the same period stylistically, the intense years from 1867 to 1869 when Pater was experiencing a climax of aesthetic self-discovery. He brought to them an enthusiasm generated and perfected by his study of Winckelmann in relation to Goethe, an enthusiasm for the liberating effect of the Hellenic ideal. He saw that Hellenic ideal working in Morris in a poetically salutary way, and through seeing how it worked there, he discovered how it should work, on what terms any imaginative ideal of the past can be brought into the service of the present imaginative need. Rossetti, on the other hand, never discovered the secret of the Hellenic ideal. In consequence, he was imprisoned in a refined medieval ideal, and though he crafted out of its weightiness of outlook and "grandeur of literary workmanship" a "great style," he suffered the "defect of its quality" and was unable to liberate himself from what ultimately became a malignant force in his imaginative life.

Wordsworth is to APPRECIATIONS what *Leonardo da Vinci* is to THE RENAISSANCE, a portrait of the artist who embodies what was deepest and most characteristic in the spirit of the age and who drew upon imaginative resources that we all share in our individual degree to transform life into an ideal sensuous form that persists as a model for our own self-modeling. Pater treats the discoverer and founder of the true poetic motive of modernism in a way that not only enables us to understand how Wordsworth succeeded in bringing his natural fondness for metaphysical ideas under the rule of art—how, like Leonardo, he resolved the struggle between the mind and its ideas and the senses and their love of beauty— but also helps us to recognize how much of what we consider beautiful and eminently worthwhile in our own lives has its correspondences in him. To understand the magnitude of Pater's critical achievement in the essay, it is important to notice that in the early 1870s when Pater underwent his influence so profoundly, Wordsworth's reputation was at a low ebb and that, though much of what Pater says about Wordsworth's poetry seems to have become conventional in the century or so since he wrote it, what Pater meant by what he said has by no means become standard fare in Wordsworth criticism. Pater's Wordsworth is a great *aesthetic* prophet, and modern Wordsworthians have either not exactly understood Pater or have chosen to dismiss and/or override him.

The *Wordsworth* essay was written under the influence of THE RENAISSANCE when its aesthetic ideals and the critical approach implicit in it had gone through the process of maturation clearly marked by the sharp contrast between the exposition/argument of the *Preface* and the incantation/exhortation of the *Conclusion*. Pater had from the beginning used Wordsworth as a critical point of reference, but the character and prominence of his remarks on him in the *Preface* suggest that he was in the process of a more deliberate and comprehensive testing both of Wordsworth and of his own aesthetic ideals. His question in *Wordsworth*, "What is Wordsworth's poetry to *me?*" demands more than a private answer. He asks it both personally and in his public role as a critic, for himself and for the age, and he seeks an "absolutely sincere apprehension" of what is, or ideally should be, true for both.

In the penultimate paragraph of the essay, Pater says, "To treat life in the spirit of art, is to make life a thing in which means and ends are identified: to encourage such treatment, the true moral significance of art and poetry." Drawing extensively on Wordsworth's *Preface* to LYRICAL BALLADS and echoing ideas and phrases he knows his readers will recognize as quintessentially Arnoldian, Pater goes on to speak of "the aim of all culture" as the fixing of man's thoughts, "with appropriate emotions," on the "spectacle" of the great facts of his existence and of poetry like Wordsworth's as a "great nourisher and stimulant" of those emotions in such a context. It is the same solution to the same problem addressed in the *Conclusion* to THE RENAISSANCE; what is different is the intonation. Pater is no longer reacting directly to the exotic influence of Morris mastering through art the rebellious tensions of a certain late phase of medievalism; he is under the soberer, more tranquil spell of the "divine possession" Wordsworth brought to the "soul of apparently little or familiar things." "To burn always with this hard gemlike flame, to maintain this ecstasy" has yielded to "impassioned contemplation." The thought has not changed, only the attitude toward the thought. How we read the *Preface* to THE RENAISSANCE is also modified by juxtaposition to it of the *Wordsworth* essay. "What is this song or picture . . . to *me?*" loses the quality of defiant subjectivity and wholly personal impressionism some readers see it as authorizing. Rather, it asserts the qualitative principle that one's opinion be worth having. Wordsworth's writings are the "central and elementary expression" of "what is strongest and most attractive in modern literature," and if they are not that "to *me,*" then perhaps I should consider whether or not I have undergone the "sort of training towards the things of art and poetry" that those very writings provide. In short, Pater has made an advance on Pater, has in a sense grown up, and the conscientious reader must allow that advance, not always push him back to tones of voice and phrase that, though inherently sound, seem to have an effect on some readers that perpetually undercuts that soundness. Wordsworth, like the Plato of *Plato and Platonism,* had a crucial maturing effect on Pater.

Pater himself virtually acknowledges that he made those advances in maturity as a result of Wordsworth's example and influence. He speaks as one converted going out to convert. Having

been privileged to experience the *"disciplina arcani"* of Wordsworth's poetry, he is reporting its salutary effects to others. The
secret lies in the very "duality" of the Wordsworth canon; its
alternation of "lower and higher moods," or of merely fanciful
and genuinely imaginative poetry, tests in an exemplary way the
reader's capacity to distinguish between the mere appearance of
poetry and its reality, to "look below the surface" and separate
what is "organic, animated, expressive" from what is "only conventional, derivative, inexpressive." Though he had always
known and acknowledged such a distinction, he had really never
understood its profound aesthetic implications until he saw the
way it actually worked in Wordsworth. The true aesthetic Wordsworth—the "more powerful and original poet, hidden away, in
part, under those weaker elements"—had simply altered his way
of seeing the world, making it sharper, firmer, giving it a newer,
more intense reality, and had shown him how powerful thought
can be that is both wholly sincere and wholly poetic.

The true aesthetic Wordsworth, not the metaphysical Wordsworth twentieth-century criticism's curious love affair with metaphysics has fostered, is Pater's subject. He is the Wordsworth who
has a quality in common with Giorgione and the Venetian school,
namely, the artist's recognition that in the most direct, immediate, earthly reality, there is an image of an ideal secular world—
clear, just, splendid, exquisitely refined and refining. Wordsworth
and Giorgione expressed themselves in different mediums and
images, but in both, sights and sounds have that "bare, abstract"
reality the artist transforms, as if by a touch, into a metaphor of
the ideal. Like Giorgione, Wordsworth "has a power . . . of realising, and conveying to the consciousness of the reader [or viewer],
abstract and elementary expressions—silence, darkness, motionlessness, or, again, the whole complex sentiment of a particular
place, the *abstract expression* of desolation in the long white
road, of peacefulness in a particular folding of the hills" (emphasis added). "A chance expression is overheard and placed in a new
connexion, the sudden memory of a thing long past occurs to him,
a distant object relieved for a while by a random gleam of light."
The restrospective connection thus made between Wordsworth's
poetry and the art of Giorgione and the Venetian school enables

us in turn to make a prospective connection between it and the paintings of the abstract expressionists of the mid-twentieth century. When Pater speaks of incidents in *Resolution and Independence*, he means such "precise and vivid incidents" as "the pliant harebell swinging in the breeze/On some grey rock" and "the green corn all day . . . rustling in thine ears." Those "'particular spots' of time" that have "a presence in one's history" may be made memorable by "the happy light" upon a "special day or hour." Natural objects have a "moral or spiritual life," are "full of expression, of inexplicable affinities and delicacies of intercourse with man," by virtue of the motion in leaves or water or the sudden rising into view of a "distant peak of the hills" as the result of a change of perspective or "the passing space of light across the plain" or a "lichened Druidic stone." This mysterious but profoundly affective reciprocation between what is and what the eye sees, as in painting, or between what sound is and how the ear hears it, as in music, is what Wordsworth made us conscious of. These are images, certainly, sharp and firm, but through the aesthetic power of the poet, they become ideal forms—not metaphysical ideas, but actual realities, as individual and knowable as a person.

But though Pater's Wordsworth depends for some of his primary aesthetic effects on the authority of the eye and ear and uses language to create sensuous forms comparable to those created by a painter, he is yet a poet with poetry's distinctive imaginative laws. Poetry may, like the plastic arts variously and like music, recall "color, form, sound," and "the profound, joyous sensuousness of motion," but poetry is, in its essence, the art of "thought or sentiment," "discourse and action." Its imaginative power inheres finally in them; they are the means and ends, the stimulus and the goal, of its aesthetic form and interest. Pater's Wordsworth is, therefore, a poet of thought and action, capable of altering profoundly his reader's sense of himself and of the "awful forms and powers" in whose midst he dwells.

Wordsworth is at his best in this complex endeavor when "matter and form" are entirely fused, a "really poetical motive" uniting "with absolute justice, the word and the idea." It is here, too, that the "duality" in his poetry becomes most visible and most potentially damaging. At times, Wordsworth only skirts the borders of great "philosophical imaginings," is caught up only in the preliminary excitement that belongs to large "imaginative theories;" at other times his writing, lacking a "true poetical motive," becomes prosaic and tedious. Despite the claims made for it by a class of minds that confounds poetry with philosophy, art with ideas, this is not the poetry of Wordsworth that, through a peculiarly intense and mind-altering pleasure, has pointed and accelerated modern man's changing sense of himself.

The difference between these two "higher and lower moods" in Wordsworth's poetry—a difference Wordsworth himself designated by the metaphysical terms *Imagination* and *Fancy*—does not turn upon speculation. Speculation is common to them both. It is a difference of poetic motive—what sets the speculation in motion, what "inward presentation" the poet is attempting to give indirect expression to. The very boldest "trains of speculative thought" may be triggered by a "chance expression . . . overheard," "the sudden memory of a thing long past," "a distant object . . . relieved . . . by a random gleam of light," "the humble graves and lowly arches of 'the little rock-like pile' of a Westmoreland church." Such casual incidents, unplanned and seemingly negligible, may suddenly find profound echoes in a mind deeply conscious of its own history and release "strange reminiscences and forebodings, which seem to make our lives stretch before and behind us, beyond where we can see or touch anything, or trace the lines of connexion."

The "mysterious notion" of an "ideal childhood" around which Wordsworth shapes *Ode: Intimations of Immortality*, *Tintern Abbey*, and various passages of *The Prelude* is an example of a poetic motive at its best, as are those moments of "profound, imaginative power, in which the outward object appears to take colour and expression, a new nature almost, from the prompting of the observant mind" and in "those periods of intense susceptibility, in which he appeared to himself as but the passive recipient of external influences, he was attracted by the thought of a spirit of life in outward things, a single, all-pervading mind in them, of which man, and even the poet's imaginative energy, are but moments." Speculation has, of course, a very large presence in such poems, but what makes them poetical is their motive. They emerge naturally out of a cultivated, self-examined poet's mind stimulated by an external incident that, though accidental, he has become habitually and profoundly susceptible to. The thought or intuition at their center is not abstract or theoretical or even consistent, but personal and experiential, and it is only the great but secondary means to a greater, more primary end, namely, a perfectly faithful and sincere representation of the mysterious possibilities, transformed for the moment into an imaginative affirmation, that man in his most exalted state has access to the essential truth of himself and his universe. The intensity of the "imaginative flame" that makes such moments possible burns out all impure elements, making expression "faultless" and setting on "philosophical imaginings" the limits that "true poetry" demands.

Such faultless expression was no accident, of course. Like the poet's mind, the poet's language was also searched and cultivated. Wordsworth's very career as a poet was built on the renewal of language, on the "subtle adjustment of the elementary sounds of words themselves to the image or feeling they convey" and on the purer forms of language to be found in "older English literature"—in Shakespeare, for example, and in the "racy idiom" of language close to its origins, the "old English language" and "the language used by the simplest people under strong excitement." Thus when Wordsworth's moments of inspiration came, he had a language equal to their needs.

In the end, however, a great poet's impact on an individual and on an age is greater than the sum of its parts, and that is the practical result to which Pater's method finally leads him. Wordsworth's poetry, "like all great art and poetry," is a "continual protest" against the "predominance of machinery" in our lives. It is a metaphor to which Arnold had given reiterative attention in the years when Pater was examining his thoughts and shaping his craft as a critic, but though Pater was obviously willing to acknowledge Arnold's influence on this theme both in himself and in the critical consciousness of the age, he created around the metaphor a distinctive context. He focused on the machinery of the mind rather than on external machinery, on man's habit of imprisoning himself in moral structures which he finds satisfying and even high-minded but which are not only stifling but also often lead to moral ambiguity or iniquity and dispossess the human spirit of the freedom, actions, and excitement of which Wordsworth's poetry is a thoroughly English and a universally available instance.

Pater was shyer than Arnold about using criticism of art and poetry to point lessons to his readers. Ultimately, however, he could not deny either that people in fact seek moral insight or that art, however aesthetically determined the artist or the critic may be, inevitably projects it. It is a question of *how* rather than *what*, as it always is in art—how to convey value without vulgarity, to strengthen the spirit without mechanizing the means. That is the force and the purpose of the trope Pater chose to identify the ultimate "lesson" of Wordsworth, "impassioned contemplation," *"being"* something rather than *"doing"* something. It expressed an all-encompassing, wholly non-sectarian vision of man's moral life in a age that, being more reform-minded than revolutionary, was eagerly dismantling the past only to institutionalize the future. The effect of Wordsworth's poetry is to return man to basics and enable him to see that a perception of change requires a perception of permanence, that how one perceives *what may be* depends on how one perceives *what is*, and that how one perceives is itself the immediate result of what one is. As a poet, Wordsworth expressed this by converting the "actual form of life" into the form of poetry, thus making its ends one with its means. As an aesthetic critic, Pater expressed it by translating the actual form of art into a model of the ideal form required for genuine success in life, and by doing so, he made criticism itself an art form.

6. IMAGINARY PORTRAITS

In 1878, Pater published the first pure example of a new species of writing that showed not only that he had creative intuitions that were inadequately satisfied by even the most imaginative reaches of conventional criticism, but also that prose literature itself lacked a precisely appropriate form for the expression of certain kinds of awarenesses that were being pressed upon the imaginative consciousness by mutually reinforcing developments in modern thought and in modern man's need to announce his spiritual whereabouts. Like Browning in THE RING AND THE BOOK immediately before him and Hardy in THE DYNASTS soon after, Pater recognized that "the modern expression of a modern outlook" required, if not an absolutely new literary form, a new formal adaptation and a new voice. *The Child in the House* was Pater's exemplary response to this need for a creative alternative—exemplary in that he wrote of it, "Child in the House: voilà, the germinating, original, source, specimen, of all my *imaginative* work."

Pater's "imaginary portraits," as he called his new literary adaptation, are non-fictional fictions and critical non-criticisms. Often described as autobiographical in the more or less literal sense, they rather suggest that, to the imagination, even one's personal experience is not peculiarly one's own and that literal autobiography is history with blinkers on. Although the subject of each portrait is studied against a particular historical background, it is imaginary, even historical figures like the painter Anthony Watteau being perceived largely from an imaginary perspective and mythic figures like Dionysus and Apollo redivivus moving across the landscape as naturally as contemporary characters. The major difference between the critical essays and these critical fictions is that in the latter Pater is freed from the necessity of working under the restrictions of the facts of a particular individual's life and works and known relations to his times. That was a necessity he had accepted in his critical essays, and he had shown that, working under those restrictions, he could yet create metaphoric visions or images, works of criticism that mean "beyond the facts." However, mirrored in his very success in reconstituting that conventional form of criticism was the idea for an alternative form that would be an oblique gloss or comment on it. The imaginary portraits gave Pater the freedom to create his own myths or to put inherited fictions like those of Dionysus, Hippolytus, and Apollo to new mythological uses. At the same time, the natural growth from the one to the other, and the retention in the later form of such elements as criticism and history from the earlier form, suggest that though the mythic element became, through handling, more explicit in the later form, it was also an implicit assumption of the earlier, myth being the imaginative common-denominator between them.

A writer's reason for creating a new literary form is presumably to give himself more imaginative freedom than the form he has previously been using provides. Thus the very existence of the imaginary portraits seems to be an invitation to read them as imaginatively as possible, more imaginatively, for example, than even the most ingenious and cunning sort of autobiographical reading allows for, since at some level literal fact is necessarily an assumption of autobiography. Myth, on the other hand, encourages us to see things whole and to value them at their "eternal worth," literal fact having only so much interest as our imaginative sense invests in it.

If *The Child in the House* is the normative "specimen" of Pater's imaginary portraits, supplying a paradigm of how to read them, then a mythic reading is certainly appropriate. *The Child in the House* is the fictive portrait of an imaginary but representative character named Florian Deleal as related by a narrator whose identity is implicit in the peculiarities—facts, interpretations, attitudes, needs—of what he tells. Thus it fully qualifies, not as verifiable fact, but as self-verifying myth. The "poor aged man" whom Florian Deleal at the age of approximately forty-two helps with his burden along the road "one hot afternoon," the boy Florian Deleal who is "the child in the house" denotatively, the Florian who has grown into middle life bearing the unremitting weight of "an agony of homesickness" that has been the result of an eager anticipation realized "almost thirty years ago," and the middle-aged man who must look forward to the prospect of an old age weary with the road, burdened with what he carries, and in need of human sympathy—they are all one person, and *The Child in the House* is the poetic myth of man in this world whose house is furnished forever in the first twelve years of his life. It is his "material shrine or sanctuary of sentiment" that knits his affections to the earth; it is the paradise from which his very eagerness to depart visits on him a piercing and eternal sense of loss.

In determining the meaning or emblematic content of *The Child in the House*, one should keep in mind two things: its character as myth and its artistic motive, the former being an organic outgrowth of the latter. The motive is to make us "sympathetic, begetting. . .the power of entering, by all sorts of finer ways, into the intimate recesses of other minds"; the myth, a fictive configuration of such a representative process, is the result. Transformation is, I suggest, the emblematic content of *The Child in the House*. Despite its markings as a representative example of Romantic Modernism, Pater's first imaginary portrait finds its literary models in THE GOLDEN ASS of Apuleius and the METAMORPHOSES of Ovid. It is a tale of transformation or metamorphosis, and, as in the case of Pater's classical predecessors, its myth is its meaning. Like those of its mythic models, the story-line is very simple. A younger man helps a "poor aged man" who is overtasked along the way "one hot afternoon." The old man tells him "his story," and though they are strangers, he finds they have a common place of origin. This has the effect, at once natural and magical, of putting him in mind of the place where he was born and of enabling him to review and penetrate his early life there for the first time. Thus his reward for having taken pity on the old man's plight is self-knowledge, and although, like all Apollonian gifts, it has its price—the sorrow born of knowledge born of disposition and need—it better enables him to enter into the joys and pains of others, to feel less caged and abandoned in the "hot afternoon" of his life, and to moderate in his mind the extremes of joy and sorrow to which he seems temperamentally susceptible. As his psyche undergoes formation in this highly favored retrospect, he begins to understand that rich and curious thing called life as mirrored in his own individuality. The illusion of simplicity in the story draws us into a process of "brainbuilding" or psyche-formation in which "little accidents have their consequnce" and such seemingly negligible things as "floating thistle-down and chance straws" get themselves compacted as "the house of thought in which we live."

As the myth of *The Child in the House* is, through its delicate formal appointments, distanced and directed away from "the state of [Pater's] own mind," so is its meaning. It is much larger than the *Bildung* of an authorial house of thought; Pater is personally complicit in it, of course, but only in the generic sense in which Flaubert exclaimed, "*Emma Bovary, c'est moi!*"

A Prince of Court Painters is unique among the portraits in several respects. It is the only one narrated by a woman, specifically a woman very conscious of her female character and status, and it alone uses the autobiography of one person to relate the biography of another in such a way as to pose in a provocative way the question of who is the told-of, who the teller, or who is the portrait's real protagonist and what is its real subject. No other portrait is based as it is on wholly historical personages, and in none of the others does Pater make such substantial use of his extraordinary talents for art criticism. Each of these distinctive elements plays a considerable part in the way Pater works out the portrait's myth.

A Prince of Court Painters creates the illusion that we have taken an intimate look into the very soul of a so-called "court painter" who devoted himself to the depiction of scenes and personalities "bathed in [the] aura of privilege" associated in our minds with the Court of Louis XIV. Knowing something of his personal life, we think, we understand why he was unhappy and indeed may wonder if, despite the insight his incomparable style gives us into the truth of him in relation to his times, it would not have been better had he never seen "that impossible or forbidden world. . .through the closed gateways of the enchanted garden," but had remained relatively unknown and at peace in his native Flanders. Much mystery remains, and our insights are more like supended judgments than firm conclusions, but we seem to have sufficient if select grounds for thinking we understand Anthony Watteau.

In actual fact, however, it is almost all illusion, created by the critical imagination of Pater out of his subjective-objective penetration of Watteau's works themselves projected through a myth that rests on the barest minimum of known facts. That is not to say that the portrait is false; its essential truth has been confirmed by a century of increasingly sophisticated art history and art criticism. It does suggest, however, that no system or theory or method composed of ingredients external to the works themselves and to the absolutely sincere and discriminating way someone felt or thought about them would have made the portrait as true and complete as it is. *A Prince of Court Painters* objectifies mythically Pater's most distinctive principle of aesthetic criticism, that of knowing the object through knowing one's impression of the object. Marie-Marguerite is so full and precise an embodiment of that principle that, even if Pater were not deliberately attempting to illustrate it, he was surely conscious of its applicability to the role in which he cast her. In fact, it was a brilliant strategy on his part to have created a story with two protagonists—an artist with a real history and a critic whose character is almost wholly imaginary—to activate that particular principle of aesthetic criticism. She is the teller, he the told-of, but the subject of the tale, its myth or action, is larger than both of them. Each reader must judge for himself whether or not Watteau's mastery of an environment he despised was worth his sacrifice to it of any chance for health and happiness. Some degree of suspended judgment is a significant part of the effect Pater sought to achieve in this portrait.

To enable the portrait to work, one should not conclude so quickly and easily as some critics have done that the narrator, Marie-Marguerite, is literally "in love" with Watteau or that she is a drab, visionless person imprisoned in "representational fixity." She has too much subjective-objective empathy and measures Watteau's personal pain and artistic achievement too impeccably to justify such a patronizing view of her. Though she describes herself as "a tame, unambitious soul," that is an expression of her modesty of character and of her acute consciousness of her role as a woman in a man's world. That she sometimes feels her spirit stagnating within her and compelled to "bury" herself in the work of her brother—like her, exiled for mysterious reasons from the royal presence—is also consistent with her character and her role and suggests that to "possess" Watteau romantically has been less her aspiration than to bask in the glory of his fame and to save him some degree of the pain that is the price of his temperament and his gift. She is torn between applause of his Parisian success and her recognition of the feverish, unfulfilled state of his soul, "agitated, exigent, unsatisfying," "like a woman with some nervous malady." Watteau's life as much as hers—indeed, life itself—is glossed by the incident of the entrapped bird. Though she is not herself an artist, she is a lover of art and an enabler of artists. She has the artist's authority of the eye and recognizes "in what one is to *see*—in the outsides of things . . . something, a sign, a memento, at the least, of what makes life really valuable." That is the talent she shares with Watteau, and though it brings them to different external views of life—him to an elegant disdain of what he sees with luminous "purity," her to a profound pity that is yet compatible with personal tranquility and an undisturbed religious faith—it enables her to look through "the *Watteau* style" at the thing signified by it. It is a "fairy arrangement . . . like a piece of 'chamber-music' . . . part answering to part; while no trenchant note is allowed to break through the delicate harmony of white and pale red and little golden touches." It has a "sort of *moral* purity," but its morality is all "in the *forms* and *colours* of things." While he casts upon his scenes an "unreal, imaginary light," there is yet "a poetry" in the way "they group themselves with such a perfect fittingness" that without his help we would never have seen. Tragedy inheres in his comedy, however: "The storm is always brooding through the massy splendour of the trees, above those sundried glades or lawns, where delicate children may be trusted thinly clad; and the secular trees themselves will hardly outlast another generation."

In short, the originality, delicacy, and precision of *A Prince of Court Painters* depend on Pater's handling and our understanding of Marie-Marguerite as the narrative persona. That is what makes the portrait mythic and enables it to work as history transformed into poetry.

The creative principle behind *Denys L'Auxerrois* is imaginative metamorphosis, especially visual metamorphosis, as signaled by the architectural theme, the "large and brilliant fragment of stained glass," the multiple variations on the central character in the series of antique tapestries, and the narrator's sense of actually *seeing* his "tortured figure . . . in the streets" of Auxerre. Denys's influence is particularly felt in "those arts which address themselves first of all to sight." The story itself is an imaginative transformation of the images of the tapestries into a verbal portrait that follows "the successive phases or fashions" of the three "humours he had determined"—first, "wild gaiety," second, "the satiric, the grotesque and coarse," and, third, "a well-assured seriousness," especially "in the precise sort of expression that should be induced upon it." Finally, as Denys's effects are "to be seen most clearly in the rich miniature work of the manuscripts . . . a marvellous Ovid especially, upon the pages of which those old loves and sorrows seemed to come to life again in medieval costume," so is it too in the modern story, for which Ovid remains the creative model. The imaginative excitement of *Denys L'Auxerrois* is the *formal* excitement of how it gets itself told, of how "the figure in the stained glass explained itself." The "quaint legend" or myth is removed from "the usual vagueness of dreams" and furnished forth "with details enough"—gay, riotous, earthy details, grotesque, coarse details, the serious details of a beautiful pagan god undergoing the torture of a profoundly melancholy age—to enable us to gain genuine critical perspective on our sentimental dreams of a return to a "golden age."

The hilarious game of ball played in the cathedral on Easter Day at which Denys makes his appearance in his first phase of "wild gaiety" is barometric. While the ecclesiastical ceremony is absurdly solemn, silent, and decorous, the metamorphosis Denys brings about, while proportionate to the preceding absurdity, is disproportionate to the ideal of such an occasion, being riotous, clamorous, and wholly indecorous. That is the revelation of this first revolutionary phase: it is so temptingly attractive, so seemingly free, sensuous, and intoxicating, so flexible, natural, funloving, and ecstatic, that only the rarest individual can look through the substance to the thing it signifies. The "gaily-painted chariot" and "soft silken raiment" of the " 'morality' " pageant or "stage-play" are so immediately alluring to most that they ignore the ominous implications of the "strange elephant-scalp with gilded tusks." The "sage monk Hermes" is a cautionary exception. He recognizes that Denys's gifts are "perhaps more than natural," and he would like to understand them "for the friendly purpose of explaining to the lad himself" how they might be profitably rather than unprofitably cultivated.

Denys–Dionysus is an embodiment of the primitive, immature pleasure principle, benign beyond measure in a world all green and gold with fertility and abundance, but stealthy, malignant, and ferocious at the first frost-bite of pain. A child of both seduction and violent wrath, he has also a "dark or antipathetic side"; as the "wise monk Hermes" recognizes, he is "like a double creature, of two natures, difficult or impossible to harmonize." In his second, grotesque phase, everything that was golden is more than matched by everything that is grim, even his much-vaunted pity being transformed to ghastly horror. The idea that, like the Wine-god whose part he "had played so well," Denys "had been in hell" is a "satiric" or "grotesque" idea. It is an *"after-thought"* in pagan poetry that the monk Hermes remembers "whimsically." To make the journey to hell and return requires in both pagan and Christian literature a heroic, god-like capacity to confront and survive with tempered strength the awful truth of crime and punishment, of evil and the suffering due to evil, grossly under-developed in Denys. He is "manifestly a sufferer," but the sight of the "dwindled body" of the exhumed patron saint, "shrunken inconceivably, but still with every feature of the face traceable in a sudden, oblique ray of a ghastly dawn," throws him into such a demon-ridden fit that he becomes in an exaggerated form the very thing he had sought to transform in the first phase, "a subdued, silent, melancholy creature." Even Denys's final penitential undertaking in this grotesque phase—to carry "the music of the pipe" beyond its earlier modes of simple, homely pastoral and "wild, savage din" to "sweeter purposes" "tamed, ruled, united"—has its deeply ironic note. "Apollo, with his lyre in his hand, as lord of the strings," is waiting in the wings with thoughts of Marsyas, the hapless faun whom he defeated in a musical competition and flayed alive for punishment.

In his third and final phase, Denys is the object of community hatred. Whether one perceives him as the victim of his own "sins" and thus of poetic justice or the scapegoat of those who would purge their own guilt by making a vicarious sacrifice of him, he is the central figure in a quaint legend whose artistic function is to remind us of our own divided and distressed humanity. He is the erstwhile vintner caught in the crush of the winepress, the organ-builder who, at the very moment he would devote himself to "sweeter purposes," becomes the victim of the "wild, savage din" that he himself has authored; he is the traveler from the warm

South and exotic East who transforms for a brief moment a melancholy Midland people who turn upon him with the unholy, barbarian passions of the heathmen of the "golden age" of the North.

It was as if the disturbing of that timeworn masonry let out the dark spectres of departed times. Deep down, at the core of the central pile, a painful object was exposed—the skeleton of a child, placed there alive . . . in the superstitious belief that, by way of vicarious substitution, its death would secure the safety of all who should pass over.

That, by analogy, is what the dream of a return of a "golden age" ultimately comes to when it is removed from the vagueness of dreams and furnished forth "with details enough" by a critical consciousness fully and imaginatively awake. It is not a moral judgment, but an imaginative portrait of a probable reality insofar as the "imaginative reason" can intuit probability, and the killing off of the dream with what some commentators see as perverse relish may seem to others a necessary and proportionate price to pay for the imaginative revelation of what might be unimaginably devastating if it were ever in fact to be transformed from the dream to the reality. Denys's heart is buried "under a stone, marked with a cross . . . in a dark corner of the cathedral aisle" because such legends—of which dreams of personal immortality is also one—"will hardly be forgotten, however prosaic the world may become, while man himself remains the aspiring, never quite contented being he is."

The subject of *Sebastian van Storck* is disengagement—its motives, man's capacity for it, its practical results. The fact that there is something about the myth and what it bodes to which the epithet *monstrous* applies is both masked and accentuated by the narrator's manner. He is as analytical, non-judgmental, matter-of-fact, and thorough as one can be who is as much fascinated by the historical moment as by the mythohistorical man and empathizes at a well-marked distance with the inconsistent consistency, the faulted but honorable distress, of an unusual yet representative modern man. It is the mythic situation that is monstrous, not the man, and no moral judgment is passed on him.

Neither does the narrator suggest any therapy for the psychological *"phthisis"* or tubercular-like wasting away of "people grown somewhat over-delicate in their nature by the effects of modern luxury" when, by the accident of their moment in historical time, they contract a certain virulent strain of thought. The myth does suggest a number of implicit reassurances—its characterization as a disease, the immunity to its more fatal manifestations of all but the unhappy few, the intimation that, since it appears to be an aberration of the mind, the mind itself will correct it, the hint that inherent in the very extremes of its selfishness there is some promise of a heroic selflessness. Nonetheless, it is a terrifying element that has invaded the phenomenology of the modern mind through the gateway of theological scientism and may take a more general and threatening course after its monkish associations have disappeared.

Art and religion are persistent reference-points in the portrait. It is his flight from everything that art "represents" in the double entendre of that term that drives Sebastian toward the "cold-blooded transcendentalism" that is his ultimate undoing. The early part of the text is flooded with the names of artists who are riding the crest of Dutch prosperity and "helping" the Dutch nation "to a full consciousness of the genial yet delicate homeliness it loved." Prettiness, neatness, flattering colors, comfort amidst countless symbols of solid, well-earned worldly success mark their taste. "Those innumerable *genre* pieces—conversation, music, play—were in truth the equivalent of novel-reading for that day; its own actual life, in its own proper circumstances, reflected in various degrees of idealisation, with no diminution of the sense of reality (that is to say) but with more and more purged and perfected delightfulness of interest." The irony is elegant but cutting, and one can hardly help contrasting the magnificent chance-taking of Renaissance artists like Leonardo and Michelangelo with "the kind of quaint new Atticism" that characterizes this vacuous, ceremonious, gracious self-flattery, or help noting the vast difference between this "kind of natural religiousness" and the grandeur with which Leonardo rejected as Michelangelo accepted the religion of their day. This is the atmosphere that is suffocating Sebastian, and he rejects the art that is ever concentrating his consciousness of it: "in truth the arts were a matter he could but just tolerate. Why add, by a forced and artificial production, to the monotonous tide of competing, fleeting experience?" "Poetic" as used to characterize the "rigidly logical" method of Sebastian's inferences and "beauty" to characterize his "youthful enthusiasm for an abstract theorem" are given a special connotation that empties them of everything sensuously valuable, like a body from which the life has flown.

Spinoza is used glancingly but repeatedly to define the tendency of Sebastian's self-consuming thought. One "bold" thought of Spinoza's is considered by Sebastian to be especially "fine"— "That who so loveth God truly must not expect to be loved by him in return"—and though it is certainly true that Spinoza cannot with objective fairness be "read" in the self-confirming way Sebastian reads him, it is also certainly true that the "cold-blooded transcendentalism" that carries Sebastian to destruction is a plausible way of characterizing Spinoza's intellectual scheme of things. The "ideal of an intellectual disinterestedness, of a domain of unimpassioned mind" that attracts Sebastian so exclusively and for which he finds the support of a kindred spirit in Spinoza is represented by the narrator as "a constant tradition" in Western thought, as a "haunting recurrent voice of the human soul itself, and as such sealed with natural truth." But he represents it, too, as an "accident" of the times and of the individual temperament that this ideal should have taken such a negative turn, at once egotistical and suicidal, in Sebastian. In others such as Plato and Wordsworth it has worked lovingly and poetically, but in Sebastian it has taken an opposite turn. For immersion, he substitutes detachment, for heat cold, for intimacy distance, for sympathy or love rejection, for the finite the infinite, for existence annihilation.

Sebastian undertakes his final journey in the vain hope that an extended visit to one of his favorite haunts will enable him to free himself of the realization that his intellectual position is morally faulted at its very center, that *he* is sincerely false. His realization is of an "absolute selfishness, which could not, if it would, pass beyond the circumference of itself." The only way he can get free of his impossible situation is to get free of himself, and that, symbolically, is what he does. He brings to safety a little child through considerable personal struggle before being drowned himself. The Sebastian that has reached the inevitable end of his line of thought dies after assisting at the birth of an alternative Sebastian. The little child is, imaginatively or expressionistically, Sebastian himself reincarnate. This sudden expressionistic leap, though startling, has been in some sense prepared for by the suddenness and inexplicability of the contagion with which his spirit is infected in the first place and by the series of inconsistencies evident even in his relentless pursuit of theorem and corollary. There is a little child under all of his display of intellectual fearlessness, and though Sebastian can admit it least when he is most vigorous in pursuing his self-conscious goals, he has inarticulate intimations of it even then, and in his final "victory" over life—or his ultimate defeat—he acknowledges it symbolically. He uses what energy he has left to make the little child safe and secure and thus commits his last and most endearing inconsistency.

As *Denys L'Auxerrois* brings a penetrating consciousness, critical as well as imaginative, to bear upon man's vague but persistent dreams of a return of a "golden age," *Duke Carl of Rosenmold* suffuses the earliest stirrings of a historical awakening, also both critical and imaginative, with a gently amusing, thoroughly affectionate spirit of irony. The nearest analogue of the former is late-medieval gothic, that of the latter, Romantic-Modern fairy tale. The mythic persona who supplies the imaginative energy and sets the critical parameters of *Denys L'Auxerrois* is Dionysus-cum-Bacchus, the Greek god of wine, revelry, and fertility in his degenerate Roman manifestation—"a double creature, of two natures, difficult or impossible to harmonize." Apollo, god of music, poetry, and all things bright and beautiful, is the spiritual patron of the naturally pagan soul of young Duke Carl of Rosenmold.

That the *éclaircissement* or *Aufklärung* that actually took place in Germany in the eighteenth century, channeling itself through such "precursors" as Lessing and Herder and climaxing in the life and works of Goethe at the beginning of the nineteenth, is a real dimension but not the imaginatively controlling intuition of *Duke Carl of Rosenmold* is made clear by the portrait's "coda" or "tag." The very explicitness of its critical statement and the analytical manner of its use of historical documentation suggest that, though that aspect is true, clever, and intellectually rewarding, it is subordinate to the myth's primary imaginative character. Duke Carl is not a "little Goethe" or even a precursor in Goethe's direct line of endeavor. He is one of a thousand unsung persons, in that time and place as well as in other times and places, "awakening each other to the permanent reality of a poetic ideal in human life" and, by desiring it, becoming its "'forecast of capacity'" in the "public consciousness." Young Duke Carl's imagined place in early-eighteenth-century German history is a poetic metaphor of the pioneering possibilities of all youths whose imaginations are set aglow and who struggle against the encumbered lethargy of the past and the deceptions of the present long enough to discover that poetry is rooted in nature, not in custom, and that the poetry of nature is in themselves in their time and place or nowhere. He is a Prince Charming in search of a Sleeping Beauty in the fabulous kingdom of artificial roses. The fairy-tale mode of the story is itself a metaphor, a metaphor of form that has absorbed substance—has been informed by substance and has in turn *trans*formed substance into itself. That is the magic or miracle of the imagination, and fairy tales are only the imagination's way of showing how essentially natural and universal miracles really are.

Duke Carl's staging of his own funeral is his fantastic way of claiming his selfhood, dying to the identity that the cumulative conventional wisdom of others would impose on him and returning as the self he aspires to and is determined that, given the necessary freedom, he shall be. But there is a journey that a person with a cultural or spiritual legacy to which it has been necessary to die must take, the journey into an alternative reality, into empirical verification that the beauty he has had intuitions of is a "true truth," not merely an illusion. Carl thinks it is a physical journey, and thus only by making the physical journey can he discover that it is a state of mind or, in a more hieratic trope, a state of grace. As he gradually travels farther from home, he gradually learns some very fundamental home truths, perceiving that he does not need, literally, to go so far as Greece or even Italy.

Traveling along the beautiful Rhine and other national rivers, he views what seem to him "outpost[s] of some far-off . . . land" of the fancy or imagination as "pledge[s] of the reality of such." As he travels through Germany, the conviction comes with the force of a divine revelation that, "'For you, France, Italy, Hellas, is here!'" Having recognized that he has been "journeying partly in search of physical heat," he extrapolates this analogically: if Germany can provide physical heat sufficient to a German, is Germany's light not sufficient too, requiring interpretation rather than importation? It may be different from Hellenic light, hyperborean perhaps, but Apollonian still. What Germany needs— what any national art, poetry, literature, philosophy needs—is informed interpretation of "the vast accumulated material of which it is in possession," and the only qualified interpreter is one who has an informed, critical, imaginative "understanding of the past, of nature, of one's self—an understanding of all beside through the knowledge of one's self." Having arrived at this point of illumination, Duke Carl has no need to travel farther afield. He understands the inner source of the "poetry of nature" and is ready to turn home again. At the climax of his journey, he has one of those spectacularly mystical experiences of nature at the physical apex of Europe, but his real *éclaircissement* or *Aufklärung* is critical-imaginative: "Straight through life, straight through nature and man, with one's self-knowledge as a light thereon, not by way of geographical Italy or Greece, lay the road to the new Hellas, to be realised now as the outcome of home-born German genius."

Duke Carl carries his natural idealism ("'Go straight to life!'") into his domestic arrangements, choosing for his bride the "beggar-girl" who had "half detected" him in his funeral masquerade, and he shows his reconciliation with his Romantic homeland by choosing for their honeymoon an "old grange or hunting-lodge" rich only in the "charm of remoteness and romance." Finally, he insists that his betrothed play-act a Romantic folktale about the place, a peculiarly German instance of the principle of metamorphosis. However, both their romantic conversion to man and wife and the Romantic transformation, under his faithful pledge, of the rich, fierce, aged wizard Germany into

a beautiful youth are suddenly cut short by the enemy of all
idealism, the violent, mindless brutality of war.

Hippolytus Veiled has two main structural parts—an unusually
elaborate historical-critical introduction and the action or myth
of Hippolytus—and these are integrated into a single, unified
whole through the character and role of Theseus, the mythological hero of Athens, the center of Greek civilization in its most
advanced, "modern" development. He is both the tyrant who, as a
vigorous exponent of "the modern spirit" of his day, did most to
threaten the "picturesque, intensely localised" "early Attic
deme-life"—the subject of the historical-critical introduction—
and the agent of catastrophe in the myth of Hippolytus. Thus
Theseus becomes one of the principals in an action that mirrors a
way of life that from unexamined motives manipulated by others
he seeks to destroy. Through this structural or formal technique,
Pater achieves in *Hippolytus Veiled* a dynamic integration of criticism and creation. His judgment that certain phases of so-called
primitive art possess a "permanent attractiveness in themselves,
being often, indeed, the true maturity of certain amiable artistic
qualities" is confirmed by example in the myth of Hippolytus
upon which Euripides based his play.

The basic contrast is between the modern, progressive, cen-
tralized life of Athens and the ancient, conservative, localized
life of the demes or townships into which Attica was officially
divided around 500 B.C. but which had grown up in the form of
towns and villages from time immemorial. King Theseus, "a kind
of mythic shorthand for civilization," dooms the old deme-life to
decay by his uncompromising emphasis on Athens, and when he
wants to "veil" his mistake or crime toward Antiope, he puts her
and their illegitimate son away in one of those "doomed, decaying
villages." On the other hand, it is from being "veiled" in that
ancient village life that Hippolytus develops his seemingly preter-
natural placidity, a contentment so complete as to have
"something unearthly" about it; it also provides suitable conditions for studiousness and for the simple regimen by which he
"devotes himself—his immaculate body and soul"—to his virgin

mother, Artemis-Persephone, undifferentiated daughters of Demeter in whom virginity is associated with death.

Hippolytus Veiled depends on its private rather than its public
face for its literary distinction. The final unravelling of the public
myth is relatively unimportant compared with the fine, picturesque way in which Hippolytus converts his austere private life
into a work of art. For that the critic-creator had to depend on his
own imagination, details of that kind being almost entirely miss-
ing from such meagre facts as history itself supplied. And this
brings us as close as we can get to the portrait's true subject and
the author's initiating intuition. In those "crumbling little
towns" such as that in which Theseus placed Antiope and Hippolytus, the supernatural life "lingered on . . . into the heroic," as
at a later time the "heroic life . . . lingered on into the actual,"
and unless we can somehow penetrate the innermost secrets of
that phase of our development, we will have lost something of
ourselves. History helps some, but imagination helps inestimably
more. Through imagination we can restore what history has left
but a meagre record of because imagination makes it possible for
us to get in touch with and examine the secrets of our own inner
consciousness and to discover there such vestigial patterns as will
enable us to recognize and reconstruct the spiritual history that
we continue to share with representative inhabitants of those
"crumbling little towns" in ancient Attica.

The structure of *Emerald Uthwart* is determined by the myth of
the return that is its subject. Emerald is "carelessly plucked" out
of a hereditary paradise marked by nothing so stern and peremptory as a moral imperative; he brings back to it "the charm of an
exquisite character" that fills those who minister to him with
reverential awe. The story has an architectural unity—a beginning, middle, and end in which the conclusion is implicit in the
introduction and a central turning that looks both backward and
forward—but its texture is that of a Flemish tapestry in which
everything has a representational as well as a symbolic content
and the theme is restated with numerous variations. It is the
tragic story of a type of youth who from the beginning knows that
he is doomed to catastrophe and is strangely refined and solem-

nized by the manner in which he comports himself under the influence of that knowledge. It is a reversal of the usual expectation of "'the younger part of us'" that we "'shall live forever,'" that the "'past years of our life are absolutely beyond proportion small in comparison with those which certainly remain to us,'" and its ideal result is a "Hellenic fitness" that makes even "'Golden-haired Apollo'" an inadequate gloss upon it. It is "better" than that because, in its "expressiveness," its lines of "delicate meaning," it registers thousands of historically incremental "touches, traces, complex influences" on the person of a "real" youth that make the "old Greek god" appear simply "theatrical" by comparison. Such youths as Emerald Uthwart have, as Hardy was to say, occupied a "meditative world" that is "older, more invidious, more quizzical," and therefore their deaths in the flower of youth mirror back an older, more terrible beauty.

Emerald is a "splitter"—one divided against himself in the way he apprehends life and conducts himself within its rules. Therein lies the inner correspondence or origin of his doom, according to whether one explains life metaphysically or phenomenologically. Part of it is the result of such numberless external forces as the accident of his place within an ancient family, the institutions that have been forming for centuries to receive and impress him, chance events, and the way others exert their power over him. But much of it comes from within—the seemingly innate ambivalence of his response to events, his "genius" for "submissiveness," his exceptional tendency to take all things, "not to heart, but rather to mind," and to ponder them, the "original, active, personal" way in which he internalizes the sense that all high things are "'things too high for *me*!'" He possesses in harmonious combination all the "qualities proper to a large and varied community of youths of nineteen or twenty," and he is completely free of any "note" or "accent" of a vulgarizing egotism.

Emerald Uthwart is an educational portrait in the manner of the German *Bildungsroman*. Its *Bildung* or development portion takes place at school; Emerald's "gifts" and "good-fortune" reach their zenith there and during his brief period at Oxford, and the narrator has much to say about the steadfastness of English ideals of classical education. However, such applause of the regimen and results of the English public schools as presented is persistently undercut. Emerald is a thrall who thinks, and his thoughts subvert almost everything held to be virtuous about the English system of classical education. Though he is the ideal product of an institution that charges its students "to make moral philosophy one of [their] acquirements . . . and to systematise [their] vagrant [selves]," Emerald seems to succeed only because he brings to it a profound conviction of guilt and exile from his natural home, and what he learns there, frankly and precisely pondered, deprives him forever of the sentimental dreams by which reconciliation and redemption are customarily effected.

How Emerald copes with catastrophe, with the "last four years of doom," is the crux of his myth's "meaning." We are told that on the morning of the execution he had looked into the grave and established "a sort of fraternal familiarity to death" and had "in a few weeks' time" "fought out" the battle of fate so far as death as an inevitable fact made imminent was concerned. All men die, and he had shaped his life under a perpetual premonition of doom. The problem, then, is with life itself. Driven home by dejection, he makes a holiday of the time remaining. He immerses himself in pure sensuous delight, touching others and being touched by them with exquisite softness. The closer he comes to the infinite unknown, the more he clings to the "beloved finite." The pagan naturalism he has learned from the classics serves him well: he seizes the day and is glad for what is. When the judgment of "dismissal from the army with disgrace" is reversed and he receives the offer of a commission, however, he ceases to cling to life and welcomes death with a kind of enthusiasm in which no sentimental myths are involved.

The narrator repeatedly draws our attention to the "funny belief" that Emerald " 'never shed tears and was incapable of pain' " and makes pointed reference to the two occasions on which he wept. The first was when he returned to the scene of his disgrace and could not find the unmarked grave of his friend Stokes; the second was when he received the offer of a commission. These are the nadir-zenith points in Emerald's relentless determination, within the myth's total action, to see life as life in fact is. He weeps the first time in recognition of the terrifying possibility that he has not just been exiled from home but actually erased from the face of the earth, that his life has no meaning at all. The second time he weeps it is in recognition that he was wrong, that life as he knows it is complete if he is complete. He directs that the bullet be removed from his heart, wrapped in the letter of commission, and placed in the breast pocket of his old soldier's coat; then the coat is to be put back on his body, the whole covered with the flowers he loved best, and the lid screwed on his coffin without further notice of who he was. He would have liked to return to the earth as all the "proper creatures of the earth" do—the flowers, the grass, the dear departed pets—but he accepts the harmony and propriety of the churchyard, consoled by the recognition that it houses the memory of the one soldierly ancestor who had given mythic content to a life to which he has been true and which he has lived long enough to complete.

Emerald Uthwart is a man of exquisite character and irresistible personal style, but such existential solace as he finds in life is nakedly secular, as secular as that of all "proper creatures of the earth" with this addition: he must cope with the attribute of an emotional, intellectual, and moral consciousness that tempts him, in modern life's inevitable divisions, with mythic sentimentality or existential despair. He is determined not to succumb to the former, and though his doom brings him to the very brink of the latter, he survives his "long-agony" and finds peace in being simply and precisely what he *is*.

Even more explicitly than the other imaginary portraits, *Apollo in Picardy* has as its subject critical-creative reading itself: how it is read is made a deliberate concern of its meaning.

Like *Denys L'Auxerrois*, it takes Heine's gods-in-exile theme and provides for it a new myth set in the late Middle Ages. In the background, underscoring its literature-made-of-literature or "palimpsest" motif, is, besides Heine's *Gods in Exile*, the classical myth of Apollo, including but by no means restricted to the death of Hyacinth in the discus-throwing episode. In the foreground are two literary texts. One is a commentary by "a writer of Teutonic proclivities" on Apollo "'as a god definitely in exile'" in both time and place; the other is "a certain manuscript volume taken from an old monastic library in France at the Revolution." The former sets forth a thesis about Apollo's "'sad fortunes'" north of the Alps in the Middle Ages that, despite some evidence of classical learning, is highly Romantic and vestigially medieval in its sympathies. Apollo is seen as a sort of Byronic hero with "'a divine or titanic regret, a titanic revolt in his heart'" that makes him vengeful rather than "'beneficent'" toward man; he "'is in fact a devil!'" The latter supplies the internal evidence upon which the narrator erects an imaginary portrait that brings the Apollo-in-exile theme to a specific critical case. Viewing the form and content of the old monastic manuscript in the context of the author's life and times, he creates a historical fiction that is imaginative in the best critical sense: the protagonist is thoroughly personalized, a complex human being coping in his fashion with a fundamental crisis of life, while at the same time the portrait is "ideal" or typical, a fictive configuration of representative human experience in one of its fascinating specialized manifestations. The narrator acknowledges that, like the Teutonic commentator, the reader ("you") "might fancy" that "Devilry, devil's work" is the import of the old manuscript, and he does not set himself in blank confrontation with such a view. Rather, he interests himself in the "fine gradations and subtly linked conditions," the "delicate and fugitive details," that "are more precious than anything else" to the critical-creative spirit of writer and reader alike. Instead of some "vague scholastic abstraction" like that of the Teutonic commentator, he gives us an "interpolated page" in the great ongoing story of human life in a voice that declines to press moral judgment beyond a point of delicately poised suggestiveness.

To resist the tendency of the ingratiating character of Hyacinth and the re-telling of the Apollo-Hyacinthus episode from the classical myth to divert attention from the portrait's organizing intuition, the reader must keep his critical eye on Prior Saint-Jean, whose tragic metamorphosis is the focus of the story's structure and its central revelation. Apollo himself is subjugated to a particular time and place of which Prior Saint-Jean is the symbolic embodiment, and Hyacinth's youthful capacity to bridge the gulf between the Christian and the pagan is important but ancillary. Without such a critical focus, the portrait's principle of composition would be lost and the reader perhaps tempted to view it too moralistically or as merely an example of picturesque antiquarianism.

The tragic death of Hyacinth in the discus-throwing is, however, the episode that integrates the two myths of the portrait—the pristine classical myth of Apollo and the myth of Prior Saint-Jean, which is imaginatively supported by the classical myth. In the classical myth, Apollo and Hyacinth play the discus-throwing game with equal relish, and the accident that brings about Hyacinth's death has an external explanation, the interference of Zephyr or Boreas. There is no malign intent on Apollo's part and no culpable recklessness. His grief at the loss of the beloved youth is enormous, and he immortalizes his memory with perfect fitness, with blue flowers, "the colour of hope," as Prior Saint-Jean says with Christianizing intent, "of merciful omnipresent deity."

In the myth of Prior Saint-Jean, Apollo and Hyacinth play surrogate roles. Apollo returns the aging, ailing monk to health and high spirits and reveals to him the true meaning of music, the law of the universe that reaches beyond time and space and is wholly constructive and creative in its significance for mankind. But Apollo's gift always has its price, and it is unthinkable that one who has lived so long by "hard and abstract" rules as the aging Prior has should make the conversion to Pythagorean harmony without great inner turmoil. His "battle between light and darkness" is very turbulent indeed, sometimes lifting him to giddy heights—"light, simple, and absolute"—and sometimes making him seem, "with a sign of disgust, of self-reproach, to be his old unimpassioned monastic self once more." In the end, however, he strikes a bargain with Apollo—"to draw down the moon from the sky, for some shameful price, known to the magicians of that day." Apollyon has become to Prior Saint-Jean what Mephistopheles is to Faust.

That is where the Hyacinth of the medieval myth comes in. The charming youth has found "his true self," and though he relishes the vigorous sport with his "beloved playmate," his mind is not, like the Prior's, "divide[d] hopelessly against itself" by Apollyon's influence. He tries to find a means of getting the Prior away or of getting away himself to carry the distressful news back to the monastery. Apollyon, however, "quietly obstructs any movement of that kind." The death of Hyacinth follows immediately from this point, and though it appears to be accidental in the Apollo myth, in the myth of Prior Saint-Jean it leads to the charge of the Prior's "having caused the death of his young server by violence, in a fit of mania, induced by dissolute living in that solitary place."

By its very nature, Pater's imaginative interplay of myths defies reduction to a harsh allegorical interpretation that would satisfy the scientific historian. The duplication of variables makes positive proof impossible. However, if one accepts the portrait's "imaginary" premises—that its appeal is primarily poetic and only secondarily historical, its mythic outlines both firm and suggestive, and its substance incidental to its significance—then it is easier to accept the charge against Prior Saint-Jean as true and to accept it as essentially an act of violence against himself.

As Apollyon-Apollo is the mythic surrogate of one part of his inner nature, Hyacinth is the surrogate of another part. Hyacinth is the "hope," the "merciful omnipresent deity," that was his companion even in the early days in the monastery when, though willing to grow along spiritual lines, he was still naturally rebellious and resistant to conformity, and even afterwards, when conformity became a hard fact based on an abstract theory, the hope persisted as a delightful or "pet" dream—no longer real, perhaps, but still clung to in some secret quarter. When, as a result of personal depletion brought on by prolonged excess in one approach to reality, Prior Saint-Jean is forced to overcome his great anxiety and go to a distant Grange in search of physical and spiritual repair, he is quite naturally accompanied by his pet dream, and in the first stages of his recovery, the dream quickly becomes its "true self" again, the original hope. However, what is is no longer what might have been, and the Prior's desire for recovery and return is gradually replaced by a desire to follow this new approach to reality to its utmost extremes, leading him to make bargains with magical powers beyond ordinary human ken and thus repeating his former pattern of excess. In the meantime, however, the hope embodied in his young companion has been restored to its original, authentic state and becomes a threat to his new obsessions. He does what he can to obstruct its well-founded maneuvers, and then one night in a state of exaltation and panic ("in a fit of mania") brought on by the extravagant hopes and fears obsessing his mind ("by dissolute living in that solitary place"), he crushes to death the one youthful hope that might have served to save him from catastrophe ("caused the death of his young server by violence"). Brought back to the monastery and confined to his quarters as a madman ("*'deliquio animi'*"), he longs only to return to the Grange where he enjoyed his one adult experience of authentic hope, and the preparation for his doing so is simultaneous with his death, "standing upright with an effort to gaze forth once more" into the "blue distance" in which he sees "blue flowers, . . . hyacinths." Though some of his brethren think of him as damned, the myth itself makes no such judgment but is instead suffused with a critically detached understanding or empathy that completes and confirms *Apollo in Picardy* as an imaginative exercise in critical reading.

Apollo in Picardy is a fitting conclusion to what Pater called his "*imaginative* work." A critical-creative reading of art is, he believed, the first step toward a critical-creative reading of life. The great artists and poets are humanity's true prophets—those who not only see things as they in fact are, but also create a form, a style, a life-giving principle that frees mankind from the infinity of details that enslave his spirit and make his days hectic and insignificant. There is nothing unctuous or morally high-minded or merely dilettantish about Pater's view of the constructive relationship between art and life. It is based on a wide-ranging study of the history of the human mind and of his own mind, is supported by a disciplined logical structure, and is indifferent to conventional moral considerations. To make one's life a work of art means simply to be perpetually becoming something in which what one does is an ever finer thread of what one is, the greatest lives being those in which we see modeled "something of the soul of humanity" within "the great structure of human life." The persons in the history of man who have devoted themselves most fully and successfully to the study of such modeling are the artists and poets; they are its experts. Therefore, it is only reasonable that one should look to their example for both the clearest motive and the most direct and efficacious way to achieve it.

A Pater Chronology

1839   Born August 4, the second son of Richard Glode
            Pater, a physician, and Maria Hill. There were three
            other children, William Thompson (1835–1887),
            Hester Maria (1837–1922), and Clara Ann
            (1841–1910)

1842   Father died January 28; family moved to Chase Side,
            Enfield, where Pater attended Enfield Grammar
            School

1853–1858   Attended King's School, Canterbury

1854   Mother died February 25

1858–1862   Attended Queen's College, Oxford, graduating with
            second-class honors in Literae Humaniores

1863   Elected to Old Mortality, an Oxford Literary
            Society

1864   Elected probationary fellow of Brasenose College,
            Oxford; read *Diaphanéitè*, his earliest extant essay,
            to Old Mortality

1865   Traveled to Italy, visiting Ravenna, Pisa, and
            Florence

1866   *Coleridge's Writings*, his first publication, appeared
            anonymously in the *Westminster Review* (January)

1867   *Winckelmann* appeared anonymously in the *West-
            minster Review* (October); became lecturer at
            Brasenose

1868   Traveled abroad; *Poems by William Morris* appeared
            anonymously in the *Westminster Review* (October)

1869   Established a household with his sisters in Bradmore
            Road, Oxford; *Notes on Leonardo da Vinci* appeared
            in the *Fortnightly Review* (November) with his
            name, as did all remaining pieces listed unless oth-
            erwise indicated

1870   *A Fragment on Sandro Botticelli* appeared in the *Fortnightly Review* (August)

1871   *Pico della Mirandola* (October) and *The Poetry of Michelangelo* (November) appeared in the *Fortnightly Review*

1872   Review of Sidney Colvin's *Children in Italian and English Design* appeared in the *Academy* (July 15)

1873   *Studies in the History of the Renaissance* published (February 15)

1874   *On Wordsworth* (April) and *A Fragment on "Measure for Measure"* (November) appeared in the *Fortnightly Review*

1875   Review of John Addington Symonds's *Renaissance in Italy: The Age of the Despots* appeared in the *Academy* (July 31)

1876   Satirized as "Mr. Rose" in W. H. Mallock's *The New Republic; The Myth of Demeter and Persephone* appeared in the *Fortnightly Review* (January and February); *Romanticism* appeared in *Macmillan's Magazine* (November); *A Study of Dionysus. I. The Spiritual Form of Fire and Dew* appeared in the *Fortnightly Review* (December)

1877   *The Renaissance: Studies in Art and Poetry*, 2nd edition, published (May 24), omitting the *Conclusion; The School of Giorgione* appeared in the *Fortnightly Review* (October)

1878   *Imaginary Portraits I. The Child in the House* appeared in *Macmillan's Magazine* (August); *The Character of the Humourist. Charles Lamb* appeared in the *Fortnightly Review* (October); *On "Love's Labours Lost"* appeared in *Macmillan's Magazine* (December); cancelled in proof a volume entitled *Dionysus and Other Studies;* lectured on classical archaeology at Oxford

1880   *The Beginnings of Greek Sculpture. I. The Heroic Age of Greek Art* (February), *II. The Age of Graven Images* (March), and *The Marbles of Aegina* (April) appeared in the *Fortnightly Review*

1882   Traveled in Italy, spending most of his time in Rome

1883   Resigned his tutorship but kept his fellowship at Brasenose College; *Samuel Taylor Coleridge* and

Dante Gabriel Rossetti appeared in T. H. Ward's *The English Poets,* Vol. IV

1885   *Marius the Epicurean: His Sensations and Ideas* published in 2 vols. (February); *A Prince of Court Painters. Extracts from an Old French Journal* appeared in *Macmillan's Magazine* (October); second revised edition of *Marius the Epicurean* published (November); in the summer established a London residence with his sisters at 12 Earl's Terrace, Kensington

1886   *Sir Thomas Browne* appeared in *Macmillan's Magazine* (May); review of *Amiel's "Journal Intime,"* with an introduction and notes by Mrs. Humphry Ward, appeared anonymously in the *Guardian* (March); *Sebastian van Storck* (March), *Denys L'Auxerrois* (November), and an anonymous review of *M. Feuillet's "La Morte"* (December) appeared in *Macmillan's Magazine*

1887   *Duke Carl of Rosenmold* appeared in *Macmillan's Magazine* (May); *Imaginary Portraits* published (June); review of *M. Lemaitre's "Serenus, and Other Tales"* appeared anonymously in *Macmillan's Magazine* (November)

1888   *The Renaissance,* 3rd edition, published, adding *The School of Giorgione* and restoring the *Conclusion;* review of Mrs. Humphry Ward's *Robert Elsmere* appeared anonymously in the *Guardian* (March); first five chapters of *Gaston de Latour* appeared in *Macmillan's Magazine* (June–October); review of *The Life and Letters of Gustave Flaubert* appeared in the *Pall Mall Gazette; Style* appeared in the *Fortnightly Review* (December)

1889   *Shakespeare's English Kings* appeared in *Scribner's Magazine* (April); *Hippolytus Veiled. A Study from Euripides* appeared in *Macmillan's Magazine* (August); *Giordano Bruno. Paris: 1586* appeared in the *Fortnightly Review* (November); *Appreciations. With an Essay on Style* published (December)

1890   *Art Notes in Northern Italy* appeared in the *New Review* (November); *Prosper Mérimée* appeared in the *Fortnightly Review* (November); *Appreciations,*

2nd edition, published, substituting *Feuillet's "La Morte"* for *Æsthetic Poetry*

1892   *The Genius of Plato* appeared in the *Contemporary Review* (February); *A Chapter on Plato* [*Plato and the Doctrine of Motion*] appeared in *Macmillan's Magazine* (May); *Lacedaemon* appeared in the *Contemporary Review* (June); *Emerald Uthwart* appeared in the *New Review* (June and July); *Marius the Epicurean*, 3rd edition, published (August); *Raphael* appeared in the *Fortnightly Review* (October)

1893   *Plato and Platonism. A Series of Lectures* published (February); *Apollo in Picardy* appeared in *Harper's New Monthly Magazine* (November); *The Renaissance*, 4th edition, published (December); in the summer, re-established with his sisters a residence at St. Giles', Oxford

1894   *The Age of Athletic Prizemen* appeared in the *Contemporary Review* (February); *Some Great Churches in France. Notre-Dame d'Amiens* appeared in the *Nineteenth Century* (March); *Some Great Churches in France. Vézelay* appeared in the *Nineteenth Century* (June); died July 30, in Oxford

1895   *Greek Studies. A Series of Essays* published (January 11); *Pascal* appeared in the *Contemporary Review* (February); *Miscellaneous Studies. A Series of Essays* published (October 11)

1896   *Gaston de Latour. An Unfinished Romance* published (October 6); *Essays from "The Guardian"* published

1900–1901   *The Works of Walter Pater*, Edition de Luxe, in 8 vols., published

1910   *The Works of Walter Pater*, New Library Edition, in 10 vols., published

Suggestions for Further Study

The great present need is for a modern scholarly biography. Thomas Wright's two-volume *Life of Walter Pater* (London: Everett, 1907) is sometimes factually imprecise and often insensitive and imperceptive; it has remained more or less standard for its massiveness and the lack of a suitable alternative. In 1978, Michael Levey published *The Case of Walter Pater* (London: Thames and Hudson), a serious, well-written study in biographical form. Levey adds considerable detail to our knowledge of Pater's childhood and family, and his expertise as an art critic and historian is useful, but his book is not the literary biography we need. Lawrance Evans's edition of the *Letters* (London: Oxford University Press, 1970) helps us to be more secure about the publishing history, but Pater was customarily frugal about personal details. The convincing modern biographer will have to be as imaginative and persuasive as Pater himself in recovering the internal evidence of the life and works.

Four recent books have put the study of Pater's writings on a more objective basis than has frequently obtained. R. M. Seiler's *Walter Pater: The Critical Heritage* (London: Routledge) and Franklin E. Court's *Walter Pater: An Annotated Bibliography of Writings about Him* (De Kalb: Northern Illinois University Press), both published in 1980, make it possible to trace Pater's reputation among his contemporaries and to identify and weigh the successive critical fashions to which his writings have been subjected in this century. The books are timely since more serious persons are more seriously interested in Pater at the present time than ever before. Donald L. Hill's fine 1980 edition of *The Renaissance* (Berkeley: University of California Press) and Billie Andrew Inman's 1981 scholarly study of *Walter Pater's Reading* (New York:

Garland Publishing) also reinforce each other. Hill's extensive "Critical and Explanatory Notes" and Inman's detailed account of the books Pater read, especially in the decade preceding the publication of *The Renaissance,* make it abundantly clear that Pater's thought was profoundly influenced by the best philosophical and historical criticism of the century. His so-called impressionism was thoroughly informed and conscientiously balanced as well as distinctive.

At mid-century, Graham Hough (*The Last Romantics* [London: Duckworth, 1949]), Frank Kermode (*Romantic Image* [London: Routledge and Kegan Paul, 1957]), and Iain Fletcher (*Walter Pater* [London: Longmans, 1959, 1971]) made admirable contributions to our understanding of what Pater accomplished in himself and for a whole new phase of Romantic Modernism. In 1969, David DeLaura (*Hebrew and Hellene in Victorian England* [Austin: University of Texas Press]) linked Pater with Newman and Arnold in the most impressive history-of-ideas approach to his works we have.

Currently, Harold Bloom exercises, through his critical writings and the graduate students he has inspired, a large and controversial influence on Pater studies. Besides his introduction to *Selected Writings of Walter Pater* (New York: New American Library, 1974; New York: Columbia University Press, 1981), entitled "The Crystal Man," he has a vigorous essay on "Late Victorian Poetry and Pater" in *Yeats* (New York: Oxford University Press, 1970) and a revision of his introduction to *Marius the Epicurean* (1970) in *The Ringers in the Tower: Studies in Romantic Tradition* (Chicago: University of Chicago Press, 1971). Gerald Monsman, our most prolific commentator on Pater at the present time, frankly acknowledges his debt to Bloom (and to J. Hillis Miller) and sees it as the way to the future in Pater studies. In his latest book, *Walter Pater's Art of Autobiography* (New Haven: Yale University Press, 1980), Monsman identifies and offers "a formula for pulling together all [Pater's] varied writings . . . under the rubric of criticism-as-creative-self-portraiture." A more varied profile of the present state of Pater studies can be found in *Walter Pater: An Imaginative Sense of Fact,* edited by Philip Dodd (London: Frank Cass, 1981)—papers from the first International Pater Conference held at Oxford in 1980.

THE RENAISSANCE:
STUDIES IN ART AND POETRY

In his edition of *The Renaissance*, the text of which is used here, Donald L. Hill makes one emendation and nine corrections: p. 73: critic for critique; pp. 96–97: Villa of Careggi for Villa Careggi; p. 107: *La Città di Vita* for *La Città Vita*; p. 126: ante-natal for anti-natal; p. 147: A hundred anecdotes for Effective anecdotes; p. 160: narrowly examined for narrowly explained; p. 182: *œillets* for *œlliets*; p. 186: 1748 for 1784; p. 191: insert phrase — words spoken on so high an occasion— after *soi-même*; p. 212: 1786 for 1876.

Preface

Many attempts have been made by writers on art and poetry to define beauty in the abstract, to express it in the most general terms, to find some universal formula for it. The value of these attempts has most often been in the suggestive and penetrating things said by the way. Such discussions help us very little to enjoy what has been well done in art or poetry, to discriminate between what is more and what is less excellent in them, or to use words like beauty, excellence, art, poetry, with a more precise meaning than they would otherwise have. Beauty, like all other qualities presented to human experience, is relative; and the definition of it becomes unmeaning and useless in proportion to its abstractness. To define beauty, not in the most abstract but in the most concrete terms possible, to find, not its universal formula, but the formula which expresses most adequately this or that special manifestation of it, is the aim of the true student of æsthetics.

"To see the object as in itself it really is," has been justly said to be the aim of all true criticism whatever; and in æsthetic criticism the first step towards seeing one's object as it really is, is to know one's own impression as it really is, to discriminate it, to realise it distinctly. The objects with which æsthetic criticism deals—music, poetry, artistic and accomplished forms of human life—are indeed receptacles of so many powers or forces: they possess, like the products of nature, so many virtues or qualities. What is this song or picture, this engaging personality presented in life or in a book, to *me*? What effect does it really produce on me? Does it give me pleasure? and if so, what sort or degree of pleasure? How is my nature modified by its presence, and under its influence? The answers to these questions are the original facts with which the æsthetic critic has to do; and, as in the study of light, of morals, of number, one must realise such primary data for one's self, or not at all. And he who experiences these impressions strongly, and drives directly at the discrimination and analysis of them, has no need to trouble himself with the abstract question what beauty is in itself, or what its exact relation to truth or experience—metaphysical questions, as unprofitable as metaphysical questions elsewhere. He may pass them all by as being, answerable or not, of no interest to him.

The æsthetic critic, then, regards all the objects with which he has to do, all works of art, and the fairer forms of nature and human life, as powers or forces producing pleasurable sensations, each of a more or less peculiar or unique kind. This influence he feels, and wishes to explain, by analysing and reducing it to its elements. To him, the picture, the landscape, the engaging personality in life or in a book, *La Gioconda*, the hills of Carrara, Pico of Mirandola, are valuable for their virtues, as we say, in speaking of a herb, a wine, a gem; for the property each has of affecting one with a special, a unique, impression of pleasure. Our education becomes complete in proportion as our susceptibility to these impressions increases in depth and variety. And the function of the æsthetic critic is to distinguish, to analyse, and separate from its adjuncts, the virtue by which a picture, a landscape, a fair personality in life or in a book, produces this special impression of beauty or pleasure, to indicate what the source of that impression is, and under what conditions it is experienced. His end is reached when he has disengaged that virtue, and noted it, as a chemist notes some natural element, for himself and others; and the rule for those who would reach this end is stated with great exactness in the words of a recent critique of Sainte-Beuve:—*De se borner à connaître de près les belles choses, et à s'en nourrir en exquis amateurs, en humanistes accomplis.*

What is important, then, is not that the critic should possess a correct abstract definition of beauty for the intellect, but a certain kind of temperament, the power of being deeply moved by the presence of beautiful objects. He will remember always that beauty exists in many forms. To him all periods, types, schools of taste, are in themselves equal. In all ages there have been some excellent workmen, and some excellent work done. The question he asks is always:—In whom did the stir, the genius, the sentiment of the period find itself? where was the receptacle of its refinement, its elevation, its taste? "The ages are all equal," says William Blake, "but genius is always above its age."

Often it will require great nicety to disengage this virtue from the commoner elements with which it may be found in combination. Few artists, not Goethe or Byron even, work quite cleanly, casting off all *débris*, and leaving us only what the heat of their imagination has wholly fused and transformed. Take, for instance, the writings of Wordsworth. The heat of his genius, entering into the substance of his work, has crystallised a part, but only a part, of it; and in that great mass of verse there is much which might well be forgotten. But scattered up and down it, sometimes fusing and transforming entire compositions, like the Stanzas on *Resolution and Independence*, or the *Ode on the Recollections of Childhood*, sometimes, as if at random, depositing a fine crystal here or there, in a matter it does not wholly search through and transmute, we trace the action of his unique, incommunicable faculty, that strange, mystical sense of a life in natural things, and of man's life as a part of nature, drawing strength and colour and character from local influences, from the hills and streams, and from natural sights and sounds. Well! that is the *virtue*, the active principle in Wordsworth's poetry; and then the function of the critic of Wordsworth is to follow up that active principle, to disengage it, to mark the degree in which it penetrates his verse.

The subjects of the following studies are taken from the history of the *Renaissance*, and touch what I think the chief points in that complex, many-sided movement. I have explained in the first of them what I understand by the word, giving it a much wider scope than was intended by those who originally used it to denote that revival of classical antiquity in the fifteenth century which was only one of many results of a general excitement and enlightening of the human mind, but of which the great aim and achievements of what, as Christian art, is often falsely opposed to the Renaissance, were another result. This outbreak of the human spirit may be traced far into the middle age itself, with its motives

already clear pronounced, the care for physical beauty, the worship of the body, the breaking down of those limits which the
religious system of the middle age imposed on the heart and the
imagination. I have taken as an example of this movement, this
earlier Renaissance within the middle age itself, and as an expression of its qualities, two little compositions in early French;
not because they constitute the best possible expression of them,
but because they help the unity of my series, inasmuch as the
Renaissance ends also in France, in French poetry, in a phase of
which the writings of Joachim du Bellay are in many ways the
most perfect illustration. The Renaissance, in truth, put forth in
France an aftermath, a wonderful later growth, the products of
which have to the full that subtle and delicate sweetness which
belongs to a refined and comely decadence, as its earliest phases
have the freshness which belongs to all periods of growth in art,
the charm of *ascêsis*, of the austere and serious girding of the loins
in youth.

But it is in Italy, in the fifteenth century, that the interest of the
Renaissance mainly lies,—in that solemn fifteenth century which
can hardly be studied too much, not merely for its positive results
in the things of the intellect and the imagination, its concrete
works of art, its special and prominent personalities, with their
profound æsthetic charm, but for its general spirit and character,
for the ethical qualities of which it is a consummate type.

The various forms of intellectual activity which together make
up the culture of an age, move for the most part from different
starting-points, and by unconnected roads. As products of the
same generation they partake indeed of a common character, and
unconsciously illustrate each other; but of the producers themselves, each group is solitary, gaining what advantage or disadvantage there may be in intellectual isolation. Art and poetry,
philosophy and the religious life, and that other life of refined
pleasure and action in the conspicuous places of the world, are
each of them confined to its own circle of ideas, and those who
prosecute either of them are generally little curious of the thoughts
of others. There come, however, from time to time, eras of more
favourable conditions, in which the thoughts of men draw nearer
together than is their wont, and the many interests of the intel-

lectual world combine in one complete type of general culture. The fifteenth century in Italy is one of these happier eras, and what is sometimes said of the age of Pericles is true of that of Lorenzo:—it is an age productive in personalities, many-sided, centralised, complete. Here, artists and philosophers and those whom the action of the world has elevated and made keen, do not live in isolation, but breathe a common air, and catch light and heat from each other's thoughts. There is a spirit of general elevation and enlightenment, in which all alike communicate. The unity of this spirit gives unity to all the various products of the Renaissance; and it is to this intimate alliance with mind, this participation in the best thoughts which that age produced, that the art of Italy in the fifteenth century owes much of its grave dignity and influence.

I have added an essay on Winckelmann, as not incongruous with the studies which precede it, because Winckelmann, coming in the eighteenth century, really belongs in spirit to an earlier age. By his enthusiasm for the things of the intellect and the imagination for their own sake, by his Hellenism, his life-long struggle to attain to the Greek spirit, he is in sympathy with the humanists of a previous century. He is the last fruit of the Renaissance, and explains in a striking way its motive and tendencies.

1873.

Two Early French Stories

The history of the Renaissance ends in France, and carries us away from Italy to the beautiful cities of the country of the Loire. But it was in France also, in a very important sense, that the Renaissance had begun. French writers, who are fond of connecting the creations of Italian genius with a French origin, who tell us how Saint Francis of Assissi took not his name only, but all those notions of chivalry and romantic love which so deeply penetrated his thoughts, from a French source, how Boccaccio borrowed the outlines of his stories from the old French *fabliaux*, and how Dante himself expressly connects the origin of the art of miniature-painting with the city of Paris, have often dwelt on this notion of a Renaissance in the end of the twelfth and the beginning of the thirteenth century, a Renaissance within the limits of the middle age itself—a brilliant, but in part abortive effort to do for human life and the human mind what was afterwards done in the fifteenth. The word *Renaissance*, indeed, is now generally used to denote not merely the revival of classical antiquity which took place in the fifteenth century, and to which the word was first applied, but a whole complex movement, of which that revival of classical antiquity was but one element or symptom. For us the Renaissance is the name of a many-sided but yet united movement, in which the love of the things of the intellect and the imagination for their own sake, the desire for a more liberal and comely way of conceiving life, make themselves felt, urging those who experience this desire to search out first one and then another means of intellectual or imaginative enjoyment, and directing them not only to the discovery of old and forgotten sources of this enjoyment, but to the divination of fresh sources thereof—

new experiences, new subjects of poetry, new forms of art. Of such feeling there was a great outbreak in the end of the twelfth and the beginning of the following century. Here and there, under rare and happy conditions, in pointed architecture, in the doctrines of romantic love, in the poetry of Provence, the rude strength of the middle age turns to sweetness; and the taste for sweetness generated there becomes the seed of the classical revival in it, prompting it constantly to seek after the springs of perfect sweetness in the Hellenic world. And coming after a long period in which this instinct had been crushed, that true "dark age," in which so many sources of intellectual and imaginative enjoyment had actually disappeared, this outbreak is rightly called a Renaissance, a revival.

Theories which bring into connexion with each other modes of thought and feeling, periods of taste, forms of art and poetry, which the narrowness of men's minds constantly tends to oppose to each other, have a great stimulus for the intellect, and are almost always worth understanding. It is so with this theory of a Renaissance within the middle age, which seeks to establish a continuity between the most characteristic work of that period, the sculpture of Chartres, the windows of Le Mans, and the work of the later Renaissance, the work of Jean Cousin and Germain Pilon, thus healing that rupture between the middle age and the Renaissance which has so often been exaggerated. But it is not so much the ecclesiastical art of the middle age, its sculpture and painting—work certainly done in a great measure for pleasure's sake, in which even a secular, a rebellious spirit often betrays itself—but rather its profane poetry, the poetry of Provence, and the magnificent after-growth of that poetry in Italy and France, which those French writers have in view when they speak of this medieval Renaissance. In that poetry, earthly passion, with its intimacy, its freedom, its variety—the liberty of the heart— makes itself felt; and the name of Abelard, the great scholar and the great lover, connects the expression of this liberty of heart with the free play of human intelligence around all subjects presented to it, with the liberty of the intellect, as that age understood it.

Every one knows the legend of Abelard, a legend hardly less

passionate, certainly not less characteristic of the middle age, than the legend of Tannhäuser; how the famous and comely clerk, in whom Wisdom herself, self-possessed, pleasant, and discreet, seemed to sit enthroned, came to live in the house of a canon of the church of *Notre-Dame*, where dwelt a girl, Heloïse, believed to be the old priest's orphan niece; how the old priest had testified his love for her by giving her an education then unrivalled, so that rumour asserted that, through the knowledge of languages, enabling her to penetrate into the mysteries of the older world, she had become a sorceress, like the Celtic druidesses; and how as Abelard and Heloïse sat together at home there, to refine a little further on the nature of abstract ideas, "Love made himself of the party with them." You conceive the temptations of the scholar, who, in such dreamy tranquillity, amid the bright and busy spectacle of the "Island," lived in a world of something like shadows; and that for one who knew so well how to assign its exact value to every abstract thought, those restraints which lie on the consciences of other men had been relaxed. It appears that he composed many verses in the vulgar tongue: already the young men sang them on the quay below the house. Those songs, says M. de Rémusat, were probably in the taste of the *Trouvères*, "of whom he was one of the first in date, or, so to speak, the predecessor." It is the same spirit which has moulded the famous "letters," written in the quaint Latin of the middle age.

At the foot of that early Gothic tower, which the next generation raised to grace the precincts of Abelard's school, on the "Mountain of Saint Geneviève," the historian Michelet sees in thought "a terrible assembly; not the hearers of Abelard alone, fifty bishops, twenty cardinals, two popes, the whole body of scholastic philosophy; not only the learned Heloïse, the teaching of languages, and the Renaissance; but Arnold of Brescia—that is to say, the revolution." And so from the rooms of this shadowy house by the Seine side we see that spirit going abroad, with its qualities already well defined, its intimacy, its languid sweetness, its rebellion, its subtle skill in dividing the elements of human passion, its care for physical beauty, its worship of the body, which penetrated the early literature of Italy, and finds an echo even in Dante.

That Abelard is not mentioned in the *Divine Comedy* may appear a singular omission to the reader of Dante, who seems to have inwoven into the texture of his work whatever had impressed him as either effective in colour or spiritually significant among the recorded incidents of actual life. Nowhere in his great poem do we find the name, nor so much as an allusion to the story of one who had left so deep a mark on the philosophy of which Dante was an eager student, of whom in the *Latin Quarter*, and from the lips of scholar or teacher in the University of Paris, during his sojourn among them, he can hardly have failed to hear. We can only suppose that he had indeed considered the story and the man, and abstained from passing judgment as to his place in the scheme of "eternal justice."

In the famous legend of Tannhäuser, the erring knight makes his way to Rome, to seek absolution at the centre of Christian religion. "So soon," thought and said the Pope, "as the staff in his hand should bud and blossom, so soon might the soul of Tannhäuser be saved, and no sooner;" and it came to pass not long after that the dry wood of a staff which the Pope had carried in his hand was covered with leaves and flowers. So, in the cloister of Godstow, a petrified tree was shown of which the nuns told that the fair Rosamond, who had died among them, had declared that, the tree being then alive and green, it would be changed into stone at the hour of her salvation. When Abelard died, like Tannhäuser, he was on his way to Rome. What might have happened had he reached his journey's end is uncertain; and it is in this uncertain twilight that his relation to the general beliefs of his age has always remained. In this, as in other things, he prefigures the character of the Renaissance, that movement in which, in various ways, the human mind wins for itself a new kingdom of feeling and sensation and thought, not opposed to but only beyond and independent of the spiritual system then actually realised. The opposition into which Abelard is thrown, which gives its colour to his career, which breaks his soul to pieces, is a no less subtle opposition than that between the merely professional, official, hireling ministers of that system, with their ignorant worship of system for its own sake, and the true child of light, the humanist, with reason and heart and senses quick, while theirs were almost dead. He reaches out towards, he attains, modes of ideal living, beyond the prescribed limits of that system, though in essential germ, it may be, contained within it. As always happens, the adherents of the poorer and narrower culture had no sympathy with, because no understanding of, a culture richer and more ample than their own. After the discovery of wheat they would still live upon acorns—*après l'invention du blé ils voulaient encore vivre du gland;* and would hear of no service to the higher needs of humanity with instruments not of their forging.

But the human spirit, bold through those needs, was too strong for them. Abelard and Heloïse write their letters—letters with a wonderful outpouring of soul—in medieval Latin; and Abelard, though he composes songs in the vulgar tongue, writes also in Latin those treatises in which he tries to find a ground of reality below the abstractions of philosophy, as one bent on trying all things by their congruity with human experience, who had felt the hand of Heloïse, and looked into her eyes, and tested the resources of humanity in her great and energetic nature. Yet it is only a little later, early in the thirteenth century, that French prose romance begins; and in one of the pretty volumes of the *Bibliothèque Elzevirienne* some of the most striking fragments of it may be found, edited with much intelligence. In one of these thirteenth-century stories, *Li Amitiez de Ami et Amile,* that free play of human affection, of the claims of which Abelard's story is an assertion, makes itself felt in the incidents of a great friendship, a friendship pure and generous, pushed to a sort of passionate exaltation, and more than faithful unto death. Such comradeship, though instances of it are to be found everywhere, is still especially a classical motive; Chaucer expressing the sentiment of it so strongly in an antique tale, that one knows not whether the love of both Palamon and Arcite for Emelya, or of those two for each other, is the chiefer subject of the *Knight's Tale—*

> *He cast his eyen upon Emelya,*
> *And therewithal he bleynte and cried, ah!*
> *As that he stongen were unto the herte.*

What reader does not refer something of the bitterness of that cry to the spoiling, already foreseen, of the fair friendship, which had made the prison of the two lads sweet hitherto with its daily offices?

The friendship of Amis and Amile is deepened by the romantic circumstances of an entire personal resemblance between the two heroes, through which they pass for each other again and again, and thereby into many strange adventures; that curious interest of the *Doppelgänger*, which begins among the stars with the Dioscuri, being entwined in and out through all the incidents of the story, like an outward token of the inward similitude of their souls. With this, again, is connected, like a second reflexion of that inward similitude, the conceit of two marvellously beautiful cups, also exactly like each other—children's cups, of wood, but adorned with gold and precious stones. These two cups, which by their resemblance help to bring the friends together at critical moments, were given to them by the Pope, when he baptised them at Rome, whither the parents had taken them for that purpose, in gratitude for their birth. They cross and recross very strangely in the narrative, serving the two heroes almost like living things, and with that well-known effect of a beautiful object, kept constantly before the eye in a story or poem, of keeping sensation well awake, and giving a certain air of refinement to all the scenes into which it enters. That sense of fate, which hangs so much of the shaping of human life on trivial objects, like Othello's strawberry handkerchief, is thereby heightened, while witness is borne to the enjoyment of beautiful handiwork by a primitive people, their simple wonder at it, so that they give it an oddly significant place among the factors of a human history.

Amis and Amile, then, are true to their comradeship through all trials; and in the end it comes to pass that at a moment of great need Amis takes the place of Amile in a tournament for life or death. "After this it happened that a leprosy fell upon Amis, so that his wife would not approach him, and wrought to strangle him. He departed therefore from his home, and at last prayed his servants to carry him to the house of Amile;" and it is in what follows that the curious strength of the piece shows itself:—

His servants, willing to do as he desired, carried him to the place where Amile was; and they began to sound their rattles before the court of

Amile's house, as lepers are accustomed to do. And when Amile heard the
noise he commanded one of his servants to carry meat and bread to the
sick man, and the cup which was given to him at Rome filled with good
wine. And when the servant had done as he was commanded, he returned
and said, Sir, if I had not thy cup in my hand, I should believe that the cup
which the sick man has was thine, for they are alike, the one to the other,
in height and fashion. And Amile said, Go quickly and bring him to me.
And when Amis stood before his comrade Amile demanded of him who he
was, and how he had gotten that cup. I am of Briquain le Chastel, answered Amis, and the cup was given to me by the Bishop of Rome, who
baptised me. And when Amile heard that, he knew that it was his comrade Amis, who had delivered him from death, and won for him the
daughter of the King of France to be his wife. And straightway he fell
upon him, and began weeping greatly, and kissed him. And when his wife
heard that, she ran out with her hair in disarray, weeping and distressed
exceedingly, for she remembered that it was he who had slain the false
Ardres. And thereupon they placed him in a fair bed, and said to him,
Abide with us until God's will be accomplished in thee, for all we have is
at thy service. So he and the two servants abode with them.

And it came to pass one night, when Amis and Amile lay in one chamber without other companions, that God sent His angel Raphael to Amis,
who said to him, Amis, art thou asleep? And he, supposing that Amile had
called him, answered and said, I am not asleep, fair comrade! And the
angel said to him, Thou hast answered well, for thou art the comrade of
the heavenly citizens.—I am Raphael, the angel of our Lord, and am come
to tell thee how thou mayest be healed; for thy prayers are heard. Thou
shalt bid Amile, thy comrade, that he slay his two children and wash thee
in their blood, and so thy body shall be made whole. And Amis said to
him, Let not this thing be, that my comrade should become a murderer for
my sake. But the angel said, It is convenient that he do this. And thereupon the angel departed.

And Amile also, as if in sleep, heard those words; and he awoke and
said, Who is it, my comrade, that hath spoken with thee? And Amis
answered, No man; only I have prayed to our Lord, as I am accustomed.
And Amile said, Not so! but some one hath spoken with thee. Then he
arose and went to the door of the chamber; and finding it shut he said, Tell
me, my brother, who it was said those words to thee to-night. And Amis
began to weep greatly, and told him that it was Raphael, the angel of the
Lord, who had said to him, Amis, our Lord commands thee that thou bid
Amile slay his two children, and wash thee in their blood, and so thou
shalt be healed of thy leprosy. And Amile was greatly disturbed at those
words, and said, I would have given to thee my man-servants and my
maid-servants and all my goods, and thou feignest that an angel hath
spoken to thee that I should slay my two children. And immediately Amis
began to weep, and said, I know that I have spoken a terrible thing, but
constrained thereto; I pray thee cast me not away from the shelter of thy

house. And Amile answered that what he had convenanted with him, that he would perform, unto the hour of his death: But I conjure thee, said he, by the faith which there is between me and thee, and by our comradeship, and by the baptism we received together at Rome, that thou tell me whether it was man or angel said that to thee. And Amis answered again, So truly as an angel hath spoken to me this night, so may God deliver me from my infirmity!

Then Amile began to weep in secret, and thought within himself: If this man was ready to die before the king for me, shall I not for him slay my children? Shall I not keep faith with him who was faithful to me even unto death? And Amile tarried no longer, but departed to the chamber of his wife, and bade her go hear the Sacred Office. And he took a sword, and went to the bed where the children were lying, and found them asleep. And he lay down over them and began to weep bitterly and said, Hath any man yet heard of a father who of his own will slew his children? Alas, my children! I am no longer your father, but your cruel murderer.

And the children awoke at the tears of their father, which fell upon them; and they looked up into his face and began to laugh. And as they were of the age of about three years, he said, Your laughing will be turned into tears, for your innocent blood must now be shed, and therewith he cut off their heads. Then he laid them back in the bed, and put the heads upon the bodies, and covered them as though they slept: and with the blood which he had taken he washed his comrade, and said, Lord Jesus Christ! who has commanded men to keep faith on earth, and didst heal the leper by Thy word! cleanse now my comrade, for whose love I have shed the blood of my children.

Then Amis was cleansed of his leprosy. And Amile clothed his companion in his best robes; and as they went to the church to give thanks, the bells, by the will of God, rang of their own accord. And when the people of the city heard that, they ran together to see the marvel. And the wife of Amile, when she saw Amis and Amile coming, asked which of the twain was her husband, and said, I know well the vesture of them both, but I know not which of them is Amile. And Amile said to her, I am Amile, and my companion is Amis, who is healed of his sickness. And she was full of wonder, and desired to know in what manner he was healed. Give thanks to our Lord, answered Amile, but trouble not thyself as to the manner of the healing.

Now neither the father nor the mother had yet entered where the children were; but the father sighed heavily, because they were dead, and the mother asked for them, that they might rejoice together; but Amile said, Dame! let the children sleep. And it was already the hour of Tierce. And going in alone to the children to weep over them, he found them at play in the bed; only, in place of the sword-cuts about their throats was as it were a thread of crimson. And he took them in his arms and carried them to his wife and said, Rejoice greatly, for thy children whom I had slain by the commandment of the angel are alive, and by their blood is Amis healed.

There, as I said, is the strength of the old French story. For the Renaissance has not only the sweetness which it derives from the classical world, but also that curious strength of which there are great resources in the true middle age. And as I have illustrated the early strength of the Renaissance by the story of Amis and Amile, a story which comes from the North, in which a certain racy Teutonic flavour is perceptible, so I shall illustrate that other element, its early sweetness, a languid excess of sweetness even, by another story printed in the same volume of the *Bibliothèque Elzevirienne*, and of about the same date, a story which comes, characteristically, from the South, and connects itself with the literature of Provence.

The central love-poetry of Provence, the poetry of the *Tenson* and the *Aubade*, of Bernard de Ventadour and Pierre Vidal, is poetry for the few, for the elect and peculiar people of the kingdom of sentiment. But below this intenser poetry there was probably a wide range of literature, less serious and elevated, reaching, by lightness of form and comparative homeliness of interest, an audience which the concentrated passion of those higher lyrics left untouched. This literature has long since perished, or lives only in later French or Italian versions. One such version, the only representative of its species, M. Fauriel thought he detected in the story of *Aucassin and Nicolette*, written in the French of the latter half of the thirteenth century, and preserved in a unique manuscript, in the national library of Paris; and there were reasons which made him divine for it a still more ancient ancestry, traces in it of an Arabian origin, as in a leaf lost out of some early *Arabian Nights*[1].

The little book loses none of its interest through the criticism which finds in it only a traditional subject, handed on by one people to another; for after passing thus from hand to hand, its

[1] Recently, *Aucassin and Nicolette* has been edited and translated into English, with much graceful scholarship, by Mr. F. W. Bourdillon. Still more recently we have had a translation—a poet's translation—from the ingenious and versatile pen of Mr. Andrew Lang. The reader should consult also the chapter on "The Outdoor Poetry," in Vernon Lee's most interesting *Euphorion; being Studies of the Antique and Mediæval in the Renaissance*, a work abounding in knowledge and insight on the subjects of which it treats.

outline is still clear, its surface untarnished; and, like many other stories, books, literary and artistic conceptions of the middle age, it has come to have in this way a sort of personal history, almost as full of risk and adventure as that of its own heroes. The writer himself calls the piece a *cantefable*, a tale told in prose, but with its incidents and sentiment helped forward by songs, inserted at irregular intervals. In the junctions of the story itself there are signs of roughness and want of skill, which make one suspect that the prose was only put together to connect a series of songs—a series of songs so moving and attractive that people wished to heighten and dignify their effect by a regular framework or setting. Yet the songs themselves are of the simplest kind, not rhymed even, but only imperfectly assonant, stanzas of twenty or thirty lines apiece, all ending with a similar vowel sound. And here, as elsewhere in that early poetry, much of the interest lies in the spectacle of the formation of a new artistic sense. A novel art is arising, the music of rhymed poetry, and in the songs of Aucassin and Nicolette, which seem always on the point of passing into true rhyme, but which halt somehow, and can never quite take flight, you see people just growing aware of the elements of a new music in their possession, and anticipating how pleasant such music might become.

The piece was probably intended to be recited by a company of trained performers, many of whom, at least for the lesser parts, were probably children. The songs are introduced by the rubric, *Or se cante (ici on chante)* and each division of prose by the rubric, *Or dient et content et fabloient (ici on conte)*. The musical notes of a portion of the songs have been preserved; and some of the details are so descriptive that they suggested to M. Fauriel the notion that the words had been accompanied throughout by dramatic action. That mixture of simplicity and refinement which he was surprised to find in a composition of the thirteenth century, is shown sometimes in the turn given to some passing expression or remark; thus, "the Count de Garins was old and frail, his time was over"—*Li quens Garins de Beaucaire estoit vix et frales; si avoit son tans trespassé.* And then all is so realised! One sees the ancient forest, with its disused roads grown deep with grass, and the place where seven roads meet—*u a forkeut set cemin qui s'en vont par le païs;* we hear the light-hearted country-people calling each other by their rustic names, and putting forward, as their spokesman, one among them who is more eloquent and ready than the rest—*li un qui plus fu enparlés des autres;* for the little book has its burlesque element also, so that one hears the faint, far-off laughter still. Rough as it is, the piece certainly possesses this high quality of poetry, that it aims at a purely artistic effect. Its subject is a great sorrow, yet it claims to be a thing of joy and refreshment, to be entertained not for its matter only, but chiefly for its manner; it is *cortois*, it tells us, *et bien assis.*

For the student of manners, and of the old French language and literature, it has much interest of a purely antiquarian order. To say of an ancient literary composition that it has an antiquarian interest, often means that it has no distinct æsthetic interest for the reader of to-day. Antiquarianism, by a purely historical effort, by putting its object in perspective, and setting the reader in a certain point of view, from which what gave pleasure to the past is pleasurable for him also, may often add greatly to the charm we receive from ancient literature. But the first condition of such aid must be a real, direct, æsthetic charm in the thing itself. Unless it has that charm, unless some purely artistic quality went to its original making, no merely antiquarian effort can ever give it an æsthetic value, or make it a proper subject of æsthetic criticism. This quality, wherever it exists, it is always pleasant to define, and discriminate from the sort of borrowed interest which an old play, or an old story, may very likely acquire through a true antiquarianism. The story of Aucassin and Nicolette has something of this quality. Aucassin, the only son of Count Garins of Beaucaire, is passionately in love with Nicolette, a beautiful girl of unknown parentage, bought of the Saracens, whom his father will not permit him to marry. The story turns on the adventures of these two lovers, until at the end of the piece their mutual fidelity is rewarded. These adventures are of the simplest sort, adventures which seem to be chosen for the happy occasion they afford of keeping the eye of the fancy, perhaps the outward eye, fixed on pleasant objects, a garden, a ruined tower, the little hut of flowers which Nicolette constructs in the forest whither she escapes from her enemies, as a token to Aucassin that she has passed that way. All the charm of the piece is in its details, in a turn of peculiar lightness and grace given to the situations and traits of sentiment, especially in its quaint fragments of early French prose.

All through it one feels the influence of that faint air of over-wrought delicacy, almost of wantonness, which was so strong a characteristic of the poetry of the Troubadours. The Troubadours themselves were often men of great rank; they wrote for an exclusive audience, people of much leisure and great refinement, and they came to value a type of personal beauty which has in it but little of the influence of the open air and sunshine. There is a languid Eastern deliciousness in the very scenery of the story, the full-blown roses, the chamber painted in some mysterious manner where Nicolette is imprisoned, the cool brown marble, the almost nameless colours, the odour of plucked grass and flowers. Nicolette herself well becomes this scenery, and is the best illustration of the quality I mean—the beautiful, weird, foreign girl, whom the shepherds take for a fay, who has the knowledge of simples, the healing and beautifying qualities of leaves and flowers, whose skilful touch heals Aucassin's sprained shoulder, so that he suddenly leaps from the ground; the mere sight of whose white flesh, as she passed the place where he lay, healed a pilgrim stricken with sore disease, so that he rose up, and returned to his own country. With this girl Aucassin is so deeply in love that he forgets all knightly duties. At last Nicolette is shut up to get her out of his way, and perhaps the prettiest passage in the whole piece is the fragment of prose which describes her escape:—

Aucassin was put in prison, as you have heard, and Nicolette remained shut up in her chamber. It was summer-time, in the month of May, when the days are warm and long and clear, and the nights coy and serene.

One night Nicolette, lying on her bed, saw the moon shine clear through the little window, and heard the nightingale sing in the garden, and then came the memory of Aucassin, whom she so much loved. She thought of the Count Garins of Beaucaire, who mortally hated her, and, to be rid of her, might at any moment cause her to be burned or drowned. She perceived that the old woman who kept her company was asleep; she rose and put on the fairest gown she had; she took the bedclothes and the towels, and knotted them together like a cord, as far as they would go. Then she tied the end to a pillar of the window, and let herself slip down quite softly into the garden, and passed straight across it, to reach the town.

Her hair was yellow in small curls, her smiling eyes blue-green, her face clear and feat, the little lips very red, the teeth small and white; and the daisies which she crushed in passing, holding her skirt high behind and before, looked dark against her feet; the girl was so white!

She came to the garden-gate and opened it, and walked through the streets of Beaucaire, keeping on the dark side of the way to be out of the light of the moon, which shone quietly in the sky. She walked as fast as she could, until she came to the tower where Aucassin was. She pressed herself against one of the pillars, wrapped herself closely in her mantle, and putting her face to a chink in the tower, which was old and ruined, she heard Aucassin crying bitterly within, and when she had listened awhile she began to speak.—

But scattered up and down through this lighter matter, always tinged with humour and often passing into burlesque, which makes up the general substance of the piece, there are morsels of a different quality, touches of some intenser sentiment, coming it would seem from the profound and energetic spirt of the Provençal poetry itself, to which the inspiration of the book has been referred. Let me gather up these morsels of deeper colour, these expressions of the ideal intensity of love, the motive which really unites together the fragments of the little composition. Dante, the perfect flower of ideal love, has recorded how the tyranny of that "Lord of terrible aspect" became actually physical, blinding his senses, and suspending his bodily forces. In this, Dante is but the central expression and type of experiences known well enough to the initiated, in that passionate age. Aucassin represents this ideal intensity of passion—

> *Aucassin, li biax, li blons,*
> *Li gentix, li amorous;—*

slim, tall, debonair, *dansellon*, as the singers call him, with his curled yellow hair, and eyes of *vair*, who faints with love, as Dante fainted, who rides all day through the forest in search of Nicolette, while the thorns tear his flesh, so that one might have traced him by the blood upon the grass, and who weeps at eventide because he has not found her, who has the malady of his love, and neglects all knightly duties. Once he is induced to put himself at the head of his people, that they, seeing him before them, might have more heart to defend themselves; then a song relates how the sweet, grave figure goes forth to battle, in dainty, tight-laced armour. It is the very image of the Provençal love-god, no longer a child, but grown to pensive youth, as Pierre Vidal met him, riding on a white horse, fair as the morning, his vestment embroidered with flowers. He rode on through the gates into the open plain beyond. But as he went, that great malady of his love came upon him. The bridle fell from his hands; and like one who sleeps walking, he was carried on into the midst of his enemies, and heard them talking together how they might most conveniently kill him.

One of the strongest characteristics of that outbreak of the reason and the imagination, of that assertion of the liberty of the heart, in the middle age, which I have termed a medieval Renaissance, was its antinomianism, its spirit of rebellion and revolt against the moral and religious ideas of the time. In their search after the pleasures of the senses and the imagination, in their care for beauty, in their worship of the body, people were impelled beyond the bounds of the Christian ideal; and their love became sometimes a strange idolatry, a strange rival religion. It was the return of that ancient Venus, not dead, but only hidden for a time in the caves of the Venusberg, of those old pagan gods still going to and fro on the earth, under all sorts of disguises. And this element in the middle age, for the most part ignored by those writers who have treated it preeminently as the "Age of Faith"—this rebellious and antinomian element, the recognition of which has made the delineation of the middle age by the writers of the Romantic school in France, by Victor Hugo for instances in *Notre-Dame de Paris*, so suggestive and exciting—is found alike in the history of Abelard and the legend of Tannhäuser. More and more, as we come to mark changes and distinctions of temper in what is often in one all-embracing confusion called the middle age, that rebellion, that sinister claim for liberty of heart and thought, comes to the surface. The Albigensian-movement, connected so strangely with the history of Provençal poetry, is deeply tinged with it. A touch of it makes the Franciscan order, with its poetry, its mysticism, its "illumination," from the point of view of religious authority, justly suspect. It influences the thoughts of those obscure prophetical writers, like Joachim of Flora, strange dreamers in a world of flowery rhetoric of that third and final dispensation of a "spirit of freedom," in which law shall have passed away. Of this spirit *Aucassin and Nicolette* contains perhaps the most famous expression: it is the answer Aucassin gives when he is threatened with the pains of hell, if he makes Nicolette his mistress. A creature wholly of affection and the senses, he sees on the way to paradise only a feeble and worn-out company of aged priests, "clinging day and night to the chapel altars," barefoot or in patched sandals. With or even without Nicolette, "his sweet mistress whom he so much loves," he, for his part, is ready to start on the way to hell, along with "the good scholars," as he says, and the actors, and the fine horsemen dead in battle, and the men of fashion[1], and "the fair courteous ladies who had two or three chevaliers apiece beside their own true lords," all gay with music, in their gold, and silver, and beautiful furs—"the vair and the grey."

But in the *House Beautiful* the saints too have their place; and the student of the Renaissance has this advantage over the student of the emancipation of the human mind in the Reformation, or the French Revolution, that in tracing the footsteps of humanity to higher levels, he is not beset at every turn by the inflexibilities and antagonisms of some well-recognised controversy, with rigidly defined opposites, exhausting the intelligence and limiting one's sympathies. The opposition of the professional defenders of a mere system to that more sincere and generous play of the forces of human mind and character, which I have noted as the secret of Abelard's struggle, is indeed always powerful. But the incompatibility with one another of souls really "fair" is not essential; and within the enchanted region of the Renaissance, one needs not be for ever on one's guard. Here are no fixed parties,

---

[1]*Parage*, peerage:—which came to signify all that ambitious youth affected most on the outside of life, in that old world of the Troubadours, with whom this term is of frequent recurrence.

no exclusions: all breathes of that unity of culture in which "whatsoever things are comely" are reconciled, for the elevation and adorning of our spirits. And just in proportion as those who took part in the Renaissance become centrally representative of it, just so much the more is this condition realised in them. The wicked popes, and the loveless tyrants, who from time to time became its patrons, or mere speculators in its fortunes, lend themselves easily to disputations, and, from this side or that, the spirit of controversy lays just hold upon them. But the painter of the *Last Supper*, with his kindred, lives in a land where controversy has no breathing-place. They refuse to be classified. In the story of *Aucassin and Nicolette*, in the literature which it represents, the note of defiance, of the opposition of one system to another, is sometimes harsh. Let me conclude then with a morsel from *Amis and Amile*, in which the harmony of human interests is still entire. For the story of the great traditional friendship, in which, as I said, the liberty of the heart makes itself felt, seems, as we have it, to have been written by a monk:—*La vie des saints martyrs Amis et Amile*. It was not till the end of the seventeenth century that their names were finally excluded from the martyrology; and their story ends with this monkish miracle of earthly comradeship, more than faithful unto death.—

For, as God had united them in their lives in one accord, so they were not divided in their death, falling together side by side, with a host of other brave men, in battle for King Charles at Mortara, so called from that great slaughter. And the bishops gave counsel to the king and queen that they should bury the dead, and build a church in that place; and their counsel pleased the king greatly. And there were built two churches, the one by commandment of the king in honour of Saint Oseige, and the other by commandment of the queen in honour of Saint Peter.

And the king caused the two chests of stone to be brought in the which the bodies of Amis and Amile lay; and Amile was carried to the church of Saint Peter, and Amis to the church of Saint Oseige; and the other corpses were buried, some in one place and some in the other. But lo! next morning, the body of Amile in his coffin was found lying in the church of Saint Oseige, beside the coffin of Amis his comrade. Behold then this wondrous amity, which by death could not be dissevered!

This miracle God did, who gave to His disciples power to remove mountains. And by reason of this miracle the king and queen remained in that place for a space of thirty days, and performed the offices of the dead who were slain, and honoured the said churches with great gifts. And the bishop ordained many clerks to serve in the church of Saint Oseige, and commanded them that they should guard duly, with great devotion, the bodies of the two companions, Amis and Amile.

1872.

Pico della Mirandola

No account of the Renaissance can be complete without some
notice of the attempt made by certain Italian scholars of the
fifteenth century to reconcile Christianity with the religion of
ancient Greece. To reconcile forms of sentiment which at first
sight seem incompatible, to adjust the various products of the
human mind to one another in one many-sided type of intellectual culture, to give humanity, for heart and imagination to feed
upon, as much as it could possibly receive, belonged to the generous instincts of that age. An earlier and simpler generation had
seen in the gods of Greece so many malignant spirits, the defeated
but still living centres of the religion of darkness, struggling, not
always in vain, against the kingdom of light. Little by little, as the
natural charm of pagan story reasserted itself over minds emerg-
ing out of barbarism, the religious significance which had once
belonged to it was lost sight of, and it came to be regarded as the
subject of a purely artistic or poetical treatment. But it was inevitable that from time to time minds should arise, deeply enough
impressed by its beauty and power to ask themselves whether the
religion of Greece was indeed a rival of the religion of Christ; for
the older gods had rehabilitated themselves, and men's allegiance
was divided. And the fifteenth century was an impassioned age,
so ardent and serious in its pursuit of art that it consecrated everything with which art had to do as a religious object. The restored
Greek literature had made it familiar, at least in Plato, with a
style of expression concerning the earlier gods, which had about
it something of the warmth and unction of a Christian hymn. It
was too familiar with such language to regard mythology as a
mere story; and it was too serious to play with a religion.

"Let me briefly remind the reader"—says Heine, in the *Gods in Exile*, an essay full of that strange blending of sentiment which is characteristic of the traditions of the middle age concerning the pagan religions—

how the gods of the older world, at the time of the definite triumph of Christianity, that is, in the third century, fell into painful embarrassments, which greatly resembled certain tragical situations of their earlier life. They now found themselves beset by the same troublesome necessities to which they had once before been exposed during the primitive ages, in that revolutionary epoch when the Titans broke out of the custody of Orcus, and, piling Pelion on Ossa, scaled Olympus. Unfortunate gods! They had then to take flight ignominiously, and hide themselves among us here on earth, under all sorts of disguises. The larger number betook themselves to Egypt, where for greater security they assumed the forms of animals, as is generally known. Just in the same way, they had to take flight again, and seek entertainment in remote hiding-places, when those iconoclastic zealots, the black brood of monks, broke down all the temples, and pursued the gods with fire and curses. Many of these unfortunate emigrants, now entirely deprived of shelter and ambrosia, must needs take to vulgar handicrafts, as a means of earning their bread. Under these circumstances, many whose sacred groves had been confiscated, let themselves out for hire as woodcutters in Germany, and were forced to drink beer instead of nectar. Apollo seems to have been content to take service under graziers, and as he had once kept the cows of Admetus, so he lived now as a shepherd in Lower Austria. Here, however, having become suspected on account of his beautiful singing, he was recognized by a learned monk as one of the old pagan gods, and handed over to the spiritual tribunal. On the rack he confessed that he was the god Apollo; and before his execution he begged that he might be suffered to play once more upon the lyre, and to sing a song. And he played so touchingly, and sang with such magic, and was withal so beautiful in form and feature, that all the women wept, and many of them were so deeply impressed that they shortly afterwards fell sick. Some time afterwards the people wished to drag him from the grave again, that a stake might be driven through his body, in the belief that he had been a vampire, and that the sick women would by this means recover. But they found the grave empty.

The Renaissance of the fifteenth century was, in many things, great rather by what it designed than by what it achieved. Much which it aspired to do, and did but imperfectly or mistakenly, was accomplished in what is called the *éclaircissement* of the eighteenth century, or in our own generation; and what really belongs to the revival of the fifteenth century is but the leading instinct, the curiosity, the initiatory idea. It is so with this very question of the reconciliation of the religion of antiquity with the religion of Christ. A modern scholar occupied by this problem might observe that all religions may be regarded as natural products, that, at least in their origin, their growth, and decay, they have common laws, and are not to be isolated from the other movements of the human mind in the periods in which they respectively prevailed; that they arise spontaneously out of the human mind, as expressions of the varying phases of its sentiment concerning the unseen world; that every intellectual product must be judged from the point of view of the age and the people in which it was produced. He might go on to observe that each has contributed something to the development of the religious sense, and ranging them as so many stages in the gradual education of the human mind, justify the existence of each. The basis of the reconciliation of the religions of the world would thus be the inexhaustible activity and creativeness of the human mind itself, in which all religions alike have their root, and in which all alike are reconciled; just as the fancies of childhood and the thoughts of old age meet and are laid to rest, in the experience of the individual.

Far different was the method followed by the scholars of the fifteenth century. They lacked the very rudiments of the historic sense, which, by an imaginative act, throws itself back into a world unlike one's own, and estimates every intellectual creation in its connexion with the age from which it proceeded. They had no idea of development, of the differences of ages, of the process by which our race has been "educated." In their attempts to reconcile the religions of the world, they were thus thrown back upon the quicksand of allegorical interpretation. The religions of the world were to be reconciled, not as successive stages in a regular development of the religious sense, but as subsisting side by side, and substantially in agreement with one another. And here the first necessity was to misrepresent the language, the conceptions, the sentiments, it was proposed to compare and reconcile. Plato and Homer must be made to speak agreeably to Moses. Set side by side, the mere surfaces could never unite in any harmony of design. Therefore one must go below the surface, and bring up the supposed secondary, or still more remote meaning,—that diviner signification held in reserve, *in recessu divinius aliquid*, latent in some stray touch of Homer, or figure of speech in the books of Moses.

And yet as a curiosity of the human mind, a "madhouse-cell," if you will, into which we may peep for a moment, and see it at work weaving strange fancies, the allegorical interpretation of the fifteenth century has its interest. With its strange web of imagery, its quaint conceits, its unexpected combinations and subtle moralising, it is an element in the local colour of a great age. It illustrates also the faith of that age in all oracles, its desire to hear all voices, its generous belief that nothing which had ever interested the human mind could wholly lose its vitality. It is the counterpart, though certainly the feebler counterpart, of that practical truce and reconciliation of the gods of Greece with the Christian religion, which is seen in the art of the time. And it is for his share in this work, and because his own story is a sort of analogue or visible equivalent to the expression of this purpose in his writings, that something of a general interest still belongs to the name of Pico della Mirandola, whose life, written by his nephew Francis, seemed worthy, for some touch of sweetness in it, to be translated out of the original Latin by Sir Thomas More, that great lover of Italian culture, among whose works the life of Pico, *Earl of Mirandola, and a great lord of Italy*, as he calls him, may still be read, in its quaint, antiquated English.

Marsilio Ficino has told us how Pico came to Florence. It was the very day—some day probably in the year 1482—on which Ficino had finished his famous translation of Plato into Latin, the work to which he had been dedicated from childhood by Cosmo de' Medici, in furtherance of his desire to resuscitate the knowledge of Plato among his fellow-citizens. Florence indeed, as M. Renan has pointed out, had always had an affinity for the mystic and dreamy philosophy of Plato, while the colder and more practical philosophy of Aristotle had flourished in Padua, and other cities of the north; and the Florentines, though they knew perhaps very little about him, had had the name of the great idealist often on their lips. To increase this knowledge, Cosmo had founded the Platonic academy, with periodical discussions at the Villa of

Careggi. The fall of Constantinople in 1453, and the council in 1438 for the reconciliation of the Greek and Latin Churches, had brought to Florence many a needy Greek scholar. And now the work was completed, the door of the mystical temple lay open to all who could construe Latin, and the scholar rested from his labour; when there was introduced into his study, where a lamp burned continually before the bust of Plato, as other men burned lamps before their favourite saints, a young man fresh from a journey, "of feature and shape seemly and beauteous, of stature goodly and high, of flesh tender and soft, his visage lovely and fair, his colour white, intermingled with comely reds, his eyes grey, and quick of look, his teeth white and even, his hair yellow and abundant," and trimmed with more than the usual artifice of the time.

It is thus that Sir Thomas More translates the words of the biographer of Pico, who, even in outward form and appearance, seems an image of that inward harmony and completeness, of which he is so perfect an example. The word *mystic* has been usually derived from a Greek word which signifies *to shut*, as if one *shut one's lips*, brooding on what cannot be uttered; but the Platonists themselves derive it rather from the act of *shutting the eyes*, that one may see the more, inwardly. Perhaps the eyes of the mystic Ficino, now long past the midway of life, had come to be thus half-closed; but when a young man, not unlike the archangel Raphael, as the Florentines of that age depicted him in his wonderful walk with Tobit, or Mercury, as he might have appeared in a painting by Sandro Botticelli or Piero di Cosimo, entered his chamber, he seems to have thought there was something not wholly earthly about him; at least, he ever afterwards believed that it was not without the co-operation of the stars that the stranger had arrived on that day. For it happened that they fell into a conversation, deeper and more intimate than men usually fall into at first sight. During this conversation Ficino formed the design of devoting his remaining years to the translation of Plotinus, that new Plato, in whom the mystical element in the Platonic philosophy had been worked out to the utmost limit of vision and ecstasy; and it is in dedicating this translation to Lorenzo d'Medici that Ficino has recorded these incidents.

It was after many wanderings, wanderings of the intellect as well as physical journeys, that Pico came to rest at Florence. Born in 1463, he was then about twenty years old. He was called Giovanni at baptism, Pico, like all his ancestors, from Picus, nephew of the Emperor Constantine, from whom they claimed to be descended, and Mirandola from the place of his birth, a little town afterwards part of the duchy of Modena, of which small territory his family had long been the feudal lords. Pico was the youngest of the family, and his mother, delighting in his wonderful memory, sent him at the age of fourteen to the famous school of law at Bologna. From the first, indeed, she seems to have had some presentiment of his future fame, for, with a faith in omens characteristic of her time, she believed that a strange circumstance had happened at the time of Pico's birth—the appearance of a circular flame which suddenly vanished away, on the wall of the chamber where she lay. He remained two years at Bologna; and then, with an inexhaustible, unrivalled thirst for knowledge, the strange, confused, uncritical learning of that age, passed through the principal schools of Italy and France, penetrating, as he thought, into the secrets of all ancient philosophies, and many eastern languages. And with this flood of erudition came the generous hope, so often disabused, of reconciling the philosophers with one another, and all alike with the Church. At last he came to Rome. There, like some knight-errant of philosophy, he offered to defend nine hundred bold paradoxes, drawn from the most opposite sources, against all comers. But the pontifical court was led to suspect the orthodoxy of some of these propositions, and even the reading of the book which contained them was forbidden by the Pope. It was not until 1493 that Pico was finally absolved, by a brief of Alexander the Sixth. Ten years before that date he had arrived at Florence; an early instance of those who, after following the vain hope of an impossible reconciliation from system to system, have at last fallen back unsatisfied on the simplicities of their childhood's belief.

The oration which Pico composed for the opening of this philosophical tournament still remains; its subject is the dignity of human nature, the greatness of man. In common with nearly all medieval speculation, much of Pico's writing has this for its drift;

and in common also with it, Pico's theory of that dignity is founded on a misconception of the place in nature both of the earth and of man. For Pico the earth is the centre of the universe: and around it, as a fixed and motionless point, the sun and moon and stars revolve, like diligent servants or ministers. And in the midst of all is placed man, *nodus et vinculum mundi*, the bond or copula of the world, and the "interpreter of nature": that famous expression of Bacon's really belongs to Pico. *Tritum est in scholis*, he says, *esse hominem minorem mundum, in quo mixtum ex elementis corpus et spiritus coelestis et plantarum anima vegetalis et brutorum sensus et ratio et angelica mens et Dei similitudo conspicitur:*—"It is a commonplace of the schools that man is a little world, in which we may discern a body mingled of earthy elements, and ethereal breath, and the vegetable life of plants, and the senses of the lower animals, and reason, and the intelligence of angels, and a likeness to God."

A commonplace of the schools! But perhaps it had some new significance and authority, when men heard one like Pico reiterate it; and, false as its basis was, the theory had its use. For this high dignity of man, thus bringing the dust under his feet into sensible communion with the thoughts and affections of the angels, was supposed to belong to him, not as renewed by a religious system, but by his own natural right. The proclamation of it was a counterpoise to the increasing tendency of medieval religion to depreciate man's nature, to sacrifice this or that element in it, to make it ashamed of itself, to keep the degrading or painful accidents of it always in view. It helped man onward to that reassertion of himself, that rehabilitation of human nature, the body, the senses, the heart, the intelligence, which the Renaissance fulfils. And yet to read a page of one of Pico's forgotten books is like a glance into one of those ancient sepulchres, upon which the wanderer in classical lands has sometimes stumbled, with the old disused ornaments and furniture of a world wholly unlike ours still fresh in them. That whole conception of nature is so different from our own. For Pico the world is a limited place, bounded by actual crystal walls, and a material firmament; it is like a painted toy, like that map or system of the world, held, as a great target or shield, in the hands of the creative *Logos*, by whom the Father made all things, in one of the earlier frescoes of the *Campo Santo* at Pisa. How different from this childish dream is our own conception of nature, with its unlimited space, its innumerable suns, and the earth but a mote in the beam; how different the strange new awe, or superstition, with which it fills our minds! "The silence of those infinite spaces," says Pascal, contemplating a starlight night, "the silence of those infinite spaces terrifies me:"—*Le silence éternel de ces espaces infinis m'effraie.*

He was already almost wearied out when he came to Florence. He had loved much and been beloved by women, "wandering over the crooked hills of delicious pleasure;" but their reign over him was over, and long before Savonarola's famous "bonfire of vanities," he had destroyed those love-songs in the vulgar tongue, which would have been so great a relief to us, after the scholastic prolixity of his Latin writings. It was in another spirit that he composed a Platonic commentary, the only work of his in Italian which has come down to us, on the "Song of Divine Love"— *secondo la mente ed opinione dei Platonici*—"according to the mind and opinion of the Platonists," by his friend Hieronymo Beniveni, in which, with an ambitious array of every sort of learning, and a profusion of imagery borrowed indifferently from the astrologers, the Cabala, and Homer, and Scripture, and Dionysius the Areopagite, he attempts to define the stages by which the soul passes from the earthly to the unseen beauty. A change indeed had passed over him, as if the chilling touch of the abstract and disembodied beauty Platonists profess to long for were already upon him. Some sense of this, perhaps, coupled with that overbrightness which in the popular imagination always betokens an early death, made Camilla Rucellai, one of those prophetic women whom the preaching of Savonarola had raised up in Florence, declare, seeing him for the first time, that he would depart in the time of lilies—prematurely, that is, like the field-flowers which are withered by the scorching sun almost as soon as they are sprung up. He now wrote down those thoughts on the religious life which Sir Thomas More turned into English, and which another English translator thought worthy to be added to the books of the *Imitation.* "It is not hard to know God, provided one will not force oneself to define Him:"—has been thought a great saying of Joubert's. "Love God," Pico writes to Angelo Politian, "we rather may, than either know Him, or by speech utter Him. And yet had men liefer by knowledge never find that which they seek, than by love possess that thing, which also without love were in vain found."

Yet he who had this fine touch for spiritual things did not—and in this is the enduring interest of his story—even after his conversion, forget the old gods. He is one of the last who seriously and sincerely entertained the claim on men's faith of the pagan religions; he is anxious to ascertain the true significance of the obscurest legend, the lightest tradition concerning them. With many thoughts and many influences which led him in that direction, he did not become a monk; only he became gentle and patient in disputation; retaining "somewhat of the old plenty, in dainty viand and silver vessel," he gave over the greater part of his property to his friend, the mystical poet Beniveni, to be spent by him in works of charity, chiefly in the sweet charity of providing marraige-dowries for the peasant girls of Florence. His end came in 1494, when, amid the prayers and sacraments of Savonarola, he died of fever, on the very day on which Charles the Eighth entered Florence, the seventeenth of November, yet in the time of lilies— the lilies of the shield of France, as the people now said, remembering Camilla's prophecy. He was buried in the conventual church of Saint Mark, in the hood and white frock of the Dominican order.

It is because the life of Pico, thus lying down to rest in the Dominican habit, yet amid thoughts of the older gods, himself like one of those comely divinities, reconciled indeed to the new religion, but still with a tenderness for the earlier life, and desirous literally to "bind the ages each to each by natural piety"—it is because this life is so perfect a parallel to the attempt made in his writings to reconcile Christianity with the ideas of paganism, that Pico, in spite of the scholastic character of those writings, is really interesting. Thus, in the *Heptaplus, or Discourse on the Seven Days of the Creation,* he endeavours to reconcile the accounts which pagan philosophy had given of the origin of the world with the account given in the books of Moses—the *Timœus* of Plato with the book of *Genesis.* The *Heptaplus* is dedicated to

Lorenzo the Magnificent, whose interest, the preface tells us, in the secret wisdom of Moses is well known. If Moses seems in his writings simple and even popular, rather than either a philosopher or a theologian, that is because it was an institution with the ancient philosophers, either not to speak of divine things at all, or to speak of them dissemblingly: hence their doctrines were called mysteries. Taught by them, Pythagoras became so great a "master of silence," and wrote almost nothing, thus hiding the words of God in his heart, and speaking wisdom only among the perfect. In explaining the harmony between Plato and Moses, Pico lays hold on every sort of figure and analogy, on the double meanings of words, the symbols of the Jewish ritual, the secondary meanings of obscure stories in the later Greek mythologists. Everywhere there is an unbroken system of correspondences. Every object in the terrestrial world is an analogue, a symbol or counterpart, of some higher reality in the starry heavens, and this again of some law of the angelic life in the world beyond the stars. There is the element of fire in the material world; the sun is the fire of heaven; and in the super-celestial world there is the fire of the seraphic intelligence. "But behold how they differ! The elementary fire burns, the heavenly fire vivifies, the super-celestial fire loves." In this way, every natural object, every combination of natural forces, every accident in the lives of men, is filled with higher meanings. Omens, prophecies, supernatural coincidences, accompany Pico himself all through life. There are oracles in every tree and mountain-top, and a significance in every accidental combination of the events of life.

This constant tendency to symbolism and imagery gives Pico's work a figured style, by which it has some real resemblance to Plato's, and he differs from other mystical writers of his time by a genuine desire to know his authorities at first hand. He reads Plato in Greek, Moses in Hebrew, and by this his work really belongs to the higher culture. Above all, we have a constant sense in reading him, that his thoughts, however little their positive value may be, are connected with springs beneath them of deep and passionate emotion; and when he explains the grades or steps by which the soul passes from the love of a physical object to the love of unseen beauty, and unfolds the analogies between this process and other movements upward of human thought, there is a glow and vehemence in his words which remind one of the manner in which his own brief existence flamed itself away.

I said that the Renaissance of the fifteenth century was, in many things, great rather by what it designed or aspired to do, than by what it actually achieved. It remained for a later age to conceive the true method of effecting a scientific reconciliation of Christian sentiment with the imagery, the legends, the theories about the world, of pagan poetry and philosophy. For that age the only possible reconciliation was an imaginative one, and resulted from the efforts of artists, trained in Christian schools, to handle pagan subjects; and of this artistic reconciliation work like Pico's was but the feebler counterpart. Whatever philosophers had to say on one side or the other, whether they were successful or not in their attempts to reconcile the old to the new, and to justify the expenditure of so much care and thought on the dreams of a dead faith, the imagery of the Greek religion, the direct charm of its story, were by artists valued and cultivated for their own sake. Hence a new sort of mythology, with a tone and qualities of its own. When the ship-load of sacred earth from the soil of Jerusalem was mingled with the common clay in the *Campo Santo* at Pisa, a new flower grew up from it, unlike any flower men had seen before, the anemone with its concentric rings of strangely blended colour, still to be found by those who search long enough for it, in the long grass of the Maremma. Just such a strange flower was that mythology of the Italian Renaissance, which grew up from the mixture of two traditions, two sentiments, the sacred and the profane. Classical story was regarded as so much imaginative material to be received and assimilated. It did not come into men's minds to ask curiously of science, concerning the origin of such story, its primary form and import, its meaning for those who projected it. The thing sank into their minds, to issue forth again with all the tangle about it of medieval sentiment and ideas. In the *Doni* Madonna in the *Tribune* of the *Uffizii*, Michelangelo actually brings the pagan religion, and with it the unveiled human form, the sleepy-looking fauns of a Dionysiac revel, into the presence of the Madonna, as simpler painters had introduced there other products of the earth, birds or flowers, while he has given to that Madonna herself much of the uncouth energy of the older and more primitive "Mighty Mother."

This picturesque union of contrasts, belonging properly to the art of the close of the fifteenth century, pervades, in Pico della Mirandola, an actual person, and that is why the figure of Pico is so attractive. He will not let one go; he wins one on, in spite of one's self, to turn again to the pages of his forgotten books, although we know already that the actual solution proposed in them will satisfy us as little as perhaps it satisfied him. It is said that in his eagerness for mysterious learning he once paid a great sum for a collection of cabalistic manuscripts, which turned out to be forgeries; and the story might well stand as a parable of all he ever seemed to gain in the way of actual knowledge. He had sought knowledge, and passed from system to system, and hazarded much; but less for the sake of positive knowledge than because he believed there was a spirit of order and beauty in knowledge, which would come down and unite what men's ignorance had divided, and renew what time had made dim. And so, while his actual work has passed away, yet his own qualities are still active, and himself remains, as one alive in the grave, *caesiis et vigilibus oculis*, as his biographer describes him, and with that sanguine, clear skin, *decenti rubore interspersa*, as with the light of morning upon it; and he has a true place in that group of great Italians who fill the end of the fifteenth century with their names, he is a true *humanist*. For the essence of humanism is that belief of which he seems never to have doubted, that nothing which has ever interested living men and women can wholly lose its vitality—no language they have spoken, nor oracle beside which they have hushed their voices, no dream which has once been entertained by actual human minds, nothing about which they have ever been passionate, or expended time and zeal.

1871.

Sandro Botticelli

In Leonardo's treatise on painting only one contemporary is mentioned by name—Sandro Botticelli. This pre-eminence may be
due to chance only, but to some will rather appear a result of
deliberate judgment; for people have begun to find out the charm
of Botticelli's work, and his name, little known in the last century, is quietly becoming important. In the middle of the fifteenth
century he had already anticipated much of that meditative subtlety, which is sometimes supposed peculiar to the great imaginative workmen of its close. Leaving the simple religion which had
occupied the followers of Giotto for a century, and the simple
naturalism which had grown out of it, a thing of birds and flowers
only, he sought inspiration in what to him were works of the
modern world, the writings of Dante and Boccaccio, and in new
readings of his own of classical stories: or, if he painted religious
incidents, painted them with an under-current of original sentiment, which touches you as the real matter of the picture through
the veil of its ostensible subject. What is the peculiar sensation,
what is the peculiar quality of pleasure, which his work has the
property of exciting in us, and which we cannot get elsewhere?
For this, especially when he has to speak of a comparatively unknown artist, is always the chief question which a critic has to
answer.

In an age when the lives of artists were full of adventure, his life
is almost colourless. Criticism indeed has cleared away much of
the gossip which Vasari accumulated, has touched the legend of
Lippo and Lucrezia, and rehabilitated the character of Andrea del
Castagno. But in Botticelli's case there is no legend to dissipate.
He did not even go by his true name: Sandro is a nickname, and his

true name is Filipepi, Botticelli being only the name of the gold-smith who first taught him art. Only two things happened to him, two things which he shared with other artists:—he was invited to Rome to paint in the Sistine Chapel, and he fell in later life under the influence of Savonarola, passing apparently almost out of men's sight in a sort of religious melancholy, which lasted till his death in 1515, according to the received date. Vasari says that he plunged into the study of Dante, and even wrote a comment on the *Divine Comedy*. But it seems strange that he should have lived on inactive so long; and one almost wishes that some document might come to light, which, fixing the date of his death earlier, might relieve one, in thinking of him, of his dejected old age.

He is before all things a poetical painter, blending the charm of story and sentiment, the medium of the art of poetry, with the charm of line and colour, the medium of abstract painting. So he becomes the illustrator of Dante. In a few rare examples of the edition of 1481, the blank spaces, left at the beginning of every canto for the hand of the illuminator, have been filled, as far as the nineteenth canto of the *Inferno*, with impressions of engraved plates, seemingly by way of experiment, for in the copy in the Bodleian Library, one of the three impressions it contains has been printed upside down, and much awry, in the midst of the luxurious printed page. Giotto, and the followers of Giotto, with their almost childish religious aim, had not learned to put that weight of meaning into outward things, light, colour, everyday gesture, which the poetry of the *Divine Comedy* involves, and before the fifteenth century Dante could hardly have found an illustrator. Botticelli's illustrations are crowded with incident, blending, with a naïve carelessness of pictorial propriety, three phases of the same scene into one plate. The grotesques, so often a stumbling-block to painters, who forget that the words of a poet, which only feebly present an image to mind, must be lowered in key when translated into visible form, make one regret that he has not rather chosen for illustration the more subdued imagery of the *Purgatorio*. Yet in the scene of those who "go down quick into hell," there is an inventive force about the fire taking hold on the upturned soles of the feet, which proves that the design is no mere translation of Dante's words, but a true painter's vision;

while the scene of the Centaurs wins one at once, for, forgetful of the actual circumstances of their appearance, Botticelli has gone off with delight on the thought of the Centaurs themselves, bright, small creatures of the woodland, with arch baby faces and mignon forms, drawing tiny bows.

Botticelli lived in a generation of naturalists, and he might have been a mere naturalist among them. There are traces enough in his work of that alert sense of outward things, which, in the pictures of that period, fills the lawns with delicate living creatures, and the hillsides with pools of water, and the pools of water with flowering reeds. But this was not enough for him; he is a visionary painter, and in his visionariness he resembles Dante. Giotto, the tried companion of Dante, Masaccio, Ghirlandajo even, do but transcribe, with more or less refining, the outward image; they are dramatic, not visionary painters; they are almost impassive spectators of the action before them. But the genius of which Botticelli is the type usurps the data before it as the exponent of ideas, moods, visions of its own; in this interest it plays fast and loose with those data, rejecting some and isolating others, and always combining them anew. To him, as to Dante, the scene, the colour, the outward image or gesture, comes with all its incisive and importunate reality; but awakes in him, moreover, by some subtle law of his own structure, a mood which it awakes in no one else, of which it is the double or repetition, and which it clothes, that all may share it, with visible circumstance.

But he is far enough from accepting the conventional orthodoxy of Dante which, referring all human action to the simple formula of purgatory, heaven and hell, leaves an insoluble element of prose in the depths of Dante's poetry. One picture of his, with the portrait of the donor, Matteo Palmieri, below, had the credit or discredit of attracting some shadow of ecclesiastical censure. This Matteo Palmieri, (two dim figures move under that name in contemporary history,) was the reputed author of a poem, still unedited, *La Città di Vita*, which represented the human race as an incarnation of those angels who, in the revolt of Lucifer, were neither for Jehovah nor for His enemies, a fantasy of that earlier Alexandrian philosophy about which the Florentine intellect in that century was so curious. Botticelli's picture may have been only one of those familiar compositions in which religious reverie has recorded its impressions of the various forms of beatified existence—*Glorias*, as they were called, like that in which Giotto painted the portrait of Dante; but somehow it was suspected of embodying in a picture the wayward dream of Palmieri, and the chapel where it hung was closed. Artists so entire as Botticelli are usually careless about philosophical theories, even when the philosopher is a Florentine of the fifteenth century, and his work a poem in *terza rima*. But Botticelli, who wrote a commentary on Dante, and became the disciple of Savonarola, may well have let such theories come and go across him. True or false, the story interprets much of the peculiar sentiment with which he infuses his profane and sacred persons, comely, and in a certain sense like angels, but with a sense of displacement or loss about them—the wistfulness of exiles, conscious of a passion and energy greater than any known issue of them explains, which runs through all his varied work with a sentiment of ineffable melancholy.

So just what Dante scorns as unworthy alike of heaven and hell, Botticelli accepts, that middle world in which men take no side in great conflicts, and decide no great causes, and make great refusals. He thus sets for himself the limits within which art, undisturbed by any moral ambition, does its most sincere and surest work. His interest is neither in the untempered goodness of Angelico's saints, nor the untempered evil of Orcagna's *Inferno*; but with men and women, in their mixed and uncertain condition, always attractive, clothed sometimes by passion with a character of loveliness and energy, but saddened perpetually by the shadow upon them of the great things from which they shrink. His morality is all sympathy; and it is this sympathy, conveying into his work somewhat more than is usual of the true complexion of humanity, which makes him, visionary as he is, so forcible a realist.

It is this which gives to his Madonnas their unique expression and charm. He has worked out in them a distinct and peculiar type, definite enough in his own mind, for he has painted it over and over again, sometimes one might think almost mechanically, as a pastime during that dark period when his thoughts were so heavy upon him. Hardly any collection of note is without one of these circular pictures, into which the attendant angels depress their heads so naïvely. Perhaps you have sometimes wondered why those peevish-looking Madonnas, conformed to no acknowledged or obvious type of beauty, attract you more and more, and often come back to you when the Sistine Madonna and the Virgins of Fra Angelico are forgotten. At first, contrasting them with those, you may have thought that there was something in them mean or abject even, for the abstract lines of the face have little nobleness, and the colour is wan. For with Botticelli she too, though she holds in her hands the "Desire of all nations," is one of those who are neither for Jehovah nor for His enemies; and her choice is on her face. The white light on it is cast up hard and cheerless from below, as when snow lies upon the ground, and the children look up with surprise at the strange whiteness of the ceiling. Her trouble is in the very caress of the mysterious child, whose gaze is always far from her, and who has already that sweet look of devotion which men have never been able altogether to love, and which still makes the born saint an object almost of suspicion to his earthly brethren. Once, indeed, he guides her hand to transcribe in a book the words of her exaltation, the *Ave*, and the *Magnificat*, and the *Gaude Maria*, and the young angels, glad to rouse her for a moment from her dejection, are eager to hold the inkhorn and to support the book. But the pen almost drops from her hand, and the high cold words have no meaning for her, and her true children are those others, among whom, in her rude home, the intolerable honour came to her, with that look of wistful inquiry on their irregular faces which you see in startled animals—gipsy children, such as those who, in Apennine villages, still hold out their long brown arms to beg of you, but on Sundays become *enfants du chœur*, with their thick black hair nicely combed, and fair white linen on their sunburnt throats.

What is strangest is that he carries this sentiment into classical subjects, its most complete expression being a picture in the *Uffizii*, of Venus rising from the sea, in which the grotesque emblems of the middle age, and a landscape full of its peculiar feeling, and even its strange draperies, powdered all over in the Gothic manner with a quaint conceit of daisies, frame a figure that reminds you of the faultless nude studies of Ingres. At first, perhaps, you are attracted only by a quaintness of design, which seems to recall all at once whatever you have read of Florence in the fifteenth century; afterwards you may think that this quaintness must be incongruous with the subject, and that the colour is cadaverous or at least cold. And yet, the more you come to understand what imaginative colouring really is, that all colour is no mere delightful quality of natural things, but a spirit upon them by which they become expressive to the spirit, the better you will like this peculiar quality of colour; and you will find that quaint design of Botticelli's a more direct inlet into the Greek temper than the works of the Greeks themselves even of the finest period. Of the Greeks as they really were, of their difference from ourselves, of the aspects of their outward life, we know far more than Botticelli, or his most learned contemporaries; but for us long familiarity has taken off the edge of the lesson, and we are hardly conscious of what we owe to the Hellenic spirit. But in pictures like this of Botticelli's you have a record of the first impression made by it on minds turned back towards it, in almost painful aspiration, from a world in which it had been ignored so long; and in the passion, the energy, the industry of realisation, with which Botticelli carries out his intention, is the exact measure of the legitimate influence over the human mind of the imaginative system of which this is perhaps the central subject. The light is indeed cold—mere sunless dawn; but a later painter would have cloyed you with sunshine; and you can see the better for that quietness in the morning air each long promontory, as it slopes down to the water's edge. Men go forth to their labours until the evening; but she is awake before them, and you might think that the sorrow in her face was at the thought of the whole long day of love yet to come. An emblematical figure of the wind blows hard across the grey water, moving forward the dainty-lipped shell on which she sails, the sea "showing his teeth," as it moves, in thin lines of foam, and sucking in, one by one, the falling roses, each severe in outline, plucked off short at the stalk, but embrowned a little, as Botticelli's flowers always are. Botticelli meant all this imagery to be altogether pleasurable; and it was partly an incompleteness of resources, inseparable from the art of that time,

that subdued and chilled it. But his predilection for minor tones
counts also; and what is unmistakable is the sadness with which
he has conceived the goddess of pleasure, as the depository of a
great power over the lives of men.

I have said that the peculiar character of Botticelli is the result
of a blending in him of a sympathy for humanity in its uncertain
condition, its attractiveness, its investiture at rarer moments in a
character of loveliness and energy, with his consciousness of the
shadow upon it of the great things from which it shrinks, and that
this conveys into his work somewhat more than painting usually
attains of the true complexion of humanity. He paints the story of
the goddess of pleasure in other episodes besides that of her birth
from the sea, but never without some shadow of death in the grey
flesh and wan flowers. He paints Madonnas, but they shrink from
the pressure of the divine child, and plead in unmistakable under-
tones for a warmer, lower humanity. The same figure—tradition
connects it with Simonetta, the mistress of Giuliano de' Medici—
appears again as Judith, returning home across the hill country,
when the great deed is over, and the moment of revulsion come,
when the olive branch in her hand is becoming a burthen; as
Justice, sitting on a throne, but with a fixed look of self-hatred
which makes the sword in her hand seem that of a suicide; and
again as *Veritas*, in the allegorical picture of *Calumnia*, where
one may note in passing the suggestiveness of an accident which
identifies the image of Truth with the person of Venus. We might
trace the same sentiment through his engravings; but his share in
them is doubtful, and the object of this brief study has been attained, if I have defined aright the temper in which he worked.

But, after all, it may be asked, is a painter like Botticelli—a
secondary painter, a proper subject for general criticism? There
are a few great painters, like Michelangelo or Leonardo, whose
work has become a force in general culture, partly for this very
reason that they have absorbed into themselves all such workmen
as Sandro Botticelli; and, over and above mere technical or antiquarian criticism, general criticism may be very well employed in
that sort of interpretation which adjusts the position of these men
to general culture, whereas smaller men can be the proper subjects only of technical or antiquarian treatment. But, besides

those great men, there is a certain number of artists who have a distinct faculty of their own by which they convey to us a peculiar quality of pleasure which we cannot get elsewhere; and these too have their place in general culture, and must be interpreted to it by those who have felt their charm strongly, and are often the object of a special diligence and a consideration wholly affectionate, just because there is not about them the stress of a great name and authority. Of this select number Botticelli is one. He has the freshness, the uncertain and diffident promise, which belong to the earlier Renaissance itself, and make it perhaps the most interesting period in the history of the mind. In studying his work one begins to understand to how great a place in human culture the art of Italy had been called.

1870.

Luca della Robbia

The Italian sculptors of the earlier half of the fifteenth century are more than mere forerunners of the great masters of its close, and often reach perfection, within the narrow limits which they chose to impose on their work. Their sculpture shares with the paintings of Botticelli and the churches of Brunelleschi that profound expressiveness, that intimate impress of an indwelling soul, which is the peculiar fascination of the art of Italy in that century. Their works have been much neglected, and often almost hidden away amid the frippery of modern decoration, and we come with some surprise on the places where their fire still smoulders. One longs to penetrate into the lives of the men who have given expression to so much power and sweetness. But it is part of the reserve, the austere dignity and simplicity of their existence, that their histories are for the most part lost, or told but briefly. From their lives, as from their work, all tumult of sound and colour has passed away. Mino, the Raphael of sculpture, Maso del Rodario, whose works add a further grace to the church of Como, Donatello even,—one asks in vain for more than a shadowy outline of their actual days.

Something more remains of Luca della Robbia; something more of a history, of outward changes and fortunes, is expressed through his work. I suppose nothing brings the real air of a Tuscan town so vividly to mind as those pieces of pale blue and white earthenware, by which he is best known, like fragments of the milky sky itself, fallen into the cool streets, and breaking into the darkened churches. And no work is less imitable: like Tuscan wine, it loses its savour when moved from its birthplace, from the crumbling walls where it was first placed. Part of the charm of this work, its grace and purity and finish of expression, is common to all Tuscan sculptors of the fifteenth century; for Luca was first of all a worker in marble, and his works in *terra cotta* only transfer to a different material the principles of his sculpture.

These Tuscan sculptors of the fifteenth century worked for the most part in low relief, giving even to their monumental effigies something of its depression of surface, getting into them by this means a pathetic suggestion of the wasting and etherealisation of death. They are haters of all heaviness and emphasis, of strongly-opposed light and shade, and seek their means of delineation among those last refinements of shadow, which are almost invisible except in a strong light, and which the finest pencil can hardly follow. The whole essence of their work is *expression*, the passing of a smile over the face of a child, the ripple of the air on a still day over the curtain of a window ajar.

What is the precise value of this system of sculpture, this low relief? Luca della Robbia, and the other sculptors of the school to which he belongs, have before them the universal problem of their art; and this system of low relief is the means by which they meet and overcome the special limitation of sculpture.

That limitation results from the material, and other necessary conditions, of all sculptured work, and consists in the tendency of such work to a hard realism, a one-sided presentment of mere form, that solid material frame which only motion can relieve, a thing of heavy shadows, and an individuality of expression pushed to caricature. Against this tendency to the hard presentment of mere form trying vainly to compete with the reality of nature itself, all noble sculpture constantly struggles; each great system of sculpture resisting it in its own way, etherealising, spiritualising, relieving, its stiffness, its heaviness, and death. The use of colour in sculpture is but an unskilful contrivance to effect, by borrowing from another art, what the nobler sculpture effects by strictly appropriate means. To get not colour, but the equivalent of colour; to secure the expression and the play of life; to expand the too firmly fixed individuality of pure, unrelieved, uncoloured form:—this is the problem which the three great styles in sculpture have solved in three different ways.

Allgemeinheit—breadth, generality, universality—is the word chosen by Winckelmann, and after him by Goethe and many German critics, to express that law of the most excellent Greek sculptors, of Pheidias and his pupils, which prompted them constantly to seek the type in the individual, to abstract and express only what is structural and permanent, to purge from the individual all that belongs only to him, all the accidents, the feelings and actions of the special moment, all that (because in its own nature it endures but for a moment) is apt to look like a frozen thing if one arrests it.

In this way their works came to be like some subtle extract or essence, or almost like pure thoughts or ideas: and hence the breadth of humanity in them, that detachment from the conditions of a particular place or people, which has carried their influence far beyond the age which produced them, and insured them universal acceptance.

That was the Greek way of relieving the hardness and unspirituality of pure form. But it involved to a certain degree the sacrifice of what we call *expression;* and a system of abstraction which aimed always at the broad and general type, at the purging away from the individual of what belonged only to him, and of the mere accidents of a particular time and place, imposed upon the range of effects open to the Greek sculptor limits somewhat narrowly defined. When Michelangelo came, therefore, with a genius spiritualised by the reverie of the middle age, penetrated by its spirit of inwardness and introspection, living not a mere outward life like the Greek, but a life full of intimate experiences, sorrows, consolations, a system which sacrificed so much of what was inward and unseen could not satisfy him. To him, lover and student of Greek sculpture as he was, work which did not bring what was inward to the surface, which was not concerned with individual expression, with individual character and feeling, the special history of the special soul, was not worth doing at all.

And so, in a way quite personal and peculiar to himself, which often is, and always seems, the effect of accident, he secured for his work individuality and intensity of expression, while he avoided a too heavy realism, that tendency to harden into caricature which the representation of feeling in sculpture is apt to display. What time and accident, its centuries of darkness under the furrows of the "little Melian farm," have done with singular felicity of touch for the Venus of Melos, fraying its surface and softening its lines, so that some spirit in the thing seems always on the point of breaking out, as though in it classical sculpture had advanced already one step into the mystical Christian age, its expression being in the whole range of ancient work most like that of Michelangelo's own:—this effect Michelangelo gains by leaving nearly all his sculpture in a puzzling sort of incompleteness, which suggests rather than realises actual form. Something of the wasting of that snow-image which he moulded at the command of Piero de' Medici, when the snow lay one night in the court of the *Pitti* palace, almost always lurks about it, as if he had determined to make the quality of a task, exacted from him half in derision, the pride of all his work. Many have wondered at that incompleteness, suspecting, however, that Michelangelo himself loved and was loath to change it, and feeling at the same time that they too would lose something if the half-realised form ever quite emerged from the stone, so rough-hewn here, so delicately finished there; and they have wished to fathom the charm of this incompleteness. Well! that incompleteness is Michelangelo's equivalent for colour in sculpture; it is his way of etherealising pure form, of relieving its stiff realism, and communicating to it breath, pulsation, the effect of life. It was a characteristic too which fell in with his peculiar temper and mode of living, his disappointments and hesitations. And it was in reality perfect finish. In this way he combines the utmost amount of passion and intensity with the sense of a yielding and flexible life: he gets not vitality merely, but a wonderful force, of expression.

Midway between these two systems—the system of the Greek sculptors and the system of Michelangelo—comes the system of Luca della Robbia and the other Tuscan sculptors of the fifteenth century, partaking both of the *Allgemeinheit* of the Greeks, their way of extracting certain select elements only of pure form and sacrificing all the rest, and the studied incompleteness of Michelangelo, relieving that sense of intensity, passion, energy, which might otherwise have stiffened into caricature. Like Michelangelo, these sculptors fill their works with intense and individualised expression. Their noblest works are the careful sepulchral portraits of particular persons—the monument of Conte Ugo in the *Badía* of Florence, of the youthful Medea Colleoni, with the wonderful, long throat, in the chapel on the cool north side of the Church of *Santa Maria Maggiore* at Bergamo— monuments such as abound in the churches of Rome, inexhaustible in suggestions of repose, of a subdued sabbatic joy, a kind of sacred grace and refinement. And these elements of tranquillity, of repose, they unite to an intense and individual expression by a system of conventionalism as skilful and subtle as that of the Greeks, repressing all such curves as indicate solid form, and throwing the whole into low relief.

The life of Luca, a life of labour and frugality, with no adventure and no excitement except what belongs to the trial of new artistic processes, the struggle with new artistic difficulties, the solution of purely artistic problems, fills the first seventy years of the fifteenth century. After producing many works in marble for the *Duomo* and the *Campanile* of Florence, which place him among the foremost masters of the sculpture of his age, he became desirous to realise the spirit and manner of that sculpture, in a humbler material, to unite its science, its exquisite and expressive system of low relief, to the homely art of pottery, to introduce those high qualities into common things, to adorn and cultivate daily household life. In this he is profoundly characteristic of the Florence of that century, of that in it which lay below its superficial vanity and caprice, a certain old-world modesty and seriousness and simplicity. People had not yet begun to think that what was good art for churches was not so good, or less fitted, for their own houses. Luca's new work was in plain white earthenware at first, a mere rough imitation of the costly, laboriously wrought marble, finished in a few hours. But on this humble path he found his way to a fresh success, to another artistic grace. The fame of the oriental pottery, with its strange bright colours—colours of art, colours not to be attained in the natural stone—mingled with the tradition of the old Roman pottery of the neighbourhood. The little red, coral-like jars of Arezzo, dug up in that district from time to time, are much prized. These colours haunted Luca's fancy. "He still continued seeking something more," his biographer says of him; "and instead of making his figures of baked earth simply white, he added the further invention of giving them colour, to the astonishment and delight of all who beheld them"—*Cosa singolare, e multo utile per la state!*—a curious thing, and very useful for summer-time, full of coolness and repose for hand and eye. Luca loved the forms of various fruits, and wrought them into all sorts of marvellous frames and garlands, giving them their natural colours, only subdued a little, a little paler than nature.

I said that the art of Luca della Robbia possessed in an unusual measure that special characteristic which belongs to all the workmen of his school, a characteristic which, even in the absence of much positive information about their actual history, seems to bring those workmen themselves very near to us. They bear the impress of a personal quality, a profound expressiveness, what the French call *intimité*, by which is meant some subtler sense of originality—the seal on a man's work of what is most inward and peculiar in his moods, and manner of apprehension: it is what we call *expression*, carried to its highest intensity of degree. That characteristic is rare in poetry, rarer still in art, rarest of all in the abstract art of sculpture; yet essentially, perhaps, it is the quality which alone makes work in the imaginative order really worth having at all. It is because the works of the artists of the fifteenth century possess this quality in an unmistakable way that one is anxious to know all that can be known about them, and explain to one's self the secret of their charm.

1872.

The Poetry of Michelangelo

Critics of Michelangelo have sometimes spoken as if the only
characteristic of his genius were a wonderful strength, verging, as
in the things of the imagination great strength always does, on
what is singular or strange. A certain strangeness, something of
the blossoming of the aloe, is indeed an element in all true works
of art: that they shall excite or surprise us is indispensable. But
that they shall give pleasure and exert a charm over us is indispensable too; and this strangeness must be sweet also—a lovely
strangeness. And to the true admirers of Michelangelo this is the
true type of the Michelangelesque—sweetness and strength, pleasure with surprise, an energy of conception which seems at every
moment about to break through all the conditions of comely
form, recovering, touch by touch, a loveliness found usually only
in the simplest natural things—*ex forti dulcedo*.

In this way he sums up for them the whole character of medieval art itself in that which distinguishes it most clearly from
classical work, the presence of a convulsive energy in it, becoming in lower hands merely monstrous or forbidding, and felt, even
in its most graceful products, as a subdued quaintness or grotesque. Yet those who feel this grace or sweetness in Michelangelo
might at the first moment be puzzled if they were asked wherein
precisely such quality resided. Men of inventive temperament—
Victor Hugo, for instance, in whom, as in Michelangelo, people
have for the most part been attracted or repelled by the strength,
while few have understood his sweetness—have sometimes relieved conceptions of merely moral or spiritual greatness, but
with little æsthetic charm of their own, by lovely accidents or
accessories, like the butterfly which alights on the blood-stained

barricade in *Les Misérables*, or those sea-birds for whom the monstrous Gilliatt comes to be as some wild natural thing, so that they are no longer afraid of him, in *Les Travailleurs de la Mer*. But the austere genius of Michelangelo will not depend for its sweetness on any mere accessories like these. The world of natural things has almost no existence for him; "When one speaks of him," says Grimm, "woods, clouds, seas, and mountains disappear, and only what is formed by the spirit of man remains behind;" and he quotes a few slight words from a letter of his to Vasari as the single expression in all he has left of a feeling for nature. He has traced no flowers, like those with which Leonardo stars over his gloomiest rocks; nothing like the fretwork of wings and flames in which Blake frames his most startling conceptions. No forest-scenery like Titian's fills his backgrounds, but only blank ranges of rock, and dim vegetable forms as blank as they, as in a world before the creation of the first five days.

Of the whole story of the creation he has painted only the creation of the first man and woman, and, for him at least, feebly, the creation of light. It belongs to the quality of his genius thus to concern itself almost exclusively with the making of man. For him it is not, as in the story itself, the last and crowning act of a series of developments, but the first and unique act, the creation of life itself in its supreme form, off-hand and immediately, in the cold and lifeless stone. With him the beginning of life has all the characteristics of resurrection; it is like the recovery of suspended health or animation, with its gratitude, its effusion, and eloquence. Fair as the young men of the Elgin marbles, the Adam of the Sistine Chapel is unlike them in a total absence of that balance and completeness which express so well the sentiment of a self-contained, independent life. In that languid figure there is something rude and satyr-like, something akin to the rugged hillside on which it lies. His whole form is gathered into an expression of mere expectancy and reception; he has hardly strength enough to lift his finger to touch the finger of the creator; yet a touch of the finger-tips will suffice.

This creation of life—life coming always as relief or recovery, and always in strong contrast with the rough-hewn mass in which it is kindled—is in various ways the motive of all his work, whether its immediate subject be pagan or Christian, legend or allegory; and this, although at least one-half of his work was designed for the adornment of tombs—the tomb of Julius, the tombs of the Medici. Not the Judgment but the Resurrection is the real subject of his last work in the Sistine Chapel; and his favourite pagan subject is the legend of Leda, the delight of the world breaking from the egg of a bird. As I have already pointed out, he secures that ideality of expression which in Greek sculpture depends on a delicate system of abstraction, and in early Italian sculpture on lowness of relief, by an incompleteness, which is surely not always undesigned, and which, as I think, no one regrets, and trusts to the spectator to complete the half-emergent form. And as his persons have something of the unwrought stone about them, so, as if to realise the expression by which the old Florentine records describe a sculptor—*master of live stone*—with him the very rocks seem to have life. They have but to cast away the dust and scurf that they may rise and stand on their feet. He loved the very quarries of Carrara, those strange grey peaks which even at mid-day convey into any scene from which they are visible something of the solemnity and stillness of evening, sometimes wandering among them month after month, till at last their pale ashen colours seem to have passed into his painting; and on the crown of the head of the *David* there still remains a morsel of uncut stone, as if by one touch to maintain its connexion with the place from which it was hewn.

And it is in this penetrative suggestion of life that the secret of that sweetness of his is to be found. He gives us indeed no lovely natural objects like Leonardo or Titian, but only the coldest, most elementary shadowing of rock or tree; no lovely draperies and comely gestures of life, but only the austere truths of human nature; "simple persons"—as he replied in his rough way to the querulous criticism of Julius the Second, that there was no gold on the figures of the Sistine Chapel—"simple persons, who wore no gold on their garments;" but he penetrates us with a feeling of that power which we associate with all the warmth and fulness of the world, the sense of which brings into one's thoughts a swarm of birds and flowers and insects. The brooding spirit of life itself is there; and the summer may burst out in a moment.

He was born in an interval of a rapid midnight journey in March, at a place in the neighbourhood of Arezzo, the thin, clear air of which was then thought to be favourable to the birth of children of great parts. He came of a race of grave and dignified men, who, claiming kinship with the family of Canossa, and some colour of imperial blood in their veins, had, generation after generation, received honourable employment under the government of Florence. His mother, a girl of nineteen years, put him out to nurse at a country-house among the hills of Settignano, where every other inhabitant is a worker in the marble-quarries, and the child early became familiar with that strange first stage in the sculptor's art. To this succeeded the influence of the sweetest and most placid master Florence had yet seen, Domenico Ghirlandajo. At fifteen he was at work among the curiosities of the garden of the Medici, copying and restoring antiques, winning the condescending notice of the great Lorenzo. He knew too how to excite strong hatreds; and it was at this time that in a quarrel with a fellow-student he received a blow on the face which deprived him for ever of the comeliness of outward form.

It was through an accident that he came to study those works of the early Italian sculptors which suggested much of his own grandest work, and impressed it with so deep a sweetness. He believed in dreams and omens. One of his friends dreamed twice that Lorenzo, then lately dead, appeared to him in grey and dusty apparel. To Michelangelo this dream seemed to portend the troubles which afterwards really came, and with the suddenness which was characteristic of all his movements, he left Florence. Having occasion to pass through Bologna, he neglected to procure the little seal of red wax which the stranger entering Bologna must carry on the thumb of his right hand. He had no money to pay the fine, and would have been thrown into prison had not one of the magistrates interposed. He remained in this man's house a whole year, rewarding his hospitality by readings from the Italian poets whom he loved. Bologna, with its endless colonnades and fantastic leaning towers, can never have been one of the lovelier cities in Italy. But about the portals of its vast unfinished churches and its dark shrines, half hidden by votive flowers and candles, lie some of the sweetest works of the early Tuscan sculptors, Giovanni da Pisa and Jacopo della Quercia, things as winsome as flowers; and the year which Michelangelo spent in copying these works was not a lost year. It was now, on returning to Florence, that he put forth that unique presentment of Bacchus, which expresses, not the mirthfulness of the god of wine, but his sleepy seriousness, his enthusiasm, his capacity for profound dreaming. No one ever expressed more truly than Michelangelo the notion of inspired sleep, of faces charged with dreams. A vast fragment of marble had long lain below the *Loggia* of Orcagna, and many a sculptor had had his thoughts of a design which should just fill this famous block of stone, cutting the diamond, as it were, without loss. Under Michelangelo's hand it became the *David* which stood till lately on the steps of the *Palazzo Vecchio*, when it was replaced below the *Loggia*. Michelangelo was now thirty years old, and his reputation was established. Three great works fill the remainder of his life—three works often interrupted, carried on through a thousand hesitations, a thousand disappointments, quarrels with his patrons, quarrels with his family, quarrels perhaps most of all with himself—the Sistine Chapel, the Mausoleum of Julius the Second, and the Sacristy of *San Lorenzo*.

In the story of Michelangelo's life the strength, often turning to bitterness, is not far to seek. A discordant note sounds throughout it which almost spoils the music. He "treats the Pope as the King of France himself would not dare to treat him:" he goes along the streets of Rome "like an executioner," Raphael says of him. Once he seems to have shut himself up with the intention of starving himself to death. As we come, in reading his life, on its harsh, untempered incidents, the thought again and again arises that he is one of those who incur the judgment of Dante, as having "wilfully lived in sadness." Even his tenderness and pity are embittered by their strength. What passionate weeping in that mysterious figure which, in the *Creation of Adam*, crouches below the image of the Almighty, as he comes with the forms of things to be, woman and her progeny, in the fold of his garment! What a sense of wrong in those two captive youths, who feel the chains like scalding water on their proud and delicate flesh! The idealist who became a reformer with Savonarola, and a republican superintending the fortification of Florence—the nest where he was born, *il nido ove naqqu'io*, as he calls it once, in a sudden throb of affection—in its last struggle for liberty, yet believed always that he had imperial blood in his veins and was of the kindred of the great Matilda, had within the depths of his nature some secret spring of indignation or sorrow. We know little of his youth, but all tends to make one believe in the vehemence of its passions. Beneath the Platonic calm of the sonnets there is latent a deep delight in carnal form and colour. There, and still more in the madrigals, he often falls into the language of less tranquil affections; while some of them have the colour of penitence, as from a wanderer returning home. He who spoke so decisively of the supremacy in the imaginative world of the unveiled human form had not been always, we may think, a mere Platonic lover. Vague and wayward his loves may have been; but they partook of the strength of his nature, and sometimes, it may be, would by no means become music, so that the comely order of his days was quite put out: *par che amaro ogni mio dolce io senta.*

But his genius is in harmony with itself; and just as in the products of his art we find resources of sweetness within their exceeding strength, so in his own story also, bitter as the ordinary sense of it may be, there are select pages shut in among the rest— pages one might easily turn over too lightly, but which yet sweeten the whole volume. The interest of Michelangelo's poems is that they make us spectators of this struggle; the struggle of a strong nature to adorn and attune itself; the struggle of a desolating passion, which yearns to be resigned and sweet and pensive, as Dante's was. It is a consequence of the occasional and informal character of his poetry, that it brings us nearer to himself, his own mind and temper, than any work done only to support a literary reputation could possibly do. His letters tell us little that is worth knowing about him—a few poor quarrels about money and commissions. But it is quite otherwise with these songs and sonnets, written down at odd moments, sometimes on the margins of his sketches, themselves often unfinished sketches, arresting some salient feeling or unpremeditated idea as it passed. And it happens that a true study of these has become within the last few years for the first time possible. A few of the sonnets circulated widely in manuscript, and became almost within Michelangelo's own lifetime a subject of academical discourses. But they were first collected in a volume in 1623 by the great-nephew of Michelangelo, Michelangelo Buonarroti the younger. He omitted much, re-wrote the sonnets in part, and sometimes compressed two or more compositions into one, always losing something of the force and incisiveness of the original. So the book remained, neglected even by Italians themselves in the last century, through the influence of that French taste which despised all compositions of the kind, as it despised and neglected Dante. "His reputation will ever be on the increase, because he is so little read," says Voltaire of Dante.—But in 1858 the last of the Buonarroti bequeathed to the municipality of Florence the curiosities of his family. Among them was a precious volume containing the autograph of the sonnets. A learned Italian, Signor Cesare Guasti, undertook to collate this autograph with other manuscripts at the Vatican and elsewhere, and in 1863 published a true version of Michelangelo's poems, with dissertations and a paraphrase[1].

People have often spoken of these poems as if they were a mere cry of distress, a lover's complaint over the obduracy of Vittoria Colonna. But those who speak thus forget that though it is quite possible that Michelangelo had seen Vittoria, that somewhat shadowy figure, as early as 1537, yet their closer intimacy did not begin till about the year 1542, when Michelangelo was nearly seventy years old. Vittoria herself, an ardent neo-catholic, vowed to perpetual widowhood since the news had reached her, seventeen years before, that her husband, the youthful and princely Marquess of Pescara, lay dead of the wounds he had received in the battle of Pavia, was then no longer an object of great passion. In a dialogue written by the painter, Francesco d'Ollanda, we catch a glimpse of them together in an empty church at Rome, one Sunday afternoon, discussing indeed the characteristics of various schools of art, but still more the writings of Saint Paul, already following the ways and tasting the sunless pleasures of weary people, whose care for external things is slackening. In a

[1] The sonnets have been translated into English, with much skill, and poetic taste, by Mr. J. A. Symonds.

letter still extant he regrets that when he visited her after death he had kissed her hands only. He made, or set to work to make, a crucifix for her use, and two drawings, perhaps in preparation for it, are now in Oxford. From allusions in the sonnets, we may divine that when they first approached each other he had debated much with himself whether this last passion would be the most unsoftening, the most desolating of all—*un dolce amaro, un sì e no mi muovi.* Is it carnal affection, or, *del suo prestino stato* (of Plato's ante-natal state) *il raggio ardente?* The older, conventional criticism, dealing with the text of 1623, had lightly assumed that all or nearly all the sonnets were actually addressed to Vittoria herself; but Signor Guasti finds only four, or at most five, which can be so attributed on genuine authority. Still, there are reasons which make him assign the majority of them to the period between 1542 and 1547, and we may regard the volume as a record of this resting-place in Michelangelo's story. We know how Goethe escaped from the stress of sentiments too strong for him by making a book about them; and for Michelangelo, to write down his passionate thoughts at all, to express them in a sonnet, was already in some measure to command, and have his way with them—

> *La vita del mia amor non è il cor mio,*
> *Ch'amor, di quel ch'io t'amo, è senza córe.*

It was just because Vittoria raised no great passion that the space in his life where she reigns has such peculiar suavity; and the spirit of the sonnets is lost if we once take them out of that dreamy atmosphere in which men have things as they will, because the hold of all outward things upon them is faint and uncertain. Their prevailing tone is a calm and meditative sweetness. The cry of distress is indeed there, but as a mere residue, a trace of bracing chalybeate salt, just discernible in the song which rises like a clear, sweet spring from a charmed space in his life.

This charmed and temperate space in Michelangelo's life, without which its excessive strength would have been so imperfect, which saves him from the judgment of Dante on those who "wilfully lived in sadness," is then a well-defined period there, reaching from the year 1542 to the year 1547, the year of Vittoria's death. In it the lifelong effort to tranquillise his vehement emotions by withdrawing them into the region of ideal sentiment, becomes successful; and the significance of Vittoria is, that she realises for him a type of affection which even in disappointment may charm and sweeten his spirit.

In this effort to tranquillise and sweeten life by idealising its vehement sentiments, there were two great traditional types, either of which an Italian of the sixteenth century might have followed. There was Dante, whose little book of the *Vita Nuova* had early become a pattern of imaginative love, maintained somewhat feebly by the later followers of Petrarch; and, since Plato had become something more than a name in Italy by the publication of the Latin translation of his works by Marsilio Ficino, there was the Platonic tradition also. Dante's belief in the resurrection of the body, through which, even in heaven, Beatrice loses for him no tinge of flesh-colour, or fold of raiment even; and the Platonic dream of the passage of the soul through one form of life after another, with its passionate haste to escape from the burden of bodily form altogether; are, for all effects of art or poetry, principles diametrically opposite. Now it is the Platonic tradition rather than Dante's that has moulded Michelangelo's verse. In many ways no sentiment could have been less like Dante's love for Beatrice than Michelangelo's for Vittoria Colonna. Dante's comes in early youth; Beatrice is a child, with the wistful, ambiguous vision of a child, with a character still unaccentuated by the influence of outward circumstances, almost expressionless. Vittoria, on the other hand, is a woman already weary, in advanced age, of grave intellectual qualities. Dante's story is a piece of figured work, inlaid with lovely incidents. In Michelangelo's poems, frost and fire are almost the only images— the refining fire of the goldsmith; once or twice the phoenix; ice melting at the fire; fire struck from the rock which it afterwards consumes. Except one doubtful allusion to a journey, there are almost no incidents. But there is much of the bright, sharp, unerring skill, with which in boyhood he gave the look of age to the head of a faun by chipping a tooth from its jaw with a single stroke of the hammer. For Dante, the amiable and devout materialism of the middle age sanctifies all that is presented by hand and eye; while Michelangelo is always pressing forward from the outward beauty—*il bel del fuor che agli occhi piace*, to apprehend the unseen beauty; *trascenda nella forma universale*—that abstract form of beauty, about which the Platonists reason. And this gives the impression in him of something flitting and unfixed, of the houseless and complaining spirit, almost clairvoyant through the frail and yielding flesh. He accounts for love at first sight by a previous state of existence—*la dove io t'amai prima*.

And yet there are many points in which he is really like Dante, and comes very near to the original image, beyond those later and feebler followers in the wake of Petrarch. He learns from Dante rather than from Plato, that for lovers, the surfeiting of desire—*ove gran desir gran copia affrena*, is a state less happy than poverty with abundance of hope—*una miseria di speranza piena*. He recalls him in the repetition of the words *gentile* and *cortesia*, in the personification of *Amor*, in the tendency to dwell minutely on the physical effects of the presence of a beloved object on the pulses and the heart. Above all, he resembles Dante in the warmth and intensity of his political utterances, for the lady of one of his noblest sonnets was from the first understood to be the city of Florence; and he avers that all must be asleep in heaven, if she, who was created "of angelic form" for a thousand lovers, is appropriated by one alone, some Piero, or Alessandro de' Medici. Once and again he introduces Love and Death, who dispute concerning him. For, like Dante and all the nobler souls of Italy, he is much occupied with thoughts of the grave, and his true mistress is death,—death at first as the worst of all sorrows and disgraces, with a clod of the field for its brain; afterwards, death in its high distinction, its detachment from vulgar needs, the angry stains of life and action escaping fast.

Some of those whom the gods love die young. This man, because the gods loved him, lingered on to be of immense, patriarchal age, till the sweetness it had taken so long to secrete in him was found at last. Out of the strong came forth sweetness, *ex forti dulcedo*. The world had changed around him. The "new catholicism" had taken the place of the Renaissance. The spirit of the Roman

Church had changed: in the vast world's cathedral which his skill
had helped to raise for it, it looked stronger than ever. Some of the
first members of the *Oratory* were among his intimate associates.
They were of a spirit as unlike as possible from that of Lorenzo, or
Savonarola even. The opposition of the Reformation to art has
been often enlarged upon; far greater was that of the Catholic
revival. But in thus fixing itself in a frozen orthodoxy, the Roman
Church had passed beyond him, and he was a stranger to it. In
earlier days, when its beliefs had been in a fluid state, he too
might have been drawn into the controversy. He might have been
for spiritualising the papal sovereignty, like Savonarola; or for
adjusting the dreams of Plato and Homer with the words of Christ,
like Pico of Mirandola. But things had moved onward, and such
adjustments were no longer possible. For himself, he had long
since fallen back on that divine ideal, which above the wear and
tear of creeds has been forming itself for ages as the possession of
nobler souls. And now he began to feel the soothing influence
which since that time the Roman Church has often exerted over
spirits too independent to be its subjects, yet brought within the
neighbourhood of its action; consoled and tranquillised, as a traveller might be, resting for one evening in a strange city, by its
stately aspect and the sentiment of its many fortunes, just because with those fortunes he has nothing to do. So he lingers on; a
revenant, as the French say, a ghost out of another age, in a world
too coarse to touch his faint sensibilities very closely; dreaming,
in a worn-out society, theatrical in its life, theatrical in its art,
theatrical even in its devotion, on the morning of the world's
history, on the primitive form of man, on the images under which
the primitive world had conceived of spiritual forces.

I have dwelt on the thought of Michelangelo as thus lingering
beyond his time in a world not his own, because, if one is to
distinguish the peculiar savour of his work, he must be approached, not through his followers, but through his predecessors;
not through the marbles of *Saint Peter's*, but through the work of
the sculptors of the fifteenth century over the tombs and altars of
Tuscany. He is the last of the Florentines, of those on whom the
peculiar sentiment of the Florence of Dante and Giotto de-

scended: he is the consummate representative of the form that sentiment took in the fifteenth century with men like Luca Signorelli and Mino da Fiesole. Up to him the tradition of sentiment is unbroken, the progress towards surer and more mature methods of expressing that sentiment continuous. But his professed disciples did not share this temper; they are in love with his strength only, and seem not to feel his grave and temperate sweetness. Theatricality is their chief characteristic; and that is a quality as little attributable to Michelangelo as to Mino or Luca Signorelli. With him, as with them, all is serious, passionate, impulsive.

This discipleship of Michelangelo, this dependence of his on the tradition of the Florentine schools, is nowhere seen more clearly than in his treatment of the *Creation*. The *Creation of Man* had haunted the mind of the middle age like a dream; and weaving it into a hundred carved ornaments of capital or doorway, the Italian sculptors had early impressed upon it that pregnancy of expression which seems to give it many veiled meanings. As with other artistic conceptions of the middle age, its treatment became almost conventional, handed on from artist to artist, with slight changes, till it came to have almost an independent and abstract existence of its own. It was characteristic of the medieval mind thus to give an independent traditional existence to a special pictorial conception, or to a legend, like that of *Tristram* or *Tannhäuser*, or even to the very thoughts and substance of a book, like the *Imitation*, so that no single workman could claim it as his own, and the book, the image, the legend, had itself a legend, and its fortunes, and a personal history; and it is a sign of the medievalism of Michelangelo, that he thus receives from tradition his central conception, and does but add the last touches, in transferring it to the frescoes of the Sistine Chapel.

But there was another tradition of those earlier, more serious Florentines, of which Michelangelo is the inheritor, to which he gives the final expression, and which centres in the sacristy of *San Lorenzo*, as the tradition of the *Creation* centres in the Sistine Chapel. It has been said that all the great Florentines were preoccupied with death. *Outre-tombe! Outre-tombe!*—is the burden of their thoughts, from Dante to Savonarola. Even the gay and licentious Boccaccio gives a keener edge to his stories by putting them in the mouths of a party of people who had taken refuge in a country-house from the danger of death by plague. It was to this inherited sentiment, this practical decision that to be preoccupied with the thought of death was in itself dignifying, and a note of high quality, that the seriousness of the great Florentines of the fifteenth century was partly due; and it was reinforced in them by the actual sorrows of their times. How often, and in what various ways, had they seen life stricken down, in their streets and houses. *La bella Simonetta* dies in early youth, and is borne to the grave with uncovered face. The young Cardinal Jacopo di Portogallo dies on a visit to Florence—*insignis formâ fui et mirabili modestiâ*—his epitaph dares to say. Antonio Rossellino carves his tomb in the church of San Miniato, with care for the shapely hands and feet, and sacred attire; Luca della Robbia puts his skyiest works there; and the tomb of the youthful and princely prelate became the strangest and most beautiful thing in that strange and beautiful place. After the execution of the Pazzi conspirators, Botticelli is employed to paint their portraits. This preoccupation with serious thoughts and sad images might easily have resulted, as it did, for instance, in the gloomy villages of the Rhine, or in the overcrowded parts of medieval Paris, as it still does in many a village of the Alps, in something merely morbid or grotesque, in the *Danse Macabre* of many French and German painters, or the grim inventions of Dürer. From such a result the Florentine masters of the fifteenth century were saved by the nobility of their Italian culture, and still more by their tender pity for the thing itself. They must often have leaned over the lifeless body, when all was at length quiet and smoothed out. After death, it is said, the traces of slighter and more superficial dispositions disappear; the lines become more simple and dignified; only the abstract lines remain, in a great indifference. They came thus to see death in its distinction. Then following it perhaps one stage further, dwelling for a moment on the point where all this transitory dignity must break up, and discerning with no clearness a new body, they paused just in time, and abstained, with a sentiment of profound pity.

Of all this sentiment Michelangelo is the achievement; and, first of all, of pity. *Pietà*, pity, the pity of the Virgin Mother over the dead body of Christ, expanded into the pity of all mothers over all dead sons, the entombment, with its cruel "hard stones":—this is the subject of predilection. He has left it in many forms, sketches, half-finished designs, finished and unfinished groups of sculpture; but always as a hopeless, rayless, almost heathen sorrow—no divine sorrow, but mere pity and awe at the stiff limbs and colourless lips. There is a drawing of his at Oxford, in which the dead body has sunk to the earth between the mother's feet, with the arms extended over her knees. The tombs in the sacristy of *San Lorenzo* are memorials, not of any of the nobler and greater Medici, but of Giuliano, and Lorenzo the younger, noticeable chiefly for their somewhat early death. It is mere human nature therefore which has prompted the sentiment here. The titles assigned traditionally to the four symbolical figures, *Night* and *Day*, *The Twilight* and *The Dawn*, are far too definite for them; for these figures come much nearer to the mind and spirit of their author, and are a more direct expression of his thoughts, than any merely symbolical conceptions could possibly have been. They concentrate and express, less by way of definite conceptions than by the touches, the promptings of a piece of music, all those vague fancies, misgivings, presentiments, which shift and mix and are defined and fade again, whenever the thoughts try to fix themselves with sincerity on the conditions and surroundings of the disembodied spirit. I suppose no one would come to the sacristy of San Lorenzo for consolation; for seriousness, for solemnity, for dignity of impression, perhaps, but not for consolation. It is a place neither of consoling nor of terrible thoughts, but of vague and wistful speculation. Here, again, Michelangelo is the disciple not so much of Dante as of the Platonists. Dante's belief in immortality is formal, precise, and firm, almost as much so as that of a child, who thinks the dead will hear if you cry loud enough. But in Michelangelo you have maturity, the mind of the grown man, dealing cautiously and dispassionately with serious things; and what hope he has is based on the consciousness of ignorance—ignorance of man, ignorance of the nature of the mind, its origin and capacities. Michelangelo is so ignorant of the spiritual world, of the new body and its laws, that he does not surely know whether the consecrated Host may not be the body of Christ. And of all that range of sentiment he is the poet, a poet still alive, and in possession of our inmost thoughts—dumb inquiry over the relapse after death into the formlessness which preceded life, the change, the revolt from that change, then the correcting, hallowing, consoling rush of pity; at last, far off, thin and vague, yet not more vague than the most definite thoughts men have had through three centuries on a matter that has been so near their hearts, the new body—a passing light, a mere intangible, external effect, over those too rigid, or too formless faces; a dream that lingers a moment, retreating in the dawn, incomplete, aimless, helpless; a thing with faint hearing, faint memory, faint power of touch; a breath, a flame in the doorway, a feather in the wind.

The qualities of the great masters in art or literature, the combination of those qualities, the laws by which they moderate, support, relieve each other, are not peculiar to them; but most often typical standards, or revealing instances of the laws by which certain æsthetic effects are produced. The old masters indeed are simpler; their characteristics are written larger, and are easier to read, than the analogues of them in all the mixed, confused productions of the modern mind. But when once we have succeeded in defining for ourselves those characteristics, and the law of their combination, we have acquired a standard or measure which helps us to put in its right place many a vagrant genius, many an unclassified talent, many precious though imperfect products of art. It is so with the components of the true character of Michelangelo. That strange interfusion of sweetness and strength is not to be found in those who claimed to be his followers; but it is found in many of those who worked before him, and in many others down to our own time, in William Blake, for instance, and Victor Hugo, who, though not of his school, and unaware, are his true sons, and help us to understand him, as he in turn interprets and justifies them. Perhaps this is the chief use in studying old masters.

1871.

Leonardo da Vinci

Homo minister et interpres naturæ

In Vasari's life of Leonardo da Vinci as we now read it there are
some variations from the first edition. There, the painter who has
fixed the outward type of Christ for succeeding centuries was a
bold speculator, holding lightly by other men's beliefs, setting
philosophy above Christianity. Words of his, trenchant enough to
justify this impression, are not recorded, and would have been out
of keeping with a genius of which one characteristic is the tendency to lose itself in a refined and graceful mystery. The suspicion was but the time-honoured mode in which the world stamps
its appreciation of one who has thoughts for himself alone, his
high indifference, his intolerance of the common forms of things;
and in the second edition the image was changed into something
fainter and more conventional. But it is still by a certain mystery
in his work, and something enigmatical beyond the usual measure of great men, that he fascinates, or perhaps half repels. His
life is one of sudden revolts, with intervals in which he works not
at all, or apart from the main scope of his work. By a strange
fortune the pictures on which his more popular fame rested disappeared early from the world, like the *Battle of the Standard*; or are
mixed obscurely with the product of meaner hands, like the *Last
Supper*. His type of beauty is so exotic that it fascinates a larger
number than it delights, and seems more than that of any other
artist to reflect ideas and views and some scheme of the world
within; so that he seemed to his contemporaries to be the possessor of some unsanctified and secret wisdom; as to Michelet and
others to have anticipated modern ideas. He trifles with his ge-

nius, and crowds all his chief work into a few tormented years of later life; yet he is so possessed by his genius that he passes unmoved through the most tragic events, overwhelming his country and friends, like one who comes across them by chance on some secret errand.

His *legend*, as the French say, with the anecdotes which every one remembers, is one of the most brilliant chapters of Vasari. Later writers merely copied it, until, in 1804, Carlo Amoretti applied to it a criticism which left hardly a date fixed, and not one of those anecdotes untouched. The various questions thus raised have since that time become, one after another, subjects of special study, and mere antiquarianism has in this direction little more to do. For others remain the editing of the thirteen books of his manuscripts, and the separation by technical criticism of what in his reputed works is really his, from what is only half his, or the work of his pupils. But a lover of strange souls may still analyse for himself the impression made on him by those works, and try to reach through it a definition of the chief elements of Leonardo's genius. The *legend*, as corrected and enlarged by its critics, may now and then intervene to support the results of this analysis.

His life has three divisions—thirty years at Florence, nearly twenty years at Milan, then nineteen years of wandering, till he sinks to rest under the protection of Francis the First at the *Château de Clou*. The dishonour of illegitimacy hangs over his birth. Piero Antonio, his father, was of a noble Florentine house, of Vinci in the *Val d'Arno*, and Leonardo, brought up delicately among the true children of the house, was the love-child of his youth, with the keen, puissant nature such children often have. We see him in his boyhood fascinating all men by his beauty, improvising music and songs, buying the caged birds and setting them free, as he walked the streets of Florence, fond of odd bright dresses and spirited horses.

From his earliest years he designed many objects, and constructed models in relief, of which Vasari mentions some of women smiling. His father, pondering over this promise in the child, took him to the workshop of Andrea del Verrocchio, then the most famous artist in Florence. Beautiful objects lay about there—reliquaries, pyxes, silver images for the pope's chapel at Rome, strange fancy-work of the middle age, keeping odd company with fragments of antiquity, then but lately discovered. Another student Leonardo may have seen there—a lad into whose soul the level light and aerial illusions of Italian sunsets had passed, in after days famous as Perugino. Verrocchio was an artist of the earlier Florentine type, carver, painter, and worker in metals, in one; designer, not of pictures only, but of all things for sacred or household use, drinking-vessels, ambries, instruments of music, making them all fair to look upon, filling the common ways of life with the reflexion of some far-off brightness; and years of patience had refined his hand till his work was now sought after from distant places.

It happened that Verrocchio was employed by the brethren of Vallombrosa to paint the Baptism of Christ, and Leonardo was allowed to finish an angel in the left-hand corner. It was one of those moments in which the progress of a great thing—here, that of the art of Italy—presses hard on the happiness of an individual, through whose discouragement and decrease, humanity, in more fortunate persons, comes a step nearer to its final success.

For beneath the cheerful exterior of the mere well-paid craftsman, chasing brooches for the copes of *Santa Maria Novella*, or twisting metal screens for the tombs of the Medici, lay the ambitious desire to expand the destiny of Italian art by a larger knowledge and insight into things, a purpose in art not unlike Leonardo's still unconscious purpose; and often, in the modelling of drapery, or of a lifted arm, or of hair cast back from the face, there came to him something of the freer manner and richer humanity of a later age. But in this *Baptism* the pupil had surpassed the master; and Verrocchio turned away as one stunned, and as if his sweet earlier work must thereafter be distasteful to him, from the bright animated angel of Leonardo's hand.

The angel may still be seen in Florence, a space of sunlight in the cold, laboured old picture; but the legend is true only in sentiment, for painting had always been the art by which Verrocchio set least store. And as in a sense he anticipates Leonardo, so, to the last Leonardo recalls the studio of Verrocchio, in the love of beautiful toys, such as the vessel of water for a mirror, and lovely needlework about the implicated hands in the *Modesty and Vanity*, and of reliefs, like those cameos which in the *Virgin of the Balances* hang all round the girdle of Saint Michael, and of bright variegated stones, such as the agates in the *Saint Anne*, and in a hieratic preciseness and grace, as of a sanctuary swept and garnished. Amid all the cunning and intricacy of his Lombard manner this never left him. Much of it there must have been in that lost picture of *Paradise*, which he prepared as a cartoon for tapestry, to be woven in the looms of Flanders. It was the perfection of the older Florentine style of miniature-painting, with patient putting of each leaf upon the trees and each flower in the grass, where the first man and woman were standing.

And because it was the perfection of that style, it awoke in Leonardo some seed of discontent which lay in the secret places of his nature. For the way to perfection is through a series of disgusts; and this picture—all that he had done so far in his life at Florence—was after all in the old slight manner. His art, if it was to be something in the world, must be weighted with more of the meaning of nature and purpose of humanity. Nature was "the true mistress of higher intelligences." He plunged, then, into the study of nature. And in doing this he followed the manner of the older students; he brooded over the hidden virtues of plants and crystals, the lines traced by the stars as they moved in the sky, over the correspondences which exist between the different orders of living things, through which, to eyes opened, they interpret each other, and for years he seemed to those about him as one listening to a voice, silent for other men.

He learned here the art of going deep, of tracking the sources of expression to their subtlest retreats, the power of an intimate presence in the things he handled. He did not at once or entirely desert his art; only he was no longer the cheerful, objective painter, through whose soul, as through clear glass, the bright figures of Florentine life, only made a little mellower and more pensive by the transit, passed on to the white wall. He wasted many days in curious tricks of design, seeming to lose himself in the spinning of intricate devices of line and colour. He was smitten with a love of the impossible—the perforation of mountains, changing the course of rivers, raising great buildings, such as the church of *San Giovanni*, in the air; all those feats for the perform-ance of which natural magic professed to have the key. Later writers, indeed, see in these efforts an anticipation of modern mechanics; in him they were rather dreams, thrown off by the overwrought and labouring brain. Two ideas were especially con-firmed in him, as reflexes of things that had touched his brain in childhood beyond the depth of other impressions—the smiling of women and the motion of great waters.

And in such studies some interfusion of the extremes of beauty and terror shaped itself, as an image that might be seen and touched, in the mind of this gracious youth, so fixed that for the rest of his life it never left him. As if catching glimpses of it in the strange eyes or hair of chance people, he would follow such about the streets of Florence till the sun went down, of whom many sketches of his remain. Some of these are full of a curious beauty, that remote beauty which may be apprehended only by those who have sought it carefully; who, starting with acknowledged types of beauty, have refined as far upon these, as these refine upon the world of common forms. But mingled inextricably with this there is an element of mockery also; so that, whether in sorrow or scorn, he caricatures Dante even. Legions of grotesques sweep under his hand; for has not nature too her grotesques—the rent rock, the distorting lights of evening on lonely roads, the unveiled structure of man in the embryo, or the skeleton?

All these swarming fancies unite in the *Medusa* of the *Uffizii*. Vasari's story of an earlier Medusa, painted on a wooden shield, is perhaps an invention; and yet, properly told, has more of the air of truth about it than anything else in the whole legend. For its real subject is not the serious work of a man, but the experiment of a child. The lizards and glowworms and other strange small crea-tures which haunt an Italian vineyard bring before one the whole picture of a child's life in a Tuscan dwelling—half castle, half farm—and are as true to nature as the pretended astonishment of the father for whom the boy has prepared a surprise. It was not in play that he painted that other Medusa, the one great picture which he left behind him in Florence. The subject has been treated in various ways; Leonardo alone cuts to its centre; he alone realises it as the head of a corpse, exercising its powers through all the circumstances of death. What may be called the fascination of corruption penetrates in every touch its exquisitely finished beauty. About the dainty lines of the cheek the bat flits unheeded. The delicate snakes seem literally strangling each other in terrified struggle to escape from the Medusa brain. The hue which violent death always brings with it is in the features; features singularly massive and grand, as we catch them inverted, in a dexterous foreshortening, crown foremost, like a great calm stone against which the wave of serpents breaks.

The science of that age was all divination, clairvoyance, unsubjected to our exact modern formulas, seeking in an instant of vision to concentrate a thousand experiences. Later writers, thinking only of the well-ordered treatise on painting which a Frenchman, Raffaelle du Fresne, a hundred years afterwards, compiled from Leonardo's bewildered manuscripts, written strangely, as his manner was, from right to left, have imagined a rigid order in his inquiries. But this rigid order would have been little in accordance with the restlessness of his character; and if we think of him as the mere reasoner who subjects design to anatomy, and composition to mathematical rules, we shall hardly have that impression which those around Leonardo received from him. Poring over his crucibles, making experiments with colour, trying, by a strange variation of the alchemist's dream, to discover the secret, not of an elixir to make man's natural life immortal, but of giving immortality to the subtlest and most delicate effects of painting, he seemed to them rather the sorcerer or the magician, possessed of curious secrets and a hidden knowledge, living in a world of which he alone possessed the key. What his philosophy seems to have been most like is that of Paracelsus or Cardan; and much of the spirit of the older alchemy still hangs about it, with its confidence in short cuts and odd byways to knowledge. To him philosophy was to be something giving strange swiftness and double sight, divining the sources of springs beneath the earth or of expression beneath the human countenance, clairvoyant of occult gifts in common or uncommon things, in the reed at the brookside, or the star which draws near to us but once in a century. How, in this way, the clear purpose was overclouded, the fine chaser's hand perplexed, we but dimly see; the mystery which at no point quite lifts from Leonardo's life is deepest here. But it is certain that at one period of his life he had almost ceased to be an artist.

The year 1483—the year of the birth of Raphael and the thiry-first of Leonardo's life—is fixed as the date of his visit to Milan by the letter in which he recommends himself to Ludovico Sforza, and offers to tell him, for a price, strange secrets in the art of war. It was that Sforza who murdered his young nephew by slow poison, yet was so susceptible of religious impressions that he blended mere earthly passion with a sort of religious sentimentalism, and who took for his device the mulberry-tree—symbol, in its long delay and sudden yielding of flowers and fruit together, of a wisdom which economises all forces for an opportunity of sudden and sure effect. The fame of Leonardo had gone before him, and he was to model a colossal statue of Francesco, the first Duke of Milan. As for Leonardo himself, he came not as an artist it all, or careful of the fame of one; but as a player on the harp, a strange harp of silver of his own construction, shaped in some curious likeness to a horse's skull. The capricious spirit of Ludovico was susceptible also to the power of music, and Leonardo's nature had a kind of spell in it. Fascination is always the word descriptive of him. No portrait of his youth remains; but all tends to make us believe that up to this time some charm of voice and aspect, strong enough to balance the disadvantage of his birth, had played about him. His physical strength was great; it was said that he could bend a horse-shoe like a coil of lead.

The *Duomo*, work of artists from beyond the Alps, so fantastic to the eye of a Florentine used to the mellow, unbroken surfaces of Giotto and Arnolfo, was then in all its freshness; and below, in the streets of Milan, moved a people as fantastic, changeful, and dreamlike. To Leonardo least of all men could there be anything poisonous in the exotic flowers of sentiment which grew there. It was a life of brilliant sins and exquisite amusements: Leonardo became a celebrated designer of pageants; and it suited the quality of his genius, composed, in almost equal parts, of curiosity and the desire of beauty, to take things as they came.

Curiosity and the desire of beauty—these are the two elementary forces in Leonardo's genius; curiosity often in conflict with the desire of beauty, but generating, in union with it, a type of subtle and curious grace.

The movement of the fifteenth century was two-fold; partly the Renaissance, partly also the coming of what is called the "modern spirit," with its realism, its appeal to experience. It comprehended a return to antiquity, and a return to nature. Raphael represents the return to antiquity, and Leonardo the return to nature. In this return to nature, he was seeking to satisfy a boundless curiosity by her perpetual surprises, a microscopic sense of finish by her *finesse*, or delicacy of operation, that *subtilitas naturæ* which Bacon notices. So we find him often in intimate relations with men of science,—with Fra Luca Paccioli the mathematician, and the anatomist Marc Antonio della Torre. His observations and experiments fill thirteen volumes of manuscript; and those who can judge describe him as anticipating long before, by rapid intuition, the later ideas of science. He explained the obscure light of the unilluminated part of the moon, knew that the sea had once covered the mountains which contain shells, and of the gathering of the equatorial waters above the polar.

He who thus penetrated into the most secret parts of nature preferred always the more to the less remote, what, seeming exceptional, was an instance of law more refined, the construction about things of a peculiar atmosphere and mixed lights. He paints flowers with such curious felicity that different writers have attributed to him a fondness for particular flowers, as Clement the cyclamen, and Rio the jasmin; while, at Venice, there is a stray leaf from his portfolio dotted all over with studies of violets and the wild rose. In him first appears the taste for what is *bizarre* or *recherché* in landscape; hollow places full of the green shadow of bituminous rocks, ridged reefs of trap-rock which cut the water into quaint sheets of light,—their exact antitype is in our own western seas; all the solemn effects of moving water. You may follow it springing from its distant source among the rocks on the heath of the *Madonna of the Balances*, passing, as a little fall, into the treacherous calm of the *Madonna of the Lake*, as a goodly river next, below the cliffs of the *Madonna of the Rocks*, washing the white walls of its distant villages, stealing out in a network of divided streams in *La Gioconda* to the seashore of the *Saint Anne*

—that delicate place, where the wind passes like the point of some fine etcher over the surface, and the untorn shells are lying thick upon the sand, and the tops of the rocks, to which the waves never rise, are green with grass, grown fine as hair. It is the land-scape, not of dreams or of fancy, but of places far withdrawn, and hours selected from a thousand with a miracle of *finesse*. Through Leonardo's strange veil of sight things reach him so; in no ordinary night or day, but as in faint light of eclipse, or in some brief interval of falling rain at daybreak, or through deep water.

And not into nature only; but he plunged also into human personality, and became above all a painter of portraits; faces of a modelling more skilful than has been seen before or since, embodied with a reality which almost amounts to illusion, on the dark air. To take a character as it was, and delicately sound its stops, suited one so curious in observation, curious in invention. He painted thus the portraits of Ludovico's mistresses, Lucretia Crivelli and Cecilia Galerani the poetress, of Ludovico himself, and the Duchess Beatrice. The portrait of Cecilia Galerani is lost, but that of Lucretia Crivelli has been identified with *La Belle Feronière* of the Louvre, and Ludovico's pale, anxious face still remains in the Ambrosian Library. Opposite is the portrait of Beatrice d'Este, in whom Leonardo seems to have caught some presentiment of early death, painting her precise and grave, full of the refinement of the dead, in sad earth-coloured raiment, set with pale stones.

Sometimes this curiosity came in conflict with the desire of beauty; it tended to make him go too far below that outside of things in which art really begins and ends. This struggle between the reason and its ideas, and the senses, the desire of beauty, is the key to Leonardo's life at Milan—his restlessness, his endless retouchings, his odd experiments with colour. How much must he leave unfinished, how much recommence! His problem was the transmutation of ideas into images. What he had attained so far had been the mastery of that earlier Florentine style, with its naïve and limited sensuousness. Now he was to entertain in this narrow medium those divinations of a humanity too wide for it, that larger vision of the opening world, which is only not too much for the great, irregular art of Shakespeare; and everywhere the effort is visible in the work of his hands. This agitation, this perpetual delay, give him an air of weariness and *ennui*. To others he seems to be aiming at an impossible effect, to do something that art, that painting, can never do. Often the expression of physical beauty at this or that point seems strained and marred in the effort, as in those heavy German foreheads—too heavy and German for perfect beauty.

For there was a touch of Germany in that genius which, as Goethe said, had "thought itself weary"—*müde sich gedacht.* What an anticipation of modern Germany, for instance, in that debate on the question whether sculpture or painting is the nobler art[1]! But there is this difference between him and the German, that, with all that curious science, the German would have thought nothing more was needed. The name of Goethe himself reminds one how great for the artist may be the danger of overmuch science; how Goethe, who, in the *Elective Affinities* and the first part of *Faust*, does transmute ideas into images, who wrought many such transmutations, did not invariably find the spell-word, and in the second part of *Faust* presents us with a mass of science which has almost no artistic character at all. But Leonardo will never work till the happy moment comes—that moment of *bien-être*, which to imaginative men is the moment of invention. On this he waits with a perfect patience; other moments are but a preparation, or after-taste of it. Few men distinguish between them as jealously as he. Hence, so many flaws even in the choicest work. But for Leonardo the distinction is absolute, and, in the moment of *bien-être*, the alchemy complete: the idea is stricken into colour and imagery: a cloudy mysticism is refined to a subdued and graceful mystery, and painting pleases the eye while it satisfies the soul.

This curious beauty is seen above all in his drawings, and in these chiefly in the abstract grace of the bounding lines. Let us take some of these drawings, and pause over them awhile; and, first, one of those at Florence—the heads of a woman and a little child, set side by side, but each in its own separate frame. First of

---

[1] How princely, how characteristic of Leonardo, the answer, *Quanto più un' arte porta seco fatica di corpo tanto più è vile!*

all, there is much pathos in the reappearance, in the fuller curves of the face of the child, of the sharper, more chastened lines of the worn and older face, which leaves no doubt that the heads are those of a little child and its mother. A feeling for maternity is indeed always characteristic of Leonardo; and this feeling is further indicated here by the half-humorous pathos of the diminutive, rounded shoulders of the child. You may note a like pathetic power in drawings of a young man, seated in a stooping posture, his face in his hands, as in sorrow; of a slave sitting in an uneasy inclined attitude, in some brief interval of rest; of a small Madonna and Child, peeping sideways in half-reassured terror, as a mighty griffin with batlike wings, one of Leonardo's finest *inventions*, descends suddenly from the air to snatch up a great wild beast wandering near them. But note in these, as that which especially belongs to art, the contour of the young man's hair, the poise of the slave's arm above his head, and the curves of the head of the child, following the little skull within, thin and fine as some seashell worn by the wind.

Take again another head, still more full of sentiment, but of a different kind, a little drawing in red chalk which every one will remember who has examined at all carefully the drawings by old masters at the Louvre. It is a face of doubtful sex, set in the shadow of its own hair, the cheek-line in high light against it, with something voluptuous and full in the eyelids and the lips. Another drawing might pass for the same face in childhood, with parched and feverish lips, but much sweetness in the loose, short-waisted childish dress, with necklace and *bulla*, and in the daintily bound hair. We might take the thread of suggestion which these two drawings offer, when thus set side by side, and, following it through the drawings at Florence, Venice, and Milan, construct a sort of series, illustrating better than anything else Leonardo's type of womanly beauty. Daughters of Herodias, with their fantastic head-dresses knotted and folded so strangely to leave the dainty oval of the face disengaged, they are not of the Christian family, or of Raphael's. They are the clairvoyants, through whom, as through delicate instruments, one becomes aware of the subtler forces of nature, and the modes of their action, all that is magnetic in it, all those finer conditions wherein material things rise to that subtlety of operation which constitutes them spiritual, where only the finer nerve and the keener touch can follow. It is as if in certain significant examples we actually saw those forces at their work on human flesh. Nervous, electric, faint always with some inexplicable faintness, these people seem to be subject to exceptional conditions, to feel powers at work in the common air unfelt by others, to become, as it were, the receptacle of them, and pass them on to us in a chain of secret influences.

But among the more youthful heads there is one at Florence which Love chooses for its own—the head of a young man, which may well be the likeness of Andrea Salaino, beloved of Leonardo for his curled and waving hair—*belli capelli ricci e inanellati*—and afterwards his favourite pupil and servant. Of all the interests in living men and women which may have filled his life at Milan, this attachment alone is recorded. And in return Salaino identified himself so entirely with Leonardo, that the picture of *St. Anne*, in the Louvre, has been attributed to him. It illustrates Leonardo's usual choice of pupils, men of some natural charm of person or intercourse like Salaino, or men of birth and princely habits of life like Francesco Melzi—men with just enough genius to be capable of initiation into his secret, for the sake of which they were ready to efface their own individuality. Among them, retiring often to the villa of the Melzi at *Canonica al Vaprio*, he worked at his fugitive manuscripts and sketches, working for the present hour, and for a few only, perhaps chiefly for himself. Other artists have been as careless of present or future applause, in self-forgetfulness, or because they set moral or political ends above the ends of art; but in him this solitary culture of beauty seems to have hung upon a kind of self-love, and a carelessness in the work of art of all but art itself. Out of the secret places of a unique temperament he brought strange blossoms and fruits hitherto unknown; and for him, the novel impression conveyed, the exquisite effect woven, counted as an end in itself—a perfect end.

And these pupils of his acquired his manner so thoroughly, that though the number of Leonardo's authentic works is very small indeed, there is a multitude of other men's pictures through which we undoubtedly see him, and come very near to his genius.

Sometimes, as in the little picture of the *Madonna of the Balances*, in which, from the bosom of His mother, Christ weighs the pebbles of the brook against the sins of men, we have a hand, rough enough by contrast, working upon some fine hint or sketch of his. Sometimes, as in the subjects of the *Daughter of Herodias* and the *Head of John the Baptist*, the lost originals have been re-echoed and varied upon again and again by Luini and others. At other times the original remains, but has been a mere theme or motive, a type of which the accessories might be modified or changed; and these variations have but brought out the more the purpose, or expression of the original. It is so with the so-called *Saint John the Baptist* of the Louvre—one of the few naked figures Leonardo painted—whose delicate brown flesh and woman's hair no one would go out into the wilderness to seek, and whose treacherous smile would have us understand something far beyond the outward gesture or circumstance. But the long, reedlike cross in the hand, which suggests Saint John the Baptist, becomes faint in a copy at the Ambrosian Library, and disappears altogether in another version, in the *Palazzo Rosso* at Genoa. Returning from the latter to the original, we are no longer surprised by Saint John's strange likeness to the *Bacchus* which hangs near it, and which set Théophile Gautier thinking of Heine's notion of decayed gods, who, to maintain themselves, after the fall of paganism, took employment in the new religion. We recognise one of those symbolical inventions in which the ostensible subject is used, not as matter for definite pictorial realisation, but as the starting-point of a train of sentiment, subtle and vague as a piece of music. No one ever ruled over the mere *subject* in hand more entirely than Leonardo, or bent it more dexterously to purely artistic ends. And so it comes to pass that though he handles sacred subjects continually, he is the most profane of painters; the given person or subject, Saint John in the Desert, or the Virgin on the knees of Saint Anne, is often merely the pretext for a kind of work which carries one altogether beyond the range of its conventional associations.

About the *Last Supper*, its decay and restorations, a whole literature has risen up, Goethe's pensive sketch of its sad fortunes being perhaps the best. The death in child-birth of the Duchess

Beatrice was followed in Ludovico by one of those paroxysms of religious feeling which in him were constitutional. The low, gloomy Dominican church of *Saint Mary of the Graces* had been the favourite oratory of Beatrice. She had spent her last days there, full of sinister presentiments; at last it had been almost necessary to remove her from it by force; and now it was here that mass was said a hundred times a day for her repose. On the damp wall of the refectory, oozing with mineral salts, Leonardo painted the *Last Supper*. A hundred anecdotes were told about it, his retouchings and delays. They show him refusing to work except at the moment of invention, scornful of anyone who supposed that art could be a work of mere industry and rule, often coming the whole length of Milan to give a single touch. He painted it, not in fresco, where all must be *impromptu*, but in oils, the new method which he had been one of the first to welcome, because it allowed of so many after-thoughts, so refined a working-out of perfection. It turned out that on a plastered wall no process could have been less durable. Within fifty years it had fallen into decay. And now we have to turn back to Leonardo's own studies, above all to one drawing of the central head at the *Brera*, which, in a union of tenderness and severity in the face-lines, reminds one of the monumental work of Mino da Fiesole, to trace it as it was.

Here was another effort to lift a given subject out of the range of its traditional associations. Strange, after all the mystic developments of the middle age, was the effort to see the Eucharist, not as the pale Host of the altar, but as one taking leave of his friends. Five years afterwards the young Raphael, at Florence, painted it with sweet and solemn effect in the refectory of Saint Onofrio; but still with all the mystical unreality of the school of Perugino. Vasari pretends that the central head was never finished. But finished or unfinished, or owing part of its effect to a mellowing decay, the head of Jesus does but consummate the sentiment of the whole company—ghosts through which you see the wall, faint as the shadows of the leaves upon the wall on autumn afternoons. This figure is but the faintest, the most spectral of them all.

The *Last Supper* was finished in 1497; in 1498 the French entered Milan, and whether or not the Gascon bowmen used it as a mark for their arrows, the model of Francesco Sforza certainly did not survive. What, in that age, such work was capable of being—of what nobility, amid what racy truthfulness to fact—we may judge from the bronze statue of Bartolomeo Colleoni on horseback, modelled by Leonardo's master, Verrocchio, (he died of grief, it was said, because, the mould accidentally failing, he was unable to complete it,) still standing in the *piazza* of Saint John and Saint Paul at Venice. Some traces of the thing may remain in certain of Leonardo's drawings, and perhaps also, by a singular circumstance, in a far-off town of France. For Ludovico became a prisoner, and ended his days at Loches in Touraine. After many years of captivity in the dungeons below, where all seems sick with barbarous fuedal memories, he was allowed at last, it is said, to breathe fresher air for awhile in one of the rooms of the great tower still shown, its walls covered with strange painted arabesques, ascribed by tradition to his hand, amused a little, in this way, through the tedious years. In those vast helmets and human faces and pieces of armour, among which, in great letters, the motto *Infelix Sum* is woven in and out, it is perhaps not too fanciful to see the fruit of a wistful after-dreaming over Leonardo's sundry experiments on the armed figure of the great duke, which had occupied the two so much during the days of their good fortune in Milan.

The remaining years of Leonardo's life are more or less years of wandering. From his brilliant life at court he had saved nothing, and he returned to Florence a poor man. Perhaps necessity kept his spirit excited: the next four years are one prolonged rapture or ecstasy of invention. He painted now the pictures of the Louvre, his most authentic works, which came there straight from the cabinet of Francis the First, at Fontainebleau. One picture of his, the *Saint Anne*—not the *Saint Anne* of the Louvre, but a simple cartoon, now in London—revived for a moment a sort of appreciation more common in an earlier time, when good pictures had still seemed miraculous. For two days a crowd of peole of all qualities passed in naïve excitement through the chamber where it hung, and gave Leonardo a taste of the "triumph" of Cimabue. But his work was less with the saints than with the living women of Florence. For he lived still in the polished society that he loved, and in the houses of Florence, left perhaps a little subject to light thoughts by the death of Savonarola—the latest gossip (1869) is of an undraped Monna Lisa, found in some out-of-the-way corner of the late *Orleans* collection—he saw Ginevra di Benci, and Lisa, the young third wife of Francesco del Giocondo. As we have seen him using incidents of sacred story, not for their own sake, or as mere subjects for pictorial realisation, but as a cryptic language for fancies all his own, so now he found a vent for his thought in taking one of these languid women, and raising her, as Leda or Pomona, as Modesty or Vanity, to the seventh heaven of symbolical expression.

La Gioconda is, in the truest sense, Leonardo's masterpiece, the revealing instance of his mode of thought and work. In suggestiveness, only the *Melancholia* of Dürer is comparable to it; and no crude symbolism disturbs the effect of its subdued and graceful mystery. We all know the face and hands of the figure, set in its marble chair, in that circle of fantastic rocks, as in some faint light under sea. Perhaps of all ancient pictures time has chilled it least[1]. As often happens with works in which invention seems to reach its limit, there is an element in it given to, not invented by, the master. In that inestimable folio of drawings, once in the possession of Vasari, were certain designs by Verrocchio, faces of such impressive beauty that Leonardo in his boyhood copied them many times. It is hard not to connect with these designs of the elder, by-past master, as with its germinal principle, the unfathomable smile, always with a touch of something sinister in it, which plays over all Leonardo's work. Besides, the picture is a portrait. From childhood we see this image defining itself on the fabric of his dreams; and but for express historical testimony, we might fancy that this was but his ideal lady, embodied and beheld at last. What was the relationship of a living Florentine to this creature of his thought? By what strange affinities had the dream and the person grown up thus apart, and yet so closely together? Present from the first incorporeally in Leonardo's brain, dimly traced in the designs of Verrocchio, she is found present at last in

[1]Yet for Vasari there was some further magic of crimson in the lips and cheeks, lost for us.

Il Giocondo's house. That there is much of mere portraiture in the picture is attested by the legend that by artificial means, the presence of mimes and flute-players, that subtle expression was protracted on the face. Again, was it in four years and by renewed labour never really completed, or in four months and as by stroke of magic, that the image was projected?

The presence that rose thus so strangely beside the waters, is expressive of what in the ways of a thousand years men had come to desire. Hers is the head upon which all "the ends of the world are come," and the eyelids are a little weary. It is a beauty wrought out from within upon the flesh, the deposit, little cell by cell, of strange thoughts and fantastic reveries and exquisite passions. Set it for a moment beside one of those white Greek goddesses or beautiful women of antiquity, and how would they be troubled by this beauty, into which the soul with all its maladies has passed! All the thoughts and experience of the world have etched and moulded there, in that which they have of power to refine and make expressive the outward form, the animalism of Greece, the lust of Rome, the mysticism of the middle age with its spiritual ambition and imaginative loves, the return of the Pagan world, the sins of the Borgias. She is older than the rocks among which she sits; like the vampire, she has been dead many times, and learned the secrets of the grave; and has been a diver in deep seas, and keeps their fallen day about her; and trafficked for strange webs with Eastern merchants: and, as Leda, was the mother of Helen of Troy, and, as Saint Anne, the mother of Mary; and all this has been to her but as the sound of lyres and flutes, and lives only in the delicacy with which it has moulded the changing lineaments, and tinged the eyelids and the hands. The fancy of a perpetual life, sweeping together ten thousand experiences, is an old one; and modern philosophy has conceived the idea of humanity as wrought upon by, and summing up in itself, all modes of thought and life. Certainly Lady Lisa might stand as the embodiment of the old fancy, the symbol of the modern idea.

During these years at Florence Leonardo's history is the history of his art; for himself, he is lost in the bright cloud of it. The outward history begins again in 1502, with a wild journey through central Italy, which he makes as the chief engineer of Cæsar

Borgia. The biographer, putting together the stray jottings of his manuscripts, may follow him through every day of it, up the strange tower of Siena, elastic like a bent bow, down to the sea-shore at Piombino, each place appearing as fitfully as in a fever dream.

One other great work was left for him to do, a work all trace of which soon vanished, *The Battle of the Standard*, in which he had Michelangelo for his rival. The citizens of Florence, desiring to decorate the walls of the great council-chamber, had offered the work for competition, and any subject might be chosen from the Florentine wars of the fifteenth century. Michelangelo chose for his cartoon an incident of the war with Pisa, in which the Florentine soldiers, bathing in the Arno, are surprised by the sound of trumpets, and run to arms. His design has reached us only in an old engraving, which helps us less perhaps than our remembrance of the background of his *Holy Family* in the *Uffizii* to imagine in what superhuman form, such as might have beguiled the heart of an earlier world, those figures ascended out of the water. Leonardo chose an incident from the battle of Anghiari, in which two parties of soldiers fight for a standard. Like Michelangelo's, his cartoon is lost, and has come to us only in sketches, and in a fragment of Rubens. Through the accounts given we may discern some lust of terrible things in it, so that even the horses tore each other with their teeth. And yet one fragment of it, in a drawing of his at Florence, is far different—a waving field of lovely armour, the chased edgings running like lines of sunlight from side to side. Michelangelo was twenty-seven years old; Leonardo more than fifty; and Raphael, then nineteen years of age, visiting Florence for the first time, came and watched them as they worked.

We catch a glimpse of Leonardo again, at Rome in 1514, surrounded by his mirrors and vials and furnaces, making strange toys that seemed alive of wax and quicksilver. The hesitation which had haunted him all through life, and made him like one under a spell, was upon him now with double force. No one had ever carried political indifferentism further; it had always been his philosophy to "fly before the storm"; he is for the Sforzas, or against them, as the tide of their fortune turns. Yet now, in the political society of Rome, he came to be suspected of secret

French sympathies. It paralysed him to find himself among enemies; and he turned wholly to France, which had long courted him.

France was about to become an Italy more Italian than Italy itself. Francis the First, like Lewis the Twelfth before him, was attracted by the *finesse* of Leonardo's work; *La Gioconda* was already in his cabinet, and he offered Leonardo the little *Château de Clou*, with its vineyards and meadows, in the pleasant valley of the Masse, just outside the walls of the town of Amboise, where, especially in the hunting season, the court then frequently resided. *A Monsieur Lyonard, peinteur du Roy pour Amboyse:* —so the letter of Francis the First is headed. It opens a prospect, one of the most interesting in the history of art, where, in a peculiarly blent atmosphere, Italian art dies away as a French exotic.

Two questions remain, after much busy antiquarianism, concerning Leonardo's death—the question of the exact form of his religion, and the question whether Francis the First was present at the time. They are of about equally little importance in the estimate of Leonardo's genius. The directions in his will concerning the thirty masses and the great candles for the church of Saint Florentin are things of course, their real purpose being immediate and practical; and on no theory of religion could these hurried offices be of much consequence. We forget them in speculating how one who had been always so desirous of beauty, but desired it always in such precise and definite forms, as hands or flowers or hair, looked forward now into the vague land, and experienced the last curiosity.

1869.

The School of Giorgione

It is the mistake of much popular criticism to regard poetry, music, and painting—all the various products of art—as but translations into different languages of one and the same fixed quantity of imaginative thought, supplemented by certain technical qualities of colour, in painting; of sound, in music; of rhythmical words, in poetry. In this way, the sensuous element in art, and with it almost everything in art that is essentially artistic, is made a matter of indifference; and a clear apprehension of the opposite principle—that the sensuous material of each art brings with it a special phase or quality of beauty, untranslatable into the forms of any other, an order of impressions distinct in kind—is the beginning of all true æsthetic criticism. For, as art addresses not pure sense, still less the pure intellect, but the "imaginative reason" through the senses, there are differences of kind in æsthetic beauty, corresponding to the differences in kind of the gifts of sense themselves. Each art, therefore, having its own peculiar and untranslatable sensuous charm, has its own special mode of reaching the imagination, its own special responsibilities to its material. One of the functions of æsthetic criticism is to define these limitations; to estimate the degree in which a given work of art fulfils its responsibilities to its special material; to note in a picture that true pictorial charm, which is neither a mere poetical thought or sentiment, on the one hand, nor a mere result of communicable technical skill in colour or design, on the other; to define in a poem that true poetical quality, which is neither descriptive nor meditative merely, but comes of an inventive handling of rhythmical language, the element of song in the singing; to note in music the musical charm, that essential music, which presents no words, no matter of sentiment or thought, separable from the special form in which it is conveyed to us.

To such a philosophy of the variations of the beautiful, Lessing's analysis of the spheres of sculpture and poetry, in the *Laocoon*, was an important contribution. But a true appreciation of these things is possible only in the light of a whole system of such art-casuistries. Now painting is the art in the criticism of which this truth most needs enforcing, for it is in popular judgments on pictures that the false generalisation of all art into forms of poetry is most prevalent. To suppose that all is mere technical acquirement in delineation or touch, working through and addressing itself to the intelligence, on the one side, or a merely poetical, or what may be called literary interest, addressed also to the pure intelligence, on the other:—this is the way of most spectators, and of many critics, who have never caught sight all the time of that true pictorial quality which lies between, unique pledge, as it is, of the possession of the pictorial gift, that inventive or creative handling of pure line and colour, which, as almost always in Dutch painting, as often also in the works of Titian or Veronese, is quite independent of anything definitely poetical in the subject it accompanies. It is the *drawing*—the design projected from that peculiar pictorial temperament or constitution, in which, while it may possibly be ignorant of true anatomical proportions, all things whatever, all poetry, all ideas however abstract or obscure, float up as visible scene or image: it is the *colouring*—that weaving of light, as of just perceptible gold threads, through the dress, the flesh, the atmosphere, in Titian's *Lace-girl*, that staining of the whole fabric of the thing with a new, delightful physical quality. This *drawing*, then—the arabesque traced in the air by Tintoret's flying figures, by Titian's forest branches; this colouring—the magic conditions of light and hue in the atmosphere of Titian's *Lace-girl*, or Rubens's *Descent from the Cross*:—these essential pictorial qualities must first of all delight the sense, delight it as directly and sensuously as a fragment of Venetian glass; and through this delight alone become the vehicle of whatever poetry or science may lie beyond them in the intention of the composer. In its primary aspect, a great picture has no more definite message for us than an accidental play of sunlight and shadow for a few

moments on the wall or floor: is itself, in truth, a space of such
fallen light, caught as the colours are in an Eastern carpet, but
refined upon, and dealt with more subtly and exquisitely than by
nature itself. And this primary and essential condition fulfilled,
we may trace the coming of poetry into painting, by fine gradations upwards; from Japanese fan-painting, for instance, where
we get, first, only abstract colour; then, just a little interfused
sense of the poetry of flowers; then, sometimes, perfect flower-
painting; and so, onwards, until in Titian we have, as his poetry
in the *Ariadne*, so actually a touch of true childlike humour in
the diminutive, quaint figure with its silk gown, which ascends
the temple stairs, in his picture of the *Presentation of the Virgin*,
at Venice.

But although each art has thus its own specific order of impressions, and an untranslatable charm, while a just apprehension of
the ultimate differences of the arts is the beginning of æsthetic
criticism; yet it is noticeable that, in its special mode of handling
its given material, each art may be observed to pass into the
condition of some other art, by what German critics term an
Andersstreben—a partial alienation from its own limitations,
through which the arts are able, not indeed to supply the place of
each other, but reciprocally to lend each other new forces.

Thus, some of the most delightful music seems to be always
approaching to figure, to pictorial definition. Architecture,
again, though it has its own laws—laws esoteric enough, as the
true architect knows only too well—yet sometimes aims at fulfilling the conditions of a picture, as in the *Arena* chapel; or of
sculpture, as in the flawless unity of Giotto's tower at Florence;
and often finds a true poetry, as in those strangely twisted stair-
cases of the *châteaux* of the country of the Loire, as if it were
intended that among their odd turnings the actors in a theatrical
mode of life might pass each other unseen; there being a poetry
also of memory and of the mere effect of time, by which architecture often profits greatly. Thus, again, sculpture aspires out of the
hard limitation of pure form towards colour, or its equivalent;
poetry also, in many ways, finding guidance from the other arts,
the analogy between a Greek tragedy and a work of Greek sculpture, between a sonnet and a relief, of French poetry generally

with the art of engraving, being more than mere figures of speech; and all the arts in common aspiring towards the principle of music; music being the typical, or ideally consummate art, the object of the great *Anders-streben* of all art, of all that is artistic, or partakes of artistic qualities.

All art constantly aspires towards the condition of music. For while in all other kinds of art it is possible to distinguish the matter from the form, and the understanding can always make this distinction, yet it is the constant effort of art to obliterate it. That the mere matter of a poem, for instance, its subject, namely, its given incidents or situation—that the mere matter of a picture, the actual circumstances of an event, the actual topography of a landscape—should be nothing without the form, the spirit, of the handling, that this form, this mode of handling, should become an end in itself, should penetrate every part of the matter: this is what all art constantly strives after, and achieves in different degrees.

This abstract language becomes clear enough, if we think of actual examples. In an actual landscape we see a long white road, lost suddenly on the hill-verge. That is the matter of one of the etchings of M. Alphonse Legros: only, in this etching, it is informed by an indwelling solemnity of expression, seen upon it or half-seen, within the limits of an exceptional moment, or caught from his own mood perhaps, but which he maintains as the very essence of the thing, throughout his work. Sometimes a momentary hint of stormy light may invest a homely or too familiar scene with a character which might well have been drawn from the deep places of the imagination. Then we might say that this particular effect of light, this sudden inweaving of gold thread through the texture of the haystack, and the poplars, and the grass, gives the scene artistic qualities, that it is like a picture. And such tricks of circumstance are commonest in landscape which has little salient character of its own; because, in such scenery, all the material details are so easily absorbed by that informing expression of passing light, and elevated, throughout their whole extent, to a new and delightful effect by it. And hence the superiority, for most conditions of the picturesque, of a river-side in France to a Swiss valley, because, on the French river-side, mere topography, the simple material, counts for so little, and, all being very pure, untouched, and tranquil in itself, mere light and shade have such easy work in modulating it to one dominant tone. The Venetian landscape, on the other hand, has in its material conditions much which is hard, or harshly definite; but the masters of the Venetian school have shown themselves little burdened by them. Of its Alpine background they retain certain abstracted elements only, of cool colour and tranquillising line; and they use its actual details, the brown windy turrets, the straw-coloured fields, the forest arabesques, but as the notes of a music which duly accompanies the presence of their men and women, presenting us with the spirit or essence only of a certain sort of landscape—a country of the pure reason or half-imaginative memory.

Poetry, again, works with words addressed in the first instance to the pure intelligence; and it deals, most often, with a definite subject or situation. Sometimes it may find a noble and quite legitimate function in the conveyance of moral or political aspiration, as often in the poetry of Victor Hugo. In such instances it is easy enough for the understanding to distinguish between the matter and the form, however much the matter, the subject, the element which is addressed to the mere intelligence, has been penetrated by the informing, artistic spirit. But the ideal types of poetry are those in which this distinction is reduced to its *minimum*; so that lyrical poetry, precisely because in it we are least able to detach the matter from the form, without a deduction of something from that matter itself, is, at least artistically, the highest and most complete form of poetry. And the very perfection of such poetry often appears to depend, in part, on a certain suppression or vagueness of mere subject, so that the meaning reaches us through ways not distinctly traceable by the understanding as in some of the most imaginative compositions of William Blake, and often in Shakespeare's songs, as preeminently in that song of Mariana's page in *Measure for Measure*, in which the kindling force and poetry of the whole play seems to pass for a moment into an actual strain of music.

And this principle holds good of all things that partake in any degree of artistic qualities, of the furniture of our houses, and of dress, for instance, of life itself, of gesture and speech, and the details of daily intercourse; these also, for the wise, being susceptible of a suavity and charm, caught from the way in which they are done, which gives them a worth in themselves. Herein, again, lies what is valuable and justly attractive, in what is called the fashion of a time, which elevates the trivialities of speech, and manner, and dress, into "ends in themselves," and gives them a mysterious grace and attractiveness in the doing of them.

Art, then, is thus always striving to be independent of the mere intelligence, to become a matter of pure perception, to get rid of its responsibilities to its subject or material; the ideal examples of poetry and painting being those in which the constituent elements of the composition are so welded together, that the material or subject no longer strikes the intellect only; nor the form, the eye or the ear only; but form and matter, in their union or identity, present one single effect to the "imaginative reason," that complex faculty for which every thought and feeling is twinborn with its sensible analogue or symbol.

It is the art of music which most completely realises this artistic ideal, this perfect identification of matter and form. In its consummate moments, the end is not distinct from the means, the form from the matter, the subject from the expression; they inhere in and completely saturate each other; and to it, therefore, to the condition of its perfect moments, all the arts may be supposed constantly to tend and aspire. In music, then, rather than in poetry, is to be found the true type or measure of perfected art. Therefore, although each art has its incommunicable element, its untranslatable order of impressions, its unique mode of reaching the "imaginative reason," yet the arts may be represented as continually struggling after the law or principle of music, to a condition which music alone completely realises; and one of the chief functions of æsthetic criticism, dealing with the products of art, new or old, is to estimate the degree in which each of those products approaches, in this sense, to musical law.

By no school of painters have the necessary limitations of the art of painting been so unerringly though instinctively apprehended, and the essence of what is pictorial in a picture so justly con-

ceived, as by the school of Venice; and the train of thought suggested in what has been now said is, perhaps, a not unfitting
introduction to a few pages about Giorgione, who, though much
has been taken by recent criticism from what was reputed to be
his work, yet, more entirely than any other painter, sums up, in
what we know of himself and his art, the spirit of the Venetian
school.

The beginnings of Venetian painting link themselves to the last,
stiff, half-barbaric splendours of Byzantine decoration, and are
but the introduction into the crust of marble and gold on the
walls of the *Duomo* of Murano. or of *Saint Mark's*, of a little more
of human expression. And throughout the course of its later development, always subordinate to architectural effect, the work
of the Venetian school never escaped from the influence of its
beginnings. Unassisted, and therefore unperplexed, by naturalism, religious mysticism, philosophical theories, it had no Giotto,
no Angelico, no Botticelli. Exempt from the stress of thought and
sentiment, which taxed so severely the resources of the generations of Florentine artists, those earlier Venetian painters, down
to Carpaccio and the Bellini, seem never for a moment to have
been so much as tempted to lose sight of the scope of their art in
its strictness, or to forget that painting must be before all things
decorative, a thing for the eye, a space of colour on the wall, only
more dexterously blent than the marking of its precious stone or
the chance interchange of sun and shade upon it:—this, to begin
and end with; whatever higher matter of thought, or poetry, or
religious reverie might play its part therein, between. At last,
with final mastery of all the technical secrets of his art, and with
somewhat more than "a spark of the divine fire" to his share,
comes Giorgione. He is the inventor of *genre*, of those easily mov-
able pictures which serve neither for uses of devotion, nor of allegorical or historic teaching—little groups of real men and women,
amid congruous furniture or landscape—morsels of actual life,
conversation or music or play, but refined upon or idealised, till
they come to seem like glimpses of life from afar. Those spaces of
more cunningly blent colour, obediently filling their places, hitherto, in a mere architectural scheme, Giorgione detaches from the
wall. He frames them by the hands of some skilful carver, so that

people may move them readily and take with them where they go, as one might a poem in manuscript, or a musical instrument, to be used, at will, as a means of self-education, stimulus or solace, coming like an animated presence, into one's cabinet, to enrich the air as with some choice aroma, and, like persons, live with us, for a day or a lifetime. Of all art such as this, art which has played so large a part in men's culture since that time, Giorgione is the initiator. Yet in him too that old Venetian clearness or justice, in the apprehension of the essential limitations of the pictorial art, is still undisturbed. While he interfuses his painted work with a high-strung sort of poetry, caught directly from a singularly rich and high-strung sort of life, yet in his selection of subject, or phase of subject, in the subordination of mere subject to pictorial design, to the main purpose of a picture, he is typical of that aspiration of all the arts towards music, which I have endeavoured to explain,—towards the perfect identification of matter and form.

Born so near to Titian, though a little before him, that these two companion pupils of the aged Giovanni Bellini may almost be called contemporaries, Giorgione stands to Titian in something like the relationship of Sordello to Dante, in Browning's poem. Titian, when he leaves Bellini, becomes, in turn, the pupil of Giorgione. He lives in constant labour more than sixty years after Giorgione is in his grave; and with such fruit, that hardly one of the greater towns of Europe is without some fragment of his work. But the slightly older man, with his so limited actual product (what remains to us of it seeming, when narrowly examined, to reduce itself to almost one picture, like Sordello's one fragment of lovely verse) yet expresses, in elementary motive and principle, that spirit—itself the final acquisition of all the long endeavours of Venetian art—which Titian spreads over his whole life's activity.

And, as we might expect, something fabulous and illusive has always mingled itself in the brilliancy of Giorgione's fame. The exact relationship to him of many works—drawings, portraits, painted idylls—often fascinating enough, which in various collections went by his name, was from the first uncertain. Still, six or eight famous pictures at Dresden, Florence and the Louvre, were with no doubt attributed to him, and in these, if anywhere, something of the splendour of the old Venetian humanity seemed to have been preserved. But of those six or eight famous pictures it is now known that only one is certainly from Giorgione's hand. The accomplished science of the subject has come at last, and, as in other instances, has not made the past more real for us, but assured us only that we possess less of it than we seemed to possess. Much of the work on which Giorgione's immediate fame depended, work done for instantaneous effect, in all probability passed away almost within his own age, like the frescoes on the façade of the *fondaco dei Tedeschi* at Venice, some crimson traces of which, however, still give a strange additional touch of splendour to the scene of the *Rialto*. And then there is a barrier or borderland, a period about the middle of the sixteenth century, in passing through which the tradition miscarries, and the true outlines of Giorgione's work and person are obscured. It became fashionable for wealthy lovers of art, with no critical standard of authenticity, to collect so-called works of Giorgione, and a multitude of imitations came into circulation. And now, in the "new Vasari[1]," the great traditional reputation, woven with so profuse demand on men's admiration, has been scrutinised thread by thread; and what remains of the most vivid and stimulating of Venetian masters, a live flame, as it seemed, in those old shadowy times, has been reduced almost to a name by his most recent critics.

Yet enough remains to explain why the legend grew up above the name, why the name attached itself, in many instances, to the bravest work of other men. The *Concert* in the *Pitti* Palace, in which a monk, with cowl and tonsure, touches the keys of a harpsichord, while a clerk, placed behind him, grasps the handle of a viol, and a third, with cap and plume, seems to wait upon the true interval for beginning to sing, is undoubtedly Giorgione's. The outline of the lifted finger, the trace of the plume, the very threads of the fine linen, which fasten themselves on the memory, in the moment before they are lost altogether in that calm unearthly glow, the skill which has caught the waves of wandering sound, and fixed them for ever on the lips and hands—these are

[1]Crowe and Cavalcaselle: *History of Painting in North Italy.*

indeed the master's own; and the criticism which, while dismissing so much hitherto believed to be Giorgione's, has established
the claims of this one picture, has left it among the most precious
things in the world of art.

It is noticeable that the "distinction" of this *Concert*, its sustained evenness of perfection, alike in design, in execution, and
in choice of personal type, becomes for the "new Vasari" the
standard of Giorgione's genuine work. Finding here sufficient to
explain his influence, and the true seal of mastery, its authors
assign to Pellegrino da San Daniele the *Holy Family* in the
Louvre, in consideration of certain points where it comes short of
this standard. Such shortcoming however will hardly diminish
the spectator's enjoyment of a singular charm of liquid air, with
which the whole picture seems instinct, filling the eyes and lips,
the very garments, of its sacred personages, with some wind-
searched brightness and energy; of which fine air the blue peak,
clearly defined in the distance, is, as it were, the visible pledge.
Similarly, another favourite picture in the Louvre, subject of a
delightful sonnet by a poet[1] whose own painted work often comes
to mind as one ponders over these precious things—the *Fête
Champêtre*, is assigned to an imitator of Sebastian del Piombo;
and the *Tempest*, in the Academy at Venice, to Paris Bordone, or
perhaps to "some advanced craftsman of the sixteenth century."
From the gallery at Dresden, the *Knight embracing a Lady*, where
the knight's broken gauntlet seems to mark some well-known
pause in a story we would willingly hear the rest of, is conceded to
"a Brescian hand," and *Jacob meting Rachel* to a pupil of Palma.
And then, whatever their charm, we are called on to give up the
Ordeal, and the *Finding of Moses* with its jewel-like pools of
water, perhaps to Bellini.

Nor has the criticism, which thus so freely diminishes the number of his authentic works, added anything important to the well-
known outline of the life and personality of the man: only, it has
fixed one or two dates, one or two circumstances, a little more
exactly. Giorgione was born before the year 1477, and spent his
childhood at Castelfranco, where the last crags of the Venetian

[1]Dante Gabriel Rossetti.

Alps break down romantically, with something of a park-like grace, to the plain. A natural child of the family of the Barbarelli by a peasant-girl of Vedelago, he finds his way early into the circle of notable persons—people of courtesy. He is initiated into those differences of personal type, manner, and even dress, which are best understood there—that "distinction" of the *Concert* of the *Pitti* Palace. Not far from his home lives Catherine of Cornara, formerly Queen of Cyprus; and, up in the towers still remain, Tuzio Costanzo, the famous *condottiere*, a picturesque remnant of medieval manners, amid a civilisation rapidly changing. Giorgione paints their portraits; and when Tuzio's son, Matteo, dies in early youth, adorns in his memory a chapel in the church of Castelfranco, painting on this occasion, perhaps, the altar-piece, foremost among his authentic works, still to be seen there, with the figure of the warrior-saint, Liberale, of which the original little study in oil, with the delicately gleaming, silver-grey armour, is one of the greater treasures of the National Gallery. In that figure, as in some other knightly personages attributed to him, people have supposed the likeness of the painter's own presumably gracious presence. Thither, at last, he is himself brought home from Venice, early dead, but celebrated. It happened, about his thirty-fourth year, that in one of those parties at which he entertained his friends with music, he met a certain lady of whom he became greatly enamoured, and "they rejoiced greatly," says Vasari, "the one and the other, in their loves." And two quite different legends concerning it agree in this, that it was through this lady he came by his death; Ridolfi relating that, being robbed of her by one of his pupils, he died of grief at the double treason; Vasari, that she being secretly stricken of the plague, and he making his visits to her as usual, Giorgione took the sickness from her mortally, along with her kisses, and so briefly departed.

But, although the number of Giorgione's extant works has been thus limited by recent criticism, all is not done when the real and the traditional elements in what concerns him have been discriminated; for, in what is connected with a great name, much that is not real is often very stimulating. For the æsthetic philosopher, therefore, over and above the real Giorgione and his authentic extant works, there remains the *Giorgionesque* also—an influence, a spirit or type in art, active in men so different as those to whom many of his supposed works are really assignable. A veritable school, in fact, grew together out of all those fascinating works rightly or wrongly attributed to him; out of many copies from, or variations on him, by unknown or uncertain workmen, whose drawings and designs were, for various reasons, prized as his; out of the immediate impression he made upon his contemporaries, and with which he continued in men's minds; out of many traditions of subject and treatment, which really descend from him to our own time, and by retracing which we fill out the original image. Giorgione thus becomes a sort of impersonation of Venice itself, its projected reflex or ideal, all that was intense or desirable in it crystallising about the memory of this wonderful young man.

And now, finally, let me illustrate some of the characteristics of this *School of Giorgione*, as we may call it, which, for most of us, notwithstanding all that negative criticism of the "new Vasari," will still identify itself with those famous pictures at Florence, at Dresden and Paris. A certain artistic ideal is there defined for us— the conception of a peculiar aim and procedure in art, which we may understand as the *Giorgionesque*, wherever we find it, whether in Venetian work generally, or in work of our own time. Of this the *Concert*, that undoubted work of Giorgione in the *Pitti* Palace, is the typical instance, and a pledge authenticating the connexion of the school, and the spirit of the school, with the master.

I have spoken of a certain interpenetration of the matter or subject of a work of art with the form of it, a condition realised absolutely only in music, as the condition to which every form of art is perpetually aspiring. In the art of painting, the attainment of this ideal condition, this perfect interpenetration of the subject with the elements of colour and design, depends, of course, in great measure, on dexterous choice of that subject, or phase of subject; and such choice is one of the secrets of Giorgione's school. It is the school of *genre*, and employs itself mainly with "painted idylls," but, in the production of this pictorial poetry, exercises a wonderful tact in the selecting of such matter as lends itself most readily and entirely to pictorial form, to complete expression by drawing and colour. For although its productions are painted poems, they belong to a sort of poetry which tells itself without an articulated story. The master is pre-eminent for the resolution, the ease and quickness, with which he reproduces instantaneous motion—the lacing-on of armour, with the head bent back so stately—the fainting lady—the embrace, rapid as the kiss, caught with death itself from dying lips—some momentary conjunction of mirrors and polished armour and still water, by which all the sides of a solid image are exhibited at once, solving that casuistical question whether painting can present an object as completely as sculpture. The sudden act, the rapid transition of thought, the passing expression—these he arrests with that vivacity which Vasari has attributed to him, *il fuoco Giorgionesco*, as he terms it. Now it is part of the ideality of the highest sort of dramatic poetry, that it presents us with a kind of profoundly significant and animated instants, a mere gesture, a look, a smile, perhaps—some brief and wholly concrete moment—into which, however, all the motives, all the interests and effects of a long history, have condensed themselves, and which seem to absorb past and future in an intense consciousness of the present. Such ideal instants the school of Giorgione selects, with its admirable tact, from that feverish, tumultuously coloured world of the old citizens of Venice—exquisite pauses in time, in which, arrested thus, we seem to be spectators of all the fulness of existence, and which are like some consummate extract or quintessence of life.

It is to the law or condition of music, as I said, that all art like this is really aspiring; and, in the school of Giorgione, the perfect moments of music itself, the making or hearing of music, song or its accompaniment, are themselves prominent as subjects. On that background of the silence of Venice, so impressive to the modern visitor, the world of Italian music was then forming. In choice of subject, as in all besides, the *Concert* of the *Pitti* Palace is typical of everything that Giorgione, himself an admirable musician, touched with his influence. In sketch or finished picture, in various collections, we may follow it through many intricate variations—men fainting at music; music at the pool-side while people fish, or mingled with the sound of the pitcher in the well, or heard across running water, or among the flocks; the tuning of instruments; people with intent faces, as if listening, like those described by Plato in an ingenious passage of the Republic, to detect the smallest interval of musical sound, the smallest undulation in the air, or feeling for music in thought on a stringless instrument, ear and finger refining themselves infinitely, in the appetite for sweet sound; a momentary touch of an instrument in the twilight, as one passes through some unfamiliar room, in a chance company.

In these then, the favourite incidents of Giorgione's school, music or the musical intervals in our existence, life itself is conceived as a sort of listening—listening to music, to the reading of Bandello's novels, to the sound of water, to time as it flies. Often such moments are really our moments of play, and we are surprised at the unexpected blessedness of what may seem our least important part of time; not merely because play is in many instances that to which people really apply their own best powers, but also because at such times, the stress of our servile, everyday attentiveness being relaxed, the happier powers in things without are permitted free passage, and have their way with us. And so, from music, the school of Giorgione passes often to the play which is like music; to those masques in which men avowedly do but play at real life, like children "dressing-up," disguised in the strange old Italian dresses, parti-coloured, or fantastic with embroidery and furs, of which the master was so curious a designer, and which, above all the spotless white linen at wrist and throat, he painted so dexterously.

But when people are happy in this thirsty land water will not be far off; and in the school of Giorgione, the presence of water—the well, or marble-rimmed pool, the drawing or pouring of water, as the woman pours it from a pitcher with her jewelled hand in the *Fête Champêtre*, listening, perhaps, to the cool sound as it falls, blent with the music of the pipes—is as characteristic, and almost as suggestive, as that of music itself. And the landscape feels, and is glad of it also—a landscape full of clearness, of the effects of water, of fresh rain newly passed through the air, and collected into the grassy channels. The air, moreover, in the school of

Giorgione, seems as vivid as the people who breathe it, and literally empyrean, all impurities being burnt out of it, and no taint,
no floating particle of anything but its own proper elements allowed to subsist within it.

Its scenery is such as in England we call "park scenery," with
some elusive refinement felt about the rustic buildings, the
choice grass, the grouped trees, the undulations deftly econo-
mised for graceful effect. Only, in Italy all natural things are as it
were woven through and through with gold thread, even the
cypress revealing it among the folds of its blackness. And it is with
gold dust, or gold thread, that these Venetian painters seem to
work, spinning its fine filaments, through the solemn human
flesh, away into the white plastered walls of the thatched huts.
The harsher details of the mountains recede to a harmonious distance, the one peak of rich blue above the horizon remaining but
as the sensible warrant of that due coolness which is all we need
ask here of the Alps, with their dark rains and streams. Yet what
real, airy space, as the eye passes from level to level, through the
long-drawn valley in which Jacob embraces Rachel among the
flocks! Nowhere is there a truer instance of that balance, that
modulated unison of landscape and persons—of the human image
and its accessories—already noticed as characteristic of the Venetian school, so that, in it, neither personage nor scenery is ever a
mere pretext for the other.

Something like this seems to me to be the *vraie vérité* about
Giorgione, if I may adopt a serviceable expression, by which the
French recognise those more liberal and durable impressions
which, in respect of any really considerable person or subject,
anything that has at all intricately occupied men's attention, lie
beyond, and must supplement, the narrower range of the strictly
ascertained facts about it. In this, Giorgione is but an illustration
of a valuable general caution we may abide by in all criticism. As
regards Giorgione himself, we have indeed to take note of all
those negations and exceptions, by which, at first sight, a "new
Vasari" seems merely to have confused our apprehension of a delightful object, to have explained away in our inheritance from
past time what seemed of high value there. Yet it is not with a full

understanding even of those exceptions that one can leave off just at this point. Properly qualified, such exceptions are but a salt of genuineness in our knowledge; and beyond all those strictly ascertained facts, we must take note of that indirect influence by which one like Giorgione, for instance, enlarges his permanent efficacy and really makes himself felt in our culture. In a just impression of that, is the essential truth, the *vraie vérité*, concerning him.

1877.

Joachim du Bellay

In the middle of the sixteenth century, when the spirit of the Renaissance was everywhere, and people had begun to look back with distaste on the works of the middle age, the old Gothic manner had still one chance more, in borrowing something from the rival which was about to supplant it. In this way there was produced, chiefly in France, a new and peculiar phase of taste with qualities and a charm of its own, blending the somewhat attenuated grace of Italian ornament with the general outlines of northern design. It created the *Château de Gaillon*, as you may still see it in the delicate engravings of Isräel Silvestre—a Gothic donjon veiled faintly by a surface of dainty Italian traceries—Chenonceaux, Blois, Chambord, and the church of Brou. In painting, there came from Italy workmen like *Maître Roux* and the masters of the school of Fontainebleau, to have their later Italian voluptuousness attempered by the naïve and silvery qualities of the native style; and it was characteristic of these painters that they were most successful in painting on glass, an art so essentially medieval. Taking it up where the middle age had left it, they found their whole work among the last subtleties of colour and line; and keeping within the true limits of their material, they got quite a new order of effects from it, and felt their way to refinements on colour never dreamed of by those older workmen, the glass-painters of Chartres or Le Mans. What is called the *Renaissance in France* is thus not so much the introduction of a wholly new taste ready-made from Italy, but rather the finest and subtlest phase of the middle age itself, its last fleeting splendour and temperate Saint Martin's summer. In poetry, the Gothic spirit in France had produced a thousand songs; so in the Renaissance,

French poetry too did but borrow something to blend with a native growth, and the poems of Ronsard, with their ingenuity, their delicately figured surfaces, their slightness, their fanciful combinations of rhyme, are the correlative of the traceries of the house of Jacques Cœur at Bourges, or the *Maison de Justice* at Rouen.

There was indeed something in the native French taste naturally akin to that Italian *finesse*. The characteristic of French work had always been a certain nicety, a remarkable daintiness of hand, *une netteté remarquable d'exécution*. In the paintings of François Clouet, for example, or rather of the Clouets—for there was a whole family of them—painters remarkable for their resistance to Italian influences, there is a silveriness of colour and a clearness of expression which distinguish them very definitely from their Flemish neighbours, Hemling or the Van Eycks. And this nicety is not less characteristic of old French poetry. A light, aerial delicacy, a simple elegance—*une netteté remarquable d'exécution:* these are essential characteristics alike of Villon's poetry, and of the *Hours of Anne of Brittany*. They are characteristic too of a hundred French Gothic carvings and traceries. Alike in the old Gothic cathedrals, and in their counterpart, the old Gothic *chansons de geste*, the rough and ponderous mass becomes, as if by passing for a moment into happier conditions, or through a more gracious stratum of air, graceful and refined, like the carved ferneries on the granite church at Folgoat, or the lines which describe the fair priestly hands of Archbishop Turpin, in the song of Roland; although below both alike there is a fund of mere Gothic strength, or heaviness[1].

Now Villon's songs and Clouet's painting are like these. It is the higher touch making itself felt here and there, betraying itself, like nobler blood in a lower stock, by a fine line or gesture or expression, the turn of a wrist, the tapering of a finger. In Ronsard's time that rougher element seemed likely to predominate. No one can turn over the pages of Rabelais without feeling how much need there was of softening, of castigation. To effect this

[1]The purely artistic aspects of this subject have been interpreted, in a work of great taste and learning, by Mrs. Mark Pattison.—*The Renaissance of Art in France.*

softening is the object of the revolution in poetry which is connected with Ronsard's name. Casting about for the means of thus
refining upon and saving the character of French literature, he
accepted that influx of Renaissance taste, which, leaving the
buildings, the language, the art, the poetry of France, at bottom,
what they were, old French Gothic still, gilds their surfaces with
a strange, delightful, foreign aspect passing over all that northern
land, in itself neither deeper nor more permanent than a chance
effect of light. He reinforces, he doubles the French daintiness by
Italian *finesse*. Thereupon, nearly all the force and all the seriousness of French work disappear; only the elegance, the aerial
touch, the perfect manner remain. But this elegance, this manner, this daintiness of execution are consummate, and have an
unmistakable æsthetic value.

So the old French *chanson*, which, like the old northern Gothic
ornament, though it sometimes refined itself into a sort of weird
elegance, was often, in its essence, something rude and formless,
became in the hands of Ronsard a Pindaric ode. He gave it structure, a sustained system, *strophe* and *antistrophe*, and taught it a
changefulness and variety of metre which keep the curiosity always excited, so that the very aspect of it, as it lies written on the
page, carries the eye lightly onwards, and of which this is a good
instance:—

> *Avril, la grace, et le ris*
> *De Cypris,*
> *Le flair et la douce haleine;*
> *Avril, le parfum des dieux,*
> *Qui, des cieux,*
> *Sentent l'odeur de la plaine;*
>
> *C'est toy, courtois et gentil,*
> *Qui, d'exil*
> *Retire ces passageres,*
> *Ces arondelles qui vont,*
> *Et qui sont*
> *Du printemps les messageres.*

That is not by Ronsard, but by Remy Belleau, for Ronsard soon
came to have a school. Six other poets threw in their lot with him

in his literary revolution,—this Remy Belleau, Antoine de Baïf, Pontus de Tyard, Étienne Jodelle, Jean Daurat, and lastly Joachim du Bellay; and with that strange love of emblems which is characteristic of the time, which covered all the works of Francis the First with the salamander, and all the works of Henry the Second with the double crescent, and all the works of Anne of Brittany with the knotted cord, they called themselves the *Pleiad*; seven in all, although, as happens with the celestial Pleiad, if you scrutinise this constellation of poets more carefully you may find there a great number of minor stars.

The first note of this literary revolution was struck by Joachim du Bellay in a little tract written at the early age of twenty-four, which coming to us through three centuries seems of yesterday, so full is it of those delicate critical distinctions which are sometimes supposed peculiar to modern writers. The piece has for its title *La Deffense et Illustration de la langue Françoyse*; and its problem is how to illustrate or ennoble the French language, to give it lustre. We are accustomed to speak of the varied critical and creative movement of the fifteenth and sixteenth centuries as the *Renaissance*, and because we have a single name for it we may sometimes fancy that there was more unity in the thing itself than there really was. Even the Reformation, that other great movement of the fifteenth and sixteenth centuries, had far less unity, far less of combined action, than is at first sight supposed; and the Renaissance was infinitely less united, less conscious of combined action, than the Reformation. But if anywhere the Renaissance became conscious, as a German philosopher might say, if ever it was understood as a systematic movement by those who took part in it, it is in this little book of Joachim du Bellay's, which it is impossible to read without feeling the excitement, the animation, of change, of discovery. "It is a remarkable fact," says M. Sainte-Beuve, "and an inversion of what is true of other languages, that, in French, prose has always had the precedence over poetry." Du Bellay's prose is perfectly transparent, flexible, and chaste. In many ways it is a more characteristic example of the culture of the *Pleiad* than of any of its verse; and those who love the whole movement of which the *Pleiad* is a part, for a weird foreign grace in it, and may be looking about for a true specimen of it, cannot have a better than Joachim du Bellay and this little treatise of his.

Du Bellay's object is to adjust the existing French culture to the rediscovered classical culture; and in discussing this problem, and developing the theories of the *Pleiad*, he has lighted upon many principles of permanent truth and applicability. There were some who despaired of the French language altogether, who thought it naturally incapable of the fulness and the elegance of Greek and Latin—*cette élégance et copie qui est en la langue Greque et Romaine*—that science could be adequately discussed, and poetry nobly written, only in the dead languages. "Those who speak thus," says du Bellay, "make me think of the relics which one may only see through a little pane of glass, and must not touch with one's hands. That is what these people do with all branches of culture, which they keep shut up in Greek and Latin books, not permitting one to see them otherwise, or transport them out of dead words into those which are alive, and wing their way daily through the mouths of men." "Languages," he says again, "are not born like plants and trees, some naturally feeble and sickly, others healthy and strong and apter to bear the weight of men's conceptions, but all their virture is generated in the world of choice and men's freewill concerning them. Therefore, I cannot blame too strongly the rashness of some of our countrymen, who being anything rather than Greeks or Latins, depreciate and reject with more than stoical disdain everything written in French; nor can I express my surprise at the odd opinion of some learned men who think that our vulgar tongue is wholly incapable of erudition and good literature."

It was an age of translations. Du Bellay himself translated two books of the *Æneid*, and other poetry, old and new, and there were some who thought that the translation of the classical literature was the true means of *ennobling* the French language:—strangers are ever favourites with us—*nous favorisons toujours les étrangers*. Du Bellay moderates their expectations. "I do not believe that one can learn the right use of them"—he is speaking of figures and ornament in language—"from translations, because it is impossible to reproduce them with the same grace with which the original author used them. For each language has I know not what peculiarity of its own; and if you force yourself to express the naturalness *(le naïf)* of this in another language, observing the law of translation,—not to expatiate beyond the limits of the author himself, your words will be constrained, cold and ungraceful." Then he fixes the test of all good translations:—"To prove this, read me Demosthenes and Homer in Latin, Cicero and Virgil in French, and see whether they produce in you the same affections which you experience in reading those authors in the original."

In this effort to ennoble the French language, to give it grace, number, perfection, and as painters do to their pictures, that last, so desirable, touch—*ette dernière main que nous désirons*—what du Bellay is really pleading for is his mother-tongue, the language, that is, in which one will have the utmost degree of what is moving and passionate. He recognised of what force the music and dignity of languages are, how they enter into the inmost part of things; and in pleading for the cultivation of the French language, he is pleading for no merely scholastic interest, but for freedom, impulse, reality, not in literature only, but in daily communion of speech. After all, it was impossible to have this impulse in Greek and Latin, dead languages shut up in books as in reliquaries—*péris et mises en reliquaires de livres.* By aid of this starveling stock—*pauvre plante et vergette*—of the French language, he must speak delicately, movingly, if he is ever to speak so at all: that, or none, must be for him the medium of what he calls, in one of his great phrases, *le discours fatal des choses mondaines* —that discourse about affairs which decides men's fates. And it is his patriotism not to despair of it; he sees it already perfect in all elegance and beauty of words—*parfait en toute élégance et vénusté de paroles.*

Du Bellay was born in the disastrous year 1525, the year of the battle of Pavia, and the captivity of Francis the First. His parents died early, and to him, as the younger son, his mother's little estate, *ce petit Liré,* the beloved place of his birth, descended. He was brought up a brother only a little older than himself; and left to themselves, the two boys passed their lives in daydreams of military glory. Their education was neglected; "The time of my youth," says du Bellay, "was lost, like the flower which no shower waters, and no hand cultivates." He was just twenty years old when the elder brother died, leaving Joachim to be the guardian of his child. It was with regret, with a shrinking sense of incapacity, that he took upon him the burden of this responsibility. Hitherto he had looked forward to the profession of a soldier, hereditary in his family. But at this time a sickness attacked him which brought him cruel sufferings, and seemed likely to be mortal. It was then for the first time that he read the Greek and Latin poets. These studies came too late to make him what he so much desired to be, a trifler in Greek and Latin verse, like so many others of his time now forgotten; instead, they made him a lover of his own homely native tongue, that poor starveling stock of the French language. It was through this fortunate shortcoming in his education that he became national and modern; and he learned afterwards to look back on that wild garden of his youth with only a half-regret. A certain Cardinal du Bellay was the successful member of the family, a man often employed in high official business. To him the thoughts of Joachim turned when it became necessary to choose a profession, and in 1552 he accompanied the Cardinal to Rome. He remained there nearly five years, burdened with the weight of affairs, and languishing with homesickness. Yet it was under these circumstances that his genius yielded its best fruits. From Rome, so full of pleasurable sensation for men of an imaginative temperament such as his, with all the curiosities of the Renaissance still fresh in it, his thoughts went back painfully, longingly, to the country of the Loire, with its wide expanse of waving corn, its homely pointed roofs of grey slate, and its far-off scent of the sea. He reached home at last, but only to die there, quite suddenly, one wintry day, at the early age of thirty-five.

Much of du Bellay's poetry illustrates rather the age and school to which he belonged than his own temper and genius. As with the writings of Ronsard and the other poets of the *Pleiad*, its interest depends not so much on the impress of individual genius upon it, as on the circumstance that it was once poetry *à la mode*, that it is part of the manner of a time—a time which made much of manner, and carried it to a high degree of perfection. It is one of the decorations of an age which threw a large part of its energy into the work of decoration. We feel a pensive pleasure in gazing on these faded adornments, and observing how a group of actual men and women pleased themselves long ago. Ronsard's poems are a kind of epitome of his age. Of one side of that age, it is true, of the strenuous, the progressive, the serious movement, which was then going on, there is little; but of the catholic side, the losing side, the forlorn hope, hardly a figure is absent. The Queen of Scots, at whose desire Ronsard published his Odes, reading him in her northern prison, felt that he was bringing back to her the true flavour of her early days in the court of Catherine at the Louvre, with its exotic Italian gaieties. Those who disliked that poetry, disliked it because they found that age itself distasteful. The poetry of Malherbe came, with its sustained style and weighty sentiment, but with nothing that set people singing; and the lovers of such poetry saw in the poetry of the *Pleiad* only the latest trumpery of the middle age. But the time arrived when the school of Malherbe also had had its day; and the *Romanticists*, who in their eagerness for excitement, for strange music and imagery, went back to the works of the middle age, accepted the *Pleiad* too with the rest; and in that new middle age which their genius has evoked, the poetry of the *Pleiad* has found its place. At first, with Malherbe, you may think it, like the architecture, the whole mode of life, the very dresses of that time, fantastic, faded, *rococo*. But if you look long enough to understand it, to conceive its sentiment, you will find that those wanton lines have a spirit guiding their caprices. For there is *style* there; one temper has shaped the whole; and everything that has style, that has been done as no other man or age could have done it, as it could never, for all our trying, be done again, has its true value and interest. Let us dwell upon it for a moment, and try to gather from it that special flower, *ce fleur particulier*, which Ronsard himself tells us every garden has.

It is poetry not for the people, but for a confined circle, for courtiers, great lords and erudite persons, people who desire to be humoured, to gratify a certain refined voluptuousness they have in them. Ronsard loves, or dreams that he loves, a rare and peculiar type of beauty, *la petite pucelle Angevine*, with golden hair and dark eyes. But he has the ambition not only of being a courtier and a lover, but a great scholar also; he is anxious about orthography, about the letter *è Grecque*, the true spelling of Latin names in French writing, and the restoration of the letter *i* to its primitive liberty—*del' i voyelle en sa première liberté*. His poetry is full of quaint, remote learning. He is just a little pedantic, true always to his own express judgment, that to be natural is not enough for one who in poetry desires to produce work worthy of immortality. And therewithal a certain number of Greek words, which charmed Ronsard and his circle by their gaiety and daintiness, and a certain air of foreign elegance about them, crept into the French language; as there were other strange words which the poets of the *Pleiad* forged for themselves, and which had only an ephemeral existence.

With this was united the desire to taste a more exquisite and various music than that of the older French verse, or of the classical poets. The music of the measured, scanned verse of Latin and Greek poetry is one thing; the music of the rhymed, unscanned verse of Villon and the old French poets, *la poésie chantée*, is another. To combine these two kinds of music in a new school of French poetry, to make verse which should scan and rhyme as well, to search out and harmonise the measure of every syllable, and unite it to the swift, flitting, swallow-like motion of rhyme, to penetrate their poetry with a double music—this was the ambition of the *Pleiad*. They are insatiable of music, they cannot have enough of it; they desire a music of greater compass perhaps than words can possibly yield, to drain out the last drops of sweetness which a certain note or accent contains.

It was Goudimel, the serious and protestant Goudimel, who set Ronsard's songs to music; but except in this eagerness for music the poets of the *Pleiad* seem never quite in earnest. The old Greek and Roman mythology, which the great Italians had found a motive so weighty and severe, becomes with them a mere toy. That "Lord of terrible aspect," *Amor*, has become Love the boy, or the babe. They are full of fine railleries; they delight in diminutives, *ondelette, fontelette, doucelette, Cassandrette*. Their loves are only half real, a vain effort to prolong the imaginative loves of the middle age beyond their natural lifetime. They write love-poems for hire. Like that party of people who tell the tales in Boccaccio's *Decameron*, they form a circle which in an age of great troubles, losses, anxieties, can amuse itself with art, poetry, intrigue. But they amuse themselves with wonderful elegance. And sometimes their gaiety becomes satiric, for, as they play, real passions insinuate themselves, and at least the reality of death. Their dejection at the thought of leaving this fair abode of our common daylight—*le beau sejour du commun jour*—is expressed by them with almost wearisome reiteration. But with this sentiment too they are able to trifle. The imagery of death serves for delicate ornament, and they weave into the airy nothingness of their verses their trite reflexions on the vanity of life. Just so the grotesque details of the charnel-house nest themselves, together with birds and flowers and the fancies of the pagan mythology, in the traceries of the architecture of that time, which wantons in its graceful arabesques with the images of old age and death.

Ronsard became deaf at sixteen; and it was this circumstance which finally determined him to be a man of letters instead of a diplomatist, significantly, one might fancy, of a certain premature agedness, and of the tranquil, temperate sweetness appropriate to that, in the school of poetry which he founded. Its charm is that of a thing not vigorous or original, but full of the grace which comes of long study and reiterated refinements, and many steps repeated, and many angles worn down, with an exquisite faintness, *une fadeur exquise*, a certain tenuity and caducity, as for those who can bear nothing vehement or strong; for princes weary of love, like Francis the First, or of pleasure, like Henry the Third, or of action, like Henry the Fourth. Its merits are those of the old,—grace and finish, perfect in minute detail. For these people are a little jaded, and have a constant desire for a subdued and delicate excitement, to warm their creeping fancy a little. They love a constant change of rhyme in poetry, and in their houses that strange, fantastic interweaving of thin, reed-like lines, which are a kind of rhetoric in architecture.

But the poetry of the *Pleiad* is true not only to the physiognomy of its age, but also to its country, *ce pays du Vendomois*, the names and scenery of which so often recur in it:—the great Loire, with its long spaces of white sand; the little river Loir; the heathy, upland country, with its scattered pools of water and waste roadsides, and retired manors, with their crazy old feudal defences half fallen into decay; *La Beauce*, where the vast rolling fields seem to anticipate the great western sea itself. It is full of the traits of that country. We see du Bellay and Ronsard gardening, or hunting with their dogs, or watch the pastimes of a rainy day; and with all this is connected a domesticity, a homeliness and simple goodness, by which the northern country gains upon the south. They have the love of the aged for warmth, and understand the poetry of winter; for they are not far from the Atlantic, and the west wind which comes up from it, turning the poplars white, spares not this new Italy in France. So the fireside often appears, with the pleasures of the frosty season, about the vast embla-zoned chimneys of the time, and with a *bonhomie* as of little children, or old people.

It is in du Bellay's *Olive*, a collection of sonnets in praise of a half-imaginary lady, *Sonnetz a la louange d'Olive*, that these characteristics are most abundant. Here is a perfectly crystallised example:—

> *D'Amour, de grace, et de haulte valeur*
> *Les feux divins estoient ceinctz et les cieulx*
> *S'estoient vestuz d'un manteau precieux*
> *A raiz ardens de diverse couleur:*
> *Tout estoit plein de beauté, de bonheur,*
> *La mer tranquille, et le vent gracieulx,*
> *Quand celle la nasquit en ces bas lieux*
> *Qui a pillé du monde tout l'honneur.*
> *Ell' prist son teint des beaux lyz blanchissans,*
> *Son chef de l'or, ses deux levres des rozes,*
> *Et du soleil ses yeux resplandissans:*
> *Le ciel usant de liberalité,*
> *Mist en l'esprit ses semences encloses,*
> *Son nom des Dieux prist l'immortalité.*

That he is thus a characteristic specimen of the poetical taste of that age, is indeed du Bellay's chief interest. But if his work is to have the highest sort of interest, if it is to do something more than satisfy curiosity, if it is to have an æsthetic as distinct from an historical value, it is not enough for a poet to have been the true child of his age, to have conformed to its æsthetic conditions, and by so conforming to have charmed and stimulated that age; it is necessary that there should be perceptible in his work something individual, inventive, unique, the impress there of the writer's own temper and personality. This impress M. Sainte-Beuve thought he found in the *Antiquités de Rome*, and the *Regrets*, which he ranks as what has been called *poésie intime*, that intensely modern sort of poetry in which the writer has for his aim the portraiture of his own most intimate moods, and to take the reader into his confidence. That age had other instances of this intimacy of sentiment: Montaigne's *Essays* are full of it, the carvings of the church of Brou are full of it. M. Sainte-Beuve has perhaps exaggerated the influence of this quality in du Bellay's *Regrets*; but the very name of the book has a touch of Rousseau about it, and reminds one of a whole generation of self-pitying poets in modern times. It was in the atmosphere of Rome, to him so strange and mournful, that these pale flowers grew up. For that journey to Italy, which he deplored as the greatest misfortune of his life, put him in full possession of his talent, and brought out all its originality. And in effect you do find intimacy, *intimité*, here. The trouble of his life is analysed, and the sentiment of it conveyed directly to our minds; not a great sorrow or passion, but only the sense of loss in passing days, the *ennui* of a dreamer who must plunge into the world's affairs, the opposition between actual life and the ideal, a longing for rest, nostalgia, home-sickness—that pre-eminently childish, but so suggestive sorrow, as significant of the final regret of all human creatures for the familiar earth and limited sky.

The feeling for landscape it often described as a modern one; still more so is that for antiquity, the sentiment of ruins. Du Bellay has this sentiment. The duration of the hard, sharp outlines of things is a grief to him, and passing his wearisome days among the ruins of ancient Rome, he is consoled by the thought that all must one day end, by the sentiment of the grandeur of nothingness—*la grandeur du rien*. With a strange touch of far-off mysticism, he thinks that the great whole—*le grand tout*—into which all other things pass and lose themselves, ought itself sometimes to perish and pass away. Nothing less can relieve his weariness. From the stately aspects of Rome his thoughts went back continually to France, to the smoking chimneys of his little village, the longer twilight of the north, the soft climate of Anjou—

le douceur Angevine; yet not so much to the real France, we may be sure, with its dark streets and roofs of rough-hewn slate, as to that other country, with slenderer towers, and more winding rivers, and trees like flowers, and with softer sunshine on more gracefully-proportioned fields and ways, which the fancy of the exile, and the pilgrim, and of the schoolboy far from home, and of those kept at home unwillingly, everywhere builds up before or behind them.

He came home at last, through the *Grisons*, by slow journeys; and there, in the cooler air of his own country, under its skies of milkier blue, the sweetest flower of his genius sprang up. There have been poets whose whole fame has rested on one poem, as Gray's on the *Elegy in a Country Churchyard*, or Ronsard's, as many critics have thought, on the eighteen lines of one famous ode. Du Bellay has almost been the poet of one poem; and this one poem of his is an Italian product transplanted into that green country of Anjou; out of the Latin verses of Andrea Navagero, into French. But it is a composition in which the matter is almost nothing, and the form almost everything; and the form of the poem as it stands, written in old French, is all du Bellay's own. It is a song which the winnowers are supposed to sing as they winnow the corn, and they invoke the winds to lie lightly on the grain.

D'UN VANNEUR DE BLE AUX VENTS[1].

> *A vous trouppe legère*
> *Qui d'aile passagère*
> *Par le monde volez,*
> *Et d'un sifflant murmure*
> *L'ombrageuse verdure*
> *Doulcement esbranlez.*
>
> *J'offre ces violettes,*
> *Ces lis & ces fleurettes,*
> *Et ces roses icy,*
> *Ces vermeillettes roses*

[1]A graceful translation of this and some other poems of the *Pleiad* may be found in *Ballads and Lyrics of Old France*, by Mr. Andrew Lang.

Sont freschement écloses,
Et ces œillets aussi.

De vostre doulce haleine
Eventez ceste plaine
Eventez ce sejour;
Ce pendant que j'ahanne
A mon blé que je vanne
A la chaleur du jour.

That has, in the highest degree, the qualities, the value, of the whole *Pleiad* school of poetry, of the whole phase of taste from which that school derives—a certain silvery grace of fancy, nearly all the pleasure of which is in the surprise at the happy and dexterous way in which a thing slight in itself is handled. The sweetness of it is by no means to be got at by crushing, as you crush wild herbs to get at their perfume. One seems to hear the measured motion of the fans, with a child's pleasure on coming across the incident for the first time, in one of those great barns of du Bellay's own country, *La Beauce*, the granary of France. A sudden light transfigures some trivial thing, a weather-vane, a windmill, a winnowing-fan, the dust in the barn door. A moment—and the thing has vanished, because it was pure effect; but it leaves a relish behind it, a longing that the accident may happen again.

1872.

Winckelmann

Et ego in Arcadia fui

Goethe's fragments of art-criticism contain a few pages of strange
pregnancy on the character of Winckelmann. He speaks of the
teacher who had made his career possible, but whom he had never
seen, as of an abstract type of culture, consummate, tranquil,
withdrawn already into the region of ideals, yet retaining colour
from the incidents of a passionate intellectual life. He classes him
with certain works of art, possessing an inexhaustible gift of suggestion, to which criticism may return again and again with renewed freshness. Hegel, in his lectures on the *Philosophy of Art*,
estimating the work of his predecessors, has also passed a remarkable judgment on Winckelmann's writings:—"Winckelmann, by
contemplation of the ideal works of the ancients, received a sort
of inspiration, through which he opened a new sense for the study
of art. He is to be regarded as one of those who, in the sphere of
art, have known how to initiate a new organ for the human
spirit." That it has given a new sense, that it has laid open a new
organ, is the highest that can be said of any critical effort. It is
interesting then to ask what kind of man it was who thus laid
open a new organ. Under what conditioons was that effected?

Johann Joachim Winckelmann was born at Stendal, in Brandenburg, in the year 1717. The child of a poor tradesman, he passed
through many struggles in early youth, the memory of which ever
remained in him as a fitful cause of dejection. In 1763, in the full
emancipation of his spirit, looking over the beautiful Roman prospect, he writes—"One gets spoiled here; but God owed me this; in
my youth I suffered too much." Destined to assert and interpret

the charm of the Hellenic spirit, he served first a painful apprenticeship in the tarnished intellectual world of Germany in the
earlier half of the eighteenth century. Passing out of that into the
happy light of the antique, he had a sense of exhilaration almost
physical. We find him as a child in the dusky precincts of a German school, hungrily feeding on a few colourless books. The master of this school grows blind; Winckelmann becomes his *famulus*.
The old man would have had him study theology. Winckelmann,
free of the master's library, chooses rather to become familiar
with the Greek classics. Herodotus and Homer win, with their
"vowelled" Greek, his warmest enthusiasm; whole nights of fever
are devoted to them; disturbing dreams of an Odyssey of his own
come to him. "He felt in himself," says Madame de Staël, "an
ardent attraction towards the south. In German imaginations
even now traces are often to be found of that love of the sun,
that weariness of the north (*cette fatigue du nord*) which carried the northern peoples away into the countries of the south. A
fine sky brings to birth sentiments not unlike the love of one's
Fatherland."

To most of us, after all our steps towards it, the antique world,
in spite of its intense outlines, its own perfect self-expression, still
remains faint and remote. To him, closely limited except on the
side of the ideal, building for his dark poverty "a house not made
with hands," it early came to seem more real than the present. In
the fantastic plans of foreign travel continually passing through
his mind, to Egypt, for instance, and to France, there seems always to be rather a wistful sense of something lost to be regained,
than the desire of discovering anything new. Goethe has told us
how, in his eagerness actually to handle the antique, he became
interested in the insignificant vestiges of it which the neighbourhood of Strasburg afforded. So we hear of Winckelmann's boyish
antiquarian wanderings among the ugly Brandenburg sandhills.
Such a conformity between himself and Winckelmann, Goethe
would have gladly noted.

At twenty-one he enters the University of Halle, to study theology, as his friends desire; instead, he becomes the enthusiastic
translator of Herodotus. The condition of Greek learning in German schools and universities had fallen, and there were no pro-
fessors at Halle who could satisfy his sharp, intellectual craving.

Of his professional education he always speaks with scorn, claiming to have been his own teacher from first to last. His appointed teachers did not perceive that a new source of culture was within their hands. *Homo vagus et inconstans!*—one of them pedantically reports of the future pilgrim to Rome, unaware on which side his irony was whetted. When professional education confers nothing but irritation on a Schiller, no one ought to be surprised; for Schiller, and such as he, are primarily spiritual adventurers. But that Winckelmann, the votary of the gravest of intellectual traditions, should get nothing but an attempt at suppression from the professional guardians of learning, is what may well surprise us.

In 1743 he became master of a school at Seehausen. This was the most wearisome period of his life. Notwithstanding a success in dealing with children, which seems to testify to something simple and primeval in his nature, he found the work of teaching very depressing. Engaged in this work, he writes that he still has within him a longing desire to attain to the knowledge of beauty—*sehnlich wünschte zur Kenntniss des Schönen zu gelangen.* He had to shorten his nights, sleeping only four hours, to gain time for reading. And here Winckelmann made a step forward in culture. He multiplied his intellectual force by detaching from it all flaccid interests. He renounced mathematics and law, in which his reading had been considerable, all but the literature of the arts. Nothing was to enter into his life unpenetrated by its central enthusiasm. At this time he undergoes the charm of Voltaire. Voltaire belongs to that flimsier, more artificial, classical tradition, which Winckelmann was one day to supplant, by the clear ring, the eternal outline, of the genuine antique. But it proves the authority of such a gift as Voltaire's that it allures and wins even those born to supplant it. Voltaire's impression on Winckelmann was never effaced; and it gave him a consideration for French literature which contrasts with his contempt for the literary products of Germany. German literature transformed, siderealised, as we see it in Goethe, reckons Winckelmann among its initiators. But Germany at that time presented nothing in which he could have anticipated *Iphigenie,* and the formation of an effective classical tradition in German literature.

Under this purely literary influence, Winckelmann protests

against Christian Wolff and the philosophers. Goethe, in speaking of this protest, alludes to his own obligations to Emmanuel Kant. Kant's influence over the culture of Goethe, which he tells us could not have been resisted by him without loss, consisted in a severe limitation to the concrete. But he adds, that in born antiquaries, like Winckelmann, a constant handling of the antique, with its eternal outline, maintains that limitation as effectually as a critical philosophy. Plato, however, saved so often for his redeeming literary manner, is excepted from Winckelmann's proscription of the philosophers. The modern student most often meets Plato on that side which seems to pass beyond Plato into a world no longer pagan, and based upon the conception of a spiritual life. But the element of affinity which he presents to Winckelmann is that which is wholly Greek, and alien from the Christian world, represented by that group of brilliant youths in the *Lysis*, still uninfected by any spiritual sickness, finding the end of all endeavour in the aspects of the human form, the continual stir and motion of a comely human life.

This new-found interest in Plato's dialogues could not fail to increase his desire to visit the countries of the classical tradition. "It is my misfortune," he writes, "that I was not born to great place, wherein I might have had cultivation, and the opportunity of following my instinct and forming myself." A visit to Rome probably was already designed, and he silently preparing for it. Count Bünau, the author of a historical work then of note, had collected at Nöthenitz a valuable library, now part of the library of Dresden. In 1748 Winckelmann wrote to Bünau in halting French:—He is emboldened, he says, by Bünau's indulgence for needy men of letters. He desires only to devote himself to study, having never allowed himself to be dazzled by favourable prospects in the Church. He hints at his doubtful position "in a metaphysical age, by which humane literature is trampled under foot. At present," he goes on, "little value is set on Greek literature, to which I have devoted myself so far as I could penetrate, when good books are so scarce and expensive." Finally, he desires a place in some corner of Bünau's library. "Perhaps, at some future time, I shall become more useful to the public, if, drawn from obscurity in whatever way, I can find means to maintain myself in the capital."

Soon afterwards we find Winckelmann in the library at Nöthenitz. Thence he made many visits to the collection of antiquities at Dresden. He became acquainted with many artists, above all with Oeser, Goethe's future friend and master, who, uniting a high culture with the practical knowledge of art, was fitted to minister to Winckelmann's culture. And now a new channel of communion with the Greek life was opened for him. Hitherto he had handled the words only of Greek poetry, stirred indeed and roused by them, yet divining beyond the words some unexpressed pulsation of sensuous life. Suddenly he is in contact with that life, still fervent in the relics of plastic art. Filled as our culture is with the classical spirit, we can hardly imagine how deeply the human mind was moved, when, at the Renaissance, in the midst of a frozen world, the buried fire of ancient art rose up from under the soil. Winckelmann here reproduces for us the earlier sentiment of the Renaissance. On a sudden the imagination feels itself free. How facile and direct, it seems to say, is this life of the senses and the understanding, when once we have apprehended it! Here, surely, is that more liberal mode of life we have been seeking so long, so near to us all the while. How mistaken and round-about have been our efforts to reach it by mystic passion, and monastic reverie; how they have deflowered the flesh; how little have they really emancipated us! Hermione melts from her stony posture, and the lost proportions of life right themselves. Here, then, in vivid realisation, we see the native tendency of Winckelmann to escape from abstract theory to intuition, to the exercise of sight and touch. Lessing, in the *Laocoon*, has theorised finely on the relation of poetry to sculpture; and philosophy may give us theoretical reasons why not poetry but sculpture should be the most sincere and exact expression of the Greek ideal. By a happy, unperplexed dexterity, Winckelmann solves the question in the concrete. It is what Goethe calls his *Gewahrwerden der griechischen Kunst*, his *finding* of Greek art.

Through the tumultuous richness of Goethe's culture, the influence of Winckelmann is always discernible, as the strong, regulative under-current of a clear, antique motive. "One learns nothing from him," he says to Eckermann, "but one becomes something." If we ask what the secret of this influence was, Goethe himself will tell us—wholeness, unity with one's self, intellectual integrity. And yet these expressions, because they fit Goethe, with his universal culture, so well, seem hardly to describe the narrow, exclusive interest of Winckelmann. Doubtless Winckelmann's perfection is a narrow perfection: his feverish nursing of the one motive of his life is a contrast to Goethe's various energy. But what affected Goethe, what instructed him and ministered to his culture, was the integrity, the truth to its type, of the given force. The development of this force was the single interest of Winckelmann, unembarrassed by anything else in him. Other interests, practical or intellectual, those slighter talents and motives not supreme, which in most men are the waste part of nature, and drain away their vitality, he plucked out and cast from him. The protracted longing of his youth is not a vague, romantic longing: he knows what he longs for, what he wills. Within its severe limits his enthusiasm burns like lava. "You know," says Lavater, speaking of Winckelmann's countenance, "that I consider ardour and indifference by no means incompatible in the same character. If ever there was a striking instance of that union, it is in the countenance before us." "A lowly childhood," says Goethe, "insufficient instruction in youth, broken, distracted studies in early manhood, the burden of school-keeping! He was thirty years old before he enjoyed a single favour of fortune: but so soon as he had attained to an adequate condition of freedom, he appears before us consummate and entire, complete in the ancient sense."

But his hair is turning grey, and he has not yet reached the south. The Saxon court had become Roman Catholic, and the way to favour at Dresden was through Roman ecclesiastics. Probably the thought of a profession of the papal religion was not new to Winckelmann. At one time he had thought of begging his way to Rome, from cloister to cloister, under the pretence of a disposition to change his faith. In 1751, the papal *nuncio*, Archinto, was one of the visitors at Nöthenitz. He suggested Rome as the fitting stage for Winckelmann's accomplishments, and held out the hope of a place in the pope's library. Cardinal Passionei, charmed with Winckelmann's beautiful Greek writing, was ready to play the part of Mæcenas, if the indispensable change were made. Winckelmann accepted the bribe, and visited the *nuncio* at Dresden. Unquiet still at the word "profession," not without a struggle, he joined the Roman Church, July the 11th, 1754.

Goethe boldly pleads that Winckelmann was a pagan, that the landmarks of Christendom meant nothing to him. It is clear that he intended to deceive no one by his disguise; fears of the inquisition are sometimes visible during his life in Rome; he entered Rome notoriously with the works of Voltaire in his possession; the thought of what Count Bünau might be thinking of him seems to have been his greatest difficulty. On the other hand, he my have had a sense of a certain antique and as it were pagan grandeur in the Roman Catholic religion. Turning from the crabbed Protestantism, which had been the *ennui* of his youth, he might reflect that while Rome had reconciled itself to the Renaissance, the Protestant principle in art had cut off Germany from the supreme tradition of beauty. And yet to that transparent nature, with its simplicity as of the earlier world, the loss of absolute sincerity must have been a real loss. Goethe understands that Winckelmann had made this sacrifice. Yet at the bar of the highest criticism, perhaps, Winckelmann may be absolved. The insincerity of his religious profession was only one incident of a culture in which the moral instinct, like the religious or political, was merged in the artistic. But then the artistic interest was that, by desperate faithfulness to which Winckelmann was saved from a mediocrity, which, breaking through no bounds, moves ever in a bloodless routine, and misses its one chance in the life of the spirit and the intellect. There have been instances of culture developed by every high motive in turn, and yet intense at every point; and the aim of our culture should be to attain not only as intense but as complete a life as possible. But often the higher life is only possible at all, on condition of the selection of that in which one's motive is native and strong; and this selection involves the renunciation of a crown reserved for others. Which is better?—to lay open a new sense, to initiate a new organ for the human spirit, or to cultivate many types of perfection up to a point which leaves us still beyond the range of their transforming power? Savonarola is one type of success; Winckelmann is another; criticism can reject neither, because each is true to itself. Winckelmann himself explains the motive of his life when he says, "It will be my highest reward, if posterity acknowledges that I have written worthily."

For a time he remained at Dresden. There his first book appeared, *Thoughts on the Imitation of Greek Works of Art in Paint-ing and Sculpture*. Full of obscurities as it was, obscurities which baffled but did not offend Goethe when he first turned to art-criticism, its purpose was direct—an appeal from the artificial classicism of the day to the study of the antique. The book was well received, and a pension supplied through the king's con-fessor. In September 1755 he started for Rome, in the company of a young Jesuit. He was introduced to Raphael Mengs, a painter then of note, and found a home near him, in the artists' quarter, in a place where he could "overlook, far and wide, the eternal city." At first he was perplexed with the sense of being a stranger on what was to him, spiritually, native soil. "Unhappily," he cries in French, often selected by him as the vehicle of strong feeling, "I am one of those whom the Greeks call ὀψιμαθεῖς.—I have come into the world and into Italy too late." More than thirty years afterwards, Goethe also, after many aspirations and severe prepa-ration of mind, visited Italy. In early manhood, just as he too was *finding* Greek art, the rumour of that true artist's life of Winckelmann in Italy had strongly moved him. At Rome, spend-ing a whole year drawing from the antique, in preparation for *Iphigenie*, he finds the stimulus of Winckelmann's memory ever active. Winckelmann's Roman life was simple, primeval, Greek. His delicate constitution permitted him the use only of bread and wine. Condemned by many as a renegade, he had no desire for places of honour, but only to see his merits acknowledged, and existence assured to him. He was simple without being niggardly, he desired to be neither poor nor rich.

Winckelmann's first years in Rome present all the elements of an intellectual situation of the highest interest. The beating of the soul against its bars, the sombre aspect, the alien traditions, the still barbarous literature of Germany, are afar off. Before him are adequate conditions of culture, the sacred soil itself, the first tokens of the advent of the new German literature, with it broad horizons, its boundless intellectual promise. Dante, passing from the darkness of the *Inferno*, is filled with a sharp and joyful sense of light, which makes him deal with it, in the opening of the *Purgatorio*, in a wonderfully touching and penetrative way. Hellenism, which is the principle pre-eminently of intellectual light, (our modern culture may have more colour, the medieval spirit greater heat and profundity, but Hellenism is preeminent for light), has always been most effectively conceived by those who have crept into it out of an intellectual world in which the sombre elements predominate. So it had been in the ages of the Renaissance. This repression, removed at last, gave force and glow to Winckelmann's native affinity to the Hellenic spirit. "There had been known before him," says Madame de Staël, "learned men who might be consulted like books; but no one had, if I may say so, made himself a pagan for the purpose of penetrating antiquity." "One is always a poor executant of conceptions not one's own."—*On exécute mal ce qu'on n'a pas conçu soi-même*[1]—words spoken on so high an occasion—are true in their measure of every genuine enthusiasm. Enthusiasm,—that, in the broad Platonic sense of the *Phaedrus*, was the secret of his divinatory power over the Hellenic world. This enthusiasm, dependent as it is to a great degree on bodily temperament, has a power of reinforcing the purer emotions of the intellect with an almost physical excitement. That his affinity with Hellenism was not merely intellectual, that the subtler threads of temperament were inwoven in it, is proved by his romantic, fervent friendships with young men. He has known, he says, many young men more beautiful than Guido's archangel. These friendships, bringing him into contact with the pride of human form, and staining the thoughts with its bloom, perfected his reconciliation to the spirit of Greek sculpture. A letter on taste, addressed from Rome to a young nobleman, Friedrich von Berg, is the record of such a friendship.

"I shall excuse my delay," he begins,

in fulfilling my promise of an essay on the taste for beauty in works of art, in the words of Pindar. He says to Agesidamus, a youth of Locri—ἰδέα τε καλόν, ὥρᾳ τε κεκραμένον—whom he had kept waiting for an intended ode, that a debt paid with usury is the end of reproach. This may win your good-nature on behalf of my present essay, which has turned out far more detailed and circumstantial than I had at first intended.

It is from yourself that the subject is taken. Our intercourse has been short, too short both for you and me; but the first time I saw you, the

[1] Words of Charlotte Corday before the *Convention*.

affinity of our spirits was revealed to me: your culture proved that my hope was not groundless; and I found in a beautiful body a soul created for nobleness, gifted with the sense of beauty. My parting from you was therefore one of the most painful in my life; and that this feeling continues our common friend is witness, for your separation from me leaves me no hope of seeing you again. Let this essay be a memorial of our friendship, which, on my side, is free from every selfish motive, and ever remains subject and dedicate to yourself alone.

The following passage is characteristic—

As it is confessedly the beauty of man which is to be conceived under one general idea, so I have noticed that those who are observant of beauty only in women, and are moved little or not at all by the beauty of men, seldom have an impartial, vital, inborn instinct for beauty in art. To such persons the beauty of Greek art will ever seem wanting, because its supreme beauty is rather male than female. But the beauty of art demands a higher sensibility than the beauty of nature, because the beauty of art, like tears shed at a play, gives no pain, is without life, and must be awakened and repaired by culture. Now, as the spirit of culture is much more ardent in youth than in manhood, the instinct of which I am speaking must be exercised and directed to what is beautiful, before that age is reached, at which one would be afraid to confess that one had no taste for it.

Certainly, of that beauty of living form which regulated Winckelmann's friendships, it could not be said that it gave no pain. One notable friendship, the fortune of which we may trace through his letters, begins with an antique, chivalrous letter in French, and ends noisily in a burst of angry fire. Far from reaching the quietism, the bland indifference of art, such attachments are nevertheless more susceptible than any others of equal strength of a purely intellectual culture. Of passion, of physical excitement, they contain only just so much as stimulates the eye to the finest delicacies of colour and form. These friendships, often the caprices of a moment, make Winckelmann's letters, with their troubled colouring, an instructive but bizarre addition to the *History of Art*, that shrine of grave and mellow light around the mute Olympian family. The impression which Winckelmann's literary life conveyed to those about him, was that of excitement, intuition, inspiration, rather than the contemplative evolution of general principles. the quick, susceptible enthusiast, betraying his temperament even in appearance, by his olive complexion, his deep-seated, piercing eyes, his rapid movements, apprehended the subtlest principles of the Hellenic manner, not through the understanding, but by instinct or touch. A German biographer of Winckelmann has compared him to Columbus. That is not the aptest of comparisons; but it reminds one of a passage in which Edgar Quinet describes the great discoverer's famous voyage. His science was often at fault; but he had a way of estimating at once the slightest indication of land, in a floating weed or passing bird; he seemed actually to come nearer to nature than other men. And that world in which others had moved with so much embarrassment, seems to call out in Winckelmann new senses fitted to deal with it. He is in touch with it; it penetrates him, and becomes part of his temperament. He remodels his writings with constant renewal of insight; he catches the thread of a whole sequence of laws in some hollowing of the hand, or dividing of the hair; he seems to realise that fancy of the reminiscence of a forgotten knowledge hidden for a time in the mind itself; as if the mind of one, lover and philosopher at once in some phase of pre-existence—φιλοσοφήσας ποτὲ μέτ᾽ ἔρωτος—fallen into a new cycle, were beginning its intellectual career over again, yet with a certain power of anticipating its results. And so comes the truth of Goethe's judgments on his works; they are a life, a living thing, designed for those who are alive—*ein Lebendiges für die Lebendigen geschrieben, ein Leben selbst.*

In 1758 Cardinal Albani, who had formed in his Roman villa a precious collection of antiquities, became Winckelmann's patron. Pompeii had just opened its treasures; Winckelmann gathered its first-fruits. But his plan of a visit to Greece remained unfulfilled. From his first arrival in Rome he had kept the *History of Ancient Art* ever in view. All his other writings were a preparation for that. It appeared, finally, in 1764; but even after its publication Winckelmann was still employed in perfecting it. It is since his time that many of the most significant examples of Greek art have been submitted to criticism. He had seen little or nothing of what we ascribe to the age of Pheidias; and his conception of Greek art tends, therefore, to put the mere elegance of the

imperial society of ancient Rome in place of the severe and chastened grace of the *palaestra*. For the most part he had to penetrate
to Greek art through copies, imitations, and later Roman art itself; and it is not surprising that this turbid medium has left in
Winckelmann's actual results much that a more privileged criticism can correct.

He had been twelve years in Rome. Admiring Germany had
made many calls to him. At last, in 1768, he set out to revisit the
country of his birth; and as he left Rome, a strange, inverted
home-sickness, a strange reluctance to leave it at all, came over
him. He reached Vienna. There he was loaded with honours and
presents: other cities were awaiting him. Goethe, then nineteen
years old, studying art at Leipsic, was expecting his coming, with
that wistful eagerness which marked his youth, when the news of
Winckelmann's murder arrived. All his "weariness of the north"
had revived with double force. He left Vienna, intending to hasten
back to Rome, and at Trieste a delay of a few days occurred. With
characteristic openness, Winckelmann had confided his plans to a
fellow-traveller, a man named Arcangeli, and had shown him the
gold medals received at Vienna. Arcangeli's avarice was roused.
One morning he entered Winckelmann's room, under pretence of
taking leave. Winckelmann was then writing "memoranda for the
future editor of the *History of Art*," still seeking the perfection of
his great work. Arcangeli begged to see the medals once more. As
Winckelmann stooped down to take them from the chest, a cord
was thrown round his neck. Some time afterwards, a child with
whose companionship Winckelmann had beguiled his delay,
knocked at the door, and receiving no answer, gave the alarm.
Winckelmann was found dangerously wounded, and died a few
hours later, after receiving the last sacraments. It seemed as if the
gods, in reward for his devotion to them, had given him a death
which, for its swiftness and its opportunity, he might well have
desired. "He has," says Goethe, "the advantage of figuring in the
memory of posterity, as one eternally able and strong; for the
image in which one leaves the world, is that in which one moves
among the shadows." Yet, perhaps, it is not fanciful to regret that
his proposed meeting with Goethe never took place. Goethe, then
in all the pregnancy of his wonderful youth, still unruffled by the

"press and storm" of his earlier manhood, was awaiting Winckelmann with a curiosity of the worthiest kind. As it was, Winckelmann became to him something like what Virgil was to Dante. And Winckelmann, with his fiery friendships, had reached that age and that period of culture at which emotions hitherto fitful, sometimes concentrate themselves in a vital, unchangeable relationship. German literary history seems to have lost the chance of one of those famous friendships, the very tradition of which becomes a stimulus to culture, and exercises an imperishable influence.

In one of the frescoes of the Vatican, Raphael has commemorated the tradition of the Catholic religion. Against a space of tranquil sky, broken in upon by the beatific vision, are ranged the great personages of Christian history, with the Sacrament in the midst. Another fresco of Raphael in the same apartment presents a very different company, Dante alone appearing in both. Surrounded by the muses of Greek mythology, under a thicket of laurel, sits Apollo, with the sources of Castalia at his feet. On either side are grouped those on whom the spirit of Apollo descended, the classical and Renaissance poets, to whom the waters of Castalia come down, a river making glad this other "City of God." In this fresco it is the classical tradition, the orthodoxy of taste, that Raphael commemorates. Winckelmann's intellectual history authenticates the claims of this tradition in human culture. In the countries where that tradition arose, where it still lurked about its own artistic relics, and changes of language had not broken its continuity, national pride might sometimes light up anew in enthusiasm for it. Aliens might imitate that enthusiasm, and classicism become from time to time an intellectual fashion. But Winckelmann was not further removed by language, than by local aspects and associations, from those vestiges of the classical spirit; and he lived at a time when, in Germany, classical studies were out of favour. Yet, remote in time and place, he feels after the Hellenic world, divines those channels of ancient art, in which its life still circulates, and, like Scyles, the half-barbarous yet Hellenising king, in the beautiful story of Herodotus, is irresistibly attracted by it. This testimony to the authority of the

Hellenic tradition, its fitness to satisfy some vital requirement of the intellect, which Winckelmann contributes as a solitary man of genius, is offered also by the general history of the mind. The spiritual forces of the past, which have prompted and informed the culture of a succeeding age, live, indeed, within that culture, but with an absorbed, underground life. The Hellenic element alone has not been so absorbed, or content with this underground life; from time to time it has started to the surface; culture has been drawn back to its sources to be clarified and corrected. Hellenism is not merely an absorbed element in our intellectual life; it is a conscious tradition in it.

Again, individual genius works ever under conditions of time and place: its products are coloured by the varying aspects of nature, and type of human form, and outward manners of life. There is thus an element of change in art; criticism must never for a moment forget that "the artist is the child of his time." But besides these conditions of time and place, and independent of them, there is also an element of permanence, a standard of taste, which genius confesses. This standard is maintained in a purely intellectual tradition. It acts upon the artist, not as one of the influences of his own age, but through those artistic products of the previous generation which first excited, while they directed into a particular channel, his sense of beauty. The supreme artistic products of succeeding generations thus form a series of elevated points, taking each from each the reflexion of a strange light, the source of which is not in the atmosphere around and above them, but in a stage of society remote from ours. The standard of taste, then, was fixed in Greece, at a definite historical period. A tradition for all succeeding generations, it originates in a spontaneous growth out of the influences of Greek society. What were the conditions under which this ideal, this standard of artistic orthodoxy, was generated? How was Greece enabled to force its thought upon Europe?

Greek art, when we first catch sight of it, is entangled with Greek religion. We are accustomed to think of Greek religion as the religion of art and beauty, the religion of which the Olympian Zeus and the Athene Polias are the idols, the poems of Homer the sacred books. Thus Cardinal Newman speaks of "the classical

polytheism which was gay and graceful, as was natural in a civil-
ised age." Yet such a view is only a partial one. In it the eye is
fixed on the sharp, bright edge of high Hellenic culture, but loses
sight of the sombre world across which it strikes. Greek religion,
where we can observe it most distinctly, is at once a magnificent
ritualistic system, and a cycle of poetical conceptions. Religions,
as they grow by natural laws out of man's life, are modified by
whatever modifies his life. They brighten under a bright sky, they
become liberal as the social range widens, they grow intense and
shrill in the clefts of human life, where the spirit is narrow and
confined, and the stars are visible at noonday; and a fine analysis
of these differences is one of the gravest functions of religious
criticism. Still, the broad foundation, in mere human nature, of
all religions as they exist for the greatest number, is a universal
pagan sentiment, a paganism which existed before the Greek religion, and has lingered far onward into the Christian world, ineradicable, like some persistent vegetable growth, because its
seed is an element of the very soil out of which it springs.

This pagan sentiment measures the sadness with which the human mind is filled, whenever its thoughts wander far from what is
here, and now. It is beset by notions of irresistible natural powers,
for the most part ranged against man, but the secret also of his
fortune, making the earth golden and the grape fiery for him. He
makes gods in his own image, gods smiling and flower-crowned, or
bleeding by some sad fatality, to console him by their wounds,
never closed from generation to generation. It is with a rush of
home-sickness that the thought of death presents itself. He would
remain at home for ever on the earth if he could. As it loses its
colour and the senses fail, he clings ever closer to it; but since the
mouldering of bones and flesh must go on to the end, he is careful
for charms and talismans, which may chance to have some
friendly power in them, when the inevitable shipwreck comes.
Such sentiment is a part of the eternal basis of all religions, modified indeed by changes of time and place, but indestructible, because its root is so deep in the earth of man's nature. The breath of
religious initiators passes over them; a few "rise up with wings as
eagles," but the broad level of religious life is not permanently
changed. Religious progress, like all purely spiritual progress, is

confined to a few. This sentiment attaches itself in the earliest times to certain usages of patriarchal life, the kindling of fire, the washing of the body, the slaughter of the flock, the gathering of harvest, holidays and dances. Here are the beginnings of a ritual, at first as occasional and unfixed as the sentiment which it expresses, but destined to become the permanent element of religious life. The usages of patriarchal life change; but this germ of ritual remains, promoted now with a consciously religious motive, losing its domestic character, and therefore becoming more and more inexplicable with each generation. Such pagan worship, in spite of local variations, essentially one, is an element in all religions. It is the anodyne which the religious principle, like one administering opiates to the incurable, has added to the law which makes life sombre for the vast majority of mankind.

More definite religious conceptions come from other sources, and fix themselves upon this ritual in various ways, changing it, and giving it new meanings. In Greece they were derived from mythology, itself not due to a religious source at all, but developing in the course of time into a body of religious conceptions, entirely human in form and character. To the unprogressive ritual element it brought these conceptions, itself—ἡ πτεροῦ δύναμις, the power of the wing—an element of refinement, of ascension, with the promise of an endless destiny. While the ritual remains unchanged, the æsthetic element, only accidentally connected with it, expands with the freedom and mobility of the things of the intellect. Always, the fixed element is the religious observance; the fluid, unfixed element is the myth, the religious conception. This religion is itself pagan, and has in any broad view of it the pagan sadness. It does not at once, and for the majority, become the higher Hellenic religion. The country people, of course, cherish the unlovely idols of an earlier time, such as those which Pausanias found still devoutly preserved in Arcadia. Athenæus tells the story of one who, coming to a temple of Latona, had expected to find some worthy presentment of the mother of Apollo, and laughed on seeing only a shapeless wooden figure. The wilder people have wilder gods, which, however, in Athens, or Corinth, or Lacedæmon, changing ever with the worshippers in whom they live and move and have their being, borrow something of the lordliness and distinction of human nature there.

Greek religion too has its mendicants, its purifications, its antinomian mysticism, its garments offered to the gods, its statues worn
with kissing, its exaggerated superstitions for the vulgar only, its
worship of sorrow, its *addolorata*, its mournful mysteries.
Scarcely a wild or melancholy note of the medieval church but
was anticipated by Greek polytheism! What should we have
thought of the vertiginous prophetess at the very centre of Greek
religion? The supreme Hellenic culture is a sharp edge of light
across this gloom. The fiery, stupefying wine becomes in a happier climate clear and exhilarating. The Dorian worship of
Apollo, rational, chastened, debonair, with his unbroken
daylight, always opposed to the sad Chthonian divinities, is the
aspiring element, by force and spring of which Greek religion
sublimes itself. Out of Greek religion, under happy conditions,
arises Greek art, to minister to human culture. It was the privilege of Greek religion to be able to transform itself into an artistic ideal.

For the thoughts of the Greeks about themselves, and their relation to the world generally, were ever in the happiest readiness to
be transformed into objects for the senses. In this lies the main
distinction between Greek art and the mystical art of the Christian middle age, which is always struggling to express thoughts
beyond itself. Take, for instance, a characteristic work of the middle age, Angelico's *Coronation of the Virgin*, in the cloister of
Saint Mark's at Florence. In some strange halo of a moon Jesus
and the Virgin Mother are seated, clad in mystical white raiment,
half shroud, half priestly linen. Jesus, with rosy nimbus and the
long pale hair—*tanquam lana alba et tanquam nix*—of the figure
in the Apocalypse, with slender finger-tips is setting a crown of
pearl on the head of Mary, who, corpse-like in her refinement, is
bending forward to receive it, the light lying like snow upon her
forehead. Certainly, it cannot be said of Angelico's fresco that it
throws into a sensible form our highest thoughts about man and
his relation to the world; but it did not do this adequately even for
Angelico. For him, all that is outward or sensible in his work—the
hair like wool, the rosy nimbus, the crown of pearl—is only the
symbol or type of a really inexpressible world, to which he wishes
to direct the thoughts; he would have shrunk from the notion that
what the eye apprehended was all. Such forms of art, then, are

inadequate to the matter they clothe; they remain ever below its level. Something of this kind is true also of oriental art. As in the middle age from an exaggerated inwardness, so in the East from a vagueness, a want of definition, in thought, the matter presented to art is unmanageable, and the forms of sense struggle vainly with it. The many-headed gods of the East, the orientalised, many-breasted Diana of Ephesus, like Angelico's fresco, are at best overcharged symbols, a means of hinting at an idea which art cannot fitly or completely express, which still remains in the world of shadows.

But take a work of Greek art,—the Venus of Melos. That is in no sense a symbol, a suggestion, of anything beyond its own victorious fairness. The mind begins and ends with the finite image, yet loses no part of the spiritual motive. This motive is not lightly and loosely attached to the sensuous form, as its meaning to an allegory, but saturates and is identical with it. The Greek mind had advanced to a particular stage of self-reflexion, but was careful not to pass beyond it. In oriental thought there is a vague conception of life everywhere, but no true appreciation of itself by the mind, no knowledge of the distinction of man's nature: in its consciousness of itself, humanity is still confused with the fantastic, indeterminate life of the animal and vegetable world. In Greek thought, on the other hand, the "lordship of the soul" is recognised; that lordship gives authority and divinity to human eyes and hands and feet; inanimate nature is thrown into the background. But just there Greek thought finds its happy limit; it has not yet become too inward; the mind has not yet learned to boast its independence of the flesh; the spirit has not yet absorbed everything with its emotions, nor reflected its own colour everywhere. It has indeed committed itself to a train of reflexion which must end in defiance of form, of all that is outward, in an exaggerated idealism. But that end is still distant: it has not yet plunged into the depths of religious mysticism.

This ideal art, in which the thought does not outstrip or lie beyond the proper range of its sensible embodiment, could not have arisen out of a phase of life that was uncomely or poor. That delicate pause in Greek reflexion was joined, by some supreme good luck, to the perfect animal nature of the Greeks. Here are the two conditions of an artistic ideal. The influences which perfected the animal nature of the Greeks are part of the process by which "the ideal" was evolved. Those "Mothers" who, in the second part of *Faust*, mould and remould the typical forms that appear in human history, preside, at the beginning of Greek culture, over such a concourse of happy physical conditions as ever generates by natural laws some rare type of intellectual or spiritual life. That delicate air, "nimbly and sweetly recommending itself" to the senses, the finer aspects of nature, the finer lime and clay of the human form, and modelling of the dainty framework of the human countenance:—these are the good luck of the Greek when he enters upon life. Beauty becomes a distinction, like genius, or noble place.

"By no people," says Winckelmann,

has beauty been so highly esteemed as by the Greeks. The priests of a youthful Jupiter at Ægae, of the Ismenian Apollo, and the priest who at Tanagra led the procession of Mercury, bearing a lamb upon his shoulders, were always youths to whom the prize of beauty had been awarded. The citizens of Egesta erected a monument to a certain Philip who was not their fellow-citizen, but of Croton, for his distinguished beauty; and the people made offerings at it. In an ancient song, ascribed to Simonides or Epicharmus, of four wishes, the first was health, the second beauty. And as beauty was so longed for and prized by the Greeks, every beautiful person sought to become known to the whole people by this distinction, and above all to approve himself to the artists, because they awarded the prize; and this was for the artists an occasion for having supreme beauty ever before their eyes. Beauty even gave a right to fame; and we find in Greek histories the most beautiful people distinguished. Some were famous for the beauty of one single part of their form; as Demetrius Phalereus, for his beautiful eyebrows, was called *Charito-blepharos*. It seems even to have been thought that the procreation of beautiful children might be promoted by prizes. This is shown by the existence of contests for beauty, which in ancient times were established by Cypselus, King of Arcadia, by the river Alpheus; and, at the feast of Apollo of Philæ, a prize was offered to the youths for the deftest kiss. This was decided by an umpire; as also at Megara, by the grave of Diocles. At Sparta, and at Lesbos, in the temple of Juno, and among the Parrhasii, there were contests for beauty among women. The general esteem for beauty went so far, that the Spartan women set up in their bedchambers a Nireus, a Narcissus, or a Hyacinth, that they might bear beautiful children.

So, from a few stray antiquarianisms, a few faces cast up sharply from the waves, Winckelmann, as his manner was, divines the

temperament of the antique world, and that in which it had delight. It has passed away with that distant age, and we may venture to dwell upon it. What sharpness and reality it has is the
sharpness and reality of suddenly arrested life. The Greek system
of gymnastics originated as part of a religious ritual. The worshipper was to recommend himself to the gods by becoming fleet and
fair, white and red, like them. The beauty of the *palæstra*, and
the beauty of the artist's workshop, reacted on one another. The
youth tried to rival his gods; and his increased beauty passed back
into them.—"I take the gods to witness, I had rather have a fair
body than a king's crown"—῎Ομνυμι πάντας θεοὺς μὴ ἑλέσθαι ἂν
τὴν βασιλέως ἀρχὴν ἀντὶ τοῦ καλὸς εἶναι—that is the form in which
one age of the world chose the higher life.—A perfect world, if the
gods could have seemed for ever only fleet and fair, white and red!
Let us not regret that this unperplexed youth of humanity, satisfied with the vision of itself, passed, at the due moment, into a
mournful maturity; for already the deep joy was in store for the
spirit, of finding the ideal of that youth still red with life in the
grave.

It followed that the Greek ideal expressed itself preeminently in
sculpture. All art has a sensuous element, colour, form, sound—
in poetry a dexterous recalling of these, together with the profound, joyful sensuousness of motion, and each of them may be a
medium for the ideal: it is partly accident which in any individual case makes the born artist, poet, or painter rather than sculptor. But as the mind itself has had an historical development, one
form of art, by the very limitations of its material, may be more
adequate than another for the expression of any one phase of that
development. Different attitudes of the imagination have a native
affinity with different types of sensuous form, so that they combine together, with completeness and ease. The arts may thus be
ranged in a series, which corresponds to a series of developments
in the human mind itself. Architecture, which begins in a practical need, can only express by vague hint or symbol, the spirit or
mind of the artist. He closes his sadness over him, or wanders in
the perplexed intricacies of things, or projects his purpose from
him clean-cut and sincere, or bares himself to the sunlight. But
these spiritualities, felt rather than seen, can but lurk about ar-

chitectural form as volatile effects, to be gathered from it by reflexion. Their expression is, indeed, not really sensuous at all. As
human form is not the subject with which it deals, architecture is
the mode in which the artistic effort centres, when the thoughts
of man concerning himself are still indistinct, when he is still
little preoccupied with those harmonies, storms, victories, of the
unseen and intellectual world, which, wrought out into the
bodily form, give it an interest and significance communicable to
it alone. The art of Egypt, with its supreme architectural effects,
is, according to Hegel's beautiful comparison, a Memnon waiting
for the day, the day of the Greek spirit, the humanistic spirit, with
its power of speech.

Again, painting, music, and poetry, with their endless power of
complexity, are the special arts of the romantic and modern ages.
Into these, with the utmost attenuation of detail, may be translated every delicacy of thought and feeling, incidental to a consciousness brooding with delight over itself. Through their
gradations of shade, their exquisite intervals, they project in an
external form that which is most inward in passion or sentiment.
Between architecture and those romantic arts of painting, music,
and poetry, comes sculpture, which, unlike architecture, deals
immediately with man, while it contrasts with the romantic arts,
because it is not self-analytical. It has to do more exclusively
than any other art with the human form, itself one entire medium
of spiritual expression, trembling, blushing, melting into dew,
with inward excitement. That spirituality which only lurks
about architecture as a volatile effect, in sculpture takes up the
whole given material, and penetrates it with an imaginative motive; and at first sight sculpture, with its solidity of form, seems a
thing more real and full than the faint, abstract world of poetry or
painting. Still the fact is the reverse. Discourse and action show
man as he is, more directly than the play of the muscles and the
moulding of the flesh; and over these poetry has command. Painting, by the flushing of colour in the face and dilatation of light in
the eye—music, by its subtle range of tones—can refine most delicately upon a single moment of passion, unravelling its subtlest
threads.

But why should sculpture thus limit itself to pure form? Because, by this limitation, it becomes a perfect medium of expression for one peculiar motive of the imaginative intellect. It therefore renounces all those attributes of its material which do not forward that motive. It has had, indeed, from the beginning an unfixed claim to colour; but this element of colour in it has always been more or less conventional, with no melting or modulation of tones, never permitting more than a very limited realism. It was maintained chiefly as a religious tradition. In proportion as the art of sculpture ceased to be merely decorative, and subordinate to architecture, it threw itself upon pure form. It renounces the power of expression by lower or heightened tones. In it, no member of the human form is more significant than the rest; the eye is wide, and without pupil; the lips and brow are hardly less significant than hands, and breasts, and feet. But the limitation of its resources is part of its pride: it has no backgrounds, no sky or atmosphere, to suggest and interpret a train of feeling; a little of suggested motion, and much of pure light on its gleaming surfaces, with pure form—only these. And it gains more than it loses by this limitation to its own distinguishing motives; it unveils man in the repose of his unchanging characteristics. That white light, purged from the angry, bloodlike stains of action and passion, reveals, not what is accidental in man, but the tranquil godship in him, as opposed to the restless accidents of life. The art of sculpture records the first naïve, unperplexed recognition of man by himself; and it is a proof of the high artistic capacity of the Greeks, that they apprehended and remained true to these exquisite limitations, yet, in spite of them, gave to their creations, a mobile, a vital, individuality.

Heiterkeit—blitheness or repose, and *Allgemeinheit*—generality or breadth, are, then, the supreme characteristics of the Hellenic ideal. But that generality or breadth has nothing in common with the lax observation, the unlearned thought, the flaccid execution, which have sometimes claimed superiority in art, on the plea of being "broad" or "general." Hellenic breadth and generality come of a culture minute, severe, constantly renewed, rectifying and concentrating its impressions into certain pregnant types.

The basis of all artistic genius lies in the power of conceiving humanity in a new and striking way, of putting a happy world of its own creation in place of the meaner world of our common days, generating around itself an atmosphere with a novel power of refraction, selecting, transforming, recombining the images it transmits, according to the choice of the imaginative intellect. In exercising this power, painting and poetry have a variety of subject almost unlimited. The range of characters or persons open to them is as various as life itself; no character, however trivial, misshapen, or unlovely, can resist their magic. That is because those arts can accomplish their function in the choice and development of some special situation, which lifts or glorifies a character, in itself not poetical. To realise this situation, to define, in a chill and empty atmosphere, the focus where rays, in themselves pale and impotent, unite and begin to burn, the artist may have, indeed, to employ the most cunning detail, to complicate and refine upon thought and passion a thousandfold. Let us take a brilliant example from the poems of Robert Browning. His poetry is pre-eminently the poetry of situations. The characters themselves are always of secondary importance; often they are characters in themselves of little interest; they seem to come to him by strange accidents from the ends of the world. His gift is shown by the way in which he accepts such a character, throws it into some situation, or apprehends it in some delicate pause of life, in which for a moment it becomes ideal. In the poem entitled *Le Byron de nos Jours*, in his *Dramatis Personæ*, we have a single moment of passion thrown into relief after this exquisite fashion. Those two jaded Parisians are not intrinsically interesting: they begin to interest us only when thrown into a choice situation. But to discriminate that moment, to make it appreciable by us, that we may "find" it, what a cobweb of allusions, what double and treble reflexions of the mind upon itself, what an artificial light is constructed and broken over the chosen situation: on how fine a needle's point that little world of passion is balanced! Yet, in spite of this intricacy, the poem has the clear ring of a central motive. We receive from it the impression of one imaginative tone, of a single creative act.

To produce such effects at all requires all the resources of painting, with its power of indirect expression, of subordinate but significant detail, its atmosphere, its foregrounds and backgrounds. To produce them in a pre-eminent degree requires all the resources of poetry, language in its most purged form, its remote associations and suggestions, its double and treble lights. These appliances sculpture cannot command. In it, therefore, not the special situation, but the type, the general character of the subject to be delineated, is all-important. In poetry and painting, the situation predominates over the character; in sculpture, the character over the situation. Excluded by the proper limitation of its material from the development of exquisite situations, it has to choose from a select number of types intrinsically interesting— interesting, that is, independently of any special situation into which they may be thrown. Sculpture finds the secret of its power in presenting these types, in their broad, central, incisive lines. This it effects not by accumulation of detail, but by abstracting from it. All that is accidental, all that distracts the simple effect upon us of the supreme types of humanity, all traces in them of the commonness of the world, it gradually purges away.

Works of art produced under this law, and only these, are really characterised by Hellenic generality or breadth. In every direction it is a law of restraint. It keeps passion always below that degree of intensity at which it must necessarily be transitory, never winding up the features to one note of anger, or desire, or surprise. In some of the feebler allegorical designs of the middle age, we find isolated qualities portrayed as by so many masks; its religious art has familiarised us with faces fixed immovably into blank types of placid reverie. Men and women, again, in the hurry of life, often wear the sharp impress of one absorbing motive, from which it is said death sets their features free. All such instances may be ranged under the *grotesque;* and the Hellenic ideal has nothing in common with the grotesque. It allows passion to play lightly over the surface of the individual form, losing thereby nothing of its central impassivity, its depth and repose. To all but the highest culture, the reserved faces of the gods will ever have something of insipidity.

Again, in the best Greek sculpture, the archaic immobility has been stirred, its forms are in motion; but it is a motion ever kept in reserve, and very seldom committed to any definite action.

Endless as are the attitudes of Greek sculpture, exquisite as is the invention of the Greeks in this direction, the actions or situations it permits are simple and few. There is no Greek Madonna; the goddesses are always childless. The actions selected are those which would be without significance, except in a divine person— binding on a sandal, or preparing for the bath. When a more complex and significant action is permitted, it is most often represented as just finished, so that eager expectancy is excluded, as in the image of Apollo just after the slaughter of the Python, or of Venus with the apple of Paris already in her hand. The *Laocoon*, with all that patient science through which it has triumphed over an almost unmanageable subject, marks a period in which sculpture has begun to aim at effects legitimate, because delightful, only in painting.

The hair, so rich a source of expression in painting, because, relatively to the eye or the lip, it is mere drapery, is withdrawn from attention; its texture, as well as its colour, is lost, its arrangement but faintly and severely indicated, with no broken or enmeshed light. The eyes are wide and directionless, not fixing anything with their gaze, not riveting the brain to any special external object, the brows without hair. Again, Greek sculpture deals almost exclusively with youth, where the moulding of the bodily organs is still as if suspended between growth and completion; indicated but not emphasised; where the transition from curve to curve is so delicate and elusive, that Winckelmann compares it to a quiet sea, which, although we understand it to be in motion, we nevertheless regard as an image of repose; where, therefore, the exact degree of development is so hard to apprehend. If a single product only of Hellenic art were to be saved in the wreck of all beside, one might choose perhaps from the "beautiful multitude" of the Panathenaic frieze, that line of youths on horseback, with their level glances, their proud, patient lips, their chastened reins, their whole bodies in exquisite service. This colourless, unclassified purity of life, with its blending and interpenetration of intellectual, spiritual, and physical elements, still folded together, pregnant with the possibilities of a whole world closed within it, is the highest expression of the indifference which lies beyond all that is relative or partial.

Everywhere there is the effect of an awaking, of a child's sleep just disturbed. All these effects are united in a single instance—the *adorante* of the museum of Berlin, a youth who has gained the wrestler's prize, with hands lifted and open, in praise for the victory. Fresh, unperplexed, it is the image of man as he springs first from the sleep of nature, his white light taking no colour from any one-sided experience. He is characterless, so far as *character* involves subjection to the accidental influences of life.

"This sense," says Hegel,

for the consummate modelling of divine and human forms was pre-eminently at home in Greece. In its poets and orators, its historians and philosophers, Greece cannot be conceived from a central point, unless one brings, as a key to the understanding of it, an insight into the ideal forms of sculpture, and regards the images of statesmen and philosophers, as well as epic and dramatic heroes, from the artistic point of view. For those who act, as well as those who create and think, have, in those beautiful days of Greece, this plastic character. They are great and free, and have grown up on the soil of their own individuality, creating themselves out of themselves, and moulding themselves to what they were, and willed to be. The age of Pericles was rich in such characters; Pericles himself, Pheidias, Plato, above all Sophocles, Thucydides also, Xenophon and Socrates, each in his own order, the perfection of one remaining undiminished by that of the others. They are ideal artists of themselves, cast each in one flawless mould, works of art, which stand before us as an immortal presentment of the gods. Of this modelling also are those bodily works of art, the victors in the Olympic games; yes! and even Phryne, who, as the most beautiful of women, ascended naked out of the water, in the presence of assembled Greece.

This key to the understanding of the Greek spirit, Winckelmann possessed in his own nature, itself like a relic of classical antiquity, laid open by accident to our alien, modern atmosphere. To the criticism of that consummate Greek modelling he brought not only his culture but his temperament. We have seen how definite was the leading motive of that culture; how, like some central root-fibre, it maintained the well-rounded unity of his life through a thousand distractions. Interests not his, nor meant for him, never disturbed him. In morals, as in criticism, he followed the clue of instinct, of an unerring instinct. Penetrating into the antique world by his passion, his temperament, he enunciated no formal principles, always hard and one-sided. Minute and anxious as his culture was, he never became one-sidedly self-analytical. Occupied ever with himself, perfecting himself and developing his genius, he was not content, as so often happens with such natures, that the atmosphere between him and other minds should be thick and clouded; he was ever jealously refining his meaning into a form, express, clear, objective. This temperament he nurtured and invigorated by friendships which kept him always in direct contact with the spirit of youth. The beauty of Greek statues was a sexless beauty: the statues of the gods had the least traces of sex. Here there is a moral sexlessness, a kind of ineffectual wholeness of nature, yet with a true beauty and significance of its own.

One result of this temperament is a serenity—*Heiterkeit*—which characterises Winckelmann's handling of the sensuous side of Greek art. This serenity is, perhaps, in great measure, a negative quality: it is the absence of any sense of want, or corruption, or shame. With the sensuous element in Greek art he deals in the pagan manner; and what is implied in that? It has been sometimes said that art is a means of escape from "the tyranny of the senses." It may be so for the spectator: he may find that the spectacle of supreme works of art takes from the life of the senses something of its turbid fever. But this is possible for the spectator only because the artist, in producing those works, has gradually sunk his intellectual and spiritual ideas in sensuous form. He may live, as Keats lived, a pure life; but his soul, like that of Plato's false astronomer, becomes more and more immersed in sense, until nothing which lacks the appeal to sense has interest for him. How could such an one ever again endure the greyness of the ideal or spiritual world? The spiritualist is satisfied as he watches the escape of the sensuous elements from his conceptions; his interest grows, as the dyed garment bleaches in the keener air. But the artist steeps his thought again and again into the fire of colour. To the Greek this immersion is the sensuous was, religiously, at least, indifferent. Greek sensuousness, therefore, does not fever the conscience: it is shameless and childlike. Christian asceticism, on the other hand, discrediting the slightest touch of sense, has from time to time provoked into strong emphasis the contrast or antagonism to itself, of the artistic life, with its inevitable sensuousness.—*I did but taste a little honey with the end of the rod that was in mine hand, and lo! I must die.*—It has sometimes seemed hard to pursue that life without something of conscious disavowal of a spiritual world; and this imparts to genuine artistic interests a kind of intoxication. From this intoxication Winckelmann is free: he fingers those pagan marbles with unsinged hands, with no sense of shame or loss. That is to deal with the sensuous side of art in the pagan manner.

The longer we contemplate that Hellenic ideal, in which man is at unity with himself, with his physical nature, with the outward world, the more we may be inclined to regret that he should ever have passed beyond it, to contend for a perfection that makes the blood turbid, and frets the flesh, and discredits the actual world about us. But if he was to be saved from the *ennui* which ever attaches itself to realisation, even the realisation of the perfect life, it was necessary that a conflict should come, that some sharper note should grieve the existing harmony, and the spirit chafed by it beat out at last only a larger and profounder music. In Greek tragedy this conflict has begun: man finds himself face to face with rival claims. Greek tragedy shows how such a conflict may be treated with serenity, how the evolution of it may be a spectacle of the dignity, not of the impotence, of the human spirit. but it is not only in tragedy that the Greek spirit showed itself capable of thus bringing joy out of matter in itself full of discouragements. Theocritus too strikes often a note of romantic sadness. But what a blithe and steady poise, above these discouragements, in a clear and sunny stratum of the air!

Into this stage of Greek achievement Winckelmann did not enter. Supreme as he is where his true interest lay, his insight into the typical unity and repose of the highest sort of sculpture seems to have involved limitation in another direction. His conception of art excludes that bolder type of it which deals confidently and serenely with life, conflict, evil. Living in a world of exquisite but abstract and colourless form, he could hardly have conceived of the subtle and penetrative, yet somewhat grotesque art of the modern world. What would he have thought of Gilliatt, in Victor Hugo's *Travailleurs de la Mer*, or of the bledding mouth of Fantine in the first part of *Les Misérables*, penetrated as those books are with a sense of beauty, as lively and transparent as that of a Greek? Nay, a sort of preparation for the romantic temper is noticeable even within the limits of the Greek ideal itself, which for his part Winckelmann failed to see. For Greek religion has not merely its mournful mysteries of Adonis, of Hyacinthus, of Demeter, but it is conscious also of the fall of earlier divine dynasties. Hyperion gives way to Apollo, Oceanus to Poseidon. Around the feet of that tranquil Olympian family still crowd the weary shadows of an earlier, more formless, divine world. The placid minds even of Olympian gods are troubled with thoughts of a limit to duration, of inevitable decay, of dispossession. Again, the supreme and colourless abstraction of those divine forms, which is the secret of their repose, is also a premonition of the fleshless, consumptive refinements of the pale, medieval artists. That high indifference to the outward, that impassivity, has already a touch of the corpse in it: we see already Angelico and the *Master of the Passion* in the artistic future. The suppression of the sensuous, the shutting of the door upon it, the ascetic interest, may be even now foreseen. Those abstracted gods, "ready to melt out their essence fine into the winds," who can fold up their flesh as a garment, and still remain themselves, seem already to feel that bleak air, in which, like Helen of Troy, they wander as the spectres of the middle age.

Gradually, as the world came into the church, an artistic interest, native in the human soul, reasserted its claims. But Christian art was still dependent on pagan examples, building the shafts of pagan temples into its churches, perpetuating the form of the *basilica*, in later times working the disused amphitheatres as stone-quarries. The sensuous expression of ideas which unreservedly discredit the world of sense, was the delicate problem which Christian art had before it. If we think of medieval painting, as it ranges from the early German schools, still with something of the air of the charnel-house about them, to the clear loveliness of Perugino, we shall see how that problem was solved. In the very "worship of sorrow" the native blitheness of art asserted itself. The religious spirit, as Hegel says, "smiled through its tears." So perfectly did the young Raphael infuse that *Heiterkeit*, that pagan blitheness, into religious works, that his picture of Saint Agatha at Bologna became to Goethe a step in the evolution of *Iphigenie*[1]. But in proportion as the gift of smiling was found once more, there came also an aspiration towards that lost antique art, some relics of which Christian art had buried in itself, ready to work wonders when their day came.

The history of art has suffered as much as any history by trenchant and absolute divisions. Pagan and Christian art are sometimes harshly opposed, and the Renaissance is represented as a fashion which set in at a definite period. That is the superficial view: the deeper view is that which preserves the identity of European culture. The two are really continuous; and there is a sense in which it may be said that the Renaissance was an uninterrupted effort of the middle age, that it was ever taking place. When the actual relics of the antique were restored to the world, in the view of the Christian ascetic it was as if an ancient plague-pit had been opened. All the world took the contagion of the life of nature and of the senses. And now it was seen that the medieval spirit too had done something for the new fortunes of the antique. By hastening the decline of art, by withdrawing interest from it and yet keeping unbroken the thread of its traditions, it had suffered the human mind to repose itself, that when day came it might awake, with eyes refreshed, to those ancient, ideal forms.

The aim of a right criticism is to place Winckelmann in an intellectual perspective, of which Goethe is the foreground. For, after all, he is infinitely less than Goethe; and it is chiefly because at certain points he comes in contact with Goethe, that criticism entertains consideration of him. His relation to modern culture is a peculiar one. He is not of the modern world; nor is he wholly of the eighteenth century, although so much of his outer life is characteristic of it. But that note of revolt against the eighteenth century, which we detect in Goethe, was struck by Winckelmann. Goethe illustrates a union of the Romantic spirit, in its adventure, its variety, its profound subjectivity of soul, with Hellenism, in its transparency, its rationality, its desire of beauty—that mar-

---

[1] *Italiänische Reise. Bologna, 19 Oct. 1786.*

riage of Faust and Helena, of which the art of the nineteenth century is the child, the beautiful lad Euphorion, as Goethe conceives him, on the crags, in the "splendour of battle and in harness as for victory," his brows bound with light[1]. Goethe illustrates, too, the preponderance in this marriage of the Hellenic element; and that element, in its true essence, was made known to him by Winckelmann.

Breadth, centrality, with blitheness and repose, are the marks of Hellenic culture. Is such culture a lost art? The local, accidental colouring of its own age has passed from it; and the greatness that is dead looks greater when every link with what is slight and vulgar has been severed. We can only see it at all in the reflected, refined light which a great education creates for us. Can we bring down that ideal into the gaudy, perplexed light of modern life?

Certainly, for us of the modern world, with its conflicting claims, its entangled interests, distracted by so many sorrows, with many preoccupations, so bewildering an experience, the problem of unity with ourselves, in blitheness and repose, is far harder than it was for the Greek within the simple terms of antique life. Yet, not less than ever, the intellect demands completeness, centrality. It is this which Winckelmann imprints on the imagination of Goethe, at the beginning of life, in its original and simplest form, as in a fragment of Greek art itself, stranded on that littered, indeterminate shore of Germany in the eighteenth century. In Winckelmann, this type comes to him, not as in a book or a theory, but more importunately, because in a passionate life, in a personality. For Goethe, possessing all modern interests, ready to be lost in the perplexed currents of modern thought, he defines, in clearest outline, the eternal problem of culture—balance, unity with one's self, consummate Greek modelling.

It could no longer be solved, as in Phryne ascending naked out of the water, by perfection of bodily form, or any joyful union with the external world: the shadows had grown too long, the light too solemn, for that. It could hardly be solved, as in Pericles or Pheidias, by the direct exercise of any single talent: amid the manifold claims of our modern intellectual life, that could only

[1] *Faust, Th. ii. Act. 3.*

have ended in a thin, one-sided growth. Goethe's Hellenism was of another order, the *Allgemeinheit* and *Heiterkeit*, the completeness and serenity, of a watchful, exigent intellectualism. *Im Ganzen, Guten, Wahren, resolut zu leben:*—is Goethe's description of his own higher life; and what is meant by life in the whole—*im Ganzen?* It means the life of one for whom, over and over again, what was once precious has become indifferent. Every one who aims at the life of culture is met by many forms of it, arising out of the intense, laborious, one-sided development of some special talent. They are the brightest enthusiasms the world has to show: and it is not their part to weigh the claims which this or that alien form of genius makes upon them. But the proper instinct of self-culture cares not so much to reap all that those various forms of genius can give, as to find in them its own strength. The demand of the intellect is to feel itself alive. It must see into the laws, the operation, the intellectual reward of every divided form of culture; but only that it may measure the relation between itself and them. It struggles with those forms till its secret is won from each, and then lets each fall back into its place, in the supreme, artistic view of life. With a kind of passionate coldness, such natures rejoice to be away from and past their former selves, and above all, they are jealous of that abandonment to one special gift which really limits their capabilities. It would have been easy for Goethe, with the gift of a sensuous nature, to let it overgrow him. It comes easily and naturally, perhaps, to certain "other-worldly" natures to be even as the *Schöne Seele*, that ideal of gentle pietism, in *Wilhelm Meister:* but to the large vision of Goethe, this seemed to be a phase of life that a man might feel all round, and leave behind him. Again, it is easy to indulge the commonplace metaphysical instinct. But a taste for metaphysics may be one of those things which we must renounce, if we mean to mould our lives to artistic perfection. Philosophy serves culture, not by the fancied gift of absolute or transcendental knowledge, but by suggesting questions which help one to detect the passion, and strangeness, and dramatic contrasts of life.

But Goethe's culture did not remain "behind the veil": it ever emerged in the practical functions of art, in actual production. For him the problem came to be:—Can the blitheness and universality of the antique ideal be communicated to artistic productions, which shall contain the fulness of the experience of the modern world? We have seen that the development of the various forms of art has corresponded to the development of the thoughts of man concerning humanity, to the growing revelation of the mind to itself. Sculpture corresponds to the unperplexed, emphatic outlines of Hellenic humanism; painting to the mystic depth and intricacy of the middle age; music and poetry have their fortune in the modern world.

Let us understand by poetry all literary production which attains the power of giving pleasure by its form, as distinct from its matter. Only in this varied literary form can art command that width, variety, delicacy of resources, which will enable it to deal with the conditions of modern life. What modern art has to do in the service of culture is so to rearrange the details of modern life, so to reflect it, that it may satisfy the spirit. And what does the spirit need in the face of modern life? The sense of freedom. That naïve, rough sense of freedom, which supposes man's will to be limited, if at all, only by a will stronger than his, he can never have again. The attempt to represent it in art would have so little verisimilitude that it would be flat and uninteresting. The chief factor in the thoughts of the modern mind concerning itself is the intricacy, the universality of natural law, even in the moral order. For us, necessity is not, as of old, a sort of mythological personage without us, with whom we can do warfare. It is rather a magic web woven through and through us, like that magnetic system of which modern science speaks, penetrating us with a network, subtler than our subtlest nerves, yet bearing in it the central forces of the world. Can art represent men and women in these bewildering toils so as to give the spirit at least an equivalent for the sense of freedom? Certainly, in Goethe's romances, and even more in the romances of Victor Hugo, we have high examples of modern art dealing thus with modern life, regarding that life as the modern mind must regard it, yet reflecting upon it blitheness and repose. Natural laws we shall never modify, embarrass us as they may; but there is still something in the nobler or less noble attitude with which we watch their fatal combinations. In those romances of Goethe and Victor Hugo, in some excellent work done *after* them, this entanglement, this network of law, becomes the tragic situation, in which certain groups of noble men and women work out for themselves a supreme *dénouement*. Who, if he saw through all, would fret against the chain of circumstance which endows one at the end with those great experiences?

1867.

Conclusion[1]

Λέγει που Ἡράκλειτος ὅτι πάντα χωρεῖ καὶ οὐδὲν μένει

To regard all things and principles of things as inconstant modes or fashions has more and more become the tendency of modern thought. Let us begin with that which is without—our physical life. Fix upon it in one of its more exquisite intervals, the moment, for instance, of delicious recoil from the flood of water in summer heat. What is the whole physical life in that moment but a combination of natural elements to which science gives their names? But those elements, phosphorus and lime and delicate fibres, are present not in the human body alone: we detect them in places most remote from it. Our physical life is a perpetual motion of them—the passage of the blood, the waste and repairing of the lenses of the eye, the modification of the tissues of the brain under every ray of light and sound—processes which science reduces to simpler and more elementary forces. Like the elements of which we are composed, the action of these forces extends beyond us: it rusts iron and ripens corn. Far out on every side of us those elements are broadcast, driven in many currents; and birth and gesture and death and the springing of violets from the grave are but a few out of ten thousand resultant combinations. That clear, perpetual outline of face and limb is but an image of ours,

---

[1]This brief "Conclusion" was omitted in the second edition of this book, as I conceived it might possibly mislead some of those young men into whose hands it might fall. On the whole, I have thought it best to reprint it here, with some slight changes which bring it closer to my original meaning. I have dealt more fully in *Marius the Epicurean* with the thoughts suggested by it.

under which we group them—a design in a web, the actual threads of which pass out beyond it. This at least of flame-like our life has, that it is but the concurrence, renewed from moment to moment, of forces parting sooner or later on their ways.

Or if we begin with the inward world of thought and feeling, the whirlpool is still more rapid, the flame more eager and devouring. There it is no longer the gradual darkening of the eye, the gradual fading of colour from the wall—movements of the shore-side, where the water flows down indeed, though in apparent rest—but the race of the midstream, a drift of momentary acts of sight and passion and thought. At first sight experience seems to bury us under a flood of external objects, pressing upon us with a sharp and importunate reality, calling us out of ourselves in a thousand forms of action. But when reflexion begins to play upon those objects they are dissipated under its influence; the cohesive force seems suspended like some trick of magic; each object is loosed into a group of impressions—colour, odour, texture—in the mind of the observer. And if we continue to dwell in thought on this world, not of objects in the solidity with which language invests them, but of impressions, unstable, flickering, inconsistent, which burn and are extinguished with our consciousness of them, it contracts still further: the whole scope of observation is dwarfed into the narrow chamber of the individual mind. Experience, already reduced to a group of impressions, is ringed round for each one of us by that thick wall of personality through which no real voice has ever pierced on its way to us, or from us to that which we can only conjecture to be without. Every one of those impressions is the impression of the individual in his isolation, each mind keeping as a solitary prisoner its own dream of a world. Analysis goes a step further still, and assures us that those impressions of the individual mind to which, for each one of us, experience dwindles down, are in perpetual flight; that each of them is limited by time, and that as time is infinitely divisible, each of them is infinitely divisible also; all that is actual in it being a single moment, gone while we try to apprehend it, of which it may ever be more truly said that it has ceased to be than that it is. To such a tremulous wisp constantly re-forming itself on the stream, to a single sharp impression, with a sense in it, a relic more or less fleeting, of such moments gone by, what is real in our life fines itself down. It is with this movement, with the passage and dissolution of impressions, images, sensations, that analysis leaves off—that continual vanishing away, that strange, perpetual, weaving and unweaving of ourselves.

Philosophiren, says Novalis, *ist dephlegmatisiren, vivificiren*. The service of philosophy, of speculative culture, towards the human spirit, is to rouse, to startle it to a life of constant and eager observation. Every moment some form grows perfect in hand or face; some tone on the hills or the sea is choicer than the rest; some mood of passion or insight or intellectual excitement is irresistibly real and attractive to us,—for that moment only. Not the fruit of experience, but experience itself, is the end. A counted number of pulses only is given to us of a variegated, dramatic life. How may we see in them all that is to be seen in them by the finest senses? How shall we pass most swiftly from point to point, and be present always at the focus where the greatest number of vital forces unite in their purest energy?

To burn always with this hard, gem-like flame, to maintain this ecstasy, is success in life. In a sense it might even be said that our failure is to form habits: for, after all, habit is relative to a stereotyped world, and meantime it is only the roughness of the eye that makes any two persons, things, situations, seem alike. While all melts under our feet, we may well grasp at any exquisite passion, or any contribution to knowledge that seems by a lifted horizon to set the spirit free for a moment, or any stirring of the senses, strange dyes, strange colours, and curious odours, or work of the artist's hands, or the face of one's friend. Not to discriminate every moment some passionate attitude in those about us, and in the very brilliancy of their gifts some tragic dividing of forces on their ways, is, on this short day of frost and sun, to sleep before evening. With this sense of the splendour of our experience and of its awful brevity, gathering all we are into one desperate effort to see and touch, we shall hardly have time to make theories about the things we see and touch. What we have to do is to be for ever curiously testing new opinions and courting new impressions, never acquiescing in a facile orthodoxy, of Comte, or of Hegel, or of our own. Philosophical theories or ideas, as points of view, instruments of criticism, may help us to gather up what might otherwise pass unregarded by us. "Philosophy is the microscope of thought." The theory or idea or system which requires of us the sacrifice of any part of this experience, in consideration of some interest into which we cannot enter, or some abstract theory we have not identified with ourselves, or of what is only conventional, has no real claim upon us.

One of the most beautiful passages of Rousseau is that in the sixth book of the *Confessions*, where he describes the awakening in him of the literary sense. An undefinable taint of death had clung always about him, and now in early manhood he believed himself smitten by mortal disease. He asked himself how he might make as much as possible of the interval that remained; and he was not biassed by anything in his previous life when he decided that it must be by intellectual excitement, which he found just then in the clear, fresh writings of Voltaire. Well! we are all *condamnés*, as Victor Hugo says: we are all under sentence of death but with a sort of indefinite reprieve—*les hommes sont tous condamnés à mort avec des sursis indéfinis:* we have an interval, and then our place knows us no more. Some spend this interval in listlessness, some in high passions, the wisest, at least among "the children of this world," in art and song. For our one chance lies in expanding that interval, in getting as many pulsations as possible into the given time. Great passions may give us this quickened sense of life, ecstasy and sorrow of love, the various forms of enthusiastic activity, disinterested or otherwise, which come naturally to many of us. Only be sure it is passion—that it does yield you this fruit of a quickened, multiplied consciousness. Of such wisdom, the poetic passion, the desire of beauty, the love of art for its own sake, has most. For art comes to you proposing frankly to give nothing but the highest quality to your moments as they pass, and simply for those moments' sake.

1868.

THE END

IMAGINARY
PORTRAITS

The Child in the House

As Florian Deleal walked, one hot afternoon, he overtook by the wayside a poor aged man, and, as he seemed weary with the road, helped him on with the burden which he carried, a certain distance. And as the man told his story, it chanced that he named the place, a little place in the neighbourhood of a great city, where Florian had passed his earliest years, but which he had never since seen, and, the story told, went forward on his journey comforted. And that night, like a reward for his pity, a dream of that place came to Florian, a dream which did for him the office of the finer sort of memory, bringing its object to mind with a great clearness, yet, as sometimes happens in dreams raised a little above itself, and above ordinary retrospect. The true aspect of the place, especially of the house there in which he had lived as a child, the fashion of its doors, its hearths, its windows, the very scent upon the air of it, was with him in sleep for a season; only, with tints more musically blent on wall and floor, and some finer light and shadow running in and out along its curves and angles, and with all its little carvings daintier. He awoke with a sigh at the thought of almost thirty years which lay between him and that place, yet with a flutter of pleasure still within him at the fair light, as if it were a smile, upon it. And it happened that this accident of his dream was just the thing needed for the beginning of a certain design he then had in view, the noting, namely, of some things in the story of his spirit—in that process of brain-building by which we are, each one of us, what we are. With the image of the place so clear and favourable upon him, he fell to thinking of himself therein, and how his thoughts had grown up to him. In that half-spiritualised house he could watch the better, over again, the gradual expansion of the soul which had come to be there—of which indeed, through the law which makes the material objects about them so large an element in children's lives, it had actually become a part; inward and outward being woven through and through each other into one inextricable texture—half, tint and trace and accident of homely colour and form, from the wood and the bricks; half, mere soul-stuff, floated thither from who knows how far. In the house and garden of his dream he saw a child moving, and could divide the main streams at least of the winds that had played on him, and study so the first stage in that mental journey.

The *old house*, as when Florian talked of it afterwards he always called it, (as all children do, who can recollect a change of home, soon enough but not too soon to mark a period in their lives) really was an old house; and an element of French descent in its inmates—descent from Watteau, the old court-painter, one of whose gallant pieces still hung in one of the rooms—might explain, together with some other things, a noticeable trimness and comely whiteness about everything there—the curtains, the couches, the paint on the walls with which the light and shadow played so delicately; might explain also the tolerance of the great poplar in the garden, a tree most often despised by English people, but which French people love, having observed a certain fresh way its leaves have of dealing with the wind, making it sound, in never so slight a stirring of the air, like running water.

The old-fashioned, low wainscoting went round the rooms, and up the staircase with carved balusters and shadowy angles, landing half-way up at a broad window, with a swallow's nest below the sill, and the blossom of an old pear-tree showing across it in late April, against the blue, below which the perfumed juice of the find of fallen fruit in autumn was so fresh. At the next turning came the closet which held on its deep shelves the best china. Little angel faces and reedy flutings stood out round the fireplace of the children's room. And on the top of the house, above the large attic, where the white mice ran in the twilight—an infinite, unexplored wonderland of childish treasures, glass beads, empty scent-bottles still sweet, thrum of coloured silks, among its lumber—a flat space of roof, railed round, gave a view of the neighbouring steeples; for the house, as I said, stood near a great city, which sent up heavenwards, over the twisting weather-vanes, not seldom, its beds of rolling cloud and smoke, touched with storm or sunshine. But the child of whom I am writing did not hate the fog because of the crimson lights which fell from it sometimes upon the chimneys, and the whites which gleamed through its openings, on summer mornings, on turret or pavement. For it is false to suppose that a child's sense of beauty is dependent on any choiceness or special fineness, in the objects which present themselves to it, though this indeed comes to be the rule with most of us in later life; earlier, in some degree, we see inwardly; and the child finds for itself, and with unstinted delight, a difference for the sense, in those whites and reds through the smoke on very homely buildings, and in the gold of the dandelions at the road-side, just beyond the houses, where not a handful of earth is virgin and untouched, in the lack of better ministries to its desire of beauty.

This house then stood not far beyond the gloom and rumours of the town, among high garden-wall, bright all summer-time with Golden-rod, and brown-and-golden Wall-flower—*Flos Parietis*, as the children's Latin-reading father taught them to call it, while he was with them. Tracing back the threads of his complex spiritual habit, as he was used in after years to do, Florian found that he owed to the place many tones of sentiment afterwards customary with him, certain inward lights under which things most naturally presented themselves to him. The coming and going of travellers to the town along the way, the shadow of the streets, the sudden breath of the neighbouring gardens, the singular brightness of bright weather there, its singular darknesses which linked themselves in his mind to certain engraved illustrations in the old big Bible at home, the coolness of the dark, cavernous shops round the great church, with its giddy winding stair up to the pigeons and the bells—a citadel of peace in the heart of the trouble—all this acted on his childish fancy, so that ever afterwards the like aspects and incidents never failed to throw him into a well-recognised imaginative mood, seeming actually to have become a part of the texture of his mind. Also, Florian could trace home to this point a pervading preference in himself for a kind of comeliness and dignity, an *urbanity* literally, in modes of life, which he connected with the pale people of towns, and which made him susceptible to a kind of exquisite satisfaction in the trimness and well-considered grace of certain things and persons he afterwards met with, here and there, in his way through the world.

So the child of whom I am writing lived on there quietly; things without thus ministering to him, as he sat daily at the window with the birdcage hanging below it, and his mother taught him to read, wondering at the ease with which he learned, and at the quickness of his memory. The perfume of the little flowers of the lime-tree fell through the air upon them like rain; while time seemed to move ever more slowly to the murmur of the bees in it, till it almost stood still on June afternoons. How insignificant, at the moment, seem the influences of the sensible things which are tossed and fall and lie about us, so, or so, in the environment of early childhood. How indelibly, as we afterwards discover, they affect us; with what capricious attractions and associations they figure themselves on the white paper, the smooth wax, of our ingenuous souls, as "with lead in the rock for ever," giving form and feature, and as it were assigned house-room in our memory, to early experiences of feeling and thought, which abide with us ever afterwards, thus, and not otherwise. The realities and passions, the rumours of the greater world without, steal in upon us, each by its own special little passage-way, through the wall of custom about us; and never afterwards quite detach themselves from this or that accident, or trick, in the mode of their first entrance to us. Our susceptibilities, the discovery of our powers, manifold experiences—our various experiences of the coming and going of bodily pain, for instance—belong to this or the other well-remembered place in the material habitation—that little white room with the window across which the heavy blossoms could beat so peevishly in the wind, with just that particular catch or throb, such a sense of teasing in it, on gusty mornings; and the early habitation thus gradually becomes a sort of material shrine or sanctuary of sentiment; a system of visible symbolism interweaves itself through all our thoughts and passions; and irresistibly, little shapes, voices, accidents—the angle at which the sun in the morning fell on the pillow—become parts of the great chain wherewith we are bound.

Thus far, for Florian, what all this had determined was a peculiarly strong sense of home—so forcible a motive with all of us—prompting to us our customary love of the earth, and the larger part of our fear of death, that revulsion we have from it, as from something strange, untried, unfriendly; though life-long imprisonment, they tell you, and final banishment from home is a thing bitterer still; the looking forward to but a short space, a mere childish *goûter* and dessert of it, before the end, being so great a resource of effort to pilgrims and wayfarers, and the soldier in distant quarters, and lending, in lack of that, some power of solace to the thought of sleep in the home churchyard, at least—dead cheek by dead cheek, and with the rain soaking in upon one from above.

So powerful is this instinct, and yet accidents like those I have been speaking of so mechanically determine it; its essence being indeed the early familiar, as constituting our ideal, or typical conception, of rest and security. Out of so many possible conditions, just this for you and that for me, brings ever the unmistakeable realisation of the delightful *chez soi*; this for the Englishman, for me and you, with the closely-drawn white curtain and the shaded lamp; that, quite other, for the wandering Arab, who folds his tent every morning, and makes his sleeping-place among haunted ruins, or in old tombs.

With Florian then the sense of home became singularly intense, his good fortune being that the special character of his home was in itself so essentially home-like. As after many wanderings I have come to fancy that some parts of Surrey and Kent are, for Englishmen, the true landscape, true home-counties, by right, partly, of a certain earthy warmth in the yellow of the sand below their gorse-bushes, and of a certain grey-blue mist after rain, in the hollows of the hills there, welcome to fatigued eyes, and never seen farther south; so I think that the sort of house I have described, with precisely those proportions of red-brick and green, and with a just perceptible monotony in the subdued order of it, for its distinguishing note, is for Englishmen at least typically home-life. And so for Florian that general human instinct was reinforced by this special home-likeness in the place his wandering soul had happened to light on, as, in the second degree, its body and earthly tabernacle; the sense of harmony between his

soul and its physical environment became, for a time at least, like
perfectly played music, and the life led there singularly tranquil
and filled with a curious sense of self-possession. The love of security, of an habitually undisputed standing-ground or sleeping-
place, came to count for much in the generation and correcting of
his thoughts, and afterwards as a salutary principle of restraint in
all his wanderings of spirit. The wistful yearning towards home,
in absence from it, as the shadows of evening deepened, and he
followed in thought what was doing there from hour to hour,
interpreted to him much of a yearning and regret he experienced
afterwards, towards he knew not what, out of strange ways of
feeling and thought in which, from time to time, his spirit found
itself alone; and in the tears shed in such absences there seemed
always to be some soul-subduing foretaste of what his last tears
might be.

And the sense of security could hardly have been deeper, the
quiet of the child's soul being one with the quiet of its home, a
place "inclosed" and "sealed." But upon this assured place, upon
the child's assured soul which resembled it, there came floating in
from the larger world without, as at windows left ajar un-
knowingly, or over the high garden walls, two streams of impressions, the sentiments of beauty and pain—recognitions of the
visible, tangible, audible loveliness of things, as a very real and
somewhat tyrannous element in them—and of the sorrow of the
world, of grown people and children and animals, as a thing not
to be put by in them. From this point he could trace two predominant processes of mental change in him—the growth of an almost
diseased sensibility to the spectacle of suffering, and, parallel
with this, the rapid growth of a certain capacity of fascination by
bright colour and choice form—the sweet curvings, for instance,
of the lips of those who seemed to him comely persons, modulated
in such delicate unison to the things they said or sang,—marking
early the activity in him of a more than customary sensuousness,
"the lust of the eye," as the Preacher says, which might lead him,
one day, how far! Could he have foreseen the weariness of the
way! In music sometimes the two sorts of impressions came together, and he would weep, to the surprise of older people. Tears of
joy too the child knew, also to older people's surprise; real tears,

once, of relief from long-strung, childish expectation, when he found returned at evening, with new roses in her cheeks, the little sister who had been to a place where there was a wood, and brought back for him a treasure of fallen acorns, and black crow's feathers, and his peace at finding her again near him mingled all night with some intimate sense of the distant forest, the rumour of its breezes, with the glossy blackbirds aslant and the branches lifted in them, and of the perfect nicety of the little cups that fell. So those two elementary apprehensions of the tenderness and of the colour in things grew apace in him, and were seen by him afterwards to send their roots back into the beginnings of life.

Let me note first some of the occasions of his recognition of the element of pain in things—incidents, now and again, which seemed suddenly to awake in him the whole force of that sentiment which Goethe has called the *Weltschmerz*, and in which the concentrated sorrow of the world seemed suddenly to lie heavy upon him. A book lay in an old book-case, of which he cared to remember one picture—a woman sitting, with hands bound behind her, the dress, the cap, the hair, folded with a simplicity which touched him strangely, as if not by her own hands, but with some ambiguous care at the hands of others—Queen Marie Antoinette, on her way to execution—we all remember David's drawing, meant merely to make her ridiculous. The face that had been so high had learned to be mute and resistless; but out of its very resistlessness, seemed now to call on men to have pity, and forbear; and he took note of that, as he closed the book, as a thing to look at again, if he should at any time find himself tempted to be cruel. Again, he would never quite forget the appeal in the small sister's face, in the garden under the lilacs, terrified at a spider lighted on her sleeve. He could trace back to the look then noted a certain mercy he conceived always for people in fear, even of little things, which seemed to make him, though but for a moment, capable of almost any sacrifice of himself. Impressible, susceptible persons, indeed, who had had their sorrows, lived about him; and this sensibility was due in part to the tacit influence of their presence, enforcing upon him habitually the fact that there are those who pass their days, as a matter of course, in a sort of "going quietly." Most poignantly of all he could recall, in unfading minutest circumstance, the cry on the stair, sounding bitterly through the house, and struck into his soul for ever, of an aged woman, his father's sister, come now to announce his death in distant India; how it seemed to make the aged woman like a child again; and, he knew not why, but this fancy was full of pity to him. There were the little sorrows of the dumb animals too—of the white angora, with a dark tail like an ermine's, and a face like a flower, who fell into a lingering sickness, and became quite delicately human in its valetudinarianism, and came to have a hundred different expressions of voice—how it grew worse and worse, till it began to feel the light too much for it, and at last, after one wild morning of pain, the little soul flickered away from the body, quite worn to death already, and now but feebly retaining it.

So he wanted another pet; and as there were starlings about the place, which could be taught to speak, one of them was caught, and he meant to treat it kindly; but in the night its young ones could be heard crying after it, and the responsive cry of the mother-bird towards them; and at last, with the first light, though not till after some debate with himself, he went down and opened the cage, and saw a sharp bound of the prisoner up to her nestlings; and therewith came the sense of remorse,—that he too was become an accomplice in moving, to the limit of his small power, the springs and handles of that great machine in things, constructed so ingeniously to play pain-fugues on the delicate nerve-work of living creatures.

I have remarked how, in the process of our brain-building, as the house of thought in which we live gets itself together, like some airy bird's-nest of floating thistle-down and chance straws, compact at last, little accidents have their consequence; and thus it happened that, as he walked one evening, a garden gate, usually closed, stood open; and lo! within, a great red hawthorn in full flower, embossing heavily the bleached and twisted trunk and branches, so aged that there were but few green leaves thereon—a plumage of tender, crimson fire out of the heart of the dry wood. The perfume of the tree had now and again reached him, in the currents of the wind, over the wall, and he had wondered what might be behind it, and was now allowed to fill his arms with the flowers—flowers enough for all the old blue-china pots along the chimney-piece, making *fête* in the children's room. Was it some periodic moment in the expansion of soul within him, or mere trick of heat in the heavily-laden summer air? But the beauty of the thing struck home to him feverishly; and in dreams all night he loitered along a magic roadway of crimson flowers, which seemed to open ruddily in thick, fresh masses about his feet, and fill softly all the little hollows in the banks on either side. Always afterwards, summer by summer, as the flowers came on, the blossom of the red hawthorn still seemed to him absolutely the reddest of all things; and the goodly crimson, still alive in the works of old Venetian masters or old Flemish tapestries, called out always from afar the recollection of the flame in those perishing little petals, as it pulsed gradually out of them, kept long in the drawers of an old cabinet. Also then, for the first time, he seemed to experience a passionateness in his relation to fair outward objects, an inexplicable excitement in their presence, which disturbed him, and from which he half longed to be free. A touch of regret or desire mingled all night with the remembered presence of the red flowers, and their perfume in the darkness about him; and the longing for some undivined, entire possession of them was the beginning of a revelation to him, growing ever clearer, with the coming of the gracious summer guise of fields and trees and persons in each succeeding year, of a certain, at times seemingly exclusive, predominance in his interests, of beautiful physical things, a kind of tyranny of the senses over him.

In later years he came upon philosophies which occupied him much in the estimate of the proportion of the sensuous and the ideal elements in human knowledge, the relative parts they bear in it; and, in his intellectual scheme, was led to assign very little to the abstract thought, and much to its sensible vehicle or occasion. Such metaphysical speculation did but reinforce what was instinctive in his way of receiving the world, and for him, everywhere, that sensible vehicle or occasion became, perhaps only too surely, the necessary concomitant of any perception of things, real enough to be of any weight or reckoning, in his house of thought. There were times when he could think of the necessity he was under of associating all thoughts to touch and sight, as a sympathetic link between himself and actual, feeling, living objects; a protest in favour of real men and women against mere grey, unreal abstractions; and he remembered gratefully how the Christian religion, hardly less than the religion of the ancient Greeks, translating so much of its spiritual verity into things that may be seen, condescends in part to sanction this infirmity, if so it be, of our human existence, wherein the world of sense is so much with us, and welcomed this thought as a kind of keeper and sentinel over his soul therein. But certainly, he came more and more to be unable to care for, or think of soul but as in an actual body, or of any world but that wherein are water and trees, and where men and women look, so or so, and press actual hands. It was the trick even his pity learned, fastening those who suffered in anywise to his affections by a kind of sensible attachments. He would think of Julian, fallen into incurable sickness, as spoiled in the sweet blossom of his skin like pale amber, and his honey-like hair; of Cecil, early dead, as cut off from the lilies, from golden summer days, from women's voices; and then what comforted him a little was the thought of the turning of the child's flesh to violets in the turf above him. And thinking of the very poor, it was not the things which most men care most for that he yearned to give them; but fairer roses, perhaps, and power to taste quite as they will, at their ease and not task-burdened, a certain desirable, clear light in the new morning, through which sometimes he had noticed them, quite unconscious of it, on their way to their early toil.

So he yielded himself to these things, to be played upon by them like a musical instrument, and began to note with deepening watchfulness, but always with some puzzled, unutterable longing in his enjoyment, the phases of the seasons and of the growing or waning day, down even to the shadowy changes wrought on bare wall or ceiling—the light cast up from the snow, bringing out their darkest angles; the brown light in the cloud, which meant rain; that almost too austere clearness, in the protracted light of the lengthening day, before warm weather began, as if it lingered but to make a severer workday, with the school-books opened earlier and later; that beam of June sunshine, at last, as he lay awake before the time, a way of gold-dust across the darkness; all the humming, the freshness, the perfume of the garden seemed to lie upon it—and coming in one afternoon in September, along the red gravel walk, to look for a basket of yellow crab-apples left in the cool, old parlour, he remembered it the more, and how the colours struck upon him, because a wasp on one bitten apple stung him, and he felt the passion of sudden, severe pain. For this too brought its curious reflexions; and, in relief from it, he would wonder over it—how it had then been with him—puzzled at the depth of the charm or spell over him, which lay, for a little while at least, in the mere absence of pain; once, especially, when an older boy taught him to make flowers of sealing-wax, and he had burnt his hand badly at the lighted taper, and been unable to sleep. He remembered that also afterwards, as a sort of typical thing—a white vision of heat about him, clinging closely, through the languid scent of the ointments put upon the place to make it well.

Also, as he felt this pressure upon him of the sensible world, then, as often afterwards, there would come another sort of curious questioning how the last impressions of eye and ear might happen to him, how they would find him—the scent of the last flower, the soft yellowness of the last morning, the last recognition of some object of affection, hand or voice; it could not be but that the latest look of the eyes, before their final closing, would be strangely vivid; one would go with the hot tears, the cry, the touch of the wistful bystander, impressed how deeply on one! or would it be, perhaps, a mere frail retiring of all things, great or little, away from one, into a level distance?

For with this desire of physical beauty mingled itself early the fear of death—the fear of death intensified by the desire of beauty. Hitherto he had never gazed upon dead faces, as sometimes, afterwards, at the *Morgue* in Paris, or in that fair cemetery at Munich, where all the dead must go and lie in state before burial, behind glass windows, among the flowers and incense and holy candles— the aged clergy with their sacred ornaments, the young men in their dancing-shoes and spotless white linen—after which visits, those waxen, resistless faces would always live with him for many days, making the broadest sunshine sickly. The child had heard indeed of the death of his father, and how, in the Indian station, a fever had taken him, so that though not in action he had yet died as a soldier; and hearing of the "resurrection of the just," he could think of him as still abroad in the world, somehow, for his protection—a grand, though perhaps rather terrible figure, in beautiful soldier's things, like the figure in the picture of Joshua's Vision in the Bible—and of that, round which the mourners moved so softly, and afterwards with such solemn singing, as but a worn-out garment left at a deserted lodging. So it was, until on a summer day he walked with his mother through a fair churchyard. In a bright dress he rambled among the graves, in the gay weather, and so came, in one corner, upon an open grave for a child—a dark space on the brilliant grass—the black mould lying heaped up round it, weighing down the little jewelled branches of the dwarf rose-bushes in flower. And therewith came, full-grown, never wholly to leave him, with the certainty that even children do sometimes die, the physical horror of death, with its wholly selfish recoil from the association of lower forms of life, and the suffocating weight above. No benign, grave figure in beautiful soldier's things any longer abroad in the world for his protection! only a few poor, piteous bones; and above them, possibly, a certain sort of figure he hoped not to see. For sitting one day in the garden below an open window, he heard people talking, and could not but listen, how, in a sleepless hour, a sick woman had seen one of the dead sitting beside her, come to call her hence; and from the broken talk evolved with much clearness the notion that not all those dead people had really departed to the churchyard, nor were quite so motionless as they looked, but led a secret, half-fugitive life in their old homes, quite free by night, though sometimes visible in the day, dodging from room to room, with no great goodwill towards those who shared the place with them. All night the figure sat beside him in the reveries of his broken sleep, and was not quite gone in the morning—an odd, irreconcileable new member of the household, making the sweet familiar chambers unfriendly and suspect by its uncertain presence. He could have hated the dead he had pitied so, for being thus. Afterwards he came to think of those poor, home-returning ghosts, which all men have fancied to themselves—the *revenants*—pathetically, as crying, or beating with vain hands at the doors, as the wind came, their cries indistinguishable in it as a wilder inner note. But, always making death more unfamiliar still, that old experience would ever, from time to time, return to him; even in the living he sometimes caught its likeness; at any time or place, in a moment, the faint atmosphere of the chamber of death would be breathed around him, and the image with the bound chin, the quaint smile, the straight, stiff feet, shed itself across the air upon the bright carpet, amid the gayest company, or happiest communing with himself.

To most children the sombre questionings to which impressions like these attach themselves, if they come at all, are actually suggested by religious books, which therefore they often regard with much secret distaste, and dismiss, as far as possible, from their habitual thoughts as a too depressing element in life. To Florian such impressions, these misgivings as to the ultimate tendency of the years, of the relationship between life and death, had been suggested spontaneously in the natural course of his mental growth by a strong innate sense for the soberer tones in things, further strengthened by actual circumstances; and re-ligious sentiment, that system of biblical ideas in which he had been brought up, presented itself to him as a thing that might soften and dignify, and light up as with a "lively hope," a melan-choly already deeply settled in him. So he yielded himself easily to religious impressions, and with a kind of mystical appetite for sacred things; the more as they came to him through a saintly person who loved him tenderly, and believed that this early pre-occupation with them already marked the child out for a saint. He began to love, for their own sakes, church lights, holy days, all that belonged to the comely order of the sanctuary, the secrets of its white linen, and holy vessels, and fonts of pure water; and its hieratic purity and simplicity became the type of something he desired always to have about him in actual life. He pored over the pictures in religious books, and knew by heart the exact mode in which the wrestling angel grasped Jacob, how Jacob looked in his mysterious sleep, how the bells and pomegranates were attached to the hem of Aaron's vestment, sounding sweetly as he glided over the turf of the holy place. His way of conceiving religion came then to be in effect what it ever afterwards remained—a sacred history indeed, but still more a sacred ideal, a transcendent version or representation, under intenser and more expressive light and shade, of human life and its familiar or exceptional incidents, birth, death, marriage, youth, age, tears, joy, rest, sleep, waking—a mirror, towards which men might turn away their eyes from vanity and dullness, and see themselves therein as angels, with their daily meat and drink, even, become a kind of sacred transaction—a complementary strain or burden, applied to our every-day existence, whereby the stray snatches of music in it re-set themselves, and fall into the scheme of some higher and more consistent harmony. A place adumbrated itself in his thoughts, wherein those sacred personalities, which are at once the reflex and the pattern of our nobler phases of life, housed themselves; and this region in his intellectual scheme all subsequent experience did but tend still further to realise and define. Some ideal, hieratic persons he would always need to occupy it and keep a warmth there. And he could hardly understand those who felt no such need at all, finding themselves quite happy without such heavenly companionship, and sacred double of their life, beside them.

Thus a constant substitution of the typical for the actual took place in his thoughts. Angels might be met by the way, under English elm or beech-tree; mere messengers seemed like angels, bound on celestial errands; a deep mysticity brooded over real meetings and partings; marriages were made in heaven; and deaths also, with hands of angels thereupon, to bear soul and body quietly asunder, each to its appointed rest. All the acts and accidents of daily life borrowed a sacred colour and significance; the very colours of things became themselves weighty with meanings like the sacred stuffs of Moses' tabernacle, full of penitence or peace. Sentiment, congruous in the first instance only with those divine transactions, the deep, effusive unction of the House of Bethany, was assumed as the due attitude for the reception of our every-day existence; and for a time he walked through the world in a sustained, not unpleasurable awe, generated by the habitual recognition, beside every circumstance and event of life, of its celestial correspondent.

Sensibility—the desire of physical beauty—a strange biblical awe, which made any reference to the unseen act on him like solemn music—these qualities the child took away with him, when, at about the age of twelve years, he left the old house, and was taken to live in another place. He had never left home before, and, anticipating much from this change, had long dreamed over it, jealously counting the days till the time fixed for departure should come; had been a little careless about others even, in his strong desire for it—when Lewis fell sick, for instance, and they must wait still two days longer. At last the morning came, very fine; and all things—the very pavement with its dust, at the road-side—seemed to have a white, pearl-like lustre in them. They were to travel by a favourite road on which he had often walked a certain distance, and on one of those two prisoner days, when Lewis was sick, had walked farther than ever before, in his great desire to reach the new place. They had started and gone a little way when a pet bird was found to have been left behind, and must even now—so it presented itself to him—have already all the appealing fierceness and wild self-pity at heart of one left by others to perish of hunger in a closed house; and he returned to fetch it, himself in hardly less stormy distress. But as he passed in search of it from room to room, lying so pale, with a look of meekness in their denudation, and at last through that little, stripped white room, the aspect of the place touched him like the face of one dead; and a clinging back towards it came over him, so intense that he knew it would last long, and spoiling all his pleasure in the realisation of a thing so eagerly anticipated. And so, with the bird found, but himself in an agony of home-sickness, thus capriciously sprung up within him, he was driven quickly away, far into the rural distance, so fondly speculated on, of that favourite country-road.

[1878]

A Prince of Court Painters

Extracts From an Old French Journal

Valenciennes, *September* 1701.

They have been renovating my father's large workroom. That delightful, tumble-down old place has lost its moss-grown tiles and
the green weather-stains we have known all our lives on the high
whitewashed wall, opposite which we sit, in the little sculptor's
yard, for the coolness, in summertime. Among old Watteau's
work-people came his son, "the genius," my father's godson and
namesake, a dark-haired youth, whose large, unquiet eyes seemed
perpetually wandering to the various drawings which lie exposed
here. My father will have it that he is a genius indeed, and a
painter born. We have had our September Fair in the *Grande
Place*, a wonderful stir of sound and colour in the wide, open
space beneath our windows. And just where the crowd was busi-
est young Antony was found, hoisted into one of those empty
niches of the old *Hôtel de Ville*, sketching the scene to the life,
but with a kind of grace—a marvellous tact of omission, as my
father pointed out to us, in dealing with the vulgar reality seen
from one's own window—which has made trite old Harlequin,
Clown, and Columbine, seem like people in some fairyland; or
like infinitely clever tragic actors, who, for the humour of the
thing, have put on motley for once, and are able to throw a world
of serious innuendo into their burlesque looks, with a sort of comedy which shall be but tragedy seen from the other side. He
brought his sketch to our house to-day, and I was present when
my father questioned him and commended his work. But the lad

seemed not greatly pleased, and left untasted the glass of old Malaga which was offered to him. His father will hear nothing of educating him as a painter. Yet he is not ill-to-do, and has lately built himself a new stone house, big and grey and cold. Their old plastered house with the black timbers, in the *Rue des Cardinaux*, was prettier; dating from the time of the Spaniards, and one of the oldest in Valenciennes.

October 1701.

Chiefly through the solicitations of my father, old Watteau has consented to place Antony with a teacher of painting here. I meet him betimes on the way to his lessons, as I return from Mass; for he still works with the masons, but making the most of late and early hours, of every moment of liberty. And then he has the feast-days, of which there are so many in this old-fashioned place. Ah! such gifts as his, surely, may once in a way make much industry seem worth while. He makes a wonderful progress. And yet, far from being set-up, and too easily pleased with what, after all, comes to him so easily, he has, my father thinks, too little self-approval for ultimate success. He is apt, in truth, to fall out too hastily with himself and what he produces. Yet here also there is the "golden mean." Yes! I could fancy myself offended by a sort of irony which sometimes crosses the half-melancholy sweetness of manner habitual with him; only that as I can see, he treats himself to the same quality.

October 1701.

Antony Watteau comes here often now. It is the instinct of a natural fineness in him, to escape when he came from that blank stone house, with so little to interest, and that homely old man and woman. The rudeness of his home has turned his feeling for even the simpler graces of life into a physical want, like hunger or thirst, which might come to greed; and methinks he perhaps over-values these things. Still, made as he is, his hard fate in that rude place must needs touch one. And then, he profits by the experience of my father, who has much knowledge in matters of art beyond his own art of sculpture; and Antony is not unwelcome to him. In these last rainy weeks especially, when he can't sketch out of doors, when the wind only half dries the pavement before another torrent comes, and people stay at home, and the only sound from without is the creaking of a restless shutter on its hinges, or the march across the *Place* of those weary soldiers, coming and going so interminably, one hardly knows whether to or from battle with the English and the Austrians, from victory or defeat:—Well! he has become like one of our family. "He will go far!" my father declares. He would go far, in the literal sense, if he might—to Paris, to Rome. It must be admitted that our Valenciennes is a quiet, nay! a sleepy place; sleepier than ever since it became French, and ceased to be so near the frontier. The grass is growing deep on our old ramparts, and it is pleasant to walk there—to walk there and muse; pleasant for a tame, unambitious soul such as mine.

December 1702.

Antony Watteau left us for Paris this morning. It came upon us quite suddenly. They amuse themselves in Paris. A scene-painter we have here, well known in Flanders, has been engaged to work in one of the Parisian play-houses; and young Watteau, of whom he had some slight knowledge, has departed in his company. He doesn't know it was I who persuaded the scene-painter to take him; that he would find the lad useful. We offered him our little presents—fine thread-lace of our own making for his ruffles, and the like; for one must make a figure in Paris, and he is slim and well-formed. For myself, I presented him with a silken purse I had long ago embroidered for another. Well! we shall follow his fortunes (of which I for one feel quite sure) at a distance. Old Watteau didn't know of his departure, and has been here in great anger.

December 1703.

Twelve months to-day since Antony went to Paris! The first struggle must be a sharp one for an unknown lad in that vast, overcrowded place, even if he be as clever as young Antony Watteau. We may think, however, that he is on the way to his chosen end, for he returns not home; though, in truth, he tells those poor old people very little of himself. The apprentices of the M. Méta-yer for whom he works, labour all day long, each at a single part only,—*coiffure*, or robe, or hand,—of the cheap pictures of religion or fantasy he exposes for sale at a low price along the footways of the *Pont Notre-Dame*. Antony is already the most skilful of them, and seems to have been promoted of late to work on church pictures. I like the thought of that. He receives three *livres* a week for his pains, and his soup daily.

May 1705.

Antony Watteau has parted from the dealer in pictures *à bon marché*, and works now with a painter of furniture pieces (those headpieces for doors and the like, now in fashion) who is also *concierge* of the Palace of the Luxembourg. Antony is actually lodged somewhere in that grand place, which contains the king's collection of the Italian pictures he would so willingly copy. Its gardens also are magnificent, with something, as we understand from him, altogether of a novel kind in their disposition and embellishment. Ah! how I delight myself, in fancy at least, in those beautiful gardens, freer and trimmed less stiffly than those of other royal houses. Me-thinks I see him there, when his long summerday's work is over, enjoying the cool shade of the stately, broad-foliaged trees, each of which is a great courtier, though it has its way almost as if it belonged to that open and unbuilt country beyond, over which the sun is sinking.

His thoughts, however, in the midst of all this, are not wholly away from home, if I may judge by the subject of a picture he hopes to sell for as much as sixty *livres*—*Un Départ de Troupes*, Soldiers Departing—one of those scenes of military life one can study so well here at Valenciennes.

June 1705.

Young Watteau has returned home—proof, with a character so independent as his, that things have gone well with him; and (it is agreed!) stays with us, instead of in the stone-mason's house. The old people suppose he comes to us for the sake of my father's instruction. French people as we are become, we are still old Flemish, if not at heart, yet on the surface. Even in *French* Flanders, at Douai and Saint Omer, as I understand, in the churches and in people's houses, as may be seen from the very streets, there is noticeable a minute and scrupulous air of care-taking and neatness. Antony Watteau remarks this more than ever on returning to Valenciennes, and savours greatly, after his lodging in Paris, our Flemish cleanliness, lover as he is of distinc-tion and elegance. Those worldly graces he seemed when a young lad almost to hunger and thirst for, as though truly the mere adornments of life were its necessaries, he already takes as if he had been always used to them. And there is something noble— shall I say?—in his half-disdainful way of serving himself with what he still, as I think, secretly values over-much. There is an air of seemly thought—*le bel sérieux*—about him, which makes me think of one of those grave old Dutch statesmen in their youth, such as that famous William the Silent. And yet the effect of this first success of his (of more importance than its mere money value, as insuring for the future the full play of his natural powers) I can trace like the bloom of a flower upon him; and he has, now and then, the gaieties which from time to time, surely, must refresh all true artists, however hard-working and "painful."

July 1705.

The charm of all this—his physiognomy and manner of being— has touched even my young brother, Jean-Baptiste. He is greatly taken with Antony, clings to him almost too attentively, and will be nothing but a painter, though my father would have trained him to follow his own profession. It may do the child good. He needs the expansion of some generous sympathy or sentiment in that close little soul of his, as I have thought, watching some-times how his small face and hands are moved in sleep. A child of ten who cares only to save and possess, to hoard his tiny savings! Yet he is not otherwise selfish, and loves us all with a warm heart. Just now it is the moments of Antony's company he counts, like a little miser. Well! that may save him perhaps from developing a certain meanness of character I have sometimes feared for him.

August 1705.

We returned home late this summer evening—Antony Watteau, my father and sisters, young Jean-Baptiste, and myself—from an excursion to Saint-Amand, in celebration of Antony's last day with us. After visiting the great abbey-church and its range of chapels, with their costly encumbrance of carved shrines and golden reliquaries and funeral scutcheons in the coloured glass, half seen through a rich enclosure of marble and brasswork, we supped at the little inn in the forest. Antony, looking well in his new-fashioned, long-skirted coat, and taller than he really is, made us bring our cream and wild strawberries out of doors, ranging ourselves according to his judgment (for a hasty sketch in that big pocket-book he carries) on the soft slope of one of those fresh spaces in the wood, where the trees unclose a little, while Jean-Baptiste and my youngest sister danced a minuet on the grass, to the notes of some strolling lutanist who had found us out. He is visibly cheerful at the thought of his return to Paris, and became for a moment freer and more animated than I have ever yet seen him, as he discoursed to us about the paintings of Peter Paul Rubens in the church here. His words, as he spoke of them, seemed full of a kind of rich sunset with some moving glory within it. Yet I like far better than any of these pictures of Rubens a work of that old Dutch master, Peter Porbus, which hangs, though almost out of sight indeed, in our church at home. The patron saints, simple, and standing firmly on either side, present two homely old people to Our Lady enthroned in the midst, with the look and attitude of one for whom, amid her "glories" (depicted in dim little circular pictures, set in the openings of a chaplet of pale flowers around her) all feelings are over, except a great pitifulness. Her robe of shadowy blue suits my eyes better far than the hot flesh-tints of the Medicean ladies of the great Peter Paul, in spite of that amplitude and royal ease of action under their stiff court costumes, at which Antony Watteau declares himself in dismay.

August 1705.

I am just returned from early Mass. I lingered long after the office was ended, watching, pondering how in the world one could help a small bird which had flown into the church but could find no way out again. I suspect it will remain there, fluttering round and round distractedly, far up under the arched roof, till it dies exhausted. I seem to have heard of a writer who likened man's life to a bird passing just once only, on some winter night, from window to window, across a cheerfully-lighted hall. The bird, taken captive by the ill-luck of a moment, re-tracing its issueless circle till it expires within the close vaulting of that great stone church:—human life may be like that bird too!

Antony Watteau returned to Paris yesterday. Yes!—Certainly, great heights of achievement would seem to lie before him; access to regions whither one may find it increasingly hard to follow him even in imagination, and figure to one's self after what manner his life moves therein.

January 1709.

Antony Watteau has competed for what is called the *Prix de Rome*, desiring greatly to profit by the grand establishment founded at Rome by King Lewis the Fourteenth, for the encouragement of French artists. He obtained only the second place, but does not renounce his desire to make the journey to Italy. Could I save enough by careful economies for that purpose? It might be conveyed to him in some indirect way that would not offend.

February 1712.

We read, with much pleasure for all of us, in the *Gazette* to-day, among other events of the great world, that Antony Watteau had been elected to the Academy of Painting under the new title of *Peintre des Fêtes Galantes*, and had been named also *Peintre du Roi*. My brother, Jean-Baptiste, ran to tell the news to old Jean-Philippe and Michelle Watteau.

A new manner of painting! The old furniture of people's rooms must needs be changed throughout, it would seem, to accord with this painting; or rather, the painting is designed exclusively to suit one particular kind of apartment. A manner of painting greatly prized, as we understand, by those Parisian judges who have had the best opportunity of acquainting themselves with whatever is most enjoyable in the arts:—such is the achievement of the young Watteau! He looks to receive more orders for his work than he will be able to execute. He will certainly relish—he, so elegant, so hungry for the colours of life—a free intercourse with those wealthy lovers of the arts, M. de Crozat, M. de Julienne, the Abbé de la Roque, the Count de Caylus, and M. Gersaint, the famous dealer in pictures, who are so anxious to lodge him in their fine *hôtels*, and to have him of their company at their country houses. Paris, we hear, has never been wealthier and more luxurious than now: and the great ladies outbid each other to carry his work upon their very fans. Those vast fortunes, however, seem to change hands very rapidly. And Antony's new manner? I am unable even to divine it—to conceive the trick and effect of it—at all. Only, something of lightness and coquetry I discern there, at variance, methinks, with his own singular gravity and even sadness of mien and mind, more answerable to the stately apparelling of the age of Henry the Fourth, or of Lewis the Thirteenth, in these old, sombre Spanish houses of ours.

March 1713.

We have all been very happy,—Jean-Baptiste as if in a delightful dream. Antony Watteau, being consulted with regard to the lad's training as a painter, has most generously offered to receive him for his own pupil. My father, for some reason unknown to me, seemed to hesitate at the first; but Jean-Baptiste, whose enthusiasm for Antony visibly refines and beautifies his whole nature, has won the necessary permission, and this dear young brother will leave us tomorrow. Our regrets and his, at his parting from us for the first time, overtook our joy at his good fortune by surprise, at the last moment, just as we were about to bid each other goodnight. For a while there had seemed to be an uneasiness under our

cheerful talk, as if each one present were concealing something
with an effort; and it was Jean-Baptiste himself who gave way at
last. And then we sat down again, still together, and allowed free
play to what was in our hearts, almost till morning, my sisters
weeping much. I know better how to control myself. In a few days
that delightful new life will have begun for him: and I have made
him promise to write often to us. With how small a part of my
whole life shall I be really living at Valenciennes!

January 1714.

Jean-Philippe Watteau has received a letter from his son to-day.
Old Michelle Watteau, whose sight is failing, though she still
works (half by touch, indeed) at her pillow-lace, was glad to hear
me read the letter aloud more than once. It recounts—how modestly, and almost as a matter of course!—his late successes. And
yet!—does he, in writing to these old people, purposely underrate
his great good fortune and seeming happiness, not to shock them
too much by the contrast between the delicate enjoyments of the
life he now leads among the wealthy and refined, and that bald
existence of theirs in his old home? A life, agitated, exigent, unsatisfying! That is what this letter really discloses, below so attractive a surface. As his gift expands so does that incurable
restlessness one supposed but the humour natural to a promising
youth who had still everything to do. And now the only realised
enjoyment he has of all this might seem to be the thought of the
independence it has purchased him, so that he can escape from
one lodging-place to another, just as it may please him. He has
already deserted, somewhat incontinently, more than one of
those fine houses, the liberal air of which he used so greatly to
affect, and which have so readily received him. Has he failed
truly to grasp the fact of his great success and the rewards that lie
before him? At all events, he seems, after all, not greatly to value
that dainty world he is now privileged to enter, and has certainly
but little relish for his own works—those works which I for one so
thirst to see.

March 1714.

We were all—Jean-Philippe, Michelle Watteau, and ourselves—
half in expectation of a visit from Antony; and to-day, quite suddenly, he is with us. I was lingering after early Mass this morning
in the church of Saint Vaast. It is good for me to be there. Our
people lie under one of the great marble slabs before the *jubé*,
some of the memorial brass balusters of which are engraved with
their names and the dates of their decease. The settle of carved
oak which runs all round the wide nave is my father's own work.
The quiet spaciousness of the place is itself like a meditation, an
"act of recollection," and clears away the confusions of the heart.
I suppose the heavy droning of the *carillon* had smothered the
sound of his footsteps, for on my turning round, when I supposed
myself alone, Antony Watteau was standing near me. Constant
observer as he is of the lights and shadows of things, he visits
places of this kind at odd times. He has left Jean-Baptiste at work
in Paris, and will stay this time with the old people, not at our
house; though he has spent the better part of to-day in my father's
workroom. He hasn't yet put off, in spite of all his late intercourse
with the great world, his distant and preoccupied manner—a
manner, it is true, the same to every one. It is certainly not
through pride in his success, as some might fancy, for he was thus
always. It is rather as if, with all that success, life and its daily
social routine were somewhat of a burden to him.

April 1714.

At last we shall undertand something of that new style of his—the
Watteau style—so much relished by the fine people at Paris. He
has taken it into his kind head to paint and decorate our chief
salon—the room with the three long windows, which occupies
the first floor of the house.

The room was a landmark, as we used to think, an inviolable
milestone and landmark, of old Valenciennes fashion—that
sombre style, indulging much in contrasts of black or deep brown
with white, which the Spaniards left behind them here. Doubtless

their eyes had found its shadows cool and pleasant, when they
shut themselves in from the cutting sunshine of their own country. But in our country, where we must needs economise not the
shade but the sun, its grandiosity weighs a little on one's spirits.
Well! the rough plaster we used to cover as well as might be with
morsels of old figured arras-work, is replaced by dainty panelling
of wood, with mimic columns, and a quite aerial scrollwork
around sunken spaces of a pale-rose stuff and certain oval openings—two over the doors, opening on each side of the great couch
which faces the windows, one over the chimney-piece, and one
above the buffet which forms its *vis-à-vis*—four spaces in all, to
be filled by and by with "fantasies" of the Four Seasons, painted
by his own hand. He will send us from Paris arm-chairs of a new
pattern he has devised, suitably covered, and a painted *clavecin*,
Our old silver candlesticks look well on the chimney-piece. Odd,
faint-coloured flowers fill coquettishly the little empty spaces
here and there, like ghosts of nosegays left by visitors long ago,
which paled thus, sympathetically, at the decease of their old
owners; for, in spite of its new-fashionedness, all this array is
really less like a new thing than the last surviving result of all the
more lightsome adornments of past times. Only, the very walls
seem to cry out:—No! to make delicate insinuation, for a music, a
conversation, nimbler than any we have known, or are likely to
find here. For himself, he converses well, but very sparingly. He
assures us, indeed, that the "new style" is in truth a thing of old
days, of his own old days here in Valenciennes, when, working
long hours as a mason's boy, he in fancy reclothed the walls of this
or that house he was employed in, with this fairy arrangement—
itself like a piece of "chamber-music," methinks, part answering
to part; while no too trenchant note is allowed to break through
the delicate harmony of white and pale red and little golden
touches. Yet it is all very comfortable also, it must be confessed;
with an elegant open place for the fire, instead of the big old stove
of brown tiles. The ancient, heavy furniture of our grandparents
goes up, with difficulty, into the garrets, much against my father's inclination. To reconcile him to the change, Antony is
painting his portrait in a vast *perruque*, and with more vigorous
massing of light and shadow than he is wont to permit himself.

June 1714.

He has completed the ovals:—The Four Seasons. Oh! the summerlike grace, the freedom and softness, of the "Summer"—a hayfield such as we visited to-day, but boundless, and with touches of level Italian architecture in the hot, white, elusive distance, and wreaths of flowers, fairy hayrakes and the like, suspended from tree to tree, with that wonderful lightness which is one of the charms of his work. I can understand through this, at last, what it is he enjoys, what he selects by preference, from all that various world we pass our lives in. I am struck by the purity of the room he has re-fashioned for us—a sort of *moral* purity; yet, in the *forms* and *colours* of things. Is the actual life of Paris, to which he will soon return, equally pure, that it relishes this kind of thing so strongly? Only, methinks 'tis a pity to incorporate so much of his work, of himself, with objects of use, which must perish by use, or disappear, like our own old furniture, with mere change of fashion.

July 1714.

On the last day of Antony Watteau's visit we made a party to Cambrai. We entered the cathedral church: it was the hour of Vespers, and it happened that *Monseigneur le Prince de Cambrai*, the author of *Télémaque*, was in his place in the choir. He appears to be of great age, assists but rarely at the offices of religion, and is never to be seen in Paris; and Antony had much desired to behold him. Certainly it was worth while to have come so far only to see him, and hear him give his pontifical blessing, in a voice feeble but of infinite sweetness, and with an inexpressibly graceful movement of the hands. A veritable *grand seigneur!* His refined old age, the impress of genius and honours, even his disappointments, concur with natural graces to make him seem too distinguished (a fitter word fails me) for this world. *Omnia vanitas!* he seems to say, yet with a profound resignation, which makes the things we are most of us so fondly occupied with look petty enough. *Omnia vanitas!* Is that indeed the proper comment on our lives, coming, as it does in this case, from one who might have made his own all that life has to bestow? Yet he was never to be seen at court, and has lived here almost as an exile. Was our "Great King Lewis" jealous of a true *grand seigneur* or *grand monarque* by natural gift and the favour of heaven, that he could not endure his presence?

July 1714.

⅄ My own portrait remains unfinished at his sudden departure. I sat for it in a walking-dress, made under his direction—a gown of a peculiar silken stuff, falling into an abundance of small folds, giving me "a certain air of piquancy" which pleases him, but is far enough from my true self. My old Flemish *faille*, which I shall always wear, suits me better.

I notice that our good-hearted but sometimes difficult friend said little of our brother Jean-Baptiste, though he knows us so anxious on his account—spoke only of his constant industry, cautiously, and not altogether with satisfaction, as if the sight of it wearied him.

September 1714.

Will Antony ever accomplish that long-pondered journey to Italy? For his own sake, I should be glad he might. Yet it seems desolately far, across those great hills and plains. I remember how I formed a plan for providing him with a sum sufficient for the purpose. But that he no longer needs.

With myself, how to get through time becomes sometimes the question,—unavoidably; though it strikes me as a thing unspeakably sad in a life so short as ours. The sullenness of a long wet day is yielding just now to an outburst of watery sunset, which strikes from the far horizon of this quiet world of ours, over fields and willow-woods, upon the shifty weather-vanes and long-pointed windows of the tower on the square—from which the *Angelus* is sounding—with a momentary promise of a fine night. I prefer the *Salut* at Saint Vaast. The walk thither is a longer one, and I have a fancy always that I may meet Antony Watteau there again, any time; just as, when a child, having found one day a tiny box in the shape of a silver coin, for long afterwards I used to try every piece of money that came into my hands, expecting it to open.

September 1714.

We were sitting in the *Watteau* chamber for the coolness, this sultry evening. A sudden gust of wind ruffled the lights in the sconces on the walls: the distant rumblings, which had continued all the afternoon, broke out at last; and through the driving rain, a coach, rattling across the *Place*, stops at our door: in a moment Jean-Baptiste is with us once again; but with bitter tears in his eyes;—dismissed!

October 1714.

Jean-Baptiste! he too, rejected by Antony! It makes our friendship and fraternal sympathy closer. And still as he labours, not less sedulously than of old, and still so full of loyalty to his old master, in that *Watteau* chamber, I seem to see Antony himself, of whom Jean-Baptiste dares not yet speak,—to come very near his work, and understand his great parts. So Jean-Baptiste's work, in its nearness to his, may stand, for the future, as the central interest of my life. I bury myself in that.

February 1715.

If I understand anything of these matters, Antony Watteau paints that delicate life of Paris so excellently, with so much spirit, partly because, after all, he looks down upon it or despises it. To persuade myself of that, is my womanly satisfaction for his prefer-ence—his apparent preference—for a world so different from mine. Those coquetries, those vain and perishable graces, can be rendered so perfectly, only through an intimate understanding of them. For him, to understand must be to despise them; while (I think I know why) he nevertheless undergoes their fascination. Hence that discontent with himself, which keeps pace with his fame. It would have been better for him—he would have enjoyed a purer and more real happiness—had he remained here, obscure; as it might have been better for me!

It is altogether different with Jean-Baptiste. He approaches that life, and all its pretty nothingness, from a level no higher than its own; and beginning just where Antony Watteau leaves off in disdain, produces a solid and veritable likeness of it and of its ways.

March 1715.

There are points in his painting (I apprehend this through his own persistently modest observations) at which he works out his purpose more excellently than Watteau; of whom he has trusted himself to speak at last, with a wonderful self-effacement, pointing out in each of his pictures, for the rest so just and true, how Antony would have managed this or that, and, with what an easy superiority, have done the thing better—done the impossible.

February 1716.

There are good things, attractive things, in life, meant for one and not for another—not meant perhaps for me; as there are pretty clothes which are not suitable for every one. I find a certain immobility of disposition in me, to quicken or interfere with which is like physical pain. He, so brilliant, petulant, mobile! I am better far beside Jean-Baptiste—in contact with his quiet, even labour, and manner of being. At first he did the work to which he had set himself, sullenly; but the mechanical labour of it has cleared his mind and temper at last, as a sullen day turns quite clear and fine by imperceptible change. With the earliest dawn he enters his workroom, the *Watteau* chamber, where he remains at work all day. The dark evenings he spends in industrious preparation with the *crayon* for the pictures he is to finish during the hours of daylight. His toil is also his amusement: he goes but rarely into the society whose manners he has to re-produce. The animals in his pictures, pet animals, are mere toys: he know it. But he finishes a large number of works, door-heads, *clavecin* cases, and the like. His happiest, his most genial moments, he puts, like savings of fine gold, into one particular picture (true *opus magnum*, as he hopes), *The Swing*. He has the secret of surprising effects with a certain pearl-grey silken stuff of his predilection; and it must be confessed that he paints hands—which a draughtsman, of course, should understand at least twice as well as all other people—with surpassing expression.

March 1716.

Is it the depressing result of this labour, of a too exacting labour? I know not. But at times (it is his one melancholy!) he expresses a strange apprehension of poverty, of penury and mean surroundings in old age; reminding me of that childish disposition to hoard, which I noticed in him of old. And then—inglorious Watteau, as he is!—at times that steadiness, in which he is so great a contrast to Antony, as it were accumulates, changes, into a ray of genius, a grace, an inexplicable touch of truth, in which all his heaviness leaves him for a while, and he actually goes beyond the master; as himself protests to me, yet modestly. And still, it is precisely at those moments that he feels most the difference between himself and Antony Watteau. "In *that* country, *all* the pebbles are golden nuggets," he says; with perfect good-humour.

June 1716.

'Tis truly in a delightful abode that Antony Watteau is just now lodged—the *hôtel*, or townhouse of M. de Crozat, which is not only a comfortable dwelling-place, but also a precious museum lucky people go far to see. Jean-Baptiste, too, has seen the place, and describes it. The antiquities, beautiful curiosities of all sorts—above all, the original drawings of those old masters Antony so greatly admires—are arranged all around one there, that the influence, the genius, of those things may imperceptibly play upon and enter into one, and form what one does. The house is situated near the *Rue Richelieu*, but has a large garden about it. M. de Crozat gives his musical parties there, and Antony Watteau has painted the walls of one of the apartments with the Four Seasons, after the manner of ours, but doubtless improved by second thoughts. This beautiful place is now Antony's home for a while. The house has but one story, with attics in the *mansard* roofs, like those of a farmhouse in the country. I fancy Antony fled thither for a few moments, from the visitors who weary him; breathing the freshness of that dewy garden in the very midst of Paris. As for me, I suffocate this summer afternoon in this pretty *Watteau* chamber of ours, where Jean-Baptiste is at work so contentedly.

May 1717.

In spite of all that happened, Jean-Baptiste has been looking forward to a visit to Valenciennes which Antony Watteau had proposed to make. He hopes always—has a patient hope—that Anthony's former patronage of him may be revived. And now he is among us, actually at his work—restless and disquieting, meagre, like a woman with some nervous malady. Is it pity, then, pity only, one must feel for the brilliant one? He has been criticising the work of Jean-Baptiste, who takes his judgments generously, gratefully. Can it be that, after all, he despises and is no true lover of his own art, and is but chilled by an enthusiasm for it in another, such as that of Jean-Baptiste? as if Jean-Baptiste over-valued it, or as if some ignobleness or blunder, some sign that he has really missed his aim, started into sight from his work at the sound of praise—as if such praise could hardly be altogether sincere.

June 1717.

And at last one has actual sight of his work—what it is. He has brought with him certain long-cherished designs to finish here in quiet, as he protests he has never finished before. That charming *Noblesse*—can it be really so distinguished to the minutest point, so naturally aristocratic? Half in masquerade, playing the drawing-room or garden comedy of life, these persons have upon them, not less than the landscape he composes, and among the accidents of which they group themselves with such a perfect fittingness, a certain light we should seek for in vain upon anything real. For their framework they have around them a veritable architecture—a tree-architecture—to which those moss-grown bal-usters, *termes*, statues, fountains, are really but accessories. Only, as I gaze upon those windless afternoons, I find myself always saying to myself involuntarily, "The evening will be a wet one." The storm is always brooding through the massy splendour of the trees, above those sun-dried glades or lawns, where delicate children may be trusted thinly clad; and the secular trees themselves will hardly outlast another generation.

July 1717.

There has been an exhibition of his pictures in the Hall of the Academy of Saint Luke; and all the world has been to see.

Yes! Besides that unreal, imaginary light upon these scenes, these persons, which is pure gift of his, there was a light, a poetry, in those persons and things themselves, close at hand *we* had not seen. He has enabled us to see it: we are so much the better-off thereby, and I, for one, the better. The world he sets before us so engagingly has its care for purity, its cleanly preferences, in what one is to *see*—in the outsides of things—and there is something, a sign, a memento, at the least, of what makes life really valuable, even in that. There, is my simple notion, wholly womanly per-haps, but which I may hold by, of the purpose of the arts.

August 1717.

And yet! (to read my mind, my experience, in somewhat different terms) methinks Antony Watteau reproduces that gallant world, those patched and powdered ladies and fine cavaliers, so much to its own satisfaction, partly because he despises it; if this be a possible condition of excellent artistic production. People talk of a new era now dawning upon the world, of fraternity, liberty, humanity, of a novel sort of social freedom in which men's natu-ral goodness of heart will blossom at a thousand points hitherto repressed, of wars disappearing from the world in an infinite, be-nevolent ease of life—yes! perhaps of infinite littleness also. And it is the outward manner of that, which, partly by anticipation, and through pure intellectual power, Antony Watteau has caught, together with a flattering something of his own, added thereto. Himself really of the old time—that serious old time which is passing away, the impress of which he carries on his physiognomy—he dignifies, by what in him is neither more nor less than a profound melancholy, the essential insignificance of what he *wills* to touch in all that, transforming its mere pettiness into grace. It looks certainly very graceful, fresh animated, "piquant," as they love to say—yes! and withal, I repeat, perfectly pure, and may well congratulate itself on the loan of a fallacious grace, not its own. For in truth Antony Watteau is still the mason's boy, and deals with that world under a fascination, of the nature of which he is half-conscious methinks, puzzled at "the queer trick he possesses," to use his own phrase. You see him growing ever more and more meagre, as he goes through the world and its applause. Yet he reaches with wonderful sagacity the secret of an adjustment of colours, a *coiffure*, a toilette, setting I know not what air of real superiority on such things. He will never overcome his early training; and these light things will possess for him always a kind of representative or borrowed worth, as characterising that impossible or forbidden world which the mason's boy saw through the closed gateways of the enchanted garden. Those trifling and petty graces, the *insignia* to him of that nobler world of aspiration and idea, even now that he is aware, as I conceive, of their true littleness, bring back to him, by the power of association, all the old magical exhilaration of his dream—his dream of a better world than the real one. There, is the formula, as I apprehend, of his success—of his extraordinary hold on things so alien from himself. And I think there is more real hilarity in my brother's *fêtes champêtres*—more truth to life, and therefore less distinction. Yes! the world profits by such reflection of its poor, coarse self, in one who renders all its caprices from the height of a Corneille. That is my way of making up to myself for the fact that I think *his* days, too, would have been really happier, had he remained obscure at Valenciennes.

September 1717.

My own poor likeness, begun so long ago, still remains unfinished on the easel, at his departure from Valenciennes—perhaps for ever; since the old people departed this life in the hard winter of last year, at no distant time from each other. It is pleasanter to him to sketch and plan than to paint and finish; and he is often out of humour with himself because he cannot project into a picture the life and spirit of his first thought with the *crayon*. He would fain begin where that famous master Gerard Dow left off, and snatch, as it were with a single stroke, what in him was the result of infinite patience. It is the sign of this sort of promptitude that he values solely in the work of another. To my thinking there is a kind of greed or grasping in that humour; as if things were not to last very long, and one must snatch opportunity. And often he succeeds. The old Dutch painter cherished with a kind of piety his colours and pencils. Antony Watteau, on the contrary, will hardly make any preparations for his work at all, or even clean his palette, in the dead-set he makes at improvisation. 'Tis the contrast perhaps between the staid Dutch genius and the petulant, sparkling French temper of this new era, into which he has thrown himself. Alas! it is already apparent that the result also loses something of longevity, of durability—the colours fading or changing, from the first, somewhat rapidly, as Jean-Baptiste notes. 'Tis true, a mere trifle alters or produces the expression. But then, on the other hand, in pictures the whole effect of which lies in a kind of harmony, the treachery of a single colour must needs involve the failure of the whole to outlast the fleeting grace of those social conjunctions it is meant to perpetuate. This is what has happened, in part, to that portrait on the easel. Meantime, he has commanded Jean-Baptiste to finish it; and so it must be.

October 1717.

Anthony Watteau is an excellent judge of literature, and I have been reading (with infinite surprise!) in my afternoon walks in the little wood here, a new book he left behind him—a great favourite of his; as it has been a favourite with large numbers in Paris.[1] Those pathetic shocks of fortune, those sudden alterna-

[1] Possibly written at this date, but almost certainly not printed till many years later.—*Note in Second Edition.*

tions of pleasure and remorse, which must always lie among the very conditions of an irregular and guilty love, as in sinful games of chance:—they have begun to talk of these things in Paris, to amuse themselves with the spectacle of them, set forth here, in the story of poor Manon Lescaut—for whom fidelity is impossible, so vulgarly eager for the money which can buy pleasures such as hers—with an art like Watteau's own, for lightness and grace. Incapacity of truth, yet with such tenderness, such a gift of tears, on the one side: on the other, a faith so absolute as to give to an illicit love almost the regularity of marriage! And this is the book those fine ladies in Watteau's "conversations," who look so exquisitely pure, lay down on the cushion when the children run up to have their laces righted. Yet the pity of it! What floods of weeping! There is a tone about it which strikes me as going well with the grace of these leafless birch-trees against the sky, the pale silver of their bark, and a certain delicate odour of decay which rises from the soil. It is all one half-light; and the heroine, nay! the hero himself also, that dainty Chevalier des Grieux, with all his fervour, have, I think, but a half-life in them truly, from the first. And I could fancy myself almost of their condition sitting here alone this evening, in which a premature touch of winter makes the world look but an inhospitable place of entertainment for one's spirit. With so little genial warmth to hold it there, one feels that the merest accident might detach that flighty guest altogether. So chilled at heart things seem to me, as I gaze on that glacial point in the motionless sky, like some mortal spot whence death begins to creep over the body!

And yet, in the midst of this, by mere force of contrast, comes back to me, very vividly, the true colour, ruddy with blossom and fruit, of the past summer, among the streets and gardens of some of our old towns we visited; when the thought of cold was a luxury, and the earth dry enough to sleep on. The summer was indeed a fine one; and the whole country seemed bewitched. A kind of infectious sentiment passed upon us, like an efflux from its flowers and flower-like architecture—flower-like to me at least, but of which I never felt the beauty before.

And as I think of that, certainly I have to confess that there is a wonderful reality about this lovers' story; an accordance between themselves and the conditions of things around them, so deep as to make it seem that the course of their lives could hardly have been other than it was. That impression comes, perhaps, wholly of the writer's skill; but, at all events, I must read the book no more.

June 1718.

And he has allowed that Mademoiselle Rosalba—"*ce bel esprit*"—who can discourse upon the arts like a master, to paint his portrait: has painted hers in return! She holds a lapful of white roses with her two hands. *Rosa Alba*—himself has inscribed it! It will be engraved, to circulate and perpetuate it the better.

One's journal, here in one's solitude, is of service at least in this, that it affords an escape for vain regrets, angers, impatience. One puts this and that angry spasm into it, and is delivered from it so.

And then, it was at the desire of M. de Crozat that the thing was done. One must oblige one's patrons. The lady also, they tell me, is consumptive, like Antony himself, and like to die. And he, who has always lacked either the money or the spirits to make that long-pondered, much-desired journey to Italy, has found in her work the veritable accent and colour of those old Venetian masters he would so willingly have studied under the sunshine of their own land. Alas! How little peace have his great successes given him; how little of that quietude of mind, without which, methinks, one fails in true dignity of character.

November 1718.

His thirst for change of place has actually driven him to England, that veritable home of the consumptive. Ah me! I feel it may be the finishing stroke. To have run into the native country of consumption! Strange caprice of that desire to travel, which he has really indulged so little in his life—of the restlessness which, they tell me, is itself a symptom of this terrible disease!

January 1720.

As once before, after long silence, a token has reached us, a slight token that he remembers—an etched plate, one of very few he has executed, with that old subject: *Soldiers on the March.* And the weary soldier himself is returning once more to Valenciennes, on his way from England to Paris.

February 1720.

Those sharply-arched brows, those restless eyes which seem larger than ever—something that seizes on one, and is almost terrible, in his expression—speak clearly, and irresistibly set one on the thought of a summing-up of his life. I am reminded of the day when, already with that air of seemly thought, *le bel sérieux,* he was found sketching, with so much truth to the inmost mind in them, those picturesque mountebanks at the Fair in the *Grande Place;* and I find, throughout his course of life, something of the essential melancholy of the comedian. He, so fastidious and cold, and who has never "ventured the representation of passion," does but amuse the gay world; and is aware of that, though certainly unamused himself all the while. Just now, however, he is finishing a very different picture—that too, full of humour—an English family-group, with a little girl riding a wooden horse: the father, and the mother holding his tobacco-pipe, stand in the centre.

March 1720.

To-morrow he will depart finally. And this evening the Syndics of the Academy of Saint Luke came with their scarves and banners to conduct their illustrious fellow-citizen, by torch-light, to supper in their Guildhall, where all their beautiful old corporation plate will be displayed. The *Watteau salon* was lighted up to receive them. There is something in the payment of great honours to the living which fills one with apprehension, especially when the recipient of them looks so like a dying man. God have mercy on him!

April 1721.

We were on the point of retiring to rest last evening when a messenger arrived post-haste with a letter on behalf of Antony Watteau, desiring Jean-Baptiste's presence at Paris. We did not go to bed that night; and my brother was on his way before daylight, his heart full of a strange conflict of joy and apprehension.

May 1721.

A letter at last! from Jean-Baptiste, occupied with cares of all sorts at the bedside of the sufferer. Antony fancying that the air of the country might do him good, the Abbé Haranger, one of the canons of the Church of Saint Germain l'Auxerrois, where he was in the habit of hearing Mass, has lent him a house at Nogent-sur-Marne. There he receives a few visitors. But in truth the places he once liked best, the people, nay! the very friends, have become to him nothing less than insupportable. Though he still dreams of change, and would fain try his native air once more, he is at work constantly upon his art; but solely by way of a teacher, instructing (with a kind of remorseful diligence, it would seem) Jean-Baptiste, who will be heir to his unfinished work, and take up many of his pictures where he has left them. He seems now anxious for one thing only, to give his old "dismissed" disciple what remains of himself, and the last secrets of his genius. His property—9000 livres only—goes to his relations. Jean-Baptiste has found these last weeks immeasurably useful.

For the rest, bodily exhaustion perhaps, and this new interest in an old friend, have brought him tranquillity at last, a tranquillity in which he is much occupied with matters of religion. Ah! it was ever so with me. And one *lives* also most reasonably so.—With women, at least, it is thus, quite certainly. Yet I know not what there is of a pity which strikes deep, at the thought of a man, a while since so strong, turning his face to the wall from the things which most occupy men's lives. 'Tis that homely, but honest *curé* of Nogent he has caricatured so often, who attends him.

July 1721.

Our incomparable Watteau is no more! Jean-Baptiste returned un-expectedly. I heard his hasty footstep on the stairs. We turned together into that room; and he told his story there. Antony Wat-teau departed suddenly, in the arms of M. Gersaint, on one of the late hot days of July. At the last moment he had been at work upon a crucifix for the good *curé* of Nogent, liking little the very rude one he possessed. He died with all the sentiments of religion.

He has been a sick man all his life. He was always a seeker after something in the world that is there is no satisfying measure, or not at all.

[1885]

Denys L'Auxerrois

Almost every people, as we know, has had its legend of a "golden age" and of its return—legends which will hardly be forgotten, however prosaic the world may become, while man himself remains the aspiring, never quite contented being he is. And yet in truth, since we are no longer children, we might well question the advantage of the return to us of a condition of life in which, by the nature of the case, the values of things would, so to speak, lie wholly on their surfaces, unless we could regain also the childish consciousness, or rather unconsciousness, in ourselves, to take all that adroitly and with the appropriate lightness of heart. The dream, however, has been left for the most part in the usual vagueness of dreams: in their waking hours people have been too busy to furnish it forth with details. What follows is a quaint legend, with detail enough, of such a return of a golden or poetically-gilded age (a denizen of old Greece itself actually finding his way back again among men) as it happened in an ancient town of medieval France.

Of the French town, properly so called, in which the products of successive ages, not without lively touches of the present, are blended together harmoniously, with a beauty *specific*—a beauty cisalpine and northern, yet at the same time quite distinct from the massive German picturesque of Ulm, or Freiburg, or Augsburg, and of which Turner has found the ideal in certain of his studies of the rivers of France, a perfectly happy conjunction of river and town being of the essence of its physiognomy—the town of Auxerre is perhaps the most complete realisation to be found by the actual wanderer. Certainly, for picturesque expression it is the most memorable of a distinguished group of three in these

parts,—Auxerre, Sens, Troyes,—each gathered, as if with deliberate aim at such effect, about the central mass of a huge grey
cathedral.

Around Troyes the natural picturesque is to be sought only in
the rich, almost coarse, summer colouring of the Champagne
country, of which the very tiles, the plaster and brickwork of its
tiny villages and great, straggling, village-like farms have caught
the warmth. The cathedral, visible far and wide over the fields
seemingly of loose wild-flowers, itself a rich mixture of all the
varieties of the Pointed style down to the latest *Flamboyant*, may
be noticed among the greater French churches for breadth of proportions internally, and is famous for its almost unrivalled treasure of stained glass, chiefly of a florid, elaborate, later type, with
much highly conscious artistic contrivance in design as well as in
colour. In one of the richest of its windows, for instance, certain
lines of pearly white run hither and thither, with delightful distant effect, upon ruby and dark blue. Approaching nearer you
find it to be a Travellers' window, and those odd lines of white the
long walking-staves in the hands of Abraham, Raphael, the Magi,
and the other saintly patrons of journeys. The appropriate provincial character of the *bourgeoisie* of Champagne is still to be seen,
it would appear, among the citizens of Troyes. Its streets, for the
most part in timber and pargeting, present more than one unaltered specimen of the ancient *hôtel* or town-house, with fore-
court and garden in the rear; and its more devout citizens would
seem even in their church-building to have sought chiefly to
please the eyes of those occupied with mundane affairs and out of
doors, for they have finished, with abundant outlay, only the
vast, useless portals of their parish churches, of surprising height
and lightness, in a kind of wildly elegant Gothic-on-stilts, giving
to the streets of Troyes a peculiar air of the grotesque, as if in some
quaint nightmare of the Middle Age.

At Sens, thirty miles away to the west, a place of far graver
aspect, the name of Jean Cousin denotes a more chastened temper, even in these sumptuous decorations. Here all is cool and
composed, with an almost English austerity. The first growth of
the Pointed style in England—the hard "early English" of Canterbury—is indeed the creation of William, a master reared in the

architectural school of Sens; and the severity of his taste might seem to have acted as a restraining power on all the subsequent changes of manner in this place—changes in themselves for the most part towards luxuriance. In harmony with the atmosphere of its great church is the cleanly quiet of the town, kept fresh by little channels of clear water circulating through its streets, derivatives of the rapid Vanne which falls just below into the Yonne. The Yonne, bending gracefully, link after link, through a never-ending rustle of poplar trees, beneath lowly vine-clad hills, with relics of delicate woodland here and there, sometimes close at hand, sometimes leaving an interval of broad meadow, has all the lightsome characteristics of French river-side scenery on a smaller scale than usual, and might pass for the child's fancy of a river, like the rivers of the old miniature-painters, blue, and full to a fair green margin. One notices along its course a greater proportion than elsewhere of still untouched old seignorial residences, larger or smaller. The range of old gibbous towns along its banks, expanding their gay quays upon the water-side, have a common character—Joigny, Villeneuve, Saint Julien-du-Sault—yet tempt us to tarry at each and examine its relics, old glass and the like, of the Renaissance or the Middle Age, for the acquisition of real though minor lessons on the various arts which have left themselves a central monument at Auxerre.—Auxerre! A slight ascent in the winding road! and you have before you the prettiest town in France—the broad framework of vineyard sloping upwards gently to the horizon, with distant white cottages inviting one to walk: the quiet curve of river below, with all the river-side details: the three great purple-tiled masses of Saint Germain, Saint Pierre, and the cathedral of Saint Étienne, rising out of the crowded houses with more than the usual abruptness and irregularity of French building. Here, that rare artist, the susceptible painter of architecture, if he understands the value alike of line and mass of broad masses and delicate lines, has "a subject made to his hand."

A veritable country of the vine, its presents nevertheless an expression peaceful rather than radiant. Perfect type of that happy mean between northern earnestness and the luxury of the south, for which we prize midland France, its physiognomy is not

quite happy—attractive in part for its melancholy. Its most characteristic atmosphere is to be seen when the tide of light and
distant cloud is travelling quickly over it, when rain is not far off,
and every touch of art or of time on its old building is defined in
clear grey. A fine summer ripens its grapes into a valuable wine;
but in spite of that it seems always longing for a larger and more
continuous allowance of the sunshine which is so much to its
taste. You might fancy something querulous or plaintive in that
rustling movement of the vine-leaves, as blue-frocked Jacques
Bonhomme finishes his day's labour among them.

To beguile one such afternoon when the rain set in early and
walking was impossible, I found my way to the shop of an old
dealer in *bric-à-brac*. It was not a monotonous display, after the
manner of the Parisian dealer, of a stock-in-trade the like of which
one has seen many times over, but a discriminate collection of
real curiosities. One seemed to recognise a provincial school of
taste in various relics of the housekeeping of the last century,
with many a gem of earlier times from the old churches and religious houses of the neighborhood. Among them was a large and
brilliant fragment of stained glass which might have come from
the cathedral itself. Of the very finest quality in colour and design, it presented a figure not exactly conformable to any recognised ecclesiastical type; and it was clearly part of a series. On my
eager inquiry for the remainder, the old man replied that no more
of it was known, but added that the priest of a neighbouring village was the possessor of an entire set of tapestries, apparently intended for suspension in church, and designed to portray the whole
subject of which the figure in the stained glass was a portion.

Next afternoon accordingly I repaired to the priest's house, in
reality a little Gothic building, part perhaps of an ancient manor-
house, close to the village church. In the front garden, flower-
garden and *potager* in one, the bees were busy among the autumn
growths—many-coloured asters, bignonias, scarlet-beans, and
the old-fashioned parsonage flowers. The courteous owner readily
showed me his tapestries, some of which hung on the walls of his
parlour and staircase by way of a background for the display of the
other curiosities of which he was a collector. Certainly, those
tapestries and the stained glass dealt with the same theme. In

both were the same musical instruments—pipes, cymbals, long reed-like trumpets. The story, indeed, included the building of an organ, just such an instrument, only on a larger scale, as was standing in the old priest's library, though almost soundless now, whereas in certain of the woven pictures the hearers appear as if transported, some of them shouting rapturously to the organ music. A sort of mad vehemence prevails, indeed, throughout the delicate bewilderments of the whole series—giddy dances, wild animals leaping, above all perpetual wreathings of the vine, connecting, like some mazy arabesque, the various presentations of one oft-repeated figure, translated here out of the clear-coloured glass into the sadder, somewhat opaque and earthen hues of the silken threads. The figure was that of the organ-builder himself, a flaxen and flowery creature, sometimes wellnigh naked among the vine-leaves, sometimes muffled in skins against the cold, sometimes in the dress of a monk, but always with a strong impress of real character and incident from the veritable streets of Auxerre. What is it? Certainly, notwithstanding its grace, and wealth of graceful accessories, a suffering, tortured figure. With all the regular beauty of a pagan god, he has suffered after a manner of which we must suppose pagan gods incapable. It was as if one of those fair, triumphant beings had cast in his lot with the creatures of an age later than his own, people of larger spiritual capacity and assuredly of a larger spiritual capacity and assuredly of a larger capacity for melancholy. With this fancy in my mind, by the help of certain notes, which lay in the priest's curious library, upon the history of the works at the cathedral during the period of its finishing, and in repeated examination of the old tapestried designs, the story shaped itself at last.

Towards the middle of the thirteenth century the cathedral of Saint Étienne was complete in its main outlines: what remained was the building of the great tower, and all that various labour of final decoration which it would take more than one generation to accomplish. Certain circumstances, however, not wholly explained, led to a somewhat rapid finishing, as it were out of hand, yet with a marvellous fulness at once and grace. Of the result much has perished, or been transferred elsewhere; a portion is still visible in sumptuous relics of stained windows, and, above all, in the reliefs which adorn the western portals, very delicately carved in a fine, firm stone from Tonnerre, of which time has only browned the surface, and which, for early mastery in art, may be compared with the contemporary work of Italy. They come nearer than the art of that age was used to do to the expression of life; with a feeling for reality, in no ignoble form, caught, it might seem, from the ardent and full-veined existence then current in these actual streets and houses. Just then Auxerre had its turn in that political movement which broke out sympathetically, first in one, then in another of the towns of France, turning their narrow, feudal institutions into a free, communistic life—a movement of which those great centres of popular devotion, the French cathedrals, are in many instances the monument. Closely connected always with the assertion of individual freedom, alike in mind and manners, at Auxerre this political stir was associated also, as cause or effect, with the figure and character of a particular personage, long remembered. He was the very genius, it would appear, of that new, free, generous manner in art, active and potent as a living creature.

As the most skilful of the band of carvers worked there one day, with a labour he could never quite make equal to the vision within him, a finely-sculptured Greek coffin of stone, which had been made to serve for some later Roman funeral, was unearthed by the masons. Here, it might seem, the thing was indeed done, and art achieved, as far as regards those final graces, and harmonies of execution, which were precisely what lay beyond the hand of the medieval workman, who for his part had largely at command a seriousness of conception lacking in the old Greek. Within the coffin lay an object of a fresh and brilliant clearness among the ashes of the dead—a flask of lively green glass, like a great emerald. It might have been "the wondrous vessel of the Grail." Only, this object seemed to bring back no ineffable purity, but rather the riotous and earthy heat of old paganism itself. Coated within, and, as some were persuaded, still redolent with the tawny sediment of the Roman wine it had held so long ago, it was set aside for use at the supper which was shortly to celebrate the completion of the mason's work. Amid much talk of the great age of gold, and some random expressions of hope that it might return again, fine old wine of Auxerre was sipped in small glasses from the precious flask as supper ended. And, whether or not the opening of the buried vessel had anything to do with it, from that time a sort of golden age seemed indeed to be reigning there for a while, and the triumphant completion of the great church was contemporary with a series of remarkable wine seasons. The vintage of those years was long remembered. Fine and abundant wine was to be found stored up even in poor men's cottages; while a new beauty, a gaiety, was abroad, as all the conjoint arts branched out exuberantly in a reign of quiet, delighted labour, at the prompting, as it seemed, of the singular being who came suddenly and oddly to Auxerre to be the centre of so pleasant a period, though in truth he made but a sad ending.

A peculiar usage long perpetuated itself at Auxerre. On Easter Day the canons, in the very centre of the great church, played solemnly at ball. Vespers being sung, instead of conducting the bishop to his palace, they proceeded in order into the nave, the people standing in two long rows to watch. Girding up their skirts a little way, the whole body of clerics awaited their turn in silence, while the captain of the singing-boys cast the ball into the air, as high as he might, along the vaulted roof of the central aisle to be caught by any boy who could, and tossed again with hand or foot till it passed on to the portly chanters, the chaplains, the canons themselves, who finally played out the game with all the decorum of an ecclesiastical ceremony. It was just then, just as the canons took the ball to themselves so gravely, that Denys— Denys l'Auxerrois, as he was afterwards called—appeared for the first time. Leaping in among the timid children, he made the thing really a game. The boys played like boys, the men almost like madmen, and all with a delightful glee which became contagious, first in the clerical body, and then among the spectators. The aged Dean of the Chapter, Protonotary of his Holiness, held up his purple skirt a little higher, and stepping from the ranks with an amazing levity, as if suddenly relieved of his burden of eighty years, tossed the ball with his foot to the venerable capitular Homilist, equal to the occasion. And then, unable to stand inactive any longer, the laity carried on the game among themselves, with shouts of not too boisterous amusement; the sport

continuing till the flight of the ball could no longer be traced
along the dusky aisles.

Though the home of his childhood was but a humble one—one
of those little cliff-houses cut out in the low chalky hillside, such
as are still to be found with inhabitants in certain districts of
France—there were some who connected his birth with the story
of a beautiful country girl, who, about eighteen years before, had
been taken from her own people, not unwillingly, for the pleasure
of the Count of Auxerre. She had wished indeed to see the great
lord, who had sought her privately, in the glory of his own house;
but, terrified by the strange splendours of her new abode and
manner of life, and the anger of the true wife, she had fled suddenly from the place during the confusion of a violent storm, and
in her flight given birth prematurely to a child. The child, a singularly fair one, was found alive, but the mother dead, by light-
ning-stroke as it seemed, not far from her lord's chamber-door,
under the shelter of a ruined ivy-clad tower. Denys himself certainly was a joyous lad enough. At the cliff-side cottage, nestling
actually beneath the vineyards, he came to be an unrivalled gardener, and, grown to manhood, brought his produce to market,
keeping a stall in the great cathedral square for the sale of melons
and pomegranates, all manner of seeds and flowers (*omnia spec-
iosa camporum*), honey also, wax tapers, sweetmeats hot from
the frying-pan, rough home-made pots and pans from the little
pottery in the wood, loaves baked by the aged woman in whose
house he lived. On that Easter Day he had entered the great
church for the first time, for the purpose of seeing the game.

And from the very first, the women who saw him at his business, or watering his plants in the cool of the evening, idled for
him. The men who noticed the crowd of women at his stall, and
how even fresh young girls from the country, seeing him for the
first time, always loitered there, suspected—who could tell what
kind of powers? hidden under the white veil of that youthful form;
and pausing to ponder the matter, found themselves also fallen
into the snare. The sight of him made old people feel young again.
Even the sage monk Hermes, devoted to study and experiment,
was unable to keep the fruit-seller out of his mind, and would fain
have discovered the secret of his charm, partly for the friendly

purpose of explaining to the lad himself his perhaps more than natural gifts with a view to their profitable cultivation.

It was a period, as older men took note, of young men and their influence. They took fire, no one could quite explain how, as if at his presence, and asserted a wonderful amount of volition, of insolence, yet as if with the consent of their elders, who would themselves sometimes lose their balance, a little comically. That revolution in the temper and manner of individuals concurred with the movement then on foot at Auxerre, as in other French towns, for the liberation of the *commune* from its old feudal superiors. Denys they called *Frank*, among many other nicknames. Young lords prided themselves on saying that labour should have its ease, and were almost prepared to take freedom, plebeian freedom (of course duly decorated, at least with wild-flowers) for a bride. For in truth Denys at his stall was turning the grave, slow movement of politic heads into a wild social license, which for a while made life like a stage-play. He first led those long processions, through which by and by "the little people," the discontented, the despairing, would utter their minds. One man engaged with another in talk in the market-place; a new influence came forth at the contact; another and then another adhered; at last a new spirit was abroad everywhere. The hot nights were noisy with swarming troops of dishevelled women and youths with red-stained limbs and faces, carrying their lighted torches over the vine-clad hills, or rushing down the streets, to the horror of timid watchers, towards the cool spaces by the river. A shrill music, a laughter at all things, was everywhere. And the new spirit repaired even to church to take part in the novel offices of the Feast of Fools. Heads flung back in ecstasy—the morning sleep among the vines, when the fatigue of the night was over—drew-drenched garments—the serf lying at his ease at last: the artists, then so numerous at the place, caught what they could, something, at least, of the richness, the flexibility of the visible aspects of life, from all this. With them the life of seeming idleness, to which Denys was conducting the youth of Auxerre so pleasantly, counted but as the cultivation, for their due service to man, of delightful natural things. And the powers of nature concurred. It seemed there would be winter no more. The planet Mars drew

nearer to the earth than usual, hanging in the low sky like a fiery
red lamp. A massive but well-nigh lifeless vine on the wall of the
cloister, allowed to remain there only as a curiosity on account of
its immense age, in that *great* season, as it was long after called,
clothed itself with fruit once more. The culture of the grape
greatly increased. The sunlight fell for the first time on many a
spot of deep woodland cleared for vine-growing; though Denys, a
lover of trees, was careful to leave a stately specimen of forest
growth here and there.

When his troubles came, one characteristic that had seemed
most amiable in his prosperity was turned against him—a fondness for oddly grown or even misshappen, yet potentially happy,
children; for odd animals also: he sympathised with them all, was
skilful in healing their maladies, saved the hare in the chase, and
sold his mantle to redeem a lamb from the butcher. He taught the
people not to be afraid of the strange, ugly creatures which the
light of the moving torches drew from their hiding-places, nor
think it a bad omen that they approached. He tamed a veritable
wolf to keep him company like a dog. It was the first of many
ambiguous circumstances about him, from which, in the minds of
an increasing number of people, a deep suspicion and hatred began to define itself. The rich *bestiary*, then compiling in the library of the great church, became, through his assistance,
nothing less than a garden of Eden—the garden of Eden grown
wild. The owl alone he abhorred. A little later, almost as if in
revenge, alone of all animals it clung to him, haunting him persistently among the dusky stone towers, when grown gentler than
ever he dared not kill it. He moved unhurt in the famous
ménagerie of the castle, of which the common people were so
much afraid, and let out the lions, themselves timid prisoners
enough, through the streets during the fair. The incident suggested to the somewhat barren penmen of the day a "morality"
adapted from the old pagan books—a stage-play in which the God
of Wine should return in triumph from the East. In the cathedral
square the pageant was presented, amid an intolerable noise of
every kind of pipe-music, with Denys in the chief part, upon a
gaily-painted chariot, in soft silken raiment, and, for headdress, a
strange elephant-scalp with gilded tusks.

And that unrivalled fairness and freshness of aspect:—how did he alone preserve it untouched, through the wind and heat? In truth, it was not by magic, as some said, but by a natural simplicity in his living. When that dark season of his troubles arrived he was heard begging querulously one wintry night, "Give me wine, meat; dark wine and brown meat!"—come back to the rude door of his old home in the cliff-side. Till that time the great vine-dresser himself drank only water; he had lived on spring-water and fruit. A lover of fertility in all its forms, in what did but suggest it, he was curious and penetrative concerning the habits of water, and had the secret of the divining-rod. Long before it came he could detect the scent of rain from afar, and would climb with delight to the great scaffolding on the unfinished tower to watch its coming over the thirsty vine-land, till it rattled on the great tiled roof of the church below; and then, throwing off his mantle, allow it to bathe his limbs freely, clinging firmly against the tempestuous wind among the carved imageries of dark stone.

It was on his sudden return after a long journey (one of many inexplicable disappearances), coming back changed somewhat, that he ate flesh for the first time, tearing the hot, red morsels with his delicate fingers in a kind of wild greed. He had fled to the south from the first forbidding days of a hard winter which came at last. At the great seaport of Marseilles he had trafficked with sailors from all parts of the world, from Arabia and India, and bought their wares, exposed now for sale, to the wonder of all, at the Easter fair—richer wines and incense than had been known in Auxerre, seeds of marvellous new flowers, creatures wild and tame, new pottery painted in raw gaudy tints, the skins of animals, meats fried with unheard-of condiments. His stall formed a strange, unwonted patch of colour, found suddenly displayed in the hot morning.

The artists were more delighted than ever, and frequented his company in the little manorial habitation, deserted long since by its owners and haunted, so that the eyes of many looked evil upon it, where he had taken up his abode, attracted, in the first instance, by its rich though neglected garden, a tangle of every kind of creeping, vine-like plant. Here, surrounded in abundance by the pleasant materials of his trade, the vine-dresser as it were

turned pedant and kept school for the various artists, who learned
here an art supplementary to their own,—that gay magic, namely
(art or trick) of his existence, till they found themselves grown
into a kind of aristocracy, like veritable *gens fleur-de-lisés*, as
they worked together for the decoration of the great church and a
hundred other places beside. And yet a darkness had grown upon
him. The kind creature had lost something of his gentleness.
Strange motiveless misdeeds had happened; and, at a loss for
other causes, not the envious only would fain have traced the
blame to Denys. He was making the younger world mad. Would
he make himself Count of Auxerre? The lady Ariane, deserted by
her former lover, had looked kindly upon him; was ready to make
him son-in-law to the old count her father, old and not long for
this world. The wise monk Hermes bethought him of certain old
readings in which the Wine-god, whose part Denys had played so
well, had his contrast, his dark or antipathetic side; was like a
double creature, of two natures, difficult or impossible to harmonise. And in truth the much-prized wine of Auxerre has itself but
a fugitive charm, being apt to sicken and turn gross long before
the bottle is empty, however carefully sealed; as it goes indeed,
at its best, by hard names, among those who grow it, such as
Chainette and *Migraine*.

   A kind of degeneration, of coarseness—the coarseness of satiety,
and shapeless, battered-out appetite—with an almost savage
taste for carnivorous diet, had come over the company. A rumour
went abroad of certain women who had drowned, in mere wantonness, their newborn babes. A girl with child was found hanged
by her own act in a dark cellar. Ah! if Denys also had not felt
himself mad! But when the guilt of a murder, committed with a
great vine-axe far out among the vineyards, was attributed
vaguely to him, he could but wonder whether it had been indeed
thus, and the shadow of a fancied crime abode with him. People
turned against their favourite, whose former charms must now be
counted only as the fascinations of witchcraft. It was as if the
wine poured out for them had soured in the cup. The golden age
had indeed come back for a while:—golden was it, or gilded only,
after all? and they were too sick, or at least too serious, to carry
through their parts in it. The monk Hermes was whimsically re-

minded of that *after-thought* in pagan poetry, of a Wine-god who had been in hell. Denys certainly, with all his flaxen fairness about him, was manifestly a sufferer. At first he thought of departing secretly to some other place. Alas! his wits were too far gone for certainty of success in the attempt. He feared to be brought back a prisoner. Those fat years were over. It was a time of scarcity. The working people might not eat and drink of the good things they had helped to store away. Tears rose in the eyes of needy children, of old or weak people like children, as they woke up again and again to sunless, frost-bound, ruinous mornings; and the little hungry creatures went prowling after scattered hedge-nuts or dried vine-tendrils. Mysterious, dark rains prevailed throughout the summer. The great offices of Saint John were fumbled through in a sudden darkness of unseasonable storm, which greatly damaged the carved ornaments of the church, the bishop reading his mid-day Mass by the light of the little candle at his book. And then, one night, the night which seemed literally to have swallowed up the shortest day in the year, a plot was contrived by certain persons to take Denys as he went and kill him privately for a sorcerer. He could hardly tell how he escaped, and found himself safe in his earliest home, the cottage in the cliff-side, with such a big fire as he delighted in burning upon the hearth. They made a little feast as well as they could for the beautiful hunted creature, with abundance of waxlights.

And at last the clergy bethought themselves of a remedy for this evil time. The body of one of the patron saints had lain neglected somewhere under the flagstones of the sanctuary. This must be piously exhumed, and provided with a shrine worthy of it. The goldsmiths, the jewellers and lapidaries, set diligently to work, and no long time after, the shrine, like a little cathedral with portals and tower complete, stood ready, its chiselled gold framing panels of rock crystal, on the great altar. Many bishops arrived, with King Lewis the Saint himself accompanied by his mother, to assist at the search for and disinterment of the sacred relics. In their presence, the Bishop of Auxerre, with vestments of deep red in honour of the relics, blessed the new shrine, according to the office *De benedictione capsarum pro reliquiis.* The pavement of the choir, removed amid a surging sea of lugubrious

chants, all persons fasting, discovered as if it had been a bat-
tlefield of mouldering human remains. Their odour rose plainly
above the plentiful clouds of incense, such as was used in the
king's private chapel. The search for the Saint himself continued
in vain all day and far into the night. At last from a little narrow
chest, into which the remains had been almost crushed together,
the bishop's red-gloved hands drew the dwindled body, shrunken
inconceivably, but still with every feature of the face traceable in
a sudden oblique ray of ghastly dawn.

That shocking sight, after a sharp fit as though a demon were
going out of him, as he rolled on the turf of the cloister to which
he had fled alone from the suffocating church, where the crowd
still awaited the Procession of the relics and the Mass *De reliquiis
quæ continentur in Ecclesiis,* seemed indeed to have cured the
madness of Denys, but certainly did not restore his gaiety. He was
left a subdued, silent, melancholy creature. Turning now, with an
odd revulsion of feeling, to gloomy objects, he picked out a ghastly
shred from the common bones on the pavement to wear about his
neck, and in a little while found his way to the monks of Saint
Germain, who gladly received him into their workshop, though
secretly, in fear of his foes.

The busy tribe of variously gifted artists, labouring rapidly at
the many works on hand for the final embellishment of the cathedral of St. Étienne, made those conventual buildings just then
cheerful enough to lighten a melancholy, heavy even as that of
our friend Denys. He took his place among the workmen, a conventual novice; a novice also as to whatever concerns any actual
handicraft. He could but compound sweet incense for the sanctuary. And yet, again by merely visible presence, he made himself
felt in all the varied exercise around him of those arts which
address themselves first of all to sight. Unconsciously he defined a
peculiar manner, alike of feeling and expression, to those skilful
hands at work day by day with the chisel, the pencil, or the needle, in many an enduring form of exquisite fancy. In three successive phases or fashions might be traced, especially in the carved
work, the humours he had determined. There was first wild
gaiety, exuberant in a wreathing of life-like imageries, from
which nothing really present in nature was excluded. That, as the

soul of Denys darkened, had passed into obscure regions of the satiric, the grotesque and coarse. But from this time there was manifest, with no loss of power or effect, a well-assured seriousness, somewhat jealous and exclusive, not so much in the selection of the material on which the arts were to work, as in the precise sort of expression that should be induced upon it. It was as if the gay old pagan world had been *blessed* in some way; with effects to be seen most clearly in the rich miniature work of the manuscripts of the capitular library,—a marvellous Ovid especially, upon the pages of which those old loves and sorrows seemed to come to life again in medieval costume, as Denys, in cowl now and with tonsured head, leaned over the painter, and led his work, by a kind of visible sympathy, often unspoken, rather than by any formal comment.

Above all, there was a desire abroad to attain the instruments of a freer and more various sacred music than had been in use hitherto—a music that might express the whole compass of souls now grown to manhood. Auxerre, indeed, then as afterwards, was famous for its liturgical music. It was Denys, at last, to whom the thought occurred of combining in a fuller tide of music all the instruments then in use. Like the Wine-god of old, he had been a lover and patron especially of the music of the pipe, in all its varieties. Here, too, there had been evident those three fashions or "modes":—first, the simple and pastoral, the homely note of the pipe, like the piping of the wind itself from off the distant fields; then, the wild, savage din, that had cost so much to quiet people, and driven excitable people mad. Now he would compose all this to sweeter purposes; and the building of the first organ became like the book of his life: it expanded to the full compass of his nature, in its sorrow and delight. In long, enjoyable days of wind and sun by the river-side, the seemingly half-witted "brother" sought and found the needful varieties of reed. The carpenters, under his instruction, set up the great wooden passages for the thunder; while the little pipes of pasteboard simulated the sound of the human voice singing to the victorious notes of the long metal trumpets. At times this also, as people heard night after night those wandering sounds, seemed like the work of a madman, though they awoke sometimes in wonder at snatches

of a new, an unmistakable new music. It was the triumph of all
the various modes of the power of the pipe, tamed, ruled, united.
Only, on the painted shutters of the organ-case Apollo with his
lyre in his hand, as lord of the strings, seemed to look askance on
the music of the reed, in all the jealousy with which he put Marsyas to death so cruelly.

Meantime, the people, even his enemies, seemed to have forgotten him. Enemies, in truth, they still were, ready to take his life
should the opportunity come; as he perceived when at last he
ventured forth on a day of public ceremony. The bishop was to
pronounce a blessing upon the foundations of a new bridge, designed to take the place of the ancient Roman bridge which, repaired in a thousand places, had hitherto served for the chief
passage of the Yonne. It was as if the disturbing of that time-worn
masonry let out the dark spectres of departed times. Deep down,
at the core of the central pile, a painful object was exposed—the
skeleton of a child, placed there alive, it was rightly surmised, in
the superstitious belief that, by way of vicarious substitution, its
death would secure the safety of all who should pass over. There
were some who found themselves, with a little surprise, looking
round as if for a similar pledge of security in their new undertaking. It was just then that Denys was seen plainly, standing, in all
essential features precisely as of old, upon one of the great stones
prepared for the foundation of the new building. For a moment he
felt the eyes of the people upon him full of that strange humour,
and with characteristic alertness, after a rapid gaze over the grey
city in its broad green framework of vineyards, best seen from this
spot, flung himself down into the water and disappeared from
view where the stream flowed most swiftly below a row of flour-
mills. Some indeed fancied they had seen him emerge again safely
on the deck of one of the great boats, loaded with grapes and
wreathed triumphantly with flowers like a floating garden,
which were then bringing down the vintage from the country; but
generally the people believed their strange enemy now at last
departed for ever. Denys in truth was at work again in peace at
the cloister, upon his house of reeds and pipes. At times his fits
came upon him again; and when they came, for his cure he would
dig eagerly, turned sexton now, digging, by choice, graves for the

dead in the various churchyards of the town. There were those who had seen him thus employed (that form seeming still to carry something of real sun-gold upon it) peering into the darkness, while his tears fell sometimes among the grim relics his mattock had disturbed.

In fact, from the day of the exhumation of the body of the Saint in the great church, he had had a wonderful curiosity for such objects, and one wintry day bethought him of removing the body of his mother from the unconsecrated ground in which it lay, that he might bury it in the cloister, near the spot where he was now used to work. At twilight he came over the frozen snow. As he passed through the stony barriers of the place the world around seemed curdled to the centre—all but himself, fighting his way across it, turning now and then rightabout from the persistent wind, which dealt so roughly with his blond hair and the purple mantle whirled about him. The bones, hastily gathered, he placed, awefully but without ceremony, in a hollow space pre-pared secretly within the grave of another.

Meantime the winds of his organ were ready to blow; and with difficulty he obtained grace from the Chapter for a trial of its powers on a notable public occasion, as follows. A singular guest was expected at Auxerre. In recompense for some service ren-dered to the Chapter in times gone by, the Sire de Chastellux had the hereditary dignity of a canon of the church. On the day of his reception he presented himself at the entrance of the choir in surplice and amice, worn over the military habit. The old count of Chastellux was lately dead, and the heir had announced his coming, according to custom, to claim his ecclesiastical priv-ilege. There had been long feud between the houses of Chastellux and Auxerre; but on this happy occasion an offer of peace came with a proposal for the hand of the Lady Ariane.

The goodly young man arrived, and, duly arrayed, was received into his stall at vespers, the bishop assisting. It was then that the people heard the music of the organ, rolling over them for the first time, with various feelings of delight. But the performer on and author of the instrument was forgotten in his work, and there was no re-instatement of the former favourite. The religious ceremony was followed by a civic festival, in which Auxerre welcomed its future lord. The festival was to end at nightfall with a somewhat rude popular pageant, in which the person of Winter would be hunted blindfold through the streets. It was the sequel to that earlier stage-play of the *Return from the East* in which Denys had been the central figure. The old forgotten player saw his past before him, and, as if mechanically, fell again into the chief place, monk's dress and all. It might restore his popularity: who could tell? Hastily he donned the ashen-grey mantle, the rough haircloth about the throat, and went through the preliminary matter. And it happened that a point of the haircloth scratched his lip deeply, with a long trickling of blood upon the chin. It was as if the sight of blood transported the spectators with a kind of mad rage, and suddenly revealed to them the truth. The pretended hunting of the unholy creature became a real one, which brought out, in rapid increase, men's evil passions. The soul of Denys was already at rest, as his body, now borne along in front of the crowd, was tossed hither and thither, torn at last limb from limb. The men stuck little shreds of his flesh, or, failing that, of his torn raiment, into their caps; the women lending their long hairpins for the purpose. The monk Hermes sought in vain next day for any remains of the body of his friend. Only, at nightfall, the heart of Denys was brought to him by a stranger, still entire. It must long since have mouldered into dust under the stone, marked with a cross, where he buried it in a dark corner of the cathedral aisle.

So the figure in the stained glass explained itself. To me, Denys seemed to have been a real resident at Auxerre. On days of a certain atmosphere, when the trace of the Middle Age comes out, like old marks in the stones in rainy weather, I seemed actually to have seen the tortured figure there—to have met Denys l'Auxerrois in the streets.

[1886]

Sebastian van Storck

It was a winter-scene, by Adrian van de Velde, or by Isaac van Ostade. All the delicate poetry together with all the delicate comfort of the frosty season was in the leafless branches turned to silver, the furred dresses of the skaters, the warmth of the red-brick housefronts under the gauze of white fog, the gleams of pale sunlight on the cuirasses of the mounted soldiers as they receded into the distance. Sebastian van Storck, confessedly the most graceful performer in all that skating multitude, moving in endless maze over the vast surface of the frozen water-meadow, liked best this season of the year for its expression of a perfect impassivity, or at least of a perfect repose. The earth was, or seemed to be, at rest, with a breathlessness of slumber which suited the young man's peculiar temper. The heavy summer, as it dried up the meadows now lying dead below the ice, set free a crowded and competing world of life, which, while it gleamed very pleasantly russet and yellow for the painter Albert Cuyp, seemed wellnigh to suffocate Sebastian van Storck. Yet with all his appreciation of the national winter, Sebastian was not altogether a Hollander. His mother, of Spanish descent and Catholic, had given a richness of tone and form to the healthy freshness of the Dutch physiognomy, apt to preserve its youthfulness of aspect far beyond the period of life usual with other peoples. This mixed expression charmed the eye of Isaac van Ostade, who had painted his portrait from a sketch taken at one of those skating parties, with his plume of squirrel's tail and fur muff, in all the modest pleasantness of boyhood. When he returned home lately from his studies at a place far inland, at the proposal of his tutor, to recover, as the tutor suggested, a certain loss of robustness, something more than that cheerful indifference of early youth had passed away. The learned man, who held, as was alleged, the doctrines of a surprising new philosophy, reluctant to disturb too early the fine intelligence of the pupil entrusted to him, had found it, perhaps, a matter of honesty to send back to his parents one likely enough to catch from others any sort of theoretic light; for the letter he wrote dwelt much on the lad's intellectual fearlessness. "At present," he had written, "he is influenced more by curiosity than by a care for truth, according to the character of the young. Certainly, he differs strikingly from his equals in age, by his passion for a vigorous intellectual gymnastic, such as the supine character of their minds renders distasteful to most young men, but in which he shows a fearlessness that at times makes me fancy that his ultimate destination may be the military life; for indeed the rigidly logical tendency of his mind always leads him out upon the practical. Don't misunderstand me! At present, he is strenuous only intellectually; and has given no definite sign of preference, as regards a vocation in life. But he seems to me to be one practical in this sense, that his theorems will shape life for him, directly; that he will always seek, as a matter of course, the effective equivalent to—the line of being which shall be the proper continuation of—his line of thinking. This intellectual rectitude, or candour, which to my mind has a kind of beauty in it, has reacted upon myself. I confess, with a searching quality." That "searching quality," indeed, many others also, people far from being intellectual, had experienced—an agitation of mind in his neighbourhood, oddly at variance with the composure of the young man's manner and surrounding, so jealously preserved.

In the crowd of spectators at the skating, whose eyes followed, so well-satisfied, the movements of Sebastian van Storck, were the mothers of marriageable daughters, who presently became the suitors of this rich and distinguished youth, introduced to them, as now grown to man's estate, by his delighted parents. Dutch aristocracy had put forth all its graces to become the winter morn: and it was characteristic of the period that the artist tribe was there, on a grand footing,—in waiting, for the lights and shadows they liked best. The artists were, in truth, an important body just then, as a natural consequence of the nation's hard-won prosperity; helping it to a full consciousness of the genial yet delicate homeliness it loved, for which it had fought so bravely, and was ready at any moment to fight anew, against man or the sea. Thomas de Keyser, who understood better than any one else the kind of quaint new Atticism which had found its way into the world over those waste salt marshes, wondering whether quite its finest type as he understood it could ever actually be seen there, saw it at last, in lively motion, in the person of Sebastian van Storck, and desired to paint his portrait. A little to his surprise, the young man declined the offer; not graciously, as was thought.

Holland, just then, was reposing on its laurels after its long contest with Spain, in a short period of complete wellbeing, before troubles of another kind should set in. That a darker time might return again, was clearly enough felt by Sebastian the elder—a time like that of William the Silent, with its insane civil animosities, which would demand similarly energetic personalities, and offer them similar opportunities. And then, it was part of his honest geniality of character to admire those who "get on" in the world. Himself had been, almost from boyhood, in contact with great affairs. A member of the States-General which had taken so hardly the kingly airs of Frederick Henry, he had assisted at the Congress of Munster, and figures conspicuously in Terburgh's picture of that assembly, which had finally established Holland as a first-rate power. The heroism by which the national wellbeing had been achieved was still of recent memory—the air full of its reverberation, and great movement. There was a tradition to be maintained; the sword by no means resting in its sheath. The age was still fitted to evoke a generous ambition; and this son, from whose natural gifts there was so much to hope for, might play his part, at least as a diplomatist, if the present quiet continued. Had not the learned man said that his natural disposition would lead him out always upon practice? And in truth, the memory of that Silent hero had its fascination for the youth. When, about this time, Peter de Keyser, Thomas's brother, unveiled at last his tomb of wrought bronze and marble in the *Nieuwe Kerk* at Delft, the young Sebastian was one of a small company present, and relished much the cold and abstract simplicity of the monument, so conformable to the great, abstract, and unuttered force of the hero who slept beneath.

In complete contrast to all that is abstract or cold in art, the home of Sebastian, the family mansion of the Storcks—a house, the front of which still survives in one of those patient architectural pieces by Jan van der Heyde—was, in its minute and busy wellbeing, like an epitome of Holland itself with all the good-fortune of its "thriving genius" reflected, quite spontaneously, in the national taste. The nation had learned to content itself with a religion which told little, or not at all, on the outsides of things. But we may fancy that something of the religious spirit had gone, according to the law of the transmutation of forces, into the scrupulous care for cleanliness, into the grave, old-world, conservative beauty of Dutch houses, which meant that the life people maintained in them was normally affectionate and pure.

The most curious florists of Holland were ambitious to supply the Burgomaster van Storck with the choicest products of their skill for the garden spread below the windows on either side of the portico, and along the central avenue of hoary beeches which led to it. Naturally this house, within a mile of the city of Haarlem, became a resort of the artists, then mixing freely in great society, giving and receiving hints as to the domestic picturesque. Creatures of leisure—of leisure on both sides—they were the appropriate complement of Dutch prosperity, as it was understood just then. Sebastian the elder could almost have wished his son to be one of them: it was the next best thing to being an influential publicist or statesman. The Dutch had just begun to see what a picture their country was—its canals, and *boompjis*, and endless, broadly-lighted meadows, and thousands of miles of quaint water-side: and their painters, the first true masters of landscape for its own sake, were further informing them in the matter. They were bringing proof, for all who cared to see, of the wealth of colour there was all around them in this, supposably, sad land. Above all, they developed the old Low-country taste for interiors. Those innumerable *genre* pieces—conversation, music, play—were in truth the equivalent of novel-reading for that day; its own actual life, in its own proper circumstances, reflected in various degrees of idealisation, with no diminution of the sense of reality (that is to say) but with more and more purged and perfected delightfulness of interest. Themselves illustrating, as every student of their history knows, the good-fellowship of family life, it was the ideal of that life which these artists depicted; the ideal of home in a country where the preponderant interest of life, after all, could not well be out of doors. Of the earth earthy—genuine red earth of the old Adam—it was an ideal very different from that which the sacred Italian painters had evoked from the life of Italy, yet, in its best types, was not without a kind of natural religiousness. And in the achievement of a type of beauty so national and vernacular, the votaries of purely Dutch art might well feel that the Italianisers, like Berghem, Boll, and Jan Weenix went so far afield in vain.

The fine organisation and acute intelligence of Sebastian would have made him an effective connoisseur of the arts, as he showed by the justice of his remarks in those assemblies of the artists which his father so much loved. But in truth the arts were a matter he could but just tolerate. Why add, by a forced and artificial production, to the monotonous tide of competing, fleeting existence? Only, finding so much fine art actually about him, he was compelled (so to speak) to adjust himself to it; to ascertain and accept that in it which should least collide with, or might even carry forward a little, his own characteristic tendencies. Obviously somewhat jealous of his intellectual interests, he loved inanimate nature, it might have been thought, better than man. He cared nothing, indeed, for the warm sandbanks of Wynants, nor for those eerie relics of the ancient Dutch woodland which survive in Hobbema and Ruysdael, still less for the highly-coloured sceneries of the academic band at Rome, in spite of the escape they provide one into clear breadth of atmosphere. For though Sebastian van Storck refused to travel, he loved the distant—enjoyed the sense of things seen from a distance, carrying us, as on wide wings of space itself, far out of one's actual surrounding. His preference in the matter of art was, therefore, for those prospects *à vol a'oiseau*—of the caged bird on the wing at last—of which Rubens had the secret, and still more Philip de Koninck, four of whose choicest works occupied the four walls of his chamber; visionary escapes, north, south, east, and west, into a wide-open though, it must be confessed, a somewhat sullen land. For the fourth of them he had exchanged with his mother a marvellously vivid Metsu, lately bequeathed to him, in which she herself was presented. They were the sole ornaments he permitted himself. From the midst of the busy and busy-looking house, crowded with the furniture and the pretty little toys of many generations, a long passage led the rare visitor up a winding staircase, and (again at the end of a long passage) he found himself as if shut off from the whole talkative Dutch world, and in the embrace of that wonderful quiet which is also possible in Holland at its height all around him. It was here that Sebastian could yield himself, with the only sort of love he had ever felt, to the supremacy of his difficult thoughts.—A kind of *empty* place! Here, you felt, all had been mentally put to rights by the working-out of a long equation, which had zero is equal to zero for its result. Here one did, and perhaps felt, nothing; one only thought. Of living creatures only birds came there freely, the sea-birds especially, to attract and detain which there were all sorts of ingenious contrivances about the windows, such as one may see in the cottage sceneries of Jan Steen and others. There was something, doubtless, of his passion for distance in this welcoming of the creatures of the air. An extreme simplicity in their manner of life was, indeed, characteristic of many a distinguished Hollander— William the Silent, Baruch de Spinosa, the brothers de Witt. But the simplicity of Sebastian van Storck was something different from that, and certainly nothing democratic. His mother thought him like one disembarrassing himself carefully, and little by little, of all impediments, habituating himself gradually to make shift with as little as possible, in preparation for a long journey.

The Burgomaster van Storck entertained a party of friends, consisting chiefly of his favourite artists, one summer evening. The guests were seen arriving on foot in the fine weather, some of them accompanied by their wives and daughters, against the light of the low sun, falling red on the old trees of the avenue and the faces of those who advanced along it:—Willem van Aelst, expecting to find hints for a flower-portrait in the exotics which would decorate the banqueting-room; Gerard Dow, to feed his eye, amid all that glittering luxury, on the combat between candle-light and the last rays of the departing sun; Thomas de Keyser, to catch by stealth the likeness of Sebastian the younger. Albert Cuyp was there, who, developing the latent gold in Rembrandt, had brought into his native Dordrecht a heavy wealth of sunshine, as exotic as those flowers or the eastern carpets on the Burgomaster's tables, with Hooch, the indoor Cuyp, and Willem van de Velde, who painted those shorepieces with gay ships of war, such as he loved, for his patron's cabinet. Thomas de Keyser came, in company with his brother Peter, his niece, and young Mr. Nicholas Stone from England, pupil of that brother Peter, who afterwards married the niece. For the life of Dutch artists, too, was exemplary in matters of domestic relationship, its history telling many a cheering story of mutual faith in misfortune. Hardly less exemplary was the comradeship which they displayed among themselves, obscuring their own best gifts sometimes, one in the mere accessories of another man's work, so that they came together to-night with no fear of falling out, and spoiling the musical interludes of Madame van Storck in the large back parlour. A little way behind the other guests, three of them together, son, grandson, and the grandfather, moving slowly, came the Hondecoeters—Giles, Gybrecht, and Melchoir. They led the party before the house was entered, by fading light, to see the curious poultry of the Burgomaster go to roost; and it was almost night when the supper-room was reached at last. The occasion was an important one to Sebastian, and to others through him. For (was it the music of the duets? he asked himself next morning, with a certain distaste as he remembered it all, or the heady Spanish wines poured out so freely in those narrow but deep Venetian glasses?) on this evening he approached more nearly than he had ever yet done to Mademoiselle van Westrheene, as she sat there beside the *clavecin* looking very ruddy and fresh in her white satin, trimmed with glossy crimson swans-down.

So genially attempered, so warm, was life become, in the land of which Pliny had spoken as scarcely dry land at all. And, in truth, the sea which Sebastian so much loved, and with so great a satisfaction and sense of wellbeing in every hint of its nearness, is never far distant in Holland. Invading all places, stealing under one's feet, insinuating itself everywhere along an endless network of canals (by no means such formal channels as we understand by the name, but picturesque rivers, with sedgy banks and haunted by innumerable birds) its incidents present themselves oddly even in one's park or woodland walks; the ship in full sail appearing suddenly among the great trees or above the garden wall, where we had no suspicion of the presence of water. In the very conditions of life in such a country there was a standing force of pathos. The country itself shared the uncertainty of the individual human life; and there was pathos also in the constantly renewed, heavily-taxed labour, necessary to keep the native soil, fought for so unselfishly, there at all, with a warfare that must still be maintained when that other struggle with the Spaniard was over. But though Sebastian liked to breathe, so nearly, the sea and its influences, those were considerations he scarcely entertained. In his passion for *Schwindsucht*—we haven't the word—he found it pleasant to think of the resistless element which left one hardly a foot-space amidst the yielding sand; of the old beds of lost rivers, surviving now only as deeper channels in the sea; of the remains of a certain ancient town, which within men's memory had lost its few remaining inhabitants, and, with its already empty tombs, dissolved and disappeared in the flood.

It happened, on occasion of an exceptionally low tide, that some remarkable relics were exposed to view on the coast of the island of Vleeland. A countryman's waggon overtaken by the tide, as he returned with merchandise from the shore! you might have supposed, but for a touch of grace in the construction of the thing—lightly wrought timber-work, united and adorned by a multitude of brass fastenings, like the work of children for their simplicity, while the rude, stiff chair, or throne, set upon it, seemed to distinguish it as a chariot of state. To some antiquarians it told the story of the overwhelming of one of the chiefs of the old primeval people of Holland, amid all his gala array, in a great storm. But it was another view which Sebastian preferred; that this object was sepulchral, namely, in its motive—the one surviving relic of a grand burial, in the ancient manner, of a king or hero, whose very tomb was wasted away.—*Sunt metis metæ!* There came with it the odd fancy that he himself would like to have been dead and gone as long ago, with a kind of envy of those whose deceasing was so long since over.

On more peaceful days he would ponder Pliny's account of those primeval forefathers, but without Pliny's contempt for them. A cloyed Roman might despise their humble existence, fixed by necessity from age to age, and with no desire of change, as "the ocean poured in its flood twice a day, making it uncertain whether the country was a part of the continent or of the sea." But for his part Sebastian found something of poetry in all that, as he conceived what thoughts the old Hollander might have had at his fishing, with nets themselves woven of seaweed, waiting carefully for his drink on the heavy rains, and taking refuge, as the flood rose, on the sand-hills, in a little hut constructed but airily on tall stakes, conformable to the elevation of the highest tides, like a navigator, thought the learned writer, when the sea was risen, like a shipwrecked mariner when it was retired. For the fancy of Sebastian he lived with great breadths of calm light above and around him, influenced by, and, in a sense, living upon them, and surely might well complain, though to Pliny's so infinite surprise, on being made a Roman citizen.

And certainly Sebastian van Storck did not felicitate his people on the luck which, in the words of another old writer, "hath disposed them to so thriving a genius." Their restless ingenuity in making and maintaining dry land where nature had willed the sea, was even more like the industry of animals than had been that life of their forefathers. Away with that tetchy, feverish, unworthy agitation! with this and that, all too importunate, motive of interest! And then, "My son!" said his father, "be stimulated to action!" he, too, thinking of that heroic industry which had triumphed over nature precisely where the contest had been most difficult.

Yet, in truth, Sebastian was forcibly taken by the simplicity of a great affection, as set forth in an incident of real life of which he heard just then. The eminent Grotius being condemned to perpetual imprisonment, his wife determined to share his fate, alleviated only by the reading of books sent by friends. The books, finished, were returned in a great chest. In this chest the wife enclosed the husband, and was able to reply to the objections of the soldiers who carried it complaining of its weight, with a self-control, which she maintained till the captive was in safety, herself remaining to face the consequences; and there was a kind of absoluteness of affection in that, which attracted Sebastian for a while to ponder on the practical forces which shape men's lives. Had he turned, indeed, to a practical career it would have been less in the direction of the military or political life than of another form of enterprise popular with his countrymen. In the eager, gallant life of that age, if the sword fell for a moment into its sheath, they were for starting off on perilous voyages to the regions of frost and snow in search after that "North-Western passage," for the discovery of which the States-General had offered large rewards. Sebastian, in effect, found a charm in the thought of that still, drowsy, spellbound world of perpetual ice, as in art and life he could always tolerate the sea. Admiral-general of Holland, as painted by Van der Helst, with a marine background by Backhuizen:—at moments his father could fancy him so.

There was still another very different sort of character to which Sebastian would let his thoughts stray, without check, for a time. His mother, whom he much resembled outwardly, a Catholic from Brabant, had had saints in her family, and from time to time the mind of Sebastian had been occupied on the subject of monastic life, its quiet, its negation. The portrait of a certain Carthusian prior, which, like the famous statue of Saint Bruno, the first Carthusian, in the church of Santa Maria degli Angeli at Rome, could it have spoken, would have said, "Silence!" kept strange company with the painted visages of men of affairs. A great theological strife was then raging in Holland. Grave ministers of religion assembled sometimes, as in the painted scene by Rembrandt, in the Burgomaster's house, and once, not however in their company, came a renowned young Jewish divine, Baruch de Spinosa, with whom, most unexpectedly, Sebastian found himself in sympathy, meeting the young Jew's far-reaching thoughts half-way, to the confirmation of his own; and he did not know that his visitor, very ready with the pencil, had taken his likeness as they talked on the fly-leaf of his note-book. Alive to that theological disturbance in the air all around him, he refused to be moved by it, as essentially a strife on small matters, anticipating a vagrant regret which may have visited many other minds since, the regret, namely, that the old, pensive, use-and-wont Catholicism, which had accompanied the nation's earlier struggle for existence, and consoled it therein, had been taken from it. And for himself, indeed, what impressed him in that old Catholicism was a kind of lull in it—a lulling power—like that of the monotonous organ-music, which Holland, Catholic or not, still so greatly loves. But what he could not away with in the Catholic religion was its unfailing drift towards the concrete—the positive imageries of a faith, so richly beset with persons, things, historical incidents.

Rigidly logical in the method of his inferences, he attained the poetic quality only by the audacity with which he conceived the whole sublime extension of his premises. The contrast was a strange one between the careful, the almost petty fineness of his personal surrounding—all the elegant conventionalities of life, in that rising Dutch family—and the mortal coldness of a temperament, the intellectual tendencies of which seemed to necessitate straight-forward flight from all that was positive. He seemed, if one may say so, in love with death; preferring winter to summer; finding only a tranquillising influence in the thought of the earth beneath our feet cooling down for ever from its old cosmic heat; watching pleasurably how their colours fled out of things, and the long sand-bank in the sea, which had been the rampart of a town, was washed down in its turn. One of his acquaintance, a penurious young poet, who, having nothing in his pockets but the imaginative or otherwise barely potential gold of manuscript verses, would have grasped so eagerly, had they lain within his reach, at the elegant outsides of life, thought the fortunate Sebastian, possessed of every possible opportunity of that kind, yet bent only on dispensing with it, certainly a most puzzling and comfortless creature. A few only, half discerning what was in his mind, would fain have shared his intellectual clearness, and found a kind of beauty in this youthful enthusiasm for an abstract theorem. Extremes meeting, his cold and dispassionate detachment from all that is most attractive to ordinary minds came to have the impressiveness of a great passion. And for the most part, people had loved him; feeling instinctively that somewhere there must be the justification of his difference from themselves. It was like being in love: or it was an intellectual malady, such as pleaded for forbearance, like bodily sickness, and gave at times a resigned and touching sweetness to what he did and said. Only once, at a moment of the wild popular excitement which at that period was easy to provoke in Holland, there was a certain group of persons who would have shut him up as no well-wisher to, and perhaps a plotter against, the common-weal. A single traitor might cut the dykes in an hour, in the interest of the English or the French. Or, had he already committed some treasonable act, who was so anxious to expose no writing of his that he left his very letters unsigned, and there were little stratagems to get specimens of his fair manuscript? For with all his breadth of mystic intention, he was persistent, as the hours crept on, to leave all the inevitable details of life at least in order, in equation. And all his singularities appeared to be summed up in his refusal to take his place in the life-sized family group (*très distingué et très soigné*, remarks a modern critic of the work) painted about this time. His mother expostulated with him on the matter:—she must needs feel, a little icily, the emptiness of hope, and something more than the due measure of cold in things for a woman of her age, in the presence of a son who desired but to fade out of the world like a breath—and she suggested filial duty. "Good mother," he answered, "there are duties towards the intellect also, which women can but rarely understand."

The artists and their wives were come to supper again, with the Burgomaster van Storck. Mademoiselle van Westrheene was also come, with her sister and mother. The girl was by this time fallen in love with Sebastian; and she was one of the few who, in spite of his terrible coldness, really loved him for himself. But though of good birth she was poor, while Sebastian could not but perceive that he had many suitors of his wealth. In truth, Madame van Westrheene, her mother, did wish to marry this daughter into the great world, and plied many arts to that end, such as "daughterful" mothers use. Her healthy freshness of mien and mind, her ruddy beauty, some showy presents that had passed, were of a piece with the ruddy colouring of the very house these people lived in; and for a moment the cheerful warmth that may be felt in life seemed to come very close to him,—to come forth, and enfold him. Meantime the girl herself taking note of this, that on a former occasion of their meeting he had seemed likely to respond to her inclination, and that his father would readily consent to such a marriage, surprised him on the sudden with those coquetries and importunities, all those little arts of love, which often succeed with men. Only, to Sebastian they seemed opposed to that absolute nature we suppose in love. And while, in the eyes of all around him to-night, this courtship seemed to promise him, thus early in life, a kind of quiet happiness, he was coming to an estimate of the situation, with strict regard to that ideal of a calm, intellectual indifference, of which he was the sworn chevalier. Set in the cold, hard light of that ideal, this girl, with the pronounced personal views of her mother, and in the very effectiveness of arts prompted by a real affection, bringing the warm life they prefigured so close to him, seemed vulgar! And still he felt himself bound in honour; or judged from their manner that she and those about them thought him thus bound. He did not reflect on the inconsistency of the feeling of honour (living, as it does essentially, upon the concrete and minute detail of social relationship) for one who, on principle, set so slight a value on anything whatever that is merely relative in its character.

The guests, lively and late, were almost pledging the betrothed in the rich wine. Only Sebastian's mother knew; and at that advanced hour, while the company were thus intently occupied, drew away the Burgomaster to confide to him the misgiving she felt, grown to a great height just then. The young man had slipped from the assembly; but certainly not with Mademoiselle van Westrheene, who was suddenly withdrawn also. And she never appeared again in the world. Already, next day, with the rumour that Sebastian had left his home, it was known that the expected marriage would not take place. The girl, indeed, alleged something in the way of a cause on her part; but seemed to fade away continually afterwards, and in the eyes of all who saw her was like one perishing of wounded pride. But to make a clean breast of her poor girlish worldliness, before she became a *béguine*, she confessed to her mother the receipt of the letter—the cruel letter that had killed her. And in effect, the first copy of this letter, written with a very deliberate fineness, rejecting her—accusing her, so natural, and simply loyal! of a vulgar coarseness of character—was found, oddly tacked on, as their last word, to the studious record of the abstract thoughts which had been the real business of Sebastian's life, in the room whither his mother went to seek him next day, littered with the fragments of the one portrait of him in existence.

The neat and elaborate manuscript volume, of which this letter formed the final page (odd transition! by which a train of thought so abstract drew its conclusion in the sphere of action) afforded at length to the few who were interested in him a much-coveted insight into the curiosity of his existence; and I pause just here to indicate in outline the kind of reasoning through which, making the "Infinite" his beginning and his end, Sebastian had come to think all definite forms of being, the warm pressure of life, the cry of nature itself, no more than a troublesome irritation of the surface of the one absolute mind, a passing vexatious thought or uneasy dream there, at its height of petulant importunity in the eager, human creature.

The volume was, indeed, a kind of treatise to be:—a hard, systematic, well-concatenated train of thought, still implicated in the circumstances of a journal. Freed from the accidents of that particular literary form with its unavoidable details of place and occasion, the theoretic strain would have been found mathematically continuous. The already so weary Sebastian might perhaps never have taken in hand, or succeeded in, this detachment of his thoughts; every one of which, beginning with himself, as the peculiar and intimate apprehension of this or that particular day and hour, seemed still to protest against such disturbance, as if reluctant to part from those accidental associations of the personal history which had prompted it, and so become a purely intellectual abstraction.

The series began with Sebastian's boyish enthusiasm for a strange, fine saying of Doctor Baruch de Spinosa, concerning the Divine Love:—That whoso loveth God truly must not expect to be loved by him in return. In mere reaction against an actual surrounding of which every circumstance tended to make him a finished egotist, that bold assertion defined for him the ideal of an intellectual disinterestedness, of a domain of unimpassioned mind, with the desire to put one's subjective side out of the way, and let pure reason speak.

And what pure reason affirmed in the first place, as the "beginning of wisdom," was that the world is but a thought, or a series of thoughts: that it exists, therefore, solely in mind. It showed him, as he fixed the mental eye with more and more of self-absorption on the phenomena of his intellectual existence, a picture or vision of the universe as actually the product, so far as he really knew it, of his own lonely thinking power—of himself, there, thinking: as being zero without him: and as possessing a perfectly homogeneous unity in that fact. "Things that have nothing in common with each other," said the axiomatic reason, "cannot be understood or explained by means of each other." But to pure reason things discovered themselves as being, in their essence, thoughts:—all things, even the most opposite things, mere transmutations of a single power, the power of thought. All was but conscious mind. Therefore, all the more exclusively, he must minister to mind, to the intellectual power, submitting himself to the sole direction of that, whithersoever it might lead him. Everything must be referred to, and, as it were, changed into the terms of that, if its essential value was to be ascertained. "Joy," he said, anticipating Spinosa—that, for the attainment of which men are ready to surrender all beside—"is but the name of a passion in which the mind passes to a greater perfection or power of thinking; as grief is the name of the passion in which it passes to a less."

Looking backward for the generative source of that creative power of thought in him, from his own mysterious intellectual being to its first cause, he still reflected, as one can but do, the enlarged pattern of himself into the vague region of hypothesis. In this way, some, at all events, would have explained his mental process. To him that process was nothing less than the apprehension, the revelation, of the greatest and most real of ideas—the true substance of all things. He, too, with his vividly-coloured existence, with this picturesque and sensuous world of Dutch art and Dutch reality all around that would fain have made him the prisoner of its colours, its genial warmth, its struggle for life, its selfish and crafty love, was but a transient perturbation of the one absolute mind; of which, indeed, all finite things whatever, time itself, the most durable achievements of nature and man, and all that seems most like independent energy, are no more than petty accidents or affections. Theorem and corollary! Thus they stood: *"There can be only one substance:* (corollary) it is the greatest of errors to think that the nonexistent, the world of finite things seen and felt, really is: (theorem): *for, whatever is, is but in that:* (practical corollary): one's wisdom, therefore, consists in hastening, so far as may be, the action of those forces which tend to the restoration of equilibrium, the calm surface of the absolute, untroubled mind, to *tabula rasa*, by the extinction in one's self of all that is but correlative to the finite illusion—by the suppression of ourselves."

In the loneliness which was gathering round him, and, oddly enough, as a somewhat surprising thing, he wondered whether there were, or had been, others possessed of like thoughts, ready to welcome any such as his veritable compatriots. And in fact he became aware just then, in readings difficult indeed, but which from their all-absorbing interest seemed almost like an illicit pleasure, a sense of kinship with certain older minds. The study of many an earlier adventurous theorist satisfied his curiosity as the record of daring physical adventure, for instance, might satisfy the curiosity of the healthy. It was a tradition—a constant tradition—that daring thought of his; an echo, or haunting recurrent voice of the human soul itself, and as such sealed with natural truth, which certain minds would not fail to heed; discerning also, if they were really loyal to themselves, its practical conclusion.—The one alone is: and all things beside are but its passing affections, which have no necessary or proper right to be.

As but such "accidents" or "affections," indeed, there might have been found, within the circumference of that one infinite creative thinker, some scope for the joy and love of the creature. There have been dispositions in which that abstract theorem has only induced a renewed value for the finite interests around and within us. Centre of heat and light, truly nothing has seemed to lie beyond the touch of its perpetual summer. It has allied itself to the poetical or artistic sympathy, which feels challenged to acquaint itself with and explore the various forms of finite existence all the more intimately, just because of that sense of one lively spirit circulating through all things—a tiny particle of the one soul, in the sunbeam, or the leaf. Sebastian van Storck, on the contrary, was determined, perhaps by some inherited satiety or fatigue in his nature, to the opposite issue of the practical dilemma. For him, that one abstract being was as the pallid Arctic sun, disclosing itself over the dead level of a glacial, a barren and absolutely lonely sea. The lively purpose of life had been frozen out of it. What he must admire, and love if he could, was "equilibrium," the void, the *tabula rasa*, into which, through all those apparent energies of man and nature, that in truth are but forces of disintegration, the world was really settling. And, himself a mere circumstance in a fatalistic series, to which the clay of the potter was no sufficient parallel, he could not expect to be "loved in return." At first, indeed, he had a kind of delight in his thoughts—in the eager pressure forward, to whatsoever conclusion, of a rigid intellectual gymnastic, which was like the making of Euclid. Only, little by little, under the freezing influence of such propositions, the theoretic energy itself, and with it his old eagerness for truth, the care to track it from proposition to proposition, was chilled out of him. In fact, the conclusion was there already, and might have been foreseen, in the premises. By a singular perversity, it seemed to him that every one of those passing "affections"—he too, alas! at times—was for ever trying to be, to assert *itself*, to maintain its isolated and petty self, by a kind of practical lie in things; although through every incident of its hypothetic existence it had protested that its proper function was to die. Surely! those transient affections marred the freedom, the truth, the beatific calm, of the absolute selfishness, which could not, if it would, pass beyond the circumference of itself; to which, at times, with a fantastic sense of wellbeing, he was capable of a sort of fanatical devotion. And those, as he conceived, were his moments of genuine theoretic insight, in which, under the abstract "perpetual light," he died to self; while the intellect, after all, had attained a freedom of its own through the vigorous act which assured him that, as nature was but a thought of his, so himself also was but the passing thought of God.

No! rather a puzzle only, an anomaly, upon that one, white, unruffled consciousness! His first principle once recognised, all the rest, the whole array of propositions down to the heartless practical conclusion, must follow of themselves. Detachment: to hasten hence: to fold up one's whole self, as a vesture put aside: to anticipate, by such individual force as he could find in him, the slow disintegration by which nature herself is levelling the eternal hills:—here would be the secret of peace, of such dignity and truth as there could be in a world which after all was essentially an illusion. For Sebastian at least, the world and the individual alike had been divested of all effective purpose. The most vivid of finite objects, the dramatic episodes of Dutch history, the brilliant personalities which had found their parts to play in them, that golden art, surrounding us with an ideal world, beyond which the real world is discernible indeed, but etherealised by the medium through which it comes to one: all this, for most men so powerful a link to existence, only set him on the thought of escape—means of escape—into a formless and nameless infinite world, quite evenly grey. The very emphasis of those objects, their importunity to the eye, the ear, the finite intelligence, was but the measure of their distance from what really is. One's personal presence, the presence, such as it is, of the most incisive things and persons around us, could only lessen by so much, that which really is. To restore *tabula rasa*, then, by a continual effort at self-effacement! Actually proud at times of his curious, well-reasoned nihilism, he could but regard what is called the business of life as no better than a trifling and wearisome delay. Bent on making sacrifice of the rich existence possible for him, as he would readily have sacrificed that of other people, to the bare and formal logic of the answer to a query (never proposed at all to entirely healthy minds) regarding the remote conditions and tendencies of that existence, he did not reflect that if others had inquired as curiously as himself the world could never have come so far at all—that the fact of its having come so far was itself a weighty exception to his hypothesis. His odd devotion, soaring or sinking into fanaticism, into a kind of religious mania, with what was really a vehement assertion of his individual will, he had formulated duty as the principle to hinder as little as possible what he called the restoration of equilibrium, the restoration of the primary consciousness to itself—its relief from that uneasy, tetchy, unworthy dream of a world, made so ill, or dreamt so weakly—to forget, to be forgotten.

   And at length this dark fanaticism, losing the support of his pride in the mere novelty of a reasoning so hard and dry, turned round upon him, as our fanaticism will, in black melancholy. The theoretic or imaginative desire to urge Time's creeping footsteps, was felt now as the physical fatigue which leaves the book or the

letter unfinished, or finishes eagerly out of hand, for mere finishing's sake, unimportant business. Strange! that the presence to
the mind of a metaphysical abstraction should have had this
power over one so fortunately endowed for the reception of the
sensible world. It could hardly have been so with him but for the
concurrence of physical causes with the influences proper to a
mere thought. The moralist, indeed, might have noted that a
meaner kind of pride, the morbid fear of vulgarity, lent secret
strength to the intellectual prejudice, which realised duty as the
renunciation of all finite objects, the fastidious refusal to be or do
any limited thing. But besides this it was legible in his own admis-
sions from time to time, that the body, following, as it does with
powerful temperaments, the lead of mind and the will, the intellectual consumption (so to term it) had been concurrent with,
had strengthened and been strengthened by, a vein of physical
phthisis—by a merely physical accident, after all, of his bodily
constitution, such as might have taken a different turn, had another accident fixed his home among the hills instead of on the
shore. Is it only the result of disease? he would ask himself sometimes with a sudden suspicion of his intellectual cogency—this
persuasion that myself, and all that surrounds me, are but a diminution of that which really is?—this unkindly melancholy?

The journal, with that "cruel" letter to Mademoiselle van Westrheene coming as the last step in the rigid process of theoretic
deduction, circulated among the curious; and people made their
judgments upon it. There were some who held that such opinions
should be suppressed by law; that they were, or might become,
dangerous to society. Perhaps it was the confessor of his mother
who thought of the matter most justly. The aged man smiled,
observing how, even for minds by no means superficial, the mere
dress it wears alters the look of a familiar thought; with a happy
sort of smile, as he added (reflecting that such truth as there was
in Sebastian's theory was duly covered by the propositions of his
own creed, and quoting Sebastian's favourite pagan wisdom from
the lips of Saint Paul) "in Him, we live, and move, and have our
being."

Next day, as Sebastian escaped to the sea under the long, monotonous line of wind-mills, in comparative calm of mind—reaction of that pleasant morning from the madness of the night

before—he was making light, or trying to make light, with some success, of his late distress. He would fain have thought it a small matter, to be adequately set at rest for him by certain well-tested influences of external nature, in a long visit to the place he liked best: a desolate house, amid the sands of the Helder, one of the old lodgings of his family, property now, rather, of the sea-birds, and almost surrounded by the encroaching tide, though there were still relics enough of hardy, sweet things about it, to form what was to Sebastian the most perfect garden in Holland. Here he could make "equation" between himself and what was not himself, and set things in order, in preparation towards such deliberate and final change in his manner of living as circumstances so clearly necessitated.

As he stayed in this place, with one or two silent serving people, a sudden rising of the wind altered, as it might seem, in a few dark, tempestuous hours, the entire world around him. The strong wind changed not again for fourteen days, and its effect was a permanent one; so that people might have fancied that an enemy had indeed cut the dykes somewhere—a pin-hole enough to wreck the ship of Holland, or at least this portion of it, which underwent an inundation of the sea the like of which had not occurred in that province for half a century. Only, when the body of Sebastian was found, apparently not long after death, a child lay asleep, swaddled warmly in his heavy furs, in an upper room of the old tower, to which the tide was almost risen; though the building still stood firmly, and still with the means of life in plenty. And it was in the saving of this child, with a great effort, as certain circumstances seemed to indicate, that Sebastian had lost his life.

His parents were come to seek him, believing him bent on self-destruction, and were almost glad to find him thus. A learned physician, moreover, endeavoured to comfort his mother by remarking that in any case he must certainly have died ere many years were passed, slowly, perhaps painfully, of a disease then coming into the world; disease begotten by the fogs of that country—waters, he observed, not in their place, "above the firmament"—on people grown somewhat over-delicate in their nature by the effects of modern luxury.

[1886]

Duke Carl of Rosenmold

One stormy season about the beginning of the present century, a
great tree came down among certain moss-covered ridges of old
masonry which break the surface of the Rosenmold heath, exposing, together with its roots, the remains of two persons. Whether
the bodies (male and female, said German bone-science) had
been purposely buried there was questionable. They seemed
rather to have been hidden away by the accident, whatever it
was, which had caused death—crushed, perhaps, under what had
been the low wall of a garden—being much distorted, and lying,
though neatly enough discovered by the upheaval of the soil, in
great confusion. People's attention was the more attracted to the
incident because popular fancy had long run upon a tradition of
buried treasures, golden treasures, in or about the antiquated
ruin which the garden boundary enclosed; the roofless shell of a
small but solidly-built stone house, burnt or overthrown, perhaps
in the time of the wars at the beginning of the eighteenth century.
Many persons went to visit the remains lying out on the dark,
wild *plateau*, which stretches away above the tallest roofs of the
old grand-ducal town, very distinctly outlined, on that day, in
deep fluid grey against a sky still heavy with coming rain. No
treasure, indeed, was forthcoming among the masses of fallen
stone. But the tradition was so far verified, that the bones had
rich golden ornaments about them; and for the minds of some
long-remembering people their discovery set at rest an old query.
It had never been precisely known what was become of the young
Duke Carl, who disappeared from the world just a century before,
about the time when a great army passed over those parts, at a
political crisis, one result of which was the final absorption of his
small territory in a neighbouring dominion. Restless, romantic,

eccentric, had he passed on with the victorious host, and taken the chances of an obscure soldier's life? Certain old letters hinted at a different ending—love-letters which provided for a secret meeting, preliminary perhaps to the final departure of the young Duke (who, by the usage of his realm, could only with extreme difficulty go whither, or marry whom, he pleased) to whatever worlds he had chosen, not of his own people. The minds of those still interested in the matter were now at last made up, the disposition of the remains suggesting to them the lively picture of a sullen night, the unexpected passing of the great army, and the two lovers rushing forth wildly at the sudden tumult outside their cheerful shelter, caught in the dark and trampled out so, surprised and unseen, among the horses and heavy guns.

Time, at the court of the Grand-duke of Rosenmold, at the beginning of the eighteenth century might seem to have been standing still almost since the Middle Age—since the days of the Emperor Charles the Fifth, at which period, by the marriage of the hereditary Grand-duke with a princess of the Imperial house, a sudden tide of wealth, flowing through the grand-ducal exchequer, had left a kind of golden architectural splendour on the place, always too ample for its population. The sloping Gothic roofs for carrying off the heavy snows still indented the sky—a world of tiles, with space uncurtailed for the awkward gambols of that very German goblin, Hans Klapper, on the long, slumberous, northern nights. Whole quarryfuls of wrought stone had been piled along the streets and around the squares, and were now grown, in truth, like nature's self again, in their rough, time-worn massiveness, with weeds and wild flowers where their decay accumulated, blossoming, always the same, beyond people's memories, every summer, as the storks came back to their platforms on the remote chimney-tops. Without, all was as it had been on the eve of the Thirty Years' War: the venerable dark-green mouldiness, priceless pearl of architectural effect, was unbroken by a single new gable. And within, human life—its thoughts, its habits, above all, its etiquette—had been put out by no matter of excitement, political or intellectual, ever at all, one might say, at any time. The rambling grand-ducal palace was full to overflowing with furniture, which, useful or useless, was all ornamental, and none of it new. Suppose the various objects, especially the contents of the haunted old lumber-rooms, duly arranged and ticketed, and their Highnesses would have had a historic museum, after which those famed "Green Vaults" at Dresden would hardly have counted as one of the glories of Augustus the Strong. An immense heraldry, that truly German vanity, had grown, expatiating, florid, eloquent, over everything, without and within—windows, house-fronts, church walls, and church floors. And one-half of the male inhabitants were big or little State functionaries, mostly of a *quasi* decorative order—the treble-singer to the town-council, the court organist, the court poet, and the like—each with his deputies and assistants, maintaining, all unbroken, a sleepy ceremonial, to make the hours just noticeable as they slipped away. At court, with a continuous round of ceremonies, which, though early in the day, must always take place under a jealous exclusion of the sun, one seemed to live in perpetual candle-light.

It was in a delightful rummaging of one of those lumber-rooms, escaped from that candle-light into the broad day of the uppermost windows, that the young Duke Carl laid his hand on an old volume of the year 1486, printed in heavy type, with frontispiece, perhaps, by Albert Dürer—*Ars Versificandi: The Art of Versification:* by Conrad Celtes. Crowned poet of the Emperor Frederick the Third, he had the right to speak on that subject; for while he vindicated as best he might old German literature against the charge of barbarism, he did also a man's part towards reviving in the Fatherland the knowledge of the poetry of Greece and Rome; and for Carl, the pearl, the golden nugget, of the volume was the Sapphic ode with which it closed—*To Apollo, praying that he would come to us from Italy, bringing his lyre with him: Ad Apollinem, ut ab Italis cum lyra ad Germanos veniat.* The god of light, coming to Germany from some more favoured world beyond it, over leagues of rainy hill and mountain, making soft day there: that had ever been the dream of the ghost-ridden yet deep-feeling and certainly meek German soul; of the great Dürer, for instance, who had been the friend of this Conrad Celtes, and himself, all German as he was, like a gleam of real day amid that hyperborean German darkness—a darkness which clave to him, too, at that dim time, when there were violent robbers, nay, real live devils, in every German wood. And it was precisely the aspiration of Carl himself. Those verses, coming to the boy's hand at the right moment, brought a beam of effectual daylight to a whole magazine of observation, fancy, desire, stored up from the first impressions of childhood. To bring Apollo with his lyre to Germany! It was precisely that he, Carl, desired to do—was, as he might flatter himself, actually doing.

The daylight, the Apolline aurora, which the young Duke Carl claimed to be bringing to his candle-lit people, came in the somewhat questionable form of the contemporary French ideal, in matters of art and literature—French ideal, in matters of art and literature—French plays, French architecture, French looking-glasses—Apollo in the dandified costume of Lewis the Fourteenth. Only, confronting the essentially aged and decrepit graces of his model with his own essentially youthful temper, he invigorated what he borrowed; and with him as aspiration towards the classical ideal, so often hollow and insincere, lost all its affectation. His doating grandfather, the reigning Grand-duke, afforded readily enough, from the great store of inherited wealth which would one day be the lad's, the funds necessary for the completion of the vast unfinished Residence, with "pavilions" (after the manner of the famous Mansard) uniting its scattered parts; while a wonderful flowerage of architectural fancy, with broken attic roofs, passed over and beyond the earlier fabric; the later and lighter forms being in part carved adroitly out of the heavy masses of the old, honest, "stump Gothic" tracery. One fault only Carl found in his French models, and was resolute to correct. He would have, at least within, real marble in place of stucco, and, if he might, perhaps solid gold for gilding. There was something in the sanguine, floridly handsome youth, with his alertness of mind turned wholly, amid the vexing preoccupations of an age of war, upon embellishment and the softer things of life, which soothed the testy humours of the old Duke, like the quiet physical warmth of a fire or the sun. He was ready to preside with all ceremony at a presentation of Marivaux's *Death of Hannibal*, played in the original, with such imperfect mastery of the French accent as the lovers of new light in Rosenmold had at command, in a theatre copied from that at Versailles, lined with pale yellow satin, and with a picture, amid the stucco braveries of the ceiling, of the Septentrional Apollo himself, in somewhat watery red and blue. Innumerable wax lights in cut-glass lustres were a thing of course. Duke Carl himself, attired after the newest French fashion, played the part of Hannibal. The old Duke, indeed, at a council-board devoted hitherto to matters of state, would nod very early in certain long discussions on matters of art—magnificent schemes, from this or that eminent contractor, for spending his money tastefully, distinguishings of the *rococo* and the *baroque*. On the other hand, having been all his life in close intercourse with select humanity, self-conscious and arrayed for presentation, he was a helpful judge of portraits and the various degrees of the attainment of truth therein—a phase of fine art which the grandson could not value too much. The sergeant-painter and the deputy sergeant-painter were, indeed, conventional performers enough; as mechanical in their dispensation of wigs, finger-rings, ruffles, and simpers, as the figure of the armed knight who struck the bell in the Residence tower. But scattered through its half-deserted rooms, state bed-chambers and the like, hung the works of more genuine masters, still as unadulterate as the hock, known to be two generations old, in the grand-ducal cellar. The youth had even his scheme of inviting the illustrious Antony Coppel to the court; to live there, if he would, with the honours and emoluments of a prince of the blood. The illustrious Mansard had actually promised to come, had not his sudden death taken him away from earthly glory.

And at least, if one must forgo the masters, masterpieces might be had for their price. For ten thousand marks—day ever to be remembered!—a genuine work of "the Urbinate," from the cabinet of a certain commercially-minded Italian grand-duke, was on its way to Rosenmold, anxiously awaited as it came over rainy mountain-passes, and along the rough German roads, through doubtful weather. The tribune, the throne itself, were made ready in the presence-chamber, with hangings in the grand-ducal colours, laced with gold, together with a speech and an ode. Late at night, at last, the waggon was heard rumbling into the courtyard, with the guest arrived in safety, but, if one must confess one's self,

perhaps forbidding at first sight. From a comfortless portico, with
all the grotesqueness of the Middle Age, supported by brown, aged
bishops, whose meditations no incident could distract, Our Lady
looked out no better than an unpretending nun, with nothing to
say the like of which one was used to hear. Certainly one was not
stimulated by, enwrapped, absorbed in the great master's doings;
only, with much private disappointment, put on one's mettle to
defend him against critics notoriously wanting in sensibility, and
against one's self. In truth, the painter whom Carl most unaffectedly enjoyed, the real vigour of his youthful and somewhat animal taste finding here its proper sustenance, was Rubens—Rubens
reached, as he is reached at his best, in well-preserved family
portraits, fresh, gay, ingenious, as of privileged young people who
could never grown old. Had not he, too, brought something of the
splendour of a "better land" into those northern regions; if not the
glowing gold of Titian's Italian sun, yet the carnation and yellow
of roses or tulips, such as might really grow there with cultivation, even under rainy skies? And then, about this time something
was heard at the grand-ducal court of certain mysterious experiments in the making of porcelain; veritable alchemy, for the turning of clay into gold. The reign of Dresden china was at hand,
with one's own world of little men and women more delightfully
diminutive still, amid imitations of artificial flowers. The young
Duke braced himself for a plot to steal the gifted Herr Böttcher
from his enforced residence, as if in prison, at the fortress of
Meissen. Why not bring pots and wheels to Rosenmond, and prosecute his discoveries there? The Grand-duke, indeed, preferred his
old service of gold plate, and would have had the lad a *virtuoso* in
nothing less costly than gold—gold snuff-boxes.

For, in truth, regarding what belongs to art or culture, as elsewhere, we may have a large appetite and little to feed on. Only, in
the things of the mind, the appetite itself counts for so much, at
least in hopeful, unobstructed youth, with the world before it.
"You are the Apollo you tell us of, the northern Apollo," people
were beginning to say to him, surprised from time to time by a
mental purpose beyond their guesses—expressions, liftings, softly
gleaming or vehement lights, in the handsome countenance of
the youth, and his effective speech, as he roamed, inviting all

about him to share the honey, from music to painting, from painting to the drama, all alike florid in style, yes! and perhaps third-
rate. And so far consistently throughout he had held that the
centre of one's intellectual system must be understood to be in
France. He had thoughts of proceeding to that country, secretly,
in person, there to attain the very impress of its genius.

Meantime, its more portable flowers came to order in abundance. That the roses, so to put it, were but excellent artificial
flowers, redolent only of musk, neither disproved for Carl the
validity of his ideal nor for our minds the vocation of Carl himself
in these matters. In art, as in all other things of the mind, again,
much depends on the receiver; and the higher informing capacity,
if it exist within, will mould an unpromising matter to itself, will
realise itself by selection, and the preference of the better in what
is bad or indifferent, asserting its prerogative under the most unlikely conditions. People had in Carl, could they have understood
it, the spectacle, under those superficial braveries, of a really
heroic effort of mind at a disadvantage. That *rococo* seventeenth-
century French imitation of the true Renaissance, called out in
Carl a boundless enthusiasm, as the Italian original had done
two centuries before. He put into his reception of the æsthetic
achievements of Lewis the Fourteenth what young France had felt
when Francis the First brought home the great Da Vinci and his
works. It was but himself truly, after all, that he had found, so
fresh and real, among those artificial roses.

He was thrown the more upon such outward and sensuous products of mind—architecture, pottery, presently on music—because
for him, with so large intellectual capacity, there was, to speak
properly, no literature in his mother-tongue. Books there were,
German books, but of a dulness, a distance from the actual interests of the warm, various, coloured life around and within him, to
us hardly conceivable. There was more entertainment in the natural train of his own solitary thoughts, humoured and rightly
attuned by pleasant visible objects, than in all the books he had
hunted through so carefully for that all-searching intellectual
light, of which a passing gleam of interest gave fallacious promise
here or there. And still, generously, he held to the belief, urging
him to fresh endeavour, that the literature which might set heart

and mind free must exist somewhere, though court librarians could not say where. In search for it he spent many days in those old book-closets where he had lighted on the Latin ode of Conrad Celtes. Was German literature always to remain no more than a kind of penal apparatus for the teasing of the brain? Oh! for a literature set free, conterminous with the interests of life itself.

In music, it might be thought, Germany had already vindicated its spiritual liberty. One and another of those North-german towns were already aware of the youthful Sebastian Bach. The first notes had been heard of a music not borrowed from France, but flowing, as naturally as springs from their sources, out of the ever musical soul of Germany itself. And the Duke Carl was a sincere lover of music, himself playing melodiously on the violin to a delighted court. That new Germany of the spirit would be builded, perhaps, to the sound of music. In those other artistic enthusiasms, as the prophet of the French drama or the architectural taste of Lewis the Fourteenth, he had contributed himself generously, helping out with his own good-faith the inadequacy of their appeal. Music alone hitherto had really helped *him*, and taken him out of himself. To music, instinctively, more and more he was dedicate; and in his desire to refine and organise the court music, from which, by leave of absence to official performers enjoying their salaries at a distance, many parts had literally fallen away, like the favourite notes of a wornout spinet, he was ably seconded by a devoted youth, the deputy organist of the grand-ducal chapel. A member of the Roman Church amid a people chiefly of the Reformed religion, Duke Carl would creep sometimes into the curtained court pew of the Lutheran Church, to which he had presented its massive golden crucifix, to listen to the *chorales*, the execution of which he had managed to time to his liking, relishing, he could hardly explain why, those passages of a pleasantly monotonous and, as it might seem, unending melody—which certainly never came to what could rightly be called an ending here on earth; and having also a sympathy with the cheerful genius of Dr. Martin Luther, with his good tunes, and that ringing laughter which sent dull goblins flitting.

At this time, then, his mind ran eagerly for awhile on the project of some musical and dramatic development of a fancy suggested by that old Latin poem of Conrad Celtes—the hyperborean Apollo, sojourning, in the revolutions of time, in the sluggish north for a season, yet Apollo still, prompting art, music, poetry, and the philosophy which interprets man's life, making a sort of intercalary day amid the natural darkness; not meridian dry, of course, but a soft derivative daylight, good enough for us. It would be necessarily a mystic piece, abounding in fine touches, suggestions, innuendoes. His vague proposal was met half-way by the very practical executant power of his friend or servant, the deputy organist, already pondering, with just a satiric flavour (suppressible in actual performance, if the time for that should ever come) a musical work on Duke Carl himself; *Balder, an Interlude*. He was contented to re-cast and enlarge the part of the northern god of light, with a now wholly serious intention. But still, the near, the real and familiar, gave precision to, or actually superseded, the distant and the ideal. The soul of the music was but a transfusion from the fantastic but so interesting creature close at hand. And Carl was certainly true to his proposed part in that he gladdened others by an intellectual radiance which had ceased to mean warmth or animation for himself. For him the light was still to seek in France, in Italy, above all in old Greece, amid the precious things which might yet be lurking there unknown, in art, in poetry, perhaps in very life, till Prince Fortunate should come.

Yes! it was thither, to Greece, that his thoughts were turned during those romantic classical musings while the opera was made ready. That, in due time, was presented, with sufficient success. Meantime, his purpose was grown definite to visit that original country of the Muses, from which the pleasant things of Italy had been but derivative; to brave the difficulties in the way of leaving home at all, the difficulties also of access to Greece, in the present condition of the country.

At times the fancy came that he must really belong by descent to a southern race, that a physical cause might lie beneath this strange restlessness, like the imperfect reminiscence of something that had passed in earlier life. The aged ministers of heraldry were set to work (actually prolonging their days by an unexpected revival of interest in their too well-worn function) at the search for some obscure rivulet of Greek descent—later Byzantine Greek, perhaps,—in the Rosenmold genealogy. No! with a hundred quarterings, they were as indigenous, incorruptible heraldry reasserted, as the old yewtrees asquat on the heath.

And meantime those dreams of remote and probably adventurous travel lent the youth, still so healthy of body, a wing for more distant expeditions than he had ever yet inclined to, among his own wholesome German woodlands. In long rambles, afoot or on horseback, by day and night, he flung himself, for the resettling of his sanity, on the cheerful influences of their simple imagery; the hawks, as if asleep on the air below him; the bleached crags, evoked by late sunset among the dark oaks; the waterwheels, with their pleasant murmur, in the foldings of the hillside.

Clouds came across his heaven, little sudden clouds, like those which in this northern latitude, where summer is at best but a flighty visitor, chill out the heart, though but for a few minutes at a time, of the warmest afternoon. He had fits of the gloom of other people—their dull passage through and exit from the world, the threadbare incidents of their lives, their dismal funerals—which, unless he drove them away immediately by strenuous exercise, settled into a gloom more properly his own. Yet as such times outward things also would seem to concur unkindly in deepening the mental shadow about him, almost as if there were indeed animation in the natural world, elfin spirits in those inaccessible hillsides and dark ravines, as old German poetry pretended, cheerfully assistant sometimes, but for the most part troublesome, to their human kindred. Of late these fits had come somewhat more frequently, and had continued. Often it was a weary, deflowered face that his favourite mirrors reflected. Yes! people were prosaic, and their lives threadbare:—all but himself and organist Max, perhaps, and Fritz the treble-singer. In return, the people in actual contact with him thought him a little mad, though still ready to flatter his madness, as he could detect. Alone with the doating old grandfather in their stiff, distant, alien world of etiquette, he felt surrounded by flatterers, and would fain have tested the sincerity even of Max, and Fritz who said, echoing the words of the other, "Yourself, Sire, are the Apollo of Germany!"

It was his desire to test the sincerity of the people about him,

and unveil flatterers, which in the first instance suggested a trick
he played upon the court, upon all Europe. In that complex but
wholly Teutonic genealogy lately under research, lay a much-
prized thread of descent from the fifth Emperor Charles, and Carl,
under direction, read with much readiness to be impressed all
that was attainable concerning the great ancestor, finding there
in truth little enough to reward his pains. One hint he took, however. He determined to assist at his own obsequies.

That he might in this way facilitate that much-desired journey
occurred to him almost at once as an accessory motive, and in a
little while definite motives were engrossed in the dramatic interest, the pleasing gloom, the curiosity, of the thing itself. Certainly, amid the living world in Germany, especially in old, sleepy
Rosenmold, death made great parade of itself. Youth even, in its
sentimental mood, was ready to indulge in the luxury of decay,
and amuse itself with fancies of the tomb; as in periods of decadence or suspended progress, when the world seems to nap for a
time, artifices for the arrest or disguise of old age are adopted as a
fashion, and become the fopperies of the young. The whole body
of Carl's relations, saving the drowsy old grandfather, already lay
buried beneath their expansive heraldries: at times the whole
world almost seemed buried thus—made and re-made of the
dead—its entire fabric of politics, of art, of custom, being essentially heraldic "achievements," dead men's mementoes such as
those. You see he was a sceptical young man, and his kinsmen
dead and gone had passed certainly, in his imaginations of them,
into no other world, save, perhaps, into some stiffer, slower, sleepier, and more pompous phase of ceremony—the last degree of
court etiquette—as they lay there in the great, low-pitched,
grand-ducal vault, in their coffins, dusted once a year for All
Souls' Day, when the court officials descended thither, and Mass
for the dead was sung, amid an array of dropping crape and cob-
webs. The lad, with his full red lips and open blue eyes, coming as
with a great cup in his hands to life's feast, revolted from the like
of that, as from suffocation. And still the suggestion of it was
everywhere. In the garish afternoon, up to the wholesome heights
of the Heiligenberg suddenly from one of the villages of the plain
came the grinding death-knell. It seemed to come out of the ugly

grave itself, and enjoyment was dead. On his way homeward sadly, an hour later, he enters by chance the open door of a village church, half buried in the tangle of its churchyard. The rude coffin is lying there of a labourer who had but a hovel to live in. The enemy dogged one's footsteps! The young Carl seemed to be flying, not from death simply, but from assassination.

And as these thoughts sent him back in the rebounding power of youth, with renewed appetite, to life and sense, so, grown at last familiar, they gave additional purpose to his fantastic experiment. Had it not been said by a wise man that after all the offence of death was in its trappings Well! he would, as far as might be, try the thing, while, presumably, a large reversionary interest in life was still his. He would purchase his freedom, at least of those gloomy "trappings," and listen while he was spoken of as dead. The mere preparations gave pleasant proof of the devotion to him of a certain number, who entered without question into his plans. It is not difficult to mislead the world concerning what happens to those who live at the artificial distance from it of a court, with its high wall of etiquette. However the matter was managed, no one doubted, when, with a blazon of ceremonious words, the court news went forth that, after a brief illness, according to the way of his race, the hereditary Grand-duke was deceased. In momentary regret, bethinking them of the lad's taste for splendour, those to whom the arrangement of such matters belonged (the grandfather now sinking deeper into bare quiescence) backed by the popular wish, determined to give him a funeral with even more than grand-ducal measure of lugubrious magnificence. The place of his repose was marked out for him as officiously as if it had been the delimitation of a kingdom, in the ducal burial vault, through the cobwebbed windows of which, from the garden where he played as a child, the young Duke had often peered at the faded glories of the immense coroneted coffins, the oldest shedding their velvet tatters around them. Surrounded by the whole official world of Rosenmold, arrayed for the occasion in almost forgotten dresses of ceremony as if for a masquerade, the new coffin glided from the fragrant chapel where the *Requiem* was sung, down the broad staircase lined with peach-colour and yellow marble, into the shadows below. Carl himself, disguised as a strolling musician, had followed it across the square through a drenching rain, on which circumstance he overheard the old people congratulate the "blessed" dead within, had listened to a dirge of his own composing brought out on the great organ with much *bravura* by his friend, the new court organist, who was in the secret, and that night turned the key of the garden entrance to the vault, and peeped in upon the sleepy, painted, and bewigged young pages whose duty it would be for a certain number of days to come to watch beside their late master's couch.

And a certain number of weeks afterwards it was known that "the mad Duke" had reappeared, to the dismay of court marshals. Things might have gone hard with the youth had the strange news, at first as fantastic rumour, then as matter of solemn enquiry, lastly as ascertained fact, pleasing or otherwise, been less welcome than it was to the grandfather, too old, indeed, to sorrow deeply, but grown so decrepit as to propose that ministers should possess themselves of the person of the young Duke, proclaim him of age and regent. From those dim travels, presenting themselves to the old man, who had never been fifty miles away from home, as almost lunar in their audacity, he would come back—come back "in time," he murmured faintly, eager to feel that youthful, animating life on the stir about him once more.

Carl himself, now the thing was over, greatly relishing its satiric elements, must be forgiven the trick of the burial and his still greater enormity in coming to life again. And then, duke or no duke, it was understood that he willed that things should in no case be precisely as they had been. He would never again be quite so near people's lives as in the past—a fitful, intermittent visitor—almost as if he had been properly dead; the empty coffin remaining as a kind of symbolical "coronation incident," setting forth his future relations to his subjects. Of all those who believed him dead one human creature only, save the grandfather, had sincerely sorrowed for him; a woman, in tears as the funeral train passed by, with whom he had sympathetically discussed his own merits. Till then he had forgotten the incident which had exhibited him to her as the very genius of goodness and strength; how, one day, driving with her country produce into the market, and, embarrassed by the crowd, she had broken one of a hundred little

police rules, whereupon the officers were about to carry her away
to be fined, or worse, amid the jeers of the bystanders, always
ready to deal hardly with "the gipsy," at which precise moment
the tall Duke Carl, like the flash of a trusty sword, had leapt from
the palace stair and caused her to pass on in peace. She had half
detected him through his disguise; in due time news of his reappearance had been ceremoniously carried to her in her little cottage, and the remembrance of her hung about him not ungrate-
fully, as he went with delight upon his way.

The first long stage of his journey over, in headlong flight night
and day, he found himself one summer morning under the heat of
what seemed a southern sun, at last really at large on the
Bergstrasse, with the rich plain of the Palatinate on his left hand;
on the right hand vineyards, seen now for the first time, sloping
up into the crisp beeches of the Odenwald. By Weinheim only an
empty tower remained of the Castle of Windeck. He lay for the
night in the great whitewashed guest-chamber of the Capuchin
convent.

The national rivers, like the national woods, have a family
likeness: the Main, the Lahn, the Moselle, the Neckar, the Rhine.
By help of such accommodation as chance afforded, partly on the
stream itself, partly along the banks, he pursued the leisurely
winding course of one of the prettiest of these, tarrying for awhile
in the towns, grey, white, or red, which came in his way, tasting
their delightful native "little" wines, peeping into their old over-
loaded churches, inspecting the church furniture, or trying the
organs. For three nights he slept, warm and dry, on the hay stored
in a deserted cloister, and, attracted into the neighbouring mins-
ter for a snatch of church music, narrowly escaped detection. By
miraculous chance the grimmest lord of Rosenmold was there
within, recognised the youth and his companions—visitors naturally conspicuous, amid the crowd of peasants around them—and
for some hours was upon their traces. After unclean town streets
the country air was a perfume by contrast, or actually scented
with pinewoods. One seemed to breathe with it fancies of the
woods, the hills, and water—of a sort of souls in the landscape,
but cheerful and genial now, happy souls! A distant group of pines
on the verge of a great upland awoke a violent desire to be there—

seemed to challenge one to proceed thither. Was their infinite view thence? It was like an outpost of some far-off fancy land, a pledge of the reality of such. Above Cassel, the airy hills curved in one black outline against a glowing sky, pregnant, one could fancy, with weird forms, which might be at their old *diableries* again on those remote places ere night was quite come there. At last in the streets, the hundred churches, of Cologne, he feels something of a "Gothic" enthusiasm, and all a German's enthusiasm for the Rhine.

Through the length and breadth of the Rhine country the vintage was begun. The red ruins on the heights, the white-walled villages, white Saint Nepomuc upon the bridges, were but isolated high notes of contrast in a landscape, sleepy and indistinct under the flood of sunshine, with a headiness in it like that of must, of the new wine. The noise of the vineyards came through the lovely haze, still, at times, with the sharp sound of a bell—death-bell, perhaps, or only a crazy summons to the vintagers. And amid those broad, willowy reaches of the Rhine at length, from Bingen to Mannheim, where the brown hills wander into airy, blue distance, like a little picture of paradise, he felt that France was at hand. Before him lay the road thither, easy and straight.—That well of light so close! But, unexpectedly, the capricious incidence of his own humour with the opportunity did not suggest, as he would have wagered it must, "Go, drink at once!" Was it that France had come to be of no account at all, in comparison of Italy, of Greece? or that, as he passed over the German land, the conviction had come, "For you, France, Italy, Hellas, is here!"—that some recognition of the untried spiritual possibilities of meek Germany had for Carl transferred the ideal land out of space beyond the Alps or the Rhine, into future time, whither he must be the leader? A little chilly of humour, in spite of his manly strength, he was journeying partly in search of physical heat. To-day certainly, in this great vineyard, physical heat was about him in measure sufficient, at least for a German constitution. Might it be not otherwise with the imaginative, the intellectual, heat and light; the real need being that of an interpreter—Apollo, illuminant rather as the revealer than as the bringer of light? With large belief that the *Éclaircissement*, the

Aufklärung (he had already found the name for the thing) would indeed come, he had been in much bewilderment whence and how. Here, he began to see that it could be in no other way than by action of informing thought upon the vast accumulated material of which Germany was in possession: art, poetry, fiction, an entire imaginative world, following reasonably upon a deeper understanding of the past, of nature, of one's self—an understanding of all beside through the knowledge of one's self. To understand, would be the indispensable first step towards the enlargement of the great past, of one's little present, by criticism, by imagination. Then, the imprisoned souls of nature would speak as of old. The Middle Age, in Germany, where the past has had such generous reprisals, never far from us, would reassert its mystic spell, for the better understanding of our Raffaelle. The spirits of distant Hellas would reawake in the men and women of little German towns. Distant times, the most alien thoughts, would come near together, as elements in a great historic symphony. A kind of ardent, new patriotism awoke in him, sensitive for the first time at the words *national* poesy, *national* art and literature, *German* philosophy. To the resources of the past, of himself, of what was possible for German mind, more and more his mind opens as he goes on his way. A free, open space had been determined, which something now to be created, created by him, must occupy. "Only," he thought, "if I had coadjutors! If these thoughts would awake in but one other mind!"

At Strasbourg, with its mountainous goblin houses, nine stories high, grouped snugly, in the midst of that inclement plain, like a great stork's nest around the romantic red steeple of its cathedral, Duke Carl became fairly captive to the Middle Age. Tarrying there week after week he worked hard, but (without a ray of light from others) in one long mistake, at the chronology and history of the coloured windows. Antiquity's very self seemed expressed there, on the visionary images of king or patriarch, in the deeply incised marks of character, the hoary hair, the massive proportions, telling of a length of years beyond what is lived now. Surely, past ages, could one get at the historic soul of them, were not dead but living, rich in company, for the entertainment, the expansion, of the present: and Duke Carl was still without suspicion of the cynic afterthought that such historic soul was but an arbitrary substitution, a generous loan of one's self.

The mystic soul of Nature laid hold on him next, saying, "Come! understand, interpret me!" He was awakened one morning by the jingle of sledge-bells along the street beneath his windows. Winter had descended betimes from the mountains: the pale Rhine below the bridge of boats on the long way to Kehl was swollen with ice, and for the first time he realised that Switzerland was at hand. On a sudden he was captive to the enthusiasm of the mountains, and hastened along the valley of the Rhine by Alt Breisach and Basle, unrepelled by a thousand difficulties, to Swiss farmhouses and lonely villages, solemn still, and untouched by strangers. At Grindelwald, sleeping at last in the close neighbourhood of the greater Alps, he had the sense of an overbrooding presence, of some strange new companions around him. Here one might yield one's self to the unalterable imaginative appeal of the elements in their highest force and simplicity— light, air, water, earth. On very early spring days a mantle was suddenly lifted; the Alps were an apex of natural glory, towards which, in broadening spaces of light, the whole of Europe sloped upwards. Through them, on the right hand, as he journeyed on, were the doorways to Italy, to Como or Venice, from yonder peak Italy's self was visible!—as, on the left hand, in the South-german towns, in a high-toned, artistic fineness, in the dainty, flowered ironwork for instance, the overflow of Italian genius was traceable. These things presented themselves at last only to remind him that, in a new intellectual hope, he was already on his way home. Straight through life, straight through nature and man, with one's own self-knowledge as a light thereon, not by way of the geographical Italy or Greece, lay the road to the new Hellas, to be realised now as the outcome of home-born German genius. At times, in that early fine weather, looking now not southwards, but towards Germany, he seemed to trace the outspread of a faint, now wholly natural, aurora over the dark northern country. And it was in an actual sunrise that the news came which finally put him on the directest road homewards. One hardly dared breathe in the rapid uprise of all-embracing light which seemed like the intellectual rising of the Fatherland, when up the straggling path

to his high beech-grown summit (was one safe nowhere?) protesting over the roughness of the way, came the too familiar voices
(*ennui* itself made audible) of certain high functionaries of
Rosenmold, come to claim their new sovereign, close upon the
runaway.

Bringing news of the old Duke's decease! With a real grief at his
heart, he hastened now over the ground which lay between him
and the bed of death, still trying, at quieter intervals, to snatch
profit by the way; peeping, at the most unlikely hours, on the
objects of his curiosity, waiting for a glimpse of dawn through
glowing church windows, penetrating into old church treasures
by candle-light, taxing the old courtiers to pant up, for "the
view," to this or that conspicuous point in the world of hilly
woodland. From one such at last, in spite of everything with pleasure to Carl, old Rosenmold was visible—the attic windows of the
Residence, the storks on the chimneys, the green copper roofs
baking in the long, dry German summer. The homeliness of true
old Germany! He too felt it, and yearned towards his home.

And the "beggar-maid" was there. Thoughts of her had haunted
his mind all the journey through, as he was aware, not unpleased,
graciously overflowing towards any creature he found dependent
upon him. The mere fact that she was awaiting him, at his disposition, meekly, and as though through his long absence she had
never quitted the spot on which he had said farewell, touched his
fancy, and on a sudden concentrated his wavering preference into
a practical decision. "King Cophetua" would be hers. And his
goodwill sunned her wild-grown beauty into majesty, into a kind
of queenly richness. There was natural majesty in the heavy
waves of golden hair folded closely above the neck, built a little
massively; and she looked kind, beseeching also, capable of sorrow. She was like clear sunny weather, with bluebells and the
green leaves, between rainy days, and seemed to embody *Die Ruh
auf dem Gipfel*—all the restful hours he had spent of late in the
wood-sides and on the hilltops. One June day, on which she
seemed to have withdrawn into herself all the tokens of summer,
brought decision to our lover of artificial roses, who had cared so
little hitherto for the like of her. Grand-duke perforce, he would
make her his wife, and had already re-assured her with lively

mockery of his horrified ministers. "Go straight to life!" said his new poetic code; and here was the opportunity;—here, also, the real "adventure," in comparison of which his previous efforts that way seemed childish theatricalities, fit only to cheat a little the profound *ennui* of actual life. In a hundred stolen interviews she taught the hitherto indifferent youth the art of love.

Duke Carl had effected arrangements for his marriage, secret, but complete and soon to be made public. Long since he had cast complacent eyes on a strange architectural relic, an old grange or hunting-lodge on the heath, with he could hardly have defined what charm of remoteness and old romance. Popular belief amused itself with reports of the wizard who inhabited or haunted the place, his fantastic treasures, his immense age. His windows might be seen glittering afar on stormy nights, with a glaze of golden ornaments, said the more adventurous loiterer. It was not because he was suspicious still, but in a kind of wantonness of affection, and as if by way of giving yet greater zest to the luxury of their mutual trust that Duke Carl added to his announcement of the purposed place and time of the event a pretended test of the girl's devotion. He tells her the story of the aged wizard, meagre and wan, to whom she must find her way alone for the purpose of asking a question all-important to himself. The fierce old man will try to escape with terrible threats, will turn, or half turn, into repulsive animals. She must cling the faster; at last the spell will be broken; he will yield, he will become a youth once more, and give the desired answer.

The girl, otherwise so self-denying, and still modestly anxious for a private union, not to shame his high position in the world, had wished for one thing at least—to be loved amid the splendours habitual to him. Duke Carl sends to the old lodge his choicest personal possessions. For many days the public is aware of something on hand; a few get delightful glimpses of the treasures on their way to "the place on the heath." Was he preparing against contingencies, should the great army, soon to pass through these parts, not leave the country as innocently as might be desired?

The short grey day seemed a long one to those who, for various reasons, were waiting anxiously for the darkness; the court peo-

ple fretful and on their mettle, the townsfolk suspicious, Duke
Carl full of amorous longing. At her distant cottage beyond the
hills, Gretchen kept herself ready for the trial. It was expected
that certain great military officers would arrive that night, com-
manders of a victorious host making its way across Northern Germany, with no great respect for the rights of neutral territory,
often dealing with life and property too rudely to find the coveted
treasure. It was but one episode in a cruel war. Duke Carl did not
wait for the grandly illuminated supper prepared for their reception. Events precipitated themselves. Those officers came as practically victorious occupants, sheltering themselves for the night
in the luxurious rooms of the great palace. The army was in fact
in motion close behind its leaders, who (Gretchen warm and
happy in the arms, not of the aged wizard, but of the youthful
lover) are discussing terms for the final absorption of the duchy
with those traitorous old councillors. At their delicate supper
Duke Carl amuses his companion with caricature, amid cries of
cheerful laughter, of the sleepy courtiers entertaining their martial guests in all their pedantic politeness, like people in some
farcical dream. A priest, and certain chosen friends to witness the
marriage, were to come ere nightfall to the grange. The lovers
heard, as they thought, the sound of distant thunder. The hours
passed as they waited, and what came at last was not the priest
with his companions. Could they have been detained by the
storm? Duke Carl gently re-assures the girl—bids her believe in
him, and wait. But through the wind, grown to tempest, beyond
the sound of the violent thunder—louder than any possible
thunder—nearer and nearer comes the storm of the victorious
army, like some disturbance of the earth itself, as they flee into
the tumult, out of the intolerable confinement and suspense,
dead-set upon them.

The *Enlightening*, the *Aufklärung*, according to the aspiration of
Duke Carl, was effected by other hands; Lessing and Herder, brilliant precursors of the age of genius which centered in Goethe,
coming well within the natural limits of Carl's lifetime. As precursors Goethe gratefully recognised them, and understood that
there had been a thousand others, looking forward to a new era in

German literature with the desire which is in some sort a "forecast of capacity," awakening each other to the permanent reality of a poetic ideal in human life, slowly forming that public consciousness to which Goethe actually addressed himself. It is their aspirations I have tried to embody in the portrait of Carl.

A hard winter had covered the Main with a firm footing of ice. The liveliest social intercourse was quickened thereon. I was unfailing from early morning onwards; and, being lightly clad, found myself, when my mother drove up later to look on, fairly frozen. My mother sat in the carriage, quite stately in her furred cloak of red velvet, fastened on the breast with thick gold cord and tassels.

"Dear mother," I said, on the spur of the moment, "give me your furs, I am frozen."

She was equally ready. In a moment I had on the cloak. Falling below the knee, with its rich trimming of sables, and enriched with gold, it became me excellently. So clad I made my way up and down with a cheerful heart.

That was Goethe, perhaps fifty years later. His mother also related the incident to Betinna Brentano;—"There, skated my son, like an arrow among the groups. Away he went over the ice like a son of the gods. Anything so beautiful is not to be seen now. I clapped my hands for joy. Never shall I forget him as he darted out from one arch of the bridge, and in again under the other, the wind carrying the train behind him as he flew." In that amiable figure I seem to see the fulfilment of the Resurgam on Carl's empty coffin—the aspiring soul of Carl himself, in freedom and effective, at last.

[1887]

Hippolytus Veiled

A Study from Euripides

Centuries of zealous archæology notwithstanding, many phases of the so varied Greek genius are recorded for the modern student in a kind of shorthand only, or not at all. Even for Pausanias, visiting Greece before its direct part in affairs was quite played out, much had perished or grown dim—of its art, of the truth of its outward history, above all of its religion as a credible or practicable thing. And yet Pausanias visits Greece under conditions as favourable for observation as those under which later travellers, Addison or Eustace, proceed to Italy. For him the impress of life in those old Greek cities is not less vivid and entire than that of medieval Italy to ourselves; at Siena, for instance, with its ancient palaces still in occupation, its public edifices as serviceable as if the old republic had but just now vacated them, the tradition of their primitive worship still unbroken in its churches. Had the opportunities in which Pausanias was fortunate been ours, how many haunts of the antique Greek life unnoticed by him we should have peeped into, minutely systematic in our painstaking! how many a view would broaden out where he notes hardly anything at all on his map of Greece!

One of the most curious phases of Greek civilisation which has thus perished for us, and regarding which, as we may fancy, we should have made better use of that old traveller's facilities, is the early Attic deme-life—its picturesque, intensely localised variety, in the hollow or on the spur of mountain or sea-shore; and with it many a relic of primitive religion, many an early growth of art parallel to what Vasari records of artistic beginnings in the smaller cities of Italy. Colonus and Acharnæ, surviving still so vividly by the magic of Sophocles, of Aristophanes, are but isolated examples of a widespread manner of life, in which, amid many provincial peculiarities, the first, yet perhaps the most costly and telling steps were made in all the various departments of Greek culture. Even in the days of Pausanias, Piræus was still traceable as a distinct township, once the possible rival of Athens, with its little old covered market by the seaside, and the symbolical picture of the place, its Genius, visible on the wall. And that is but the type of what there had been to know of threescore and more village communities, each having its own altars, its special worship and place of civic assembly, its trade and crafts, its name drawn from physical peculiarity or famous incident, its body of heroic tradition. Lingering on while Athens, the great deme, gradually absorbed into itself more and more of their achievements, and passing away almost completely as political factors in the Peloponnesian war, they were still felt, we can hardly doubt, in the actual physiognomy of Greece. That variety in unity, which its singular geographical formation secured to Greece as a whole, was at its utmost in these minute reflexions of the national character, with all the relish of local difference— new art, new poetry, fresh ventures in political combination, in the conception of life, springing as if straight from the soil, like the thorn-blossom of early spring in magic lines over all that rocky land. On the other hand, it was just here that ancient habits clung most tenaciously—that old-fashioned, homely, delightful existence, to which the refugee, pent up in Athens in the years of the Peloponnesian war, looked back so fondly. If the impression of Greece generally is but enhanced by the littleness of the physical scene of events intellectually so great—such a system of grand lines, restrained within so narrow a compass, as in one of its fine coins—still more would this be true of those centres of country life. Here, certainly, was that assertion of seemingly small interests, which brings into free play, and gives his utmost value to, the individual; making his warfare, equally with his more peaceful rivalries, deme against deme, the mountain against the plain, the seashore, (as in our own Border life, but played out here by wonderfully gifted people) tangible as a personal history, to the doubling of its fascination for those whose business is with the survey of the dramatic side of life.

As with civil matters, so it was also, we may fairly suppose, with religion; the deme-life was a manifestation of religious custom and sentiment, in all their primitive local variety. As Athens, gradually drawing into itself the various elements of provincial culture, developed, with authority, the central religious position, the demes-men did but add the worship of Athene Polias, the goddess of the capital, to their own pre-existent ritual uses. Of local and central religion alike, time and circumstance had obliterated much when Pausanias came. A devout spirit, with religion for his chief interest, eager for the trace of a divine footstep, anxious even in the days of Lucian to deal seriously with what had counted for so much to serious men, he has, indeed, to lament that "Pan is dead":—"They come no longer!"—"These things happen no longer!" But the Greek—his very name also, *Hellen*, was the title of a priesthood—had been religious abundantly, sanctifying every detail of his actual life with the religious idea; and as Pausanias goes on his way he finds many a remnant of that earlier estate of religion, when, as he fancied, it had been nearer the gods, as it was certainly nearer the earth. It is marked, even in decay, with varieties of place; and is not only continuous but *in situ*. At Phigaleia he makes his offerings to Demeter, agreeably to the paternal rites of the inhabitants, wax, fruit, undressed wool "still full of the *sordes* of the sheep." A dream from heaven cuts short his notice of the mysteries of Eleusis. He sees the stone, "big enough for a little man," on which Silenus was used to sit and rest; at Athens, the tombs of the Amazons, of the purple-haired Nisus, of Deucalion;—"it is a manifest token that he had dwelt there." The worshippers of Poseidon, even at his temple among the hills, might still feel the earth fluctuating beneath their feet. And in care for divine things, he tells us, the Athenians outdid all other Greeks. Even in the days of Nero it revealed itself oddly; and it is natural to suppose that of this temper the demes, as the proper home of conservatism, were exceptionally expressive. Scattered in those remote, romantic villages, among their olives or sea-weeds, lay the heroic graves, the relics, the sacred images, often rude enough amid the delicate tribute of later art; this too oftentimes finding in such retirement its best inspirations, as in some Attic Fiesole. Like a network over the land of gracious poetic tradition, as also of undisturbed ceremonial usage surviving late for those who cared to seek it, the local religions had been never wholly superseded by the worship of the great national temples. They were, in truth, the most characteristic developments of a faith essentially earth-born or indigenous.

And how often must the student of fine art, again, wish he had the same sort of knowledge about its earlier growth in Greece, that he actually possesses in the case of Italian art! Given any development at all in this matter, there must have been phases of art, which, if immature, were also veritable expressions of power to come, intermediate discoveries of beauty, such as are by no means a mere anticipation, and of service only as explaining historically larger subsequent achievements, but of permanent attractiveness in themselves, being often, indeed, the true maturity of certain amiable artistic qualities. And in regard to Greek art at its best—the Parthenon—no less than to the art of the Renaissance at its best—the Sistine Chapel—the more instructive light would be derived rather from what precedes than what follows such central success, from the determination to apprehend the fulfilment of past effort rather than the eve of decline, in the critical, central moment which partakes of both. Of such early promise, early achievement, we have in the case of Greek art little to compare with what is extant of the youth of the arts in Italy. Overbeck's careful gleanings of its history form indeed a sorry relic as contrasted with Vasari's intimations of the beginnings of the Renaissance. Fired by certain fragments of its earlier days, of a beauty, in truth, absolute, and vainly longing for more, the student of Greek sculpture indulges the thought of an ideal of youthful energy therein, yet withal of youthful self-restraint; and again, as with survivals of old religion, the privileged home, he fancies, of that ideal must have been in those venerable Attic townships, as to a large extent it passed away with them.

The budding of new art, the survival of old religion, at isolated centres of provincial life, where varieties of human character also were keen, abundant, asserted in correspondingly effective incident—this is what irresistible fancy superinduces on historic details, themselves meagre enough. The sentiment of antiquity is indeed a characteristic of all cultivated people, even in what may seem the freshest ages, and not exclusively a humour of our later world. In the earliest notices about them, as we know, the people of Attica appear already impressed by the immense antiquity of their occupation of its soil, of which they claim to be the very first flower. Some at least of those old demesmen we may well fancy sentimentally reluctant to change their habits, fearful of losing too much of themselves in the larger stream of life, clinging to what is antiquated as the work of centralisation goes on, needful as that work was, with the great "Eastern difficulty" already ever in the distance. The fear of Asia, barbaric, splendid, hardly known, yet haunting the curious imagination of those who had borrowed thence the art in which they were rapidly excelling it, developing, as we now see, in the interest of Greek humanity, crafts begotten of tyrannic and illiberal luxury, was finally to suppress the rivalries of those primitive centres of activity, when the "invincible armada" of the common foe came into sight.

At a later period civil strife was to destroy their last traces. The old hoplite, from Rhamnus or Acharnæ, pent up in beleaguered Athens during that first summer of the Peloponnesian war, occupying with his household a turret of the wall, as Thucydides describes—one of many picturesque touches in that severe historian—could well remember the ancient provincial life which this conflict with Sparta was bringing to an end. He could recall his boyish, half-scared curiosity concerning those Persian ships, coming first as merchantmen, or with pirates on occasion, in the half-savage, wicked splendours of their decoration, the monstrous figure-heads, their glittering freightage. Men would hardly have trusted their women or children with that suspicious crew, hovering through the dusk. There were soothsayers, indeed, who had long foretold what happened soon after, giving shape to vague, supernatural terrors. And then he had crept from his hiding-place with other lads to go view the enemies' slain at Marathon, beside those belated Spartans, this new war with whom seemed to be reviving the fierce local feuds of his younger days. *Paraloi* and *Diacrioi* had ever been rivals. Very distant it all seemed now, with all the stories he could tell; for in those crumbling little towns, as heroic life had lingered on into the actual, so, at an earlier date, the supernatural into the heroic. Like mist at dawn, the last traces of its divine visitors had then vanished from the land, where, however, they had already begotten "our best and oldest families."

It was Theseus, uncompromising young master of the situation, in fearless application of "the modern spirit" of his day to every phase of life where it was applicable, who, at the expense of Attica, had given Athens a people, reluctant enough, in truth, as Plutarch suggests, to desert "their homes and religious usages and many good and gracious kings of their own" for this elect youth, who thus figures, passably, as a kind of mythic shorthand for civilisation, making roads and the like, facilitating travel, suppressing various forms of violence, but many innocent things as well. So it must needs be in a world where, even hand in hand with a god-assisted hero, Justice goes blindfold. He slays the bull of Marathon and many another local tyrant, but also exterminates that delightful creature, the Centaur. The Amazon, whom Plato will reinstate as the type of improved womanhood, has no better luck than Phæa, the sow-pig of Crommyon, foul old landed-proprietress. They exerted, however, the prerogative of poetic protest, and survive thereby. Centaur and Amazon, as we see them in the fine art of Greece, represent the regret of Athenians themselves for something that could never be brought to life again, and have their pathos. Those young heroes contending with Amazons on the frieze of the Mausoleum had best make haste with their bloody work, if young people's eyes can tell a true story. A type still of progress triumphant through injustice, set on improving things off the face of the earth, Theseus took occasion to attack the Amazons in their mountain home, not long after their ruinous conflict with Hercules, and hit them when they were down. That greater bully had laboured off on the world's highway, carrying with him the official girdle of Antiope, their queen, gift of Ares, and therewith, it would seem, the mystic secret of their strength. At sight of this new foe, at any rate, she came to a strange submission. The savage virgin had turned to very woman, and was presently a willing slave, returning on the gaily appointed ship in all haste to Athens, where in supposed wedlock she bore King Theseus a son.

With their annual visit—visit to the Gargareans!—for the purpose of maintaining their species, parting with their boys early, these husbandless women could hardly be supposed a very happy, certainly not a very joyous people. They figure rather as a sorry measure of the luck of the female sex in taking a hard natural law into their own hands, and by abnegation of all tender companionship making shift with bare independence, as a kind of second-best—the best practicable by them in the imperfect actual condition of things. But the heart-strings would ache still where the breast had been cut away. The sisters of Antiope had come, not immediately, but in careful array of battle, to bring back the captive. All along the weary roads from the Caucasus to Attica, their traces had remained in the great graves of those who died by the way. Against the little remnant, carrying on the fight to the very midst of Athens, Antiope herself had turned, all other thoughts transformed now into wild idolatry of her hero. Superstitious, or in real regret, the Athenians never forgot their tombs. As for Antiope, the conscience of her perfidy remained with her, adding the pang of remorse to her own desertion, when King Theseus, with his accustomed bad faith to women, set her, too, aside in turn. Phædra, the true wife, was there, peeping suspiciously at her arrival; and even as Antiope yielded to her lord's embraces the thought had come that a male child might be the instrument of her anger, and one day judge her cause.

In one of these doomed, decaying villages, then, King Theseus placed the woman and her babe, hidden, yet secure, within the Attic border, as men veil their mistakes or crimes. They might pass away, they and their story, together with the memory of other antiquated creatures of such places, who had had connubial dealings with the stars. The white, paved waggon-track, a by-path of the sacred way to Eleusis, zigzagged through sloping olive-yards, from the plain of silvered blue, with Athens building in the distance, and passed the door of the rude stone house, furnished scantily, which no one had ventured to inhabit of late years till they came there. On the ledges of the grey cliffs above, the laurel groves, stem and foliage of motionless bronze, had spread their tents. Travellers bound northwards were glad to repose themselves there, and take directions, or provision for their journey onwards, from the highland people, who came down hither to sell their honey, their cheese, and woollen stuff, in the tiny market-place. At dawn the great stars seemed to halt a while, burning as if for sacrifice to some pure deity, on those distant, obscurely named heights, like broken swords, the rim of the world. A little later you could just see the newly opened quarries, like streaks of snow on their russet-brown bosoms. Thither in spring-time all eyes turned from Athens, devoutly, intent till the first shaft of lightning gave signal for the departure of the sacred ship to Delos. Racing over those rocky surfaces, the virgin air descended hither with the secret of profound sleep, as the child lay in its cubicle hewn in the stone, the white fleeces heaped warmly round him. In the wild Amazon's soul, to her surprise, and at first against her will, the maternal sense had quickened from the moment of his conception, and (that burst of angry tears with which she had received him into the world once dried up), kindling more eagerly at every token of manly growth, had at length driven out every other feeling. And this animal sentiment, educating the human hand and heart in her, had become a moral one, when, King Theseus leaving her in anger, visibly unkind, the child had crept to her side, and tracing with small fingers the wrinkled lines of her woebegone brow, carved there as if by a thousand years of sorrow, had sown between himself and her the seed of an undying sympathy.

She was thus already on the watch for a host of minute recognitions on his part, of the self-sacrifice involved in her devotion to a career of which she must needs drain out the sorrow, careful that he might taste only the joy. So far, amid their spare living, the child, as if looking up to the warm broad wing of her love above him, seemed replete with comfort. Yet in his moments of childish sickness, the first passing shadows upon the deep joy of her motherhood, she teaches him betimes to soothe or cheat pain—little bodily pains only, hitherto. She ventures sadly to assure him of the harsh necessities of life: "Courage, child! Every one must take his share of suffering. Shift not thy body so vehemently. Pain, taken quietly, is easier to bear."

Carefully inverting the habits of her own rude childhood, she learned to spin the wools, white and grey, to clothe and cover him pleasantly. The spectacle of his unsuspicious happiness, though

at present a matter of purely physical conditions, awoke a strange
sense of poetry, a kind of artistic sense in her, watching, as her
own long-deferred recreation in life, his delight in the little delicacies she prepared to his liking—broiled kids' flesh, the red wine,
the mushrooms sought through the early dew—his hunger and
thirst so daintily satisfied, as he sat at table, like the first-born of
King Theseus, with two wax-lights and a fire at dawn or nightfall
dancing to the prattle and laughter, a bright child, never stupidly
weary. At times his very happiness would seem to her like a menace of misfortune to come. Was there not with herself the curse of
that unsisterly action? and not far from him, the terrible danger
of the father's, the step-mother's jealousy, the mockery of those
half-brothers to come? Ah! how perilous for happiness the sensibilities which make him so exquisitely happy now! Before they
started on their dreadful visit to the Minotaur, says Plutarch, the
women told their sons many tales and other things to encourage
them; and, even as she had furnished the child betimes with rules
for the solace of bodily pain, so now she would have brought her
own sad experience into service in precepts for the ejection of its
festering power out of any other trouble that might visit him.
Already those little disappointments which are as the shadow
beside all conscious enjoyment, were no petty things to her, but
had for her their pathos, as children's troubles will have, in spite
of the longer chance before them. They were as the first steps in a
long story of deferred hopes, or anticipations of death itself and
the end of them.

The gift of Ares gone, the mystic girdle she would fain have
transferred to the child, that bloody god of storm and battle, hereditary patron of her house, faded from her thoughts together
with the memory of her past life—the more completely, because
another familiar though somewhat forbidding deity, accepting
certainly a cruel and forbidding worship, was already in possession, and reigning in the new home when she came thither. Only,
thanks to some kindly local influence (by grace, say, of its delicate air), Artemis, this other god she had known in the Scythian
wilds, had put aside her fierce ways, as she paused awhile on her
heavenly course among these ancient abodes of men, gliding
softly, mainly through their dreams, with abundance of salutary

touches. Full, in truth, of grateful memory of some timely service at human hands! In these highland villages the tradition of celestial visitants clung fondly, of god or hero, belated or misled on long journeys, yet pleased to be among the sons of men, as their way led them up the steep, narrow, crooked street, condescending to rest a little, as one, under some sudden stress not clearly ascertained, had done here, in this very house, thereafter for ever sacred. The place and its inhabitants, of course, had been something bigger in the days of those old mythic hospitalities, unless, indeed, divine persons took kindly the will for the deed—very different, surely, from the present condition of things, for there was little here to detain a delicate traveller, even in the abode of Antiope and her son, though it had been the residence of a king.

Hard by stood the chapel of the goddess, who had thus adorned the place with her memories. The priests, indeed, were already departed to Athens, carrying with them the ancient image, the vehicle of her actual presence, as the surest means of enriching the capital at the expense of the country, where she must now make poor shift of the occasional worshipper on his way through these mountain passes. But safely roofed beneath the sturdy tiles of grey Hymettus marble, upon the walls of the little square recess enclosing the deserted pedestal, a series of crowded imageries, in the devout spirit of earlier days, were eloquent concerning her. Here from scene to scene, touched with silver among the wild and human creatures in dun bronze, with the moon's disk around her head, shrouded closely, the goddess of the chase still glided mystically through all the varied incidents of her story, in all the detail of a written book.

A book for the delighted reading of a scholar, willing to ponder at leisure, to make his way surely, and understand. Very different, certainly, from the cruel-featured little idol his mother had brought in her bundle—the old Scythian Artemis, hanging there on the wall, side by side with the forgotten Ares, blood-red,—the goddess reveals herself to the lad, poring through the dusk by taper-light, as at once a virgin, necessarily therefore the creature of solitude, yet also as the assiduous nurse of children, and patroness of the young. Her friendly intervention at the act of birth everywhere, her claim upon the nursling, among tame and wild creatures equally, among men as among gods, nay! among the stars (upon the very star of dawn), gave her a breadth of influence seemingly coextensive with the sum of things. Yes! his great mother was in touch with everything. Yet throughout he can but note her perpetual chastity, with pleasurable though half-suspicious wonder at the mystery, he knows not what, involved therein, as though he awoke suddenly in some distant, unexplored region of her person and activity. Why the lighted torch always, and that long straight vesture rolled round so formally? Was it only against the cold of these northern heights?

To her, nevertheless, her maternity, her solitude, to this virgin mother, who, with no husband, no lover, no fruit of her own, is so tender to the children of others, in a full heart he devotes himself—his immaculate body and soul. Dedicating himself thus, he has the sense also that he becomes more entirely than ever the chevalier of his mortal mother, of her sad cause. The devout, diligent hands clear away carefully the dust, the faded relics of her former worship; a worship renewed once more as the sacred spring, set free from encumbrance, in answer to his willing ministries murmurs again under the dim vault in its marble basin, work of primitive Titanic fingers—flows out through its rocky channel, filling the whole township with chaste thoughts of her.

Through much labour at length he comes to the veritable story of her birth, like a gift direct from the goddess herself to this loyal soul. There were those in later times who, like Æschylus, knew Artemis as the daughter not of Leto but of Demeter, according to the version of her history now conveyed to the young Hippolytus, together with some deepened insight into her character. The goddess of Eleusis, on a journey, in the old days when, as Plato says, men lived nearer the gods, finding herself with child by some starry inmate of those high places, had lain down in the rock-hewn cubicle of the inner chamber, and, certainly in sorrow, brought forth a daughter. Here was the secret at once of the genial, all-embracing maternity of this new strange Artemis, and of those more dubious tokens, the lighted torch, the winding-sheet, the arrow of death on the string—of sudden death, truly, which may be thought after all the kindest, as prevenient of all disgraceful sickness or waste in the unsullied limbs. For the late birth into the world of this so shadowy daughter was somehow identified with the sudden passing into Hades of her first-born, Persephone. As he scans those scenes anew, an awful surmise comes to him; his divine patroness moves there as death, surely. Still, however, gratefully putting away suspicion, he seized even in these ambiguous imageries their happier suggestions, satisfied in thinking of his new mother as but the giver of sound sleep, of the benign night, whence—mystery of mysteries!—good things are born softly, from which he awakes betimes for his healthful service to her. Either way, sister of Apollo or sister of Persephone, to him she should be a power of sanity, sweet as the flowers he offered her gathered at dawn, setting daily their purple and white frost against her ancient marbles. There was more certainly than the first breath of day in them. Was there here something of her person, her sensible presence, by way of direct response to him in his early devotion, astir for her sake before the very birds, nesting here so freely, the quail above all, in some privileged connexion with her story still unfathomed by the learned youth? Amid them he too found a voice, and sang articulately the praises of the great goddess.

Those more dubious traits, nevertheless, so lightly disposed of by Hippolytus (Hecate thus counting for him as Artemis goddess of health), became to his mother, in the light of her sad experience, the sum of the whole matter. While he drew only peaceful inducements to sleep from that two-sided figure, she reads there a volume of sinister intentions, and liked little this seemingly dead goddess, who could but move among the living banefully, stealing with her night-shade into the day where she had no proper right. The gods had ever had much to do with the shaping of her fortunes and the fortunes of her kindred; and the mortal mother felt nothing less than jealousy from the hour when the lad had first delightedly called her to share his discoveries, and learn the true story (if it were not rather the malicious counterfeit) of the new divine mother to whom he has thus absolutely entrusted himself. Was not this absolute chastity itself a kind of death? She, too, in secret makes her gruesome midnight offering with averted eyes. She dreams one night he is in danger; creeps to his cubicle to see; the face is covered, as he lies, against the cold. She traces the motionless outline, raises the coverlet; with the nice black head deep in the fleecy pillow he is sleeping quietly, he dreams of that other mother gliding in upon the moonbeam, and awaking turns sympathetically upon the living woman, is subdued in a moment to the expression of her troubled spirit, and understands.

And when the child departed from her for the first time, springing from his white bed before the dawn, to accompany the elders on their annual visit to the Eleusinian goddess, the after-sense of his wonderful happiness, tranquillising her in spite of herself by its genial power over the actual moment, stirred nevertheless a new sort of anxiety for the future. Her work in life henceforward was defined as a ministry to so precious a gift, in full consciousness of its risk; it became her religion, the centre of her pieties. She missed painfully his continual singing hovering about the place, like the earth itself made audible in all its humanities. Half-selfish for a moment, she prays that he may remain for ever a child, to her solace; welcomes now the promise of his chastity (though chastity were itself a kind of death) as the pledge of his abiding always with her. And these thoughts were but infixed more deeply by the sudden stroke of joy at his return home in ceremonial trim and grown more manly, with much increase of self-confidence in that brief absence among his fellows.

For, from the first, the unwelcome child, the outcast, had been successful, with that special good fortune which sometimes attends the outcast. His happiness, his invincible happiness, had been found engaging, perhaps by the gods, certainly by men; and when King Theseus came to take note how things went in that rough life he had assigned them, he felt a half liking for the boy, and bade him come down to Athens and see the sights, partly by way of proof to his already somewhat exacting wife of the difference between the old love and the new as measured by the present condition of their respective offspring. The fine nature, fastidious by instinct, but bred with frugality enough to find the charm of continual surprise in that delicate new Athens, draws, as he goes, the full savour of its novelties; the marbles, the space and finish, the busy gaiety of its streets, the elegance of life there, contrasting with while it adds some mysterious endearment to the thought of his own rude home. Without envy, in hope only one day to share, to win them by kindness, he gazes on the motley garden-plots, the soft bedding, the showy toys, the delicate keep of the children of Phædra, who turn curiously to their half-brother, venture to touch his long strange gown of homespun grey, like the soft coat of some wild creature who might let one stroke it. Close to their dainty existence for a while, he regards it as from afar; looks forward all day to the lights, the prattle, the laughter, the white bread, like sweet cake to him, of their ordinary evening meal; returns again and again, in spite of himself, to watch, to admire, feeling a power within him to merit the like; finds his way back at last, still light of heart, to his own poor fare, able to do without what he would enjoy so much. As, grateful for his scanty part in things—for the make-believe of a feast in the little white loaves she too has managed to come by, sipping the thin white wine, he touches her dearly, the mother is shocked with a sense of something unearthly in his contentment, while he comes and goes, singing now more abundantly than ever a new canticle to her divine rival. Were things, after all, to go grudgingly with him? Sensible of that curse on herself, with her suspicions of his kinsfolk, of this dubious goddess to whom he has devoted himself, she anticipates with more foreboding than ever his path to be, with or without a wife—her own solitude, or his—the painful heats and cold. She fears even these late successes; it were best to veil their heads. The strong as such had ever been against her and hers. The father came again; noted the boy's growth. Manliest of men, like Hercules in his cloak of lion's skin, he has after all but scant liking, feels, through a certain meanness of soul, scorn for the finer likeness of himself. Might this creature of an already vanishing world, who for all his hard rearing had a manifest distinction of character, one day become his rival, full of loyalty as he was already to the deserted mother?

To charming Athens, nevertheless, he crept back, as occasion served, to gaze peacefully on the delightful good fortune of others, waiting for the opportunity to take his own turn with the rest, driving down thither at last in a chariot gallantly, when all the town was assembled to celebrate the king's birthday. For the goddess, herself turning ever kinder, and figuring more and more exclusively as the tender nurse of all things, had transformed her young votary from a hunter into a charioteer, a rearer and driver of horses, after the fashion of his Amazon mothers before him. Thereupon, all the lad's wholesome vanity had centered on the fancy of the world-famous games then lately established, as, smiling down his mother's terrors, and grateful to his celestial mother for many a hair-breadth escape, he practised day by day, fed the animals, drove them out, amused though companionless, visited them affectionately in the deserted stone stables of the ancient king. A chariot and horses, as being the showiest outward thing the world afforded, was like the pawn he moved to represent the big demand he meant to make, honestly, generously, on the ample fortunes of life. There was something of his old miraculous kindred, alien from this busy new world he came to, about the boyish driver with the fame of a scholar, in his grey fleecy cloak and hood of soft white woollen stuff, as he drove in that morning. Men seemed to have seen a star flashing, and crowded round to examine the little mountain-bred beasts, in loud, friendly intercourse with the hero of the hour—even those usually somewhat unsympathetic half-brothers now full of enthusiasm for the outcast and his good fight for prosperity. Instinctively people admired his wonderful placidity, and would fain have shared its secret, as it were the carelessness of some fair flower upon his face. A victor in the day's race, he carried home as his prize a glittering new harness in place of the very old one he had come with. "My chariot and horses!" he says now, with his single touch of pride. Yet at home, savouring to the full his old solitary happiness, veiled again from time to time in that ancient life, he is still the student, still ponders the old writings which tell of his divine patroness. At Athens strange stories are told in turn of him, his nights upon the mountains, his dreamy sin, with that hypocritical virgin goddess, stories which set the jealous suspicions of Theseus at rest once more. For so "dream" not those who have the tangible, appraisable world in view. Even Queen Phædra looks with pleasure, as he comes, on the once despised illegitimate creature, at home now here too, singing always audaciously, so visibly happy, occupied, popular.

Encompassed by the luxuries of Athens, far from those peaceful mountain places, among people further still in spirit from their peaceful light and shade, he did not forget the kindly goddess, still sharing with his earthly mother the prizes, or what they would buy, for the adornment of their spare abode. The tombs of the fallen Amazons, the spot where they had breathed their last, he piously visited, informed himself of every circumstance of the event with devout care, and, thinking on them amid the dainties of the royal table, boldly brought them too their share of the offerings to the heroic dead. Aphrodite, indeed—Aphrodite, of whom he had scarcely so much as heard—was just then the best-served deity in Athens, with all its new wealth of colour and form, its gold and ivory, the acting, the music, the fantastic women, beneath the shadow of the great walls still rising steadily. Hippolytus would have no part in her worship; instead did what was in him to revive the neglected service of his own goddess, stirring an old jealousy. For Aphrodite too had looked with delight upon the youth, already the centre of a hundred less dangerous human rivalries among the maidens of Greece, and was by no means indifferent to his indifference, his instinctive distaste; while the sterner, almost forgotten Artemis found once more her great moon-shaped cake, set about with starry tapers, at the appointed seasons.

They know him now from afar, by his emphatic, shooting, arrowy movements; and on the day of the great chariot races "he goes in and wins." To the surprise of all he compounded his handsome prize for the old wooden image taken from the chapel at home, lurking now in an obscure shrine in the meanest quarter of the town. Sober amid the noisy feasting which followed, unashamed, but travelling by night to hide it from their mockery, warm at his bosom, he reached the passes at twilight, and through the deep peace of the glens bore it to the old resting-place, now more worthy than ever of the presence of its mistress, his mother and all the people of the village coming forth to salute her, all doors set mystically open, as she advances.

Phædra too, his step-mother, a fiery soul with wild strange blood in her veins, forgetting her fears of this illegitimate rival of her children, seemed now to have seen him for the first time, loved at last the very touch of his fleecy cloak, and would fain have had him of her own religion. As though the once neglected child had been another, she tries to win him as a stranger in his manly perfection, growing more than an affectionate mother to her husband's son. But why thus intimate and congenial, she asks, always in the wrong quarter? Why not compass two ends at once? Why so squeamishly neglect the powerful, any power at all, in a city so full of religion? He might find the image of her sprightly goddess everywhere, to his liking, gold, silver, native or stranger, new or old, graceful, or indeed, if he preferred it so, in iron or stone. By the way, she explains the delights of love, of marriage, the husband once out of the way; finds in him, with misgiving, a sort of forwardness, as she thinks, on this one matter, as if he understood her craft and despised it. He met her questions in truth with scarce so much as contempt, with laughing counter-queries, why people needed wedding at all? They might have *found* the children in the temples, or bought them, as you could buy flowers in Athens.

Meantime Phædra's young children drew from the seemingly unconscious finger the marriage-ring, set it spinning on the floor at his feet, and the staid youth places it for a moment on his own finger for safety. As it settles there, his step-mother, aware all the while, suddenly presses his hand over it. He found the ring there that night as he lay; left his bed in the darkness, and again, for safety, put it on the finger of the image, wedding once for all that so kindly mystical mother. And still, even amid his earthly mother's terrible misgivings, he seems to foresee a charming career marked out before him in friendly Athens, to the height of his desire. Grateful that he is here at all, sharing at last so freely life's banquet, he puts himself for a moment in his old place, recalling his old enjoyment of the pleasure of others; feels, just then, no different. Yet never had life seemed so sufficing as at this moment—the meat, the drink, the drives, the popularity as he comes and goes, even his step-mother's false, selfish, ostentatious gifts. But she, too, begins to feel something of the jealousy of that other divine, would-be mistress, and by way of a last effort to bring him to a better mind in regard to them both, conducts him (immeasurable privilege!) to her own private chapel.

You could hardly tell where the apartments of the adulteress ended and that of the divine courtesan began. Haunts of her long, indolent, self-pleasing nights and days, they presented everywhere the impress of Phædra's luxurious humour. A peculiar glow, such as he had never before seen, like heady lamplight, or sunshine to some sleeper in a delirious dream, hung upon, clung to, the bold, naked, shameful imageries, as his step-mother trimmed the lamps, drew forth her sickly perfumes, clad afresh in piquant change of raiment the almost formless goddess crouching there in her unclean shrine or stye, set at last her foolish wheel in motion to a low chant, holding him by the wrist, keeping close all the while, as if to catch some germ of consent in his indifferent words.

And little by little he perceives that all this is for him—the incense, the dizzy wheel, the shreds of stuff cut secretly from his sleeve, the sweetened cup he drank at her offer, unavailingly; and yes! his own features surely, in pallid wax. With a gasp of flighty laughter she ventures to point the thing out to him, full as he is at last of visible, irrepressible dislike. Ah! it was that very reluctance that chiefly stirred her. Healthily white and red, he had a marvellous air of discretion about him, as of one never to be caught unaware, as if he never could be anything but like water from the rock, or the wild flowers of the morning, or the beams of the morning star turned to human flesh. It was the self-possession of this happy mind, the purity of this virgin body, she would fain have perturbed, as a pledge to herself of her own gaudy claim to supremacy. King Theseus, as she knew, had had at least two earlier loves; for once she would be a first love; felt at moments that with this one passion once indulged, it might be happiness thereafter to remain chaste for ever. And then, by accident, yet surely reading indifference in his manner of accepting her gifts, she is ready again for contemptuous, open battle. Is he indeed but a child still, this nursling of the forbidding Amazon, of that Amazonian goddess—to be a child always? or a wily priest rather, skilfully circumventing her sorceries, with mystic precautions of his own? In truth, there is something of the priestly character in this impassible discretion, reminding her of his alleged intimacy with the rival goddess, and redoubling her curiosity, her fondness. Phædra, love-sick, feverish, in bodily sickness at last, raves of the cool woods, the chase, the steeds of Hippolytus, her thoughts running madly on what she fancies to be his secret business; with a storm of abject tears, foreseeing in one moment of recoil the weary tale of years to come, star-stricken as she declares, she dared at last to confess her longing to already half-suspicious attendants; and, awake one morning to find Hippolytus there kindly at her bidding, drove him openly forth in a tempest of insulting speech. There was a mordant there, like the menace of misfortune to come, in which the injured goddess also was invited to concur. What words! what terrible words! following, clinging to him, like acrid fire upon his bare flesh, as he hasted from Phædra's house, thrust out at last, his vesture remaining in her hands. The husband returning suddenly, she tells him a false story of violence to her bed, and is believed.

King Theseus, all his accumulated store of suspicion and dislike turning now to active hatred, flung away readily upon him, bewildered, unheard, one of three precious curses (some mystery of wasting sickness therein) with which Poseidon had indulged him. It seemed sad that one so young must call for justice, precariously, upon the gods, the dead, the very walls! Admiring youth dared hardly bid farewell to their late comrade; are generous, at most, in stolen, sympathetic glances towards the fallen star. At home, veiled once again in that ancient twilight world, his mother, fearing solely for what he may suffer by the departure of that so brief prosperity, enlarged as it had been, even so, by his grateful taking of it, is reassured, delighted, happy once more at the visible proof of his happiness, his invincible happiness. Duly he returned to Athens, early astir, for the last time, to restore the forfeited gifts, drove back his gaily painted chariot to leave there behind him, actually enjoying the drive, going home on foot poorer than ever. He takes again to his former modes of life, a little less to the horses, a little more to the old studies, the strange, secret history of his favourite goddess,—wronged surely! somehow, she too, as powerless to help him; till he lay sick at last, battling one morning, unaware of his mother's presence, with the feverish creations of the brain; the giddy, foolish wheel, the foolish song, of Phædra's chapel, spinning there with his heart bound thereto. "The curses of my progenitors are come upon me!" he cries. "And yet, why so? guiltless as I am of evil." His wholesome religion seeming to turn against him now, the trees, the streams, the very rocks, swoon into living creatures, swarming around the goddess who has lost her grave quietness. He finds solicitation, and recoils, in the wind, in the sounds of the rain; till at length delirium itself finds a note of returning health. The feverish wood-ways of his fancy open unexpectedly upon wide currents of air, lulling him to sleep; and the conflict ending suddenly altogether at its sharpest, he lay in the early light motionless among the pillows, his mother standing by, as she thought, to see him die. As if for the last time, she presses on him the things he had liked best in that eating and drinking she had found so beautiful. The eyes, the eyelids are big with sorrow; and, as he understands again, making an effort for her sake, the healthy light returns into his; a hand seizes hers gratefully, and a slow convalescence begins, the happiest period in the wild mother's life. When he longed for flowers for the goddess, she went a toilsome journey to seek them, growing close, after long neglect, wholesome and firm on their tall stalks. The singing she had longed for so despairingly hovers gaily once more within the chapel and around the house.

At the crisis of that strange illness she had supposed her long forebodings about to be realised at last; but upon his recovery feared no more, assured herself that the curses of the father, the step-mother, the concurrent ill-will of that angry goddess, have done their utmost; he will outlive her; a few years hence put her to a rest surely welcome. Her misgivings, arising always out of the actual spectacle of his profound happiness, seemed at an end in this meek bliss, the more as she observed that it was a shade less unconscious than of old. And almost suddenly he found the strength, the heart, in him, to try his fortune again with the old chariot; and those still unsatisfied curses, in truth, going on either side of him like living creatures unseen, legend tells briefly how, a competitor for pity with Adonis, and Icarus, and Hyacinth, and other doomed creatures of immature radiance in all story to come, he set forth joyously for the chariot-races, not of Athens, but of Trœzen, her rival. Once more he wins the prize; he says goodbye to admiring friends anxious to entertain him, and by night starts off homewards, as of old, like a child, returning quickly through the solitude in which he had never lacked company, and was now to die. Through all the perils of darkness he had guided the chariot safely along the curved shore; the dawn was come, and a little breeze astir, as the grey level spaces parted delicately into white and blue, when in a moment an earthquake, or Poseidon the earth-shaker himself, or angry Aphrodite awake from the deep betimes, rent the tranquil surface; a great wave leapt suddenly into the placid distance of the Attic shore, and was surging here to the very necks of the plunging horses, a moment since enjoying so pleasantly with him the caress of the morning air, but now, wholly forgetful of their old affectionate habit of obedience, dragging their leader headlong over the rough pavements. Evening and the dawn might seem to have met on that hapless day through which they drew him home entangled in the trappings of the chariot that had been his ruin, till he lay at length, grey and haggard, at the rest he had longed for dimly amid the buffeting of those murderous stones, his mother watching impassibly, sunk at once into the condition she had so long anticipated.

Later legends breaks a supernatural light over that great desolation, and would fain relieve the reader by introducing the kindly Asclepius, who presently restores the youth to life, not, however, in the old form or under familiar conditions. To her, surely, counting the wounds, the disfigurements, telling over the pains which had shot through that dear head now insensible to her touch among the pillows under the harsh broad daylight, that would have been no more of a solace than if, according to the fancy of Ovid, he flourished still, a little deity, but under a new name and veiled now in old age, in the haunted grove of Aricia, far from his old Attic home, in a land which had never seen him as he was.

[1889]

Emerald Uthwart

We smile at epitaphs—at those recent enough to be read easily;
smile, for the most part, at what for the most part is an unreal and
often vulgar branch of literature; yet a wide one, with its flowers
here or there, such as make us regret now and again not to have
gathered more carefully in our wanderings a fair average of the
like. Their very simplicity, of course, may set one's thoughts in
motion to fill up the scanty tale, and those of the young at least
are almost always worth while. At Siena, for instance, in the
great Dominican church, even with the impassioned work of So-
doma at hand, you may linger in a certain dimly lit chapel to spell
out the black-letter memorials of the German students who died
here—*œtatis flore!*—at the University, famous early in the last
century; young nobles chiefly, far from the Rhine, from Nurem-
berg, or Leipsic. Note one in particular! Loving parents and elder
brother meant to record carefully the very days of the lad's poor
life—*annos, menses, dies*; sent the order, doubtless, from the distant old castle in the Fatherland, but not quite explicitly; the
spaces for the numbers remain still unfilled; and they never came
to see. After two centuries the omission is not to be rectified; and
the young man's memorial has perhaps its propriety as it stands,
with those unnumbered, or numberless, days. "Full of affections,"
observed, once upon a time, a great lover of boys and young men,
speaking to a large company of them:—"full of affections, full of
powers, full of occupation, how naturally might the younger part
of us especially (more naturally than the older) receive the tid-
ings that there are things to be loved and things to be done which
shall never pass away. We feel strong, we feel active, we feel full
of life; and these feelings do not altogether deceive us, for we shall

live for ever. We see a long prospect before us, for which it is worth while to work, even with much labour; for we are as yet young, and the past portion of our lives is but small in comparison of that which probably remains to us. It is most true! The past years of our life are absolutely beyond proportion small in comparison with those which certainly remain to us."

In a very different neighbourhood, here at home, in a remote Sussex churchyard, you may read that Emerald Uthwart was born on such a day, "at Chase Lodge, in this parish; and died there," on a day in the year 18—, aged twenty-six. Think, thereupon, of the years of a very English existence passed without a lost week in that bloomy English place, amid its English lawns and flower-beds, its oldish brick and raftered plaster; you may see it still, not far off, on a clearing of the wooded hill-side sloping gradually to the sea. But you think wrong. Emerald Uthwart, in almost unbroken absence from his home, longed greatly for it, but left it early and came back there only to die, in disgrace, as he conceived; of which it was he died there, finding the sense of the place all around him at last, like blessed oil in one's wounds.

How they shook their musk from them!—those gardens, among which the youngest son, but not the youngest child, grew up, little considered till he returned there in those last years. The rippling note of the birds he distinguished so acutely seemed a part of this tree-less place, open freely to sun and air, such as rose and carnation loved, in the midst of the old disafforested chase. Brothers and sisters, all alike were gardeners, methodically intimate with their flowers. You need words compact rather of perfume than of colour to describe them, in nice annual order; terms for perfume, as immediate and definite as red, purple, and yellow. Flowers there were which seemed to yield their sweetest in the faint sea-salt, when the loosening wind was strong from the southwest; some which found their way slowly towards the neighbourhood of the old oaks and beech-trees. Others consorted most freely with the wall-fruit, or seemed made for *pot-pourri* to sweeten the old black mahogany furniture. The sweet-pea stacks loved the broad path through the kitchen garden; the old-fashioned garden azalea was the making of a nosegay, with its honey which clung to one's finger. There were flowers all the sweeter for a battle with the rain; a flower like aromatic medicine; another like summer lingering into winter; it ripened as fruit does; and another was like August, his own birthday time, dropped into March.

The very mould here, rich old black gardener's earth, was flower-seed; and beyond, the fields, one after another, through the white gates breaking the well-grown hedge-rows, were hardly less garden-like; little velvety fields, little with the true sweet English littleness of our little island, our land of vignettes. Here all was little; the very church where they went to pray, to sit, the ancient Uthwarts sleeping all around outside under the windows, deposited there as quietly as fallen trees on their native soil, and almost unrecorded, as there had been almost nothing to record; where however, Sunday after Sunday, Emerald Uthwart reads, wondering, the solitary memorial of one soldierly member of his race, who had,—well! who had *not* died here at home, in his bed. How wretched! how fine! how inconceivably great and difficult!—not for him! And yet, amid all its littleness, how large his sense of liberty in the place he, the cadet doomed to leave it—his birth-place, where he is also so early to die—had loved better than any one of them! Enjoying hitherto all the freedom of the almost grown-up brothers, the unrepressed noise, the unchecked hours, the old rooms, all their own way, he is literally without the con-sciousness of rule. Only, when the long irresponsible day is over, amid the dew, the odours, of summer twilight, they roll their cricket-field against to-morrow's game. So it had always been with the Uthwarts; they never went to school. In the great attic he has chosen for himself Emerald awakes;—it was a rule, sani-tary, almost medical, never to rouse the children—rises to play betimes; or, if he choose, with window flung open to the roses, the sea, turns to sleep again, deliberately, deliciously, under the fine old blankets.

A rather sensuous boy! you may suppose, amid the wholesome, natural self-indulgence of a very English home. His days began there: it closed again, after an interval of the larger number of them, indulgently, mercifully, round his end. For awhile he be-came its centre, old habits changing, the old furniture rearranged about him, for the first time in many generations, though he left it now with something like resentment in his heart, as if thrust harshly away, sent *ablactatus a matre;* made an effort thereon to snap the last thread which bound him to it. Yet it would come back upon him sometimes, amid so different a scene, as through a suddenly opened door, or a rent in the wall, with softer thoughts of his people,—there, or *not* there,—and a sudden, dutiful effort on his part to rekindle wasting affection.

The youngest of four sons, but not the youngest of the family!—you conceive the sort of negligence that creeps over even the kindest maternities, in such case; unless, perhaps, sickness, or the sort of misfortune, making the last first for the affectionate, that brought Emerald back at length to die contentedly, interferes with the way of nature. Little by little he comes to understand that, while the brothers are indulged with lessons at home, are some of them free even of these and placed already in the world, where, however, there remains no place for him, he is to go to school, chiefly for the convenience of others—they are going to be much away from home!—that now for the first time, as he says to himself, an old-English Uthwart is to pass under the yoke. The tutor in the house, meantime, aware of some fascination in the lad, teaches him, at his own irregularly chosen hours, more carefully than the others; exerts all his gifts for the purpose, winning him on almost insensibly to youthful proficiency in those difficult rudiments. See him as he stands, seemingly rooted in the spot where he has come to flower! He departs, however, a few days before the departure of the rest—some to foreign parts, the brothers, who shut up the old place, to town. For a moment, he makes an effort to figure to himself those coming absences as but exceptional intervals in his life here; he will count the days, going more quickly so; find his pleasure in watching the sands fall, as even the sands of time at school must. In fact, he was scarcely ever to lie at ease here again, till he came to take his final leave of it, lying at his length so. In brief holidays he rejoins his people, anywhere, anyhow, in a sort of hurry and makeshift:—*Flos Parietis!* thus carelessly plucked forth. Emerald Uthwart was born on such a day "at Chase Lodge, in this parish, and died there."

See him then as he stands! counting now the hours that remain, on the eve of that first emigration, and look away next at the other place, which through centuries has been forming to receive

him; from those garden-beds, now at their richest, but where all is
so winsomely little, to that place of "great matters," great stones,
great memories out of reach. Why! the Uthwarts had scarcely had
more memories than their woods, noiselessly deciduous; or their
prehistoric, entirely unprogressive, unrecording forefathers, in or
before the days of the Druids. Centuries of almost "still" life—of
birth, death, and the rest, as merely natural processes—had made
them and their home what we find them. Centuries of conscious
endeavour, on the other hand, had builded, shaped, and coloured
the place, a small cell, which Emerald Uthwart was now to occupy; a place such as our most characteristic English education
has rightly tended to "find itself a house" in—a place full, for
those who came within its influence, of a will of its own. Here
everything, one's very games, have gone by rule onwards from
the dim old monastic days, and the Benedictine school for novices
with the wholesome severities which have descended to our own
time. Like its customs,—there's a book in the cathedral archives
with the names, for centuries past, of the "scholars" who have
missed church at the proper times for going there—like its customs, well-worn yet well-preserved, time-stained, time-engrained,
time-mellowed, the venerable Norman or English stones of this
austere, beautifully proportioned place look like marble, to
which Emerald's softly nurtured being, his careless wild-growth
must now adapt itself, though somewhat painfully recoiling from
contact with what seems so hard also, and bright, and cold. From
his native world of soft garden touches, carnation and rose (they
had been everywhere in those last weeks), where every one did
just what he liked, he was passed now to this world of grey stone;
and here it was always the decisive word of command. That old
warrior Uthwart's record in the church at home, so fine, yet so
wretched, so unspeakably great and difficult! seemed written here
everywhere around him, as he stood feeling himself fit only to be
taught, to be drilled into, his small compartment; in every movement of his companions, with their quaint confining little cloth
gowns; in the keen, clear, well-authorised dominancy of some,
the instant submission of others. In fact, by one of our wise English compromises, we still teach our so modern boys the Classics;
a lesson in attention and patience, at the least. Nay! by a double

compromise, with delightful physiognomic results sometimes, we teach them their pagan Latin and Greek under the shadow of medieval churchtowers, amid the haunts, the traditions, and with something of the discipline, of monasticism; for which, as is noticeable, the English have never wholly lost an early inclination. The French and others have swept their scholastic houses empty of it, with pedantic fidelity to their theories. English pedants may succeed in doing the like. But the result of our older method has had its value so far, at least, say! for the careful æsthetic observer. It is of such diagonal influences, through complication of influence, that expression comes, in life, in our culture, in the very faces of men and boys—of these boys. Nothing could better harmonise present with past than the sight of them just here, as they shout at their games, or recite their lessons, overarched by the work of medieval priors, or pass to church meekly, into the seats occupied by the young monks before them.

If summer comes reluctantly to our English shores, it is also apt to linger with us;—its *flora* of red and gold leaves on the branches wellnigh to Christmas; the hot days that surprise you, and persist, though heralded by white mornings, hinting that it is but the year's indulgence so to deal with us. To the fanciful, such days may seem most at home in the places where England has thus preferred to locate the somewhat pensive education of its more favoured youth. As Uthwart passes through the old ecclesiastical city, upon which any more modern touch, modern door or window, seems a thing out of place through negligence, the diluted sunlight itself seems driven along with a sparing trace of gilded vane or red tile in it, under the wholesome active wind from the East coast. The long, finely weathered, leaden roof, and the great square tower, gravely magnificent, emphatic from the first view of it over the grey down above the hop-gardens, the gently-watered meadows, dwarf now everything beside; have the bigness of nature's work, seated up there so steadily amid the winds, as rain and fog and heat pass by. More and more persistently, as he proceeds, in the "Green Court" at last, they occupy the outlook. He is shown the narrow cubicle in which he is to sleep; and there it still is, with nothing else, in the window-pane, as he lies;—"our tower," the "Angel Steeple," noblest of its kind. Here, from morning to night, everything seems challenged to follow the upward lead of its long, bold, "perpendicular" lines. The very place one is in, its stone-work, its empty spaces, invade you; invade all who belong to them, as Uthwart belongs, yielding wholly from the first; seem to question you masterfully as to your purpose in being here at all, amid the great memories of the past, of this school;— challenge you, so to speak, to make moral philosophy one of your acquirements, if you can, and to systematise your vagrant self; which however will in any case be here systematised for you. In Uthwart, then, is the plain tablet, for the influences of place to inscribe. Say if you will, that he is under the power of an "embodied ideal," somewhat repellent, but which he cannot despise. He sits in the schoolroom—ancient, transformed chapel of the pilgrims; sits in the sober white and brown place, at the heavy old desks, carved this way and that, crowded as an old churchyard with forgotten names, side by side with sympathetic or antipathetic competitors, as it may chance. In a delightful, exactly measured, quarter of an hour's rest, they come about him, seem to wish to be friends at once, good and bad alike, dull and clever; wonder a little at the name, and the owner. A family name—he explains, good-humouredly; tries to tell some story no one could ever remember precisely of the ancestor from whom it came, the one story of the Uthwarts; is spared; nay! petulantly forbidden to proceed. But the name sticks the faster. Nicknames mark, for the most part, popularity. *Emerald!* so every one called Uthwart, but shortened to *Aldy.* They disperse; flock out into the court; acquaint him hastily with the curiosities of the Precincts, the "dark entry," the rich heraldries of the blackened and mouldering cloister, the ruined overgrown spaces where the old monastery stood, the stones of which furnished material for the rambling prebends houses, now "antediluvian" in their turn; are ready also to climb the scaffold-poles always to be found somewhere about the great church, or dive along the odd, secret passages of the old builders, with quite learned explanations (being proud of, and therefore painstaking about, the place) of architectural periods, of Gothic "late" and "early," layer upon layer, down to round-arched "Norman," like the famous staircase of their school.

The reader comprehends that Uthwart was come where the

genius loci was a strong one, with a claim to mould all who enter it to a perfect, uninquiring, willing or unwilling, conformity to itself. On Saturday half-holidays the scholars are taken to church in their surplices, across the court, under the lime-trees; emerge at last up the dark winding passages into the melodious, mellow-lighted space, always three days behind the temperature outside, so thick are the walls;—how warm and nice! how cool and nice! The choir, to which they glide in order to their places below the clergy, seems conspicuously cold and sad. But the empty chapels lying beyond it all about into the distance are a trap on sunny mornings for the clouds of yellow effulgence. The Angel Steeple is a lantern within, and sheds down a flood of the like just beyond the gates. You can peep up into it where you sit, if you dare to gaze about you. If at home there had been nothing great, here, to boyish sense, one seems diminished to nothing at all, amid the grand waves, wave upon wave, of patiently-wrought stone; the daring height, the daring severity, of the innumerable, long, up-ward, ruled lines, rigidly bent just at last, in due place, into the reserved grace of the perfect Gothic arch; the peculiar daylight which seemed to come from further than the light outside. Next morning they are here again. In contrast to those irregularly bro-ken hours at home, the passive length of things impresses Uthwart now. It develops patience—that tale of hours, the long chanted English service; our English manner of education is a develop-ment of patience, of decorous and mannerly patience. "It is good for a man that he bear the yoke in his youth: he putteth his mouth in the dust, he keepeth silence, because he hath borne it upon him."—They have this for an anthem; sung however to wonder-fully cheerful and sprightly music, as if one liked the thought.

The aim of a veritable community, says Plato, is not that this or that member of it should be disproportionately at ease, but that the whole should flourish; though indeed such general welfare might come round again to the loyal unit therein, and rest with him, as a privilege of his individual being after all. The social type he preferred, as we know, was conservative Sparta and its youth; whose unsparing discipline had doubtless something to do with the fact that it was the handsomest and best-formed in all Greece. A school is not made for one. It would misrepresent Uthwart's wholly unconscious humility to say that he felt the beauty of the ἄσκησις (we need that Greek word) to which he not merely finds himself subject, but as under a fascination submissively yields himself, although another might have been aware of the charm of it, half ethic, half physical, as visibly effective in him. Its peculiarity would have lain in the expression of a stress upon him and his customary daily existence, beyond what any definitely proposed issue of it, at least for the moment, explained. Something of that is involved in the very idea of a classical education, at least for such as he; in its seeming indirectness or lack of purpose, amid so much difficulty, as contrasted with forms of education more obviously useful or practical. He found himself in a system of fixed rules, amid which, it might be, some of his own tendencies and inclinations would die out of him though disuse. The confident word of command, the instantaneous obedience expected, the enforced silence, the very games that go by rule, a sort of hardness natural to wholesome English youths when they come together, but here *de rigueur* as a point of good manners;—he accepts all these without hesitation; the early hours also, naturally distasteful to him, which gave to actual morning, to all that had passed in it, when in more self-conscious mood he looked back on the morning of life, a preponderance, a disproportionate place there, adding greatly to the effect of its dreamy distance from him at this later time;—an *ideal* quality, he might have said, had he ever used such words as that.

Uthwart duly passes his examination; and, in their own chapel in the transept of the choir, lighted up late for evening prayer after the long day of trial, is received to the full privileges of a Scholar with the accustomed Latin words:—*Introitum tuum et exitum tuum custodiat Dominus!* He takes them, not to heart, but rather to mind, as few, if they so much as heard them, were wont to do; ponders them for a while. They seem scarcely meant for him—words like those! increase however his sense of responsibility to the place, of which he is now more exclusively than before a part—that he belongs to it, its great memories, great dim purposes; deepen the consciousness he had on first coming hither of a demand in the world about him, whereof the very stones are emphatic, to which no average human creature could be sufficient; of reproof, reproaches, of this or that in himself.

It was reported, there was a funny belief, at school, that Aldy

Uthwart had no feeling and was incapable of tears. They never came to him certainly, when, at nights for the most part, the very touch of home, so soft, yet so indifferent to him, reached him, with a sudden opulent rush of garden perfumes; came at the rattling of the window-pane in the wind, with anything that expressed distance from the bare white walls around him here. He thrust it from him brusquely, being of a practical turn, and, though somewhat sensuous, wholly without sentimentality. There is something however in the lad's soldier-like, impassible self-command, in his sustained expression of a certain indifference to things, which awakes suddenly all the sentiment, the poetry, latent hitherto in another—James Stokes, the prefect, his immediate superior; awakes for the first time into ample flower something of genius in a seemingly plodding scholar, and therewith also something of the waywardness popularly thought to belong to genius. *Preceptores, condiscipuli*, alike, marvel at a sort of delicacy coming into the habits, the person, of that tall, bashful, broad-shouldered, very Kentish, lad; so unaffectedly nevertheless, that it is understood after all to be but the smartness properly significant of change to early manhood, like the down on his lip. Wistful anticipations of manhood are in fact aroused in him, thoughts of the future; his ambition takes effective outline. The well-worn, perhaps conventional, beauties of their "dead" Greek and Latin books, associated directly now with the living companion beside him, really shine for him at last with their pristine freshness; seem more than to fulfil their claim upon the patience, the attention, of modern youth. He notices as never before minute points of meaning in Homer, in Virgil; points out thus, for instance, to his junior, one day in the sunshine, how the Greeks had a special word for the Fate which accompanied one who would come to a violent end. The common Destinies of men, Μοῖραι, *Mœræ*—they accompanied all men indifferently. But Κήρ, the extraordinary Destiny, one's Doom, had a scent for distant bloodshedding; and, to be in at a sanguinary death, one of their number came forth to the very cradle, followed persistently all the way, over the waves, through powder and shot, through the rose-gardens;—where not? Looking back, one might trace the red footsteps all along, side by side. (Emerald Uthwart, you remember, was to "die there," of lingering sickness, in disgrace, as he fancied, while the word glory came to be softly whispered of them and of their end.) Classic felicities, the choice expressions, with which James Stokes has so patiently stored his memory, furnish now a dainty embroidery upon every act, every change in time or place, of their daily life in common. He finds the Greek or the Latin model of their antique friendship or tries to find it, in the books they read together. None fits exactly. It is of military glory they are really thinking, amid those ecclesiastical surroundings, where however surplices and uniforms are often mingled together; how they will lie, in costly glory, costly to them, side by side, (as they work and walk and play now, side by side) in the cathedral aisle, with a tattered flag perhaps above them, and under a single epitaph, like that of those two older scholars, Ensigns, *Signiferi*, in their respective regiments, *in hac ecclesiâ pueri instituti*, with the sapphic stanza in imitation of the Horace they had learned here, written by their old master.

Horace!—he was, had been always, the idol of their school; to know him by heart, to translate him into effective English idiom, have an apt phrase of his instinctively on one's lips for every occasion. That boys should be made to spout him under penalties, would have seemed doubtless to that sensitive, vain, winsome poet, even more than to grim Juvenal, quite the sorriest of fates; might have seemed not so bad however, could he, from the "ashes" so persistently in his thoughts, have peeped on these English boys, row upon row, with black or golden heads, repeating him in the fresh morning, and observed how well for once the thing was done; how well he was understood by English James Stokes, feeling the old "fire" really "quick" still, under the influence which now in truth quickened, enlivened, everything around him. The old heathen's way of looking at things, his melodious expression of it, blends, or contrasts itself oddly with the everyday detail, with the very stones, the Gothic stones, of a world he could hardly have conceived, its medieval surroundings, their half-clerical life here. Yet not so inconsistently after all! The builders of these aisles and cloisters had known and valued as much of him as they could come by in their own un-instructed time; had built up their intellectual edifice more than they were aware of from fragments of pagan thought, as, quite consciously, they constructed their churches of old Roman bricks and pillars, or frank imitations of them. One's day, then, began with him, for all alike, Sundays of course excepted,—with an Ode, learned over-night by the prudent, who, observing how readily the words which send us to sleep cling to the brain and seem an inherent part of it next morning, kept him under their pillows. Prefects, without a book, heard the repetition of the Juniors, must be able to correct their blunders. Odes and Epodes, thus acquired, were a score of days and weeks; alcaic and sapphic verses like a bead-roll for counting off the time that intervened before the holidays. Time—that tardy servant of youthful appetite—brought them soon enough to the point where they desired in vain "to see one of" those days, erased now so willingly; and sentimental James Stokes has already a sense that this "pause 'twixt cup and lip" of life is really worth pausing over, worth deliberation:—all this poetry, yes! poetry, surely, of their alternate work and play; light and shade, call it! Had it been, after all, a life in itself less commonplace than theirs—that life, the trivial details of which their Horace had touched so daintily, gilded with real gold words?

Regular, submissive, dutiful to play also, Aldy meantime enjoys his triumphs in the Green Court; loves best however to run a paper-chase afar over the marshes, till you come in sight, or within scent, of the sea, in the autumn twilight; and his dutifulness to games at least had its full reward. A wonderful hit of his at cricket was long remembered; right over the lime-trees on to the cathedral roof, was it? or over the roof, and onward into space, circling there independently, minutely, as *Sidus Cantiorum?* A comic poem on it in Latin, and a pretty one in English, were penned by James Stokes, still not so serious but that he forgets time altogether one day, in a manner the converse of exemplary in a prefect, whereupon Uthwart, his companion as usual, manages to take all the blame, and the due penalty next morning. Stokes accepted the sacrifice the more readily, believing—he too—that Aldy was "incapable of pain." What surprised those who were in the secret was that, when it was over, he rose, and facing the headmaster—could it be insolence? or was it the sense of untruthfulness in his friendly action, or sense of the universal peccancy of all boys and men?—said submissively: "And now, sir, that I have taken my punishment, I hope you will forgive my fault."

Submissiveness!—It had the force of genius with Emerald Uthwart. In that very matter he had but yielded to a senior against his own inclination. What he felt in Horace was the sense, original, active, personal, of "things too high for *me!*", the sense, not really unpleasing to him, of an unattainable height here too, in this royal felicity of utterance, this literary art, the minute cares of which had been really designed for the minute carefulness of a disciple such as this—all attention. Well! the sense of authority, of a large intellectual authority over us, impressed anew day after day, of some impenetrable glory round "the masters of those who know," is, of course, one of the effects we look for from a classical education:—that, and a full estimate of the preponderating value of the manner of the doing of it in the thing done; which again, for ingenuous youth, is an encouragement of good manners on its part:—"I behave myself orderly." Just at those points, scholarship attains something of a religious colour. And in that place, religion, religious system, its claim to overpower one, presented itself in a way of which even the least serious by nature could not be unaware. Their great church, its customs and traditions, formed an element in that *espirt de corps* into which the boyish mind throws itself so readily. Afterwards, in very different scenes, the sentiment of that place would come back upon him, as if resentfully, by contrast with the conscious or unconscious profanities of others, crushed out about him straightway, by the shadow of awe, the minatory flash, felt around his unopened lips, in the glance, the changed manner. Not to be "occupied with great matters" recommends in heavenly places, as we know, the souls of some. Yet there were a few to whom it seemed unfortunate that religion whose flag Uthwart would have borne in hands so pure, touched him from first to last, and till his eyes were finally closed on this world, only, again, as a thing immeasurable, surely not meant for the like of him; its high claims, to which no one could be equal; its reproaches. He would scarcely have proposed to "enter into" such matters; was constitutionally shy of them. His submissiveness, you see, *was* a kind of genius; made him therefore, of course, unlike those around him; was a secret; a thing, you might say, "which no one knoweth, saving he that receiveth it."

Thus repressible, self-restrained, always concurring with the influence, the claim upon him, the rebuke, of others, in the bustle of school life he did not count even with those who knew him best, with those who taught him, for the intellectual capacity he really had. In every generation of schoolboys there are a few who find out, almost for themselves, the beauty and power of good literature, even in the literature they must read perforce; and this, in turn, is but the handsel of a beauty and power still active in the actual world, should they have the good fortune, or rather, acquire the skill, to deal with it properly. It has something of the stir and unction—this intellectual awaking with a leap—of the coming of love. So it was with Uthwart about his seventeenth year. He felt it, felt the intellectual passion, like the pressure outward of wings within him—ἡ πτεροῦ δύναμις, says Plato, in the *Phædrus*; but again, as some do with everyday love, withheld, restrained himself; the status of a freeman in the world of intellect can hardly be for him. The sense of intellectual ambition, ambitious thoughts such as sweeten the toil of some of those about him, coming to him once in a way, he is frankly recommended to put them aside, and acquiesces; puts them from him once for all, as he could do with besetting thoughts and feelings, his preferences, (as he had put aside soft thoughts of home as a disobedience to rule) and with a countenance more good-humoured than ever, an absolute placidity. It is fit he should be treated sparingly in this matter of intellectual enjoyment. He is made to understand that there is at least a score of others as good scholars as he. He will have of course all the pains, but must not expect the prizes, of his work; of his loyal, incessant, cheerful industry.

But only see him as he goes. It is as if he left music, delightfully throbbing music, or flowers, behind him, as he passes, careless of them, unconsciously, through the world, the school, the precincts, the old city. Strangers' eyes, resting on him by chance, are deterred for a while, even among the rich sights of the venerable place, as he walks out and in, in his prim gown and purple-tasselled cap; goes in, with the stream of sunlight, through the black shadows of the mouldering Gothic gateway, like youth's very self, eternal, immemorial, eternally renewed, about those immemorially ancient stones. "Young Apollo!" people say—people who have pigeon-holes for their impressions, watching the slim, trim figure with the exercise books. His very dress seems touched with Hellenic fitness to the healthy youthful form. "Golden-haired, scholar Apollo!" they repeat, foolishly, ignorantly. He was better; was more like a real portrait of a real young Greek, like *Tryphon, Son of Eutychos,* for instance, (as friends remembered him with regret, as you may see him still on his tombstone in the British Museum) alive among the paler physical and intellectual lights of modern England, under the old monastic stonework of the Middle Age. That theatrical old Greek god never took the expressiveness, the lines of delicate meaning, such as were come into the face of the English lad, the physiognomy of his race; ennobled now, as if by the writing, the signature, there, of a grave intelligence, by grave information and a subdued will, though without a touch of melancholy in this "best of play-fellows." A musical composer's notes, we know, are not themselves till the fit executant comes, who can put all they may be into them. The somewhat unmeaningly handsome facial type of the Uthwarts, moulded to a mere animal or physical perfection through wholesome centuries, is breathed on now, informed, by the touches, traces, complex influences from past and present a thousandfold, crossing each other in this late century, and yet at unity in the simple law of the system to which he is now subject. Coming thus upon an otherwise vigorous and healthy nature, an untainted physique, and limited by it, those combining mental influences leave the firm unconscious simplicity of the boyish nature still unperplexed. The sisters, their friends, when he comes rarely upon them in foreign places, are proud of the schoolboy's company—to walk at his side; the brothers, when he sees them for a day, more considerate than of old. Everywhere he leaves behind him an odd regret for his presence, as he in turn wonders sometimes at the deference paid to one so unimportant as himself by those he meets by accident perhaps; at the ease, for example, with which he attains to the social privileges denied to others.

They tell him, he knows it already, he would "do for the army."
"Yes! that would suit you," people observe at once, when he tells
them what "he is to be"—undoubtedly suit him, that dainty, military, very English kind of pride, in seeming precisely what one is,
neither more nor less. And the first mention of Uthwart's purpose
defines also the vague outlooks of James Stokes, who will be a
soldier too. Uniforms, their scarlet and white and blue, spruce
leather and steel, and gold lace, enlivening the old oak stalls at
service time—uniforms and surplices were always close together
here, where a military garrison had been established in the sub-
urbs for centuries past, and there were always sons of its officers
in the school. If you stole out of an evening, it was like a stage
scene—nay! like the Middle Age, itself, with this multitude of
soldiers mingling in the crowd which filled the unchanged,
gabled streets. A military tradition had been continuous, from
the days of crusading knights who lay humbly on their backs in
the "Warriors' Chapel" to the time of the civil wars, when a certain heroic youth of eighteen was brought to rest there, onward to
Dutch and American wars, and to Harry, and Geoffrey, and another James also, *in hac ecclesiâ pueri instituti.* It was not so long
since one of them sat on those very benches in the sixth form; had
come back and entered the school, in full uniform, to say good-
bye! Then the "colours" of his regiment had been brought, to be
deposited by Dean and Canons in the cathedral; and a few weeks
later they had passed, scholars and the rest in long procession, to
deposit Ensign ——himself there under his flag, or what remained
of it, a sorry, tattered fringe, along the staff he had borne out of
the battle at the cost of his life, as a little tablet explained. There
were others in similar terms. Alas! for that extraordinary, pecu-
liarly-named, Destiny, or Doom, appointed to walk side by side
with one or another, aware from the first, but never warning him,
till the random or well-considered shot comes.

Meantime however, the University, with work in preparation
thereto, fills up the thoughts, the hours, of these would-be soldiers, of James Stokes, and therefore of Emerald Uthwart, through
the long summer-time, till the Green Court is fragrant with lime-
blossom, and speech-day comes, on which, after their flower-
service and sermon from an old comrade, Emerald surprises mas-

ters and companions by the fine quality of a recitation; still more
when "Scholar Stokes" and he are found bracketed together as
"Victors" of the school, who will proceed together to Oxford. His
speech in the Chapter-house was from that place in Homer, where
the soul of the lad Elpenor, killed by accident, entreats Ulysses for
due burial rites. "Fix my oar over my grave," he says, "the oar I
rowed with when I lived, when I went with my companions."
And in effect what surprised, charmed the hearers was the scruple
with which those naturally graceful lips dealt with every word,
every syllable, put upon them. He seemed to be thinking only of
his author, except for just so much of self-consciousness as was
involved in the fact that he seemed also to be speaking a little
against his will; like a monk, it might be said, who sings in choir
with a really fine voice, but at the bidding of his superior, and
counting the notes all the while till his task be done, because his
whole nature revolts from so much as the bare opportunity for
personal display. It was his duty to speak on the occasion. They
had always been great in speech-making, in theatricals, from before the days when the Puritans destroyed the Dean's "Great Hall"
because "the King's Scholars had profaned it by acting plays
there"; and that peculiar note or accent, as being conspicuously
free from the egotism which vulgarises most of us, seemed to befit
the person of Emerald, impressing weary listeners pleasantly as a
novelty in that kind. Singular!—The words, because seemingly
forced from him, had been worth hearing. The cheers, the
"Kentish Fire," of their companions might have broken down the
crumbling black arches of the old cloister, or roused the dead
under foot, as the "Victors" came out of the Chapter-house side by
side; side by side also out of that delightful period of their life at
school, to proceed in due course to the University.

They left it precipitately, after brief residence there, taking advantage of a sudden outbreak of war to join the army at once,
regretted—James Stokes for his high academic promise, Uthwart
for a quality, or group of qualities, not strictly to be defined. He
seemed, in short, to harmonise by their combination in himself
all the various qualities proper to a large and varied community
of youths of nineteen or twenty, to which, when actually present
there, he was felt from hour to hour to be indispensable. In fact

school habits and standards had survived in a world not so different from that of school for those who are faithful to its type.
When he looked back upon it a little later, college seemed to him,
seemed indeed at the time, had he ventured to admit it, a strange
prolongation of boyhood, in its provisional character, the narrow
limitation of its duties and responsibility, the very divisions of
one's day, the routine of play and work, its formal, perhaps pedantic rules. The veritable plunge from youth into manhood came
when one passed finally through those old Gothic gates, from a
somewhat dreamy or problematic preparation for it, into the
world of peremptory facts. A college, like a school, is not made for
one; and as Uthwart sat there, still but a scholar, still reading
with care the books prescribed for him by others—Greek and Latin
books—the contrast between his own position and that of the
majority of his coevals already at the business of life impressed
itself sometimes with an odd sense of unreality in the place
around him. Yet the schoolboy's sensitive awe for the great things
of the intellectual world had but matured itself, and was at its
height here amid this larger competition, which left him more
than ever to find in doing his best submissively the sole reward of
so doing. He needs now in fact less repression than encouragement not to be a "passman," as he may if he likes, acquiescing in a
lowly measure of culture which certainly will not manufacture
Miltons, nor turn serge into silk, broom-blossom into verbenas,
but only, perhaps not so faultily, leave Emerald Uthwart and the
like of him essentially what they are. "He holds his book in a
peculiar way," notes in manuscript one of his tutors; "holds on to
it with both hands; clings as if from below, just as his tough little
mind clings to the sense of the Greek words he can English so
closely, precisely." Again, as at school, he had put his neck under
the yoke; though he has now also much reading quite at his own
choice; by preference, when he can come by such, about the place
where he finds himself, about the earlier youthful occupants, if it
might be, of his own quaint rooms on the second floor just below
the roof; of what he can see from his windows in the old black
front eastwards, with its inestimable *patina* of ancient smoke and
weather and natural decay (when you look close the very stone is
a composite of minute dead bodies) relieving heads like his so

effectively on summer mornings. On summer nights the scent of the hay, the wild-flowers, comes across the narrow fringe of town to right and left; seems to come from beyond the Oxford meadows, with sensitive, half-repellent thoughts from the gardens at home. He looks down upon the green square with the slim, quaint, black, young figures that cross it on the way to chapel on yellow Sunday mornings, or upwards to the dome, the spire; can watch them closely in freakish moonlight, or flickering softly by an occasional bonfire in the quadrangle behind him. Yet how hard, how forbidding sometimes, under a late stormy sky, the scheme of black, white, and grey, to which the group of ancient buildings could attune itself. And what he reads most readily is of the military life that intruded itself so oddly, during the Civil War, into these half-monastic places, till the timid old academic world scarcely knew itself. He treasures then every incident which connects a soldier's coat with any still recognisable object, wall, or tree, or garden-walk; that walk, for instance, under Merton garden where young Colonel Windebank was shot for a traitor. His body lies in Saint Mary Magdalen's courtyard. Unassociated to such incident, the mere beauties of the place counted at the moment for less than in retrospect. It was almost retrospect even now, with an anticipation of regret, in rare moments of solitude perhaps, when the oars splashed far up the narrow streamlets through the fields on May evenings among the fritillaries— does the reader know them? that strange remnant just here of a richer extinct flora—dry flowers, though with a drop of dubious honey in each. Snakes' heads, the rude call them, for their shape, scale-marked too, and in colour like rusted blood, as if they grew from some forgotten battle-field, the bodies, the rotten armour— yet delicate, beautiful, waving proudly. In truth the memory of Oxford made almost everything he saw after it seem vulgar. But he feels also nevertheless, characteristically, that such local pride (*fastus* he terms it) is proper only for those whose occupations are wholly congruous with it; for the gifted, the freemen who can enter into the genius, who possess the liberty, of the place; that it has a reproach in it for the outsider, which comes home to him.

Here again then as he passes through the world, so delightfully to others, they tell him, as if weighing him, his very self, against his merely scholastic capacity and effects, that he would "do for the army"; which he is now wholly glad to hear, for from first to last, through all his successes there, the army had still been scholar Stokes' choice, and he had no difficulty, as the reader sees, in keeping Uthwart also faithful to first intentions. Their names were already entered for commissions; but the war breaking out afresh, information reaches them suddenly one morning that they may join their regiment forthwith. Bidding good-bye therefore, gladly, hastily, they set out with as little delay as possible for Flanders; and passing the old school by their nearest road thither, stay for an hour, find an excuse for coming into the hall in uniform, with which it must be confessed they seem thoroughly satisfied—Uthwart quite perversely at ease in the stiff make of his scarlet jacket with black facings—and so pass onward on their way to Dover, Dunkirk, they scarcely know whither finally, among the featureless villages, the long monotonous lines of the windmills, the poplars, blurred with cold fogs, but marking the roads through the snow which covers the endless plain, till they come in sight at last of the army in motion, like machines moving—how little it looked on that endless plain!—pass on their rapid way to fame, to unpurchased promotion, as a matter of course to responsibility also, till, their fortune turning upon them, they miscarry in the latter fatally. They joined in fact a distinguished regiment in a gallant army, immediately after a victory in those Flemish regions; shared its encouragement as fully as if they had had a share in its perils; the high character of the young officers consolidating itself easily, pleasantly for them, till the hour of an act of thoughtless bravery, almost the sole irregular or undisciplined act of Uthwart's life, he still following his senior—criminal however to the military conscience, under the actual circumstances, and in an enemy's country. The faulty thing was done, certainly, with a scrupulous, a characteristic completeness on their part; and with their prize actually in hand, an old weather-beaten flag such as hung in the cathedral aisle at school, they bethought them for the first time of its price, with misgivings now in rapid growth, as they return to their posts as nearly as may be, for the division has been ordered forward in their brief absence, to find themselves under arrest, with that

damning proof of heroism, of guilt, in their possession, relin-
quished however along with the swords they will never handle
again—toys, idolised toys of our later youth, we weep at the
thought of them as never to be handled again!—as they enter the
prison to await summary trial next day on the charge of wantonly
deserting their posts while in position of high trust in time of war.

The full details of what had happened could have been told
only by one or other of themselves; by Uthwart best, in the somewhat matter-of-fact and prosaic journal he had managed to keep
from the first, noting there the incidents of each successive day, as
if in anticipation of its possible service by way of *pièce justi-
ficative*, should such become necessary, attesting hour by hour
their single-hearted devotion to soldierly duty. Had a draughtsman equally truthful or equally "realistic," as we say, accompanied them and made a like use of his pencil, he might have been
mistaken at home for an artist aiming at "effect," by skilful
"arrangements" to tickle people's interest in the spectacle of
war—the sudden ruin of a village street, the heap of bleeding
horses in the half-ploughed field, the gaping bridges, hand or face
of the dead peeping from a hastily made grave at the roadside,
smoke-stained rents in cottage-walls, ignoble ruin everywhere—
ignoble but for its frank expression.

But you find in Uthwart's journal, side by side with those ugly
patches, very precise and unadorned records of their common gallantry, the more effective indeed for their simplicity; and not of
gallantry only, but of the long-sustained patience also, the essential monotony of military life, even on a campaign. Peril, good-
luck, promotion, the grotesque hardships which leave them smart
as ever, (as if, so others observe, dust and mire wouldn't hold on
them, so "spick and span" they were, more especially on days of
any exceptional risk or effort) the great confidence reposed in
them at last; all is noted, till, with a little quiet pride, he records
a gun-shot wound which keeps him a month alone in hospital
wearily; and at last, its hasty but seemingly complete healing.

Following, leading, resting, sometimes perforce, amid gun-
shots, putrefying wounds, green corpses, they never lacked good
spirits, any more than the birds warbling perennially afresh, as
they will, over such gangrened places, or the grass which so soon

covers them. And at length fortune, their misfortune, perversely determined that heroism should take the form of patience under the walls of an unimportant frontier town, with old Vauban fortifications seemingly made only for appearance' sake, like the work in the trenches—gardener's work! round about the walls they are called upon to superintend day after day. It was like a calm at sea, delaying one's passage, one's purpose in being on board at all, a dead calm, yet with an awful feeling of tension, intolerable at last for those who were still all athirst for action. How dumb and stupid the place seemed, in its useless defiance of conquerors, anxious, for reasons not indeed apparent, but which they were undoubtedly within their rights in holding to, not to blow it at once into the air—the steeple, the perky weathercock— to James Stokes in particular, always eloquent in action, longing for heroic effort, and ready to pay its price, maddened now by the palpable imposture in front of him morning after morning, as he demonstrates conclusively to Uthwart, seduced at last from the clearer sense of duty and discipline, not by the demonstrated ease, but rather by the apparent difficulty of what Stokes proposes to do. They might have been deterred by recent example. Colonel ——, who, as every one knew, had actually gained a victory by disobeying orders, had not been suffered to remain in the army of which he was an ornament. It was easy in fact for both, though it seemed the heroic thing, to dash through the calm with delightful sense of active powers renewed; to pass into the beleaguered town with a handful of men, and no loss, after a manner the feasibility of which Stokes had explained acutely but in vain at headquarters. He proved it to Uthwart at all events, and a few others. Delightful heroism! delightful self-indulgence! It was delayed for a moment by orders to move forward at last, with hopes checked almost immediately after by a countermand, bringing them right round their stupid dumb enemy to the same wearisome position once again, to the trenches and the rest, but with their thirst for action only stimulated the more. How great the disappointment! encouraging a certain laxity of discipline that had prevailed about them of late. They take advantage however of a vague phrase in their instructions; determine in haste to proceed on their plan as carefully, as sparingly of the lives of others as may be;

detach a small company, hazarding thereby an algebraically certain scheme at headquarters of victory or secure retreat, which embraced the entire country in its calculations; detach themselves; finally pass into the place, and out again with their prize, themselves secure. Themselves only could have told the details—the intensely pleasant, the glorious sense of movement renewed once more; of defiance, just for once, of a seemingly stupid control; their dismay at finding their company led forward by others, their own posts deserted, their handful of men—nowhere!

In an ordinary trial at law, the motives, every detail of so irregular an act might have been weighed, changing the colour of it. Their general character would have told in their favour, but actually told against them now; they had but won an exceptional trust to betray it. Martial courts exist not for consideration, but for vivid exemplary effect and prompt punishment. "There is a kind of tribunal incidental to service in the field," writes another diarist, who may tell in his own words what remains to be told. "This court," he says, "may consist of three staff-officers only, but has the power of sentencing to death. On the —st two young officers of the —th regiment, in whom it appears unusual confidence had been placed, were brought before this court, on the charge of desertion and wantonly exposing their company to danger. They were found guilty, and the proper penalty death, to be inflicted next morning before the regiment marches. The delinquents were understood to have appealed to a general court-martial; desperately at last, to 'the judgment of their country'; but were held to have no *locus standi* whatever for an appeal under the actual circumstances. As a civilian I cannot but doubt the justice, whatever may be thought of the expediency, of such a summary process in regard to the capital penalty. The regiment to which the culprits belonged, with some others, was quartered for the night in the *faubourg* of Saint ——, recently under blockade by a portion of our forces. I was awoke at daybreak by the sound of marching. The morning was a particularly clear one, though, as the sun was not yet risen, it looked grey and sad along the empty street, up which a party of grey soldiers were passing with steady pace. I knew for what purpose.

"The whole of the force in garrison here had already marched to the place of execution, the immense courtyard of a monastery, surrounded irregularly by ancient buildings like those of some cathedral precincts I have seen in England. Here the soldiers then formed three sides of a great square, a grave having been dug on the fourth side. Shortly afterwards the funeral procession came up. First the band of the —th, playing the Dead March; next the firing party, consisting of twelve non-commissioned officers; then the coffins, followed immediately by the unfortunate prisoners, accompanied by a chaplain. Slowly and sadly did the mournful procession approach, when it passed through three sides of the square, the troops having been previously faced inwards, and then halted opposite to the grave. The proceedings of the court-martial were then read; and the elder prisoner having been blind-folded was ordered to kneel down on his coffin, which had been placed close to the grave, the firing party taking up a position exactly opposite at a few yards' distance. The poor fellow's face was deadly pale, but he had marched his last march as steadily as ever I saw a man step, and bore himself throughout most bravely, though an oddly mixed expression passed over his countenance when he was directed to remove himself from the side of his companion, shaking his hand first. At this moment there was hardly a dry eye, and several young soldiers fainted, numberless as must be the scenes of horror whch even they have witnessed during these last months. At length the chaplain, who had remained praying with the prisoner, quietly withdrew, and at a given signal, but without word of command, the muskets were levelled, a volley was fired, and the body of the unfortunate man sprang up, falling again on his back. One shot had purposely been reserved; and as the presiding officer thought he was not quite dead a musket was placed close to his head and fired. All was now over; but the troops having been formed into columns were marched close by the body as it lay on the ground, after which it was placed in one of the coffins and buried.

"I had almost forgotten his companion, the younger and more fortunate prisoner, though I could scarcely tell, as I looked at him, whether his fate was really preferable in leaving his own rough coffin unoccupied behind him there. Lieutenant (I think Edward) Uthwart, as being the younger of the two offenders, 'by the mercy of the court' had his sentence commuted to dismissal from the army with disgrace. A colour-sergeant then advanced with the former officer's sword, a remarkably fine one, which he thereupon snapped in sunder over the prisoner's head as he knelt. After this the prisoner's regimental coat was handed forward and put upon him, the epaulettes and buttons being then torn off and flung to a distance. This part of such sentences is almost invariably spared; but, I suppose through unavoidable haste, was on the present occasion somewhat rudely carried out. I shall never forget the expression of this man's countenance, though I have seen many sad things in the course of my profession. He had the sort of good looks which always rivet attention, and in most minds friendly interest; and now, amid all his pain and bewilderment, bore a look of humility and submission as he underwent those extraordinary details of his punishment, which touched me very oddly with a sort of desire (I cannot otherwise express it) to share his lot, to be actually in his place for a moment, Yet, alas!—no! say rather Thank Heaven! the nearest approach to that look I have seen has been on the face of those whom I have known from circumstances to be almost incapable at the time of any feeling whatever. I would have offered him pecuniary aid, supposing he needed it, but it was impossible. I went on with the regiment, leaving the poor wretch to shift for himself. Heaven knows how, the state of the country being what it is. He might join the enemy!"

What money Uthwart had about him had in fact passed that morning into the hands of his guards. To tell what followed would be to accompany him on a roundabout and really aimless journey, the details of which he could never afterwards recall. See him lingering for morsels of food at some shattered farmstead, or assisted by others almost as wretched as himself, sometimes without his asking. In his worn military dress he seems a part of the ruin under which he creeps for a night's rest as darkness comes on. He actually came round again to the scene of his disgrace, of the execution; looked in vain for the precise spot where he had knelt; then, almost envying him who lay there, for the unmarked grave; passed over it perhaps unrecognised for some change in that terrible place, or rather in himself; wept then as never before in his life; dragged himself on once more, till suddenly the whole country seems to move under the rumour, the very thunder, of "the crowning victory," as he is made to understand. Falling in with the tide of its heroes returning to English shores, his vagrant footsteps are at last directed homewards. He finds himself one afternoon at the gate, turning out of the quiet Sussex road, through the fields for whose safety he had fought with so much of undeniable gallantry and approval.

On that July afternoon the gardens, the woods, mounted in flawless sweetness all round him as he stood, to meet the circle of a flawless sky. Not a cloud; not a motion on the grass! At the first he had intended to return home no more; and it had been a proof of his great dejection that he sent at last, as best he could, for money. They knew his fate already by report, and were touched naturally when that had followed on the record of his honours. Had it been possible they would have set forth at any risk to meet, to seek him; were waiting now for the weary one to come to the gate, ready with their oil and wine, to speak metaphorically, and from this time forth underwent his charm to the utmost—the charm of an exquisite character, felt in some way to be inseparable from his person, his characteristic movements, touched also now with seemingly irreparable sorrow. For his part, drinking in here the last sweets of the sensible world, it was as if he, the lover of roses, had never before been aware of them at all. The original softness of his temperament, against which the sense of greater things thrust upon him had successfully reacted, asserted itself again now as he lay at ease, the ease well merited by his deeds, his sorrows. That he was going to die moved those about him to humour this mood, to soften all things to his touch; and looking back he might have pronouced those four last years of doom the happiest of his life. The memory of the grave into which he had gazed so steadily on the execution morning, into which, as he feels, one half of himself had then descended, does not lessen his shrinking from the fate before him, yet fortifies him to face it manfully, gives a sort of fraternal familiarity to death; in a few weeks' time this battle too is fought out; it is as if the thing were ended. The delightful summer heat, the freshness it enhances—he contrasts such things no longer with the sort of place to which he is hastening. The possible duration of life for him was indeed uncertain, the future to some degree indefinite; but as regarded any fairly distant date, anything like a term of years, from the first there had been no doubt at all; he would be no longer here. Meantime it was like a delightful few days' additional holiday from school, with which perforce one must be content at last; or as though he had not been pardoned on that terrible morning, but only reprieved for two or three years. Yet how large a proportion they would have seemed in the whole sum of his years. He would have liked to lie finally in the garden among departed pets, dear dead dogs and horses; faintly proposes it one day; but after a while comprehends the churchyard, with its white spots in the distant flowery view, as filling harmoniously its own proper place there. The weary soul seemed to be settling deeper into the body and the earth it came of, into the condition of the flowers, the grass, proper creatures of the earth to which he is returning. The saintly vicar visits him considerately; is repelled with politeness; goes on his way pondering inwardly what kind of place there might be, in any possible scheme of another world, for so abso-lutely unspiritual a subject. In fact, as the breath of the infinite world came about him, he clung all the faster to the beloved finite things still in contact with him; he had successfully hidden from his eyes all beside.

His reprieve however lasted long enough, after all, for a certain change of opinion of immense weight to him—a revision or rever-sal of judgment. It came about in this way. When peace was ar-ranged, with question of rewards, pensions, and the like, certain battle or incidents therein were fought over again, sometimes in the highest places of debate. On such an occasion a certain speaker cites the case of Lieutenant James Stokes and another, as being "*pessimi exempli*": whereupon a second speaker gets up, prepared with full detail, insists, brings that incidental matter to the front for an hour, tells his unfortunate friend's story so effec-tively, pathetically, that, as happens with our countrymen, they repent. The matter gets into the newspapers, and, coming thus into sympathetic public view, something like glory wins from Emerald Uthwart his last touch of animation. Just not too late he received the offer of a commission; kept the letter there open within sight. Aldy, who "never shed tears and was incapable of pain," in his great physical weakness, wept—shall we say for the second time in his life? A less excitement would have been more favourable to any chance there might be of the patient's surviving. In fact the old gun-shot wound, wrongly thought to be cured, which had caused the one illness of his life, is now drawing out what remains of it, as he feels with a kind of odd satisfaction and pride—his old glorious wound! And then, as of old, an absolute submissiveness comes over him, as he gazes round at the place, the relics of his uniform, the letter lying there. It was as if there was nothing more that could be said. Accounts thus settled, he stretched himself in the bed he had occupied as a boy, more completely at his ease than since the day when he had left home for the first time. Respited from death once, he was twice believed to be dead before the date actually registered on his tomb. "What will it matter a hundred years hence?" they used to ask by way of simple comfort in boyish troubles at school, overwhelming at the moment. Was that in truth part of a certain revelation of the inmost truth of things to "babes," such as we have heard of? What did it matter—the gifts, the good-fortune, its terrible withdrawal, the long agony ? Emerald Uthwart would have been all but a centenarian to-day.

Postscript, from the Diary of a Surgeon,
August —th, 18—.

I was summoned by letter into the country to perform an operation on the dead body of a young man, formerly an officer in the army. The cause of death is held to have been some kind of distress of mind, concurrent with the effects of an old gun-shot wound, the ball still remaining somewhere in the body. My instructions were to remove this, at the express desire, as I understood, of the deceased, rather than to ascertain the precise cause of death. This however became apparent in the course of my search for the ball, which had enveloped itself in the muscular substance in the region of the heart, and was removed with difficulty. I have known cases of this kind, where anxiety has caused incurable cardiac derangement (the deceased seems to have been actually sentenced to death for some military offence when on service in

Flanders), and such mental strain would of course have been aggravated by the presence of a foreign object in that place. On arriving at my destination, a small village in a remote part of Sussex, I proceeded through the little orderly churchyard, where however the monthly roses were blooming all their own way among the formal white marble monuments of the wealthier people of the neighbourhood. At one of these the masons were at work, picking and chipping in the otherwise absolute stillness of the summer afternoon. They were in fact opening the family burial-place of the people who summoned me hither; and the workmen pointed out their abode, conspicuous on the slope beyond, towards which I bent my steps accordingly. I was conducted to a large upper room or attic, set freely open to sun and air, and found the body lying in a coffin, almost hidden under very rich-scented cut flowers, after a manner I have never seen in this country, except in the case of one or two Catholics laid out for burial. The mother of the deceased was present, and actually assisted my operations, amid such tokens of distress, though perfectly self-controlled, as I fervently hope I may never witness again. Deceased was in his twenty-seventh year, but looked many years younger; had indeed scarcely yet reached the full condition of manhood. The extreme purity of the outlines, both of the face and limbs, was such as is usually found only in quite early youth; the brow especially, under an abundance of fair hair, finely formed, not high, but arched and full, as is said to be the way with those who have the imaginative temper in excess. Sad to think that had he lived reason must have deserted that so worthy abode of it! I was struck by the great beauty of the organic developments, in the strictly anatomic sense; those of the throat and diaphragm in particular might have been modelled for a teacher of normal physiology, or a professor of design. The flesh was still almost as firm as that of a living person; as happens when, as in this case, death comes to all intents and purposes as gradually as in old age. This expression of health and life, under my seemingly merciless doings, together with the mother's distress, touched me to a degree very unusual, I conceive, in persons of my years and profession. Though I believed myself to be acting by his express wish, I felt like a criminal. The ball, a small one, much corroded with blood, was at length removed; and I was then directed to wrap it in a partly-printed letter, or other document, and place it in the breast-pocket of a faded and much-worn scarlet soldier's coat, put over the shirt which enveloped the body. The flowers were then hastily replaced, the hands and the peak of the handsome nose remaining visible among them; the wind ruffled the fair hair a little; the lips were still red. I shall not forget it. The lid was then placed on the coffin and screwed down in my presence. There was no plate or other inscription upon it.

[1892]

Apollo in Picardy

"Consecutive upon Apollo in all his solar fervour and effulgence,"
says a writer of Teutonic proclivities, "we may discern even
among the Greeks themselves, elusively, as would be natural with
such a being, almost like a mock sun amid the mists, the northern
or ultra-northern sun-god. In hints and fragments the lexicogra-
phers and others have told us something of this Hyperborean
Apollo, fancies about him which evidence some knowledge of the
Land of the Midnight Sun, of the sun's ways among the Laplan-
ders, of a hoary summer breathing very softly on the violet beds,
or say, the London-pride and crab-apples, provided for those meagre people, somewhere amid the remoteness of their icy seas. In
such wise Apollo had already anticipated his sad fortunes in the
Middle Age as a god definitely in exile, driven north of the Alps,
and even here ever in flight before the summer. Summer indeed he
leaves now to the management of others, finding his way from
France and Germany to still paler countries, yet making or taking
with him always a certain seductive summer-in-winter, though
also with a divine or titanic regret, a titanic revolt in his heart,
and consequent inversion at times of his old beneficent and properly solar doings. For his favours, his fallacious good-humour,
which has in truth a touch of malign magic about it, he makes
men pay sometimes a terrible price, and is in fact a devil!"

Devilry, devil's work:—traces of such you might fancy were to be
found in a certain manuscript volume taken from an old monastic
library in France at the Revolution. It presented a strange example of a cold and very reasonable spirit disturbed suddenly,
thrown off its balance, as by a violent beam, a blaze of new light,

revealing, as it glanced here and there, a hundred truths un-
guessed at before, yet a curse, as it turned out, to its receiver, in
dividing hopelessly against itself the well-ordered kingdom of his
thought. Twelfth volume of a dry enough treatise on mathematics, applied, still with no relaxation of strict method, to astron-
omy and music, it should have concluded that work, and therewith
the second period of the life of its author, by drawing tight together the threads of a long and intricate argument. In effect
however, it began, or, in perturbed manner, and as with throes of
childbirth, seemed the preparation for, an argument of an entirely new and disparate species, such as would demand a new
period of life also, if it might be, for its due expansion.

But with what confusion, what baffling inequalities! How af-
flicting to the mind's eye! It was a veritable "solar storm"—this
illumination, which had burst at the last moment upon the strenuous, self-possessed, much-honoured monastic student, as he sat
down peacefully to write the last formal chapters of his work ere
he betook himself to its well-earned practical reward as superior,
with lordship and mitre and ring, of the abbey whose music and
calendar his mathematical knowledge had qualified him to reform. The very shape of Volume Twelve, pieced together of quite
irregularly formed pages, was a solecism. It could never be bound.
In truth, the man himself, and what passed with him in one particular space of time, had invaded a matter, which is nothing if
not entirely abstract and impersonal. Indirectly the volume was
the record of an episode, an interlude, an interpolated page of
life. And whereas in the earlier volumes you found by way of
illustration no more than the simplest indispensable diagrams,
the scribe's hand had strayed here into mazy borders, long spaces
of hieroglyph, and as it were veritable pictures of the theoretic
elements of his subject. Soft wintry auroras seemed to play behind
whole pages of crabbed textual writing, line and figure bending,
breathing, flaming, into lovely "arrangements" that were like
music made visible; till writing and writer changed suddenly, "to
one thing constant never," after the known manner of madmen in
such work. Finally, the whole matter broke off with an unfinished
word, as a later hand testified, adding the date of the author's
death, "*deliquio animi.*"

He had been brought to the monastery as a little child; was bred there; had never yet left it, busy and satisfied through youth and early manhood; was grown almost as necessary a part of the community as the stones of its material abode, as a pillar of the great tower he ascended to watch the movements of the stars. The structure of a fortified medieval town barred in those who belonged to it very effectively. High monastic walls intrenched the monk still further. From the summit of the tower you looked straight down into the deep narrow streets, upon the houses (in one of which Prior Saint-Jean was born) climbing as high as they dared for breathing space within that narrow compass. But you saw also the green breadth of Normandy and Picardy, this way and that; felt on your face the free air of a still wider realm beyond what was seen. The reviving scent of it, the mere sight of the flowers brought thence, of the country produce at the convent gate, stirred the ordinary monkish soul with desires, sometimes with efforts, to be sent on duty there. Prior Saint-Jean, on the other hand, shuddered at the view, at the thoughts it suggested to him; thoughts of unhallowed wild places, where the old heathen had worshipped "stocks and stones," and where their wickedness might still survive them in something worse than mischievous tricks of nature, such as you might read of in Ovid, whose verses, however, he for his part had never so much as touched with a finger. He gave thanks rather, that his vocation to the abstract sciences had kept him far apart from the whole crew of miscreant poets—Abode of demons.

Thither nevertheless he was now to depart, sent to the Grange or *Obedience* of Notre-Dame De-Pratis by the aged Abbot (about to resign in his favour) for the benefit of his body's health, a little impaired at last by long intellectual effort, yet so invaluable to the community. But let him beware! whispered his dearest friend, who shared those strange misgivings, let him "take heed to his ways" when he was come to that place. "The mere contact of one's feet with its soil might change one." And that same night, disturbed perhaps by thoughts of the coming journey with which his brain was full, Prior Saint-Jean himself dreamed vividly, as he had been little used to do. He saw the very place in which he lay (he knew it! his little inner cell, the brown doors, the white breadth of wall, the black crucifix upon it) alight, alight softly; and looking, as he fancied, from the window, saw also a low circlet of soundless flame, waving, licking daintily up the black sky, but harmless, beautiful, closing in upon that round dark space in the midst, which was the earth. He seemed to feel upon his shoulder just then the touch of his friend beside him. "It is hell-fire!" he said.

The Prior took with him a very youthful though devoted companion—Hyacinthus, the pet of the community. They laughed admiringly at the rebellious masses of his black hair, with blue in the depths of it, like the wings of the swallow, which refused to conform to the monkish pattern. It only grew twofold, crown upon crown, after the half-yearly shaving. And he was as neat and serviceable as he was delightful to be with. Prior Saint-Jean, then, and the boy started before daybreak for the long journey; onwards, till darkness, a soft twilight rather, was around them again. How unlike a winter night it seemed, the further they went through the endless, lonely, turf-grown tracts, and along the edge of a valley, at length—*vallis monachorum*, monksvale—taken aback by its sudden steepness and depth, as of an immense oval cup sunken in the grassy upland, over which a golden moon now shone broadly. Ah! there it was at last, the white Grange, the white gable of the chapel apart amid a few scattered white gravestones, the white flocks crouched about on the hoar-frost, like the white clouds, packed somewhat heavily on the horizon, and *nacrés* as the clouds of June, with their own light and heat in them, in their hollows, you might fancy.

From the very first, the atmosphere, the light, the influence of things, seemed different from what they knew; and how distant already the dark buildings of their home! Was there the breath of surviving summer blossom on the air? Now and then came a gentle, comfortable bleating from the folds, and themselves slept soundly at last in the great open upper chamber of the Grange; were awakened by the sound of thunder. Strange, in the late November night! It had parted, however, with its torrid fierceness; modulated by distance, seemed to break away into musical notes. And the lightning lingered along with it, but glancing softly; was in truth an aurora, such as persisted month after month on the northern sky as they sojourned here. Like Prospero's enchanted island, the whole place was "full of noises." The wind it might have been, passing over metallic strings, but that they were audible even when the night was breathless.

So like veritable music, however, were they on that first night that, upon reflexion, the Prior climbed softly the winding stair down which they appeared to flow, to the great *solar* among the beams of the roof, where the farm produce lay stored. A flood of moonlight now fell through the unshuttered dormer-windows; and, under the glow of a lamp hanging from the low rafters, Prior Saint-Jean seemed to be looking for the first time on the human form, on the old Adam fresh from his Maker's hand. A servant of the house, or farm-labourer, perhaps!—fallen asleep there by chance on the fleeces heaped like golden stuff high in all the corners of the place. A serf! But what unserflike ease, how lordly, or godlike rather, in the posture! Could one fancy a single curve bettered in the rich, warm, white limbs; in the haughty features of the face, with the golden hair, tied in a mystic knot, fallen down across the inspired brow? And yet what gentle sweetness also in the natural movement of the bosom, the throat, the lips, of the sleeper! Could that be diabolical, and really spotted with unseen evil, which was so spotless to the eye? The rude sandals of the monastic serf lay beside him apart, and all around was of the roughest, excepting only two strange objects lying within reach (even in their own renowned treasury Prior Saint-Jean had not seen the like of them), a harp, or some such instrument, of silver-gilt once, but the gold had mostly passed from it, and a bow, fashioned somehow of the same precious substance. The very form of these things filled his mind with inexplicable misgivings. He repeated a befitting collect, and trod softly away.

It was in truth but a rude place to which they were come. But, after life in the monastery, the severe discipline of which the Prior himself had done much to restore, there was luxury in the free, self-chosen hours, the irregular fare, in doing pretty much as one pleased, in the sweet novelties of the country; to the boy Hyacinth especially, who forgot himself, or rather found his true self for the first time. Girding up his heavy frock, which he laid aside erelong altogether to go in his coarse linen smock only, he seemed a monastic novice no longer; yet, in his natural gladness, was found more companionable than ever by his senior, surprised, delighted, for his part, at the fresh springing of his brain, the spring of his footsteps over the close greensward, as if smoothed by the art of man. Cause of his renewed health, or concurrent with its effects, the air here might have been that of a veritable paradise, still unspoiled. "Could there be unnatural magic," he asked himself again, "any secret evil, lurking in these tranquil valesides, in their sweet low pastures, in the belt of scattered woodland above them, in the rills of pure water which lisped from the open down beyond?" Making what was really a boy's experience, he had a wholly boyish delight in his holiday, and certainly did not reflect how much we beget for ourselves in what we see and feel, nor how far a certain diffused music in the very breath of the place was the creation of his own ear or brain.

That strange enigmatic owner of the harp and the bow, whom he had found sleeping so divinely, actually waited on them the next morning with all obsequiousness, stirred the great fire of peat, adjusted duly their monkish attire, laid their meal. It seemed an odd thing to be served thus, like St. Jerome by the lion, as if by some imperiously beautiful wild animal tamed. You hesitated to permit, were a little afraid of, his services. Their silent tonsured porter himself, contrast grim enough to any creature of that kind, had been so far seduced as to permit him to sleep there in the Grange, as he loved to do, instead of in ruder, rougher quarters; and, coaxed into odd garrulity on this one matter, told the new-comers the little he knew, with much also that he only suspected, about him; among other things, as to the origin of those precious objects, which might have belonged to some sanctuary or noble house, found thus in the possession of a mere labourer, who is no Frenchman, but a pagan, or gipsy, white as he looks, from far south or east, and who works or plays furtively, by night for the most part, returning to sleep awhile before daybreak. The other herdsmen of the valley are bond-servants, but he a hireling at will, though coming regularly at a certain season. He has come thus for any number of years past, though seemingly never grown older (as the speaker reflects), singing his way meagrely from farm to farm, to the sound of his harp. His name?—It was scarcely a name at all, in the diffident syllables he uttered in answer to that question, on first coming there; but of names known to them it came nearest to a malignant one in Scripture, Apollyon. Apollyon had a just discernible tonsure, but probably no right to it.

Well skilled in architecture, Prior Saint-Jean was set, by way of a holiday task, to superintend the completion of the great monastic barn then in building. The visitor admires it still; perhaps supposes it, with its noble aisle, though set north and south, to be a desecrated church. If he be an expert in such matters, he will remark a sort of classical harmony in its broad, very simple proportions, with a certain suppression of Gothic emphasis, more especially in that peculiarly Gothic feature, the buttresses, scarcely marking the unbroken, windowless walls, which rise very straight, taking the sun placidly. The silver-grey stone, cut, if it came from this neighbourhood at all, from some now forgotten quarry, has the fine, close-grained texture of antique marble. The great northern gable is almost a classic pediment. The horizontal lines of plinth and ridge and cornice are kept unbroken, the roof of sea-grey slates being pitched less angularly than is usual in this rainy clime. A welcome contrast, the Prior thought it, to the sort of architectural nightmare he came from. He found the structure already more than halfway up, the low squat pillars ready for their capitals.

Yes! it must have so happened often in the Middle Age, as you feel convinced, in looking sometimes at medieval building. Style must have changed under the very hands of men who were no wilful innovators. Thus it was here, in the later work of Prior Saint-Jean, all unconsciously. The mysterious harper sat there always, at the topmost point achieved; played, idly enough it might seem, on his precious instrument, but kept in fact the hard taxed workmen literally in tune, working for once with a ready will, and, so to speak, with really inventive hands—working expeditiously, in this favourable weather, till far into the night, as they joined unbidden in a chorus, which hushed, or rather turned to music, the noise of their chipping. It was hardly noise at all, even in the night-time. Now and again Brother Apollyon descended nimbly to surprise them, at an opportune moment, by the display of an immense strength. A great cheer exploded suddenly, as single-handed he heaved a massive stone into its place. He seemed to have no sense of weight: "Put there by the devil!" the modern villager assures you.

With a change then, not so much of style as of temper, of management, in the application of acknowledged rules, Prior Saint-Jean shaping only, adapting, simplifying, partly with a view to economy, not the heavy stones only, but the heavy manner of using them, turned light. With no pronounced ornamentation, it is as if in the upper story ponderous root and stem blossomed gracefully, blossomed in cornice and capital and pliant arch-line, as vigorous as they were graceful, and rose on high quickly. Almost suddenly tie-beam and rafter knit themselves together into the stone, and the dark, dry, roomy place was closed in securely to this day. Mere audible music, certainly, had counted for something in the operations of an art, held at its best (as we know) to be a sort of music made visible. That idle singer, one might fancy, by an art beyond art, had attracted beams and stones into their fit places. And there, sure enough, he still sits, as a final decorative touch, by way of apex on the gable which looks northward, though much weather-worn, and with an ugly gap between the shoulder and the fingers on the harp,[1] as if, literally, he had cut off his right hand and put it from him:—King David, or an angel? guesses the careless tourist. The space below has been lettered. After a little puzzling you recognise there the relics of a familiar verse from a Latin psalm: *Nisi Dominus ædificaverit domum,* and the rest: inscribed as well as may be in Greek characters. Prior Saint-Jean caused it to be so inscribed, absurdly, during his last days there.

And is not the human body, too, a building, with architectural laws, a structure, tending by the very forces which primarily held it together to drop asunder in time? Not in vain, it seemed, had Prior Saint-Jean come to this mystic place for the improvement of his body's health. Thenceforth that fleshly tabernacle had housed him, had housed his cunning, overwrought and excitable soul, ever the better day by day, and he began to feel his bodily health

[1] Or sundial, as some maintain, though turned from the south.

to be a positive quality or force, the presence near him of that singular being having surely something to do with this result. He and his fascinations, his music, himself, might at least be taken for an embodiment of all those genial influences of earth and sky, and the easy ways of living here, which made him turn, with less of an effort than he had known for many years past, to his daily tasks, and sink so regularly, so immediately, to wholesome rest on returning from them. It was as if Brother Apollyon himself abhorred the spectacle of distress, and mainly for his own satisfaction charmed away other people's maladies. The mere touch of that ice-cold hand, laid on the feverish brow, when the Prior lapsed from time to time into his former troubles, certainly calmed the respiration of a troubled sleeper. Was there magic in it, not wholly natural? The hand might have been a dead one. But then, was it surprising, after all, that the methods of curing men's maladies, as being in very deed the fruit of sin, should have something strange and unlooked-for about them, like some of those Old Testament healings and purifications which the Prior's biblical lore suggested to him? Yet Brother Apollyon, if their surly *Janitor*, in his less kindly moments, spoke truly, himself greatly needed purification, being not only a thief, but a homicide in hiding from the law. Nay, once, on his annual return from southern or eastern lands, he had been observed on his way along the streets of the great town literally scattering the seeds of disease till his serpent-skin bag was empty. And within seven days the "black death" was there, reaping its thousands. As a wise man declared, he who can best cure disease can also most cunningly engender it.

In short, these creatures of rule, these "regulars," the Prior and his companion, were come in contact for the first time in their lives with the power of untutored natural impulse, of natural inspiration. The boy experienced it immediately in the games which suited his years, but which he had never so much as seen before; as his superior was to undergo its influence by-and-by in serious study. By night chiefly, in its long, continuous twilights, Hyacinth became really a boy at last, with immense gaiety; eyes, hands and feet awake, expanding, as he raced his comrade over the turf, with the conical Druidic stone for a goal, or wrestled lithely enough with him, though as with a rock; or, taking the silver bow in hand for a moment, transfixed a mark, next a bird, on the bough, on the wing, shedding blood for the first time, with a boy's delight, a boy's remorse. Friend Apollyon seemed able to draw the wild animals too, to share their sport, yet not altogether kindly. Tired, surfeited, he destroys them when his game with them is at an end; breaks the toy; deftly snaps asunder the fragile back. Though all alike would come at his call, or the sound of his harp, he had his preferences; and warred in the night-time, as if on principle, against the creatures of the day. The small furry thing he pierced with his arrow fled to him nevertheless caressingly, with broken limb, to die palpitating in his hand. In this wonderful season, the migratory birds, from Norway, from Britain beyond the seas, came there as usual on the north wind, with sudden tumult of wings; but went that year no further, and by Christmas-time had built their nests, filling that belt of woodland around the vale with the chatter of their business and love quarrels. In turn they drew after them strangers no one here had ever known before; the like of which Hyacinth, who knew his bestiary, had never seen even in a picture. The wild-cat, the wild-swan— the boy peeped on these wonders as they floated over the vale, or glided with unwonted confidence over its turf, under the moonlight, or that frequent continuous aurora which was not the dawn. Even the modest rivulets of the hill-side felt that influence, and "lisped" no longer, but babbled as they leapt, like mountain streams, exposing their rocky bed. Were they angry, as they ran red sometimes, with blood-drops from the stricken bird caught there by rock or bough, as it fell with rent breast among the waves?

But say, think, what you might against him, the pagan outlaw was worth his hire as a herdsman; seemingly loved his sheep; was an "affectionate shepherd"; cured their diseases; brought them easily to the birth, and if they strayed afar would bring them back tenderly upon his shoulders. Monastic persons would have seen that image many times before. Yet if Apollyon looked like the great carved figure over the low doorway of their place of penitence at home, that could be but an accident, or perhaps a deceit; so closely akin to those soulless creatures did he still seem to the wondering Prior,—immersed in, or actually a part of, that irredeemable natural world he had dreaded so greatly ere he came hither. And was he after all making terms with it now, in the seductive person of this mysterious being—man or demon—suspected of murder; who has an air of unfathomable evil about him as from a distant but ineffaceable past, and a sort of heathen understanding with the dark realm of matter; who is bringing the simple people, the women and lovesick lads, back to those caves and cromlechs and blasted trees, resorts of old godless secret-telling? And still he has all his own way with beasts and man, with the Prior himself, much as all alike distrust him.

Most conspicious in the little group of buildings, a feudal tower of goodly white stone, cylindrical and smoothly polished without to hinder the ascent of creeping things, and snugly plastered within to resist the damp, was the pigeon-house—a veritable feudal tower, a veritable feudal *plaisance* of birds, which the common people dared not so much as ruffle. About a thousand of them were housed there, each in its little chamber, encouraged to grow plump, and to breed, in perfect self-content. From perch to perch of the great axle-tree in the centre, monastic feet might climb, gentle monastic hands pass round to every tiny compartment in turn. The arms of the monastery were carved on the keystone of the doorway, and the tower finished in a conical roof, with becoming aerial *gaillardise*, with pretty dormer-windows for the inmates to pass in and out, little balconies for brooding in the sun, little awnings to protect them from rough breezes, and a great weather-vane, on which the birds crowded for the chance of a ride. If the peasants of that day, whose small fields they plundered, noting all this, perhaps envied the birds dumbly, for the brethren, on the other hand, it was a constant delight to watch the feathered brotherhood, which supplied likewise their daintiest fare. Who then, what hawk, or wild-cat, or other savage beast, had ravaged it so wantonly, so very cruelly destroyed the bright creatures in a single night—broken backs, rent away limbs, pierced the wings? And what was that object there below? The silver harp surely, lying broken likewise on the sanded floor, soaking in the pale milky blood and torn plumage.

Apollyon sobbed and wept audibly as he went about his ordi-

nary doings next day, for once fully, though very sadly, awake in
it; and towards evening, when the villagers came to the Prior to
confess themselves, the Feast of the Nativity being now at hand,
he too came along with them in his place meekly, like any other
penitent, touched the lustral water devoutly, knew all the ways,
seemed to desire absolution from some guilt of blood heavier than
the slaughter of beast or bird. The Prior and his attendant, on
their side, are reminded that by this time they have wellnigh
forgotten the monastic duties still incumbent upon them, especially in that matter of the "Offices." On the vigil of the feast,
however, Brother Apollyon himself summoned the devout to Midnight Mass with the great bell, which had hung silent for a generation, wedged in immoveably by a beam of the cradle fallen out of
its place. With an immense effort of strength he relieved it,
hitched the bell back upon its wheel; the thick rust cracked on
the hinges, and the strokes tolled forth betimes, with a hundred
querulous, quaint creatures, bats and owls, circling stupidly in the
waves of sound, but allowed to settle back again undisturbedly
into their beds.

   People and priest, the Prior, vested as well as might be, with
Hyacinth as "server," come in due course, all alike amazed to find
that frozen neglected place, with its low-browed vault and narrow windows, alight, and as if warmed with flowers from a summer more radiant far than that of France, with ilex and laurel—
gilt laurel—by way of holly and box. Prior Saint-Jean felt that he
had never really seen flowers before. Somewhat later they and the
like of them seemed to have grown into and over his brain; to have
degraded the scientific and abstract outlines of things into a tangle of useless ornament. Whence were they procured? From what
height, or hellish depth perhaps? Apollyon, who entered the
chapel just then, as if quite naturally, though with a bleating
lamb in his bosom ("dropped" thus early in that wonderful season) by way of an offering, took his place at the altar's very foot,
and drawing forth his harp, now restrung, at the right moment,
turned to real silvery music the hoarse *Gloria in Excelsis* of those
rude worshippers, still shrinking from him, while they listened in
a little circle, as he stood there in his outlandish attire of skins
strangely spotted and striped. With that however the Mass broke

off unconsummated. The Prior felt obliged to desist from the sacred office, and had left the altar hurriedly.

But Brother Apollyon put his strange attire aside next day, and in a much-worn monk's frock, drawn forth from a dark corner, came with them, still like a penitent, when they turned once more to their neglected studies somewhat sadly. See them then, after a collect for "Light" repeated by Hyacinth, skull-cap in hand, seated at their desks in the little *scriptorium*, panelled off from their living-room on the first floor, while the Prior makes an effort to recover the last thought of his long-suspended work, in the execution of which the boy is to assist with his skilful pen. The great glazed windows remain open; admit, as if already on the soft air of spring, what seems like a stream of flowery odours, the entire moonlit scene, with the thorn bushes on the vale-side prematurely bursting into blossom, and the sound of birds and flocks emphasising the deep silence of the night.

Apollyon then, as if by habit, as he had shared all their occupations of late, had taken his seat beside them, meekly enough, at first with the manner of a mere suppliant for the crumbs of their high studies. But, straightway again, he surprises by more than racing forward incredibly on the road to facts, and from facts to luminous doctrine; Prior Saint-Jean himself, in comparison, seeming to lag incompetently behind. He can but wonder at this strange scholar's knowledge of a distant past, evidenced in his familiarity (it was as if he might once have spoken them) with the dead languages in which their text-books are written. There was more surely than the utmost merely natural acuteness in his guesses as to the words intended by those crabbed contractions, of their meaning, in his sense of allusions and the like. An ineffaceable memory it might rather seem of the entire world of which those languages had been the living speech, once more vividly awake under the Prior's cross-questioning, and now more than supplementing his own laborious search.

And at last something of the same kind happens with himself. Had he, on his way hither from the convent, passed unwittingly through some river or rivulet of Lethe, that had carried away from him all his so carefully accumulated intellectual baggage of fact and theory? The hard and abstract laws, or theory of the laws, of music, of the stars, of mechanical structure, in hard and abstract *formulæ*, adding to the abstract austerity of the man, seemed to have deserted him; to be revived in him again however, at the contact of this extraordinary pupil or fellow-inquirer, though in a very different guise or attitude towards himself, as matters no longer to be reasoned upon and understood, but to be seen rather, to be looked at and heard. Did not he *see* the angle of the earth's axis with the ecliptic, the deflexions of the stars from their proper orbits with fatal results here below, and the earth—wicked, un-scriptural truth!—moving round the sun, and those flashes of the eternal and unorbed light such as bring water, flowers, living things, out of the rocks, the dust? The singing of the planets: he could hear it, and might in time effect its notation. Having seen and heard, he might erelong speak also, truly and with authority, on such matters. Could one but arrest it for one's self, for final transference to others, on the written or printed page—this beam of insight, or of inspiration!

Alas! one result of its coming was that it encouraged delay. If he set hand to the page, the firm halo, here a moment since, was gone, had flitted capriciously to the wall; passed next through the window, to the wall of the garden; was dancing back in another moment upon the innermost walls of one's own miserable brain, to swell there—that astounding white light!—rising steadily in the cup, the mental receptacle, till it overflowed, and he lay faint and drowning in it. Or he rose above it, as above a great liquid surface, and hung giddily over it—light, simple, and absolute—ere he fell. Or there was a battle between light and darkness around him, with no way of escape from the baffling strokes, the lightning flashes; flashes of blindness one might rather call them. In truth, the intuitions of the night (for they worked still, or tried to work, by night) became the sickly nightmares of the day, in which Prior Saint-Jean slept, or tried to sleep, or lay sometimes in a trance without food for many hours, from which he would spring up suddenly to crowd, against time, as much as he could into his book with pen or brush; winged flowers, or stars with human limbs and faces, still intruding themselves, or mere notes of light and darkness from the actual horizon. There it all is still in the faded gold and colours of the ancient volume—"Prior Saint-

Jean's folly":—till on a sudden the hand collapses, as he becomes aware of that real, prosaic, broad daylight lying harsh upon the page, making his delicately toned auroras seem but a patch of grey, and himself for a moment, with a sigh of disgust, of self-reproach, to be his old unimpassioned monastic self once more.

The boy, for his part, was grown at last full of misgiving. He ponders how he may get the Prior away, or escape by himself, find his way back to the convent and report his master's condition, his strange loss of memory for names and the like, his illusions about himself and others. And he is more than ever distrustful now of his late beloved playmate, who quietly obstructs any movement of the kind, and has undertaken, at the Prior's entreaty, to draw down the moon from the sky, for some shameful price, known to the magicians of that day.

Yet Apollyon, at all events, would still play as gaily as ever on occasion. Hitherto they had played as young animals do; without playthings namely, applying hand or foot only to their games. But it happened about this time that a grave was dug, a grave of unusual depth, to be ready, in that fiery plaguesome weather, the first heat of veritable summer come suddenly, for the body of an ancient villager then at the point of death. In the drowsy afternoon Hyacinth awakes Apollyon, to see the strange thing he has found at the grave-side, among the gravel and yellow bones cast up there. He had wrested it with difficulty from the hands of the half-crippled gravedigger, at eighty still excitable by the mere touch of metal.

The like of it had indeed been found before, within living memory, in this place of immemorial use as a graveyard—"Devil's penny-pieces" people called them. Five such lay hidden already in a dark corner of the chapel, to keep them from superstitious employment. Today they came out of hiding at last. Apollyon knew the use of the thing at a glance; had put an expert hand to it forthwith; poises the *discus;* sets it wheeling. How easily it spins round under one's arm, in the groove of the bent fingers, slips thence smoothly like a knife flung from its sheath, as if for a course of perpetual motion! *Splendescit eundo:* it seems to burn as it goes. It is heavier many times than it looks, and sharp-edged. By night they have scoured and polished the corroded surfaces.

Apollyon promises Hyacinth and himself rare sport in the cool of the evening—an evening however, as it turned out, not less breathless than the day.

In the great heat Apollyon had flung aside, as if for ever, the last sorry remnant of his workman's attire, and challenged the boy to do the same. On the moonlit turf there, crouching, right foot foremost, and with face turned backwards to the disk in his right hand, his whole body, in that moment of rest, full of the circular motion he is about to commit to it, he seemed—beautiful pale spectre—to shine from within with a light of his own, like that of the glowworm in the thicket, or the dead and rotten roots of the old trees. And as if they had a proper motion of their own in them, the disks, the quoits, ran, amid the delighted shouts and laughter of the boy, as he follows, scarcely less swift, to score the points of their contact with the grass. Again and again they recommence, forgetful of the hours; while the death-bell cries out harshly for the grave's occupant, and the corpse itself is borne along stealthily not far from them, and, unnoticed by either, the entire aspect of things has changed. Under the overcast sky it is in darkness they are playing, by guess and touch chiefly; and suddenly an icy blast of wind has lifted the roof from the old chapel, the trees are moaning in wild circular motion, and their devil's penny-piece, when Apollyon throws it for the last time, is itself but a twirling leaf in the wind, till it sinks edgewise, sawing through the boy's face, uplifted in the dark to trace it, crushing in the tender skull upon the brain.

His shout of laughter is turned in an instant to a cry of pain, of reproach; and in that which echoed it—an immense cry, as from the very heart of ancient tragedy, over the Picard wolds—it was as if that half-extinguished deity, its proper immensity, its old greatness and power, were restored for a moment. The villagers in their beds wondered. It was like the sound of some natural catastrophe.

The storm which followed was still in possession, still moving tearfully among the poplar groves, though it had spent its heat and thunder. The last drops of the blood of Hyacinth still trickled through the thick masses of dark hair, where the tonsure had been. An abundant rain, mingling with the copious purple stream, had coloured the grass all around where the corpse lay, stealing afar in tiny channels. So it was, when Apollyon, reduced in the morning light to his smaller self, came with the other people of the Grange to gaze, to enquire, and found the Prior already there, speechless. Clearly this was no lightning stroke; and Apollyon straightway conceives certain very human fears that, coming upon those antecedent suspicions of himself, the boy's death may be thought the result of intention on his part. He proposes to bury the body at once, with no delay for religious rites, in that still uncovered grave, the bearers having fled from it in the tempest.

And next day, fulfilling his annual custom, he went his way northward, without a word of farewell to Prior Saint-Jean, whom he leaves in fact under suspicion of murder. From the profound slumber which had followed the excitements of yesterday, the Prior awoke amid the sound of voices, the voices of the peasants singing no Christian song, certainly, but a song which Apollyon himself had taught them, to dismiss him on his journey. For, strange or not as it might be, they loved him, perhaps in spite of themselves; would certainly protect him at any risk. Prior Saint-Jean arose, and looked forth—with wonder. A brief spell of sunshine amid the rain had clothed the vale with a marvel of blue flowers, if it were not rather with remnants of the blue sky itself, fallen among the woods there. But there too, in the little courtyard, the officers of justice are already in waiting to take him, on the charge of having caused the death of his young server by violence, in a fit of mania, induced by dissolute living in that solitary place. One hitherto so prosperous in life would, of course, have his enemies.

The monastic authorities, however, claim him from the secular power, to correct his offence in their own way, and with friendly interpretation of the facts. Madness, however wicked, being still madness, Prior, now simple Brother, Saint-Jean, is detained in a sufficiently cheerful apartment, in a region of the atmosphere likely to restore lost wits, whence indeed he can still see the country—*vallis monachorum*. The one desire which from time to time fitfully rouses him again to animation for a few moments is to return thither. Here then he remains in peace, ostensibly for the completion of his great work. He never again set pen to it, consistent and clear now on nothing save that longing to be once more at the Grange, that he may get well, or die and be well so. He is like the damned spirit, think some of the brethren, saying "I will return to the house whence I came out." Gazing thither daily for many hours, he would mistake mere blue distance, when that was visible, for blue flowers, for hyacinths, and wept at the sight; though blue, as he observed, was the colour of Holy Mary's gown on the illuminated page, the colour of hope, of merciful omnipresent deity. The necessary permission came with difficulty, just too late. Brother Saint-Jean died, standing upright with an effort to gaze forth once more, amid the preparations for his departure.

[1893]

APPRECIATIONS

Style

Since all progress of mind consists for the most part in differentia-
tion, in the resolution of an obscure and complex object into its
component aspects, it is surely the stupidest of losses to confuse
things which right reason has put asunder, to lose the sense of
achieved distinctions, the distinction between poetry and prose,
for instance, or, to speak more exactly, between the laws and
characteristic excellences of verse and prose composition. On the
other hand, those who have dwelt most emphatically on the distinction between prose and verse, prose and poetry, may sometimes have been tempted to limit the proper functions of prose too
narrowly; and this again is at least false economy, as being, in
effect, the renunciation of a certain means or faculty, in a world
where after all we must needs make the most of things. Critical
efforts to limit art *a priori*, by anticipations regarding the natural
incapacity of the material with which this or that artist works, as
the sculptor with solid form, or the prose-writer with the ordinary
language of men, are always liable to be discredited by the facts of
artistic production; and while prose is actually found to be a
coloured thing with Bacon, picturesque with Livy and Carlyle,
musical with Cicero and Newman, mystical and intimate with
Plato and Michelet and Sir Thomas Browne, exalted or florid, it
may be, with Milton and Taylor, it will be useless to protest that it
can be nothing at all, except something very tamely and narrowly confined to mainly practical ends—a kind of "good round-
hand;" as useless as the protest that poetry might not touch prosaic subjects as with Wordsworth, or an abstruse matter as with
Browning, or treat contemporary life nobly as with Tennyson. In
subordination to one essential beauty in all good literary style, in

all literature as a fine art, as there are many beauties of poetry so
the beauties of prose are many, and it is the business of criticism
to estimate them as such; as it is good in the criticism of verse to
look for those hard, logical, and quasi-prosaic excellences which
that too has, or needs. To find in the poem, amid the flowers, the
allusions, the mixed perspectives, of *Lycidas* for instance, the
thought, the logical structure:—how wholesome! how delightful!
as to identify in prose what we call the poetry, the imaginative power, not treating it as out of place and a kind of vagrant
intruder, but by way of an estimate of its rights, that is, of its
achieved powers, there.

Dryden, with the characteristic instinct of his age, loved to
emphasise the distinction between poetry and prose, the protest
against their confusion with each other, coming with somewhat
diminished effect from one whose poetry was so prosaic. In truth,
his sense of prosaic excellence affected his verse rather than his
prose, which is not only fervid, richly figured, poetic, as we say,
but vitiated, all unconsciously, by many a scanning line. Setting
up correctness, that humble merit of prose, as the central literary
excellence, he is really a less correct writer than he may seem,
still with an imperfect mastery of the relative pronoun. It might
have been foreseen that, in the rotations of mind, the province of
poetry in prose would find its assertor; and, a century after Dryden, amid very different intellectual needs, and with the need
therefore of great modifications in literary form, the range of the
poetic force in literature was effectively enlarged by Wordsworth.
The true distinction between prose and poetry he regarded as the
almost technical or accidental one of the absence or presence of
metrical beauty, or, say! metrical restraint; and for him the opposition came to be between verse and prose of course; but, as the
essential dichotomy in this matter, between imaginative and un-
imaginative writing, parallel to De Quincey's distinction between "the literature of power and the literature of knowledge,"
in the former of which the composer gives us not fact, but his
peculiar sense of fact, whether past or present.

Dismissing then, under sanction of Wordsworth, that harsher
opposition of poetry to prose, as savouring in fact of the arbitrary
psychology of the last century, and with it the prejudice that

there can be but one only beauty of prose style, I propose here to point out certain qualities of all literature as a fine art, which, if they apply to the literature of fact, apply still more to the literature of the imaginative sense of fact, while they apply indifferently to verse and prose, so far as either is really imaginative— certain conditions of true art in both alike, which conditions may also contain in them the secret of the proper discrimination and guardianship of the peculiar excellences of either.

The line between fact and something quite different from external fact is, indeed, hard to draw. In Pascal, for instance, in the persuasive writers generally, how difficult to define the point where, from time to time, argument which, if it is to be worth anything at all, must consist of facts or groups of facts, becomes a pleading—a theorem no longer, but essentially an appeal to the reader to catch the writer's spirit, to think with him, if one can or will—an expression no longer of fact but of his sense of it, his peculiar intuition of a world, prospective, or discerned below the faulty conditions of the present, in either case changed somewhat from the actual world. In science, on the other hand, in history so far as it conforms to scientific rule, we have a literary domain where the imagination may be thought to be always an intruder. And as, in all science, the functions of literature reduce themselves eventually to the transcribing of fact, so all the excellences of literary form in regard to science are reducible to various kinds of painstaking; this good quality being involved in all "skilled work" whatever, in the drafting of an act of parliament, as in sewing. Yet here again, the writer's sense of fact, in history especially, and in all those complex subjects which do but lie on the borders of science, will still take the place of fact, in various degrees. Your historian, for instance, with absolutely truthful intention, amid the multitude of facts presented to him must needs select, and in selecting assert something of his own humour, something that comes not of the world without but of a vision within. So Gibbon moulds his unwieldy material to a preconceived view. Livy, Tacitus, Michelet, moving full of poignant sensibility amid the records of the past, each, after his own sense, modifies—who can tell where and to what degree?—and becomes something else than a transcriber; each, as he thus modifies, passing into the domain of art proper. For just in proportion as the writer's aim, consciously or unconsciously, comes to be the transcribing, not of the world, not of mere fact, but of his sense of it, he becomes an artist, his work *fine* art; and good art (as I hope ultimately to show) in proportion to the truth of his presentment of that sense; as in those humbler or plainer functions of literature also, truth—truth to bare fact, there—is the essence of such artistic quality as they may have. Truth! there can be no merit, no craft at all, without that. And further, all beauty is in the long run only *fineness* of truth, or what we call expression, the finer accommodation of speech to that vision within.

—The transcript of his sense of fact rather than the fact, as being preferable, pleasanter, more beautiful to the writer himself. In literature, as in every other product of human skill, in the moulding of a bell or a platter for instance, wherever this sense asserts itself, wherever the producer so modifies his work as, over and above its primary use or intention, to make it pleasing (to himself, of course, in the first instance) there, "fine" as opposed to merely serviceable art, exists. Literary art, that is, like all art which is in any way imitative or reproductive of fact—form, or colour, or incident—is the representation of such fact as connected with soul, of a specific personality, in its preferences, its volition and power.

Such is the matter of imaginative or artistic literature—this transcript, not of mere fact, but of fact in its infinite variety, as modified by human preference in all its infinitely varied forms. It will be good literary art not because it is brilliant or sober, or rich, or impulsive, or severe, but just in proportion as its representation of that sense, that soul-fact, is true, verse being only one department of such literature, and imaginative prose, it may be thought, being the special art of the modern world. That imaginative prose should be the special and opportune art of the modern world results from two important facts about the latter: first, the chaotic variety and complexity of its interests, making the intellectual issue, the really master currents of the present time incalculable—a condition of mind little susceptible of the restraint proper to verse form, so that the most characteristic verse of the nineteenth century has been lawless verse; and secondly, an all-pervading naturalism, a curiosity about everything whatever as it really is, involving a certain humility of attitude, cognate to what must, after all, be the less ambitious form of literature. And prose thus asserting itself as the special and privileged artistic faculty of the present day, will be, however critics may try to narrow its scope, as varied in its excellence as humanity itself reflecting on the facts of its latest experience—an instrument of many stops, meditative, observant, descriptive, eloquent, analytic, plaintive, fervid. Its beauties will be not exclusively "pedestrian": it will exert, in due measure, all the varied charms of poetry, down to the rhythm which, as in Cicero, or Michelet, or Newman, at their best, gives its musical value to every syllable.[1]

The literary artist is of necessity a scholar, and in what he proposes to do will have in mind, first of all, the scholar and the scholarly conscience—the male conscience in this matter, as we must think it, under a system of education which still to so large an extent limits real scholarship to men. In his self-criticism, he supposes always that sort of reader who will go (full of eyes) warily, considerately, though without consideration for him, over the ground which the female conscience traverses so lightly, so amiably. For the material in which he works is no more a creation of his own than the sculptor's marble. Product of a myriad various minds and contending tongues, compact of obscure and minute association, a language has its own abundant and often recondite laws, in the habitual and summary recognition of which scholarship consists. A writer, full of a matter he is before all things anxious to express, may think of those laws, the limitations of vocabulary, structure, and the like, as a restriction, but if a real artist will find in them an opportunity. His punctilious observance of the proprieties of his medium will diffuse through all he writes

---

[1]Mr. Saintsbury, in his *Specimens of English Prose, from Malory to Macaulay*, has succeeded in tracing, through successive English prose-writers, the tradition of that severer beauty in them, of which this admirable scholar of our literature is known to be a lover. *English Prose, from Mandeville to Thackeray*, more recently "chosen and edited" by a younger scholar, Mr. Arthur Galton, of New College, Oxford, a lover of our literature at once enthusiastic and discreet, aims at a more various illustration of the eloquent powers of English prose, and is a delightful companion.

a general air of sensibility, of refined usage. *Exclusiones debitæ naturæ*—the exclusions, or rejections, which nature demands— we know how large a part these play, according to Bacon, in the science of nature. In a somewhat changed sense, we might say that the art of the scholar is summed up in the observance of those rejections demanded by the nature of his medium, the material he must use. Alive to the value of an atmosphere in which every term finds its utmost degree of expression, and with all the jealousy of a lover of words, he will resist a constant tendency on the part of the majority of those who use them to efface the distinctions of language, the facility of writers often reinforcing in this respect the work of the vulgar. He will feel the obligation not of the laws only, but of those affinities, avoidances, those mere preferences, of his language, which through the associations of literary history have become a part of its nature, prescribing the rejection of many a neology, many a license, many a gipsy phrase which might present itself as actually expressive. His appeal, again, is to the scholar, who has great experience in literature, and will show no favour to short-cuts, or hackneyed illustration, or an affectation of learning designed for the unlearned. Hence a contention, a sense of self-restraint and renunciation, having for the susceptible reader the effect of a challenge for minute consideration; the attention of the writer, in every minutest detail, being a pledge that it is worth the reader's while to be attentive too, that the writer is dealing scrupulously with his instrument, and therefore, indirectly, with the reader himself also, that he has the science of the instrument he plays on, perhaps, after all, with a freedom which in such case will be the freedom of a master.

For meanwhile, braced only by those restraints, he is really vindicating his liberty in the making of a vocabulary, an entire system of composition, for himself, his own true manner; and when we speak of the manner of a true master we mean what is essential in his art. Pedantry being only the scholarship of *le cuistre* (we have no English equivalent) he is no pedant, and does but show his intelligence of the rules of language in his freedoms with it, addition or expansion, which like the spontaneities of manner in a well-bred person will still further illustrate good taste.—The right vocabulary! Translators have not invariably seen how all-important that is in the work of translation, driving for the most part at idiom or construction; whereas, if the original be first-rate, one's first care should be with its elementary particles, Plato, for instance, being often reproducible by an exact following, with no variation in structure, of word after word, as the pencil follows a drawing under tracing-paper, so only each word or syllable be not of false colour, to change my illustration a little.

Well! that is because any writer worth translating at all has winnowed and searched through his vocabulary, is conscious of the words he would select in systematic reading of a dictionary, and still more of the words he would reject were the dictionary other than Johnson's; and doing this with his peculiar sense of the world ever in view, in search of an instrument for the adequate expression of that, he begets a vocabulary faithful to the colouring of his own spirit, and in the strictest sense original. That living authority which language needs lies, in truth, in its scholars, who recognising always that every language possesses a genius, a very fastidious genius, of its own, expand at once and purify its very elements, which must needs change along with the changing thoughts of living people. Ninety years ago, for instance, great mental force, certainly, was needed by Wordsworth, to break through the consecrated poetic associations of a century, and speak the language that was his, that was to become in a measure the language of the next generation. But he did it with the tact of a scholar also. English, for a quarter of a century past, has been assimilating the phraseology of pictorial art; for half a century, the phraseology of the great German metaphysical movement of eighty years ago; in part also the language of mystical theology: and none but pedants will regret a great consequent increase of its resources. For many years to come its enterprise may well lie in the naturalisation of the vocabulary of science, so only it be under the eye of a sensitive scholarship—in a liberal naturalisation of the ideas of science too, for after all the chief stimulus of good style is to possess a full, rich, complex matter to grapple with. The literary artist, therefore, will be well aware of physical science; science also attaining, in its turn, its true literary ideal. And then, as the scholar is nothing without the historic sense, he will be apt to restore not really obsolete or really worn-out words, but the finer edge of words still in use: *ascertain, communicate, discover*—words like these it has been part of our "business" to misuse. And still, as language was made for man, he will be no authority for correctnesses which, limiting freedom of utterance, were yet but accidents in their origin; as if one vowed not to say "*its,*" which ought to have been in Shakespeare; "*his*" and "*hers,*" for inanimate objects, being but a barbarous and really inexpressive survival. Yet we have known many things like this. Racy Saxon monosyllables, close to us as touch and sight, he will intermix readily with those long, savoursome, Latin words, rich in "second intention." In this late day certainly, no critical process can be conducted reasonably without eclecticism. Of such eclecticism we have a justifying example in one of the first poets of our time. How illustrative of monosyllabic effect, of sonorous Latin, of the phraseology of science, of metaphysic, of colloquialism even, are the writings of Tennyson; yet with what a fine, fastidious scholarship throughout!

A scholar writing for the scholarly, he will of course leave something to the willing intelligence of his reader. "To go preach to the first passer-by," says Montaigne, "to become tutor to the ignorance of the first I meet, is a thing I abhor;" a thing, in fact, naturally distressing to the scholar, who will therefore ever be shy of offering uncomplimentary assistance to the reader's wit. To really strenuous minds there is a pleasurable stimulus in the challenge for a continuous effort on their part, to be rewarded by securer and more intimate grasp of the author's sense. Self-restraint, a skilful economy of means, *ascêsis*, that too has a beauty of its own; and for the reader supposed there will be an æsthetic satisfaction in that frugal closeness of style which makes the most of a word, in the exaction from every sentence of a precise relief, in the just spacing out of word to thought, in the logically filled space connected always with the delightful sense of difficulty overcome.

Different classes of persons, at different times, make, of course, very various demands upon literature. Still, scholars, I suppose, and not only scholars, but all disinterested lovers of books, will always look to it, as to all other fine art, for a refuge, a sort of cloistral refuge, from a certain vulgarity in the actual world. A perfect poem like *Lycidas*, a perfect fiction like *Esmond*, the perfect handling of a theory like Newman's *Idea of a University*, has for them something of the uses of a religious "retreat." Here, then, with a view to the central need of a select few, those "men of a finer thread" who have formed and maintain the literary ideal, everything, every component element, will have undergone exact trial, and, above all, there will be no uncharacteristic or tarnished or vulgar decoration, permissible ornament being for the most part structural, or necessary. As the painter in his picture, so the artist in his book, aims at the production by honourable artifice of a peculiar atmosphere. "The artist," says Schiller, "may be known rather by what he *omits*"; and in literature, too, the true artist may be best recognised by his tact of omission. For to the grave reader words too are grave; and the ornamental word, the figure, the accessory form or colour or reference, is rarely content to die to thought precisely at the right moment, but will inevitably linger awhile, stirring a long "brainwave" behind it of perhaps quite alien associations.

Just there, it may be, is the detrimental tendency of the sort of scholarly attentiveness of mind I am recommending. But the true artist allows for it. He will remember that, as the very word ornament indicates what is in itself non-essential, so the "one beauty" of all literary style is of its very essence, and independent, in prose and verse alike, of all removable decoration; that it may exist in its fullest lustre, as in Flaubert's *Madame Bovary*, for instance, or in Stendhal's *Le Rouge et Le Noir*, in a composition utterly unadorned, with hardly a single suggestion of visibly beautiful things. Parallel, allusion, the allusive way generally, the flowers in the garden:—he knows the narcotic force of these upon the negligent intelligence to which any *diversion*, literally, is welcome, any vagrant intruder, because one can go wandering away with it from the immediate subject. Jealous, if he have a really quickening motive within, of all that does not hold directly to that, of the facile, the otiose, he will never depart from the strictly pedestrian process, unless he gains a ponderable something thereby. Even assured of its congruity, he will still question its serviceableness. Is it worth while, can we afford, to attend to

just that, to just that figure or literary reference, just then?—
Surplusage! he will dread that, as the runner on his muscles. For
in truth all art does but consist in the removal of surplusage, from
the last finish of the gem-engraver blowing away the last particle
of invisible dust, back to the earliest divination of the finished
work to be, lying somewhere, according to Michelangelo's fancy,
in the rough-hewn block of stone.

And what applies to figure or flower must be understood of all
other accidental or removable ornaments of writing whatever;
and not of specific ornament only, but of all that latent colour
and imagery which language as such carries in it. A lover of words
for their own sake, to whom nothing about them is unimportant,
a minute and constant observer of their physiognomy, he will be
on the alert not only for obviously mixed metaphors of course,
but for the metaphor that is mixed in all our speech, though a
rapid use may involve no cognition of it. Currently recognising
the incident, the colour, the physical elements or particles in
words like *absorb, consider, extract*, to take the first that occur,
he will avail himself of them, as further adding to the resources of
expression. The elementary particles of language will be realised
as colour and light and shade through his scholarly living in the
full sense of them. Still opposing the constant degradation of language by those who use it carelessly, he will not treat coloured
glass as if it were clear; and while half the world is using figure
unconsciously, will be fully aware not only of all that latent figurative texture in speech, but of the vague, lazy, half-formed personification—a rhetoric, depressing, and worse than nothing,
because it has no really rhetorical motive—which plays so large a
part there, and, as in the case of more ostentatious ornament,
scrupulously exact of it, from syllable to syllable, its precise
value.

So far I have been speaking of certain conditions of the literary
art arising out of the medium or material in or upon which it
works, the essential qualities of language and its aptitudes for
contingent ornamentation, matters which define scholarship as
science and good taste respectively. They are both subservient to
a more intimate quality of good style: more intimate, as coming
nearer to the artist himself. The otiose, the facile, surplusage:

why are these abhorrent to the true literary artist, except because, in literary as in all other art, structure is all-important, felt, or painfully missed, everywhere?—that architectural conception of work, which foresees the end in the beginning and never loses sight of it, and in every part is conscious of all the rest, till the last sentence does but, with undiminished vigour, unfold and justify the first—a condition of literary art, which, in contradistinction to another quality of the artist himself, to be spoken of later, I shall call the necessity of *mind* in style.

An acute philosophical writer, the late Dean Mansel (a writer whose works illustrate the literary beauty there may be in closeness, and with obvious repression or economy of a fine rhetorical gift) wrote a book, of fascinating precision in a very obscure subject, to show that all the technical laws of logic are but means of securing, in each and all of its apprehensions, the unity, the strict identity with itself, of the apprehending mind. All the laws of good writing aim at a similar unity or identity of the mind in all the processes by which the word is associated to its import. The term is right, and has its essential beauty, when it becomes, in a manner, what it signifies, as with the names of simple sensations. To give the phrase, the sentence, the structural member, the entire composition, song, or essay, a similar unity with its subject and with itself:—style is in the right way when it tends towards that. All depends upon the original unity, the vital wholeness and identity, of the initiatory apprehension or view. So much is true of all art, which therefore requires always its logic, its comprehensive reason—insight, foresight, retrospect, in simultaneous action—true, most of all, of the literary art, as being of all the arts most closely cognate to the abstract intelligence. Such logical coherency may be evidenced not merely in the lines of composition as a whole, but in the choice of a single word, while it by no means interferes with, but may even prescribe, much variety, in the building of the sentence for instance, or in the manner, argumentative, descriptive, discursive, of this or that part or member of the entire design. The blithe, crisp sentence, decisive as child's expression of its needs, may alternate with the long-contending, victoriously intricate sentence; the sentence, born with the integrity of a single word, relieving the sort of sentence in which, if

you look closely, you can see much contrivance, much adjustment, to bring a highly qualified matter into compass at one view.
For the literary architecture, if it is to be rich and expressive,
involves not only foresight of the end in the beginning, but also
development or growth of design, in the process of execution,
with many irregularities, surprises, and afterthoughts; the contingent as well as the necessary being subsumed under the unity
of the whole. As truly, to the lack of such architectural design, of
a single, almost visual, image, vigorously informing an entire,
perhaps very intricate, composition, which shall be austere, or-
nate, argumentative, fanciful, yet true from first to last to that
vision within, may be attributed those weaknesses of conscious or
unconcious repetition of word, phrase, motive, or member of the
whole matter, indicating, as Flaubert was aware, an original
structure in thought not organically complete. With such foresight, the actual conclusion will most often get itself written out
of hand, before, in the more obvious sense, the work is finished.
With some strong and leading sense of the world, the tight hold of
which secures true *composition* and not mere loose accretion, the
literary artist, I suppose, goes on considerately, setting joint to
joint, sustained by yet restraining the productive ardour, retracing the negligences of his first sketch, repeating his steps only that
he may give the reader a sense of secure and restful progress,
readjusting mere assonances even, that they may soothe the
reader, or at least not interrupt him on his way; and then, somewhere before the end comes, is burdened, inspired, with his conclusion, and betimes delivered of it, leaving off, not in weariness
and because he finds *himself* at an end, but in all the freshness of
volition. His work now structurally complete, with all the accumulating effect of secondary shades of meaning, he finishes the
whole up to the just proportion of that ante-penultimate conclusion, and all becomes expressive. The house he has built is rather
a body he has informed. And so it happens, to its greater credit,
that the better interest even of a narrative to be recounted, a story
to be told, will often be in its second reading. And though there
are instances of great writers who have been no artists, an unconscious tact sometimes directing work in which we may detect,
very pleasurably, many of the effects of conscious art, yet one of

the greatest pleasures of really good prose literature is in the critical tracing out of that conscious artistic structure, and the pervading sense of it as we read. Yet of poetic literature too; for, in truth, the kind of constructive intelligence here supposed is one of the forms of the imagination.

That is the special function of mind, in style. Mind and soul:—hard to ascertain philosophically, the distinction is real enough practically, for they often interfere, are sometimes in conflict, with each other. Blake, in the last century, is an instance of preponderating soul, embarrassed, at a loss, in an era of preponderating mind. As a quality of style, at all events, soul is a fact, in certain writers—the way they have of absorbing language, of attracting it into the peculiar spirit they are of, with a subtlety which makes the actual result seem like some inexplicable inspiration. By mind, the literary artist reaches us, through static and objective indications of design in his work, legible to all. By soul, he reaches us, somewhat capriciously perhaps, one and not another, through vagrant sympathy and a kind of immediate contact. Mind we cannot choose but approve where we recognise it; soul may repel us, not because we misunderstand it. The way in which theological interests sometimes avail themselves of language is perhaps the best illustration of the force I mean to indicate generally in literature, by the word *soul*. Ardent religious persuasion may exist, may make its way, without finding any equivalent heat in language: or, again, it may enkindle words to various degrees, and when it really takes hold of them doubles its force. Religious history presents many remarkable instances in which, through no mere phrase-worship, an unconscious literary tact has, for the sensitive, laid open a privileged pathway from one to another. "The altar-fire," people say, "has touched those lips!" The Vulgate, the English Bible, the English Prayer-Book, the writings of Swedenborg, the Tracts for the Times:—there, we have instances of widely different and largely diffused phases of religious feeling in operation as soul in style. But something of the same kind acts with similar power in certain writers of quite other than theological literature, on behalf of some wholly personal and peculiar sense of theirs. Most easily illustrated by theological literature, this quality lends to profane writers a kind of religious influence. At their best, these writers become, as we say sometimes, "prophets"; such character depending on the effect not merely of their matter, but of their matter as allied to, in "electric affinity" with, peculiar form, and working in all cases by an immediate sympathetic contact, on which account it is that it may be called soul, as opposed to mind, in style. And this too is a faculty of choosing and rejecting what is congruous or otherwise, with a drift towards unity—unity of atmosphere here, as there of design—soul securing colour (or perfume, might we say?) as mind secures form, the latter being essentially finite, the former vague or infinite, as the influence of a living person is practically infinite. There are some to whom nothing has any real interest, or real meaning, except as operative in a given person; and it is they who best appreciate the quality of soul in literary art. They seem to know a *person*, in a book, and make way by intuition: yet, although they thus enjoy the completeness of a personal information, it is still a characteristic of soul, in this sense of the word, that it does but suggest what can never be uttered, not as being different from, or more obscure than, what actually gets said, but as containing that plenary substance of which there is only one phase or facet in what is there expressed.

If all high things have their martyrs, Gustave Flaubert might perhaps rank as the martyr of literary style. In his printed correspondence, a curious series of letters, written in his twenty-fifth year, records what seems to have been his one other passion—a series of letters which, with its fine casuistries, its firmly repressed anguish, its tone of harmonious grey, and the sense of disillusion in which the whole matter ends, might have been, a few slight changes supposed, one of his own fictions. Writing to Madame X. certainly he does display, by "taking thought" mainly, by constant and delicate pondering, as in his love for literature, a heart really moved, but still more, and as the pledge of that emotion, a loyalty to his work. Madame X., too, is a literary artist, and the best gifts he can send her are precepts of perfection in art, counsels for the effectual pursuit of that better love. In his love-letters it is the pains and pleasures of art he insists on, its solaces: he communicates secrets, reproves, encourages, with a view to that. Whether the lady was dissatisfied with such divided or indirect service, the reader is not enabled to see; but sees that, on Flaubert's part at least, a living person could be no rival of what was, from first to last, his leading passion, a somewhat solitary and exclusive one.

I must scold you (he writes) for one thing, which shocks, scandalises me, the small concern, namely, you show for art just now. As regards glory be it so: there, I approve. But for art!—the one thing in life that is good and real—can you compare with it an earthly love?—prefer the adoration of a relative beauty to the *cultus* of the true beauty? Well! I tell you the truth. That is the one thing good in me: the one thing I have, to me estimable. For yourself, you blend with the beautiful a heap of alien things, the useful, the agreeable, what not?—

The only way not to be unhappy is to shut yourself up in art, and count everything else as nothing. Pride takes the place of all beside when it is established on a large basis. Work! God wills it. That, it seems to me, is clear.—

I am reading over again the *Æneid*, certain verses of which I repeat to myself to satiety. There are phrases there which stay in one's head, by which I find myself beset, as with those musical airs which are for ever returning, and cause you pain, you love them so much. I observe that I no longer laugh much, and am no longer depressed. I am ripe. You talk of my serenity, and envy me. It may well surprise you. Sick, irritated, the prey a thousand times a day of cruel pain, I continue my labour like a true working-man, who, with sleeves turned up, in the sweat of his brow, beats away at his anvil, never troubling himself whether it rains or blows, for hail or thunder. I was not like that formerly. The change has taken place naturally, though my will has counted for something in the matter.—

Those who write in good style are sometimes accused of a neglect of ideas, and of the moral end, as if the end of the physician were something else than healing, of the painter than painting—as if the end of art were not, before all else, the beautiful.

What, then, did Flaubert understand by beauty, in the art he pursued with so much fervour, with so much self-command? Let us hear a sympathetic commentator:—

Possessed of an absolute belief that there exists but one way of expressing one thing, one word to call it by, one adjective to qualify, one verb to animate it, he gave himself to superhuman labour for the discovery, in every phrase, of that word, that verb, that epithet. In this way, he believed in some mysterious harmony of expression, and when a true word seemed to him to lack euphony still went on seeking another, with invincible patience, certain that he had not yet got hold of the *unique* word. . . . A thousand preoccupations would beset him at the same moment, always with this desperate certitude fixed in his spirit: Among all the expressions in the world, all forms and turns of expression, there is but *one*—one form, one mode—to express what I want to say.

The one word for one thing, the one thought, amid the multitude of words, terms, that might just do: the problem of style was there!—the unique word, phrase, sentence, paragraph, essay, or song, absolutely proper to the single mental presentation or vision within. In that perfect justice, over and above the many contingent and removable beauties with which beautiful style may charm us, but which it can exist without, independent of them yet dexterously availing itself of them, omnipresent in good work, in function at every point, from single epithets to the rhythm of a whole book, lay the specific, indispensable, very intellectual, beauty of literature, the possibility of which constitutes it a fine art.

One seems to detect the influence of a philosophic idea there, the idea of a natural economy, of some pre-existent adaptation, between a relative, somewhere in the world of thought, and its correlative, somewhere in the world of language—both alike, rather, somewhere in the mind of the artist, desiderative, expectant, inventive—meeting each other with the readiness of "soul and body reunited," in Blake's rapturous design; and, in fact, Flaubert was fond of giving his theory philosophical expression.—

There are no beautiful thoughts (he would say) without beautiful forms, and conversely. As it is impossible to extract from a physical body the qualities which really constitute it—colour, extension, and the like—without reducing it to a hollow abstraction, in a word, without destroying it; just so it is impossible to detach the form from the idea, for the idea only exists by virtue of the form.

All the recognised flowers, the removable ornaments of literature (including harmony and ease in reading aloud, very carefully considered by him) counted, certainly; for these too are part of the actual value of what one says. But still, after all, with Flaubert, the search, the unwearied research, was not for the smooth, or winsome, or forcible word, as such, as with false

Ciceronians, but quite simply and honestly, for the word's adjustment to its meaning. The first condition of this must be, of course,
to know yourself, to have ascertained your own sense exactly.
Then, if we suppose an artist, he says to the reader,—I want you
to see precisely what I see. Into the mind sensitive to "form," a
flood of random sounds, colours, incidents, is ever penetrating
from the world without, to become, by sympathetic selection, a
part of its very structure, and, in turn, the visible vesture and
expression of that other world it sees so steadily within, nay,
already with a partial conformity thereto, to be refined, enlarged,
corrected, at a hundred points; and it is just there, just at those
doubtful points that the function of style, as tact or taste, inter-
venes. The unique term will come more quickly to one than another, at one time than another, according also to the kind of
matter in question. Quickness and slowness, ease and closeness
alike, have nothing to do with the artistic character of the true
word found at last. As there is a charm of ease, so there is also a
special charm in the signs of discovery, of effort and contention
towards a due end, as so often with Flaubert himself—in the style
which has been pliant, as only obstinate, durable metal can be, to
the inherent perplexities and recusancy of a certain difficult
thought.

If Flaubert had not told us, perhaps we should never have
guessed how tardy and painful his own procedure really was, and
after reading his confession may think that his almost endless
hesitation had much to do with diseased nerves. Often, perhaps,
the felicity supposed will be the product of a happier, a more
exuberant nature than Flaubert's. Aggravated, certainly, by a
morbid physical condition, that anxiety in "seeking the phrase,"
which gathered all the other small *ennuis* of a really quiet existence into a kind of battle, was connected with his lifelong contention against facile poetry, facile art—art, facile and flimsy;
and what constitutes the true artist is not the slowness or quickness of the process, but the absolute success of the result. As with
those labourers in the parable, the prize is independent of the
mere length of the actual day's work. "You talk," he writes, odd,
trying lover, to Madame X.—

"You talk of the exclusiveness of my literary tastes. That might have enabled you to divine what kind of a person I am in the matter of love. I grow so hard to please as a literary artist, that I am driven to despair. I shall end by not writing another line."

"Happy," he cries, in a moment of discouragement at that patient labour, which for him, certainly, was the condition of a great success—

Happy those who have no doubts of themselves! who lengthen out, as the pen runs on, all that flows forth from their brains. As for me, I hesitate, I disappoint myself, turn round upon myself in despite: my taste is augmented in proportion as my natural vigour decreases, and I afflict my soul over some dubious word out of all proportion to the pleasure I get from a whole page of good writing. One would have to live two centuries to attain a true idea of any matter whatever. What Buffon said is a big blasphemy: genius is not long-continued patience. Still, there is some truth in the statement, and more than people think, especially as regards our own day. Art! art! art! bitter deception! phantom that glows with light, only to lead one on to destruction.

Again—

I am growing so peevish about my writing. I am like a man whose ear is true but who plays falsely on the violin: his fingers refuse to reproduce precisely those sounds of which he has the inward sense. Then the tears come rolling down from the poor scraper's eyes and the bow falls from his hand.

Coming slowly or quickly, when it comes, as it came with so much labour of mind, but also with so much lustre, to Gustave Flaubert, this discovery of the word will be, like all artistic success and felicity, incapable of strict analysis: effect of an intuitive condition of mind, it must be recognised by like intuition on the part of the reader, and a sort of immediate sense. In every one of those masterly sentences of Flaubert there was, below all mere contrivance, shaping and afterthought, by some happy instantaneous concourse of the various faculties of the mind with each other, the exact apprehension of what was *needed* to carry the meaning. And that it fits with absolute justice will be a judgment of immediate sense in the appreciative reader. We all feel this in what may be called inspired translation. Well! all language involves translation from inward to outward. In literature, as in

all forms of art, there are the absolute and the merely relative or
accessory beauties; and precisely in that exact proportion of the
term to its purpose is the absolute beauty of style, prose or verse.
All the good qualities, the beauties, of verse also, are such, only
as precise expression.

In the highest as in the lowliest literature, then, the one indispensable beauty is, after all, truth:—truth to bare fact in the
latter, as to some personal sense of fact, diverted somewhat from
men's ordinary sense of it, in the former; truth there as accuracy,
truth here as expression, that finest and most intimate form of
truth, the *vraie vérité*. And what an eclectic principle this really
is! employing for its one sole purpose—that absolute accordance
of expression to idea—all other literary beauties and excellences
whatever: how many kinds of style it covers, explains, justifies,
and at the same time safeguards! Scott's facility, Falubert's deeply
pondered evocation of "the phrase," are equally good art. Say
what you have to say, what you have a will to say, in the simplest,
the most direct and exact manner possible, with no surplusage:—
there, is the justification of the sentence so fortunately born,
"entire, smooth, and round," that it needs no punctuation, and
also (that is the point!) of the most elaborate period, if it be right
in its elaboration. Here is the office of ornament: here also the
purpose of restraint in ornament. As the exponent of truth, that
austerity (the beauty, the function, of which in literature
Flaubert understood so well) becomes not the correctness or pur-
ism of the mere scholar, but a security against the otiose, a jealous exclusion of what does not really tell towards the pursuit of
relief, of life and vigour in the portraiture of one's sense. License
again, the making free with rule, if it be indeed, as people fancy, a
habit of genius, flinging aside or transforming all that opposes the
liberty of beautiful production, will be but faith to one's own
meaning. The seeming baldness of *Le Rouge et Le Noir* is nothing
in itself; the wild ornament of *Les Misérables* is nothing in itself;
and the restraint of Flaubert, amid a real natural opulence, only
redoubled beauty—the phrase so large and so precise at the same
time, hard as bronze, in service to the more perfect adaptation of
words to their matter. Afterthoughts, retouchings, finish, will be
of profit only so far as they too really serve to bring out the original, initiative, generative, sense in them.

In this way, according to the well-known saying, "The style is the man," complex or simple, in his individuality, his plenary sense of what he really has to say, his sense of the world; all cautions regarding style arising out of so many natural scruples as to the medium through which alone he can expose that inward sense of things, the purity of this medium, its laws or tricks of refraction: nothing is to be left there which might give conveyance to any matter save that. Style in all its varieties, reserved or opulent, terse, abundant, musical, stimulant, academic, so long as each is really characteristic or expressive, finds thus its justification, the sumptuous good taste of Cicero being as truly the man himself, and not another, justified, yet insured inalienably to him, thereby, as would have been his portrait by Raffaelle, in full consular splendour, on his ivory chair.

A relegation, you may say perhaps—a relegation of style to the subjectivity, the mere caprice, of the individual, which must soon transform it into mannerism. Not so! since there is, under the conditions supposed, for those elements of the man, for every lineament of the vision within, the one word, the one acceptable word, recognisable by the sensitive, by others "who have intelligence" in the matter, as absolutely as ever anything can be in the evanescent and delicate region of human language. The style, the manner, would be the man, not in his unreasoned and really uncharacteristic caprices, involuntary or affected, but in absolutely sincere apprehension of what is most real to him. But let us hear our French guide again.—

Styles (says Flaubert's commentator), *Styles*, as so many peculiar moulds, each of which bears the mark of a particular writer, who is to pour into it the whole content of his ideas, were no part of his theory. What he believed in was *Style:* that is to say, a certain absolute and unique manner of expressing a thing, in all its intensity and colour. For him the *form* was the work itself. As in living creatures, the blood, nourishing the body, determines its very contour and external aspect, just so, to his mind, the *matter*, the basis, in a work of art, imposed, necessarily, the unique, the just expression, the measure, the rhythm—the *form* in all its characteristics.

If the style be the man, in all the colour and intensity of a veritable apprehension, it will be in a real sense "impersonal."

I said, thinking of books like Victor Hugo's *Les Misérables*, that prose literature was the characteristic art of the nineteenth century, as others, thinking of its triumphs since the youth of Bach, have assigned that place to music. Music and prose literature are, in one sense, the opposite terms of art; the art of literature presenting to the imagination, through the intelligence, a range of interests, as free and various as those which music presents to it through sense. And certainly the tendency of what has been here said is to bring literature too under those conditions, by conformity to which music takes rank as the typically perfect art. If music be the ideal of all art whatever, precisely because in music it is impossible to distinguish the form from the substance or matter, the subject from the expression, then, literature, by finding its specific excellence in the absolute correspondence of the term to its import, will be but fulfilling the condition of all artistic quality in things everywhere, of all good art.

Good art, but not necessarily great art; the distinction between great art and good art depending immediately, as regards literature at all events, not on its form, but on the matter. Thackeray's *Esmond*, surely, is greater art than *Vanity Fair*, by the greater dignity of its interests. It is on the quality of the matter it informs or controls, its compass, its variety, its alliance to great ends, or the depth of the note of revolt, or the largeness of hope in it, that the greatness of literary art depends, as *The Divine Comedy*, *Paradise Lost*, *Les Misérables*, *The English Bible*, are great art. Given the conditions I have tried to explain as constituting good art;— then, if it be devoted further to the increase of men's happiness, to the redemption of the oppressed, or the enlargement of our sympathies with each other, or to such presentment of new or old truth about ourselves and our relation to the world as may ennoble and fortify us in our sojourn here, or immediately, as with Dante, to the glory of God, it will be also great art; if, over and above those qualities I summed up as mind and soul—that colour and mystic perfume, and that reasonable structure, it has something of the soul of humanity in it, and finds its logical, its architectural place, in the great structure of human life.

1888.

Wordsworth

Some English critics at the beginning of the present century had a great deal to say concerning a distinction, of much importance, as they thought, in the true estimate of poetry, between the *Fancy*, and another more powerful faculty—the *Imagination*. This metaphysical distinction, borrowed originally from the writings of German philosophers, and perhaps not always clearly apprehended by those who talked of it, involved a far deeper and more vital distinction, with which indeed all true criticism more or less directly has to do, the distinction, namely, between higher and lower degrees of intensity in the poet's perception of his subject, and in his concentration of himself upon his work. Of those who dwelt upon the metaphysical distinction between the Fancy and the Imagination, it was Wordsworth who made the most of it, assuming it as the basis for the final classification of his poetical writings; and it is in these writings that the deeper and more vital distinction, which, as I have said, underlies the metaphysical distinction, is most needed, and may best be illustrated.

For nowhere is there so perplexed a mixture as in Wordsworth's own poetry, of work touched with intense and individual power, with work of almost no character at all. He has much conventional sentiment, and some of that insincere poetic diction, against which his most serious critical efforts were directed: the reaction in his political ideas, consequent on the excesses of 1795, makes him, at times, a mere declaimer on moral and social topics; and he seems, sometimes, to force an unwilling pen, and write by rule. By making the most of these blemishes it is possible to obscure the true æsthetic value of his work, just as his life also, a life of much quiet delicacy and independence, might easily be placed in a false focus, and made to appear a somewhat tame theme in illustration of the more obvious parochial virtues. And those who wish to understand his influence, and experience his peculiar savour, must bear with patience the presence of an alien element in Wordsworth's work, which never coalesced with what is really delightful in it, nor underwent his special power. Who that values his writings most has not felt the intrusion there, from time to time, of something tedious and prosaic? Of all poets equally great, he would gain most by a skilfully made anthology. Such a selection would show, in truth, not so much what he was, or to himself or others seemed to be, as what, by the more energetic and fertile quality in his writings, he was ever tending to become. And the mixture in his work, as it actually stands, is so perplexed, that one fears to miss the least promising composition even, lest some precious morsel should be lying hidden within—the few perfect lines, the phrase, the single word perhaps, to which he often works up mechanically through a poem, almost the whole of which may be tame enough. He who thought that in all creative work the larger part was *given* passively, to the recipient mind, who waited so dutifully upon the gift, to whom so large a measure was sometimes given, had his times also of desertion and relapse; and he has permitted the impress of these too to remain in his work. And this duality there—the fitfulness with which the higher qualities manifest themselves in it, gives the effect in his poetry of a power not altogether his own, or under his control, which comes and goes when it will, lifting or lowering a matter, poor in itself; so that that old fancy which made the poet's art an enthusiasm, a form of divine possession, seems almost literally true of him.

This constant suggestion of an absolute duality between higher and lower moods, and the work done in them, stimulating one always to look below the surface, makes the reading of Wordsworth an excellent sort of training towards the things of art and poetry. It begets in those, who, coming across him in youth, can bear him at all, a habit of reading between the lines, a faith in the effect of concentration and collectedness of mind in the right appreciation of poetry, an expectation of things, in this order, coming to one by means of a right discipline of the temper as well as of the intellect. He meets us with the promise that he has much, and something very peculiar, to give us, if we will follow a certain difficult way, and seems to have the secret of a special and privileged state of mind. And those who have undergone his influence, and followed this difficult way, are like people who have passed through some initiation, a *disciplina arcani*, by submitting to which they become able constantly to distinguish in art, speech, feeling, manners, that which is organic, animated, expressive, from that which is only conventional, derivative, inexpressive.

But although the necessity of selecting these precious morsels for oneself is an opportunity for the exercise of Wordsworth's peculiar influence, and induces a kind of just criticism and true estimate of it, yet the purely literary product would have been more excellent, had the writer himself purged away that alien element. How perfect would have been the little treasury, shut between the covers of how thin a book! Let us suppose the desired separation made, the electric thread untwined, the golden pieces, great and small, lying apart together.[1] What are the peculiarities of this residue? What special sense does Wordsworth exercise, and what instincts does he satisfy? What are the subjects and the motives which in him excite the imaginative faculty? What are the qualities in things and persons which he values, the impression and sense of which he can convey to others, in an extraordinary way?

An intimate consciousness of the expression of natural things, which weighs, listens, penetrates, where the earlier mind passed roughly by, is a large element in the complexion of modern poetry. It has been remarked as a fact in mental history again and again. It reveals itself in many forms; but is strongest and most attractive in what is strongest and most attractive in modern literature. It is exemplified, almost equally, by writers as unlike each other as Senancour and Théophile Gautier: as a singular chapter in the history of the human mind, its growth might be

---

[1] Since this essay was written, such selections have been made, with excellent taste, by Matthew Arnold and Professor Knight.

traced from Rousseau to Chateaubriand, from Chateaubriand to Victor Hugo: it has doubtless some latent connexion with those pantheistic theories which locate an intelligent soul in material things, and have largely exercised men's minds in some modern systems of philosophy: it is traceable even in the graver writings of historians: it makes as much difference between ancient and modern landscape art, as there is between the rough masks of an early mosaic and a portrait by Reynolds or Gainsborough. Of this new sense, the writings of Wordsworth are the central and elementary expression: he is more simply and entirely occupied with it than any other poet, though there are fine expressions of precisely the same thing in so different a poet as Shelley. There was in his own character a certain contentment, a sort of inborn religious placidity, seldom found united with a sensibility so mobile as his, which was favourable to the quiet, habitual observation of inanimate, or imperfectly animate, existence. His life of eighty years is divided by no very profoundly felt incidents: its changes are almost wholly inward, and it falls into broad, untroubled, perhaps somewhat monotonous spaces. What it most resembles is the life of one of those early Italian or Flemish painters, who, just because their minds were full of heavenly visions, passed, some of them, the better part of sixty years in quiet, systematic industry. This placid life matured a quite unusual sensibility, really innate in him, to the sights and sounds of the natural world—the flower and its shadow on the stone, the cuckoo and its echo. The poem of *Resolution and Independence* is a storehouse of such records: for its fulness of imagery it may be compared to Keats's *Saint Agnes' Eve*. To read one of his longer pastoral poems for the first time, is like a day spent in a new country: the memory is crowded for a while with its precise and vivid incidents—

> The pliant harebell swinging in the breeze
> On some grey rock;—
>
> The single sheep and the one blasted tree
> And the bleak music from that old stone wall;—
>
> In the meadows and the lower ground
> Was all the sweetness of a common dawn;—
>
> And that green corn all day is rustling in thine ears.

Clear and delicate at once, as he is in the outlining of visible imagery, he is more clear and delicate still, and finely scrupulous, in the noting of sounds; so that he conceives of noble sound as even moulding the human countenance to nobler types, and as something actually "profaned" by colour, by visible form, or image. He has a power likewise of realising, and conveying to the consciousness of the reader, abstract and elementary impressions—silence, darkness, absolute motionlessness: or, again, the whole complex sentiment of a particular place, the abstract expression of desolation in the long white road, of peacefulness in a particular folding of the hills. In the airy building of the brain, a special day or hour even, comes to have for him a sort of personal identity, a spirit or angel given to it, by which, for its exceptional insight, or the happy light upon it, it has a presence in one's history, and acts there, as a separate power or accomplishment; and he has celebrated in many of his poems the "efficacious spirit," which, as he says, resides in these "particular spots" of time.

It is to such a world, and to a world of congruous meditation thereon, that we see him retiring in his but lately published poem of *The Recluse*—taking leave, without much count of costs, of the world of business, of action and ambition, as also of all that for the majority of mankind counts as sensuous enjoyment.[1]

---

[1] In Wordsworth's prefatory advertisement to the first edition of *The Prelude*, published in 1850, it is stated that that work was intended to be introductory to *The Recluse*; and that *The Recluse*, if completed, would have consisted of three parts. The second part is "The Excursion." The third part was only planned; but the first book of the first part was left in manuscript by Wordsworth—though in manuscript, it is said, in no great condition of forwardness for the printers. This book, now for the first time printed *in extenso* (a very noble passage from it found place in that prose advertisement to *The Excursion*), is included in the latest edition of Wordsworth by Mr. John Morley. It was well worth adding to the poet's great bequest to English literature. A true student of his work, who has formulated for himself what he supposes to be the leading characteristics of Wordsworth's genius, will feel, we think, lively interest in testing them by the various fine passages in what is here presented for the first time. Let the following serve for a sample:—

> Thickets full of songsters, and the voice
> Of lordly birds, an unexpected sound
> Heard now and then from morn to latest eve,
> Admonishing the man who walks below
> Of solitude and silence in the sky:—

And so it came about that this sense of a life in natural objects, which in most poetry is but a rhetorical artifice, is with Wordsworth the assertion of what for him is almost literal fact. To him every natural object seemed to possess more or less of a moral or spiritual life, to be capable of a companionship with man, full of expression, of inexplicable affinities and delicacies of intercourse. An emanation, a particular spirit, belonged, not to the moving leaves or water only, but to the distant peak of the hills arising suddenly, by some change of perspective, above the nearer horizon, to the passing space of light across the plain, to the lichened Druidic stone even, for a certain weird fellowship in it with the moods of men. It was like a "survival," in the peculiar intellectual temperament of a man of letters at the end of the eighteenth century, of that primitive condition, which some philosophers have traced in the general history of human culture, wherein all outward objects alike, including even the works of men's hands, were believed to be endowed with animation, and the world was "full of souls"—that mood in which the old Greek gods were first begotten, and which had many strange aftergrowths.

In the early ages, this belief, delightful as its effects on poetry often are, was but the result of a crude intelligence. But, in Wordsworth, such power of seeing life, such perception of a soul, in in-

---

These have we, and a thousand nooks of earth
Have also these, but nowhere else is found,
Nowhere (or is it fancy?) can be found
The one sensation that is here; 'tis here,
Here as it found its way into my heart
In childhood, here as it abides by day,
By night, here only; or in chosen minds
That take it with them hence, where'er they go.
—'Tis, but I cannot name it, 'tis the sense
Of majesty, and beauty, and repose,
A blended holiness of earth and sky,
Something that makes this individual spot,
This small abiding-place of many men,
A termination, and a last retreat,
A centre, come from whereso'er you will,
A whole without dependence or defect,
Made for itself, and happy in itself,
Perfect contentment, Unity entire.

animate things, came of an exceptional susceptibility to the impressions of eye and ear, and was, in its essence, a kind of sensuousness. At least, it is only in a temperament exceptionally susceptible on the sensuous side, that this sense of the expressiveness of outward things comes to be so large a part of life. That he awakened "a sort of thought in sense," is Shelley's just estimate of this element in Wordsworth's poetry.

And it was through nature, thus ennobled by a semblance of passion and thought, that he approached the spectacle of human life. Human life, indeed, is for him, at first, only an additional, accidental grace on an expressive landscape. When he thought of man, it was of man as in the presence and under the influence of these effective natural objects, and linked to them by many associations. The close connexion of man with natural objects, the habitual association of his thoughts and feelings with a particular spot of earth, has sometimes seemed to degrade those who are subject to its influence, as if it did but reinforce that physical connexion of our nature with the actual lime and clay of the soil, which is always drawing us nearer to our end. But for Wordsworth, these influences tended to the dignity of human nature, because they tended to tranquillise it. By raising nature to the level of human thought he gives it power and expression: he subdues man to the level of nature, and gives him thereby a certain breadth and coolness and solemnity. The leech-gatherer on the moor, the woman "stepping westward," are for him natural objects, almost in the same sense as the aged thorn, or the lichened rock on the heath. In this sense the leader of the "Lake School," in spite of an earnest preoccupation with man, his thoughts, his destiny, is the poet of nature. And of nature, after all, in its modesty. The English lake country has, of course, its grandeurs. But the peculiar function of Wordsworth's genius, as carrying in it a power to open out the soul of apparently little or familiar things, would have found its true test had he become the poet of Surrey, say! and the prophet of its life. The glories of Italy and Switzerland, though he did write a little about them, had too potent a material life of their own to serve greatly his poetic purpose.

Religious sentiment, consecrating the affections and natural regrets of the human heart, above all, that pitiful awe and care for the perishing human clay, of which relic-worship is but the corruption, has always had much to do with localities, with the thoughts which attach themselves to actual scenes and places. Now what is true of it everywhere, is truest of it in those secluded valleys where one generation after another maintains the same abiding-place; and it was on this side, that Wordsworth apprehended religion most strongly. Consisting, as it did so much, in the recognition of local sanctities, in the habit of connecting the stones and trees of a particular spot of earth with the great events of life, till the low walls, the green mounds, the half-obliterated epitaphs seemed full of voices, and a sort of natural oracles, the very religion of these people of the dales appeared but as another link between them and the earth, and was literally a religion of nature. It tranquillised them by bringing them under the placid rule of traditional and narrowly localised observances. "Grave livers," they seemed to him, under this aspect, with stately speech, and something of that natural dignity of manners, which underlies the highest courtesy.

And, seeing man thus as a part of nature, elevated and solemnised in proportion as his daily life and occupations brought him into companionship with permanent natural objects, his very religion forming new links for him with the narrow limits of the valley, the low vaults of his church, the rough stones of his home, made intense for him now with profound sentiment, Wordsworth was able to appreciate passion in the lowly. He chooses to depict people from humble life, because, being nearer to nature than others, they are on the whole more impassioned, certainly more direct in their expression of passion, than other men: it is for this direct expression of passion, that he values their humble words. In much that he said in exaltation of rural life, he was but pleading indirectly for that sincerity, that perfect fidelity to one's own inward presentations, to the precise features of the picture within, without which any profound poetry is impossible. It was not for their tameness, but for this passionate sincerity, that he chose incidents and situations from common life, "related in a selection of language really used by men." He constantly endeavours to bring his language near to the real language of men: to the real language of men, however, not on the dead level of their ordinary intercourse, but in select moments of vivid sensation, when this language is winnowed and ennobled by excitement. There are poets who have chosen rural life as their subject, for the sake of its passionless repose, and times when Wordsworth himself extols the mere calm and dispassionate survey of things as the highest aim of poetical culture. But it was not for such passionless calm that he preferred the scenes of pastoral life; and the meditative poet, sheltering himself, as it might seem, from the agitations of the outward world, is in reality only clearing the scene for the great exhibitions of emotion, and what he values most is the almost elementary expression of elementary feelings.

And so he has much for those who value highly the concentrated presentment of passion, who appraise men and women by their susceptibility to it, and art and poetry as they afford the spectacle of it. Breaking from time to time into the pensive spectacle of their daily toil, their occupations near to nature, come those great elementary feelings, lifting and solemnising their language and giving it a natural music. The great, distinguishing passion came to Michael by the sheepfold, to Ruth by the wayside, adding these humble children of the furrow to the true aristocracy of passionate souls. In this respect, Wordsworth's work resembles most that of George Sand, in those of her novels which depict country life. With a penetrative pathos, which puts him in the same rank with the masters of the sentiment of pity in literature, with Meinhold and Victor Hugo, he collects all the traces of vivid excitement which were to be found in that pastoral world—the girl who rung her father's knell; the unborn infant feeling about its mother's heart; the instinctive touches of children; the sorrows of the wild creatures, even—their home-sickness, their strange yearnings; the tales of passionate regret that hang by a ruined farm-building, a heap of stones, a deserted sheepfold; that gay, false, adventurous, outer world, which breaks in from time to time to bewilder and deflower these quiet homes; not "passionate sorrow" only, for the overthrow of the soul's beauty, but the loss of, or carelessness for personal beauty even, in those whom men have wronged—their pathetic wanness; the sailor "who, in his heart, was half a shepherd on the stormy seas"; the wild woman teaching her child to pray for her betrayer; incidents like the making of the shepherd's staff, or that of the young boy laying the first stone of the sheepfold;—all the pathetic episodes of their humble existence, their longing, their wonder at fortune, their poor pathetic pleasures, like the pleasures of children, won so hardly in the struggle for bare existence; their yearning towards each other, in their darkened houses, or at their early toil. A sort of biblical depth and solemnity hangs over this strange, new, passionate, pastoral world, of which he first raised the image, and the reflection of which some of our best modern fiction has caught from him.

He pondered much over the philosophy of his poetry, and reading deeply in the history of his own mind, seems at times to have passed the borders of a world of strange speculations, inconsistent enough, had he cared to note such inconsistencies, with those traditional beliefs, which were otherwise the object of his devout acceptance. Thinking of the high value he set upon customariness, upon all that is habitual, local, rooted in the ground, in matters of religious sentiment, you might sometimes regard him as one tethered down to a world, refined and peaceful indeed, but with no broad outlook, a world protected, but somewhat narrowed, by the influence of received ideas. But he is at times also something very different from this, and something much bolder. A chance expression is overheard and placed in a new connexion, the sudden memory of a thing long past occurs to him, a distant object is relieved for a while by a random gleam of light—accidents turning up for a moment what lies below the surface of our immediate experience—and he passes from the humble graves and lowly arches of "the little rock-like pile" of a Westmoreland church, on bold trains of speculative thought, and comes, from point to point, into strange contact with thoughts which have visited, from time to time, far more venturesome, perhaps errant, spirits.

He had pondered deeply, for instance, on those strange reminiscences and forebodings, which seem to make our lives stretch before and behind us, beyond where we can see or touch anything, or trace the lines of connexion. Following the soul, backwards and forwards, on these endless ways, his sense of man's dim, potential powers became a pledge to him, indeed, of a future life, but carried him back also to that mysterious notion of an earlier state of existence—the fancy of the Platonists—the old heresy of Origen. It was in this mood that he conceived those oft-reiterated regrets for a half-ideal childhood, when the relics of Paradise still clung about the soul—a childhood, as it seemed, full of the fruits of old age, lost for all, in a degree, in the passing away of the youth of the world, lost for each one, over again, in the passing away of actual youth. It is this ideal childhood which he celebrates in his famous *Ode on the Recollections of Childhood,* and some other poems which may be grouped around it, such as the lines on *Tintern Abbey,* and something like what he describes was actually truer of himself than he seems to have understood; for his own most delightful poems were really the instinctive productions of earlier life, and most surely for him, "the first diviner influence of this world" passed away, more and more completely, in his contact with experience.

Sometimes as he dwelt upon those moments of profound, imaginative power, in which the outward object appears to take colour and expression, a new nature almost, from the prompting of the observant mind, the actual world would, as it were, dissolve and detach itself, flake by flake, and he himself seemed to be the creator, and when he would the destroyer, of the world in which he lived—that old isolating thought of many a brain-sick mystic of ancient and modern times.

At other times, again, in those periods of intense susceptibility, in which he appeared to himself as but the passive recipient of external influences, he was attracted by the thought of a spirit of life in outward things, a single, all-pervading mind in them, of which man, and even the poet's imaginative energy, are but moments—that old dream of the *anima mundi,* the mother of all things and their grave, in which some had desired to lose themselves, and others had become indifferent to the distinctions of good and evil. It would come, sometimes, like the sign of the *macrocosm* to Faust in his cell: the network of man and nature was seen to be pervaded by a common, universal life: a new, bold thought lifted him above the furrow, above the green turf of the Westmoreland churchyard, to a world altogether different in its vagueness and vastness, and the narrow glen was full of the brooding power of one universal spirit.

And so he has something, also, for those who feel the fascination of bold speculative ideas, who are really capable of rising upon them to conditions of poetical thought. He uses them, indeed, always with a very fine apprehension of the limits within which alone philosophical imaginings have any place in true poetry; and using them only for poetical purposes, is not too careful even to make them consistent with each other. To him, theories which for other men bring a world of technical diction, brought perfect form and expression, as in those two lofty books of *The Prelude*, which describe the decay and the restoration of Imagination and Taste. Skirting the borders of this world of bewildering heights and depths, he got but the first exciting influence of it, that joyful enthusiasm which great imaginative theories prompt, when the mind first comes to have an understanding of them; and it is not under the influence of these thoughts that his poetry becomes tedious or loses its blitheness. He keeps them, too, always within certain ethical bounds, so that no word of his could offend the simplest of those simple souls which are always the largest portion of mankind. But it is, nevertheless, the contact of these thoughts, the speculative boldness in them, which constitutes, at least for some minds, the secret attraction of much of his best poetry—the sudden passage from lowly thoughts and places to the majestic forms of philosophical imagination, the play of these forms over a world so different, enlarging so strangely the bounds of its humble churchyards, and breaking such a wild light on the graves of christened children.

And these moods always brought with them faultless expression. In regard to expression, as with feeling and thought, the duality of the higher and lower moods was absolute. It belonged to the higher, the imaginative mood, and was the pledge of its reality, to bring the appropriate language with it. In him, when the really poetical motive worked at all, it united, with absolute justice, the word and the idea; each, in the imaginative flame, becoming inseparably one with the other, by that fusion of matter and form, which is the characteristic of the highest poetical expression. His words are themselves thought and feeling; not eloquent, or musical words merely, but that sort of creative language which carries the reality of what it depicts, directly, to the consciousness.

The music of mere metre performs but a limited, yet a very peculiar and subtly ascertained function, in Wordsworth's poetry. With him, metre is but an additional grace, accessory to that deeper music of words and sounds, that moving power, which they exercise in the nobler prose no less than in formal poetry. It is a sedative to that excitement, an excitement sometimes almost painful, under which the language, alike of poetry and prose, attains a rhythmical power, independent of metrical combination, and dependent rather on some subtle adjustment of the elementary sounds of words themselves to the image or feeling they convey. Yet some of his pieces, pieces prompted by a sort of half-playful mysticism, like the *Daffodils* and *The Two April Mornings*, are distinguished by a certain quaint gaiety of metre, and rival by their perfect execution, in this respect, similar pieces among our own Elizabethan, or contemporary French poetry. And those who take up these poems after an interval of months, or years perhaps, may be surprised at finding how well old favourites wear, how their strange, inventive turns of diction or thought still send through them the old feeling of surprise. Those who lived about Wordsworth were all great lovers of the older English literature, and oftentimes there came out in him a noticeable likeness to our earlier poets. He quotes unconsciously, but with new power of meaning, a clause from one of Shakespeare's sonnets; and, as with some other men's most famous work, the *Ode on the Recollections of Childhood* had its anticipator.[1] He drew something too from the unconscious mysticism of the old English language itself, drawing out the inward significance of its racy idiom, and the not wholly unconscious poetry of the language used by the simplest people under strong excitement—language, therefore, at its origin.

[1]Henry Vaughan, in *The Retreat*.

The office of the poet is not that of the moralist, and the first aim of Wordsworth's poetry is to give the reader a peculiar kind of pleasure. But through his poetry, and through this pleasure in it, he does actually convey to the reader an extraordinary wisdom in the things of practice. One lesson, if men must have lessons, he conveys more clearly than all, the supreme importance of contemplation in the conduct of life.

Contemplation—impassioned contemplation—that, is with Wordsworth the end-in-itself, the perfect end. We see the majority of mankind going most often to definite ends, lower or higher ends, as their own instincts may determine; but the end may never be attained, and the means not be quite the right means, great ends and little ones alike being, for the most part, distant, and the ways to them, in this dim world, somewhat vague. Meantime, to higher or lower ends, they move too often with something of a sad countenance, with hurried and ignoble gait, becoming, unconsciously, something like thorns, in their anxiety to bear grapes; it being possible for people, in the pursuit of even great ends, to become themselves thin and impoverished in spirit and temper, thus diminishing the sum of perfection in the world, at its very sources. We understand this when it is a question of mean, or of intensely selfish ends—of Grandet, or Javert. We think it bad morality to say that the end justifies the means, and we know how false to all higher conceptions of the religious life is the type of one who is ready to do evil that good may come. We contrast with such dark, mistaken eagerness, a type like that of Saint Catherine of Siena, who made the means to her ends so attractive, that she has won for herself an undying place in the *House Beautiful*, not by her rectitude of soul only, but by its "fairness"—by those quite different qualities which commend themselves to the poet and the artist.

Yet, for most of us, the conception of means and ends covers the whole of life, and is the exclusive type or figure under which we represent our lives to ourselves. Such a figure, reducing all things to machinery, though it has on its side the authority of that old Greek moralist who has fixed for succeeding generations the outline of the theory of right living, is too like a mere picture or description of men's lives as we actually find them, to be the basis of the higher ethics. It covers the meanness of men's daily lives, and much of the dexterity and the vigour with which they pursue what may seem to them the good of themselves or of others; but not the intangible perfection of those whose ideal is rather in *being* than in *doing*—not those *manners* which are, in the deepest as in the simplest sense, *morals*, and without which one cannot so much as offer a cup of water to a poor man without offence—not the part of "antique Rachel," sitting in the company of Beatrice; and even the moralist might well endeavour rather to withdraw men from the too exclusive consideration of means and ends, in life.

Against this predominance of machinery in our existence, Wordsworth's poetry, like all great art and poetry, is a continual protest. Justify rather the end by the means, it seems to say: whatever may become of the fruit, make sure of the flowers and the leaves. It was justly said, therefore, by one who had meditated very profoundly on the true relation of means to ends in life, and on the distinction between what is desirable in itself and what is desirable only as machinery, that when the battle which he and his friends were waging had been won, the world would need more than ever those qualities which Wordsworth was keeping alive and nourishing.[1]

That the end of life is not action but contemplation—*being* as distinct from *doing*—a certain disposition of the mind: is, in some shape or other, the principle of all the higher morality. In poetry, in art, if you enter into their true spirit at all, you touch this principle, in a measure: these, by their very sterility, are a type of beholding for the mere joy of beholding. To treat life in the spirit of art, is to make life a thing in which means and ends are identified: to encourage such treatment, the true moral significance of art and poetry. Wordsworth, and other poets who have been like him in ancient or more recent times, are the masters, the experts, in this art of impassioned contemplation. Their work is, not to teach lessons, or enforce rules, or even to stimulate us to noble

---

[1] See an interesting paper, by Mr. John Morley, on "The Death of Mr. Mill," *Fortnightly Review*, June 1873.

ends; but to withdraw the thoughts for a little while from the mere machinery of life, to fix them, with appropriate emotions, on the spectacle of those great facts in man's existence which no machinery affects, "on the great and universal passions of men, the most general and interesting of their occupations, and the entire world of nature,"—on "the operations of the elements and the appearances of the visible universe, on storm and sunshine, on the revolutions of the seasons, on cold and heat, on loss of friends and kindred, on injuries and resentments, on gratitude and hope, on fear and sorrow." To witness this spectacle with appropriate emotions is the aim of all culture; and of these emotions poetry like Wordsworth's is a great nourisher and stimulant. He sees nature full of sentiment and excitement; he sees men and women as parts of nature, passionate, excited, in strange grouping and connexion with the grandeur and beauty of the natural world:—images, in his own words, "of man suffering, amid awful forms and powers."

Such is the figure of the more powerful and original poet, hidden away, in part, under those weaker elements in Wordsworth's poetry, which for some minds determine their entire character; a poet somewhat bolder and more passionate than might at first sight be supposed, but not too bold for true poetical taste; an unimpassioned writer, you might sometimes fancy, yet thinking the chief aim, in life and art alike, to be a certain deep emotion; seeking most often the great elementary passions in lowly places; having at least this condition of all impassioned work, that he aims always at an absolute sincerity of feeling and diction, so that he is the true forerunner of the deepest and most passionate poetry of our own day; yet going back also, with something of a protest against the conventional fervour of much of the poetry popular in his own time, to those older English poets, whose unconscious likeness often comes out in him.

1874.

Coleridge[1]

Forms of intellectual and spiritual culture sometimes exercise their subtlest and most artful charm when life is already passing from them. Searching and irresistible as are the changes of the human spirit on its way to perfection, there is yet so much elasticity of temper that what must pass away sooner or later is not disengaged all at once, even from the highest order of minds. Nature, which by one law of development evolves ideas, hypotheses, modes of inward life, and represses them in turn, has in this way provided that the earlier growth should propel its fibres into the later, and so transmit the whole of its forces in an unbroken continuity of life. Then comes the spectacle of the reserve of the elder generation exquisitely refined by the antagonism of the new. That current of new life chastens them while they contend against it. Weaker minds fail to perceive the change: the clearest minds abandon themselves to it. To feel the change everywhere, yet not abandon oneself to it, is a situation of difficulty and contention. Communicating, in this way, to the passing stage of culture, the charm of what is chastened, high-strung, athletic, they yet detach the highest minds from the past, by pressing home its difficulties and finally proving it impossible. Such has been the charm of many leaders of lost causes in philosophy and in religion. It is the special charm of Coleridge, in connexion with those older methods of philosophic inquiry, over which the empirical philosophy of our day has triumphed.

---

[1]The latter part of this paper, like that on Dante Gabriel Rossetti, was contributed to Mr. T. H. Ward's *English Poets*.

Modern thought is distinguished from ancient by its cultivation of the "relative" spirit in place of the "absolute." Ancient philosophy sought to arrest every object in an eternal outline, to fix thought in a necessary formula, and the varieties of life in a classification by "kinds," or *genera*. To the modern spirit nothing is, or can be rightly known, except relatively and under conditions. The philosophical conception of the relative has been developed in modern times through the influence of the sciences of observation. Those sciences reveal types of life evanescing into each other by inexpressible refinements of change. Things pass into their opposites by accumulation of undefinable quantities. The growth of those sciences consists in a continual analysis of facts of rough and general observation into groups of facts more precise and minute. The faculty for truth is recognised as a power of distinguishing and fixing delicate and fugitive detail. The moral world is ever in contact with the physical, and the relative spirit has invaded moral philosophy from the ground of the inductive sciences. There it has started a new analysis of the relations of body and mind, good and evil, freedom and necessity. Hard and abstract moralities are yielding to a more exact estimate of the subtlety and complexity of our life. Always, as an organism increases in perfection, the conditions of its life become more complex. Man is the most complex of the products of nature. Character merges into temperament: the nervous system refines itself into intellect. Man's physical organism is played upon not only by the physical conditions about it, but by remote laws of inheritance, the vibration of long-past acts reaching him in the midst of the new order of things in which he lives. When we have estimated these conditions he is still not yet simple and isolated; for the mind of the race, the character of the age, sway him this way or that through the medium of language and current ideas. It seems as if the most opposite statements about him were alike true: he is so receptive, all the influences of nature and of society ceaselessly playing upon him, so that every hour in his life is unique, changed altogether by a stray word, or glance, or touch. It is the truth of these relations that experience gives us, not the truth of eternal outlines ascertained once for all, but a world of fine gradations and subtly linked conditions, shifting intricately as we ourselves change—and bids us, by a constant clearing of the organs of observation and perfecting of analysis, to make what we can of these. To the intellect, the critical spirit, just these sub-tleties of effect are more precious than anything else. What is lost in precision of form is gained in intricacy of expression. It is no vague scholastic abstraction that will satisfy the speculative in-stinct in our modern minds. Who would change the colour or curve of a rose leaf for that οὐσία ἀχρώματος, ἀσχημάτιστος, ἀναφής—that colourless, formless, intangible, being—Plato put so high? For the true illustration of the speculative temper is not the Hindoo mystic, lost to sense, understanding, individuality, but one such as Goethe, to whom every moment of life brought its contribution of experimental, individual knowledge; by whom no touch of the world of form, colour, and passion was disregarded.

Now the literary life of Coleridge was a disinterested struggle against the relative spirit. With a strong native bent towards the tracking of all questions, critical or practical, to first principles, he is ever restlessly scheming to "apprehend the absolute," to affirm it effectively, to get it acknowledged. It was an effort, surely, an effort of sickly thought, that saddened his mind, and limited the operation of his unique poetic gift.

So what the reader of our own generation will least find in Coleridge's prose writings is the excitement of the literary sense. And yet, in those grey volumes, we have the larger part of the production of one who made way ever by a charm, the charm of voice, of aspect, of language, above all by the intellectual charm of new, moving, luminous ideas. Perhaps the chief offence in Cole-ridge is an excess of seriousness, a seriousness arising not from any moral principle, but from a misconception of the perfect manner. There is a certain shade of unconcern, the perfect manner of the eighteenth century, which may be thought to mark complete culture in the handling of abstract questions. The humanist, the possessor of that complete culture, does not "weep" over the failure of "a theory of the quantification of the predicate," nor "shriek" over the fall of a philosophical formula. A kind of humour is, in truth, one of the conditions of the just mental attitude, in the criticism of bypast stages of thought. Humanity cannot afford to be too serious about them, any more than a man of good sense can afford to be too serious in looking back upon his own child-hood. Plato, whom Coleridge claims as the first of his spiritual ancestors, Plato, as we remember him, a true humanist, holds his theories lightly, glances with a somewhat blithe and naive incon-sequence from one view to another, not anticipating the burden of importance "views" will one day have for men. In reading him one feels how lately it was that Crœsus thought it a paradox to say that external prosperity was not necessarily happiness. But on Coleridge lies the whole weight of the sad reflection that has since come into the world, with which for us the air is full, which the "children in the market-place" repeat to each other. His very language is forced and broken lest some saving formula should be lost—*distinctities, enucleation, pentad of operative Christianity*; he has a whole armoury of these terms, and expects to turn the tide of human thought by fixing the sense of such expressions as "reason," "understanding," "idea." Again, he lacks the jealousy of a true artist in excluding all associations that have no colour, or charm, or gladness in them; and everywhere allows the impress of a somewhat inferior theological literature.

"I was driven from life in motion to life in thought and sensa-tion:" so Coleridge sums up his childhood, with its delicacy, its sensitiveness, and passion. But at twenty-five he was exercising a wonderful charm, and had already defined for himself his pecu-liar line of intellectual activity. He had an odd, attractive gift of conversation, or rather of monologue, as Madame de Staël ob-served of him, full of *bizarreries*, with the rapid alternations of a dream, and here or there an unexpected summons into a world strange to the hearer, abounding in images drawn from a sort of divided imperfect life, the consciousness of the opium-eater, as of one to whom the external world penetrated only in part, and, blent with all this, passages of deep obscurity, precious, if at all, only for their musical cadence, echoes in Coleridge of the elo-quence of those older English writers of whom he was so ardent a lover. And all through this brilliant early manhood we may dis-cern the power of the "Asiatic" temperament, of that voluptuous-ness, which is connected perhaps with his appreciation of the intimacy, the almost mystical communion of touch, between na-ture and man. "I am much better," he writes, "and my new and

tender health is all over me like a voluptuous feeling." And whatever fame, or charm, or life-inspiring gift he has had as a speculative thinker, is the vibration of the interest he excited then, the
propulsion into years which clouded his early promise of that first
buoyant, irresistible, self-assertion. So great is even the indirect
power of a sincere effort towards the ideal life, of even a temporary escape of the spirit from routine.

In 1798 he visited Germany, then, the only half-known,
"promised land," of the metaphysical, the "absolute," philosophy. A beautiful fragment of this period remains, describing a
spring excursion to the Brocken. His excitement still vibrates in
it. Love, all joyful states of mind, are self-expressive: they loosen
the tongue, they fill the thoughts with sensuous images, they
harmonise one with the world of sight. We hear of the "rich gra-
ciousness and courtesy" of Coleridge's manner, of the white and
delicate skin, the abundant black hair, the full, almost animal
lips—that whole physiognomy of the dreamer, already touched
with narcotism. One says, of the beginning of one of his Unitarian
sermons: "His voice rose like a stream of rich, distilled perfumes;"
another, "He talks like an angel, and does—nothing!"

The *Aids to Reflection, The Friend, The Biographia Literaria*:
those books came from one whose vocation was in the world of
the imagination, the theory and practice of poetry. And yet, perhaps, of all books that have been influential in modern times,
they are furthest from artistic form—bundles of notes; the original matter inseparably mixed up with that borrowed from others;
the whole, just that mere preparation for an artistic effect which
the finished literary artist would be careful one day to destroy.
Here, again, we have a trait profoundly characteristic of Coleridge. He sometimes attempts to reduce a phase of thought, subtle and exquisite, to conditions too rough for it. He uses a purely
speculative gift for direct moral edification. Scientific truth is a
thing fugitive, relative, full of fine gradations: he tries to fix it in
absolute formulas. The *Aids to Reflection, The Friend*, are efforts
to propagate the volatile spirit of conversation into the less ethereal fabric of a written book; and it is only here or there that the
poorer matter becomes vibrant, is really lifted by the spirit.

De Quincey said of him that "he wanted better bread than can be made with wheat:" Lamb, that from childhood he had "hungered for eternity." Yet the faintness, the continuous dissolution, whatever its cause, which soon supplanted the buoyancy of his first wonderful years, had its own consumptive refinements, and even brought, as to the "Beautiful Soul" in *Wilhelm Meister*, a faint religious ecstasy—that "singing in the sails" which is not of the breeze. Here again is one of his occasional notes:—

"In looking at objects of nature while I am thinking, as at yonder moon, dim-glimmering through the window-pane, I seem rather to be seeking, as it were asking, a symbolical language for something within me, that already and for ever exists, than observing anything new. Even when the latter is the case, yet still I have always an obscure feeling, as if that new phenomenon were the dim awaking of a forgotten or hidden truth of my inner nature. While I was preparing the pen to make this remark, I lost the train of thought which had led me to it."

What a distemper of the eye of the mind! What an almost bodily distemper there is in that!

Coleridge's intellectual sorrows were many; but he had one singular intellectual happiness. With an inborn taste for transcendental philosophy, he lived just at the time when that philosophy took an immense spring in Germany, and connected itself with an impressive literary movement. He had the good luck to light upon it in its freshness, and introduce it to his countrymen. What an opportunity for one reared on the colourless analytic English philosophies of the last century, but who feels an irresistible attraction towards bold metaphysical synthesis! How rare are such occasions of intellectual contentment! This transcendental philosophy, chiefly as systematised by the mystic Schelling, Coleridge applied with an eager, unwearied subtlety, to the questions of theology, and poetic or artistic criticism. It is in his theory of poetry, of art, that he comes nearest to principles of permanent truth and importance: that is the least fugitive part of his prose work. What, then, is the essence of his philosophy of art—of imaginative production?

Generally, it may be described as an attempt to reclaim the world of art as a world of fixed laws, to show that the creative activity of genius and the simplest act of thought are but higher and lower products of the laws of a universal logic. Criticism, feeling its own inadequacy in dealing with the greater works of art, is sometimes tempted to make too much of those dark and capricious suggestions of *genius*, which even the intellect possessed by them is unable to explain or recall. It has seemed due to the half-sacred character of those works to ignore all analogy between the productive process by which they had their birth, and the simpler processes of mind. Coleridge, on the other hand, assumes that the highest phases of thought must be more, not less, than the lower, subject to law.

With this interest, in the *Biographia Literaria*, he refines Schelling's "Philosophy of Nature" into a theory of art. "There can be no plagiarism in philosophy," says Heine:—*Es giebt kein Plagiat in der Philosophie*, in reference to the charge brought against Schelling of unacknowledged borrowing from Bruno; and certainly that which is common to Coleridge and Schelling and Bruno alike is of far earlier origin than any of them. Schellingism, the "Philosophy of Nature," is indeed a constant tradition in the history of thought: it embodies a permanent type of the speculative temper. That mode of conceiving nature as a mirror or reflex of the intelligence of man may be traced up to the first beginnings of Greek speculation. There are two ways of envisaging those aspects of nature which seem to bear the impress of reason or intelligence. There is the deist's way, which regards them merely as marks of design, which separates the informing mind from its result in nature, as the mechanist from the machine; and there is the pantheistic way, which identifies the two, which regards nature itself as the living energy of an intelligence of the same kind as though vaster in scope than the human. Partly through the influence of mythology, the Greek mind became early possessed with the conception of nature as living, thinking, almost speaking to the mind of man. This unfixed poetical prepossession, reduced to an abstract form, petrified into an idea, is the force which gives unity of aim to Greek philosophy. Little by little, it works out the substance of the Hegelian formula: "Whatever is, is according to reason: whatever is according to reason, that is." Experience, which has gradually saddened the earth's colours for us, stiffened its motions, withdrawn from it some blithe and debonair presence, has quite changed the character of the science of nature, as we understand it. The "positive" method, in truth, makes very little account of marks of intelligence in nature: in its wider view of phenonema, it sees that those instances are a minority, and may rank as happy coincidences: it absorbs them in the larger conception of universal mechanical law. But the suspicion of a mind latent in nature, struggling for release, and intercourse with the intellect of man through true ideas, has never ceased to haunt a certain class of minds. Started again and again in successive periods by enthusiasts on the antique pattern, in each case the thought may have seemed paler and more fantastic amid the growing consistency and sharpness of outline of other and more positive forms of knowledge. Still, wherever the speculative instinct has been united with a certain poetic inwardness of temperament, as in Bruno, in Schelling, there that old Greek conception, like some seed floating in the air, has taken root and sprung up anew. Coleridge, thrust inward upon himself, driven from "life in thought and sensation" to life in thought only, feels already, in his dark London school, a thread of the Greek mind on this matter vibrating strongly in him. At fifteen he is discoursing on Plotinus, as in later years he reflects from Schelling that flitting intellectual tradition. He supposes a subtle, sympathetic coordination between the ideas of the human reason and the laws of the natural world. Science, the real knowledge of that natural world, is to be attained, not by observation, experiment, analysis, patient generalisation, but by the evolution or recovery of those ideas directly from within, by a sort of Platonic "recollection"; every group of observed facts remaining an enigma until the appropriate idea is struck upon them from the mind of a Newton, or a Cuvier, the genius in whom sympathy with the universal reason becomes entire. In the next place, he conceives that this reason or intelligence in nature becomes reflective, or self-conscious. He fancies he can trace, through all the simpler forms of life, fragments of an eloquent prophecy about the human mind. The whole of nature he regards as a development of higher forms out of the lower, through shade after shade of systematic change. The dim stir of chemical atoms towards the axis of crystal form, the trance-like life of plants, the animal troubled by strange irri-

tabilities, are stages which anticipate consciousness. All through
the ever-increasing movement of life that was shaping itself;
every successive phase of life, in its unsatisfied susceptibilities,
seeming to be drawn out of its own limits by the more pronounced
current of life on its confines, the "shadow of approaching humanity" gradually deepening, the latent intelligence winning a
way to the surface. And at this point the law of development does
not lose itself in caprice: rather it becomes more constraining and
incisive. From the lowest to the very highest acts of the conscious
intelligence, there is another series of refining shades. Gradually
the mind concentrates itself, frees itself from the limitations of
the particular, the individual, attains a strange power of modifying and centralising what it receives from without, according to
the pattern of an inward ideal. At last, in imaginative genius,
ideas become effective: the intelligence of nature, all its discursive elements now connected and justified, is clearly reflected;
the interpretation of its latent purposes being embodied in the
great central products of creative art. The secret of creative genius would be an exquisitely purged sympathy with nature, with
the reasonable soul antecedent there. Those associative conceptions of the imagination, those eternally fixed types of action and
passion, would come, not so much from the conscious invention
of the artist, as from his self-surrender to the suggestions of an
abstract reason or ideality in things: they would be evolved by the
stir of nature itself, realising the highest reach of its dormant
reason: they would have a kind of prevenient necessity to rise at
some time to the surface of the human mind.

It is natural that Shakespeare should be the favourite illustration of such criticism, whether in England or Germany. The first
suggestion in Shakespeare is that of capricious detail, of a waywardness that plays with the parts careless of the impression of
the whole; what supervenes is the constraining unity of effect,
the ineffaceable impression, of Hamlet or Macbeth. His hand
moving freely is curved round as if by some law of gravitation
from within: an energetic unity or identity makes itself visible
amid an abounding variety. This unity or identity Coleridge exag-
gerates into something like the identity of a natural organism,
and the associative act which effected it into something closely

akin to the primitive power of nature itself. "In the Shakespearian drama," he says, "there is a vitality which grows and evolves itself from within."

Again—

He, too, worked in the spirit of nature, by evolving the germ from within, by the imaginative power, according to the idea. For as the power of seeing is to light, so is an idea in mind to a law in nature. They are correlatives which suppose each other.

Again—

The organic form is innate: it shapes, as it develops, itself from within, and the fulness of its development is one and the same with the perfection of its outward form. Such as the life is, such is the form. Nature, the prime, genial artist, inexhaustible in diverse powers, is equally inexhaustible in forms: each exterior is the physiognomy of the being within, and even such is the appropriate excellence of Shakespeare, himself a nature humanised, a genial understanding, directing self-consciously a power and an implicit wisdom deeper even than our consciousness.

In this late age we are become so familiarised with the greater works of art as to be little sensitive of the act of creation in them: they do not impress us as a new presence in the world. Only sometimes, in productions which realise immediately a profound influence and enforce a change in taste, we are actual witnesses of the moulding of an unforeseen type by some new principle of association; and to that phenomenon Coleridge wisely recalls our attention. What makes his view a one-sided one is, that in it the artist has become almost a mechanical agent: instead of the most luminous and self-possessed phase of consciousness, the associative act in art or poetry is made to look like some blindly organic process of assimilation. The work of art is likened to a living organism. That expresses truly the sense of a self-delighting, independent life which the finished work of art gives us: it hardly figures the process by which such work was produced. Here there is no blind ferment of lifeless elements towards the realisation of a type. By exquisite analysis the artist attains clearness of idea; then, through many stages of refining, clearness of expression. He moves slowly over his work, calculating the tenderest tone, and restraining the subtlest curve, never letting hand or fancy move at large, gradually enforcing flaccid spaces to the higher degree of expressiveness. The philosophic critic, at least, will value, even in works of imagination, seemingly the most intuitive, the power of the understanding in them, their logical process of construction, the spectacle of a supreme intellectual dexterity which they afford.

Coleridge's prose writings on philosophy, politics, religion, and criticism, were, in truth, but one element in a whole lifetime of endeavours to present the then recent metaphysics of Germany to English readers, as a legitimate expansion of the older, classical and native masters of what has been variously called the *a priori*, or absolute, or spiritual, or Platonic, view of things. His criticism, his challenge for recognition in the concrete, visible, finite work of art, of the dim, unseen, comparatively infinite, soul or power of the artist, may well be remembered as part of the long pleading of German culture for the things "behind the veil." To introduce that spiritual philosophy, as represented by the more transcendental parts of Kant, and by Schelling, into all subjects, as a system of reason in them, one and ever identical with itself, however various the matter through which it was diffused, became with him the motive of an unflagging enthusiasm, which seems to have been the one thread of continuity in a life otherwise singularly wanting in unity of purpose, and in which he was certainly far from uniformly at his best. Fragmentary and obscure, but often eloquent, and always at once earnest and ingenious, those writings, supplementing his remarkable gift of conversation, were directly and indirectly influential, even on some the furthest removed from Coleridge's own masters; on John Stuart Mill, for instance, and some of the earlier writers of the "high-church" school. Like his verse, they display him also in two other characters—as a student of words, and as a psychologist, that is, as a more minute observer or student than other men of the phenomena of mind. To note the recondite associations of words, old or new; to expound the logic, the reasonable soul, of their various uses; to recover the interest of older writers who had had a phraseology of their own—this was a vein of inquiry allied to his un-

spoken several times of the scent of the bean-field in the air:—the
tropical touches in a chilly climate; his is a nature that will make
the most of these, which finds a sort of caress in such things.
Kubla Khan, the fragment of a poem actually composed in some
certainly not quite healthy sleep, is perhaps chiefly of interest as
showing, by the mode of its composition, how physical, how
much of a diseased or valetudinarian temperament, in its moments of relief, Coleridge's happiest gift really was; and side by
side with *Kubla Khan* should be read, as Coleridge placed it, the
Pains of Sleep, to illustrate that retarding physical burden in his
temperament, that "unimpassioned grief," the source of which
lay so near the source of those pleasures. Connected also with
this, and again in contrast with Wordsworth, is the limited quantity of his poetical performance, as he himself regrets so elo-
quently in the lines addressed to Wordsworth after his recitation
of *The Prelude*. It is like some exotic plant, just managing to
blossom a little in the somewhat un-english air of Coleridge's own
south-western birthplace, but never quite well there.

In 1798 he joined Wordsworth in the composition of a volume of
poems—the *Lyrical Ballads*. What Wordsworth then wrote already vibrates with that blithe impulse which carried him to final
happiness and self-possession. In Coleridge we feel already that
faintness and obscure dejection which clung like some contagious
damp to all his work. Wordsworth was to be distinguished by a
joyful and penetrative conviction of the existence of certain latent affinities between nature and the human mind, which reciprocally gild the mind and nature with a kind of "heavenly
alchemy."

> My voice proclaims
> How exquisitely the individual mind
> (And the progressive powers, perhaps, no less
> Of the whole species) to the external world
> Is fitted; and how exquisitely, too,
> The external world is fitted to the mind;
> And the creation, by no lower name
> Can it be called, which they with blended might
> Accomplish.

In Wordsworth this took the form of an unbroken dreaming over the aspects and transitions of nature—a reflective, though altogether unformulated, analysis of them.

There are in Coleridge's poems expressions of this conviction as deep as Worthsworth's. But Coleridge could never have abandoned himself to the dream, the vision, as Wordsworth did, because the first condition of such abandonment must be an unvexed quietness of heart. No one can read the *Lines composed above Tintern* without feeling how potent the physical element was among the conditions of Wordsworth's genius—"felt in the blood and felt along the heart."

> My whole life I have lived in quiet thought!

The stimulus which most artists require of nature he can renounce. He leaves the ready-made glory of the Swiss mountains that he may reflect glory on a mouldering leaf. He loves best to watch the floating thistledown, because of its hint at an unseen life in the air. Coleridge's temperament, ἀεί ἐν σφοδρᾷ ὀρέξει, with its faintness, its grieved dejection, could never have been like that.

> My genial spirits fail;
> And what can these avail
> To lift the smothering weight from off my breast?
> It were a vain endeavour,
> Though I should gaze for ever
> On that green light that lingers in the west:
> I may not hope from outward forms to win
> The passion and the life whose fountains are within.

Wordsworth's flawless temperament, his fine mountain atmosphere of mind, that calm, sabbatic, mystic, wellbeing which De Quincey, a little cynically, connected with worldly (that is to say, pecuniary) good fortune, kept his conviction of a latent intelligence in nature within the limits of sentiment or instinct, and confined it to those delicate and subdued shades of expression which alone perfect art allows. In Coleridge's sadder, more purely intellectual, cast of genius, what with Wordsworth was sentiment or instinct became a philosophical idea, or philosophical for-

and no mere matter of theory, in him as in Wordsworth. That record of the

> green light
> Which lingers in the west,

and again, of

> the western sky,
> And its peculiar tint of yellow green,

which Byron found ludicrously untrue, but which surely needs no defence, is a characterstic example of a singular watchfulness for the minute fact and expression of natural scenery pervading all he wrote—a closeness to the exact physiognomy of nature, having something to do with that idealistic philosophy which sees in the external world no mere concurrence of mechanical agencies, but an animated body, informed and made expressive, like the body of man, by an indwelling intelligence. It was a tendency, doubtless, in the air, for Shelley too is affected by it, and Turner, with the school of landscape which followed him. "I had found," Coleridge tells us,

> That outward forms, the loftiest, still receive
> Their finer influence from the world within;
> Fair ciphers of vague import, where the eye
> Traces no spot, in which the heart may read
> History and prophecy: . . .

and this induces in him no indifference to actual colour and form and process, but such minute realism as this—

> The thin grey cloud is spread on high,
> It covers but not hides the sky.
> The moon is behind and at the full;
> And yet she looks both small and dull;

or this, which has a touch of "romantic" weirdness—

> Nought was green upon the oak
> But moss and rarest misletoe;

or this—

> There is not wind enough to twirl
> The one red leaf, the last of its clan,
> That dances as often as dance it can,
> Hanging so light, and hanging so high,
> On the topmost twig that looks up at the sky:

or this, with a weirdness, again, like that of some wild French etcher—

> Lo! the new-moon winter-bright!
> And overspread with phantom light
> (With swimming phantom light o'erspread,
> But rimmed and circled with a silver thread)
> I see the old moon in her lap, foretelling
> The coming on of rain and squally blast.

He has a like imaginative apprehension of the silent and unseen processes of nature, its "ministries" of dew and frost, for instance; as when he writes, in April—

> A balmy night! and though the stars be dim,
> Yet let us think upon the vernal showers
> That gladden the green earth, and we shall find
> A pleasure in the dimness of the stars.

Of such imaginative treatment of landscape there is no better instance than the description of *The Dell*, in *Fears in Solitude*—

> A green and silent spot amid the hills,
> A small and silent dell! O'er stiller place
> No singing skylark ever poised himself—
> But the dell,
> Bathed by the mist is fresh and delicate
> As vernal cornfield, or the unripe flax
> When, through its half-transparent stalks, at eve,
> The level sunshine glimmers with green light:—
> The gust that roared and died away
> To the distant tree—
> heard and only heard
> In this low dell, bowed not the delicate grass.

the year 1797: *The Rhyme of the Ancient Mariner* was printed as a contribution to the *Lyrical Ballads* in 1798; and these two poems belong to the great year of Coleridge's poetic production, his twenty-fifth year. In poetic quality, above all in that most poetic of all qualities, a keen sense of, and delight in beauty, the infection of which lays hold upon the reader, they are quite out of proportion to all his other compositions. The form in both is that of the ballad, with some of its terminology, and some also of its quaint conceits. They connect themselves with that revival of ballad literature, of which Percy's *Relics*, and, in another way, Macpherson's *Ossian* are monuments, and which afterwards so powerfully affected Scott—

> Young-eyed poesy
> All deftly masked as hoar antiquity.

The Ancient Mariner, as also, in its measure, *Christabel*, is a "romantic" poem, impressing us by bold invention, and appealing to that taste for the supernatural, that longing for *le frisson*, a shudder, to which the "romantic" school in Germany, and its derivations in England and France, directly ministered. In Coleridge, personally, this taste had been encouraged by his odd and out-of-the-way reading in the old-fashioned literature of the marvellous—books like Purchas's *Pilgrims*, early voyages like Hakluyt's, old naturalists and visionary moralists, like Thomas Burnet, from whom he quotes the motto of *The Ancient Mariner*, "*Facile credo, plures esse naturas invisibiles quam visibiles in rerum universitate, etc.*" Fancies of the strange things which may very well happen, even in broad daylight, to men shut up alone in ships far off on the sea, seem to have occurred to the human mind in all ages with a peculiar readiness, and often have about them, from the story of the stealing of Dionysus downwards, the fascination of a certain dreamy grace, which distinguishes them from other kinds of marvellous inventions. This sort of fascination *The Ancient Mariner* brings to its highest degree: it is the delicacy, the dreamy grace, in his presentation of the marvellous, which makes Coleridge's work so remarkable. The too palpable intruders from a spiritual world in almost all ghost literature, in Scott and Shakespeare even, have a kind of crudity or coarseness. Coleridge's power is in the very fineness with which, as by some really ghostly finger, he brings home to our inmost sense his inventions, daring as they are—the skeleton ship, the polar spirit, the inspiriting of the dead corpses of the ship's crew. *The Rhyme of the Ancient Mariner* has the plausibility, the perfect adaptation to reason and the general aspect of life, which belongs to the marvellous, when actually presented as part of a credible experience in our dreams. Doubtless, the mere experience of the opium-eater, the habit he must almost necessarily fall into of noting the more elusive phenomena of dreams, had something to do with that: in its essence, however, it is connected with a more purely intellectual circumstance in the development of Coleridge's poetic gift. Some one once asked William Blake, to whom Coleridge has many resemblances, when either is at his best (that whole episode of the re-inspiriting of the ship's crew in *The Ancient Mariner* being comparable to Blake's well-known design of the "Morning Stars singing together") whether he had ever seen a ghost, and was surprised when the famous seer, who ought, one might think, to have seen so many, answered frankly, "Only once!" His "spirits," at once more delicate, and so much more real, than any ghost—the burden, as they were the privilege, of his *temperament*—like it, were an integral element in his everyday life. And the difference of mood expressed in that question and its answer, is indicative of a change of temper in regard to the supernatural which has passed over the whole modern mind, and of which the true measure is the influence of the writings of Swedenborg. What that change is we may see if we compare the vision by which Swedenborg was "called," as he thought, to his work, with the ghost which called Hamlet, or the spells of Marlowe's *Faust* with those of Goethe's. The modern mind, so minutely self-scrutinising, if it is to be affected at all by a sense of the supernatural, needs to be more finely touched than was possible in the older, romantic presentment of it. The spectral object, so crude, so impossible, has become plausible, as

> The blot upon the brain,
> That *will* show itself without;

> A dreary sea now flows between;
> But neither heat, nor frost, nor thunder,
> Shall wholly do away, I ween,
> The marks of that which once hath been.

I suppose these lines leave almost every reader with a quickened sense of the beauty and compass of human feeling; and it is the sense of such richness and beauty which, in spite of his "dejection," in spite of that burden of his morbid lassitude, accompanies Coleridge himself through life. A warm poetic joy in everything beautiful, whether it be a moral sentiment, like the friendship of Roland and Leoline, or only the flakes of falling light from the water-snakes—this joy, visiting him, now and again, after sickly dreams, in sleep or waking, as a relief not to be forgotten, and with such a power of felicitous expression that the infection of it passes irresistibly to the reader—such is the predominant element in the matter of his poetry, as cadence is the predominant quality of its form. "We bless thee for our creation!" he might have said, in his later period of definite religious assent, "because the world is so beautiful: the world of ideas—living spirits, detached from the divine nature itself, to inform and lift the heavy mass of material things; the world of man, above all in his melodious and intelligible speech; the world of living creatures and natural scenery; the world of dreams." What he really did say, by way of *A Tombless Epitaph*, is true enough of himself—

> Sickness, 'tis true,
> Whole years of weary days, besieged him close,
> Even to the gates and inlets of his life!
> But it is true, no less, that strenuous, firm,
> And with a natural gladness, he maintained
> The citadel unconquered, and in joy
> Was strong to follow the delightful Muse.
> For not a hidden path, that to the shades
> Of the beloved Parnassian forest leads,
> Lurked undiscovered by him; not a rill
> There issues from the found of Hippocrene,
> But he had traced it upward to its source,
> Through open glade, dark glen, and secret dell,
> Knew the gay wild flowers on its banks, and culled
> Its med'cinable herbs. Yea, oft alone,

Piercing the long-neglected holy cave,
The haunt obscure of old Philosophy,
He bade with lifted torch its starry walls
Sparkle, as erst they sparkled to the flame
Of odorous lamps tended by saint and sage.
O framed for calmer times and nobler hearts!
O studious Poet, eloquent for truth!
Philosopher! contemning wealth and death,
Yet docile, childlike, full of Life and Love.

The student of empirical science asks, Are absolute principles attainable? What are the limits of knowledge? The answer he receives from science itself is not ambiguous. What the moralist asks is, Shall we gain or lose by surrendering human life to the relative spirit? Experience answers that the dominant tendency of life is to turn ascertained truth into a dead letter, to make us all the phlegmatic servants of routine. The relative spirit, by its constant dwelling on the more fugitive conditions or circumstances of things, breaking through a thousand rough and brutal classifications, and giving elasticity to inflexible principles, begets an intellectual *finesse* of which the ethical result is a delicate and tender justice in the criticism of human life. Who would gain more than Coleridge by criticism in such a spirit? We know how his life has appeared when judged by absolute standards. We see him trying to "apprehend the absolute," to stereotype forms of faith and philosophy, to attain, as he says, "fixed principles" in politics, morals, and religion, to fix one mode of life as the essence of life, refusing to see the parts as parts only; and all the time his own pathetic history pleads for a more elastic moral philosophy than his, and cries out against every formula less living and flexible than life itself.

"From his childhood he hungered for eternity." There, after all, is the incontestable claim of Coleridge. The perfect flower of any elementary type of life must always be precious to humanity, and Coleridge is a true flower of the *ennuyé*, of the type of René. More than Childe Harold, more than Werther, more than René himself, Coleridge, by what he did, what he was, and what he failed to do, represents that inexhaustible discontent, languor, and homesickness, that endless regret, the chords of which ring all through

pity in them deepened by the deeper subjectivity, the intenser and closer living with itself, which is characteristic of the temper of the later generation; and therewith, the mirth also, from the amalgam of which with pity humour proceeds, has become, in Charles Dickens, for example, freer and more boisterous.

To this more high-pitched feeling, since predominant in our literature, the writings of Charles Lamb, whose life occupies the last quarter of the eighteenth century and the first quarter of the nineteenth, are a transition; and such union of grave, of terrible even, with gay, we may note in the circumstances of his life, as reflected thence into his work. We catch the aroma of a singular, homely sweetness about his first years, spent on Thames' side, amid the red bricks and terraced gardens, with their rich historical memories of old-fashioned legal London. Just above the poorer class, deprived, as he says, of the "sweet food of academic institution," he is fortunate enough to be reared in the classical languages at an ancient school, where he becomes the companion of Coleridge, as at a later period he was his enthusiastic disciple. So far, the years go by with less than the usual share of boyish difficulties; protected, one fancies, seeing what he was afterwards, by some attraction of temper in the quaint child, small and delicate, with a certain Jewish expression in his clear, brown complexion, eyes not precisely of the same colour, and a slow walk adding to the staidness of his figure; and whose infirmity of speech, increased by agitation, is partly engaging.

And the cheerfulness of all this, of the mere aspect of Lamb's quiet subsequent life also, might make the more superficial reader think of him as in himself something slight, and of his mirth as cheaply bought. Yet we know that beneath this blithe surface there was something of the fateful domestic horror, of the beautiful heroism and devotedness too, of old Greek tragedy. His sister Mary, ten years his senior, in a sudden paroxysm of madness, caused the death of her mother, and was brought to trial for what an overstrained justice might have construed as the greatest of crimes. She was released on the brother's pledging himself to watch over her; and to this sister, from the age of twenty-one, Charles Lamb sacrificed himself, "seeking thenceforth," says his earliest biographer, "no connexion which could interfere with her supremacy in his affections, or impair his ability to sustain and comfort her." The "feverish, romantic tie of love," he cast away in exchange for the "charities of home." Only, from time to time, the madness returned, affecting him too, once; and we see the brother and sister voluntarily yielding to restraint. In estimating the humour of *Elia*, we must no more forget the strong undercurrent of this great misfortune and pity, than one could forget it in his actual story. So he becomes the best critic, almost the discoverer, of Webster, a dramatist of genius so sombre, so heavily coloured, so *macabre*. *Rosamund Grey*, written in his twenty-third year, a story with something bitter and exaggerated, an almost insane fixedness of gloom perceptible in it, strikes clearly this note in his work.

For himself, and from his own point of view, the exercise of his gift, of his literary art, came to gild or sweeten a life of monotonous labour, and seemed, as far as regarded others, no very important thing; availing to give them a little pleasure, and inform them a little, chiefly in a retrospective manner, but in no way concerned with the turning of the tides of the great world. And yet this very modesty, this unambitious way of conceiving his work, has impressed upon it a certain exceptional enduringness. For of the remarkable English writers contemporary with Lamb, many were greatly preoccupied with ideas of practice—religious, moral, political—ideas which have since, in some sense or other, entered permanently into the general consciousness; and, these having no longer any stimulus for a generation provided with a different stock of ideas, the writings of those who spent so much of themselves in their propagation have lost, with posterity, something of what they gained by them in immediate influence. Coleridge, Wordsworth, Shelley even—sharing so largely in the unrest of their own age, and made personally more interesting thereby, yet, of their actual work, surrender more to the mere course of time than some of those who may have seemed to exercise themselves hardly at all in great matters, to have been little serious, or a little indifferent, regarding them.

Of this number of the disinterested servants of literature, smaller in England than in France, Charles Lamb is one. In the making of prose he realises the principle of art for its own sake, as

the old masters. Godwin, seeing in quotation a passage from *John Woodvil*, takes it for a choice fragment of an old dramatist, and goes to Lamb to assist him in finding the author. His power of delicate imitation in prose and verse reaches the length of a fine mimicry even, as in those last essays of Elia on Popular Fallacies, with their gentle reproduction or caricature of Sir Thomas Browne, showing, the more completely, his mastery, by disinterested study, of those elements of the man which were the real source of style in that great, solemn master of old English, who, ready to say what he has to say with fearless homeliness, yet continually overawes one with touches of a strange utterance from worlds afar. For it is with the delicacies of fine literature especially, its gradations of expression, its fine judgment, its pure sense of words, of vocabulary—things, alas! dying out in the English literature of the present, together with the appreciation of them in our literature of the past—that his literary mission is chiefly concerned. And yet, delicate, refining, daintily epicurean, as he may seem, when he writes of giants, such as Hogarth or Shakespeare, though often but in a stray note, you catch the sense of veneration with which those great names in past literature and art brooded over his intelligence, his undiminished impressibility by the great effects in them. Reading, commenting on Shakespeare, he is like a man who walks alone under a grand stormy sky, and among unwonted tricks of light, when powerful spirits might seem to be abroad upon the air; and the grim humour of Hogarth, as he analyses it, rises into a kind of spectral grotesque; while he too knows the secret of fine, significant touches like theirs.

There are traits, customs, characteristics of houses and dress, surviving morsels of old life, such as Hogarth has transferred so vividly into *The Rake's Progress*, or *Marriage à la Mode*, concerning which we well understand how, common, uninteresting, or even worthless in themselves, they have come to please us at last as things picturesque, being set in relief against the modes of our different age. Customs, stiff to us, stiff dresses, stiff furniture—types of castoff fashions, left by accident, and which no one ever meant to preserve—we contemplate with more than goodnature, as having in them the veritable accent of a time, not altogether to be replaced by its more solemn and self-conscious deposits; like those tricks of individuality which we find quite tolerable in persons, because they convey to us the secret of life-like expression, and with regard to which we are all to some extent humourists. But it is part of the privilege of the genuine humourist to anticipate this pensive mood with regard to the ways and things of his own day; to look upon the tricks in manner of the life about him with that same refined, purged sort of vision, which will come naturally to those of a later generation, in observing whatever may have survived by chance of its mere external habit. Seeing things always by the light of an understanding more entire than is possible for ordinary minds, of the whole mechanism of humanity, and seeing also the manner, the outward mode or fashion, always in strict connexion with the spiritual condition which determined it, a humourist such as Charles Lamb anticipates the enchantment of distance; and the characteristics of places, ranks, habits of life, are transfigured for him, even now and in advance of time, by poetic light; justifying what some might condemn as mere sentimentality, in the effort to hand on unbroken the tradition of such fashion or accent. "The praise of beggars," "the cries of London," the traits of actors just grown "old," the spots in "town" where the country, its fresh green and fresh water, still lingered on, one after another, amidst the bustle; the quaint, dimmed, just played-out farces, he had relished so much, coming partly through them to understand the earlier English theatre as a thing once really alive; those fountains and sun-dials of old gardens, of which he entertains such dainty discourse:—he feels the poetry of these things, as the poetry of things old indeed, but surviving as an actual part of the life of the present, and as something quite different from the poetry of things flatly gone from us and antique, which come back to us, if at all, as entire strangers, like Scott's old Scotch-border personages, their oaths and armour. Such gift of appreciation depends, as I said, on the habitual apprehension of men's life as a whole—its organic wholeness, as extending even to the least things in it—of its outward manner in connexion with its inward temper; and it involves a fine perception of the congruities, the musical accordance between humanity and its environment of custom, society,

fined points of earth, of human relationship, he could throw the gleam of poetry or humour on what seemed common or thread-bare; has a care for the sighs, and the weary, humdrum preoc-cupations of very weak people, down to their little pathetic "gentilities," even; while, in the purely human temper, he can write of death, almost like Shakespeare.

And that care, through all his enthusiasm of discovery, for what is accustomed, in literature, connected thus with his close cling-ing to home and the earth, was congruous also with that love for the accustomed in religion, which we may notice in him. He is one of the last votaries of that old-world sentiment, based on the feelings of hope and awe, which may be described as the religion of men of letters (as Sir Thomas Browne has his *Religion of the Physician*) religion as understood by the soberer men of letters in the last century, Addison, Gray, and Johnson; by Jane Austen and Thackeray, later. A high way of feeling developed largely by con-stant intercourse with the great things of literature, and extended in its turn to those matters greater still, this religion lives, in the main retrospectively, in a system of recieved sentiments and be-liefs; received, like those great things of literature and art, in the first instance, on the authority of a long tradition, in the course of which they have linked themselves in a thousand complex ways to the conditions of human life, and no more questioned now than the feeling one keeps by one of the greatness—say! of Shake-speare. For Charles Lamb, such form of religion becomes the sol-emn background on which the nearer and more exciting objects of his immediate experience relieve themselves, borrowing from it an expression of calm; its necessary atmosphere being indeed a profound quiet, that quiet which has in it a kind of sacramental efficacy, working, we might say, on the principle of the *opus oper-atum*, almost without any co-operation of one's own, towards the assertion of the higher self. And, in truth, to men of Lamb's deli-cately attuned temperament mere physical stillness has its full value; such natures seeming to long for it sometimes, as for no merely negative thing, with a sort of mystical sensuality.

The writings of Charles Lamb are an excellent illustration of the value of reserve in literature. Below his quiet, his quaintness, his humour, and what may seem the slightness, the occasional or accidental character of his work, there lies, as I said at starting, as in his life, a genuinely tragic element. The gloom, reflected at its darkest in those hard shadows of *Rosamund Grey*, is always there, though not alway realised either for himself or his readers, and restrained always in utterance. It gives to those lighter matters on the surface of life and literature among which he for the most part moved, a wonderful force of expression, as if at any moment these slight words and fancies might pierce very far into the deeper soul of things. In his writing, as in his life, that quiet is not the low-flying of one from the first drowsy by choice, and needing the prick of some strong passion or worldly ambition, to stimulate him into all the energy of which he is capable; but rather the reaction of nature, after an escape from fate, dark and insane as in old Greek tragedy, following upon which the sense of mere relief becomes a kind of passion, as with one who, having narrowly escaped earthquake or shipwreck, finds a thing for grateful tears in just sitting quiet at home, under the wall, till the end of days.

He felt the genius of places; and I sometimes think he resembles the places he knew and liked best, and where his lot fell—London, sixty-five years ago, with Covent Garden and the old theatres, and the Temple gardens still unspoiled, Thames gliding down, and beyond to north and south the fields at Enfield or Hampton, to which, "with their living trees," the thoughts wander "from the hard wood of the desk"—fields fresher, and coming nearer to town then, but in one of which the present writer remembers, on a brooding early summer's day, to have heard the cuckoo for the first time. Here, the surface of things is certainly humdrum, the streets dingy, the green places, where the child goes a-maying, tame enough. But nowhere are things more apt to respond to the brighter weather, nowhere is there so much difference between rain and sunshine, nowhere do the clouds roll together more grandly; those quaint suburban pastorals gathering a certain quality of grandeur from the background of the great city, with its weighty atmosphere, and portent of storm in the rapid light on dome and bleached stone steeples.

1878.

him, any more than in the books of Burton and Fuller, or some other similar writers of that age—mental abodes, we might liken, after their own manner, to the little old private houses of some historic town grouped about its grand public structures, which, when they have survived at all, posterity is loth to part with. For, in their absolute sincerity, not only do these authors clearly exhibit themselves ("the unique peculiarity of the writer's mind," being, as Johnson says of Browne, "faithfully reflected in the form and matter of his work") but, even more than mere professionally instructed writers, they belong to, and reflect, the age they lived in. In essentials, of course, even Browne is by no means so unique among his contemporaries, and so singular, as he looks. And then, as the very condition of their work, there is an entire absence of personal restraint in dealing with the public, whose humours they come at last in a great measure to reproduce. To speak more properly, they have no sense of a "public" to deal with, at all— only a full confidence in the "friendly reader," as they love to call him. Hence their amazing pleasantry, their indulgence in their own conceits; but hence also those unpremeditated wildflowers of speech we should never have the good luck to find in any more formal kind of literature.

It is, in truth, to the literary purpose of the humourist, in the old-fashioned sense of the term, that this method of writing naturally allies itself—of the humourist to whom all the world is but a spectacle in which nothing is really alien from himself, who has hardly a sense of the distinction between great and little among things that are at all, and whose half-pitying, half-amused sympathy is called out especially by the seemingly small interests and traits of character in the things or the people around him. Certainly, in an age stirred by great causes, like the age of Browne in England, of Montaigne in France, that is not a type to which one would wish to reduce all men of letters. Still, in an age apt also to become severe, or even cruel (its eager interest in those great causes turning sour on occasion) the character of the humourist may well find its proper influence, through that serene power, and the leisure it has for conceiving second thoughts, on the tendencies, conscious or unconscious, of the fierce wills around it. Something of such a humourist was Browne—not callous to men and their fortunes; certainly not without opinions of his own about them; and yet, undisturbed by the civil war, by the fall, and then the restoration, of the monarchy, through that long quiet life (ending at last on the day himself had predicted, as if at the moment he had willed) in which "all existence," as he says, "had been but food for contemplation."

Johnson, in beginning his *Life of Browne*, remarks that Browne "seems to have had the fortune, common among men of letters, of raising little curiosity after their private life." Whether or not, with the example of Johnson himself before us, we can think just that, it is certain that Browne's works are of a kind to directly stimulate curiosity about himself—about himself, as being manifestly so large a part of those works; and as a matter of fact we know a great deal about his life, uneventful as in truth it was. To himself, indeed, his life at Norwich, as he gives us to understand, seemed wonderful enough. "Of these wonders," says Johnson, "the view that can now be taken of his life offers no appearance." But "we carry with us," as Browne writes, "the wonders we seek without us," and we may note on the other hand, a circumstance which his daughter, Mrs. Lyttleton, tells us of his childhood: "His father used to open his breast when he was asleep, and kiss it in prayers over him, as 'tis said of Origen's father, that the Holy Ghost would take possession there." It was perhaps because the son inherited an aptitude for a like profound kindling of sentiment in the taking of his life, that, uneventful as it was, commonplace as it seemed to Johnson, to Browne himself it was so full of wonders, and so stimulates the curiosity of his more careful reader of to-day. "What influence," says Johnson again, "learning has had on its possessors may be doubtful." Well! the influence of his great learning, of his constant research on Browne, was its imaginative influence—that it completed his outfit as a poetic visionary, stirring all the strange "conceit" of his nature to its depths.

Browne himself dwells, in connexion with the first publication (extorted by circumstance) of the *Religio Medici*, on the natural "inactivity of his disposition"; and he does, as I have said, pass very quietly through an exciting time. Born in the year of the Gunpowder Plot, he was not, in truth, one of those clear and

dled together, they will be error itself." And yet, congruously with a dreamy sweetness of character we may find expressed in his very features, he seems not greatly concerned at the temporary suppression of the institutions he values so much. He seems to possess some inward Platonic reality of them—church or monarchy—to hold by in idea, quite beyond the reach of Roundhead or unworthy Cavalier. In the power of what is inward and inviolable in his religion, he can still take note: "In my solitary and retired imagination (*neque enim cum porticus aut me lectulus accepit, desum mihi*) I remember I am not alone, and therefore forget not to contemplate Him and His attributes who is ever with me."

His father, a merchant of London, with some claims to ancient descent, left him early in possession of ample means. Educated at Winchester and Oxford, he visited Ireland, France, and Italy; and in the year 1633, at the age of twenty-eight, became Doctor of Medicine at Leyden. Three years later he established himself as a physician at Norwich for the remainder of his life, having married a lady, described as beautiful and attractive, and affectionate also, as we may judge from her letters and postscripts to those of her husband, in an orthography of a homeliness amazing even for that age. Dorothy Browne bore him ten children, six of whom he survived.

Their house at Norwich, even then an old one it would seem, must have grown, through long years of acquisition, into an odd cabinet of antiquities—antiquities properly so called; his old Roman, or Romanised British urns, from Walsingham or Brampton, for instance, and those natural objects which he studied somewhat in the temper of a curiosity-hunter or antiquary. In one of the old churchyards of Norwich he makes the first discovery of *adipocere*, of which grim substance "a portion still remains with him." For his multifarious experiments he must have had his laboratory. The old window-stanchions had become magnetic, proving, as he thinks, that iron "acquires verticity" from long lying in one position. Once we find him re-tiling the place. It was then, perhaps, that he made the observation that bricks and tiles also acquire "magnetic alliciency"—one's whole house, one might fancy; as indeed, he holds the earth itself to be a vast lodestone.

The very faults of his literary work, its desultoriness, the time it costs his readers, that slow Latinity which Johnson imitated from him, those lengthy leisurely terminations which busy posterity will abbreviate, all breathe of the long quiet of the place. Yet he is by no means indolent. Besides wide book-learning, experimental research at home, and indefatigable observation in the open air, he prosecutes the ordinary duties of a physician; contrasting himself indeed with other students, "whose quiet and unmolested doors afford no such distractions." To most persons of mind sensitive as his, his chosen studies would have seemed full of melancholy, turning always, as they did, upon death and decay. It is well, perhaps, that life should be something of a "meditation upon death": but to many, certainly, Browne's would have seemed too like a lifelong following of one's own funeral. A museum is seldom a cheerful place—oftenest induces the feeling that nothing could ever have been young; and to Browne the whole world is a museum; all the grace and beauty it has being of a somewhat mortified kind. Only, for him (poetic dream, or philosophic apprehension, it was this which never failed to evoke his wonderful genius for exquisitely impassioned speech) over all those ugly anatomical preparations, as though over miraculous saintly relics, there was the perpetual flicker of a surviving spiritual ardency, one day to reassert itself—stranger far than any fancied odylic gravelights!

When Browne settled at Norwich, being then about thirty-six years old, he had already completed the *Religio Medici*; a desultory collection of observations designed for himself only and a few friends, at all events with no purpose of immediate publication. It had been lying by him for seven years, circulating privately in his own extraordinarily perplexed manuscript, or in manuscript copies, when, in 1642, an incorrect printed version from one of those copies, "much corrupted by transcription at various hands," appeared anonymously. Browne, decided royalist as he was in spite of seeming indifference, connects this circumstance with the unscrupulous use of the press for political purposes, and especially against the king, at that time. Just here a romantic figure comes on the scene. Son of the unfortunate young Everard Digby who perished on the scaffold for some half-hearted participation in the Gunpowder Plot, Kenelm Digby, brought up in the reformed religion, had returned in manhood to the religion of his father. In his intellectual composition he had, in common with Browne, a scientific interest, oddly tinged with both poetry and scepticism: he had also a strong sympathy with religious reaction, and a more than sentimental love for a seemingly vanishing age of faith, which he, for one, would not think of as vanishing. A copy of that surreptitious edition of the *Religio Medici* found him a prisoner on suspicion of a too active royalism, and with much time on his hands. The Roman Catholic, although, secure in his definite orthodoxy, he finds himself indifferent on many points (on the reality of witchcraft, for instance) concerning which Browne's more timid, personally grounded faith might indulge no scepticism, forced himself, nevertheless, to detect a vein of rationalism in a book which on the whole much attracted him, and hastily put forth his "animadversions" upon it. Browne, with all his distaste for controversy, thus found himself committed to a dispute, and his reply came with the correct edition of the *Religio Medici* published at last with his name. There have been many efforts to formulate the "religion of the layman," which might be rightly understood, perhaps, as something more than what is called "natural," yet less than ecclesiastical, or "professional" religion. Though its habitual mode of conceiving experience is on a different plane, yet it would recognise the legitimacy of the traditional religious interpretation of that experience, generally and by implication; only, with a marked reserve as to religious particulars, both of thought and language, out of a real reverence or awe, as proper only for a special place. Such is the lay religion, as we may find it in Addison, in Gray, in Thackeray; and there is something of a concession—a concession, on second thoughts—about it. Browne's *Religio Medici* is designed as the expression of a mind more difficult of belief than that of the mere "layman," as above described; it is meant for the religion of the man of science. Actually, it is something less to the point, in any balancing of the religious against the worldly view of things, than the religion of the layman, as just now defined. For Browne, in spite of his profession of boisterous doubt, has no real difficulties, and his religion, certainly, nothing of the character of a concession. He holds that there has never existed an atheist. Not that he is credulous; but that his religion is only the correlative of himself, his peculiar character and education, a religion of manifold associa-tion. For him, the wonders of religion, its supernatural events or agencies, are almost natural facts or processes. "Even in this ma-terial fabric, the spirits walk as freely exempt from the affection of time, place and motion, as beyond the extremest circum-ference." Had not Divine interference designed to raise the dead, nature herself is in act to do it—to lead out the "incinerated" soul from the retreats of her dark laboratory. Certainly Browne has not, like Pascal, made the "great resolution," by the apprehension that it is just in the contrast of the moral world to the world with which science deals that religion finds its proper basis. It is from the homelessness of the world which science analyses so vic-toriously, its dark unspirituality, wherein the soul he is conscious of seems such a stranger, that Pascal "turns again to his rest," in the conception of a world of wholly reasonable and moral agen-cies. For Browne, on the contrary, the light is full, design every-where obvious, its conclusion easy to draw, all small and great things marked clearly with the signature of the "Word." The ad-hesion, the difficult adhesion, of men such as Pascal, is an im-mense contribution to religious controversy; the concession, again, of a man like Addison, of great significance there. But in the adhesion of Browne, in spite of his crusade against "vulgar errors," there is no real significance. The *Religio Medici* is a con-tribution, not to faith, but to piety; a refinement and correction, such as piety often stands in need of; a help, not so much to religious belief in a world of doubt, as to the maintenance of the religious mood amid the interests of a secular calling.

From about this time Browne's letters afford a pretty clear view of his life as it passed in the house at Norwich. Many of these letters represent him in correspondence with the singular men who shared his own half poetic, half scientific turn of mind, with that impressibility towards what one might call the thaumaturgic elements in nature which has often made men dupes, and which is certainly an element in the somewhat atrabiliar mental com-plexion of that age in England. He corresponds seriously with William Lily, the astrologer; is acquainted with Dr. Dee, who had some connexion with Norwich, and has "often heard him affirm, sometimes with oaths, that he had seen transmutation of pewter dishes and flagons into silver (at least) which the goldsmiths at Prague bought of him." Browne is certainly an honest investigator; but it is still with a faint hope of something like that upon fitting occasion, and on the alert always for surprises in nature (as if nature had a rhetoric, at times, to deliver to us, like those sudden and surprising flowers of his own poetic style) that he listens to her everyday talk so attentively. Of strange animals, strange cures, and the like, his correspondence is full. The very errors he combats are, of course, the curiosities of error—those fascinating, irresistible, popular, errors, which various kinds of people have insisted on gliding into because they like them. Even his heresies were old ones—the very fossils of capricious opinion.

It is as an industrious local naturalist that Browne comes before us first, full of the fantastic minute life in the fens and "Broads" around Norwich, its various sea and marsh birds. He is something of a vivisectionist also, and we may not be surprised at it, perhaps, in an age which, for the propagation of truth, was ready to cut off men's ears. He finds one day "a *Scarabæus capricornus odoratus*," which he takes "to be mentioned by Monfetus, folio 150. He saith, '*Nucem moschatam et cinnamomum vere spirat*'— but to me it smelt like roses, santalum, and ambergris." "*Musca tuliparum moschata*," again, "is a small bee-like fly of an excellent fragrant odour, which I have often found at the bottom of the flowers of tulips." Is this within the experience of modern entomologists?

The *Garden of Cyrus*, though it ends indeed with a passage of wonderful felicity, certainly emphasises (to say the least) the defects of Browne's literary good qualities. His chimeric fancy carries him here into a kind of frivolousness, as if he felt almost too safe with his public, and were himself not quite serious, or dealing fairly with it; and in a writer such as Browne levity must of necessity be a little ponderous. Still, like one of those stiff gardens, half-way between the medieval garden and the true "English" garden of Temple or Walpole, actually to be seen in the background of some of the conventional portraits of that day, the fantasies of this indescribable exposition of the mysteries of the quincunx form part of the complete portrait of Browne himself;

and it is in connexion with it that, once or twice, the quaintly
delightful pen of Evelyn comes into the correspondence—in connexion with the "hortulane pleasure." "Norwich," he writes to
Browne, "is a place, I understand, much addicted to the flowery
part." Professing himself a believer in the operation "of the air
and genius of gardens upon human spirits, towards virtue and
sanctity," he is all for natural gardens as against "those which
appear like gardens of paste-board and march-pane, and smell
more of paint than of flowers and verdure." Browne is in commu-
nication also with Ashmole and Dugdale, the famous antiquaries; to the latter of whom, who had written a work on the
history of the embanking of fens, he communicates the discovery
of certain coins, on a piece of ground "in the nature of an island in
the fens."

Far more interesting certainly than those curious scientific letters is Browne's "domestic correspondence." Dobson, Charles the
First's "English Tintoret," would seem to have painted a life-sized
picture of Sir Thomas Browne and his family, after the manner of
those big, urbane, family groups, then coming into fashion with
the Dutch Masters. Of such a portrait nothing is now known. But
in these old-fashioned, affectionate letters, transmitted often, in
those troublous times, with so much difficulty, we have what is
almost as graphic—a numerous group, in which, although so
many of Browne's children died young, he was happy; with Dorothy Browne, occasionally adding her charming, ill-spelt
postscripts to her husband's letters; the religious daughter who
goes to daily prayers after the Restoration, which brought Browne
the honour of knighthood; and, above all, two Toms, son and
grandson of Sir Thomas, the latter being the son of Dr. Edward
Browne, now become distinguished as a physician in London (he
attended John, Earl of Rochester, in his last illness at Woodstock)
and his childish existence as he lives away from his proper home
in London, in the old house at Norwich, two hundred years ago,
we see like a thing of to-day.

At first the two brothers, Edward and Thomas (the elder) are
together in everything. Then Edward goes abroad for his studies,
and Thomas, quite early, into the navy, where he certainly develops into a wonderfully gallant figure; passing away, however,

from the correspondence, it is uncertain how, before he was of full age. From the first he is understood to be a lad of parts. "If you practise to write, you will have a good pen and style:" and a delightful, boyish journal of his remains, describing a tour the two brothers made in September 1662 among the Derbyshire hills. "I received your two last letters," he writes to his father from aboard the *Marie Rose*, "and give you many thanks for the discourse you sent me out of Vossius: *De motu marium et ventorum*. It seemed very hard to me at first; but I have now beaten it, and I wish I had the book." His father is pleased to think that he is "like to proceed not only a good navigator, but a good scholar": and he finds the much exacting, old classical prescription for the character of the brave man fulfilled in him. On 16th July 1666 the young man writes—still from the *Marie Rose*—

If it were possible to get an opportunity to send as often as I am desirous to write, you should hear more often from me, being now so near the grand action, from which I would by no means be absent. I extremely long for that thundering day: wherein I hope you shall hear we have behaved ourselves like men, and to the honour of our country. I thank you for your directions for my ears against the noise of the guns, but I have found that I could endure it; nor is it so intolerable as most conceive; especially when men are earnest, and intent upon their business, unto whom muskets sound but like popguns. It is impossible to express unto another how a smart sea-fight elevates the spirits of a man, and makes him despise all dangers. In and after all sea-fights, I have been very thirsty.

He died, as I said, early in life. We only hear of him later in connexion with a trait of character observed in Tom the grandson, whose winning ways, and tricks of bodily and mental growth, are duly recorded in these letters: the reader will, I hope, pardon the following extracts from them:—

Little Tom is lively. . . . Frank is fayne sometimes to play him asleep with a fiddle. When we send away our letters he scribbles a paper and will have it sent to his sister, and saith she doth not know how many fine things there are in Norwich. . . . He delights his grandfather when he comes home.
Tom gives you many thanks for his clothes (from London). He has appeared very fine this King's day with them.
Tom presents his duty. A gentleman at our election asked Tom who hee

was for? and he answered, "For all four." The gentleman replied that he answered like a physician's son.

Tom would have his grandmother, his aunt Betty, and Frank, valentines: but hee conditioned with them that they should give him nothing of any kind that hee had ever had or seen before.

"Tom is just now gone to see two bears which are to be shown." "Tom, his duty. He is begging books and reading of them." "The players are at the Red Lion hard by; and Tom goes sometimes to see a play."

And then one day he stirs old memories—

The fairings were welcome to Tom. He finds about the house divers things that were your brother's (the late Edward's), and Betty sometimes tells him stories about him, so that he was importunate with her to write his life in a quarter of a sheet of paper, and read it unto him, and will have still some more added.

Just as I am writing (learnedly about a comet, 7th January 1680–81) Tom comes and tells me the blazing star is in the yard, and calls me to see it. It was but dim, and the sky not clear. . . . I am very sensible of this sharp weather.

He seems to have come to no good end, riding forth one stormy night. *Requiescat in pace!*

Of this long, leisurely existence the chief events were Browne's rare literary publications; some of his writings indeed having been left unprinted till after his death; while in the circumstances of the issue of every one of them there is something accidental, as if the world might have missed it altogether. Even the *Discourse of Vulgar Errors*, the longest and most elaborate of his works, is entirely discursive and occasional, coming to an end with no natural conclusion, but only because the writer chose to leave off just there; and few probably have been the readers of the book as a consecutive whole. At times indeed we seem to have in it observations only, or notes, preliminary to some more orderly composition. Dip into it: read, for instance, the chapter "Of the Ring-finger," or the chapters "Of the Long Life of the Deer," and on the "Pictures of Mermaids, Unicorns, and some Others," and the part will certainly seem more than the whole. Try to read it through, and you will soon feel cloyed;—miss very likely, its real worth to the fancy, the literary fancy (which finds its pleasure in inventive word and phrase) and become dull to the really vivid beauties of a book so lengthy, but with no real evolution. Though there are words, phrases, constructions innumerable, which remind one how much the work initiated in France by Madame de Rambouillet—work, done for England, we may think perhaps imperfectly, in the next century by Johnson and others—was really needed; yet the capacities of Browne's manner of writing, coming as it did so directly from the man, are felt even in his treatment of matters of science. As with Buffon, his full, ardent, sympathetic vocabulary, the poetry of his language, a poetry inherent in its elementary particles—the word, the epithet—helps to keep his eye, and the eye of the reader, on the object before it, and conduces directly to the purpose of the naturalist, the observer.

But, only one half observation, its other half consisting of very out-of-the-way book-lore, this work displays Browne still in the character of the antiquary, as that age understood him. He is a kind of Elias Ashmole, but dealing with natural objects; which are for him, in the first place, and apart from the remote religious hints and intimations they carry with them, curiosities. He seems to have no true sense of natural law, as Bacon understood it; nor even of that immanent reason in the natural world, which the Platonic tradition supposes. "Things are really true," he says, "as they correspond unto God's conception; and have so much verity as they hold of conformity unto that intellect, in whose idea they had their first determinations." But, actually, what he is busy in the record of, are matters more or less of the nature of caprices; as if things, after all, were significant of their higher verity only at random, and in a sort of surprises, like music in old instruments suddenly touched into sound by a wandering finger, among the lumber of people's houses. Nature, "the art of God," as he says, varying a little a phrase used also by Hobbes, in a work printed later—Nature, he seems to protest, is only a little less magical, its processes only a little less in the way of alchemy, than you had supposed. We feel that, as with that disturbed age in England generally (and it is here that he, with it, is so interesting, curious, old-world, and unlike ourselves) his supposed experience might at any moment be broken in upon by a hundred forms of a natural magic, only not quite so marvellous as that older sort of magic, or alchemy, he is at so much pains to expose; and the large promises of which, its large words too, he still regretfully enjoys.

And yet the *Discourse of Vulgar Errors*, seeming, as it often does, to be a serious refutation of fairy tales—arguing, for instance, against the literal truth of the poetic statement that "The pigeon hath no gall," and such questions as "Whether men weigh heavier dead than alive?" being characteristic questions—is designed, with much ambition, under its pedantic Greek title *Pseudodoxia Epidemica*, as a criticism, a cathartic, an instrument for the clarifying of the intellect. He begins from "that first error in Paradise," wondering much at "man's deceivability in his perfection,"—"at such gross deceit" He enters in this connexion, with a kind of poetry of scholasticism which may interest the student of *Paradise Lost*, into what we may call the intellectual and moral by-play of the situation of the first man and woman in Paradise, with strange queries about it. Did Adam, for instance, already know of the fall of the Angels? Did he really believe in death, till Abel died? It is from Julius Scaliger that he takes his motto, to the effect that the true knowledge of things must be had from things themselves, not from books; and he seems as seriously concerned as Bacon to dissipate the crude impressions of a false "common sense," of false science, and a fictitious authority. Inverting, oddly, Plato's theory that all learning is but reminiscence, he reflects with a sigh how much of oblivion must needs be involved in the getting of any true knowledge. "Men that adore times past, consider not that those times were once present (that is, as our own are) and ourselves unto those to come, as they unto us at present." That, surely, coming from one both by temperament and habit so great an antiquary, has the touch of something like an influence in the atmosphere of the time. That there was any actual connexion between Browne's work and Bacon's is but a surmise. Yet we almost seem to hear Bacon when Browne discourses on the "use of doubts, and the advantages which might be derived from drawing up a calendar of doubts, falsehoods, and popular errors;" and, as from Bacon, one gets the impression that men really have been very much the prisoners of their own crude or pedantic terms, notions, associations; that they have been very indolent in testing very simple matters—with a wonderful kind of "supinity," as he calls it. In Browne's chapter on the "Sources of Error," again, we may trace much resemblance to Bacon's striking doctrine of the *Idola*, the "shams" men fall down and worship. Taking source respectively, from the "common infirmity of human nature," from the "erroneous disposition of the people," from "confident adherence to authority," the errors which Browne chooses to deal with may be registered as identical with Bacon's *Idola Tribus, Fori, Theatri*; the idols of our common human nature; of the vulgar, when they get together; and of the learned, when they get together.

But of the fourth species of error noted by Bacon, the *Idola Specus*, the Idols of the Cave, that whole tribe of illusions, which are "bred amongst the weeds and tares of one's own brain," Browne tells us nothing by way of criticism; was himself, rather, a lively example of their operation. Throw those illusions, those "idols," into concrete or personal form, suppose them introduced among the other forces of an active intellect, and you have Sir Thomas Browne himself. The sceptical inquirer who rises from his cathartic, his purging of error, a believer in the supernatural character of pagan oracles, and a cruel judge of supposed witches, must still need as much as ever that elementary conception of the right method and the just limitations of knowledge, by power of which he should not just strain out a single error here or there, but make a final precipitate of fallacy.

And yet if the temperament had been deducted from Browne's work—that inherent and strongly marked way of deciding things, which has guided with so surprising effect the musings of the *Letter to a Friend*, and the *Urn-Burial*—we should probably have remembered him little. Pity! some may think, for himself at least, that he had not lived earlier, and still believed in the mandrake, for instance; its fondness for places of execution, and its human cries "on eradication, with hazard of life to them that pull it up." "In philosophy," he observes, meaning to contrast his free-thinking in that department with his orthodoxy in religion—in philosophy, "where truth seems double-faced, there is no man more paradoxical than myself:" which is true, we may think, in a further sense than he meant, and that it was the "paradoxical" that he actually preferred. Happy, at all events, he still remained—

undisturbed and happy—in a hundred native prepossessions, some certainly valueless, some of them perhaps invaluable. And while one feels that no real logic of fallacies has been achieved by him, one feels still more how little the construction of that branch of logical inquiry really helps men's minds; fallacy, like truth itself, being a matter so dependent on innate gift of apprehension, so extra-logical and personal; the original perception counting for almost everything, the mere inference for so little! Yes! "A man may be in as just possession of truth as of a city, and yet be forced to surrender," even in controversies not necessarily maladroit.

The really stirring poetry of science is not in guesses, or facile divinations about it, but in its larger ascertained truths—the order of infinite space, the slow method and vast results of infinite time. For Browne, however, the sense of poetry which so overmasters his scientific procedure, depends chiefly on its vaguer possibilities; the empirical philosophy, even after Bacon, being still dominated by a temper, resultant from the general unsettlement of men's minds at the Reformation, which may be summed up in the famous question of Montaigne—*Que sçais-je?* The cold-blooded method of observation and experiment was creeping but slowly over the domain of science; and such unreclaimed portions of it as the phenomena of magnetism had an immense fascination for men like Browne and Digby. Here, in those parts of natural philosophy "but yet in discovery," "the America and untravelled parts of truth," lay for them the true prospect of science, like the new world itself to a geographical discoverer such as Raleigh. And welcome as one of the minute hints of that country far ahead of them, the strange bird, or floating fragment of unfamiliar vegetation, which met those early navigators, there was a certain fantastic experiment, in which, as was alleged, Paracelsus had been lucky. For Browne and others it became the crucial type of the kind of agency in nature which, as they conceived, it was the proper function of science to reveal in larger operation. "The subject of my last letter," says Dr. Henry Power, then a student, writing to Browne in 1648, the last year of Charles the First, "being so high and noble a piece of chemistry, invites me once more to request an experimental eviction of it from yourself; and I hope you will not chide my importunity in this petition, or be angry at my so frequent knockings at your door to obtain a grant of so great and admirable a mystery." What the enthusiastic young student expected from Browne, so high and noble a piece of chemistry, was the "re-individualling of an incinerated plant"—a violet, turning to freshness, and smelling sweet again, out of its ashes, under some genially fitted conditions of the chemic art.

Palingenesis, resurrection, effected by orderly prescription— the "re-individualling" of an "incinerated organism"—is a subject which affords us a natural transition to the little book of the *Hydriotaphia*, or *Treatise of Urn-Burial*—about fifty or sixty pages—which, together with a very singular letter not printed till after Browne's death, is perhaps, after all, the best justification of Browne's literary reputation, as it were his own curiously figured urn, and treasure-place of immortal memory.

In its first presentation to the public this letter was connected with Browne's *Christian Morals*; but its proper and sympathetic collocation would be rather with the *Urn-Burial*, of which it is a kind of prelude, or strikes the keynote. He is writing in a very complex situation—to a friend, upon occasion of the death of a common friend. The deceased apparently had been little known to Browne himself till his recent visits, while the intimate friend to whom he is writing had been absent at the time; and the leading motive of Browne's letter is the deep impression he has received during those visits, of a sort of physical beauty in the coming of death, with which he still surprises and moves his reader. There had been, in this case, a tardiness and reluctancy in the circumstances of dissolution, which had permitted him, in the character of a physician, as it were to assist at the spiritualising of the bodily frame by natural process; a wonderful new type of a kind of mortified grace being evolved by the way. The spiritual body had anticipated the formal moment of death; the alert soul, in that tardy decay, changing its vesture gradually, and as if piece by piece. The infinite future had invaded this life perceptibly to the senses, like the ocean felt far inland up a tidal river. Nowhere, perhaps, is the attitude of questioning awe on the threshold of another life displayed with the expressiveness of this unique morsel of literature; though there is something of the same kind, in another than the literary medium, in the delicate monu-

mental sculpture of the early Tuscan School, as also in many of
the designs of William Blake, often, though unconsciously, much
in sympathy with those unsophisticated Italian workmen. With
him, as with them, and with the writer of the *Letter to a Friend
upon the occasion of the death of his intimate Friend,*—so
strangely! the visible function of death is but to refine, to detach
from aught that is vulgar. And this elfin letter, really an impromptu epistle to a friend, affords the best possible light on the
general temper of the man who could be moved by the accidental
discovery of those old urns at Walsingham—funeral relics of
"Romans, or Britons Romanised which had learned Roman
customs"—to the composition of that wonderful book the
Hydriotaphia. He had drawn up a short account of the circumstance at the moment; but it was after ten years' brooding that he
put forth the finished treatise, dedicated to an eminent collector
of ancient coins and other rarities, with congratulations that he
"can daily command the view of so many imperial faces," and (by
way of frontispiece) with one of the urns, "drawn with a coal
taken out of it and found among the burnt bones." The discovery
had resuscitated for him a whole world of latent observation,
from life, from out-of-the-way reading, from the natural world,
and fused into a composition, which with all its quaintness we
may well pronounce classical, all the heterogeneous elements of
that singular mind. The desire to "record these risen ashes and not
to let them be buried twice among us," had set free, in his manner
of conceiving things, something not wholly analysable, something that may be properly called genius, which shapes his use of
common words to stronger and deeper senses, in a way unusual in
prose writing. Let the reader, for instance, trace his peculiarly
sensitive use of the epithets *thin* and *dark,* both here and in the
Letter to a Friend.

Upon what a grand note he can begin and end chapter or paragraph!—"When the funeral pyre was out, and the last valediction
over:"—"And a large part of the earth is still in the urn unto us."
Dealing with a very vague range of feelings, it is his skill to associate them to very definite objects. Like the Soul, in Blake's design,
"exploring the recesses of the tomb," he carries a light, the light
of the poetic faith which he cannot put off him, into those dark

places, "the abode of worms and pismires," peering round with a
boundless curiosity and no fear; noting the various casuistical
considerations of men's last form of self-love; all those whims of
humanity as a "student of perpetuity," the mortuary customs of
all nations, which, from their very closeness to our human nature, arouse in most minds only a strong feeling of distaste. There
is something congruous with the impassive piety of the man in his
waiting on accident from without to take start for the work,
which, of all his work, is most truly touched by the "divine
spark." Delightsome as its eloquence is actually found to be, that
eloquence is attained out of a certain difficulty and halting crab-
bedness of expression; the wretched punctuation of the piece being not the only cause of its impressing the reader with the notion that he is but dealing with a collection of notes for a more
finished composition, and of a different kind; perhaps a purely
erudite treatise on its subject, with detachment of all personal
colour now adhering to it. Out of an atmosphere of all-pervading
oddity and quaintness—the quaintness of mind which reflects
that this disclosing of the urns of the ancients hath "left unto our
view some parts which they never beheld themselves"—arises a
work really ample and grand, nay! classical, as I said, by virtue of
the effectiveness with which it fixes a type in literature; as, indeed, at its best, romantic literature (and Browne is genuinely
romantic) in every period attains classical quality, giving true
measure of the very limited value of those well-worn critical distinctions. And though the *Urn-Burial* certainly has much of the
character of a poem, yet one is never allowed to forget that it was
designed, candidly, as a scientific treatise on one department of
ancient "culture" (as much so as Guichard's curious old French
book on *Divers Manners of Burial*) and was the fruit of much
labour, in the way especially of industrious selection from remote
and difficult writers; there being then few or no handbooks, or
anything like our modern shortcuts to varied knowledge. Quite
unaffectedly, a curious learning saturates, with a kind of grey and
aged colour most apt and congruous with the subject-matter, all
the thoughts that arise in him. His great store of reading, so freely
displayed, he uses almost as poetically as Milton; like him, profit-
ing often by the mere sonorous effect of some heroic or ancient

name, which he can adapt to that same sort of learned sweetness of cadence with which so many of his single sentences are made to fall upon the ear.

Pope Gregory, that great religious poet, requested by certain eminent persons to send them some of those relics he sought for so devoutly in all the lurking-places of old Rome, took up, it is said, a portion of common earth, and delivered it to the messengers; and, on their expressing surprise at such a gift, pressed the earth together in his hand, whereupon the sacred blood of the Martyrs was beheld flowing out between his fingers. The veneration of relics became a part of Christian (as some may think it a part of natural) religion. All over Rome we may count how much devotion in fine art is owing to it; and, through all ugliness or superstition, its intention still speaks clearly to serious minds. The poor dead bones, ghastly and forbidding:—we know what Shakespeare would have felt about them.—"Beat not the bones of the buried: when he breathed, he was a man!" And it is with something of a similar feeling that Browne is full, on the common and general ground of humanity; an awe-stricken sympathy with those, whose bones "lie at the mercies of the living," strong enough to unite all his various chords of feeling into a single strain of impressive and genuine poetry. His real interest is in what may be called the curiosities of our common humanity. As another might be moved at the sight of Alexander's bones, or Saint Edmund's, or Saint Cecilia's, so he is full of a fine poetical excitement at such lowly relics as the earth hides almost everywhere beneath our feet. But it is hardly fair to take our leave amid these grievous images of so happy a writer as Sir Thomas Browne; so great a lover of the open air, under which much of his life was passed. His work, late one night, draws to a natural close:—"To keep our eyes open longer," he bethinks himself suddenly, "were but to act our Antipodes. The huntsmen are up in America!"

What a fund of open-air cheerfulness, there! in turning to sleep. Still, even when we are dealing with a writer in whom mere style counts for so much as with Browne, it is impossible to ignore his matter; and it is with religion he is really occupied from first to last, hardly less than Richard Hooker. And his religion, too, after all, was a religion of cheerfulness: he has no great consciousness of evil in things, and is no fighter. His religion, if one may say so, was all profit to him; among other ways, in securing an absolute staidness and placidity of temper, for the intellectual work which was the proper business of his life. His contributions to "evidence," in the *Religio Medici*, for instance, hardly tell, because he writes out of view of a really philosophical criticism. What does tell in him, in this direction, is the witness he brings to men's instinct of survival—the "intimations of immortality," as Wordsworth terms them, which were natural with him in surprising force. As we said of Jean Paul, his special subject was the immortality of the soul; with an assurance as personal, as fresh and original, as it was, on the one hand, in those old half-civilised people who had deposited the urns; on the other hand, in the cynical French poet of the nineteenth century, who did not think, but knew, that *his* soul was imperishable. He lived in an age in which that philosophy made a great stride which ends with Hume; and his lesson, if we may be pardoned for taking away a "lesson" from so ethical a writer, is the force of men's temperaments in the management of opinion, their own or that of others;—that it is not merely different degrees of bare intellectual power which cause men to approach in different degrees to this or that intellectual programme. Could he have foreseen the mature result of that mechanical analysis which Bacon had applied to nature, and Hobbes to the mind of man, there is no reason to think that he would have surrendered his own chosen hypothesis concerning them. He represents, in an age, the intellectual powers of which tend strongly to agnosticism, that class of minds to which the supernatural view of things is still credible. The non-mechanical theory of nature has had its grave adherents since: to the non-mechanical theory of man—that he is in contact with a moral order on a different plane from the mechanical order— thousands, of the most various types and degrees of intellectual power, always adhere; a fact worth the consideration of all ingenuous thinkers, if (as is certainly the case with colour, music, number, for instance) there may be whole regions of fact, the recognition of which belongs to one and not to another, which people may possess in various degrees; for the knowledge of which, therefore, one person is dependent upon another; and in relation to which the appropriate means of cognition must lie among the elements of what we call individual temperament, so that what looks like a pre-judgment may be really a legitimate apprehension. "Men are what they are," and are not wholly at the mercy of formal conclusions from their formally limited premises. Browne passes his whole life in observation and inquiry: he is a genuine investigator, with every opportunity: the mind of the age all around him seems passively yielding to an almost foregone intellectual result, to a philosophy of disillusion. But he thinks all that a prejudice; and not from any want of intellectual power certainly, but from some inward consideration, some after-thought, from the antecedent gravitation of his own general character—or, will you say? from that unprecipitated infusion of fallacy in him—he fails to draw, unlike almost all the rest of the world, the conclusion ready to hand.

1886.

"Love's Labours Lost"

Love's Labours Lost is one of the earliest of Shakespeare's dramas, and has many of the peculiarities of his poems, which are also the work of his earlier life. The opening speech of the king on the immortality of fame—on the triumph of fame over death—and the nobler parts of Biron, display something of the monumental style of Shakespeare's Sonnets, and are not without their conceits of thought and expression. This connexion of *Love's Labours Lost* with Shakespeare's poems is further enforced by the actual insertion in it of three sonnets and a faultless song; which, in accordance with his practice in other plays, are inwoven into the argument of the piece and, like the golden ornaments of a fair woman, give it a peculiar air of distinction. There is merriment in it also, with choice illustrations of both wit and humour; a laughter, often exquisite, ringing, if faintly, yet as genuine laughter still, though sometimes sinking into mere burlesque, which has not lasted quite so well. And Shakespeare brings a serious effect out of the trifling of his characters. A dainty love-making is interchanged with the more cumbrous play: below the many artifices of Biron's amorous speeches we may trace sometimes the "unutterable longing;" and the lines in which Katherine describes the blighting through love of her younger sister are one of the most touching things in older literature.[1] Again, how many echoes seem awakened by those strange words, actually said in jest!—"The sweet war-man (Hector of Troy) is dead and rotten; sweet chucks, beat not the bones of the buried: when he breathed, he was a man!"—words which may remind us of Shakespeare's own

[1] Act V. Scene II.

epitaph. In the last scene, an ingenious turn is given to the action, so that the piece does not conclude after the manner of other
comedies.—

> Our wooing doth not end like an old play;
> Jack hath not Jill:

and Shakespeare strikes a passionate note across it at last, in the
entrance of the messenger, who announces to the princess that
the king her father is suddenly dead.

The merely dramatic interest of the piece is slight enough; only
just sufficient, indeed, to form the vehicle of its wit and poetry.
The scene—a park of the King of Navarre—is unaltered throughout; and the unity of the play is not so much the unity of a drama
as that of a series of pictorial groups, in which the same figures
reappear, in different combinations but on the same background.
It is as if Shakespeare had intended to bind together, by some
inventive conceit, the devices of an ancient tapestry, and give
voices to its figures. On one side, a fair palace; on the other, the
tents of the Princess of France, who has come on an embassy from
her father to the King of Navarre; in the midst, a wide space of
smooth grass. The same personages are combined over and over
again into a series of gallant scenes—the princess, the three
masked ladies, the quaint, pedantic king; one of those amiable
kings men have never loved enough, whose serious occupation
with the things of the mind seems, by contrast with the more
usual forms of kingship, like frivolity or play. Some of the figures
are grotesque merely, and all the male ones at least, a little fantastic. Certain objects reappearing from scene to scene—love-
letters crammed with verses to the margin, and lovers' toys—hint
obscurely at some story of intrigue. Between these groups, on a
smaller scale, come the slighter and more homely episodes, with
Sir Nathaniel the curate, the country-maid Jaquenetta, Moth or
Mote the elfin-page, with Hiems and Ver, who recite "the dialogue that the two learned men have compiled in praise of the owl
and the cuckoo." The ladies are lodged in tents, because the king,
like the princess of the modern poet's fancy, has taken a vow

> To make his court a little Academe,

and for three years' space no woman may come within a mile of it; and the play shows how this artificial attempt was broken through. For the king and his three fellow-scholars are of course soon forsworn, and turn to writing sonnets, each to his chosen lady. These fellow-scholars of the king—"quaint votaries of science" at first, afterwards "affection's men-at-arms"—three youthful knights, gallant, amorous, chivalrous, but also a little affected, sporting always a curious foppery of language, are, throughout, the leading figures in the foreground; one of them, in particular, being more carefully depicted than the others, and in himself very noticeable—a portrait with somewhat puzzling manner and expression, which at once catches the eye irresistibly and keeps it fixed.

Play is often that about which people are most serious; and the humourist may observe how, under all love of playthings, there is almost always hidden an appreciation of something really engaging and delightful. This is true always of the toys of children: it is often true of the playthings of grown-up people, their vanities, their fopperies even, their lighter loves; the cynic would add their pursuit of fame. Certainly, this is true without exception of the playthings of a past age, which to those who succeed it are always full of a pensive interest—old manners, old dresses, old houses. For what is called fashion in these matters occupies, in each age, much of the care of many of the most discerning people, furnishing them with a kind of mirror of their real inward refinements, and their capacity for selection. Such modes or fashions are, at their best, an example of the artistic predominance of form over matter; of the manner of the doing of it over the thing done; and have a beauty of their own. It is so with that old euphuism of the Elizabethan age—that pride of dainty language and curious expression, which it is very easy to ridicule, which often made itself ridiculous, but which had below it a real sense of fitness and nicety; and which, as we see in this very play, and still more clearly in the Sonnets, had some fascination for the young Shakespeare himself. It is this foppery of delicate language, this fashionable plaything of his time, with which Shakespeare is occupied in Love's Labours Lost. He shows us the manner in all its stages; passing from the grotesque and vulgar pedantry of Holofernes, through the extravagant but polished caricature of Armado, to become the peculiar characteristic of a real though still quaint poetry in Biron himself, who is still chargeable even at his best with just a little affectation. As Shakespeare laughs broadly at it in Holofernes or Armado, so he is the analyst of its curious charm in Biron; and this analysis involves a delicate raillery by Shakespeare himself at his own chosen manner.

This "foppery" of Shakespeare's day had, then, its really delightful side, a quality in no sense "affected," by which it satisfies a real instinct in our minds—the fancy so many of us have for an exquisite and curious skill in the use of words. Biron is the perfect flower of this manner:

> A man of fire-new words, fashion's own knight:

—as he describes Armado, in terms which are really applicable to himself. In him this manner blends with a true gallantry of nature, and an affectionate complaisance and grace. He has at times some of its extravagance or caricature also, but the shades of expression by which he passes from this to the "golden cadence" of Shakespeare's own most characteristic verse, are so fine, that it is sometimes difficult to trace them. What is a vulgarity in Holofernes, and a caricature in Armado, refines itself with him into the expression of a nature truly and inwardly bent upon a form of delicate perfection, and is accompanied by a real insight into the laws which determine what is exquisite in language, and their root in the nature of things. He can appreciate quite the opposite style—

> In russet yeas, and honest kersey noes;

he knows the first law of pathos, that

> Honest plain words best suit the ear of grief.

He delights in his own rapidity of intuition; and, in harmony with the half-sensuous philosophy of the Sonnets, exalts, a little scornfully, in many memorable expressions, the judgment of the senses, above all slower, more toilsome means of knowledge, scorning some who fail to see things only because they are so clear:

> So ere you find where light in darkness lies,
> Your light grows dark by losing of your eyes:—

as with some German commentators on Shakespeare. Appealing always to actual sensation from men's affected theories, he might seem to despise learning; as, indeed, he has taken up his deep studies partly in sport, and demands always the profit of learning in renewed enjoyment. Yet he surprises us from time to time by intuitions which could come only from a deep experience and power of observation; and men listen to him, old and young, in spite of themselves. He is quickly impressible to the slightest clouding of the spirits in social intercourse, and has his moments of extreme seriousness: his trial-task may well be, as Rosaline puts it—

> To enforce the pained impotent to smile.

But still, through all, he is true to his chosen manner: that gloss of dainty language is a second nature with him: even at his best he is not without a certain artifice: the trick of playing on words never deserts him; and Shakespeare, in whose own genius there is an element of this very quality, shows us in this graceful, and, as it seems, studied, portrait, his enjoyment of it.

As happens with every true dramatist, Shakespeare is for the most part hidden behind the persons of his creation. Yet there are certain of his characters in which we feel that there is something of self-portraiture. And it is not so much in his grander, more subtle and ingenious creations that we feel this—in *Hamlet* and *King Lear*—as in those slighter and more spontaneously developed figures, who, while far from playing principal parts, are yet distinguished by a peculiar happiness and delicate ease in the drawing of them; figures which possess, above all, that winning attractiveness which there is no man but would willingly exercise, and which resemble those works of art which, though not meant to be very great or imposing, are yet wrought of the choicest material. Mercutio, in *Romeo and Juliet*, belongs to this group of Shakespeare's characters—versatile, mercurial people, such as make good actors, and in whom the

Nimble spirits of the arteries,

the finer but still merely animal elements of great wit, predominate. A careful delineation of minor, yet expressive traits seems to mark them out as the characters of his predilection; and it is hard not to identify him with these more than with others. Biron, in *Love's Labours Lost*, is perhaps the most striking member of this group. In this character, which is never quite in touch, never quite on a perfect level of understanding, with the other persons of the play, we see, perhaps, a reflex of Shakespeare himself, when he has just become able to stand aside from and estimate the first period of his poetry.

1878.

"Measure for Measure"

In *Measure for Measure*, as in some other of his plays, Shakespeare has remodelled an earlier and somewhat rough composition to "finer issues," suffering much to remain as it had
come from the less skilful hand, and not raising the whole of his
work to an equal degree of intensity. Hence perhaps some of that
depth and weightiness which make this play so impressive, as
with the true seal of experience, like a fragment of life itself,
rough and disjointed indeed, but forced to yield in places its profounder meaning. In *Measure for Measure*, in contrast with the
flawless execution of *Romeo and Juliet*, Shakespeare has spent his
art in just enough modification of the scheme of the older play to
make it exponent of this purpose, adapting its terrible essential
incidents, so that Coleridge found it the only painful work among
Shakespeare's dramas, and leaving for the reader of to-day more
than the usual number of difficult expressions; but infusing a
lavish colour and a profound significance into it, so that under his
touch certain select portions of it rise far above the level of all but
his own best poetry, and working out of it a morality so characteristic that the play might well pass for the central expression of his
moral judgments. It remains a comedy, as indeed is congruous
with the bland, half-humorous equity which informs the whole
composition, sinking from the heights of sorrow and terror into
the rough scheme of the earlier piece; yet it is hardly less full of
what is really tragic in man's existence than if Claudio had indeed "stooped to death." Even the humorous concluding scenes
have traits of special grace, retaining in less emphatic passages a
stray line or word of power, as it seems, so that we watch to the
end for the traces where the nobler hand has glanced along, leav-

ing its vestiges, as if accidentally or wastefully, in the rising of the style.

The interest of *Measure for Measure*, therefore, is partly that of an old story told over again. We measure with curiosity that variety of resources which has enabled Shakespeare to refashion the original material with a higher motive; adding to the intricacy of the piece, yet so modifying its structure as to give the whole almost the unity of a single scene; lending, by the light of a philosophy which dwells much on what is complex and subtle in our nature, a true human propriety to its strange and unexpected turns of feeling and character, to incidents so difficult as the fall of Angelo, and the subsequent reconciliation of Isabella, so that she pleads successfully for his life. It was from Whetstone, a contemporary English writer, that Shakespeare derived the outline of Cinthio's "rare history" of *Promos and Cassandra*, one of that numerous class of Italian stories, like Boccaccio's *Tancred of Salerno*, in which the mere energy of southern passion has everything its own way, and which, though they may repel many a northern reader by a certain crudity in their colouring, seem to have been full of fascination for the Elizabethan age. This story, as it appears in Whetstone's endless comedy, is almost as rough as the roughest episode of actual criminal life. But the play seems never to have been acted, and some time after its publication Whetstone himself turned the thing into a tale, included in his *Heptameron of Civil Discourses*, where it still figures as a genuine piece, with touches of undesigned poetry, a quaint field-flower here and there of diction or sentiment, the whole strung up to an effective brevity, and with the fragrance of that admirable age of literature all about it. Here, then, there is something of the original Italian colour: in this narrative Shakespeare may well have caught the first glimpse of a composition with nobler proportions; and some artless sketch from his own hand, perhaps, putting together his first impressions, insinuated itself between Whetstone's work and the play as we actually read it. Out of these insignificant sources Shakespeare's play rises, full of solemn expression, and with a profoundly designed beauty, the new body of a higher, though sometimes remote and difficult poetry, escaping from the imperfect relics of the old story, yet not wholly transformed, and even as it stands but the preparation only, we might think, of a still more imposing design. For once we have in it a real example of that sort of writing which is sometimes described as *suggestive*, and which by the help of certain subtly calculated hints only, brings into distinct shape the reader's own half-developed imaginings. Often the quality is attributed to writing merely vague and unrealised, but in *Measure for Measure*, quite certainly, Shakespeare has directed the attention of sympathetic readers along certain channels of meditation beyond the immediate scope of his work.

Measure for Measure, therefore, by the quality of these higher designs, woven by his strange magic on a texture of poorer quality, is hardly less indicative than *Hamlet* even, of Shakespeare's reason, of his power of moral interpretation. It deals, not like *Hamlet* with the problems which beset one of exceptional temperament, but with mere human nature. It brings before us a group of persons, attractive, full of desire, vessels of the genial, seed-bearing powers of nature, a gaudy existence flowering out over the old court and city of Vienna, a spectacle of the fulness and pride of life which to some may seem to touch the verge of wantonness. Behind this group of people, behind their various action, Shakespeare inspires in us the sense of a strong tyranny of nature and circumstance. Then what shall there be on this side of it—on our side, the spectators' side, of this painted screen, with its puppets who are really glad or sorry all the time? what philosophy of life, what sort of equity?

Stimulated to read more carefully by Shakespeare's own profounder touches, the reader will note the vivid reality, the subtle interchange of light and shade, the strongly contrasted characters of this group of persons, passing across the stage so quickly. The slightest of them is at least not ill-natured: the meanest of them can put forth a plea for existence—*Truly, sir, I am a poor fellow that would live!*—they are never sure of themselves, even in the strong tower of a cold unimpressible nature: they are capable of many friendships and of a true dignity in danger, giving each other a sympathetic, if transitory, regret—one sorry that another "should be foolishly lost at a game of tick-tack." Words which seem to exhaust man's deepest sentiment concerning death and

life are put on the lips of a gilded, witless youth; and the saintly
Isabella feels fire creep along her, kindling her tongue to eloquence at the suggestion of shame. In places the shadow deepens:
death intrudes itself on the scene, as among other things "a great
disguiser," blanching the features of youth and spoiling its goodly
hair, touching the fine Claudio even with its disgraceful associations. As in Orcagna's fresco at Pisa, it comes capriciously, giving
many and long reprieves to Barnardine, who has been waiting for
it nine years in prison, taking another thence by fever, another by
mistake of judgment, embracing others in the midst of their music
and song. The little mirror of existence, which reflects to each for
a moment the stage on which he plays, is broken at last by a
capricious accident; while all alike, in their yearning for untasted enjoyment, are really discounting their days, grasping so
hastily and accepting so inexactly the precious pieces. The
Duke's quaint but excellent moralising at the beginning of the
third act does but express, like the chorus of a Greek play, the
spirit of the passing incidents. To him in Shakespeare's play, to a
few here and there in the actual world, this strange practical
paradox of our life, so unwise in its eager haste, reveals itself in
all its clearness.

The Duke disguised as a friar, with his curious moralising on
life and death, and Isabella in her first mood of renunciation, a
thing "ensky'd and sainted," come with the quiet of the cloister as
a relief to this lust and pride of life: like some grey monastic
picture hung on the wall of a gaudy room, their presence cools the
heated air of the piece. For a moment we are within the placid
conventual walls, whither they fancy at first that the Duke has
come as a man crossed in love, with Friar Thomas and Friar Peter,
calling each other by their homely, English names, or at the nun-
nery among the novices, with their little limited privileges,
where

> If you speak you must not show your face,
> Or if you show your face you must not speak.

Not less precious for this relief in the general structure of the
piece, than for its own peculiar graces is the episode of Mariana, a

creature wholly of Shakespeare's invention, told, by way of interlude, in subdued prose. The moated grange, with its dejected mistress, its long, listless, discontented days, where we hear only the voice of a boy broken off suddenly in the midst of one of the loveliest songs of Shakespeare, or of Shakespeare's school,[1] is the pleasantest of many glimpses we get here of pleasant places—the field without the town, Angelo's garden-house, the consecrated fountain. Indirectly it has suggested two of the most perfect compositions among the poetry of our own generation. Again it is a picture within a picture, but with fainter lines and a greyer atmosphere: we have here the same passions, the same wrongs, the same continuance of affection, the same crying out upon death, as in the nearer and larger piece, though softened, and reduced to the mood of a more dreamy scene.

Of Angelo we may feel at first sight inclined to say only *guarda e passa!* or to ask whether he is indeed psychologically possible. In the old story, he figures as an embodiment of pure and unmodified evil, like "Hyliogabalus of Rome or Denis of Sicyll." But the embodiment of pure evil is no proper subject of art, and Shakespeare, in the spirit of a philosophy which dwells much on the complications of outward circumstance with men's inclinations, turns into a subtle study in casuistry this incident of the austere judge fallen suddenly into utmost corruption by a momentary contact with supreme purity. But the main interest in *Measure for Measure* is not, as in *Promos and Cassandra*, in the relation of Isabella and Angelo, but rather in the relation of Claudio and Isabella.

Greek tragedy in some of its noblest products has taken for its theme the love of a sister, a sentiment unimpassioned indeed, purifying by the very spectacle of its passionlessness, but capable of a fierce and almost animal strength if informed for a moment by pity and regret. At first Isabella comes upon the scene as a tranquillising influence in it. But Shakespeare, in the development of the action, brings quite different and unexpected qualities out of her. It is his characteristic poetry to expose this cold, chastened personality, respected even by the worldly Lucio as "something ensky'd and sainted, and almost an immortal

[1]Fletcher, in the *Bloody Brother*, gives the rest of it.

spirit," to two sharp, shameful trials, and wring out of her a fiery, revealing eloquence. Thrown into the terrible dilemma of the piece, called upon to sacrifice that cloistral whiteness to sisterly affection, become in a moment the ground of strong, contending passions, she develops a new character and shows herself suddenly of kindred with those strangely conceived women, like Webster's Vittoria, who unite to a seductive sweetness something of a dangerous and tigerlike changefulness of feeling. The swift, vindictive anger leaps, like a white flame, into this white spirit, and, stripped in a moment of all convention, she stands before us clear, detached, columnar, among the tender frailties of the piece. Cassandra, the original of Isabella in Whetstone's tale, with the purpose of the Roman Lucretia in her mind, yields gracefully enough to the conditions of her brother's safety; and to the lighter reader of Shakespeare there may seem something harshly conceived, or psychologically impossible even, in the suddenness of the change wrought in her, as Claudio welcomes for a moment the chance of life through her compliance with Angelo's will, and he may have a sense here of flagging skill, as in words less finely handled than in the preceding scene. They play, though still not without traces of nobler handiwork, sinks down, as we know, at last into almost homely comedy, and it might be supposed that just here the grander manner deserted it. But the skill with which Isabella plays upon Claudio's well-recognised sense of honour, and endeavours by means of that to insure him beforehand from the acceptance of life on baser terms, indicates no coming laxity of hand just in this place. It was rather that there rose in Shakespeare's conception, as there may for the reader, as there certainly would in any good acting of the part, something of that terror, the seeking for which is one of the notes of romanticism in Shakespeare and his circle. The stream of ardent natural affection, poured as sudden hatred upon the youth condemned to die, adds an additional note of expression to the horror of the prison where so much of the scene takes place. It is not here only that Shakespeare has conceived of such extreme anger and pity as putting a sort of genius into simple women, so that their "lips drop eloquence," and their intuitions interpret that which is often too hard or fine for manlier reason; and it is Isabella with her grand imaginative diction, and that poetry laid upon the "prone and speechless dialect" there is mere youth itself, who gives utterance to the equity, the finer judgments of the piece on men and things.

From behind this group with its subtle lights and shades, its poetry, its impressive contrasts, Shakespeare, as I said, conveys to us a strong sense of the tyranny of nature and circumstance over human action. The most powerful expressions of this side of experience might be found here. The bloodless, impassible temperament does but wait for its opportunity, for the almost accidental coherence of time with place, and place with wishing, to annul its long and patient discipline, and become in a moment the very opposite of that which under ordinary conditions it seemed to be, even to itself. The mere resolute self-assertion of the blood brings to others special temptations, temptations which, as defects or over-growths, lie in the very qualities which make them otherwise imposing or attractive; the very advantage of men's gifts of intellect or sentiment being dependent on a balance in their use so delicate that men hardly maintain it always. Something also must be conceded to influences merely physical, to the complexion of the heavens, the skyey influences, shifting as the stars shift; as something also to the mere caprice of men exercised over each other in the dispensations of social or political order, to the chance which makes the life or death of Claudio dependent on Angelo's will.

The many veins of thought which render the poetry of this play so weighty and impressive unite in the image of Claudio, a flowerlike young man, whom, prompted by a few hints from Shakespeare, the imagination easily clothes with all the bravery of youth, as he crosses the stage before us on his way to death, coming so hastily to the end of his pilgrimage. Set in the horrible blackness of the prison, with its various forms of unsightly death, this flower seems the braver. Fallen by "prompture of the blood," the victim of a suddenly revived law against the common fault of youth like his, he finds his life forfeited as if by the chance of a lottery. With that instinctive clinging to life, which breaks through the subtlest casuistries of monk or sage apologising for an early death, he welcomes for a moment the chance of life through his sister's shame, though he revolts hardly less from the notion of perpetual imprisonment so repulsive to the buoyant energy of youth. Familiarised, by the words alike of friends and the indifferent, to the thought of death, he becomes gentle and subdued indeed, yet more perhaps through pride than real resignation, and would go down to darkness at last hard and unblinded. Called upon suddenly to encounter his fate, looking with keen and resolute profile straight before him, he gives utterance to some of the central truths of human feeling, the sincere, concentrated expression of the recoiling flesh. Thoughts as profound and poetical as Hamlet's arise in him; and but for the accidental arrest of sentence he would descend into the dust, a mere gilded, idle flower of youth indeed, but with what are perhaps the most eloquent of all Shakespeare's words upon his lips.

As Shakespeare in *Measure for Measure* has refashioned, after a nobler pattern, materials already at hand, so that the relics of other men's poetry are incorporated into his perfect work, so traces of the old "morality," that early form of dramatic composition which had for its function the inculcating of some moral theme, survive in it also, and give it a peculiar ethical interest. This ethical interest, though it can escape no attentive reader, yet, in accordance with that artistic law which demands the predominance of form everywhere over the mere matter or subject handled, is not to be wholly separated from the special circumstances, necessities, embarrassments, of these particular dramatic persons. The old "moralities" exemplified most often some rough-and-ready lesson. Here the very intricacy and subtlety of the moral world itself, the difficulty of seizing the true relations of so complex a material, the difficulty of just judgment, of judgment that shall not be unjust, are the lessons conveyed. Even in Whetstone's old story this peculiar vein of moralising comes to the surface: even there, we notice the tendency to dwell on mixed motives, the contending issues of action, the presence of virtues and vices alike in unexpected places, on "the hard choice of two evils," on the "imprisoning" of men's "real intents." *Measure for Measure* is full of expressions drawn from a profound experience of these casuistries, and that ethical interest becomes predominant in it: it is no longer *Promos and Cassandra*, but *Measure for Measure*, its new name expressly suggesting the subject of *poetical justice*. The action of the play, like the action of life itself for the keener observer, develops in us the conception of this poetical justice, and the yearning to realise it, the true justice of which Angelo knows nothing, because it lies for the most part beyond the limits of any acknowledged law. The idea of justice involves the idea of rights. But at bottom rights are equivalent to that which really is, to facts; and the recognition of his rights therefore, the justice he requires of our hands, or our thoughts, is the recognition of that which the person, in his inmost nature, really is; and as sympathy alone can discover that which really is in matters of feeling and thought, true justice is in its essence a finer knowledge through love.

> 'Tis very pregnant:
> The jewel that we find we stoop and take it,
> Because we see it; but what we do not see
> We tread upon, and never think of it.

It is for this finer justice, a justice based on a more delicate appreciation of the true conditions of men and things, a true respect of persons in our estimate of actions, that the people in *Measure for Measure* cry out as they pass before us; and as the poetry of this play is full of the peculiarities of Shakespeare's poetry, so in its ethics it is an epitome of Shakespeare's moral judgments. They are the moral judgments of an observer, of one who sits as a spectator, and knows how the threads in the design before him hold together under the surface: they are the judgments of the humourist also, who follows with a half-amused but always pitiful sympathy, the various ways of human disposition, and sees less distance than ordinary men between what are called respectively great and little things. It is not always that poetry can be the exponent of morality; but it is this aspect of morals which it represents most naturally, for this true justice is dependent on just those finer appreciations which poetry cultivates in us the power of making, those peculiar valuations of action and its effect which poetry actually requires.

1874.

Shakespeare's English Kings

A brittle glory shineth in this face:
As brittle as the glory is the face.

The English plays of Shakespeare needed but the completion of one unimportant interval to possess the unity of a popular chronicle from Richard the Second to Henry the Eighth, and possess, as they actually stand, the unity of a common motive in the handling of the various events and persons which they bring before us. Certain of his historic dramas, not English, display Shakespeare's mastery in the development of the heroic nature amid heroic circumstances; and had he chosen, from English history, to deal with Cœur-de-Lion or Edward the First, the innate quality of his subject would doubtless have called into play something of that profound and sombre power which in *Julius Cæsar* and *Macbeth* has sounded the depths of mighty character. True, on the whole, to fact, it is another side of kingship which he has made prominent in his English histories. The irony of kingship—average human nature, flung with a wonderfully pathetic effect into the vortex of great events; tragedy of everyday quality heightened in degree only by the conspicuous scene which does but make those who play their parts there conspicuously unfortunate; the utterance of common humanity straight from the heart, but refined like other common things for kingly uses by Shakespeare's unfailing eloquence: such, unconsciously for the most part, though palpably enough to the careful reader, is the conception under which Shakespeare has arranged the lights and shadows of the story of the English kings, emphasising merely the light and shadow inherent in it, and keeping very close to the original authorities, not simply in the general outline of these dramatic histories but sometimes in their very expression. Certainly the history itself, as he found it in Hall, Holinshed, and Stowe, those somewhat picturesque old chroniclers who had themselves an eye for the dramatic "effects" of human life, has much of this sentiment already about it. What he did not find there was the natural prerogative—such justification, in kingly, that is to say, in exceptional, qualities, of the exceptional position, as makes it practicable in the result. It is no *Henriade* he writes, and no history of the English people, but the sad fortunes of some English kings as conspicuous examples of the ordinary human condition. As in a children's story, all princes are in extremes. Delightful in the sunshine above the wall into which chance lifts the flower for a season, they can but plead somewhat more touchingly than others their everyday weakness in the storm. Such is the motive that gives unity to these unequal and intermittent contributions toward a slowly evolved dramatic chronicle, which it would have taken many days to rehearse; a not distant story from real life still well remembered in its general course, to which people might listen now and again, as long as they cared, finding human nature at least wherever their attention struck ground in it.

He begins with John, and allows indeed to the first of these English kings a kind of greatness, making the development of the play centre in the counteraction of his natural gifts—that something of heroic force about him—by a madness which takes the shape of reckless impiety, forced especially on men's attention by the terrible circumstances of his end, in the delineation of which Shakespeare triumphs, setting, with true poetic tact, this incident of the king's death, in all the horror of a violent one, amid a scene delicately suggestive of what is perennially peaceful and genial in the outward world. Like the sensual humours of Falstaff in another play, the presence of the bastard Faulconbridge, with his physical energy and his unmistakable family likeness—"those limbs which Sir Robert never holp to make"[1]—contributes to an almost coarse assertion of the force of nature, of the somewhat ironic preponderance of nature and circumstance over men's artificial arrangements, to the recognition of a certain potent natural aristocracy, which is far from being always identical with that more formal, heraldic one. And what is a coarse fact in the case of Faulconbridge becomes a motive of pathetic appeal in the wan and babyish Arthur. The magic with which nature models tiny and delicate children to the likeness of their rough fathers is no-where more justly expressed than in the words of King Philip.—

> Look here upon thy brother Geoffrey's face!
> These eyes, these brows were moulded out of his:
> This little abstract doth contain that large
> Which died in Geoffrey; and the hand of time
> Shall draw this brief into as huge a volume.

It was perhaps something of a boyish memory of the shocking end of his father that had distorted the piety of Henry the Third into superstitious terror. A frightened soul, himself touched with the contrary sort of religious madness, doting on all that was alien from his father's huge ferocity, on the genialities, the soft gilding, of life, on the genuine interests of art and poetry, to be credited more than any other person with the deep religious ex-pression of

> *Elinor.* Do you not read some tokens of my son (Cœur-de-Lion)
> In the large composition of this man?

Westminster Abbey, Henry the Third, picturesque though useless, but certainly touching, might have furnished Shakespeare, had he filled up this interval in his series, with precisely the kind of effect he tends towards in his English plays. But he found it com-pleter still in the person and story of Richard the Second, a figure —"that sweet lovely rose"—which haunts Shakespeare's mind, as it seems long to have haunted the minds of the English people, as the most touching of all examples of the irony of kingship.

Henry the Fourth—to look for a moment beyond our immediate subject, in pursuit of Shakespeare's thought—is presented, of course, in general outline, as an impersonation of "surviving force:" he has a certain amount of kingcraft also, a real fitness for great opportunity. But still true to his leading motive, Shake-speare, in *King Henry the Fourth*, has left the high-water mark of his poetry in the soliloquy which represents royalty longing

vainly for the toiler's sleep; while the popularity, the showy heroism, of Henry the Fifth, is used to give emphatic point to the old
earthy commonplace about "wild oats." The wealth of homely
humour in these plays, the fun coming straight home to all the
world, of Fluellen especially in his unconscious interview with
the king, the boisterous earthiness of Falstaff and his companions, contribute to the same effect. The keynote of Shakespeare's
treatment is indeed expressed by Henry the Fifth himself, the
greatest of Shakespeare's kings.—"Though I speak it to you," he
says *incognito*, under cover of night, to a common soldier on the
field, "I think the king is but a man, as I am: the violet smells to
him as it doth to me: all his senses have but human conditions;
and though his affections be higher mounted than ours yet when
they stoop they stoop with like wing." And, in truth, the really
kingly speeches which Shakespeare assigns to him, as to other
kings weak enough in all but speech, are but a kind of flowers,
worn for, and effective only as personal embellishment. They
combine to one result with the merely outward and ceremonial
ornaments of royalty, its pageantries, flaunting so naively, so
credulously, in Shakespeare, as in that old medieval time. And
then, the force of Hotspur is but transient youth, the common
heat of youth, in him. The character of Henry the Sixth again, *roi
fainéant*, with La Pucelle[1] for his counterfoil, lay in the direct
course of Shakespeare's design: he has done much to fix the sentiment of the "holy Henry." Richard the Third, touched, like John,
with an effect of real heroism, is spoiled like him by something of
criminal madness, and reaches his highest level of tragic expression when circumstances reduce him to terms of mere human
nature.—

A horse! A horse! My kingdom for a horse!

The Princes in the Tower recall to mind the lot of young Arthur:—

[1]Perhaps the one person of *genius* in these English plays.
        The spirit of deep prophecy she hath,
        Exceeding the nine Sibyls of old Rome:
        What's past and what's to come she can descry.

> I'll go with thee,
> And find the inheritance of this poor child,
> His little kingdom of a forced grave.

And when Shakespeare comes to Henry the Eighth, it is not the superficial though very English splendour of the king himself, but the really potent and ascendant nature of the butcher's son on the one hand, and Katharine's subdued reproduction of the sad fortunes of Richard the Second on the other, that define his central interest.[1]

With a prescience of the Wars of the Roses, of which his errors were the original cause, it is Richard who best exposes Shakespeare's own constant sentiment concerning war, and especially that sort of civil war which was then recent in English memories. The soul of Shakespeare, certainly, was not wanting in a sense of the magnanimity of warriors. The grandiose aspects of war, its magnificent apparelling, he records monumentally enough—the "dressing of the lists," the lion's heart, its unfaltering haste thither in all the freshness of youth and morning.—

> Not sick although I have to do with death—
> The sun doth gild our armour: Up, my Lords!—
> I saw young Harry with his beaver on,
> His cuisses on his thighs, gallantly arm'd,
> Rise from the ground like feather'd Mercury.

Only, with Shakespeare, the afterthought is immediate:—

> They come like sacrifices in their trim.

—Will it never be to-day? I will trot to-morrow a mile, and my way shall be paved with English faces.

This sentiment Richard reiterates very plaintively, in association with the delicate sweetness of the English fields, still sweet and

---

[1] Proposing in this paper to trace the leading sentiment in Shakespeare's English Plays as a sort of *popular dramatic chronicle*, I have left untouched the question how much (or, in the case of *Henry the Sixth* and *Henry the Eighth*, how little) of them may be really his: how far inferior hands have contributed to a result, true on the whole to the greater, that is to say, the Shakespearian elements in them.

fresh, like London and her other fair towns in that England of
Chaucer, for whose soil the exiled Bolingbroke is made to long so
dangerously, while Richard on his return from Ireland salutes it—

> That pale, that white-fac'd shore,—
> As a long-parted mother with her child.—
> So, weeping, smiling, greet I thee, my earth!
> And do thee favour with my royal hands.—

Then (of Bolingbroke)

> Ere the crown he looks for live in peace,
> Ten thousand bloody crowns of mothers' sons
> Shall ill become the flower of England's face;
> Change the complexion of her maid-pale peace
> To scarlet indignation, and bedew
> My pasture's grass with faithful English blood.—

> Why have they dared to march?—

asks York,

> So many miles upon her peaceful bosom,
> Frighting her pale-fac'd visages with war?—

waking, according to Richard,

> Our peace, which in our country's cradle,
> Draws the sweet infant breath of gentle sleep:—

bedrenching "with crimson tempest"

> The fresh green lap of fair king Richard's land:—

frighting "fair peace" from "our quiet confines," laying

> The summer's dust with showers of blood,
> Rained from the wounds of slaughter'd Englishmen:

bruising

> Her flowerets with the armed hoofs
> Of hostile paces.

Perhaps it is not too fanciful to note in this play a peculiar recoil from the mere instruments of warfare, the contact of the "rude ribs," the "flint bosom," of Barkloughly Castle or Pomfret or

Julius Cæsar's ill-erected tower:

the

Boisterous untun'd drums
With harsh-resounding trumpets' dreadful bray
And grating shock of wrathful iron arms.

It is as if the lax, soft beauty of the king took effect, at least by contrast, on everything beside.

One gracious prerogative, certainly, Shakespeare's English kings possess: they are a very eloquent company, and Richard is the most sweet-tongued of them all. In no other play perhaps is there such a flush of those gay, fresh, variegated flowers of speech—colour and figure, not lightly attached to, but fused into, the very phrase itself—which Shakespeare cannot help dispensing to his characters, as in this "play of the Deposing of King Richard the Second," an exquisite poet if he is nothing else, from first to last, in light and gloom alike, able to see all things poetically, to give a poetic turn to his conduct of them, and refreshing with his golden language the tritest aspects of that ironic contrast between the pretensions of a king and the actual necessities of his destiny. What a garden of words! With him, blank verse, infinitely graceful, deliberate, musical in inflexion, becomes indeed a true "verse royal," that rhyming lapse, which to the Shakespearian ear, at least in youth, came as the last touch of refinement on it, being here doubly appropriate. His eloquence blends with that fatal beauty, of which he was so frankly aware, so amiable to his friends, to his wife, of the effects of which on the people his enemies were so much afraid, on which Shakespeare himself dwells so attentively as the "royal blood" comes and goes in the face with his rapid changes of temper. As happens with sensitive natures, it attunes him to a congruous suavity of manners, by which anger itself became flattering: it blends with his merely youthful hopefulness and high spirits, his sympathetic love for gay people, things, apparel—"his cote of gold and stone, valued at thirty thousand marks," the novel Italian fashions he preferred, as also with those real amiabilities that made people forget the darker touches of his character, but never tire of the pathetic rehearsal of his fall, the meekness of which would have seemed merely abject in a less graceful performer.

Yet it is only fair to say that in the painstaking "revival" of *King Richard the Second*, by the late Charles Kean, those who were very young thirty years ago were afforded much more than Shakespeare's play could ever have been before—the very person of the king based on the stately old portrait in Westminster Abbey, "the earliest extant contemporary likeness of any English sovereign," the grace, the winning pathos, the sympathetic voice of the player, the tasteful archæology confronting vulgar modern London with a scenic reproduction, for once really agreeable, of the London of Chaucer. In the hands of Kean the play became like an exquisite performance on the violin.

The long agony of one so gaily painted by nature's self, from his "tragic abdication" till the hour in which he

> Sluiced out his innocent soul thro' streams of blood,

was for playwrights a subject ready to hand, and became early the theme of a popular drama, of which some have fancied surviving favourite fragments in the rhymed parts of Shakespeare's work.

> The king Richard of Yngland
> Was in his flowris then regnand:
> But his flowris efter sone
> Fadyt, and ware all undone:—

says the old chronicle. Strangely enough, Shakespeare supposes him an over-confident believer in that divine right of kings, of which people in Shakespeare's time were coming to hear so much; a general right, sealed to him (so Richard is made to think) as an ineradicable personal gift by the touch—stream rather, over head and breast and shoulders—of the "holy oil" of his consecration at Westminster; not, however, through some oversight, the genuine balm used at the coronation of his successor, given, according to legend, by the Blessed Virgin to Saint Thomas of Canterbury. Richard himself found that, it was said, among other forgotten treasures, at the crisis of his changing fortunes, and vainly sought reconsecration therewith—understood, wistfully, that it was reserved for his happier rival. And yet his coronation, by the pageantry, the amplitude, the learned care, of its order, so lengthy that the king, then only eleven years of age, and fasting, as a communicant at the ceremony, was carried away in a faint, fixed the type under which it has ever since continued. And nowhere is there so emphatic a reiteration as in *Richard the Second* of the sentiment which those singular rites were calculated to produce.

> Not all the water in the rough rude sea
> Can wash the balm from an anointed king,—

as supplementing another, almost supernatural, right.—"Edward's seven sons," of whom Richard's father was one,

> Were as seven phials of his sacred blood.

But this, too, in the hands of Shakespeare, becomes for him, like any other of those fantastic, ineffectual, easily discredited, personal graces, as capricious in its operation on men's wills as merely physical beauty, kindling himself to eloquence indeed, but only giving double pathos to insults which "barbarism itself" might have pitied—the dust in his face, as he returns, through the streets of London, a prisoner in the train of his victorious enemy.

> How soon my sorrow hath destroyed my face!

he cries, in that most poetic invention of the mirror scene, which does but reinforce again that physical charm which all confessed. The sense of "divine right" in kings is found to act not so much as a secret of power over others, as of infatuation to themselves. And of all those personal gifts the one which alone never altogether fails him is just that royal utterance, his appreciation of the poetry of his own hapless lot, an eloquent self-pity, infecting others in spite of themselves, till they too become irresistibly eloquent about him.

In the Roman Pontifical, of which the order of Coronation is really a part, there is no form for the inverse process, no rite of "degradation," such as that by which an offending priest or bishop may be deprived, if not of the essential quality of "orders," yet, one by one, of its outward dignities. It is as if Shakespeare had had in mind some such inverted rite, like those old ecclesiastical or military ones, by which human hardness, or human justice, adds the last touch of unkindness to the execution of its sentences, in the scene where Richard "deposes" himself, as in some long, agonising ceremony, reflectively drawn out, with an extraordinary refinement of intelligence and variety of piteous appeal, but also with a felicity of poetic invention, which puts these pages into a very select class, with the finest "vermeil and ivory" work of Chatterton or Keats.

> Fetch hither Richard that in common view
> He may surrender!—

And Richard more than concurs: he throws himself into the part, realises a type, falls gracefully as on the world's stage.—Why is he sent for?

> To do that office of thine own good will
> Which tired majesty did make thee offer.—
>
> Now mark me! how I will undo myself.

"Hath Bolingbroke deposed thine intellect?" the Queen asks him, on his way to the Tower:—

> Hath Bolingbroke
> Deposed thine intellect? hath he been in thy heart?

And in truth, but for that adventitious poetic gold, it would be only "plume-plucked Richard."——

> I find myself a traitor with the rest,
> For I have given here my soul's consent
> To undeck the pompous body of a king.

He is duly reminded, indeed, how

> That which in mean men we entitle patience
> Is pale cold cowardice in noble breasts.

Yet at least within the poetic bounds of Shakespeare's play, through Shakespeare's bountiful gifts, his desire seems fulfilled.—

> O! that I were as great
> As is my grief.

And his grief becomes nothing less than a central expression of all that in the revolutions of Fortune's wheel goes *down* in the world.

No! Shakespeare's kings are not, nor are meant to be, great men: rather, little or quite ordinary humanity, thrust upon greatness, with those pathetic results, the natural self-pity of the weak heightened in them into irresistible appeal to others as the net result of their royal prerogative. One after another, they seem to lie composed in Shakespeare's embalming pages, with just that touch of nature about them, making the whole world akin, which has infused into their tombs at Westminister a rare poetic grace. It is that irony of kingship, the sense that it is in its happiness child's play, in its sorrows, after all, but children's grief, which gives its finer accent to all the changeful feeling of these wonderful speeches:—the great meekness of the graceful, wild creature, tamed at last.—

> Give Richard leave to live till Richard die!

his somewhat abject fear of death, turning to acquiescence at moments of extreme weariness:—

> My large kingdom for a little grave!
> A little little grave, an obscure grave!—

his religious appeal in the last reserve, with its bold reference to the judgment of Pilate, as he thinks once more of his "anointing."

And as happens with children he attains contentment finally in the merely passive recognition of superior strength, in the naturalness of the result of the great battle as a matter of course, and

experiences something of the royal prerogative of poetry to obscure, or at least to attune and soften men's griefs. As in some
sweet anthem of Handel, the sufferer, who put finger to the organ
under the utmost pressure of mental conflict, extracts a kind of
peace at last from the mere skill with which he sets his distress to
music.—

> Beshrew thee, Cousin, that didst lead me forth
> Of that sweet way I was in to despair!

"With Cain go wander through the shades of night!"—cries the
new king to the gaoler Exton, dissimulating his share in the
murder he is thought to have suggested; and in truth there is
something of the murdered Abel about Shakespeare's Richard.
The fact seems to be that he died of "waste and a broken heart:" it
was by way of proof that his end had been a natural one that,
stifling a real fear of the face, the face of Richard, on men's
minds, with the added pleading now of all dead faces, Henry
exposed the corpse to general view; and Shakespeare, in bringing
it on the stage, in the last scene of his play, does but follow out the
motive with which he has emphasised Richard's physical beauty
all through it—that "most beauteous inn," as the Queen says
quaintly, meeting him on the way to death—residence, then soon
to be deserted, of that wayward, frenzied, but withal so affectionate soul. Though the body did not go to Westminister immediately, his tomb,

> That small model of the barren earth
> Which serves as paste and cover to our bones,[1]

the effigy clasping the hand of his youthful consort, was already
prepared there, with "rich gilding and ornaments," monument of
poetic regret, for Queen Anne of Bohemia, not of course the

---

[1]Perhaps a *double entendre:*—of any ordinary grave, as comprising, in effect, the
whole small earth now left to its occupant: or, of such a tomb as Richard's in
particular, with its actual model, or effigy, of the clay of him. Both senses are so
characteristic that it would be a pity to lose either.

"Queen" of Shakespeare, who however seems to have transferred to this second wife something of Richard's wildly proclaimed affection for the first. In this way, through the connecting link of that sacred spot, our thoughts once more associate Richard's two fallacious prerogatives, his personal beauty and his "anointing."

According to Johnson, *Richard the Second* is one of those plays which Shakespeare has "apparently revised;" and how doubly delightful Shakespeare is where he seems to have revised! "Would that he had blotted a thousand"—a thousand hasty phrases, we may venture once more to say with his earlier critic, now that the tiresome German superstition has passed away which challenged us to a dogmatic faith in the plenary verbal inspiration of every one of Shakespeare's clowns. Like some melodiously contending anthem of Handel's, I said, of Richard's meek "undoing" of himself in the mirror-scene; and, in fact, the play of *Richard the Second* does, like a musical composition, possess a certain concentration of all its parts, a simple continuity, an evenness in execution, which are rare in the great dramatist. With *Romeo and Juliet*, that perfect symphony (symphony of three independent poetic forms set in a grander one[1] which it is the merit of German criticism to have detected) it belongs to a small group of plays, where, by happy birth and consistent evolution, dramatic form approaches to something like the unity of a lyrical ballad, a lyric, a song, a single strain of music. Which sort of poetry we are to account the highest, is perhaps a barren question. Yet if, in art generally, unity of impression is a note of what is perfect, then lyric poetry, which in spite of complex structure often preserves the unity of a single passionate ejaculation, would rank higher than dramatic poetry, where, especially to the reader, as distinguished from the spectator assisting at a theatrical performance, there must always be a sense of the effort necessary to keep the various parts from flying asunder, a sense of imperfect continuity, such as the older criticism vainly sought to obviate by the rule of the dramatic "unities." It follows that a play attains artistic perfection just in proportion as it approaches that unity of lyrical

---

[1] The Sonnet: the Aubade: the Epithalamium.

effect, as if a song or ballad were still lying at the root of it, all the various expression of the conflict of character and circumstance falling at last into the compass of a single melody, or musical theme. As, historically, the earliest classic drama arose out of the chorus, from which this or that person, this or that episode, detached itself, so, into the unity of a choric song the perfect drama ever tends to return, its intellectual scope deepened, complicated, enlarged, but still with an unmistakable singleness, or identity, in its impression on the mind. Just there, in that vivid single impression left on the mind when all is over, not in any mechanical limitation of time and place, is the secret of the "unities"—the true imaginative unity—of the drama.

1889.

Æsthetic Poetry

The "æsthetic" poetry is neither a mere reproduction of Greek or medieval poetry, nor only an idealisation of modern life and sentiment. The atmosphere on which its effect depends belongs to no simple form of poetry, no actual form of life. Greek poetry, medieval or modern poetry, projects, above the realities of its time, a world in which the forms of things are transfigured. Of that transfigured world this new poetry takes possession, and sublimates beyond it another still fainter and more spectral, which is literally an artificial or "earthly paradise." It is a finer ideal, extracted from what in relation to any actual world is already an ideal. Like some strange second flowering after date, it renews on a more delicate type the poetry of a past age, but must not be confounded with it. The secret of the enjoyment of it is that inversion of home-sickness known to some, that incurable thirst for the sense of escape, which no actual form of life satisfies, no poetry even, if it be merely simple and spontaneous.

The writings of the "romantic school," of which the æsthetic poetry is an afterthought, mark a transition not so much from the pagan to the medieval ideal, as from a lower to a higher degree of passion in literature. The end of the eighteenth century, swept by vast disturbing currents, experienced an excitement of spirit of which one note was a reaction against an outworn classicism severed not more from nature than from the genuine motives of ancient art; and a return to true Hellenism was as much a part of this reaction as the sudden preoccupation with things medieval. The medieval tendency is in Goethe's *Goetz von Berlichingen*, the Hellenic in his *Iphigenie*. At first this medievalism was superficial, or at least external. Adventure, romance in the frankest

sense, grotesque individualism—that is one element in medieval
poetry, and with it alone Scott and Goethe dealt. Beyond them
were the two other elements of the medieval spirit: its mystic
religion at its apex in Dante and Saint Louis, and its mystic passion, passing here and there into the great romantic loves of rebellious flesh, of Lancelot and Abelard. That stricter, imaginative
medievalism which re-creates the mind of the Middle Age, so
that the form, the presentment grows outward from within, came
later with Victor Hugo in France, with Heine in Germany.

In the *Defence of Guenevere: and Other Poems*, published by
Mr. William Morris now many years ago, the first typical specimen of æsthetic poetry, we have a refinement upon this later,
profounder medievalism. The poem which gives its name to the
volume is a thing tormented and awry with passion, like the body
of Guenevere defending herself from the charge of adultery, and
the accent falls in strange, unwonted places with the effect of a
great cry. In truth these Arthurian legends, in their origin prior to
Christianity, yield all their sweetness only in a Christian atmosphere. What is characteristic in them is the strange suggestion of
a deliberate choice between Christ and a rival lover. That religion, monastic religion at any rate, has its sensuous side, a dangerously sensuous side, has been often seen: it is the experience of
Rousseau as well as of the Christian mystics. The Christianity of
the Middle Age made way among a people whose loss was in the
life of the senses, partly by its æsthetic beauty, a thing so profoundly felt by the Latin hymn-writers, who for one moral or
spiritual sentiment have a hundred sensuous images. And so in
those imaginative loves, in their highest expression, the Provençal poetry, it is a rival religion with a new rival *cultus* that we
see. Coloured through and through with Christian sentiment,
they are rebels against it. The rejection of one worship for another
is never lost sight of. The jealousy of that other lover, for whom
these words and images and refined ways of sentiment were first
devised, is the secret here of a borrowed, perhaps factitious colour
and heat. It is the mood of the cloister taking a new direction, and
winning so a later space of life it never anticipated.

Hereon, as before in the cloister, so now in the *château*, the
reign of reverie set in. The devotion of the cloister knew that

mood thoroughly, and had sounded all its stops. For the object of this devotion was absent or veiled, not limited to one supreme plastic form like Zeus at Olympia or Athena in the Acropolis, but distracted, as in a fever dream, into a thousand symbols and reflections. But then, the Church, that new Sibyl, had a thousand secrets to make the absent near. Into this kingdom of reverie, and with it into a paradise of ambitious refinements, the earthly love enters, and becomes a prolonged somnambulism. Of religion it learns the art of directing towards an unseen object sentiments whose natural direction is towards objects of sense. Hence a love defined by the absence of the beloved, choosing to be without hope, protesting against all lower uses of love, barren, extravagant, antinomian. It is the love which is incompatible with marriage, for the chevalier who never comes, of the serf for the *châtelaine*, of the rose for the nightingale, of Rudel for the Lady of Tripoli. Another element of extravagance came in with the feudal spirit: Provençal love is full of the very forms of vassalage. To be the servant of love, to have offended, to taste the subtle luxury of chastisement, of reconciliation—the religious spirit, too, knows that, and meets just there, as in Rousseau, the delicacies of the earthly love. Here, under this strange complex of conditions, as in some medicated air, exotic flowers of sentiment expand, among people of a remote and unaccustomed beauty, somnambulistic, frail, androgynous, the light almost shining through them. Surely, such loves were too fragile and adventurous to last more than for a moment.

That monastic religion of the Middle Age was, in fact, in many of its bearings, like a beautiful disease or disorder of the senses: and a religion which is a disorder of the senses must always be subject to illusions. Reverie, illusion, delirium: they are the three stages of a fatal descent both in the religion and the loves of the Middle Age. Nowhere has the impression of this delirium been conveyed as by Victor Hugo in *Notre Dame de Paris*. The strangest creations of sleep seem here, by some appalling licence, to cross the limit of the dawn. The English poet too has learned the secret. He has diffused through *King Arthur's Tomb* the maddening white glare of the sun, and tyranny of the moon, not tender and far-off, but close down—the sorcerer's moon, large and feverish. The col-

ouring is intricate and delirious, as of "scarlet lilies." The influence
of summer is like a poison in one's blood, with a sudden bewildered
sickening of life and all things. In *Galahad: a Mystery*, the frost
of Christmas night on the chapel stones acts as a strong narcotic:
a sudden shrill ringing pierces through the numbness: a voice pro-
claims that the Grail has gone forth through the great forest. It is
in the *Blue Closet* that this delirium reaches its height with a singular beauty, reserved perhaps for the enjoyment of the few.

A passion of which the outlets are sealed, begets a tension of
nerve, in which the sensible world comes to one with a reinforced
brilliancy and relief—all redness is turned into blood, all water
into tears. Hence a wild, convulsed sensuousness in the poetry of
the Middle Age, in which the things of nature begin to play a
strange delirious part. Of the things of nature the medieval mind
had a deep sense; but its sense of them was not objective, no real
escape to the world without us. The aspects and motions of nature
only reinforced its prevailing mood, and were in conspiracy with
one's own brain against one. A single sentiment invaded the
world: everything was infused with a motive drawn from the soul.
The amorous poetry of Provence, making the starling and the
swallow its messengers, illustrates the whole attitude of nature in
this electric atmosphere, bent as by miracle or magic to the service of human passion.

The most popular and gracious form of Provençal poetry was
the *nocturn*, sung by the lover at night at the door or under the
window of his mistress. These songs were of different kinds, according to the hour at which they were intended to be sung. Some
were to be sung at midnight—songs inviting to sleep, the *serena*,
or *serenade*; others at break of day—waking songs, the *aube* or
aubade.* This waking-song is put sometimes into the mouth of a
comrade of the lover, who plays sentinel during the night, to
watch for and announce the dawn: sometimes into the mouth of
one of the lovers, who are about to separate. A modification of it
is familiar to us all in *Romeo and Juliet*, where the lovers debate
whether the song they hear is of the nightingale or the lark; the

---

*Fauriel's *Histoire de la Poésie Provençale*, tome ii. ch. xviii.

aubade, with the two other great forms of love-poetry then floating in the world, the sonnet and the epithalamium, being here
refined, heightened, and inwoven into the structure of the play.
Those, in whom what Rousseau calls *les frayeurs nocturnes* are
constitutional, know what splendour they give to the things of
the morning; and how there comes something of relief from physical pain with the first white film in the sky. The Middle Age knew
those terrors in all their forms; and these songs of the morning
win hence a strange tenderness and effect. The crown of the English poet's book is one of these appreciations of the dawn:—

> "Pray but one prayer for me 'twixt thy closed lips,
>   Think but one thought of me up in the stars,
> The summer-night waneth, the morning light slips,
>   Faint and gray 'twixt the leaves of the aspen,
>   betwixt the cloud-bars,
> That are patiently waiting there for the dawn:
>   Patient and colourless, though Heaven's gold
> Waits to float through them along with the sun.
> Far out in the meadows, above the young corn,
>   The heavy elms wait, and restless and cold
> The uneasy wind rises; the roses are dun;
> Through the long twilight they pray for the dawn,
> Round the lone house in the midst of the corn.
>   Speak but one word to me over the corn,
>   Over the tender, bow'd locks of the corn.

It is the very soul of the bridegroom which goes forth to the bride:
inanimate things are longing with him: all the sweetness of the
imaginative loves of the Middle Age, with a superadded spirituality of touch all its own, is in that!

The *Defence of Guenevere* was published in 1858; the *Life and
Death of Jason* in 1867; to be followed by *The Earthly Paradise*;
and the change of manner wrought in the interval, entire, almost
a revolt, is characteristic of the æsthetic poetry. Here there is no
delirium or illusion, no experiences of mere soul while the body
and the bodily sense sleep, or wake with convulsed intensity at
the prompting of imaginative love; but rather the great primary
passions under broad daylight as of the pagan Veronese. This sim-
plification interests us, not merely for the sake of an individual

poet—full of charm as he is—but chiefly because it explains through him a transition which, under many forms, is one law of the life of the human spirit, and of which what we call the Renaissance is only a supreme instance. Just so the monk in his cloister, through the "open vision," open only to the spirit, divined, aspired to, and at last apprehended, a better daylight, but earthly, open only to the senses. Complex and subtle interests, which the mind spins for itself, may occupy art and poetry or our own spirits for a time; but sooner or later they come back with a sharp rebound to the simple elementary passions—anger, desire, regret, pity, and fear: and what corresponds to them in the sensuous world—bare, abstract fire, water, air, tears, sleep, silence, and what De Quincey has called the "glory of motion."

This reaction from dreamlight to daylight gives, as always happens, a strange power in dealing with morning and the things of the morning. Not less is this Hellenist of the Middle Age master of dreams, of sleep and the desire of sleep—sleep in which no one walks, restorer of childhood to men—dreams, not like Galahad's or Guenevere's, but full of happy, childish wonder as in the earlier world. It is a world in which the centaur and the ram with the fleece of gold are conceivable. The song sung always claims to be sung for the first time. There are hints at a language common to birds and beasts and men. Everywhere there is an impression of surprise, as of people first waking from the golden age, at fire, snow, wine, the touch of water as one swims, the salt taste of the sea. And this simplicity at first hand is a strange contrast to the sought-out simplicity of Wordsworth. Desire here is towards the body of nature for its own sake, not because a soul is divined through it.

And yet it is one of the charming anachronisms of a poet, who, while he handles an ancient subject, never becomes an antiquarian, but animates his subject by keeping it always close to himself, that between whiles we have a sense of English scenery as from an eye well practised under Wordsworth's influence, as from "the casement half opened on summer-nights," with the song of the brown bird among the willows, the

> "Noise of bells, such as in moonlit lanes
> Rings from the grey team on the market night."

Nowhere but in England is there such a "paradise of birds," the fern-owl, the water-hen, the thrush in a hundred sweet variations, the ger-falcon, the kestrel, the starling, the pea-fowl; birds heard from the field by the townsman down in the streets at dawn; doves everywhere, pink-footed, grey-winged, flitting about the temple, troubled by the temple incense, trapped in the snow. The sea-touches are not less sharp and firm, surest of effect in places where river and sea, salt and fresh waves, conflict.

In handling a subject of Greek's legend, anything in the way of an actual revival must always be impossible. Such vain antiquarianism in a waste of the poet's power. The composite experience of all the ages is part of each one of us: to deduct from that experience, to obliterate any part of it, to come face to face with the people of a past age, as if the Middle Age, the Renaissance, the eighteenth century had not been, is as impossible as to become a little child, or enter again into the womb and be born. But though it is not possible to repress a single phase of that humanity, which, because we live and move and have our being in the life of humanity, makes us what we are, it is possible to isolate such a phase, to throw it into relief, to be divided against ourselves in zeal for it; as we may hark back to some choice space of our own individual life. We cannot truly conceive the age: we can conceive the element it has contributed to our culture: we can treat the subjects of the age bringing that into relief. Such an attitude towards Greece, aspiring to but never actually reaching its way of conceiving life, is what is possible for art.

The modern poet or artist who treats in this way a classical story comes very near, if not to the Hellenism of Homer, yet to the Hellenism of Chaucer, the Hellenism of the Middle Age, or rather of that exquisite first period of the Renaissance within it. Afterwards the Renaissance takes its side, becomes, perhaps, exaggerated or facile. But the choice life of the human spirit is always under mixed lights, and in mixed situations, when it is not too sure of itself, is still expectant, girt up to leap forward to the promise. Such a situation there was in that earliest return from the over-wrought spiritualities of the Middle Age to the earlier, more ancient life of the senses; and for us the most attractive form of classical story is the monk's conception of it, when he escapes from the sombre atmosphere of his cloister to natural light. The fruits of this mood, which, divining more than it understands, infuses into the scenery and figures of Christian history some subtle reminiscence of older gods, or into the story of Cupid and Psyche that passionate stress of spirit which the world owes to Christianity, constitute a peculiar vein of interest in the art of the fifteenth century.

And so, before we leave *Jason* and *The Earthly Paradise*, a word must be said about their medievalisms, delicate inconsistencies, which, coming in a poem of Greek subject, bring into this white dawn thoughts of the delirious night just over and make one's sense of relief deeper. The opening of the fourth book of *Jason* describes the embarkation of the Argonauts: as in a dream, the scene shifts and we go down from Iolchos to the sea through a pageant of the Middle Age in some French or Italian town. The gilded vanes on the spires, the bells ringing in the towers, the trellis of roses at the window, the close planted with apple-trees, the grotesque undercroft with its close-set pillars, change by a single touch the air of these Greek cities and we are at Glastonbury by the tomb of Arthur. The nymph in furred raiment who seduces Hylas is conceived frankly in the spirit of Teutonic romance; her song is of a garden enclosed, such as that with which the old church glass-stainer surrounds the mystic bride of the song of songs. Medea herself has a hundred touches of the medieval sorceress, the sorceress of the Streckelberg or the Blocksberg: her mystic changes are Christabel's. It is precisely this effect, this grace of Hellenism relieved against the sorrow of the Middle Age, which forms the chief motives of *The Earthly Paradise*: with an exquisite dexterity the two threads of sentiment are here interwoven and contrasted. A band of adventurers sets out from Norway, most northerly of northern lands, where the plague is raging—the bell continually ringing as they carry the Sacrament to the sick. Even in Mr. Morris's earliest poems snatches of the sweet French tongue had always come with something of Hellenic blitheness and grace. And now it is below the very coast of France, through the fleet of Edward the Third, among the gaily painted medieval sails, that we pass to a reserved fragment of Greece, which by some divine good fortune lingers on in the western sea into the Middle Age. There the stories of *The Earthly Paradise* are told, Greek story and romantic alternating; and for the crew of the *Rose Garland*, coming across the sins of the earlier world with the sign of the cross, and drinking Rhine-wine in Greece, the two worlds of sentiment are confronted.

One characteristic of the pagan spirit the æsthetic poetry has, which is on its surface—the continual suggestion, pensive or passionate, of the shortness of life. This is contrasted with the bloom of the world, and gives new seduction to it—the sense of death and the desire of beauty: the desire of beauty quickened by the sense of death. But that complexion of sentiment is at its height in another "æsthetic" poet of whom I have to speak next, Dante Gabriel Rossetti.

1868. [1889]

Dante Gabriel Rossetti

It was characteristic of a poet who had ever something about him of mystic isolation, and will still appeal perhaps, though with a name it may seem now established in English literature, to a special and limited audience, that some of his poems had won a kind of exquisite fame before they were in the full sense published. *The Blessed Damozel*, although actually printed twice before the year 1870, was eagerly circulated in manuscript; and the volume which it now opens came at last to satisfy a long-standing curiosity as to the poet, whose pictures also had become an object of the same peculiar kind of interest. For those poems were the work of a painter, understood to belong to, and to be indeed the leader, of a new school then rising into note; and the reader of to-day may observe already; in *The Blessed Damozel*, written at the age of eighteen, a prefigurement of the chief characteristics of that school, as he will recognise in it also, in proportion as he really knows Rossetti, many of the characteristics which are most markedly personal and his own. Common to that school and to him, and in both alike of primary significance, was the quality of sincerity, already felt as one of the charms of that earliest poem—a perfect sincerity, taking effect in the deliberate use of the most direct and unconventional expression, for the conveyance of a poetic sense which recognised no conventional standard of what poetry was called upon to be. At a time when poetic originality in England might seem to have had its utmost play, here was certainly one new poet more, with a structure and music of verse, a vocabulary, an accent, unmistakably novel, yet felt to be no mere tricks of manner adopted with a view to forcing attention—an accent which might rather count as the very seal of reality on one man's own proper speech; as that speech itself was the wholly natural expression of certain wonderful things he really felt and saw. Here was one, who had a matter to present to his readers, to himself at least, in the first instance, so valuable, so real and definite, that his primary aim, as regards form or expression in his verse, would be but its exact equivalence to those *data* within. That he had this gift of transparency in language—the control of a style which did but obediently shift and shape itself to the mental motion, as a well-trained hand can follow on the tracing-paper the outline of an original drawing below it, was proved afterwards by a volume of typically perfect translations from the delightful but difficult "early Italian poets": such transparency being indeed the secret of all genuine style, of all such style as can truly belong to one man and not to another. His own meaning was always personal and even recondite, in a certain sense learned and casuistical, sometimes complex or obscure; but the term was always, one could see, deliberately chosen from many competitors, as the just transcript of that peculiar phase of soul which he alone knew, precisely as he knew it.

One of the peculiarities of *The Blessed Damozel* was a definiteness of sensible imagery, which seemed almost grotesque to some, and was strange, above all, in a theme so profoundly visionary. The gold bar of heaven from which she leaned, her hair yellow like ripe corn, are but examples of a general treatment, as naively detailed as the pictures of those early painters contemporary with Dante, who has shown a similar care for minute and definite imagery in his verse; there, too, in the very midst of profoundly mystic vision. Such definition of outline is indeed one among many points in which Rossetti resembles the great Italian poet, of whom, led to him at first by family circumstances, he was ever a lover—a "servant and singer," faithful as Dante, "of Florence and of Beatrice"—with some close inward conformities of genius also, independent of any mere circumstances of education. It was said by a critic of the last century, not wisely though agreeably to the practice of his time, that poetry rejoices in abstractions. For Rossetti, as for Dante, without question on his part, the first condition of the poetic way of seeing and presenting things is particularisation. "Tell me now," he writes, for Villon's

Dictes-moy où, n'en quel pays,
Est Flora, la belle Romaine—

Tell me now, in what hidden way is
Lady Flora the lovely Roman:

—"way," in which one might actually chance to meet her; the unmistakably poetic effect of the couplet in English being dependent on the definiteness of that single word (though actually lighted on in the search after a difficult double rhyme) for which every one else would have written, like Villon himself, a more general one, just equivalent to place or region.

And this delight in concrete definition is allied with another of his conformities to Dante, the really imaginative vividness, namely, of his personifications—his hold upon them, or rather their hold upon him, with the force of a Frankenstein, when once they have taken life from him. Not Death only and Sleep, for instance, and the winged spirit of Love, but certain particular aspects of them, a whole "populace" of special hours and places, "the hour" even "which might have been, yet might not be," are living creatures, with hands and eyes and articulate voices.

Stands it not by the door—
Love's Hour—till she and I shall meet;
With bodiless form and unapparent feet
That cast no shadow yet before,
Though round its head the dawn begins to pour
The breath that makes day sweet?—

Nay, why
Name the dead hours? I mind them well:
Their ghosts in many darkened doorways dwell
With desolate eyes to know them by.

Poetry as a *mania*—one of Plato's two higher forms of "divine" mania—has, in all its species, a mere insanity incidental to it, the "defect of its quality," into which it may lapse in its moment of weakness; and the insanity which follows a vivid poetic anthropomorphism like that of Rossetti may be noted here and there in his work, in a forced and almost grotesque materialising of abstractions, as Dante also became at times a mere subject of the scholastic realism of the Middle Age.

In *Love's Nocturn* and *The Stream's Secret*, congruously perhaps
with a certain feverishness of soul in the moods they present,
there is at times a near approach (may it be said?) to such insanity of realism—

> Pity and love shall burn
> In her pressed cheek and cherishing hands;
> And from the living spirit of love that stands
> Between her lips to soothe and yearn,
> Each separate breath shall clasp me round in turn
> And loose my spirit's bands.

But even if we concede this; even if we allow, in the very plan of
those two compositions, something of the literary conceit—what
exquisite, what novel flowers of poetry, we must admit them to
be, as they stand! In the one, what a delight in all the natural
beauty of water, all its details for the eye of a painter; in the other,
how subtle and fine the imaginative hold upon all the secret ways
of sleep and dreams! In both of them, with much the same attitude and tone, Love—sick and doubtful Love—would fain inquire
of what lies below the surface of sleep, and below the water;
stream or dream being forced to speak by Love's powerful "control"; and the poet would have it foretell the fortune, issue, and
event of his wasting passion. Such artifices, indeed, were not unknown in the old Provençal poetry of which Dante had learned
something. Only, in Rossetti at least, they are redeemed by a
serious purpose, by that sincereity of his, which allies itself readily to a serious beauty, a sort of grandeur of literary workmanship,
to a great style. One seems to hear there a really new kind of
poetic utterance, with effects which have nothing else like them;
as there is nothing else, for instance, like the narrative of Jacob's
Dream in *Genesis*, or Blake's design of the Singing of the Morning
Stars, or Addison's Nineteenth Psalm.

With him indeed, as in some revival of the old mythopœic age,
common things—dawn, noon, night—are full of human or personal expression, full of sentiment. The lovely little sceneries
scattered up and down his poems, glimpses of a landscape, not
indeed of broad open-air effects, but rather that of a painter concentrated upon the picturesque effect of one or two selected ob-

jects at a time—the "hollow brimmed with mist," or the "ruined weir," as he sees it from one of the windows, or reflected in one of the mirrors of his "house of life" (the vignettes for instance seen by Rose Mary in the magic beryl) attest, by their very freshness and simplicity, to a pictorial or descriptive power in dealing with the inanimate world, which is certainly also one half of the charm, in that other, more remote and mystic, use of it. For with Rossetti this sense of lifeless nature, after all, is translated to a higher service, in which it does but incorporate itself with some phase of strong emotion. Every one understands how this may happen at critical moments of life; what a weirdly expressive soul may have crept, even in full noonday, into "the white-flower'd elder-thicket," when Godiva saw it "gleam through the Gothic archways in the wall," at the end of her terrible ride. To Rossetti it is so always, because to him life is a crisis at every moment. A sustained impressibility towards the mysterious conditions of man's everyday life, towards the very mystery itself in it, gives a singular gravity to all his work: those matters never became trite to him. But throughout, it is the ideal intensity of love—of love based upon a perfect yet peculiar type of physical or material beauty—which is enthroned in the midst of those mysterious powers; Youth and Death, Destiny and Fortune, Fame, Poetic Fame, Memory, Oblivion, and the like. Rossetti is one of those who, in the words of Mérimée, *se passionnent pour la passion*, one of Love's lovers.

And yet, again as with Dante, to speak of his ideal type of beauty as material, is partly misleading. Spirit and matter, indeed, have been for the most part opposed, with a false contrast or antagonism by schoolmen, whose artificial creation those abstractions really are. In our actual concrete experience, the two trains of phenomena which the words *matter* and *spirit* do but roughly distinguish, play inextricably into each other. Practically, the church of the Middle Age by its æsthetic worship, its sacramentalism, its real faith in the resurrection of the flesh, had set itself against that Manichean opposition of spirit and matter, and its results in men's way of taking life; and in this, Dante is the central representative of its spirit. To him, in the vehement and impassioned heat of his conceptions, the material and the spir-

itual are fused and blent: if the spiritual attains the definite vis-
ibility of a crystal, what is material loses its earthiness and
impurity. And here again, by force of instinct, Rossetti is one with
him. His chosen type of beauty is one,

> Whose speech Truth knows not from her thought,
> Nor Love her body from her soul.

Like Dante, he knows no region of spirit which shall not be sensuous also, or material. The shadowy world, which he realises so
powerfully, has still the ways and houses, the land and water, the
light and darkness, the fire and flowers, that had so much to do in
the moulding of those bodily powers and aspects which counted
for so large a part of the soul, here.

For Rossetti, then, the great affections of persons to each other,
swayed and determined, in the case of his highly pictorial genius,
mainly by that so-called material loveliness, formed the great
undeniable reality in things, the solid resisting substance, in a
world where all beside might be but shadow. The fortunes of those
affections—of the great love so determined; its casuistries, its languor sometimes; above all, its sorrows; its fortunate or unfortunate collisions with those other great matters; how it looks, as the
long day of life goes round, in the light and shadow of them: all
this, conceived with an abundant imagination, and a deep, a
philosophic, reflectiveness, is the matter of his verse, and especially of what he designed as his chief poetic work, "a work to be
called *The House of Life*," towards which the majority of his sonnets and songs were contributions.

The dwelling-place in which one finds oneself by chance or
destiny, yet can partly fashion for oneself; never properly one's
own at all, if it be changed too lightly; in which every object has
its associations—the dim mirrors, the portraits, the lamps, the
books, the hair-tresses of the dead and visionary magic crystals in
the secret drawers, the names and words scratched on the windows, windows open upon prospects the saddest or the sweetest;
the house one must quit, yet taking perhaps, how much of its
quietly active light and colour along with us!—grown now to be a
kind of raiment to one's body, as the body, according to Sweden-

borg, is but the raiment of the soul—under that image, the whole of Rossetti's work might count as a *House of Life*, of which he is but the "Interpreter." And it is a "haunted" house. A sense of power in love, defying distance, and those barriers which are so much more than physical distance, of unutterable desire penetrating into the world of sleep, however "lead-bound," was one of those anticipative notes obscurely struck in *The Blessed Damozel*, and, in his later work, makes him speak sometimes almost like a believer in mesmerism. Dream-land, as we said, with its "phantoms of the body," deftly coming and going on love's service, is to him, in no mere fancy or figure of speech, a real country, a veritable expansion of, or addition to, our waking life; and he did well perhaps to wait carefully upon sleep, for the lack of it became mortal disease with him. One may even recognise a sort of morbid and over-hasty making-ready for death itself, which increases on him; thoughts concerning it, its imageries, coming with a frequency and importunity, in excess, one might think, of even the very saddest, quite wholesome wisdom.

And indeed the publication of his second volume of *Ballads and Sonnets* preceded his death by scarcely a twelvemonth. That volume bears witness to the reverse of any failure of power, or falling-off from his early standard of literary perfection, in every one of his then accustomed forms of poetry —the song, the sonnet, and the ballad. The newly printed sonnets, now completing *The House of Life*, certainly advanced beyond those earlier ones, in clearness; his dramatic power in the ballad, was here at its height; while one monumental, gnomic piece, *Soothsay*, testifies, more clearly even than the *Nineveh* of his first volume, to the reflective force, the dry reason, always at work behind his imaginative creations, which at no time dispensed with a genuine intellectual structure. For in matters of pure reflection also, Rossetti maintained the painter's sensuous clearness of conception; and this has something to do with the capacity, largely illustrated by his ballads, of telling some red-hearted story of impassioned action with effect.

Have there, in very deed, been ages, in which the external conditions of poetry such as Rossetti's were of more spontaneous growth than in our own? The archaic side of Rossetti's work, his preferences in regard to earlier poetry, connect him with those who have certainly thought so, who fancied they could have breathed more largely in the age of Chaucer, or of Ronsard, in one of those ages, in the words of Stendhal—*ces siècles de passions où les âmes pouvaient se livrer franchement à la plus haute exaltation, quand les passions qui font la possibilité comme les sujets des beaux arts existaient.* We may think, perhaps, that such old time as that has never really existed except in the fancy of poets; but it was to find it, that Rossetti turned so often from modern life to the chronicle of the past. Old Scotch history, perhaps beyond any other, is strong in the matter of heroic and vehement hatreds and love, the tragic Mary herself being but the perfect blossom of them; and it is from that history that Rossetti has taken the subjects of the two longer ballads of his second volume: of the three admirable ballads in it, *The King's Tragedy* (in which Rossetti has dexterously interwoven some relics of James's own exquisite early verse) reaching the highest level of dramatic success, and marking perfection, perhaps, in this kind of poetry; which, in the earlier volume, gave us, among other pieces, *Troy Town, Sister Helen,* and *Eden Bower.*

Like those earlier pieces, the ballads of the second volume bring with them the question of the poetic value of the "refrain"—

> Eden bower's in flower:
> And O the bower and the hour!

—and the like. Two of those ballads—*Troy Town* and *Eden Bower,* are terrible in theme; and the refrain serves, perhaps, to relieve their bold aim at the sentiment of terror. In *Sister Helen* again, the refrain has a real, and sustained purpose (being here duly varied also) and performs the part of a chorus, as the story proceeds. Yet even in these cases, whatever its effect may be in actual recitation, it may fairly be questioned, whether, to the mere reader their actual effect is not that of a positive interruption and drawback, at least in pieces so lengthy; and Rossetti himself, it would seem, came to think so, for in the shortest of his later ballads, *The White Ship*—that old true history of the generosity with which a youth, worthless in life, flung himself upon death—

he was contented with a single utterance of the refrain, "given out" like the keynote or tune of a chant.

In *The King's Tragedy*, Rossetti has worked upon motive, broadly human (to adopt the phrase of popular criticism) such as one and all may realise. Rossetti, indeed, with all his self-concentration upon his own peculiar aim, by no means ignored those general interests which are external to poetry as he conceived it; as he has shown here and there, in this poetic, as also in pictorial, work. It was but that, in a life to be shorter even than the average, he found enough to occupy him in the fulfilment of a task, plainly "given him to do." Perhaps, if one had to name a single composition of his to readers desiring to make acquaintance with him for the first time, one would select: *The King's Tragedy*—that poem so moving, so popularly dramatic, and lifelike. Notwithstanding this, his work, it must be conceded, certainly through no narrowness or egotism, but in the faithfulness of a true workman to a vocation so emphatic, was mainly of the esoteric order. But poetry, at all times, exercises two distinct funtions: it may reveal, it may unveil to every eye, the ideal aspects of common things, after Gray's way (though Gray too, it is well to remember, seemed in his own day, seemed even to Johnson, obscure) or it may actually add to the number of motives poetic and uncommon in themselves, by the imaginative creation of things that are ideal from their very birth. Rossetti did something, something excellent, of the former kind; but his characteristic, his really revealing work, lay in the adding to poetry of fresh poetic material, of a new order of phenomena, in the creaton of a new ideal.

1883.

Postscript

αἰνεῖ δὲ παλαιὸν μὲν οἶνον, ἄνθεα δ' ὕμνων νεωτέρων

The words, *classical* and *romantic*, although, like many other critical expressions, sometimes abused by those who have understood them too vaguely or too absolutely, yet define two real tendencies in the history of art and literature. Used in an exaggerated sense, to express a greater opposition between those tendencies than really exists, they have at times tended to divide people of taste into opposite camps. But in that *House Beautiful*, which the creative minds of all generations—the artists and those who have treated life in the spirit of art—are always building together, for the refreshment of the human spirit, these oppositions cease; and the *Interpreter* of the House Beautiful, the true æsthetic critic, uses these divisions, only so far as they enable him to enter into the peculiarities of the objects with which he has to do. The term *classical*, fixed, as it is, to a well-defined literature, and a well-defined group in art, is clear, indeed; but then it has often been used in a hard, and merely scholastic sense, by the praisers of what is old and accustomed, at the expense of what is new, by critics who would never have discovered for themselves the charm of any work, whether new or old, who value what is old, in art or literature, for its accessories, and chiefly for the conventional authority that has gathered about it—people who would never really have been made glad by any Venus fresh-risen from the sea, and who praise the Venus of old Greece and Rome, only because they fancy her grown now into something staid and tame.

And as the term, *classical*, has been used in a too absolute, and therefore in a misleading sense, so the term, *romantic*, has been

used much too vaguely, in various accidental senses. The sense in
which Scott is called a romantic writer is chiefly this; that, in
opposition to the literary tradition of the last century, he loved
strange adventure, and sought it in the Middle Age. Much later,
in a Yorkshire village, the spirit of romanticism bore a more really
characteristic fruit in the work of a young girl, Emily Brontë, the
romance of *Wuthering Heights;* the figures of Hareton Earnshaw,
of Catherine Linton, and of Heathcliffe—tearing open Catherine's
grave, removing one side of her coffin, that he may really lie
beside her in death—figures so passionate, yet woven on a background of delicately beautiful, moorland scenery, being typical
examples of that spirit. In Germany, again, that spirit is shown
less in Tieck, its professional representative, than in Meinhold,
the author of *Sidonia the Sorceress* and the *Amber-Witch.* In Germany and France, within the last hundred years, the term has
been used to describe a particular school of writers; and, conse-
quently, when Heine criticises the *Romantic School* in Germany—that movement which culminated in Goethe's *Goetz von
Berlichingen;* or when Théophile Gautier criticises the romantic
movement in France, where, indeed, it bore its most characteristic
fruits, and its play is hardly yet over where, by a certain audacity,
or *bizarrerie* of motive, united with faultless literary execution,
it still shows itself in imaginative literature, they use the word,
with an exact sense of special artistic qualities, indeed; but use it,
nevertheless, with a limited application to the manifestation of
those qualities at a particular period. But the romantic spirit is,
in reality, an everpresent, an enduring principle, in the artistic
temperament; and the qualities of thought and style which that,
and other similar uses of the word *romantic* really indicate, are
indeed but symptoms of a very continuous and widely working
influence.

Though the words *classical* and *romantic,* then, have acquired
an almost technical meaning, in application to certain developments of German and French taste, yet this is but one variation of
an old opposition, which may be traced from the very beginning
of the formation of European art and literature. From the first
formation of anything like a standard of taste in these things, the
restless curiosity of their more eager lovers necessarily made itself

felt, in the craving for new motives, new subjects of interest, new modifications of style. Hence, the opposition between the classicists and the romanticists—between the adherents, in the culture of beauty, of the principles of liberty, and authority, respectively—of strength, and order or what the Greeks called κοσμιότης.

Sainte-Beuve, in the third volume of the *Causeries du Lundi*, has discussed the question, *What is meant by a classic?* It was a question he was well fitted to answer, having himself lived through many phases of taste, and having been in earlier life an enthusiastic member of the romantic school: he was also a great master of that sort of "philosophy of literature," which delights in tracing traditions in it, and the way in which various phases of thought and sentiment maintain themselves, through successive modifications, from epoch to epoch. His aim, then, is to give the word *classic* a wider and, as he says, a more generous sense than it commonly bears, to make it expressly *grandiose et flottant;* and, in doing this, he develops, in a masterly manner, those qualities of measure, purity, temperance, of which it is the especial function of classical art and literature, whatever meaning, narrower or wider, we attach to the term, to take care.

The charm, therefore, of what is classical, in art or literature, is that of the well-known tale, to which we can, nevertheless, listen over and over again, because it is told so well. To the absolute beauty of its artistic form, is added the accidental, tranquil, charm of familiarity. There are times, indeed, at which these charms fail to work on our spirits at all, because they fail to excite us. "Romanticism," says Stendhal, "is the art of presenting to people the literary works which, in the actual state of their habits and beliefs, are capable of giving them the greatest possible pleasure; *classicism*, on the contrary, of presenting them with that which gave the greatest possible pleasure to their grandfathers." But then, beneath all changes of habits and beliefs, our love of that mere abstract proportion—of music—which what is classical in literature possesses, still maintains itself in the best of us, and what pleased our grandparents may at least tranquillise us. The "classic" comes to us out of the cool and quiet of other times, as the measure of what a long experience has shown will at least never displease us. And in the classical literature of Greece and Rome, as in the classics of the last century, the essentially classical element is that quality of order in beauty, which they possess, indeed, in a pre-eminent degree, and which impresses some minds to the exclusion of everything else in them.

It is the addition of strangeness to beauty, that constitutes the romantic character in art; and the desire of beauty being a fixed element in every artistic organisation, it is the addition of curiosity to this desire of beauty, that constitutes the romantic temper. Curiosity and the desire of beauty, have each their place in art, as in all true criticism. When one's curiosity is deficient, when one is not eager enough for new impressions, and new pleasures, one is liable to value mere academical proprieties too highly, to be satisfied with worn-out or conventional types, with the insipid ornament of Racine, or the prettiness of that later Greek sculpture, which passed so long for true Hellenic work; to miss those places where the handiwork of nature, or of the artist, has been most cunning; to find the most stimulating products of art a mere irritation. And when one's curiosity is in excess, when it overbalances the desire of beauty, then one is liable to value in works of art what is inartistic in them; to be satisfied with what is exaggerated in art, with productions like some of those of the romantic school in Germany; not to distinguish, jealously enough, between what is admirably done, and what is done not quite so well, in the writings, for instance, of Jean Paul. And if I had to give instances of these defects, then I should say, that Pope, in common with the age of literature to which he belonged, had too little curiosity, so that there is always a certain insipidity in the effect of his work, exquisite as it is; and, coming down to our own time, that Balzac had an excess of curiosity—curiosity not duly tempered with the desire of beauty.

But, however falsely those two tendencies may be opposed by critics, or exaggerated by artists themselves, they are tendencies really at work at all times in art, moulding it, with the balance sometimes a little on one side, sometimes a little on the other, generating, respectively, as the balance inclines on this side or that, two principles, two traditions, in art, and in literature so far as it partakes of the spirit of art. If there is a great overbalance of curiosity, then, we have the grotesque in art: if the union of strangeness and beauty, under very difficult and complex conditions, be a successful one, if the union be entire, then the resultant beauty is very exquisite, very attractive. With a passionate care for beauty, the romantic spirit refuses to have it, unless the condition of strangeness be first fulfilled. Its desire is for a beauty born of unlikely elements, by a profound alchemy, by a difficult initiation, by the charm which wrings it even out of terrible things; and a trace of distortion, of the grotesque, may perhaps linger, as an additional element of expression, about its ultimate grace. Its eager, excited spirit will have strength, the grotesque, first of all—the trees shrieking as you tear off the leaves; for Jean Valjean, the long years of convict life; for Redgauntlet, the quicksands of Solway Moss; then, incorporate with this strangeness, and intensified by restraint, as much sweetness, as much beauty, as is compatible with that. *Énergique, frais, et dispos*—these, according to Sainte-Beuve, are the characteristics of a genuine classic—*les ouvrages anciens ne sont pas classiques parce qu'ils sont vieux, mais parce qu'ils sont énergiques, frais, et dispos.* Energy, freshness, intelligent and masterly disposition:—these are characteristics of Victor Hugo when his alchemy is complete, in certain figures, like Marius and Cosette, in certain scenes, like that in the opening of *Les Travailleurs de la Mer*, where Déruchette writes the name of *Gilliatt* in the snow, on Christmas morning; but always there is a certain note of strangeness discernible there, as well.

The essential elements, then, of the romantic spirit are curiosity and the love of beauty; and it is only as an illustration of these qualities, that it seeks the Middle Age, because, in the overcharged atmosphere of the Middle Age, there are unworked sources of romantic effect, of a strange beauty, to be won, by strong imagination, out of things unlikely or remote.

Few, probably, now read Madame de Staël's *De l'Allemagne*, though it has its interest, the interest which never quite fades out of work really touched with the enthusiasm of the spiritual adventurer, the pioneer in culture. It was published in 1810, to introduce to French readers a new school of writers—the romantic school, from beyond the Rhine; and it was followed, twenty-three

years later, by Heine's *Romantische Schule,* as at once a supplement and a correction. Both these books, then, connect romanticism with Germany, with the names especially of Goethe and
Tieck; and, to many English readers, the idea of romanticism is
still inseparably connected with Germany—that Germany which,
in its quaint old towns, under the spire of Strasburg or the towers
of Heidelberg, was always listening in rapt inaction to the melodious, fascinating voices of the Middle Age, and which, now that it
has got Strasburg back again, has, I suppose, almost ceased to
exist. But neither Germany, with its Goethe and Tieck, nor England, with its Byron and Scott, is nearly so representative of the
romantic temper as France, with Murger, and Gautier, and Victor
Hugo. It is in French literature that its most characteristic expression is to be found; and that, as most closely derivative, historically, from such peculiar conditions, as ever reinforce it to the
utmost.

For, although temperament has much to do with the generation
of the romantic spirit, and although this spirit, with its curiosity,
its thirst for a curious beauty, may be always traceable in excellent art (traceable even in Sophocles) yet still, in a limited sense,
it may be said to be a product of special epochs. Outbreaks of this
spirit, that is, come naturally with particular periods—times,
when, in men's approaches towards art and poetry, curiosity may
be noticed to take the lead, when men come to art and poetry,
with a deep thirst for intellectual excitement, after a long *ennui,*
or in reaction against the strain of outward, practical things: in
the later Middle Age, for instance; so that medieval poetry, cen-
tering in Dante, is often opposed to Greek and Roman poetry, as
romantic poetry to the classical. What the romanticism of Dante
is, may be estimated, if we compare the lines in which Virgil
describes the hazelwood, from whose broken twigs flows the
blood of Polydorus, not without the expression of a real shudder
at the ghastly incident, with the whole canto of the *Inferno,* into
which Dante has expanded them, beautifying and softening it,
meanwhile, by a sentiment of profound pity. And it is especially
in that period of intellectual disturbance, immediately preceding
Dante, amid which the romance languages define themselves at
last, that this temper is manifested. Here, in the literature of

Provence, the very name of *romanticism* is stamped with its true
signification: here we have indeed a romantic world, grotesque
even, in the strength of its passions, almost insane in its curious
expression of them, drawing all things into its sphere, making the
birds, nay! lifeless things, its voices and messengers, yet so penetrated with the desire for beauty and sweetness, that it begets a
wholly new species of poetry, in which the *Renaissance* may be
said to begin. The last century was pre-eminently a classical age,
an age in which, for art and literature, the element of a comely
order was in the ascendant; which, passing away, left a hard battle to be fought between the classical and the romantic schools.
Yet, it is in the heart of this century, of Goldsmith and Stothard,
of Watteau and the *Siècle de Louis XIV.*—in one of its central, if
not most characteristic figures, in Rousseau—that the modern
or French romanticism really originates. But, what in the eighteenth century is but an exceptional phenomenon, breaking
through its fair reserve and discretion only at rare intervals, is the
habitual guise of the nineteenth, breaking through it perpetually,
with a feverishness, an incomprehensible straining and excitement, which all experience to some degree, but yearning also, in
the genuine children of the romantic school, to be *énergique,
frais, et dispos*—for those qualities of energy, freshness, comely
order; and often, in Murger, in Gautier, in Victor Hugo, for instance, with singular felicity attaining them.

It is in the terrible tragedy of Rousseau, in fact, that French
romanticism, with much else, begins: reading his *Confessions* we
seem actually to assist at the birth of this new, strong spirit in the
French mind. The wildness which has shocked so many, and the
fascination which has influenced almost every one, in the squalid,
yet eloquent figure, we see and hear so clearly in that book,
wandering under the apple-blossoms and among the vines of
Neuchâtel or Vevey actually give it the quality of a very successful romantic invention. His strangeness or distortion, his profound subjectivity, his passionateness—the *cor laceratum*—
Rousseau makes all men in love with these. *Je ne suis fait comme
aucun de ceux que j'ai sus. Mais si je ne vaux pas mieux, au
moins je suis autre.* —"I am not made like any one else I have ever
known: yet, if I am not better, at least I am different." These

words, from the first page of the *Confessions*, anticipate all the Werthers, Renés, Obermanns, of the last hundred years. For Rousseau did but anticipate a trouble in the spirit of the whole world; and thirty years afterwards, what in him was a peculiarity, became part of the general consciousness. A storm was coming: Rousseau, with others, felt it in the air, and they helped to bring it down: they introduced a disturbing element into French literature, then so trim and formal, like our own literature of the age of Queen Anne.

In 1815 the storm had come and gone, but had left, in the spirit of "young France," the *ennui* of an immense disillusion. In the last chapter of Edgar Quinet's *Révolution Française*, a work itself full of irony, of disillusion, he distinguishes two books, Senancour's *Obermann* and Chateaubriand's *Génie du Christianisme*, as characteristic of the first decade of the present century. In those two books we detect already the disease and the cure—in *Obermann* the irony, refined into a plaintive philosophy of "indifference"—in Chateaubriand's *Génie du Christianisme*, the refuge from a tarnished actual present, a present of disillusion, into a world of strength and beauty in the Middle Age, as at an earlier period—in *René* and *Atala*—into the free play of them in savage life. It is to minds in this spiritual situation, weary of the present, but yearning for the spectacle of beauty and strength, that the works of French romanticism appeal. They set a positive value on the intense, the exceptional; and a certain distortion is sometimes noticeable in them, as in conceptions like Victor Hugo's *Quasimodo*, or *Gwynplaine*, something of a terrible grotesque, of the *macabre*, as the French themselves call it; though always combined with perfect literary execution, as in Gautier's *La Morte Amoureuse*, or the scene of the "maimed" burial-rites of the player, dead of the frost, in his *Capitaine Fracasse*—true "flowers of the yew." It becomes grim humour in Victor Hugo's combat of Gilliatt with the devil-fish, or the incident, with all its ghastly comedy drawn out at length, of the great gun detached from its fastenings on shipboard, in *Quatre-Vingt-Trieze* (perhaps the most terrible of all the accidents that can happen by sea) and in the entire episode, in that book, of the *Convention*. Not less surely does it reach a genuine pathos; for the habit of noting and distinguishing one's own most intimate passages of sentiment makes one sympathetic, begetting, as it must, the power of entering, by all sorts of finer ways, into the intimate recesses of other minds; so that pity is another quality of romanticism, both Victor Hugo and Gautier being great lovers of animals, and charming writers about them, and Murger being unrivalled in the pathos of his *Scènes de la Vie de Jeunesse.* Penetrating so finely into all situations which appeal to pity, above all, into the special or exceptional phases of such feeling, the romantic humour is not afraid of the quaintness or singularity of its circumstances or expression, pity, indeed, being of the essence of humour; so that Victor Hugo does but turn his romanticism into practice, in his hunger and thirst after practical *Justice!*—a justice which shall no longer wrong children, or animals, for instance, by ignoring in a stupid, mere breadth of view, minute facts about them. Yet the romanticists are antinomian, too, sometimes, because the love of energy and beauty, of distinction in passion, tended naturally to become a little *bizarre*, plunging into the Middle Age, into the secrets of old Italian story. *Are we in the Inferno?*—we are tempted to ask, wondering at something malign in so much beauty. For over all a care for the refreshment of the human spirit by fine art manifests itself, a predominant sense of literary charm, so that, in their search for the secret of exquisite expression, the romantic school went back to the forgotten world of early French poetry, and literature itself became the most delicate of the arts—like "goldsmith's work," says Sainte-Beuve, of Bertrand's *Gaspard de la Nuit*—and that peculiarly French gift, the gift of exquisite speech, *argute loqui*, attained in them a perfection which it had never seen before.

Stendhal, a writer whom I have already quoted, and of whom English readers might well know much more than they do, stands between the earlier and later growths of the romantic spirit. His novels are rich in romantic quality; and his other writings—partly criticism, partly personal reminiscences—are a very curious and interesting illustration of the needs out of which romanticism arose. In his book on *Racine and Shakespeare*, Stendhal argues that all good art was romantic in its day; and this is perhaps true in Stendhal's sense. That little treatise, full of "dry light" and fertile ideas, was published in the year 1823, and its object is to defend an entire independence and liberty in the choice and treatment of subject, both in art and literature, against those who upheld the exclusive authority of precedent. In pleading the cause of romanticism, therefore, it is the novelty, both of form and of motive, in writings like the *Hernani* of Victor Hugo (which soon followed it, raising a storm of criticism) that he is chiefly concerned to justify. To be interesting and really stimulating, to keep us from yawning even, art and literature must follow the subtle movements of that nimbly-shifting *Time-Spirit*, or *Zeit-Geist*, understood by French not less than by German criticism, which is always modifying men's taste, as it modifies their manners and their pleasures. This, he contends, is what all great workmen had always understood. Dante, Shakespeare, Molière, had exercised an absolute independence in their choice of subject and treatment. To turn always with that ever-changing spirit, yet to retain the flavour of what was admirably done in past generations, in the classics, as we say—is the problem of true romanticism. "Dante," he observes, "was pre-eminently the romantic poet. He adored Virgil, yet he wrote the *Divine Comedy*, with the episode of Ugolino, which is as unlike the *Æneid* as can possibly be. And those who thus obey the fundamental principle of romanticism, one by one become classical, and are joined to that ever-increasing common league, formed by men of all countries, to approach nearer and nearer to perfection."

Romanticism, then, although it has its epochs, is in its essential characteristics rather a spirit which shows itself at all times, in various degrees, in individual workmen and their work, and the amount of which criticism has to estimate in them taken one by one, than the peculiarity of a time or a school. Depending on the varying proportion of curiosity and the desire of beauty, natural tendencies of the artistic spirit at all times, it must always be partly a matter of individual temperament. The eighteenth century in England has been regarded as almost exclusively a classical period; yet William Blake, a type of so much which breaks through what are conventionally thought the influences of that century, is still a noticeable phenomenon in it, and the reaction in favour of naturalism in poetry begins in that century, early.

There are, thus, the born romanticists and the born classicists. There are the born classicists who start with *form*, to whose minds the comeliness of the old, immemorial, well-recognised types in art and literature, have revealed themselves impressively; who will entertain no matter which will not go easily and flexibly into them; whose work aspires only to be a variation upon, or study from, the old masters. "'Tis art's decline, my son!" they are always saying, to the progressive element in their own generation; to those who care for that which in fifty years' time every one will be caring for. On the other hand, there are the born romanticists, who start with an original, untried *matter*, still in fusion; who conceive this vividly, and hold by it as the essence of their work; who, by the very vividness and heat of their conception, purge away, sooner or later, all that is not organically appropriate to it, till the whole effect adjusts itself in clear, orderly, proportionate form; which form, after a very little time, becomes classical in its turn.

The romantic or classical character of a picture, a poem, a literary work, depends, then, on the balance of certain qualities in it; and in this sense, a very real distinction may be drawn between good classical and good romantic work. But all critical terms are relative; and there is at least a valuable suggestion in that theory of Stendhal's, that all good art was romantic in its day. In the beauties of Homer and Pheidias, quiet as they now seem, there must have been, for those who confronted them for the first time, excitement and surprise, the sudden, unforeseen satisfaction of the desire of beauty. Yet the *Odyssey*, with its marvellous adventure, is more romantic than the *Iliad*, which nevertheless contains, among many other romantic episodes, that of the immortal horses of Achilles, who weep at the death of Patroclus. Æschylus is more romantic than Sophocles, whose *Philoctetes*, were it written now, might figure, for the strangeness of its motive and the perfectness of its execution, as typically romantic; while, of Euripides, it may be said, that his method in writing his plays is to sacrifice readily almost everything else, so that he may attain the fulness of a single romantic effect. These two tendencies, indeed, might be applied as a measure or standard, all through Greek and Roman art and poetry, with very illuminating results; and for an analyst of the romantic principle in art, no exercise would be more profitable, than to walk through the collection of classical antiquities at the Louvre, or the British Museum, or to examine some representative collection of Greek coins, and note how the element of curiosity, of the love of strangeness, insinuates itself into classical design, and record the effects of the romantic spirit there, the traces of struggle, of the grotesque even, though overbalanced here by sweetness; as in the sculpture of Chartres and Rheims, the real sweetness of mind in the sculptor is often overbalanced by the grotesque, by the rudeness of his strength.

Classicism, then, means for Stendhal, for that younger enthusiastic band of French writers whose unconscious method he formulated into principles, the reign of what is pedantic, conventional, and narrowly academical in art; for him, all good art is romantic. To Sainte-Beuve, who understands the term in a more liberal sense, it is the characteristic of certain epochs, of certain spirits in every epoch, not given to the exercise of original imagination, but rather to the working out of refinements of manner on some authorised matter; and who bring to their perfection, in this way, the elements of sanity, of order and beauty in manner. In general criticism, again, it means the spirit of Greece and Rome, of some phases in literature and art that may seem of equal authority with Greece and Rome, the age of Louis the Fourteenth, the age of Johnson; though this is at best an uncritical use of the term, because in Greek and Roman work there are typical examples of the romantic spirit. But explain the terms as we may, in application to particular epochs, there are these two elements always recognisable; united in perfect art—in Sophocles, in Dante, in the highest work of Goethe, though not always absolutely balanced there; and these two elements may be not inappropriately termed the classical and romantic tendencies.

Material for the artist, motives of inspiration, are not yet exhausted: our curious, complex, aspiring age still abounds in subjects for æsthetic manipulation by the literary as well as by other forms of art. For the literary art, at all events, the problem just now is, to induce order upon the contorted, proportionless accumulation of our knowledge and experience, our science and history, our hopes and disillusion, and, in effecting this, to do consciously what has been done hitherto for the most part too unconsciously, to write our English language as the Latins wrote theirs, as the French write, as scholars should write. Appealing, as he may, to precedent in this matter, the scholar will still remember that if "the style is the man" it is also the age: that the nineteenth century too will be found to have had its style, justified by necessity—a style very different, alike from the baldness of an impossible "Queen Anne" revival, and an incorrect, incondite exuberance, after the mode of Elizabeth: that we can only return to either at the price of an impoverishment of form or matter, or both, although, an intellectually rich age such as ours being necessarily an eclectic one, we may well cultivate some of the excellences of literary types so different as those: that in literature as in other matters it is well to unite as many diverse elements as may be: that the individual writer or artist, certainly, is to be estimated by the number of graces he combines, and his power of interpenetrating them in a given work. To discriminate schools, of art, of literature, is, of course, part of the obvious business of literary criticism: but, in the work of literary production, it is easy to be overmuch occupied concerning them. For, in truth, the legitimate contention is, not of one age or school of literary art against another, but of all successive schools alike, against the stupidity which is dead to the substance, and the vulgarity which is dead to form.

[1879, 1889]